"THE TYRANNY
OF PRINTERS"

Jeffersonian America

Jan Ellen Lewis and

Peter S. Onuf, Editors

Jeffrey L. Pasley

"THE TYRANNY OF PRINTERS"

Newspaper Politics in the Early American Republic

University Press of Virginia
Charlottesville and London

The University Press of Virginia
© 2001 by the Rector and Visitors of the University of Virginia
All rights reserved
Printed in the United States of America
First published 2001

∞ The paper used in this publication meets the minimum requirements of the
American National Standard for Information Sciences—Permanence of Paper for
Printed Library Materials, ANSI Z39.48-1984.

Library of Congress Cataloging-in-Publication Data

Pasley, Jeffrey L., 1964–
    "The Tyranny of printers" : newspaper politics in the early American republic /
Jeffrey L. Pasley.
        p.   cm.—(Jeffersonian America)
    Includes bibliographical references (p.) and index.
    ISBN 0-8139-2030-2 (cloth : alk paper)
        1. Journalism—United States—History—18th century.   2. Journalism—
United States—History—19th century.   3. Press and politics—United States—
History—18th century.   4. Press and politics—United States—History—
19th century.   I. Title.   II. Series.
    PN4861   .P37 2001
    071'3'09033—dc21

                                                            00-051257

For Karen, Isaac, and Owen: My family and friends

CONTENTS

❦

ILLUSTRATIONS

Maps

Figures

ACKNOWLEDGMENTS

In many ways, acknowledgment sections at the beginning of books are a futile exercise. As a working academic, giving papers and applying for jobs and fellowships, one finds oneself constantly referring to "my work," "my research," or "my book." Sitting down to acknowledge one's scholarly debts brings home the deceptiveness of that possessive pronoun. It took hundreds of people to write this book, beginning with the past and present scholars whose writings laid the groundwork for it and continuing through the myriad family members, friends, teachers, colleagues, and librarians who facilitated the researching, writing, and rewriting of it. Many of the scholars get their acknowledgments in the notes, though space constraints limited even those to authors of the most directly and obviously relevant works. Everyone else must be contented with a brief notice in these few pages, and I can only beg the forgiveness of the many who will be left out.

First and foremost on my list of honorary coauthors is my wife, Karen Kunkel Pasley. We have been married nearly as long as I have been working on this project, and I cannot imagine having survived the rigors of graduate school and young professorhood without her love and friendship. This book also benefited greatly from Karen's professional skills as an editor (and budding ones as an indexer). She has read this work almost as many times as I have, improving it immeasurably—and she still professes to find the book interesting! I cannot say that our sons, Isaac and Owen, have sped this work to completion, but they have been very effective reminders of the real purposes of life here on Earth.

Of course, I would not be here on Earth without my parents, John and Julie Pasley, and though I do want to thank them for all those years of food, clothing, shelter, love, and financial support, I would not want to blame my deeds on them. They did their best. I am sorry that my late grandfather James Pasley, who first got me interested in history, did not live to see this book published, though living to be 107 years old is a lot to ask of someone just to read a book.

I also have many, many intellectual debts. Though he hoped I would go into a very different field, it was Michael Zuckert, my mentor and friend at Carleton College, who first provided me the intellectual encouragement to pursue graduate study and an appealing example of what the life of a scholar and teacher could be. I also met Karen in one of his classes, so really just about everything that I have going now is partly traceable to Michael. (I will let him decide whether that is a good or bad thing.) Two of Michael's colleagues in the Carleton political science department, Catherine Zuckert and Steve Schier, were also good friends and role models, and I benefited greatly from the teaching and advice of numerous members of the Carleton history department. (Sadly for Carleton, Michael and Catherine have since moved on to the University of Notre Dame.)

Though a world apart from my life today, my two years of working in Washington, D.C., after college influenced me enormously, helping develop the basic perspective on political life that animates this book. For much of that time, I had the honor of serving as a reporter-researcher for *The New Republic*, a magazine I had read religiously since junior high school. I will always be grateful to *TNR*'s owner, Martin Peretz, and his editorial staff of that period, including Michael Kinsley, Dorothy Wickenden, Jefferson Morley, Charles Lane, Leon Wieseltier, Louis Menand, Morton Kondracke, and Fred Barnes, for taking a starstruck kid from the provinces seriously. Besides providing many opportunities to write, and many lessons in good writing, working at *TNR* instilled a certain attention to the internal architectural details of political life, and the role of basic human impulses in driving it, that has stood me in good stead ever since. My fellow reporter-researcher, Adam Paul Weisman, was a good friend and colleague and helped reinforce the conclusion we both reached that, interesting as Washington was, academia might be better for our long-term intellectual and emotional health.

The *TNR* connection facilitated a chance to write speeches for one of the 1988 presidential campaigns. I did not particularly enjoy the hypercompetitive atmosphere of modern campaigning, but the experience lent some needed first-person specificity to my understanding of how American politics works in the present and enabled comparisons and contrasts that have, I believe, deepened my insights into American political cultures of the past. My two closest coworkers, Bruce Reed and Jerry Mande, were excellent guides to a somewhat bizarre world, and Fred Martin, the campaign manager, was kind enough to find me employment to bridge the gap between the end of the campaign and the beginning of graduate school. Luckily, one of those employers was expert political analyst Michael Barone, whose warm encouragement, encyclopedic knowledge, and voluminous library were instrumental in preparing me for what occasionally seemed like a doomed attempt to become a professional political historian.

Certain sections of this book originated as a seminar paper and then a dissertation at Harvard University. While the project has grown and changed quite a bit since then, it never would have begun without Bernard Bailyn's interest and confidence in it. He was kind enough to take on a new student just before his retirement from teaching, and then let me pursue my own work in my own way, while keeping up just the right kinds of pressure. Besides his sterling example as a scholar, intellectual, and writer, Professor Bailyn's largest contribution to my intellectual growth was his constant attention, in dealing with all his graduate students, to the "So what?" question. Early and often, we were forced to explain what made our projects worth doing and the results worth reading. By this means, the idea was deeply ingrained that serious scholars should do important, ambitious work and address big questions for relatively wide audiences. Other Harvard faculty were also helpful or helpfully challenging: these include Drew McCoy (now at Clark University), whose course taught me everything I then knew about the Early American Republic; my second reader, William Gienapp, who did not always agree with my approach but whose comments helped to sharpen my thinking and broaden my reading and methods; and Brian Balogh (now at the University of Virginia), whose interest and approachability were great morale-builders at the time. Theda Skocpol's course and colloquium on American political development not only helped me see my own work in a new and broader perspective, but also provided some crucial "outside" encouragement. Christine McFadden, administrator of the History of American Civilization program, always made me feel there was someone in the office looking out for me, a nice feeling for a shy Midwesterner to have at a byzantine institution like Harvard.

Among my graduate student colleagues, I would like to thank Jessica Marshall, Fred Dalzell, Mike Vorenberg, Bob Allison, Tom Brown, and Richard John for their friendship and for many stimulating conversations in classes, over beers, and in what I believe we called (reflecting the angst we all felt at the time) our "dissertation support group." Richard John, in particular, probably deserves a commission on every sale of this book. He was just finishing graduate school when I was starting, and he acted as unofficial mentor and fount of historiographic information. Since then, Richard's unflagging interest in my career has been incredibly generous, adding depth to my work and bringing countless opportunities that I probably never would have pursued on my own.

Since resurfacing a few years ago from the relative isolation of early father- and assistant professorhood, I have found a wonderfully stimulating and supportive intellectual home in the Society for Historians of the Early American Republic. The friendships and working relationships that I have made or maintained through SHEAR have been extremely important in finishing this book and, more generally, in enriching my experience as a professional historian. SHEAR-ites David Waldstreicher, Andrew Robertson, Richard John, Peter Onuf, Richard E. Ellis, and John Brooke all read the manuscript and enriched it with their perspectives, while Albrecht Koschnik, Joanne Freeman, Marion Winship, Rosemarie Zagarri, William G. Shade, and many others have been helpful in other ways. Before I started attending the annual SHEAR conference, I am sure that I never grasped the true meaning of the old cliché about scholarship's being a collective enterprise. That it is, and often quite a bit of fun besides.

At the University Press of Virginia, I want to thank Dick Holway, my acquisitions editor, for his unfailing good cheer and his enthusiasm for this book, which he sometimes had to maintain in the face of different emotions on the part of the author. Gary Kessler was an extremely efficient copyeditor who had the misfortune of dealing with a somewhat rebellious author. Ellen Satrom and David Sewell handled the production of the manuscript, and answered my many questions, with great skill and expedition. I am also deeply indebted to another Charlottesville resident, the University of Virginia's Peter Onuf, for his generous support of my work and for including this book in the exciting new series that he and Jan Lewis of Rutgers are editing for the press, "Jeffersonian America." The extensive comments of Professors Thomas Leonard and Robert Gross, the once-anonymous readers for the Press, were both insightful and validating.

Thanks are also due to many of my faculty colleagues at Florida State University, where most of this book was written, for their moral and intellectual support through the vicissitudes of untenured faculty life. Here I would single out, along with their significant others, Eileen Groth Lyon, Neil Jumonville, Sally Hadden, Betty Dessants, Nathan Stoltzfus, Rod Anderson, Paul Strait, Valerie Jean Conner, and, though we never actually coincided at FSU, Edward Gray. Peter Krafft, director of cartography services for FSU's Florida Environmental and Resources Analysis Center, did a remarkable job creating beautiful maps out of my lists of towns and newspapers. My new colleagues here at the University of Missouri–Columbia have my gratitude for allowing Karen and me to finally realize our longtime goal of getting back home to the Midwest.

The process of historical research and writing also generates many debts of the more pecuniary kind. Travel and summer research grants were provided by the History of American Civilization program at Harvard, the History Department and the Council on Research and Creativity at Florida State, and the Library Company of Philadelphia. James N. Green and the Library Company staff should be singled out for special commendation. Most of my own research that summer was done at the Historical Society of Pennsylvania next door, but LCP allowed me to keep my grant even though the HSP withdrew from the program during the course of the application process. An Artemas Ward Fellowship from the Harvard History Department helped relieve me of some teaching duties during my unbelievably hectic final year in graduate school. In more recent times, a grant from the University of Missouri Research Board paid for some last-minute research and, more substantially, helped defray the costs of producing this volume.

I visited and revisited numerous libraries in my research, and must content myself with issuing collective thanks to the staffs of some of them that were particularly helpful: the microforms department at Harvard; the Clements Library at the University of Michigan; everyone I ever dealt with at America's finest historical library, the American Antiquarian Society; and the Interlibrary Loan Departments at FSU's Strozier Library and MU's Ellis Library. Finally, Chris Connelly and Cindy Burkhart, Chris Dawe, Rosie DePasquale, Jim and Jan Eisner, Jennifer and Paul Flaxman, Bernie and Harriet Goodheart, Reynolds and Catherine Lassiter, and Jeff Zack all extended their hospitality on various research trips to their respective corners of the country. Keeping in touch with old friends has turned out to be a great benefit of historical research.

A NOTE ON CONVENTIONS
AND METHODS

◈

A few technical points about this book need to be made at the outset. Most but not all of the historiographic discussions were removed from my notes in order to get this work down to what the Press considered a publishable length. The Press also preferred endnotes over footnotes, and citations in the notes are given only in shortened or abbreviated form. Full citations are available in the bibliography that follows the notes. For clarity, I have adopted the following policy regarding party names in the text and notes: The proponents and opponents of the Constitution during 1787 and 1788 are named using lowercase, "federalists" and "antifederalists," respectively, to convey the idea that these were temporary coalitions of like-minded politicians rather than ongoing parties. The longer-continuing political parties that developed after 1789 are capitalized, usually as the Federalists and Republicans, the latter being the name that Thomas Jefferson and other politicians of the 1790s most often used themselves. Exceptions to this rule occur in quotations, which have been rendered exactly as I found them, with occasional silent changes in punctuation and spelling made for clarity.

A word may also be in order regarding the research strategy that I used in creating this book. While it aims to be a national study, I make no claim to have read every political newspaper published in the early United States, nor to have fully plumbed the depths of newspaper politics in every location. Attempting to be intelligently selective, I concentrated on locations where the partisan newspaper situation seemed particularly active or intriguing, but on a wide enough range of locations to provide some interesting contrasts. The research focused on Pennsylvania, Connecticut, Virginia, and interior Massachusetts, roughly in that order, with the addition of various individual figures and newspapers in most of the other early states. (On the other hand, I did try to be comprehensive in developing my aggregate data on newspapers and editors, as explained in appendix 1.) In order to expand the scope of the study without expanding research time indefinitely, I chose to avoid performing extensive archival research on certain figures and newspapers for which comprehensive secondary accounts exist, making major exceptions for Philadelphia publishers who seemed especially important in the development of what I call "newspaper politics." Outside of Philadelphia, I tried to emphasize lesser-known newspapers and editors, in the hopes that they might be more truly representative of the ordinary newspaper politician's experience.

Finally, readers of this book should be sure to consult its companion Web site at <http://pasleybrothers.com/newspols>. Serving as an extension of the book, this site contains important supporting material that was too voluminous to be included in the published version. In particular, it presents extensive data on officeholding by newspaper printers and editors, in a form that is both more complete and more usable than a paper chart could have been.

"THE TYRANNY
OF PRINTERS"

The Newspaper-Based Political System of the Nineteenth-Century United States

❦

Here at the turn of the twenty-first century, it is common to observe that journalists have become more famous and powerful than the politicians they cover.[1] It is much less well known (outside a small circle of historical specialists) that journalists once were politicians, some of them among the most prominent candidates, officeholders, and party operatives in the nation. This was last true in the early twentieth century, appearing most starkly in the presidential election of 1920, in which the two major parties each nominated a longtime Ohio newspaper editor—Warren G. Harding for the Republicans, James M. Cox for the Democrats.[2] While an unusual circumstance, the nomination of two newspapermen was no fluke. Instead, it reflected the central role the press had been playing in American party politics since the end of the eighteenth century. The 1920 campaign was a kind of last hurrah for the old political press. The editor-candidates were not well received by reporters and columnists proud of their industry's increasing professionalism. H. L. Mencken sneered that Cox and Harding were esteemed only "by the surviving hacks of the party press."[3] President Harding's disgrace probably destroyed what little national prestige the party press had left. The news media and the parties parted ways permanently after the 1920s, ending a partnership, perhaps even a merger, that had profoundly shaped American political development. The subject of this book is how and by whom this merger was accomplished.

THE PARTISAN PRESS RECONSIDERED

Taking the old partisan press seriously requires a fairly radical shift in the typical late twentieth-century perspective on the subject of the press and politics. It requires abandoning the teleological notion that there can be only one model of a political press, namely, the modern United States—one in which journalists themselves take no role as active political partisans except on editorial pages and talk shows, and, even then, typically shun formal affiliation with political parties or candidates. It requires an openness to the possibility that newspapers might have useful functions besides gathering, writing, and disseminating news stories.[4]

Though few historians or commentators in the United States have shown this openness, the need for it in understanding the history of the American press can be seen in the fact that one of the primary missions of the modern media, the active gathering of news, emerged very slowly and very late in that history. Through most of the nineteenth century, only the largest urban dailies maintained reporting staffs. The rest delivered the "news" in a desultory, haphazard fashion, printing letters written or lent to the editor, material from other newspapers, and raw government documents. Local news, in particular, was largely absent from most smaller newspapers until well after the Civil War.[5]

Newspapers have long occupied a paradoxical place in histories of early and antebellum America. They were one of the most striking aspects of the nineteenth-century American scene to foreign commentators such as Alexis de Tocqueville. He noted in his travels that there seemed to be "hardly a hamlet in America without its newspaper" and that this ubiquitous political press made "political life circulate in every corner of that vast land."[6] Yet the partisan press is perhaps the one major institution in American society that goes virtually unmentioned in survey narratives, textbooks, and other syntheses, except for a few stereotyped, largely mythical instances of journalistic excess or heroism such as the Spanish-American War, Vietnam, and Watergate.[7]

Political and cultural historians have often used newspapers as sources, but they have rarely done justice to the press as a historical phenomenon in itself.[8] This is especially true of eighteenth- and nineteenth-century partisan newspapers, which have generally been dismissed or lamented as denizens of the "dark ages" of journalism history, a time when the press was under the thumb of political parties and maintained by pathetic "kept editors."[9]

Journalism school textbooks rehearse a standard version of newspaper history that amounts to an origin myth for the modern, commercial, "objective" news media, a myth designed (according to one critic) "to reinforce journalists' and future journalists' belief in the merit of their profession." This origin myth centers around the struggle of modern journalism to emerge from the dark ages and assume its presumably foreordained characteristics: a fundamentally commercial orientation, a primary mission of delivering information to the public as quickly as possible, an ideal of objectivity regarding all political or social controversies, a value system prizing aggressive news gathering over all else, and an adversarial relationship with political parties and the state.[10] The end of this story is the present era, in which the news media (though not necessarily the newspapers) enjoy unprecedented prosperity and penetration, wielding power that is often said to outstrip that of more overtly political institutions such as the political parties and the government.[11]

This study is not the place for a full critique of this mythology, which some recent journalism historians have begun to dispel.[12] However, as a way of putting the era of the partisan press in its proper historical perspective, it may be useful to observe that arguments for the power of the modern media rest on an oxymoronic notion of political power. Typically, political power involves the ability to exercise control, implying some direction or purpose. Yet this is not what the modern news media have, committed as they are to a policy of political valuelessness and lacking as they do the direct link that a successful political party forges between public attitudes, partisan elections, and government policies. Rather, the modern political news media is powerful more as the weather is—an awesome force that moves or destroys without purpose, motive, intention, or plan, a power that cannot direct itself toward any particular object. Hence, though surveys have always revealed national-level journalists to be heavily Democratic in their personal beliefs, the news media over the years of the late twentieth century have raised up presidencies and candidates, then smote them down again, seemingly without much regard to substantive issues or ideological affinities.[13]

In nineteenth-century America, by contrast, the newspaper press was the political system's central institution, not simply a forum or atmosphere in which politics took place. Instead, newspapers and their editors were purposeful actors in the political process, linking parties, voters, and the government together, and pursuing specific political goals. Newspapers were the "linchpin" of nineteenth-century party politics, one historian has written, though historical narratives and interpretations have rarely reflected that fact.[14] This state of affairs held with particular force nationally from the 1790s to 1860s, but it remained strong long after the Civil War, as attested by the prominence of Gilded Age journalist-politicians such as Horace Greeley, James G. Blaine, Henry Watterson, and many others. In many localities, especially outside the major eastern cities where large commercial dailies came to overwhelm the party press, the system of newspaper-based politics remained fully operational until the early twentieth century.[15]

How and why was the press so central to the nineteenth-century political system?[16] One possible argument might stress technological necessity: print was the only means of mass communication available in the age before film, radio, and television. In reality, cultural factors outweighed this technological gap, which was opened by a culturally created need. Tocqueville explained the problem in terms of the decline or absence of traditional social bonds: "When no firm and lasting ties any longer unite men, it is impossible to obtain the cooperation of any great number of them unless you can persuade every man whose help is required that he serves his private interests by voluntarily uniting his efforts to those of all the others. That cannot be done habitually and conveniently without the help of a newspaper. Only a newspaper can put the same thought at the same time before a thousand readers."[17]

More specific cultural factors were also at work. During much of the nineteenth century, prevailing political mores forbade candidates—especially presidential candidates—from campaigning for themselves. There were usually no lengthy speaking tours and few if any other public events directly involving the candidates. In this situation, newspapers conducted many if not most of the opinion-shaping activities we now call campaigning: communicating a party's message, promoting its candidates, attacking their opponents, and encouraging voters to turn out at the polls.[18]

Of course, a limited number of live-audience events and personal contacts (both often conducted by surrogates for the candidate) had been part of election seasons and political controversies since colonial times, especially in the South and the Middle Atlantic region. A candidate's "friends" (usually his personal and political clients and allies) cajoled voters at the polls and sometimes even brought them there. Southern planter-candidates treated the voters to court-day barbecues that often involved speeches, but in colonial times these were more social rituals through which local elites and their clients reaffirmed their hierarchical relationship with each other, rather than real campaign events in which candidates solicited votes. During the pre-Revolutionary crisis, countless towns and villages held meetings and issued resolutions or declarations protesting a British policy or asserting American rights. (Later the town meeting evolved into a major means of nominating candidates.)

Live campaign events became even more common after the Revolution. During the 1790s, voluntary associations and militia companies in Philadelphia held politicized celebrations on the Fourth of July and other major holidays. Often beginning with a parade, these celebrations typically ended with a serious-minded yet sodden banquet. A promising or ascendant politician would give a speech, followed by a dangerously long set of toasts (both prewritten and "volunteered" from the floor) expressing pointed political sentiments. During the nineteenth century, other, more familiar, types of campaign events would come into fashion, such as conventions, rallies, debates, speaking tours, and torchlight parades. The southern political barbecue evolved from an occasional display of noblesse oblige on the part of a local bigwig into a commercialized "barbecue circuit," staged by tavernkeepers and pork purveyors and open to all candidates willing to pay the organizers.[19]

Yet, in the nineteenth century, even live events depended on newspapers (along with other forms of print) to have any significant political impact. Newspapers helped generate an audience before an event and broadcast news of it afterwards. Southern political barbecues were heavily advertised in the newspapers, and in Maryland, where political speeches and debates became popular earlier than elsewhere, newspapers featured extensive postmortem coverage of the events. In one case, the Baltimore *Whig* carried almost daily accounts of U.S. Attorney General William Pinkney's speaking tour of rural Maryland on the eve of the 1813 state elections. This became a series of debates when local Federalist congressional candidate John Hanson Thomas decided to tag along. Under the heading of "ELECTIONEERING CAMPAIGN," the *Whig* hyperbolized extensively on the eloquence of Pinkney's rhetoric, the cogency of his arguments, and the enthusiasm of the crowds. At Frederick, it was explained, the Federalists "never received a more severe and a more genteel political drubbing in their lives. They withered under it." But if that performance was great, "At Middletown, Mr. Pinkney . . . transcended himself." He spoke for three hours, but "the audience stood as if they were riveted to the ground," tears in many eyes, as they witnessed "such a display of powers as are unparalleled in the annals of oratory." The most significant aspect of Pinkney's tour for our purposes was that it seems to have been most effective in Baltimore, where people only read about it in the newspapers. The Republicans lost the 1813 elections in the rural county where the speeches took place, but won Baltimore by a landslide.[20]

Since public events like the Pinkney-Thomas debates could be attended only by a minority of the population of one small region at any given time, even an extremely well-attended event could have few wide-reaching or lasting political effects—it could not engender wide concert of opinion or action—unless an account was printed in a newspaper. Moreover, debates and rallies and parades could only be held at intervals, and campaigns themselves were intermittent. Add the vast extent of the nation and even of some individual states and congressional districts, and we can see that party activists and voters needed "some means of talking every day without seeing one another and of acting together without meeting," especially in the critical periods between campaigns, when key policy decisions were made and party ideologies and strategies were shaped and calibrated.[21]

In early America, many live political events seem to have been held almost entirely so they could be reported in the newspapers. During the pre-Revolutionary crisis, town-meeting resolutions meant little unless they were disseminated broadly, and in any case, the intended audience was not the local community but colonists and British officials in other towns. (The same applies to many of the colonial-era legislative resolutions.) Leaders everywhere scanned the papers to learn the state of public opinion elsewhere.

During the early national period, many physical political events (such as party meetings and banquets) were held mostly to provide an occasion for printing a statement that some local politician had written in advance. Like town-meeting resolutions, banquet toasts were carefully crafted to express the particular political views of the gathering, including their opinions on current political controversies and candidates. Lists of toasts often included such detail and shadings that they functioned almost as platforms, long before official party platforms were invented. Toasts were intended for public consumption in the newspapers. Individual neighborhoods, towns, and party factions held and drew up reports of their separate banquets, and as these appeared in the newspapers, sometimes for days and weeks after a major occasion, readers used them to assess the political scene and the state of public opinion.[22] Toasts were used this way quite self-consciously, as when the Trenton *True American* printed three columns of banquet reports from various locations in New Jersey, Pennsylvania, Virginia, Georgia, and Vermont under the heading "Public Sentiment."[23] Whom or what a set of toasts failed to mention could be as significant as what they actually said. Maneuvering to get Pennsylvania governor Simon Snyder placed on the 1816 Republican presidential ticket, the Philadelphia editor and political chieftain John Binns blasted Republican state legislators for leaving the governor out of their toasts at a banquet: "He is as much forgotten as if he were in [Kamchatka] or fifty fathom underground. This will wound [his cause] deeply . . . his enemies . . . will adduce it as evidence" that the governor was unpopular even in his home state.[24]

Newspapers made one of their most important contributions to party development by linking various sectors of the polity. The most obvious link that newspapers could make was the one between the parties and the voters, who through this medium could be addressed by the hundreds or thousands, in a manner uniquely suited to a widely dispersed and increasingly individualistic society. "A newspaper is an advisor that need not be sought out," Tocqueville theorized, "but comes of its own accord and talks to you briefly about the commonweal without distracting you from your private affairs."[25]

Obviously, such linkages had their limits. Newspapers could reach only literate citizens, who were most likely to be white and male. Many working families probably could not afford a yearly subscription to a newspaper in any case, and the typical partisan journal of the early national period was usually available only by subscription. Technical and market limitations kept the circulation of individual newspapers very small, from a few hundred to a few thousand for the most successful urban papers. Yet there were many channels through which the partisan press could breach these limits and reach a relatively broad sector of the population. Newspapers were kept on hand in many public gathering places, especially taverns, coffeehouses, and hotels, where they were often read aloud or in groups. In late eighteenth-century England, where similar customs were practiced, one newspaper claimed a readership seven to twenty times its nominal circulation based on sales to public establishments. Neighbors often shared newspapers with each other, or even subscribed jointly. Information and ideas contained in newspapers moved by word of mouth, and passed hand to hand in clippings and letters. In a time when most people were still conducting most of their daily affairs through face-to-face exchanges, even a few newspaper subscribers were enough to spread the word to entire neighborhoods. By the 1830s campaigners sometimes aided the diffusion of their message by opening party reading rooms, where newspapers and other literature could be perused free of charge. At any rate, though the lack of extant circulation records prevents us from knowing exactly how far early newspapers penetrated into the American population, overwhelming anecdotal evidence suggests very deeply indeed.[26]

Foreign travelers were universally agog at the diffusion of newspapers. Passing through the backwoods of Ohio in 1831, the Transylvanian bureaucrat and reformer Alexander Bölöni Farkas marveled as the stagecoach driver hurled out settlers' newspapers right and left as they passed remote cabins along the road, through a whole day's travel. "No matter how poor a settler may be, nor how far in the wilderness he may be from the civilized world," Farkas concluded, "he will read a newspaper."[27]

Newspapers also created political linkages among different regions of the country and levels of government. They allowed parties and politicians to mediate the disjunctions among the national, state, and local political communities, to make national debates and candidates resonate with local concerns and interests. This was an especially critical task in the first third of the century, when national parties were struggling to sink roots, and state and local politics often generated more interest and excitement among the voters than national contests did.[28]

Such geographic linkage was facilitated by heavily subsidized postal rates for newspapers (including the privilege of exchanging newspapers between publishers for free). The early Congresses established these policies (many of which were based on preexisting customs) in the hope that extensive newspaper circulation would help maintain public support for the new government. But the newspaper subsidies quite inadvertently fostered the development of first an opposition movement and then an opposition political party of national scope.[29]

Another form of subsidy related to newspaper content: a newspaper publisher's ability to reprint from other periodicals without limitation or payment of any kind. There were no copyright fees, required permissions, or even well-established canons of giving credit, for the use of previously published material in newspapers. Small-town newspapers typically filled most of their nonadvertising space with freely reprinted matter from their complimentary "exchange papers." While there might be some cryptic reference to the newspaper where an item was found, often pieces were reprinted with no attribution at all. This was resented by the more ambitious editors who wrote their own material. News items were "common property," wrote a New Jersey editor, but to "transplant original matter . . . unacknowledged, is neither honest nor honorable; . . . *pillaging a paper* is equal to *picking a pocket.*"[30] However, early American newspapers relied far too heavily on reprints for the practice to be seriously regulated or curtailed, and in the heat of a political controversy or campaign, correct attribution of a newspaper item was obviously less important than the rapid spread of the ideas or information it contained. This latter cause was actually aided by the lax practices, and so they remained the norm.

At any rate, from the 1790s on, no politician dreamed of mounting a campaign, launching a new movement, or winning over a new geographic area without a newspaper. As we will see in the pages below, partisan newspapers appeared early in the Jefferson-Hamilton dispute that produced the first parties, long before those parties took any organized form, and newspapers retained their precedence in the party system for decades afterward. Through most of the nineteenth century, party factions battled furiously to control key newspapers. When political alliances fell apart, the sure sequel was the founding of a new newspaper. One of the more famous examples occurred when President Andrew Jackson broke with Vice President John C. Calhoun in the early 1830s. The split resulted in the establishment of Francis Preston Blair's *Washington Globe* to supplant the former administration paper, Duff Green's pro-Calhoun *United States Telegraph.*[31] Another instance occurred early in the Van Buren administration, when conservative Democrats bolted the party over the independent treasury issue. One of the first manifestations of the split was the founding of a new Washington newspaper, the *Madisonian,* to compete with Blair's *Globe.*[32]

New political groupings founded or secured control of newspapers before they did almost anything else, and in many cases a newspaper originated a movement nearly on its own. Antimasonry was forged into a political party largely through the work of printer-editor Thurlow Weed and his three successive newspapers, the *Rochester Telegraph,* the Rochester *Anti-Masonic Enquirer,* and the *Albany Evening Journal.*[33] The pattern extended beyond party politics into the world of reform movements such as abolitionism. Though many American abolitionists virulently abhorred party politics, they were remarkably similar to the party politicians in their reliance on newspapers. The various permutations of the abolitionist movement were closely linked to particular publications, and many of its leading figures were essentially newspaper editors by profession.

For instance, the emergence of immediate abolitionism among whites is usually dated to the founding of William Lloyd Garrison's *The Liberator* in 1831. Garrison was a practical printer by trade, who had previously edited a National Republican newspaper in Vermont and then a Baltimore abolitionist paper called *Genius of Universal Emancipation*, the centerpiece of Benjamin Lundy's gradual abolition movement. When Garrison converted to more radical views, he resigned from the *Genius* and launched a new journal called *The Liberator*. As often happened in party politics, journalism came before more conventional forms of organization: the appearance of *The Liberator* preceded the founding of Garrison's New England Anti-Slavery Society by almost a year. When black abolitionists grew weary of whites' domination of the movement, they tried to establish a national newspaper of their own, finally achieving long-term success with Frederick Douglass's *North Star* in 1847.[34]

UNEVEN POLITICAL DEVELOPMENT AND
THE ORIGINS OF THE NEWSPAPER ROLE

The prominent role of newspapers was an artifact of the American political system's uneven pattern of development. A fully functioning mass party system came into being long before the parties themselves became fully institutionalized. Excepting the period after the War of 1812, when national party competition temporarily collapsed, mass participation and partisanship in national elections climbed steadily after 1800. By the late 1830s, the so-called "second party system" had coalesced, with Whigs and Democrats competing in almost every locality and at every level of government.[35] Yet the Jacksonian-era parties were usually not legally recognized by government and possessed few permanent institutional structures, to say nothing of the office buildings and permanent staffs that major political parties possess today. The antebellum parties were organized, but they were not formal organizations in the sense that the U.S. government and the Bank of the United States and the American Fur Company were. Wilson Carey McWilliams has suggested that the nineteenth-century parties are best thought of as "civic associations," decentralized networks of allegiances and ideological congruences, causes in the truest sense.[36]

The civic association thesis does not deny the massive expansion and elaboration of the formal party organizations that occurred during the antebellum period, but it does point out the many limitations and gaps in these formal organizations. Party conventions became common at all levels in the Jacksonian period, and central committees were often appointed, but before the Civil War these bodies were evanescent. Once candidates had been nominated or campaign arrangements had been made, conventions and committees went dormant until it was time to arrange the next convention. Conventions and ad hoc campaign committees provided the party organizations with no continuing institutional presence and no ability to shape the party's responses toward new issues and ongoing events. Politically oriented clubs such as New York's Tammany Society could carry a party from election to election, but Tammany was unique. No other political club or committee in the country possessed anything approaching Tammany's long-term strength and stability, to say nothing of the palpable institutional authority suggested by the widespread practice of calling the organization "Tammany Hall," the name of the building that housed it.[37] During most of the period before the Civil War, the state and national parties typically had nothing similar: no symbolic buildings, no permanent party chairs, no party offices, no employees or spokesmen or means of communication (other than private letters) that belonged to the party organization itself. The first permanent national party committee was created by the Democrats in 1848, and the new Republican party followed suit in 1856, but even these were weak, existing "less to direct or coordinate matters than to do whatever they could to help."[38]

Newspapers filled many of the gaps left by the party system's uneven development, providing a fabric that held the parties together between elections and conventions, connected voters and activists to the larger party, and linked the different political levels and geographic regions of the country. Party newspapers thus contributed in fundamental ways to the very existence of the parties and to the creation of a sense of membership, identity, and common cause among political activists and voters. Tocqueville argued that because democratic political associations measured their success in numbers and because such large numbers of private, working citizens could never meet together, political associations could be formed only in newspapers: "Newspapers make associations, and associations make newspapers." The two were coterminous with each other.[39]

Benedict Anderson has assigned newspapers a prominent role in the formation of national identities, and they performed a similar function for the parties. According to Anderson, newspapers helped forge an "imagined community," a fundamental sense of relationship among people unknown and unconnected to each other personally. A newspaper did this by offering up a set of images or reference points that all its readers could imaginatively possess in common, forming the basis for a sense of belonging to whatever community the journal defined itself as serving.[40] Party newspapers went further, not only providing readers with a common set of candidates and electoral victories, but also providing them with a common rhetoric and common ideas. There were no "card-carrying" party members or "registered voters" in eighteenth- or nineteenth-century America, but a subscription to a party newspaper, or regular readership of one in a tavern or reading room, substituted for these more formal means of belonging. The party newspaper furnished a corporeal link to the party that could be obtained in few other ways.

This was as true for candidates as it was for voters. Since few authoritative or officially sanctioned party organizations existed (and no official ballots), a candidate's partisan identity was defined entirely by privately printed matter such as newspapers and tickets that were printed in newspaper offices. Among the local party newspaper's most important jobs were clarifying party labels and their meanings, and authenticating candidates on that basis. This was especially true before the late 1830s, when party identities hardened and party organizations became more elaborate. Before then (and afterwards, in periods such as the 1850s or 1890s when parties were in flux), labels could be fluid and nominations of uncertain provenance. In many cases, being the candidate of a particular party consisted only in making a convincing claim to being the candidate, and members of new or dying parties, or apostate factions, often had incentives to misrepresent themselves.

Thus in September 1813, the Democratic-Republican Baltimore *Whig* informed its readers that a Mr. Ridgely, running for the House of Delegates from Anne Arundel County as a Republican, was really a Federalist. The editors then proceeded to set down conditions for being considered a Republican. Among other things, a candidate should abjure "federalism of the Boston stamp" and pledge not to cooperate with "infuriated factionists," of which they appended a list. "Otherwise, he will get no republican votes," they continued, and then proceeded to identify the real Republican candidates in Anne Arundel and inserted a previously published ticket.[41]

Party newspapers embodied the parties in a quite literal sense. Since there usually was no official party meeting venue, the party newspaper office frequently served as an unofficial clubhouse for local party activists, a place where they could meet informally, discuss the day's events, and plan strategy. During Jefferson's administration, the local Democratic Republican leaders in Hudson, New York, liked to sit around the stove and talk politics on the bottom floor of the Hudson *Bee's* building. Little had changed thirty years later. When Democrats in Detroit opened the "Committee Room" in 1833, it was located in a brick building across the street from the post office, one floor below the offices of the *Democratic Free Press*. In antebellum Alabama, the state party committees often met in Montgomery newspaper offices to draft their convention plans. When patronage seekers arrived in Washington after Andrew Jackson's victory in 1828, they repaired quickly to the offices of the *United States Telegraph*.[42]

NEWSPAPER EDITORS IN NINETEENTH-CENTURY POLITICS

The central role of newspapers in nineteenth-century politics made newspaper editors the most pivotal and characteristic political figures of the era, if not necessarily the most respected or best remembered today. As with newspapers more generally, historians have been maddeningly casual on the role of newspaper editors, noting their importance without devoting much serious attention to the question.[43] For instance, M. J. Heale assigned editors "a particularly crucial role in the new [Jackson-era] system of party politics" but devoted only a few sentences to explaining it.[44] Even more strikingly, Richard P. McCormick included five newspaper editors among a list of nine politicians named as exemplars of the type to which "the new [second] party system owed its existence" but made little of that fact.[45]

Party newspaper editors occupied the nodal points of the political system. While newspapers themselves provided the medium for the linkages described above, it was the editors who controlled them, using their newspapers to direct the affairs of the party and coordinate its message. The journalism historian Gerald J. Baldasty has argued that on "the national, state, and local levels, editors frequently directed—either alone or with others—their party's day-to-day operations."[46]

Each editor was his party's principal spokesman, supplier of ideology, and enforcer of discipline in the area and political level he served. In a very real sense, he was the party's face and voice. "*The cause* is generally *identified with the Editor,"* wrote a New Jersey Democratic Republican in 1812, concerned that his local editor had become corrupt and might take the party with him. The editor and his newspaper defined the party line on issues as they arose and maintained it between party conventions and caucuses. He defended his party's candidates and officeholders and attacked its opponents. His bitter rhetoric whipped recalcitrant party members into line and punished apostates by reading them out of the party. Editors of national administration (or congressional opposition) papers such as the *Washington Globe* and *National Intelligencer* performed these functions at the federal level. They had their counterparts in every major city and town, every state capital, and most county seats.[47]

Editors also acted in more concrete areas than political ideology and rhetoric. Sometimes in their newspapers, but more often privately, they were a main channel of access between government officials and the citizens they served. In an era when elected representatives maintained no "district offices," constituents and supporters back home often turned to the local editor when they needed aid from the government or party or access to political figures higher up the chain.

In the course of carrying out their myriad duties, editors had the potential to become extremely powerful men. Some have even been characterized as party "bosses," who dictated party nominations, patronage, and policies. Often the decisions of party conventions and meetings seemed only to ratify the suggestions the editors had already made in their papers, and the editors were likely to be among the leading spirits at official party meetings in any case. An early New Jersey editor was said to have to achieved this kind of power using his power as definer of party ideology and membership; he had beaten down his rivals by "stigmatizing . . . with Federalism or apostacy . . . every Republican . . . suspected of the least hostility to his political projects."[48] (Of course, opponents sometimes exaggerated the power of an editor in order to discredit him.) Under these circumstances, editors were naturally courted by other politicians for their support, with the result that editors frequently got the chance to become officeholders in their own right. These opportunities more often arose from the political debts an editor was owed by his political colleagues than from his personal popularity with the voters, but some editors acquired personal followings as well.

Conversely, it was often those editors who largely refrained from office seeking such as the New York Whig and Republican warhorse Thurlow Weed, who became the most powerful of all. Officeholding politicians came and went, but a strong and skillful editor could command the party continuously for decades. "He was more deferred to than the Whig Governors," one of Weed's obituaries asserted. "They remained in Albany for two or four years, as he might desire, but Mr. Weed remained there always."[49] A radically different figure with a similar role was Thomas Ritchie, for decades both editor of the Richmond *Enquirer* and leader of Virginia's Republicans and then Democrats. Ritchie ostentatiously refused to run for or hold any office other than state printer, the income from which office provided his primary financial support. When Martin Van Buren made his famous proposal for the alliance of "planters of the South" and "plain Republicans of the North" that became the Democratic party, Ritchie was the man he wrote to, as head of one wing of the party to the other.[50]

A deeper reason for the political success of editors like Weed and Ritchie is that newspaper editors were the most truly professional politicians in the party system. Political communication and party management were an editor's job in a sense that was not true for most other antebellum politicians. Meeting Max Weber's definition of a professional politician, editors lived both "for" and "off of" partisan political work.[51] Like many elected officials, they lived "for" politics in that they found their primary vocations and most intense occupational interests there. However, in contrast to most elected officials, in an age when legislative sessions were short and official pay was designed to meet only the expenses of serving, editors also lived "off of" politics; they actually earned their livings from political work. Party editors were full-time, year-round politicians, running businesses devoted to politics.

Though the parties themselves usually did not sponsor or subsidize newspapers directly—the parties' lack of institutionalization made this impossible at most times in most places—the editors' major sources of income were political: subscriptions and advertisements bought by political supporters, allies, and supplicants, along with job-printing contracts and often appointive offices secured by party colleagues in government. (Even many editors who eschewed running for Congress or the legislature avidly sought positions in the custom houses and post offices.) Editors sometimes established their papers or saved them from bankruptcy with loans from wealthy local supporters, and there were some cases in which such benefactors actually owned the paper themselves and paid the editor a salary. While only a few editors made lavish incomes and many could not even manage adequate ones, they were enabled (and motivated by their personal financial interests) to concentrate their time and energy on electoral politics in a way that few others could. Thus editors came to manage day-to-day party affairs almost by default.

Political editors were professional politicians in another sense, as well. Longtime editors were experts in a specialized field, who could apply their knowledge to various political cases and problems. Some quite literally became hired pens, taking on a series of journalistic assignments, often in new localities, as the opportunities arose. Hence some leading Philadelphia Republicans brought in John Norvell, to that point the editor of two newspapers in Baltimore and one in Lexington, Kentucky, to run their floundering *Franklin Gazette* in 1819. They arranged for Norvell to buy their organ specifically because of his thirteen years' experience in the business.[52] Given that most of the early editors (including Norvell) were trained as printers, we might also think of them as political artisans or mechanics, masters of the "art and mystery" of a particular craft, who supplied their unique services to the community.

By the 1830s the status of editors as professional political operatives had become so settled that some of them began to think in terms of full, literal professionalism. Calls were issued for editorial training and standards of conduct such as lawyers, physicians, and military officers had or were developing. The *Hartford Times,* a leading regional Jacksonian paper edited by Gideon Welles (who would go on to be Abraham Lincoln's navy secretary), urged editors to behave with more professionalism, respecting their calling as a whole and limiting their personal attacks on each other:

> Why then should a class of the community [party editors], whose station and employment necessarily render them highly influential, and whose abilities, attainments, and virtues entitle them to general esteem, delight to disparage and vilify their own members? In most of the professions there is . . . an *esprit du corps,* which prompts each individual to advance the interests, and "stand up" for the respectability of the whole body; . . . We know that the duties of a political editor are of a somewhat warlike nature; that he is called frequently to attack the principles of his antagonists and sometimes to animadvert on the private character of candidates for office; and in turn he is expected valiantly to defend his party from the assaults of their enemies. But there is nothing in all this to justify the course we are condemning. The honorable examples furnished by the military and legal professions, plainly show that the most active and determined professional contests are entirely consistent with perfect personal courtesy.[53]

United States Telegraph editor Duff Green, chief promoter of John C. Calhoun's national ambitions, actually took concrete action toward the professionalization of partisan editing. Green deplored the fact that too many editors considered "themselves as *mere* printers," and hoped to upgrade the status and remuneration of editors to the point that it could attract "the first talents of the country." In 1834 he founded the Washington Institute, a school in which apprentice printers could study spelling, grammar, history, and philosophy, among other elevating subjects, while learning their trade by putting out Green's newspaper. The Washington printers' union, the Columbia Typographical Society, denounced the institute as a bid for cheap labor, and Green had to close his school of partisan journalism after only a year. Most partisan editors were perfectly comfortable with, or even relished, their self-taught political professionalism.[54]

Looking back on the underinstitutionalized party systems of the nineteenth century, Max Weber conceptualized well the former role of party newspapers and their editors in his essay, "Politics as a Vocation." Without strong political clubs or elaborate, permanent, formal party organizations, Weber wrote, the "management of politics in normal times lies in the hands of the few people constantly interested in it." Before the American Civil War, those few people were usually party newspapermen. "Only the journalist is a paid professional politician; only the management of a newspaper is a continuous political organization." Weber portrayed this state of affairs as a stage along the road to full party development.[55]

Leaving aside the more questionable notion that party systems have a "natural" course of development, the period from the late eighteenth to the late nineteenth century does seem to have formed a distinct epoch in American political history, a period in which the party system was newspaper based. Partisan newspapers and loosely organized parties (aided by government subsidies) combined to create a hitherto unrecognized institution, the newspaper-based party, which dominated the American political scene in the antebellum years, remained strong in the late nineteenth century, and did not disappear completely until the twentieth century. This manner of conducting party politics lingered especially in less-developed areas: small cities and towns, the South, the rural Midwest.[56]

The rest of this study describes how and why this new institution, which I will usually refer to simply as "newspaper politics," took shape between the 1760s and the 1830s, while also considering the larger implications of its rise. One of the most important themes to be followed is the role of newspaper politics and newspaper editors in democratizing American political life.

Democratization is a complex topic that recent scholars have been surprisingly averse to exploring.[57] The older story of democratization, holding that the elections of 1800 and 1828 heralded the rise of Jeffersonian Democracy and then Jacksonian Democracy, finally ushering in a mid-nineteenth-century Age of the Common Man, became untenable many years ago. As numerous recent scholars have argued, there were simply too many exceptions to the notions of democracy that the Jeffersonians and Jacksonians promoted to accept their claims at face value. Enacting democracy and equality for white men almost seems to have required reducing the rights and status of women and, especially, people of color.[58] Even the idea that universal white male suffrage and high voter turnouts amounted to truly "participatory democracy" for white men has come under attack.[59]

The recent criticisms follow decades of debunking aimed at the idea of Jacksonian Democracy or any real "rise of the common man." While acknowledging the expansion of the suffrage and the increase in voter participation, scholars derided the notion that any meaningful democratization of political leadership occurred in this period. According to Richard Hofstadter, Lee Benson, Edward Pessen, and many others, no major party in the early republic drew its leaders from the ranks of the common man, least of all the Jacksonian Democrats, nor did the common man's interests or welfare figure into their real agendas. The Jacksonians' populist rhetoric was merely cynical window dressing for personal enrichment or political preferment, flattery of the common man issuing from the mouths of men who were usually much more than common themselves. Sean Wilentz well captures both the basic thesis and vitriolic tone of what he calls "the great revision of Jacksonian politics": "On close examination, the leading Jacksonians were shown to be not champions of deprived workers and small farmers, but cold-blooded political entrepreneurs, often men of great wealth or men eager to become wealthy, whose main purpose was to get power and keep it."[60]

Tracing the rise of newspaper politics and the struggles of partisan newspaper editors suggests the need to question at least part of this now largely accepted interpretation. Tempering the revisionist thesis just slightly, Wilentz characterizes the major change in political leadership between the Revolution and the Jacksonian era as *"embourgeoisement"* rather than democratization. "Parties and local offices remained in the hands of the wealthy," he writes, but also "included far more men of recent wealth and standing." This observation has merit, but it fits the editors only partially and unduly minimizes the significance of the change. Party leadership and local offices did not become available to the poorest and humblest citizens, but they also did not "remain in the hands of the wealthy." Socially, newspaper editors tended to fall somewhere in between these categories, and often much closer to the humbler end of the spectrum. Categorizing them simply as "wealthy" stretches the term beyond usefulness. Measuring their status by mere wealth misses the vulgar, disreputable social identity that plainly clung even to many financially successful editor-politicians, and misreads the relationship between their wealth and their political position. Partisan editors were professional politicians: they were not the *nouveaux riches* being admitted to political leadership by an older elite, but newly minted political leaders who sometimes used their power to become newly wealthy, or at least comfortable. At the same time, financially successful partisan editors were clearly a minority of the breed before the 1830s (and quite likely continued to be so after that), while even editors who did make some money often found prosperity only a temporary or occasional condition.[61]

Some significant, if rather compartmentalized, democratization did occur in American political life before the Civil War, and one form it came in was the newspaper editors' emergence as major leaders and officeholders. Much of the narrative below follows the process by which the editors entered politics and helped transform the political system as they fought to rise, or simply survive, in it.

The rise of partisan newspaper editors constitutes one of the earliest, most important, and most concrete examples of what Ronald Formisano has termed "the much heralded replacement of traditional notables by a 'new class' of professional politicians."[62] The printer-editors of the 1790s and after truly were a "new class" in politics. One historian includes newspaper editors among the "educated professionals" in political life, but as will be documented below, this was not usually true north and west of Maryland.[63] While well-educated gentlemen did indeed come to dominate southern political journalism, in the North and West most editors came from considerably less-distinguished backgrounds. In the early part of the period, especially, most of them were recruited from the printing trade. Though their literacy and role in publication gave them more prestige than many tradesmen, printers were nonetheless artisans, craftsmen who made their living with their hands and thus lacked one of the fundamental attributes of gentility.

These partisan editors were only recent graduates (at best) from manual to intellectual labor. As such, they held a liminal, indeter-minate status. Their stratum of early American society consisted of those predisposed to intellectual pursuits but unblessed with whatever it might have taken (social distinctions, financial wherewithal, educational credentials, unusually great talents, or luck) to enter the ranks of the great. They moved among the clerks, shopkeepers, small-time professionals, and government workers of the republic, qualifying neither as "gentry" nor as "the lower sort." Even editors of undisputed gentility could not escape close association, either in their working lives or the public mind, with journeymen, apprentices, grime, clutter, and other déclassé elements that were part and parcel of printing office life. To paraphrase Stuart Blumin (writing of early "white-collar" workers more generally), the line of division in society tended to be drawn above rather than below them.[64]

By their very presence, strong printer-editors helped democratize political life. While many—perhaps most—of the printer-editors were upwardly mobile, they identified (or were identified by others) with an artisanal occupation that was not traditionally accorded a share in political leadership. Living and working among artisans, in an atmosphere suffused with the political culture of the street and the tavern, uneducated or self-educated, eking out a meager living or saddled with huge debts, it was difficult to feel like a member of any kind of social elite. As sometimes the sole public spokesmen for the contending parties, editors took the brunt of the persecution, ostracism, and violent harassment that frequently resulted from the early party battles.

Often feeling ill-used themselves, editors easily adopted a populistic tone and sometimes displayed a bitter streak of class resentment. As Joyce Appleby has argued, this was often more rooted in a resentment of invidious social categories imposed by others than in real class consciousness.[65] Yet Republican *printer*-editors especially could not be blind to the hierarchies and inequalities that pervaded their society. They worked, out of both conviction and self-interest, toward a political system and culture that respected, included, and heeded people like themselves.

Thus newspaper editors became the agents and promoters of a new and less-deferential brand of politics. Brushing aside the elaborate classical republican code that gentleman politicians of the era tried to follow, which condemned parties and eschewed political competition and self-promotion, editors tended to favor blunt rhetoric and direct methods. They aggressively appealed for popular support, using whatever weapons they thought might work.[66]

Over time, this more democratic political style involved the promotion of substantive democratic reforms. As will be shown below, the printer-editors of the late 1790s were instrumental in defeating Federalist efforts to uphold their restrictive reading of First Amendment protections on political expression and, in so doing, to suppress the growth of an active, organized opposition to the national administration. This was a battle won on the plane of newspaper politics rather than that of legal theory (although the latter has been much more heavily studied): printers simply asserted their rights, refused to back down, and successfully campaigned to sweep their oppressors from office. What is more, the failure of the Sedition Act did more to establish newspaper politics, and the competitive political culture of which it was part, than it did to change legal doctrine. The "new libertarianism" was expressed by a few Republican lawyers between 1798 and 1800, but then abandoned by most Republican leaders once they were in power.[67]

After 1800 partisan newspaper editors continued to practice and vindicate the popular, competitive politics they employed so effectively against John Adams. Some editors became leaders in state movements to reform relatively undemocratic institutions such as the legal system by subjecting them to the control (and remodeling them according to the values) of popular majorities. Somewhat later, other editors helped lead movements to expand the franchise to all or nearly all white men.

With all of these activities and more, partisan newspaper editors were also helping to create the emerging party system. If the early parties, the Republicans and Federalists, never quite generated the level of organization and ballyhoo found in mid-nineteenth-century election campaigns, the editors who were their chief spokesmen made strong demands for party loyalty, seeking and most of the time receiving broad popular support for their causes.[68] Political editors valued principled partisanship and party organization much more highly than did the statesmen whose careers they advanced. After the War of 1812, newspapermen were in the vanguard of those who sought to rejuvenate party competition in the United States, arguing that parties were not a temporary expedient or a

necessary evil, but a positive good. Most of these editors were unconnected to Martin Van Buren's New York Bucktails, who have been somewhat
misleadingly portrayed as nearly the sole inventors of modern American
party politics.[69]

Party-building and party-defending editors thus laid critical groundwork for the emergence of the new "mass" party system or "party period"
that came to fruition in the late 1830s. By statistical measures, this system
was highly participatory, and formally it was extremely democratic. However, it was also largely run by newspaper editors and other political professionals, supported now by extensive and relatively uncontested access to
government jobs, politically awarded contracts, and other forms of political income. At that point, the democratization that partisan editors
helped spearhead began to run afoul of its own success. Common men
roamed the halls of power, and they sometimes acted commonly.

Important as they are, democratization and the other themes treated
below should be considered subsidiary to the larger points of this book,
which can be put simply as the existence and great significance of newspaper-based party politics in the history of the United States. Newspapers
and their editors need to occupy a place in accounts of American political
development as central as the role they actually played in nineteenth-century political parties.

The following chapters are structured as an analytical narrative, in
hopes of engaging both scholars and general readers alike. Amid an ongoing account of newspaper politics as an aggregate phenomenon, I have
tried to provide some sense of early American politics as a lived experience, by focusing rather extensively on the careers and perspectives of individual newspaper politicians. I try to impart some sense of the view
from inside the new political world, showing the impulses that drove
some people to work in and value it, even if others did not.

After sketching the colonial antecedents of these editors in the printing
trade, I trace the changing role of printers and other newspaper editors in
politics from the Revolution to the 1820s, at the beginning of the political
upheaval that created two new political parties and saw editors such as
Francis P. Blair, Thurlow Weed, and Thomas Ritchie become their parties' most strategically placed and influential men.

Printers first became political professionals more or less against their
will during the 1790s, as the printing trade's traditionally neutral approach

became increasingly unsustainable in the overheated and polarized political atmosphere. The party struggle leading up to the election of 1800 transformed the printers' role and their conception of it, as they became indispensable public spokesmen for the new parties and surrogate campaigners for gentleman candidates who needed to avoid public displays of partisanship. After 1798 printers and other young men of similar status thronged into the editorial ranks for the chance (unprecedented for men of their class) to become important actors in the public sphere. These young editors saw political editing as an opportunity to make a living by doing good, to be defenders of the republic by occupation.

The editors' work in the election campaign of 1800 ensconced newspapers as the central institutions of the nineteenth-century American political system, but despite the new prominence of editors, it would be many years before party leaders would be willing to acknowledge fully their contribution in the form of appointments to office or personal respect. During the first decades of the new century, editors worked to fashion a newspaper-based political system that could not help but acknowledge and include them to some degree. Later, some of these early editors, along with many newcomers, formed a party-oriented newspaper network that would become the engine of Andrew Jackson's rise to the presidency. In Jackson's time, what Theodore Roosevelt called the "millennium of the minnows" would be at hand.[70]

2

The Printing Trade in
Early American Politics

◈

The origins of the political newspaper business were in the colonial printing trade. It is only from the vantage point of the colonial- and Revolutionary-period printers that we can appreciate the magnitude of the changes involved in the rise of newspaper politics. On the eve of the Revolution, printers occupied a unique and contradictory niche in American society. While the service they provided was indispensable to the political and intellectual life of their communities, they were still relegated with other artisans and laborers to a marginal role in the conduct of public affairs.

ARTISANS WITH BOOKISH INCLINATIONS:
THE COLONIAL PRINTERS

On the one hand, printers were the intellectual elite of the early American working class.[1] They needed to be literate, unlike most other artisans and laborers, and they often had the chance to edit and write their own publications. Many were brainy working-class boys such as Benjamin Franklin, who was made a printer rather than a soapmaker like his father for the greater intellectual opportunities printing seemed to afford. "From a Child I was fond of Reading, and all the little money that came into my Hands was ever laid out in Books," Franklin wrote in his autobiography. "This Bookish Inclination at length determin'd my father to make me a Printer." Printing provided many a young workingman with a substitute for the advanced education that only a tiny minority of early Americans could obtain. Printers also enjoyed a more prominent role in their communities than most artisans. In a new or growing small town, a printer's very presence could lead to local acclaim, because the possession of a press (especially one that published a newspaper) was considered an essential prerequisite to a town becoming a significant place. At the same time, a printer's daily business brought him into contact with the local ruling, thinking, and writing classes: the government officials, political leaders, lawyers, and clergymen who were most likely to produce and consume printed matter.[2]

On the other hand, greater visibility rarely translated into influence. The literary training that could be acquired in a print shop conferred neither the systematic classical learning nor the polished manners that were the mark of an eighteenth-century gentleman. Though printing had its cerebral and prestigious aspects, it was still a dirty, smelly, physically demanding job. One of the first chores that would be delegated to a young apprentice printer was preparing the sheepskin balls used to ink the type. The skins were soaked in urine, stamped on daily for added softness, and finally wrung out by hand. The work got harder from there, and only a little more pleasant. Supplies of ink were often scarce in America, so printers frequently had to make it on site, by boiling lampblack (soot) in varnish (linseed oil and rosin). If the printing-office staff survived the noxious fumes and fire hazards of making ink, their persons and equipment nevertheless spent much of the workday covered in the stuff.

Then there was the printing process itself. The production of a typical four-page early American newspaper began with as many as sixteen hours setting type, which meant standing at the "case" and reading copy while one hand selected tiny bits of metal and the other placed them with a "composing stick." Next the finished lines of type were locked by the foreman into heavy metal forms that had to be muscled over to the press. Even if the shop used one of the improved Ramage models that became popular after 1800, the typical early American printing press was a human-powered, predominantly wooden contraption that had only been refined, not essentially changed, since Gutenberg's converted winepress.

To print a newspaper, each side of each sheet of each copy had to be pressed by hand, a complex task that involved (among many other procedures) wetting the paper, "beating" the type with ink-soaked balls, and repeatedly pulling the heavy crank that lowered the platen and made the impression. Two experienced workers lifting, beating, and pulling in rhythm, like parts of the machine, could print 240 sheets, or one "token," an hour at their best. Later, the job would have to be done over again for the other side of the sheets, and still later each sheet would have to be folded into newspaper form. Thus even a rural weekly, with a barely adequate circulation of only 500 or 600, required a day and most of a night of unremitting labor to produce. Publishing a more ambitious or successful journal was commensurately harder on the staff. An apprentice for the Boston *Independent Chronicle* remembered how arduous his work became when the paper went semiweekly, meaning that the boys in the shop slept little at least two nights a week.[3]

Regardless of their relatively high status vis-à-vis other artisans, colonial printers could not escape their identity as men who worked with their hands, in a society that regarded manual labor as the province of those too dull, weak, or lowly to escape it. Status was accorded as it had been throughout human history—in inverse proportion to the amount of manual labor a person had to do to survive.[4] According to Stephen Botein, one of the printing trade's most perceptive historians, "printers had to face the hard, discouraging fact that in the eyes of their neighbors they were by training mechanics, without full legitimacy as men of independent intellect and creed." As an artisan, "a colonial printer was not generally expected to possess a mind of his own . . . this expectation was likely to undercut whatever efforts he made to influence his neighbors."[5]

Class was as much a matter of appearance, demeanor, and personal habits as it was of education and occupation, but here printers tended to do even worse. Too many years of pulling on a hand press often created physical deformities: an elongated right arm, a limping, shambling gait, severe back injuries, or all of the above. Few longtime printers could expect to cut dashing figures on the hustings or in the drawing room, even if they had left ink and type years behind them. A yet more serious problem for printers was alcoholism. Though theoretically under the parental care of their masters, apprentice printers spent their boyhoods immersed in a work culture dominated by adult journeymen. While rich in tradition and craft pride, printing office culture was built around heavy, on-the-job drinking. New apprentices and journeymen were required to treat their coworkers, and the older journeymen had to treat everyone whenever signature "o" of a work was put in the press. At eleven each morning "and too frequently afterwards," Thurlow Weed remembered, the journeymen in his office "jeffed" (that is, played a dice game with pieces of type) for beer.

While on one level printing office drinking games were a charming example of preindustrial work discipline, the toll on printers' health, pros-perity, and public image was severe. Treating and jeffing involved trips around the corner to retrieve the necessary beverages, where grocers were happy to extend credit that could absorb most of a printer's meager earn-ings. Almost all early Americans drank to what later eras would define as excess, but printers gained an especially unsavory reputation in this re-gard. Successful printers' memoirs are full of old masters, friends, and col-leagues who died young or stayed poor because of chronic intemperance.[6]

For the most part, colonial printers were under no illusions about their status. James Parker, a successful master printer in mid-eighteenth-centu-ry New York, felt that the printing trade was in "wretched Disrepute." Printers were "obliged to work like Negroes, and in general are esteemed but little better." To the stigma of manual labor was added the trade's low profitability. It was obvious to Parker that no family "of Substance would ever put their Sons to such an Art." It was only because of his own undis-tinguished origins that he ever became a printer. Masters were "obliged to take of the lowest People" for apprentices. Printers with aspirations to gentry status or political power needed to give up their trade first. Thus that apostle of hard work Benjamin Franklin retired from the trade in his forties, established himself as a gentleman of leisure and refinement, and only then began his illustrious career as a politician, diplomat, and scien-tist.[7]

If they successfully made their way through the artisanal life cycle from apprentice to journeyman to master (as fewer and fewer could over time), printers also became businessmen, operating in a market that was dis-persed, agrarian, and woefully inadequate. In colonial America even more than in later times, there were many more people willing to produce printed matter than readers able or willing to pay for it. A village printer had to please as many people as possible and could not afford to alienate potential customers in any segment of his community. Politically, this dic-tated strict nonpartisanship and a self-consciously workmanlike approach to the business. Typically, colonial printers focused on the physical prod-ucts and mechanical processes of printing rather than the content of what they printed. William Bradford, the first printer in Pennsylvania, called printing "a manufacture of the nation," and most colonial printers tried hard to operate as if their product had no more political import than the shoes, barrels, and candles that other artisans made.[8]

Benjamin Franklin outlined his trade's habitual approach to political controversy in 1731: "Printers are educated in the Belief that when Men differ in opinion, both Sides ought equally to have the Advantage of being heard by the Publick." In the language of the printing trade, liberty of the press meant something close to the modern phrase "equal access": theoretically, newspapers should be open to all political opinions. In practice, many printers opted to leave local political contention out of their papers entirely if they could, preferring to fill their columns with European news copied from distant newspapers and merchants' letters or heard from sea captains. Presented without comment or literary styling, such material was both attractive and safe: it was relevant to colonial readers as residents of the greater Atlantic world, but distant and impersonal enough not to bring any local trouble on the printer. Of course, Franklin and at least some other colonial printers did take an interest in the content of what they printed and sometimes provided it themselves, but they tried to conceal their own authorship and when challenged assumed the "mechanical" stance outlined by Franklin and Bradford.[9]

PRINT, PRINTERS, AND POLITICAL ELITES IN COLONIAL AMERICA

Colonial political leaders also held printer-effacing notions of how newspapers should operate, which was as a kind of mechanical amplifier for political and social leaders, delivering the small spectrum of thoughts and information that local elites deemed fit for broader consumption. Indeed, it can be argued that American newspapers were allowed to develop only when and if colonial oligarchs found them useful for their own purposes. In the small-scale, hierarchical society of the seventeenth-century colonies, there was little perceived or actual need for "mass communication." Information flowed down the social hierarchy through face-to-face exchanges, on a need-to-know basis, with a very tiny fraction of the population seen as needing to know or have opinions about governmental affairs. What we might call "publicity"—full knowledge and the expectation of direct participation in political affairs—was reserved for the few who were directly involved in leadership, and those few were to speak in public only in unified and authoritative terms. Thus colonial leaders rarely required printed announcements to communicate with each other, conducting their most sensitive business in letters, closed meetings, or exclusive social gatherings.

Occasionally, however, they needed to reach outside their personal networks and deliver authoritative information to large numbers of their fellow inhabitants. Print was the most obvious means of doing this, but for many decades, all that seemed necessary was the occasional pamphlet or proclamation. Significantly, the first "newspaper" in British America did not appear until what might be considered the first intercolonial political event, the multiple rebellions against the Dominion of New England that broke out in response to the Glorious Revolution of 1688–89, and even this journal was created to deliver an official announcement. Trying to calm an aroused populace, the reestablished government of Massachusetts Bay issued *The Present State of New-English Affairs,* a broadside that looked exactly like the front page of a London newspaper. It contained news of the Rev. Increase Mather's mission to London to lobby for the return of the charter that James II had confiscated in 1685. The subheading of the broadside expressed the Puritan leadership's suddenly felt need to broadcast some political information: "This is Published to Prevent False Reports."[10]

The Present State of New-English Affairs proved to be a model for colonial journalism, in the sense that only newspapers firmly under the influence of the local elites could survive. The first newspaper intended for continuous publication quickly ran afoul of the colonial authorities' jealous guardianship over political information. The publisher was Benjamin Harris, a high-minded Puritan radical who had been a journalist in England and fled James II's crackdown on the press. On 25 September 1690, Harris issued a three-page journal called *Publick Occurrences Both Forreign and Domestick,* promising to report on "The Remarkable Occurrences of Divine Providence" and "the Circumstances of Public Affairs" in both Europe and America. Harris put more information and commentary in his publication than American newspapers would again for years, including even some American news, a rarity during the colonial period. *Publick Occurrences* was to be a monthly publication, but four days after the first issue appeared, the governor and council met and declared their "high Resentment and Disallowance of said Pamphlet and order[ed] that the same be Suppressed and called in: strictly forbidding any person or persons for the future to Set forth anything in Print without License first obtained." The problem was that Harris had dared to print opinions (or more properly, interpretations of fact) without the advice or imprimatur of Massachusetts leaders, issuing the paper "without the least Privity or Countenance of Authority."[11]

Colonial publishers would rarely make that mistake again. It would be fourteen years before the newspaper format would be tried a second time, and it would survive over the long term only by taking a much more cautious approach. The first American newspaper to survive its infancy, the *Boston News-Letter,* carried the legend "Published by Authority" on its banner, and this was both a seal of approval and a general truth. The publisher of the *News-Letter,* Boston postmaster John Campbell, obtained government permission before proceeding with his project and allowed officials to vet each issue before publication. Rather than Harris's comprehensive portrait of public affairs, Campbell contented himself with English and foreign news copied from London newspapers. His goal was the much more palatable one (to the colonial elite) of connecting that elite to the metropolitan core upon which they were still culturally and politically dependent.

Campbell's intended market, in fact, appears to have been the handful of politically active colonists for whom it was useful to have such information as the names of the members of Parliament and who English nobles had recently married. After the European news, Campbell slipped in a few very brief notices of local ship arrivals, deaths, storms, and finally an advertisement or two. Subsequent publications, such as Boston's second continuous newspaper, the *Boston Gazette* (founded 1719), corrected Campbell's most egregious errors (such as printing all the foreign news clippings in strict chronological order and thus allowing them to fall years behind), but retained his basic formula.[12]

The commercialism and political subservience of colonial printers can be seen in the most famous case of newspaper partisanship before 1765, John Peter Zenger's *New-York Weekly Journal.* Zenger himself was only a bit player in the famous court case that bears his name. "Finding himself unable to subsist by other printing-work," he had no choice but to hire on with the only available customers, who happened to be a coterie of local politicians at odds with New York's crown-appointed governor, William Cosby. Zenger was paid to print—and only print, not edit or write—the *New-York Journal,* a newspaper containing sarcastic, Swiftian criticism of the Cosby regime and reprints from British republican tracts such as *Cato's Letters.*

The paper's chief contributor and real editor was the ambitious attorney James Alexander. Zenger himself was a mere front, but he proved a highly useful one. When the authorities cracked down on the *Journal,* it was Zenger they imprisoned, because his was the only name on the paper. Alexander defended Zenger, but he subordinated his client's interests to his own desire to make political hay. In court, he continued the attack on Cosby, until finally disbarred by Chief Justice James DeLancey. Zenger languished nine months in jail, until his case came to trial and the colonies' leading attorney, Andrew Hamilton, got him acquitted. Hamilton made a grandstand play for colonial rights that really had little relation to Zenger or printers, arguing that local juries rather than judges appointed by the royal governor could decide matters of law (in this case, the legal definition of libel) as well as the simple facts of the case. Zenger's pawn status was underlined by the fact that the victory celebration was held before he was even released from jail.[13]

Zenger and other controversial colonial printers, such as Benjamin Franklin's brother James, were drawn into political conflict not out of any desire for power and notoriety, but because they were underemployed tradesmen who needed any work they could get. Having endured their prosecutions, they settled down to quiet lives of merely "mechanical" and studiously noncontroversial printing. The significance of colonial newspaper controversies such as the one that victimized Zenger lies in the precedents they set for the development of newspaper politics: they were the earliest instances in which the American gentry resorted to newspapers when they had political differences with the powers that were, and the first cases in which American printers became surrogates for gentleman politicians, suffering persecutions and punishments for the words of their anonymous contributors.[14]

By midcentury there were newspapers in all the more populous colonies and multiple journals in Boston, Philadelphia, and New York. Almost all eventually adopted a format that would remain essentially unchanged until the technological improvements of the Jacksonian period. Typically, newspapers contained four pages, occasionally fewer during a week when no London newspapers or letters from "correspondents" arrived.[15] Very occasionally, an extra sheet with some late-arriving items might be attached. In a financially successful newspaper, at least one and as many as three of the four pages would be devoted to advertising (including paid government notices), with ads running without change for weeks or months at a time. An important speech, proclamation, or essay might lead off the nonadvertising columns, but many papers (especially urban dailies later in the century) put the advertising on the front page.

The news items were arranged under dated geographic headings that denoted the location, not of the events described, but of the newspaper from which the item was taken. The "London" head might include British parliamentary debates or rumors about the king of Prussia.

The items themselves usually carried no headlines, titles, or other differentiation between subjects and items. In the middle or at the end of the nonadvertising pages, there would be a heading for the town where the paper was published; here would be inserted a few brief local news items and commercial information such as ship arrivals and "prices current." Here might also be found the publisher's own comments, if any.

Format changes from the 1740s to 1820s were incremental only: type sizes shrank, the amount of certain categories of matter increased, some minor improvements in differentiating content were made (such as a literary page on the back of a paper, dividing lines or occasional short titles for individual items). The use of illustrations and decorative typefaces actually decreased a bit after the colonial period. The basic scheme, including the arrangement by uninformative geographic headings, remained in force. The lack of change is illustrated by the criticisms that a Connecticut political writer could still lodge against the newspapers he read in 1811: "I have . . . often been surprized that the most valuable communications in our papers should be in illegibly small type, while news from Leghorn, accounts of rare reptiles and thunderstorms are in long pica." It was as difficult as ever for the reader to "form some idea, when he has closed one subject & begun on another."[16]

Colonial leaders softened their attitudes toward the press considerably in the decades after Benjamin Harris's short-lived experiment. Over the eighteenth century, they increasingly bid for popular support in their struggles with royal government, gravitating to the universalist rhetoric of natural rights and liberties while claiming to speak not as members of a frustrated native-born elite but instead in the name of an outraged "public" or "people." In this context, a relatively free press came to seem more helpful than threatening to colonial politicians, who became much more likely to defend the printers who served them. Conversely, printers who departed from the political line set by local leading men were quickly disciplined. A pattern of selective press freedom emerged. Colonial printers who criticized *royal* government were generally safe—local juries would rarely indict or convict them—but those who crossed colonial assemblies, the repositories of local elite power, received swift punishment. Hence the leading characteristic of the colonial press was its close and subordinate relationship with local (as opposed to imperial) political elites.[17]

THE AMERICAN REVOLUTION AND THE
BEGINNINGS OF PARTISANSHIP

Newspapers came into their own as a political weapon during the controversies preceding the American Revolution. It was a matter of consensus, then as now, that Patriot newspapers were one of the most important factors in turning American public opinion against Great Britain.[18] The years between 1760 and the outbreak of the Revolutionary War saw the number of newspapers in the colonies more than double. This was more than a demographic coincidence. Over the period, the newspaper press was expanding nearly twice as fast as the population. Moreover, as shown in appendix 1, chart 1, the number of newspapers shot up during each individual crisis: from twenty-two to twenty-seven during 1763–65 (the Stamp and Sugar Acts), from twenty-eight to thirty-two during 1767–69 (the Townshend Acts), and from thirty-five to forty-two during the final crisis of 1773–75.

This was only the first of many historical moments over the next half century when the American press quickly expanded in response to political turmoil. A chart of the press's growth (see appendix 1, chart 2) shows massive upward spikes during the tumultuous Confederation period of the 1780s and the party conflict of the 1790s. A calculation and compari son of the growth rates of the press and the population (chart 4) shows newspapers reproducing four times faster than human beings during those decades. The beginnings of newspaper politics, the integration of the press and political activism that would dominate the nineteenth century, can thus be traced to the resistance movement of the 1760s.

The impetus toward sustained partisanship came not from printers but from rebellious gentlemen eager to use the press for their own political purposes. Among other things, the Revolution was the seizure of power by a native-born elite crowded out of the colonies' top leadership positions. This "natural," local, untitled aristocracy made the press the most reliable and powerful weapon in its arsenal. As Richard Buel has argued, Patriot leaders "saw [the press] primarily as an instrument by which the mass of the people"—or their self-appointed spokesmen—"might seek to compensate for some of the disadvantages they labored under" in the eternal struggle between aggressive executive power and the rights of the people as embodied in a legislative assembly.[19] More specifically, they saw the press as the means by which political leaders could enlist their constituents' support for resistance to Great Britain. It was assumed that there would be no conflict between the views of the mass of the people and those of their representatives, once the people were properly informed and proselytized in print. It was in these terms in which the Continental Congress recommended liberty of the press to the "inhabitants of Quebec" in 1774: "The last right we shall mention, regards the freedom of the press. The importance of this consists . . . in its diffusion of liberal sentiments on the administration of Government, its ready communication of thoughts between subjects, and its consequential promotion of union among them, whereby oppressive officers are shamed or intimidated, into more honorable and just modes of conducting affairs." This statement reflected a naive Enlightenment faith in the power of "correct" information to change minds and shape events in the direction of progress, but embedded within the idea of "promoting union" was a harder-edged political lesson: that printing (and newspapers especially) could help organize, standardize, and spread a political movement's ideas across large numbers of people and places.[20]

Such a weapon was too powerful to be allowed to fall into enemy hands. Despite their libertarian rhetoric, American resistance leaders proved unwilling to tolerate opposition from the press. Since press freedom existed for the purpose of protecting liberty, they reasoned, there should be no freedom for a press that opposed liberty. Some of the most skilled and articulate printers and publishers refused to join the resistance, and a few even became active opponents. Such insubordination was dealt with harshly, as in the case of the Boston publisher John Mein. A feistier-than-normal publication, Mein's *Boston Chronicle* exposed secret violations of the nonimportation agreement by leading Patriot merchants such as John Hancock, even publishing cargo manifests as proof of the charges. Mob violence eventually forced Mein to flee to the British, but Hancock managed to exact long-distance revenge by purchasing a £2,000 debt of Mein's and having the printer thrown into debtor's prison in England. During the war, the Loyalist press was mobbed, prosecuted, or confiscated out of existence when the British army was not around to protect it. Loyalist publishers fled for their lives when they were not banished outright.[21]

If Patriot gentlemen used the press as their political instrument, they also used it in some measure to conceal their own agency in the pre-Revolutionary upheavals. Almost all partisan essays were written anonymously;

many were signed with the names of classical heroes or invented characters such as the "Farmer in Pennsylvania" portrayed by the wealthy, sophisticated lawyer John Dickinson. Anonymous and pseudonymous writing were traditional practices in the press by this time, but they served the resistance movement in more directly political ways. Unidentified writing helped preserve the impression that newspaper essays and pamphlets were spontaneous expressions of American public opinion, and it camouflaged the sheer extent of the efforts of such prolific writers as Samuel Adams.

Though Revolutionary political culture sanctioned zealous industry in the common cause, disclosing the real identities of newspaper writers might have made the Revolutionary agitation appear to be the illegitimate machinations of a handful of conspirators. Anonymity also helped work around basic tensions in American Revolutionary ideology. As Michael Warner has argued, the central premises of the new nation's emerging constitutional republicanism—that politics and government could be separated from personal social relations, and that their operations could be supervised by a rational, critical "public" and controlled by rules that were neutral regarding the status of individual persons ("a government of laws, not men")—demanded and depended for their legitimacy on a political arena in which specific persons were absent. Printed political debate in newspapers and pamphlets provided such a depersonalized arena, what political theorists and historians have called a "public sphere."

Partly through the typical anonymity and pseudonymity of contributions to it, the eighteenth-century public sphere allowed a handful of white, male, genteel political activists to speak in the guise of the supervising "public," or to put it more prosaically, to assume the role of the "people" without calling attention to the great social and cultural distance between most political writers and the plebeian majority of the population.[22]

Anonymity also shielded from reprisal those gentleman Revolutionaries who had social or professional position to lose if they appeared too active against the British or performed badly on the public stage. A gentleman had a carefully built "character" that could be damaged by a poor performance, while an artisan was a much humbler man with no such standing to lose. Thus a printer could be a convenient surrogate for a gentleman, keeping the onus of criticism away from the actual author. Such considerations had motivated the colonial leaders who had spoken through the medium of John Peter Zenger, and they definitely entered the minds of many American resistance leaders in the 1760s and 1770s.

A good example of this desire for political camouflage occurred be-

tween Dr. Benjamin Rush and the former staymaker and tax collector
Thomas Paine, when the latter was still an obscure recent immigrant. In
1775 Rush was "preparing an address to the inhabitants of the colonies" on
the necessity of independence and of bringing "the war to a speedy and
successful issue." Yet the Philadelphia society doctor "hesitated" and
"shuddered at . . . the consequence of its not being well received." Rush
had become acquainted with Paine from frequenting Robert Aitken's political bookstore, where the new arrival was working. Rush made Paine a
proposal, asking him "what he thought of writing a pamphlet upon
[Rush's subject]. I suggested to him that he had nothing to fear from the
popular odium to which such a publication might expose him, for he
could live anywhere, but that my profession and connections, which tied
me to Philadelphia, where a great majority of the citizens and some of my
friends were hostile to a separation of our country from Great Britain,
forbad me to come forward as a pioneer in that important controversy."
Paine agreed and immediately began work on the pamphlet, for which the
doctor eventually suggested the title *Common Sense*.[23] Such partisan indirection—a respectable gentleman recruiting a mouthpiece from the ranks
of the less respectable—would be a perennial theme in subsequent American political history.

Though several made names for themselves as heroes of the Revolution, printers as a group remained stubbornly traditional throughout the
Revolutionary era, rarely straying far or willingly from their deferential
habits and basically commercial orientation. Many printers were initially
spurred to resistance by the Stamp Act, a direct threat to their business interests. Yet even that provocation was insufficient for others, and most
went back to relative impartiality once the crisis was over. In the end,
market forces were more effective in creating Revolutionary printers than
Revolutionary politics was.

For instance, in 1771 the Boston printer Isaiah Thomas opened his
Massachusetts Spy to both parties in the ongoing controversy even though
he personally supported the resistance. Thomas switched the paper over to
active "support of the whig interest" only after it became clear that impartiality was hurting his business. Loyalists had canceled their subscriptions
to protest his printing pro-resistance articles along with those supporting
their own views. At some point, most other American printers came to
similar realizations that conversion to zealous patriotism was the most
prudent and profitable course. It was impossible to please both Whigs and

Loyalists, and those publishers who followed the old policy of neutrality for too long risked not only losing customers, but being ostracized from their communities and harassed by mobs and local authorities.[24]

In addition, printers were sometimes given positive incentives to publish for the Whig cause. William Rind founded the second *Virginia Gazette* at the behest, and with the pecuniary encouragement, of Thomas Jefferson and other opponents of the royal government. "Until the beginning of our revolutionary disputes, we had but one press, and that having the whole business of the government, . . . nothing disagreeable to the governor could ever be got into it," Jefferson remembered. Therefore, he and his fellow Whigs in the House of Burgesses promised Rind the legislative printing contracts and thus "procured" him to move from Maryland and publish a "free paper" in Virginia. Here press freedom was defined only as free access for a particular group of politicians. Rind's was a common experience. Government printing contracts had always been one of the most reliable and sought-after sources of profit in the trade, and Revolutionary printers were quick to secure the printing concessions of the new Revolutionary governments.[25]

Once they did become partisan, few Revolutionary printers wrote much political material for their papers. They served the cause by "editing" in the literal sense: publishing the writings of local gentlemen and selecting public documents and items from other papers that made the Whig case. (In some cases, even the editing was done by someone other than the printer.) Their papers were more conduits for Revolutionary rhetoric than initiators of it. As one scholar of the Revolutionary press has written, perhaps unwittingly taking an eighteenth-century gentleman's view of printers' mental capacities, "Although editorials were nonexistent, their place was more than taken by the contributions of others far more intelligent than the editors."[26]

Perhaps the only consistently partisan printers in the pre-Revolutionary press corps were Benjamin Edes and John Gill of the *Boston Gazette*. They were also the printers most directly involved in the anti-British agitations. Their careers illustrate the new possibilities, as well as the ultimate limits, of the printers' role in the Revolution. Longtime printers for the local and provincial governments, Edes and Gill had grown as wealthy and respected as was usually possible for working printers. Edes held several petty local offices such as constable, scavenger, and clerk of the market in the early 1760s and was a member of the Ancient and Honorable

Artillery Company. Though evidently a man of some political fervor, Edes practiced the colonial printer's habitual deference toward the local authorities who provided so much of his business. Reprimanded by the Boston selectmen for publishing some too-speculative theological pamphlets in 1757, Edes apologized for offending and promised "to take more care for the future, & publish nothing that should give any uneasiness to any Persons whatever."[27]

During the political crises over the Sugar and Stamp Acts, the *Boston Gazette* followed its customer base into active opposition. The Boston campaign against the British ministry was financed and fomented by merchants with interests at stake. Several of them, including John Hancock and Benjamin Church, also happened to be longtime *Gazette* advertisers. Edes is reputed to have been a member of the "Loyall Nine" who controlled the Sons of Liberty. It seems doubtful that he was truly such a ringleader, but at the very least, the printer was a junior partner of Samuel Adams in the ground-level management of the movement. Certainly, Edes was present at meetings of the group's brain trust and involved in many of its activities.

The fiery political matter that filled the *Boston Gazette* came from a constellation of Boston Revolutionary leaders, including Samuel Adams, John Adams, James Otis, Josiah Quincy Jr., and Joseph Warren. These same men and their allies provided Edes and Gill with all the protection they needed from the vengeance of the royal government. When an article of Warren's finally goaded Governor Frances Bernard into prosecuting the editors for seditious libel, the *Gazette*'s writers, in their capacities as attorneys, local officials, and politicians, saw to it that both the General Court and a grand jury refused to cooperate. In an arrangement that presaged the later integration of newspapers and political groups, the *Gazette* office provided a headquarters of sorts for the Patriot leadership; for a time, Edes and Gill published the paper from rooms above Josiah Quincy's law office. John Adams remembered a Sunday night in 1769 spent with Otis, Sam Adams, and others, "preparing for the next day's newspaper ... cooking up paragraphs, articles, occurrences, &c., working the political engine." According to one legend, the perpetrators of the Boston Tea Party gathered at Edes's house before setting off on their mission.[28]

It was widely agreed after the Revolution that, in the words of Edes's competitor Thomas, "no publisher of a newspaper felt a greater interest in the establishment of ... independence ... than Benjamin Edes; and no newspaper was more instrumental in bringing forward this important event than *The Boston Gazette.*" Yet it seems clear that Edes conceived of himself as the Patriot leaders' loyal auxiliary rather than as a leader himself. In 1797, hearkening back to his glory days, Edes praised himself primarily for maintaining Adams's "political engine" rather than driving it: "Did you, my fellow-citizens, ever find the Boston Gazette deficient . . . ? Did an OTIS at that time seek in vain to declare his principles through this channel? . . . No, fellow-citizens, the Gazette of Edes & Gill, was always subservient to the cause of Freedom."[29]

Benjamin Edes's career after the 1760s is instructive. The editor's illustrious Boston cohorts became generals and statesmen, but no such high stations were proffered to Edes. Even so, the printer was unwilling to give up his new vocation as a Revolutionary politician. When war broke out, Edes fled to Watertown, a wanted man, but continued to publish a makeshift *Gazette.* Later, back in Boston, he kept the paper going during a long decline, as old contributors died, retired, or deserted the *Gazette* for larger political arenas. Edes took over much of the writing himself, and his newspaper more frequently gave voice to the divergent views and interests of his own artisan class. To the horror of old political friends following the conservative trend of postwar Massachusetts politics, Edes opposed the Federal Constitution and, later, the administrations of George Washington and former *Gazette* writer John Adams.[30]

Edes's newfound independence arose from the bitterness of his experience during and after the Revolution. Like many other artisans and farmers, Edes had nearly been ruined by the economic fluctuations arising from the war. He had amassed a small fortune in increasingly worthless paper money and Continental debt certificates paid to him by Patriot customers, and like many others, he apparently sold off his securities to speculators, at a fraction of their value, to meet immediate needs. The destruction of his wealth in this manner made Edes a bitter critic of the Hamiltonian financial system: "conscious . . . that I have served my country with faithfulness, and the most disinterested zeal, I cannot but observe with regret, that thousands have become enriched by a *base speculation* on those services which have impoverished me and many others." Edes's subscription list dwindled from a high of 2,000 before the Revolution to a few hundred in the mid-1790s, as (at least in the minds of political opponents) the *Gazette* abandoned "that soberness and dignity, that might have rendered its old age useful and respectable." The *Gazette* and the Edes family alike moved into progressively shabbier quarters until by 1801 Edes was reduced to printing shop bills with worn-out type in a room above a tinsmith's shop. A younger printer, Joseph Buckingham, found the old man setting type himself, while an elderly daughter worked the press. "The singular sight of a woman, *beating and pulling* at the press, together with the aspect of destitution, that pervaded the whole apartment, presented a scene" that remained horribly vivid in Buckingham's memory fifty years later.[31]

SERVING THE FOUNDERS: PRINTERS AND NEWSPAPERS AFTER THE REVOLUTION

Edes was unusual among the Revolutionary printers in maintaining his political activity for so long after the war. Once the war ended, the pressure to display zealous patriotism was relieved, and most Revolutionary printers who had not died or retired sank back into their old commercialism and relative neutrality. Isaiah Thomas changed the motto of his *Massachusetts Spy* (now published in Worcester) from the warlike "The noble efforts of a Virtuous, Free, and United People shall extirpate Tyranny" to the impartial "Knowledge of the World is essentially necessary for every Man" and shifted focus to the commercial publishing ventures that eventually made him a wealthy man.[32]

The younger printers who came into the business during and after the war showed the partisanizing effects of the conflict upon the trade, yet they still hewed as close to traditional policies as they could. Printers such as George Goodwin, who took over the Hartford *Connecticut Courant* in 1778, or Benjamin Russell, an apprentice of Thomas's who founded the Boston *Columbian Centinel* in 1784, were more forthright in their opinions than their colonial predecessors had been, but they settled into the role of reliable auxiliaries to the victorious Whig establishment, which was growing steadily more disenchanted with the democratic, localistic political fervor the Revolution had unleashed.[33]

In places where the Revolutionaries were more divided than Massachusetts, a somewhat more freewheeling press appeared. When the Bostonian Ebenezer Hazard visited Philadelphia in 1782, opponents and defenders of the state's radical Constitution of 1776 were locked in a savage struggle that often involved personal defamation of the leaders on both sides. Hazard wrote back home in disgust: "The papers of this place have become the most indecent publications of the kind I have ever met with.

They are now the receptacles of obscenity and filth, the vehicles of scandal, and the instruments of the most infamous abuse."[34] This was true only by contrast with the Boston press. There were only two really partisan papers in Philadelphia, Francis Bailey's *Freeman's Journal,* favored by the Constitutionalists, and Colonel Eleazer Oswald's *Independent Gazetteer,* backed by the anti-Constitution forces. Most editors of this period kept the traditional low profile, allowing their politician-sponsors to slug it out under pen names.[35]

On the whole, then, both printers and politicians tried to continue their long relationship after the Revolution. Now that the people had replaced the British king as the source of sovereignty, the press became even more vital. American political leaders expected that newspapers that had once been instruments of resistance would now be tools of governance. The press was seen as the most important means available of managing or manufacturing public opinion, the legitimating force behind the new governments. Thomas Jefferson explained this principle in 1787, giving his advice on how Shays' Rebellion might have been prevented:

> The people are the only censors of their governors; and even their errors will tend to keep these to the true principles of their institution. To punish these errors too severely would be to suppress the only safeguard of the public liberty. The way to prevent these irregular interpositions of the people is to give them full information of their affairs through the channel of the public papers, and to contrive that those papers should penetrate the whole mass of the people. The basis of our government being the opinion of the people, the first object should be to keep that right.[36]

Jefferson failed to acknowledge the tension, or saw none, between his plan of keeping the people fully informed and the underlying goal of keeping public opinion "right." As long as "right" information was transmitted, Jefferson believed, public opinion would always reach the desired conclusion.

Leaders of other nations felt less sanguine and took aggressive measures to actively guide or check public opinion. The British government had for decades, even in peacetime, used prosecution, restrictive licensing, bribery, public subsidies, and other forms of "influence" to control the flow of information on government affairs and to assure the authorities a public voice that would constantly support, explain, and apologize for their actions. In the mid-seventeenth century, it became standard practice for whoever happened to hold power in London to contract for one or more official government organs. With the Printing Act of 1662, the restored Stuart monarchy sharply limited the supply of printed matter and closely regulated its content, establishing a government monopoly on domestic political news. As mouthpieces, the Stuarts initially employed newsbooks and later the first official government publications in the larger newspaper format, the *Oxford Gazette* and its successor, the *London Gazette*.[37]

The government monopoly ended when the Printing Act lapsed in 1695, but succeeding governments devised more complex (but only slightly more subtle) methods of maintaining their influence over the press, beginning with the stamp tax imposed in 1712. The system of press management most familiar to eighteenth-century Americans was developed by the ministry of Sir Robert Walpole in the 1720s and 1730s. Following the lead of opposition noblemen who had established such newspapers as *The Craftsman* and the *London Evening Post* to pillory his ministry, Walpole began an aggressive campaign of enlisting newspapers in the government's defense. Newspapers were subsidized through direct payments, government purchase of copies, and free postage, while the services of individual journalists were purchased with appointments, sinecures, and noble titles. In some cases, opposition writers were paid to keep silent. There was even a special fund for the purpose of influencing the press, from which £50,000 was disbursed between 1731 and 1741. By these methods, Walpole kept at least four London newspapers under almost direct government control and exerted a lesser degree of influence over many others. The ministry could not completely suppress the dissemination of news and opposition political comment, but many important opposition voices were neutralized. No less a figure than Thomas Gordon, coauthor of *Cato's Letters* and *The Independent Whig*, switched from violent opposition to support of the Walpole ministry after he was appointed a commissioner of wine licenses.[38]

Regarding Walpolean corruption as a great threat to liberty and being avid followers of the British opposition press, the American Revolutionaries had little desire to re-create the mother country's "hireling" press. As it turned out, there was no need to bother. The leaders of the campaign for a stronger central government in the late 1780s found the press almost as reliable without the need of a purchase price. The American press monolithically supported the Federal Convention of 1787. Few newspapers protested the conclave's secrecy, and most heaped sycophantic praise on the great "characters" who made up the body. Many newspapers carried advance recommendations that whatever document was produced should be accepted. Though scattered articles critical of the convention were written, they were seldom reprinted in other papers. Numerous pro-convention articles, on the other hand, received nationwide exposure.[39]

In the ratification campaign that followed the convention, the federalists overwhelmingly dominated the press, with only twelve of the ninety-two periodicals published during the ratification debate admitting any significant number of antifederalist articles. The pro-Constitution forces loaded the other eighty publications with an immense mass of verbiage. James Madison and Alexander Hamilton's "Federalist" essays, written as part of this newspaper campaign, made up only a tiny fraction of the output. Newspaper editors themselves were mostly the passive recipients of these writings.[40]

In some states, such as Connecticut and New Hampshire, there was virtually no ratification "debate" at all, so one-sided was the material that filled the newspapers. The editors of both Hartford papers, the *Connecticut Courant* and the *American Mercury*, eventually found themselves at pains to deny that they were "under the direction of certain men, who exclude everything written against the new Constitution." Claiming that they had maintained the "liberty of the press" to all, George Goodwin and Elisha Babcock issued a joint statement contending that no antifederal pieces had been submitted to them and invited writers on that side to come forward. In the next few weeks, a few token opposing viewpoints were heard, but they were usually couched in highly deferential terms.[41]

The federalists showed themselves to be remarkably intolerant of contradiction in the press despite the opposition's journalistic weakness. The ill temper with which antifederalist writings were received showed the Revolutionary gentry's profound discomfort with airing its political differences in front of the people.[42] While proponents of the new system of government could not silence its critics outright, they made it clear that they regarded newspaper criticism as unwelcome, badly intended, and probably illegitimate. Many federalists saw the Constitution as a cause in which all right-thinking and well-meaning people ought to be united and suspected the motives of any who refused to join. One Pennsylvania federalist condemned those who had opposed the "noble struggle which the brave and virtuous have been . . . making to establish a new frame of government." The writer accused the antifederalists of failing to publicly avow their writings and reasoned from this premise that they were "con-

scious of the wickedness of their proceedings—that their cause is that of
the devil—and of it they are truly ashamed." This reasoning was fallacious, of course, because virtually all political essays in the period were
published anonymously, though real identities were often widely known
in local elite circles.[43]

The same feelings prompted a widespread attempt to flush out antifederalists by inducing printers to break with tradition and identify the
authors of anonymous political essays. A Massachusetts paper had announced such a policy, and "Galba" in Philadelphia suggested a modification under which only antifederalists would be required to leave their
names. The "patriotic gentleman" who wrote in favor of the Constitution
should not "be exposed to the malevolence of those wretches who pretend
to find fault with it," while the latter ought to "be justly exposed to the
contempt and indignation of their fellow citizens, as enemies and traitors
to their country."

In Georgia, an elaborate "literary register" was proposed, where writers
would leave their names so that readers could find out who the "designing,
specious demagogues" writing the antifederal articles were. Belying the
supposed openness and egalitarianism of the "public sphere" of printed
debate, the proposer of the register showed a strong interest in discovering
the social status of political writers, intending to judge arguments not by
their own merits but according to the stature of the person who made
them. He suspected that a recent article against the Constitution had
been written either by a foreigner or by some uneducated person whose
mind had been "only cultivated in a drilling squad or behind the counter
of a dram shop" and "ought rather to be employed in the manufactures
than in the politics of his country."

None of the proposals were carried out, probably because they seemed
to confirm antifederalist warnings about the Constitution's counterrevolu-
tionary tendencies. Yet the fact that they were made at all suggests the un-
happiness of at least some former leaders of the Revolution with the idea
that the press might now sometimes be used against them. The antifederalists correctly compared the proposals to expose and shame antifederal
writers to the "tar and feathers" applied to Tory journalists in previous
years.[44]

The pro-Constitution forces never escalated to the measures that
Whigs had taken against Loyalists during the Revolution, but steps were
taken to silence the Constitution's critics. The one act of violence was an

attack on Thomas Greenleaf's *New-York Journal,* which seems to have been spurred as much by an inadvertent insult to the pottery trade as by politics. Yet Greenleaf believed he was being pressured by federalists for giving their opponents an outlet, and he promptly lowered his paper's tone, with apologies, after the incident. More commonly, the federalists employed quieter measures, such as having subscriptions and advertisements withdrawn from papers that published antifederalist writings or even those that merely seemed doubtful in their political complexion. In Philadelphia, for instance, a young lawyer-editor from Jamaica named Alexander Dallas was fired from his position at the *Pennsylvania Herald,* following federalist complaints and boycotts, not for criticizing the Constitution, but for too accurately reporting the speeches on both sides in the Pennsylvania ratifying convention.[45]

A long record of subservience did not stop the Revolutionary printers from carrying an exalted self-image out of their experience.[46] The years after 1788 made their true place in the scheme of things much clearer. Instead of the power and honors that accrued to the lawyers, clergymen, and military officers who participated in the Revolution, most of the Revolutionary printers became forgotten men. There were no printers among the pantheon of Revolutionary heroes and statesmen who filled the First Congress. Successful forays into nonpolitical publishing allowed some of the veteran printers to avoid the penury of Benjamin Edes, but none retained their old political influence. Though they were proud to have served in the Revolution, it is doubtful that prosperous veterans such as Isaiah Thomas wanted or expected any very different aftermath. They were printers, not politicians, after all, and planned to remain so.

What did come as a shock to men like Thomas was the steady decline in the reputation and social position of their trade after the Revolution. This occurred partly because of a trend toward functional specialization in the commercial publishing industry, in which the entrepreneurial act of selecting and editing material became increasingly separate from the physical process of printing. Journeyman printers found it more and more difficult to meet their traditional goal of owning their own printing office. The trade became identified ever more firmly with its manual labor aspects, as the intellectual activities associated with publishing were taken over by educated editors and entrepreneurs who soon gained exclusive use of the title "publisher."

Some of the first successful commercial publishers were former printers, but by the 1830s or so, this possibility had been largely foreclosed. The vast majority of apprentices and journeymen could expect to spend their lives as wage laborers. The most striking evidence of these trends was the appearance of a rudimentary labor movement among journeyman printers as early as 1778 in New York and 1786 in Philadelphia. Formal "Typographical Societies" were formed in New York in 1795 and Philadelphia in 1802, and from there spread to many other cities. In the 1830s one organization of printers tried to convince its brethren to refuse to work for editors, publishers, and other nonprinters, who were held to be merely "speculating on the labor of printers."[47]

In the face of these economic changes in the commercial printing trade, the more eminent of the traditional printers turned to scholarship and a kind of nostalgia later in life. Isaiah Thomas published his *History of Printing* in 1810 and founded the American Antiquarian Society in 1812, in large part to preserve and memorialize the legacy of the colonial and Revolutionary printers. He and Joseph T. Buckingham, who wrote a kind of sequel to Thomas's history, were clearly commemorating what they saw as the good old days of the American printing trade.[48]

Yet, despite the melancholia of the aging Revolutionary printers, the printers' period of greatest political and cultural influence still lay ahead. During the 1790s, newspapermen would fight on the front lines, doing as much as any group to secure the right of American citizens to peacefully change their government and to implement the democratic promise of the early days of the American Revolution. Why would the traditional printers not claim this honor as well?

The answer is that both the printing trade and journalism began to split and specialize during the 1790s. Probably most printers retained their commercial and mechanical orientation, but some began to focus on publishing books and others on newspapers. The newspaper business in turn came to be divided between the profit-seeking traditionalists, serving up foreign news and commercial information to merchants, and others who specialized (or came to specialize) in political journals.[49]

Younger men, and new kinds of men, took up the newspaper business during the Federalist-Republican struggle, especially on the Republican side. These new journalists lacked or lost the trade-oriented attitude and life goals of the colonial and Revolutionary printers. They did not (or came not to) conceive of themselves as mere tradesmen whose primary goal was to earn a respectable economic "competency" to pass on to their children.[50] Not only did they fail to shy away from political controversies, they came to find their trade's chief attraction in politics. In short, many printers became professional politicians, or more precisely, political communicators by trade, working in a new sector of the publishing industry devoted to and subsisting on partisan politics.

Political publishing offered an escape route from the industrializing tendencies at work in the commercial sector of the trade. Especially in the smaller cities and towns, political newspapers would be published mostly out of traditional small-scale printing offices until well after the Civil War. In the world of political publishing, many poor boys with "bookish inclinations" could begin as apprentices and find their way not only to learning, but also to political influence, without the necessity of retiring into gentility like Franklin.

The emergence of this political publishing sector was directly linked to the creation of the new government and the new political structures and forces that it called into being. The political arena was now a national one, with results and requirements for which few Americans were prepared. Chief among these were the partisan divisions that quickly appeared in the First Congress, divisions that would soon develop into nascent national political parties. The needs and effects of those parties would eventually transform many American editors and their papers into actual working parts of the political system. The editors would in turn transform the system itself. As their brother printers slipped back into the category of "mechanics" or hewed to the trade's traditional ideal of impartiality and commercialism, the Republican journalists of the 1790s would become the mechanics of the American party system, the forerunners of the political spokesmen, manipulators, and operatives who would dominate American politics evermore.

This tortuous process began with the emergence of the first national partisan editors, whose Philadelphia newspapers became associated with the party divisions that coalesced in Congress over the competing blueprints of Alexander Hamilton and Thomas Jefferson for the national future.

3

The Two National Gazettes and the
Beginnings of Newspaper Politics

❧

The first governments under the Constitution expressed the revolutionary elite's close relationship with the press by conferring unequaled privileges on the American publishing industry. Some of the privileges came from the absence of certain common restrictions. Unlike most European nations, the United States did not lay taxes on printed matter, nor did it establish a system for monitoring the content of what was printed or sent through the mail. Further privileges were conferred, on newspapers particularly, by positive steps. Very early on, Congress established an important source of income for newspaper publishers, one that would be very helpful in sustaining partisan newspapers, by providing for newspapers to publish the laws of the United States as they were passed. In fact, the government elected to contract privately for all its printing needs, opening many more possibilities for favored printers.

A broad consensus existed in the First Congress that the postal system should be used to promote the circulation of newspapers, with the only disagreements coming over how extensive this encouragement should be. There was much support for the idea of charging newspapers no postage at all, and the agitation for that proposal delayed the decision until the Second Congress. The Post Office Act of 1792 did impose a token fee for mailing newspapers, but it also made free exchanges of newspapers between printers, previously only a custom, official government policy. The combination of exemption from postage for exchanges and the low rates for papers sent to subscribers amounted to a massive newspaper subsidy, by which letter writers footed most of the bill for a postal system that by some measures was largely devoted to shipping newspapers. By 1794 newspapers accounted for 70 percent of the mail by weight, but for only 3 percent of the postage.

Government policies also shaped the structure of the new nation's newspaper industry. In contrast to Great Britain and France, where the London and Paris newspapers dominated the press in terms of both information sources and circulation, the United States government encouraged a high level of decentralization and localization. This was partly a by-product of the way the government met its printing needs. The laws were to be printed by newspapers in each state, and other government printing expenditures were spread out as well, with many contracts and legal advertisements emanating from individual custom houses, land offices, and post offices all over the nation.

In postal policy, the government opted for decentralization quite deliberately. Congress wrested the right to establish new post routes away from the executive, and members eager to serve their constituents expanded the network quickly over the years. Similar centrifugal pressures shaped other policies. Newspapers could be put into the mail from any point in the system, rather than just at the capital, as was typical in Europe. Proposals to subsidize postage only for particular newspapers, such as those published in the capital (where access to government information was best) were quickly rejected. Instead, the favorable treatment was extended to all papers equally, even those published in the smallest rural hamlets.

The only discrimination made in the newspaper postage rates was in favor of local newspapers: one cent for papers sent less than 100 miles away, one-and-a-half cents beyond that distance. The cheapness of these rates made it practical for a small country paper to circulate over a relatively wide area, while the higher long-distance rate gave it some protection, in its own region, from competition with big-city journals with better access to information and more talented writers. Free exchanges allowed the content of the national press to penetrate everywhere, while the other policies ensured that the primary delivery points for that content would be hundreds of small-circulation newspapers published in market towns, county seats, and state capitals all over the republic.[1]

Nongovernmental factors, including the still-primitive, human-powered state of printing technology, reinforced the patterns set by government policy. Using hand presses, there was simply no way that any individual printing office could produce more than a few thousand copies of a newspaper in a timely or economical fashion.[2]

This decentralized press structure strongly influenced the way newspaper politics would develop. It created nearly insurmountable difficulties for anyone who hoped to establish a dominant, large-circulation national newspaper based in the capital or even in one of the larger cities. Instead of truly national newspaper organs, American political parties would have national newspaper networks, operating with little central direction and allowing almost any single editor, writer, or event anywhere to command a national audience.

These networks proved remarkably effective and durable devices in their time. They were almost infinitely expandable and conveniently modular, easily surviving rapid turnover in newspapers and editors, even at the national level. The networks needed to have outlets in the various capitals and cities, but while these were large and important outlets, they were not controlling powers over all the others. The decentralized structure afforded great political flexibility, allowing national coalitions to show different faces in different localities while still presenting themselves (through exchanged and reprinted items) as supralocal entities.[3] All of this would serve to amplify the role and potential power of the political editor, whose paper both embodied the party locally (in the shape he chose) and represented its political locality (through items and essays picked up by other papers) to the outside world.

Little of this was well understood or even foreseen by the members of the first national government. The decentralized structure resulted more from vague fears and general preferences than conscious, clear-cut decisions. There was strong opposition to a government-controlled "court press" such as existed in Great Britain, but there were also countervailing beliefs in the efficacy (even necessity) of newspapers for the management of public opinion and the building of allegiance to the new government. No one in authority took steps to establish an official channel of communication to the national public. The government restricted itself to the general measures for encouraging the press already mentioned. Relying on their previous experience of a strongly supportive press, Thomas Jefferson, Alexander Hamilton, and other high officials seem to have trusted that nature would take its course in a way that would meet the national government's communication needs.

DEFENDING THE STATE AND IMAGINING THE NATION:
JOHN FENNO'S *GAZETTE OF THE UNITED STATES*

As it turned out, "nature" began its work before the government was even organized. As George Washington prepared to take office, a Boston entrepreneur named John Fenno was busy planning to equip the new United States government with a newspaper voice. Fenno would succeed in establishing the *Gazette of the United States,* but he would ultimately fail in his larger goal of creating an authoritative organ for the new government that would circulate in every corner of the nation and bind it together. The story of his failure illuminates, below the level of government policies and national structures, the forces and obstacles that would shape newspaper politics. Fenno's journal must also be considered because of what its design and character helped inspire: the creation of a self-consciously and thoroughly partisan opposition newspaper, marking the beginnings of American newspaper politics.

One of the more significant aspects of John Fenno's project was that, unlike most other early American newspaper publishers, he was not a printer or any kind of artisan. He was instead a small-time businessman who spent his life trying to improve upon his plebeian family background. These aspirations to upward mobility were something he shared with many printers, of course, but Fenno stands out for his single-minded identification with the upper classes he was trying to join. Ashamed of his father, a leather dresser who ended his days in the Boston almshouse, Fenno avoided the laboring life of an artisan but never prospered greatly in any of the many nonmanual pursuits he tried, including schoolteaching, innkeeping, and shopkeeping. Sometime in the late 1780s, Fenno drifted into journalism, working for Benjamin Russell's Boston *Centinel.*[4]

Fenno's efforts defending the federal constitution in the *Centinel* brought him to the attention of the Boston area's leading political gentlemen. "His talents, as the editor of a public paper, are unrivall'd in this Commonwealth," enthused Christopher Gore, "the cause of truth, and federalism are much indebted to his pen."

With the encouragement of Gore and other wealthy federalists, Fenno decided to enlist his newfound journalistic prowess in the service of the new national government. Following the British model of government-press relations, Fenno proposed to create an organ that would unquestioningly exalt the new government and aggressively defend its legitimacy, personnel, and policies. To manage, or "conciliate," public opinion on the government's behalf would be the new paper's avowed purpose. "This publication [is] to be entirely devoted to the support of the Constitution, & the Administration formed upon its national principles," Fenno promised. Besides providing the text of congressional debates, the paper would be filled with articles "calculated to conciliate the minds of our citizens, to the proceedings of the Federal Legislature." Though popular, the new government had "many difficulties & obstacles to surmount" with public opinion, which could be "encountered . . . & obviated . . . by no method so effectually as a well-conducted press, . . . under the direction of characters who are fully in the Federal Interest, & deeply impressed with a sense of the necessity of an efficient national government." Enthusiastic about this plan, Gore and friends sent Fenno off to the seat of government armed with working capital and a trove of introduction letters so voluminous it took a week to deliver them all.[5]

Though a zealot for the new constitution, Fenno undertook the *Gazette* primarily as a commercial venture. He went to New York not to turn printer, but instead to revive his business career by seizing the most attractive opportunity that had yet come his way. The optimistic entrepreneur expected to make his fortune and retire back to Boston as a wealthy gentleman within ten years.[6] This belief betrayed both the special nature of the journal Fenno envisioned and his ignorance of (or disregard for) printing economics.

Early American newspapers were proverbial for their evanescence, operating on tiny profit margins in the relatively rare cases in which they made any money at all. The high cost of obtaining basic equipment, shortages of affordable paper, and the difficulty of collecting subscription fees were only some of the conditions that brought most newspapers to an early end: more than two-thirds of the American newspapers established before 1821 published for three years or less.[7] Benjamin Franklin's profitable *Pennsylvania Gazette* was very much the exception and owed its success to the financial advantages of its owner's positions as printer for the Pennsylvania legislature and colonial postmaster general. Nor was the newspaper necessarily Franklin's biggest seller: that honor went to his famous almanacs, of which he sold a quarter of a million copies.[8] In more typical printing operations, the newspaper's economic function was as much to advertise the shop's other products and services—which always included job printing and often a general store—as to make substantial profits on its own.[9]

Of course, Fenno did not intend to run a conventional newspaper business. His new journal was to be "A NATIONAL PAPER," based at the seat of government (wherever that happened to be) but circulated nationally, presumably by the tens of thousands, and addressed to a national audience. He hoped that such a paper would aid the difficult task of turning the disparate societies of the United States into a single unified nation, a project in which he was joined by many artists, poets, and playwrights.

Benedict Anderson has described a nation as an "imagined community," a group of people unknown to each other personally who share a fundamental sense of relationship despite potentially vast geographic, social, and economic differences. Anderson writes that even newspapers more primitive than the one Fenno envisioned, journals that flatly and apolitically reported only such mundane information as commodity prices, ship arrivals, marriages, and government appointments, "created an imagined community among a specific assemblage of readers, to whom *these* ships, brides, bishops, and prices belonged." Fenno wanted to go much further and provide a fictive space in which an imagined community of Americans could read the statements and follow the doings of their national government and their leaders.[10]

Fenno's "national" plan dictated certain highly unusual business practices. He planned to have subscriptions sold in every state capital in the Union, but he solicited no advertising, in hopes of avoiding obvious ties to the local community where the paper was printed. The absence of advertising would increase the paper's ability to bolster the newly reconstituted republic's weak sense of nationhood. Just as (according to eighteenth-century reasoning) legitimate public debate could only take place in a pseudonymous arena that was empty of specific persons, so a *national* public sphere had to be cleansed of specificity with regard to the place where it was published. The *Gazette of the United States* was to be based in New York only physically.[11]

Other unusual features of Fenno's plan had more to do with his personal ambitions than with his nationalism. Fenno decided not to offer general job printing services as other newspaper publishers did, and he arranged to avoid contact with ink, type, and journeyman printers by hiring a regular printing office to produce the paper. Rare at the time, this separation of the printing and editing functions would enable Fenno to live and work as a genteel man of letters rather as proprietor of an artisanal shop. He rested his financial hopes on immediately securing large federal printing contracts; he would take out his profit and subcontract the actual work. Without substantial "public employ," Fenno wrote, the potential profits would be too small to make the project worth his while.[12]

Fenno found the Constitution's supporters in New York receptive—Senator Rufus King "rather more than intimated that if any pecuniary aid is requisite it shall not be wanted"—but he also quickly encountered unexpected obstacles. New York's printers proved unwilling to cooperate with his scheme of comfortably subcontracting for his printing needs. Finding "the terms on which [any New York printers] would have acceded . . . beyond all calculation," Fenno had to give up this cherished aspect of his plan and sent to Boston for printer John Russell, a former associate from the *Centinel.* Fenno would have to work alongside printers and their equipment after all, to the disappointment of some of his well-heeled backers. Then troubles appeared with his projected sources of income. Strong local competitors for the government printing challenged the new arrival, while the "powerful friends" he had counted on provided little more than "a cursory attention & politeness of manners."[13]

Eventually, Fenno and his Boston friends pieced together the means and equipment to launch his newspaper without much local help. When the *Gazette of the United States* finally appeared in April 1789, its content closely reflected Fenno's intentions. The editor announced that the paper would be an "auxiliary to good government" as "Men of Sense, Property, & Principle" defined it. Toning down the original proposal's rhetoric about the need to pacify public opinion, the *Gazette* would still strive to place the new government in as magnificent a light as possible. Fenno fully shared the view of another Massachusetts man, Vice President John Adams, that a government needed "dignity and splendor" if it were to be effective; the people would never obey a government for which they felt no awe. So the editor devoted much space to descriptions of the various ceremonies held to honor new chief magistrates. These reports also aided in the task of creating an imagined national community. Fenno followed the pattern of the consolidating nation-states of Europe, especially Great Britain, in which monarchs were cast as the embodiments of their nations and royal ceremonies and personages were made the focus of public attention and pride.[14]

So *Gazette* readers were treated to a detailed description of the "cavalcade" and military salutes with which "His Excellency JOHN ADAMS, Esq. Vice President of the United States" was ushered "from his seat in Braintree, to take the chair at New-York." They were invited to applaud the construction of "an elegant Barge . . . to waft the great WASHINGTON across the Hudson, to be rowed by ten SEA-CAPTAINS." When "the Most Illustrious PRESIDENT" actually wafted into New York, Fenno found it "impossible to do justice" to the gala scene, but filled two columns of extra-small type in the attempt. For its readers' literary edification, the *Gazette* carried poetic tributes to the new government's leaders, including one on "The Vice-President" that its vain subject must have enjoyed: "WHEN Heaven resolv'd COLUMBIA should be free, / And INDEPENDENCE, spake the great decree, / Lo, ADAMS rose! a giant in debate, / And turn'd *that vote* which fix'd our empire's fate." The president himself Fenno depicted with a servility as boundless as it was comprehensive. Washington's rather perfunctory response to a public testimonial was greeted with the comment, "Reason! Patriotism! Virtue! How great your Triumph!" His tour of New England was given lavish coverage, and even the "regularity and economy" of his household arrangements was singled out for praise.[15]

These efforts at magnifying the new government were in keeping with Fenno's politics, which the opening issues of the *Gazette* made unmistakable. Despite his declaration that the paper would follow "NATIONAL, INDEPENDENT, and IMPARTIAL PRINCIPLES," his catalog of the tasks ahead of the new government reflected the commercial, centralizing, and finance-oriented outlook of such men as Alexander Hamilton, Robert Morris, and Fenno's Boston sponsors. The list committed the paper to the agenda that these "nationalists" had been pushing for most of the 1780s: "to strengthen and complete the UNION of the states—to extend and protect their COMMERCE . . . to restore and establish the PUBLICK CREDIT." Later, following Hamilton closely, the *Gazette* would add the encouragement of manufacturing and the creation of a national bank to its list of causes. When word spread of Hamilton's plan to pay the national debt at face value, a controversial measure because the debt was wildly inflated and mostly speculator held, Fenno expressed certainty that only "weak heads" would try "to frustrate such a plan of justice."[16]

Despite this firm association with a particular point of view, Fenno did not consider his *Gazette* a partisan newspaper. On the contrary, it was his view that "the printer [who] can be made the tool of a party . . . merits universal contempt." Rather, he thought of himself as a defender of constituted authority and of his paper as the instrument and exemplar of a national interest whose legitimacy was far above that of any party or controversy. Though he wrote scornfully about the "Chaff of Antifederalism" in private letters, Fenno had no idea of using his paper for partisan combat, and kept it away from elections and candidates.[17]

One reason Fenno resisted using the *Gazette* as an electioneering tool was his opposition to the very idea of competitive, democratic politics. While it was true that "people are so often suspicious of their rulers, and entertain the idea that the interest of the people and the interest of the government is unconnected," this suspicion was almost always a mistake, Fenno believed, based on a lack of information. Now that the Constitution was in place, Washington and Hamilton were in power, and the people were fully informed by his *Gazette,* there could no longer be any legitimate causes for political conflict. Any opposition to the government that did appear could be safely dismissed as the work of malcontents and office seekers beneath the notice of an "official paper."

Moreover, since the wisest and best men available already filled the nation's elective offices, vigorously contested elections were not only unnecessary but dangerous, providing opportunities for "the arts of unprincipled men" to replace incumbent officials of "worth, probity, and abilities" with parvenus who had "no right to public confidence." As the second congressional elections under the Constitution approached, Fenno editorialized against electioneering and in favor of all incumbents. "The people abuse themselves," the *Gazette* declared, "when a fickleness of mind induces them to change old and faithful servants for new ones." The *Gazette* came close to endorsing the idea that wealthy, educated gentlemen with long experience in office, such as overwhelmingly dominated the membership of the First Congress, deserved a monopoly on political power, that they had a "right" to "public confidence" that less well-placed persons lacked. In a paragraph headed "POLITICIANS," Fenno argued that though every American "seems to think himself born a Legislator," only a few were really qualified to make laws for the nation. Upon learning of a case in which the electorate turned such a qualified individual out of office, Fenno beseeched the heavens: "When will the people learn wisdom?"[18]

THE FAILURE OF FENNO'S "NATIONAL PLAN"

Despite Fenno's best efforts to have the *Gazette* play the role of "official paper," the administration was slow to do its part by officially sponsoring or supporting the journal. Fenno did not receive his first government printing contract until three months after he began publishing and promised additional contracts were slow to materialize.

By the late summer of 1789, Fenno's newspaper was bringing in only half the money he needed to support his family, to say nothing of making his fortune, and its future seemed shrouded "in thick darkness." The editor was learning the economic realities of the printing trade by hard experience. The *Gazette of the United States* was rapidly gaining subscribers, but they were not paying their bills quickly or often enough. This common problem was especially acute for Fenno, because his circulation base was national, making deadbeat subscribers very difficult to effectively dun. Like many editors before and after him, Fenno came to the conclusion that Americans considered newspaper debts lightly, but what particularly irritated him was that no one, not even enthusiastic supporters like Alexander Hamilton and Rufus King, seemed to appreciate the distinction "between the Gazette, & papers in common."[19]

By October 1789 Fenno had received a few more small printing assignments from the executive departments but had grown weary of trawling for contracts. He reached the conclusion that "this kind of aid is not altogether the thing." In what was certainly the new nation's first bid for a job as a professional political communicator, Fenno decided that he needed to be the government's in-house spokesman: "My object is to carry the publication of the paper to the fullest perfection—in order to do this—I should have aid in a line that would not divide, & distract my attention from this one great object." His long-range goals for the paper now went far beyond printing contracts or private subsidies. They were nothing less than official status for the publication and a salary for himself, steps that would "confer dignity upon the Paper & give me a reputation upon a solid basis."[20] It would also put Fenno's journal on par with one of his obvious models, the British government's *London Gazette*, "Published by Authority" and edited by an official "Gazetteer," who was paid £300 a year by the royal treasury.[21]

Fenno's hopes presaged a perennial dream for American political workers of becoming fully legitimate, openly acknowledged, and fairly remunerated participants in the political process. But he was only a precursor. Though certainly Fenno did want to earn his living from work that we can define as political—building support for the Washington administration and its Hamiltonian policies—he did not think of himself as a politician. He did not even think of politics as essentially involved in his project "to hold up the people's own government—and . . . by every exertion . . . to endear the GENERAL GOVERNMENT TO THE PEOPLE." A businessman at heart, Fenno inquired about posts in the Philadelphia banks when it looked like the *Gazette* might go under, rather than elsewhere in journalism or politics. Moreover, he took no pleasure in political disputation, asking his wife more than once not to write to him about politics in her letters. (This also had to do with the idea—very prevalent among the men of the early republic—that the public sphere usually was not a place for women.) Fenno did not live "for" politics, but he found himself trapped in what became a manifestly political occupation.[22]

Fenno toyed with making this bid for legitimacy openly, but never dared to do so, fearing that an explicit demand for sponsorship might be refused. In a country so steeped in fears of British corruption, as Fenno was probably told by some member of the administration, the creation of a "state paper" in the manner of the hated *London Gazette* would "never be supported by public opinion." The administration's cowardice disgusted Fenno. His predicament suggested that the United States was even further from national greatness than he had supposed: "Is it not a pitiful business that One Paper upon this Plan cannot find support in the United States?" (In fact, the *London Gazette* was widely disliked even in Great Britain. Samuel Johnson's *Dictionary* defined "Gazetteer" as "usually applied to wretches . . . hired to vindicate the court.")

Mounting financial pressure eventually brought Fenno to a crisis that radically changed the character of his newspaper. By October 1789 he was $400 behind in paying the *Gazette*'s various expenses and estimated he would need $500 more to get through the winter; he had also not begun to pay back the debts he had incurred in launching the paper. With great reluctance, Fenno decided in November to drop a crucial part of his plan for a "national" newspaper and begin accepting advertising, a major step toward maintaining the *Gazette* as merely a conventional urban newspaper.[23]

At the same time, the emergence of political conflict over the administration's financial policies sparked Alexander Hamilton's interest in the *Gazette* and began to generate more substantial government aid. Fenno was given all of the Senate's printing business (controlled by Senate secretary Samuel A. Otis, an acquaintance from Boston) and most of the Treasury Department's. Hamilton personally also "lent" Fenno substantial sums, without asking for repayment, on at least two occasions in 1790 and 1791.[24]

These loans and printing contracts were as close as Fenno ever came to government sponsorship and a salary. By the time of the 1793 yellow fever epidemic in Philadelphia, where the federal government had moved, his financial situation had deteriorated to the point of forcing a suspension of the *Gazette*. When the epidemic subsided in November of that year, Fenno took stock. He was now $2,000 in debt, with his major asset $4,000 in accounts receivable for subscriptions "scattered in small sums from Savannah to Portland in the district of Maine." From experience, he did not expect to "realize more than a quarter of that sum."[25]

To save his business, Fenno adopted a two-pronged strategy. First, the editor applied to Hamilton for the substantial "assistance long since promised . . . with all the pathos I am capable of giving." He asked that the secretary's supporters be solicited for donations to the *Gazette*. "Four Years & an half of my life is gone for nothing; & worse," Fenno pleaded, "if at this crisis the hand of benevolence & *patriotism* is not extended." Hamilton had hesitated to take such positive, organized steps in Fenno's behalf, but by 1793 he had endured two years of assaults from Philip Freneau's *National Gazette*. Now he responded quickly and effectively to Fenno's plea, raising money with the argument that it was critical to the "Federal cause" that Fenno "be enabled to prosecute a paper." Hamilton enlisted Rufus King to collect $1,000 in New York while he raised a like amount in Philadelphia. Among the Philadelphia contributors were officers of the embattled Bank of the United States.[26]

The success of Hamilton's fundraising enabled Fenno to employ the second prong of his strategy. This was to completely abandon his original business plan and turn the *Gazette* into a conventional urban printing establishment. The paper reappeared on 11 December 1793, now a daily entitled *Gazette of the United States & Evening Advertiser*. The new subtitle indicated the more prominent role that advertising would play in the journal. At the same time, Fenno decided "to carry on the [job] printing business extensively" for any client who could pay. He purchased enough type to avoid the need to subcontract his job printing for the government. Thus four and a half years into his project, Fenno arrived where he had tried to avoid beginning, as a printer.[27]

Fenno's experience set many patterns for the future role of newspapers in the American political system. Revolutionary scruples and adverse public opinion precluded the possibility of an out-and-out government newspaper like the *London Gazette* and severely curtailed the possibility of overt sponsorship as practiced in Great Britain. As Fenno finally concluded, other than himself and a few close friends from Boston, not another person "appeared to comprehend an idea of the kind."[28] The management of public opinion, or at least the financial risks associated with it, were to be left to privately owned newspapers, organized and funded in the conventional manner, as one aspect of a full-service printing office. Partisan newspapers would have to support themselves as newspapers always had, through the sale of printing services and advertising to government, local businesses, and citizens. Subscriptions alone were not enough.

This did not mean that government officials took no interest in influencing public opinion through the newspapers. Indeed, as the antipathy between Hamilton and Jefferson blossomed into the development of political parties, both leaders became convinced that newspapers were critical to their respective causes. Given the economics of the printing trade, it was inevitable that political publishers would require financial support. Blocked from directly sponsoring newspapers, Jefferson and Hamilton had to employ methods even more devious than the British practices. The system that developed involved subsidizing political newspapers indirectly, by giving the traditional sources of newspaper income some political direction. Printing contracts, subscriptions, the availability of financing, access to information sources, and even advertising would increasingly be determined by the political leanings of the printer, his customers, and his benefactors.

THE STATESMEN AND THEIR SURROGATE: THOMAS JEFFERSON, JAMES MADISON, AND THE ORIGINS OF THE *NATIONAL GAZETTE*

The appearance of a counterpart to the *Gazette of the United States,* Philip Freneau's *National Gazette,* coincided with the linkage of newspapers to the emerging political parties and set the pattern for several other aspects of newspaper politics. Perhaps most important was the precedent that was set for giving yet another kind of aid to political newspaper editors: government jobs. Freneau, a newspaper editor, may have been the nation's first political patronage appointee. Many an editor would dream of following—and later many would indeed follow—in his footsteps.

The Jeffersonian Republicans would be the leaders in the development of newspaper politics, but in these early years, their steps toward an organized opposition to the government were taken slowly and gingerly. For a long time, John Fenno managed to maintain cordial relations even with officials whose political ideas ran counter to his own. Among the printing contracts Fenno finally managed to acquire in the spring of 1790 was one from Thomas Jefferson's State Department for the printing of the laws.[29] Yet with time and an accretion of disagreements between himself and Alexander Hamilton, Jefferson soured on the increasingly antirepublican bent he detected in Fenno's paper. Particularly offensive to Jefferson and others were John Adams's "Discourses on Davila," in which the vice president argued for the need to grant noble titles to America's natural aristocracy in order to hold the people's respect.[30]

Jefferson's attitude toward Fenno's erstwhile national newspaper gradually changed from disagreement and distaste to positive fear and loathing. Jefferson's fears regarding the *Gazette of the United States* can only be understood in terms of his attitude toward Hamilton's entire financial and economic program. Many opponents saw the program as an attempt to reconstruct the American political economy along British lines. In 1790 and 1791, Hamilton and a compliant Congress established a British-style system of public finance (including a national bank), bound the nation much more tightly to trade and good relations with Great Britain, and seemed determined to invest the United States government with the kind of unlimited authority (to do anything it deemed "necessary and proper") that British governments were thought to enjoy. The massive speculation in government securities and Bank of the United States stock that erupted, along with the abundant evidence that members of Congress and the administration were involved, only confirmed their fears.

At the bottom of it all was the treasury secretary himself, whose relations with the Congress and President Washington reminded many of Sir Robert Walpole, the first English "prime" minister, whose money-cemented hold over both the king and Parliament had made him virtual chief of state, and, in some eyes, a tyrant. Jefferson warned Washington that, like Walpole, Hamilton had corrupted the national legislature "where there was a squadron devoted to the nod of the Treasury . . . ready to do what he should direct.[31]

In this Walpolean scenario, John Fenno's newspaper ironically played the role of the British government's sponsored press, the role that Fenno had aspired to but never attained. The faithful coverage of presidential pageantry in the *Gazette of the United States* had been annoying enough to democrats and republican purists, but column after column of essays like "Davila" and the related series "Publicola" (by John Quincy Adams) had made it seem "a paper of pure Toryism, disseminating the doctrines of monarchy, aristocracy, and the exclusion of the influence of the people." Nor did it please Jefferson that Fenno was slow to implement a pet project of his, the printing of translated excerpts from the *Gazette de Leyde,* a distinguished French-language newspaper published in the Netherlands.

The secretary of state intended these excerpts to counterbalance the anti-French slant of the London newspapers from which American printers usually copied their European news. As Fenno's *Gazette* became a willing conduit and advocate for Hamilton's side of the financial controversy, it came to seem positively sinister to Jefferson, a press "servile" to an American prime minister. "No government ought to be without censors," Jefferson protested to Washington, "and where the press is free [meaning free from executive influence], no one ever will." Jefferson's fears were hardly allayed by the fact that the leading advertisers in the *Gazette of the United States* were brokerage houses handling government securities, firms that benefited from Hamilton's policies.[32]

In the 1780s Jefferson had seen the press primarily as an effective means of keeping the people in solidarity with their leaders. With a republican form of government in place, the greatest threats to such solidarity were erroneous popular beliefs and fears arising from provincial unworldliness and lack of information about the government's activities. Rather than favoring the establishment of an authoritative press that would "conciliate" the people, à la Fenno, Jefferson had sought to encourage the broad dissemination of as many newspapers as possible. "Were it left to me to decide whether we should have a government without newspapers, or newspapers without a government," declaimed Jefferson in a famous passage, "I should not hesitate a moment to prefer the latter." This statement naturally has become a favorite with generations of American journalists, but for Jefferson it had a particular meaning. In American Indian societies, he noted, "public opinion is in the place of law, and restrains morals as powerfully as laws ever did anywhere." In a literate, typographical society, newspapers were the means by which the rule of public opinion would be put into action; if the people were provided with an accurate view of the world, then public opinion would always be a good ruler.[33]

These beliefs rested on two premises, at least one of which seemed to be vitiated by the events of the early 1790s. First, Jefferson had never doubted that a well-informed public would always arrive at political views fully in accord with his own. Second, he had never dreamed that any participant in the American Revolution would try to rule the country in an unrepublican manner. The prospect of a population intentionally misinformed by a badly intentioned government horrified him. Believing themselves to be faced with exactly such a situation in Hamilton and Fenno's *Gazette,* Jefferson and James Madison eventually resolved to take more active steps "to reclaim [the people] by enlightening them." Wide circulation of just any newspaper was no longer enough.[34]

Thus, in April 1791 Jefferson approached Benjamin Franklin Bache, the editor of the Philadelphia *General Advertiser,* about transforming that paper into a possible antidote to or replacement for the *Gazette of the United States.* Like Fenno, Jefferson wanted a national newspaper that would not be overtly tied to any local community and could thus be addressed to a national public. He suggested that Bache print his newspaper in such a way that the advertising could be torn out of it and the editorial matter only mailed to distant places.[35]

Bache demurred for unknown reasons, and Jefferson shifted to the more aggressive strategy of establishing a completely new paper. He and Madison began working to "get another *weekly* or *halfweekly* paper set up excluding advertisements, so that it might go through the states, and furnish a whig-vehicle of intelligence . . . and be generally taken instead of Fenno's [paper]."[36] Jefferson and Madison were particularly interested in a paper that could reach remote rural areas such as many parts of their own Virginia, thus providing "public information in many places not sufficiently supplied with it," not to mention more likely to be inhabited by their own supporters.[37]

Following Fenno's plan in most respects other than content, Jefferson and Madison also sought to minimize the involvement of printers in the management of their journal. Not only did they look outside the trade for an editor, they also insisted on a man of education and established reputation. Unimpressed with Fenno's intellect or journalistic skills, they sought to give their journal an edge over the *Gazette of the United States* by finding a bona fide "Man of genius." They settled on Philip Freneau, "Poet of the Revolution," sea captain, and Madison's roommate at the College of New Jersey. Unlike any previous partisan journalist (or most subsequent ones), Freneau was a reasonably eminent personage in his own right, a distinguished author with a college education. The Virginians were ecstatic at the prospect of a journal run by someone other than a slow-witted printer: "It is certain that there is not to be found in the whole catalogue of American Printers," wrote Madison, "a single name that can approach towards a rivalship." Jefferson felt Freneau would succeed easily in such project, because his "genius . . . is so superior to that of his competitors."[38]

The question arises, why did Jefferson and Madison not simply supply the editorial matter for a newspaper run by a conventional, trade-oriented printer, a political strategy that the American political elite had been employing since the time of Zenger? This was what John Adams and his friends had done for the *Boston Gazette* during the Revolution and what Madison, Hamilton, and many other federalists had done during the ratification debate. The answer is that the situation in 1791 was very different. Though Jefferson and Madison fervently believed they were acting patriotically, they had decided on an act of opposition to the regularly constituted government, a government of which they themselves were members. Though they shared the political culture's profound disdain for parties, they understood that the creation of a party was what they were contemplating. Yet the prevailing code of political morality prescribed that leaders lead in the name of the whole community and prohibited them from organizing parties or openly soliciting political support.[39]

Thus, the Virginians felt the need to turn the open, active management of their opposition—and especially the role of publicly writing and speaking in defense of it—to people outside the government, and indeed outside the coterie of Revolutionary statesmen. A talented editor such as Freneau would be able to execute the business on a high level without much help, allowing his sponsors to keep a judicious distance. They knew from Freneau's earlier work with the Philadelphia *Freeman's Journal* and the New York *Daily Advertiser* that he bitterly detested banks and speculators and could be expected to ferociously attack Hamilton's policies. As Jefferson blandly told President Washington later, he and Madison assumed that Freneau would produce a "good whig" paper. In other words, the editor needed little direction from Jefferson and Madison in order to fulfill the purpose they intended.[40] The Sage of Monticello had a gift for using people in this fashion, or rather, for allowing them to use themselves in his behalf. As Hamilton put it, nastily but well:

> That Officer [Jefferson] has had too considerable a part of his political Education amidst the intrigues of an European Court to hazard a direct personal commitment in such a case. He knows how to put a man in a situation calculated to produce all the effects he desires, without the gross and awkward formality of telling him—"Sir I mean to *hire* you for the purpose."[41]

The decision to use Freneau can also be traced to Jefferson's complicated personal relationship with newspapers. While believing in the power of political newspaper writing, he vehemently disdained engaging in it personally. In 1800 he bragged to Abigail Adams (in a claim he made repeatedly over the course of his life) that "I never in my life had, directly or indirectly, written one sentence for a newspaper," noting later to himself that this statement was "an absolute truth." This was a shockingly stark double standard even for Jefferson, given his repeated efforts to found newspapers and constant efforts to get close friends such as James Madison to write for them. At least one former newspaper editor, having defended Jefferson during the 1790s, became deeply exasperated upon reading the first published collection of Jefferson's writings decades later. Despite Jefferson's claims of great merit for not writing for newspapers, "These letters prove . . . incontestably, that he continually urged others to do it, and that he assisted in supplying both facts and arguments for the purpose. . . . There is nothing . . . wrong in this; but . . . he makes it wrong by his continued efforts to impress the public . . . that he was not in any way connected with newspapers. While, at the same time, there was not a man living who placed more . . . reliance on newspapers than Mr. Jefferson."[42]

Having settled on a strategy and the man to execute it, Jefferson and Madison then took extraordinary measures to bring their plans to fruition. Working in New York but impoverished as usual, Freneau had announced plans to publish a new paper in his rural New Jersey hometown. Mutual friends alerted Madison to the poet's distress, and enticements were offered to launch the projected newspaper in Philadelphia instead. Unsolicited, Jefferson tendered Freneau a $250-a-year position as a translator in the State Department. This was not a lavish salary for a gentleman, but the secretary of state promised that it "gives so little to do as not to interfere with any other calling the person may chuse."

Of course, the "other calling" Jefferson had in mind was editing the projected newspaper. Jefferson also offered additional assistance of both a financial and an editorial nature: the "perusal" of all the secretary of state's foreign correspondence, a large selection of foreign newspapers to copy from, all of the State Department's printing business, and a contract for printing the laws.[43] Jefferson was careful to preserve his own deniability in project. He allowed Madison, House of Representatives clerk Beckley, and Virginia governor Henry Lee to handle the actual negotiations with Freneau and never mentioned the newspaper in his own correspondence with the editor.

Initially, Freneau refused the offer to become Jefferson and Madison's surrogate in the battle for public opinion. He had been involved in newspaper publishing long enough to understand the field's financial vagaries, and his future newspaper plans revolved mostly around retiring to the life of a reclusive poet. After protracted negotiations, Freneau and Jefferson's emissaries completed an arrangement that completely absolved Freneau of financial risk for the projected opposition paper. Francis Childs, the New York publisher who had been Freneau's most recent employer, agreed to print and assume all financial responsibility for the new journal. Though the poet would not be liable for the paper's losses, he would still receive one-third of any profits.[44]

Even more remarkably, Jefferson and Madison personally assisted in building a list of subscribers for the paper. Within a month of Freneau's decision in favor of the venture, Francis Childs was on his way to Virginia, armed with a sheaf of letters from Madison, to solicit the Virginia gentry for subscriptions. Madison enlisted his own considerable prestige in their effort, inviting his fellow Virginians to regard subscribing as a personal favor to him. Madison had his own father collect subscriptions in Orange and Culpeper counties, the governor perform the task in Richmond, and a member of the powerful Carroll family do the same in Maryland. Jefferson had his neighbor Thomas Bell scour the environs of Charlottesville for subscribers. The Virginia leaders became so closely involved in Freneau's operations that several subscribers wrote to Madison rather than the editor with complaints about delivery problems.[45]

EMBODYING THE OPPOSITION: THE *NATIONAL GAZETTE* IN ACTION

The result of all these labors, the Philadelphia *National Gazette*, first appeared in October 1791. The title and the lack of advertising in the first issue announced it as a self-consciously national publication, devoted to presenting an imagined national community based on more correct republican principles than were found in Fenno's paper. Jefferson had always advocated omitting advertising, but Freneau and Childs compromised on the issue, announcing that ads would be limited to one page, one-half to one-third of what successful urban papers could usually sell. The limit turned out to be academic, since Childs never came close to selling even one page per issue. A few small shopkeepers and tradesmen purchased space occasionally, but the *National Gazette* never attracted the large-scale merchants and brokers who patronized the *Gazette of the United States*.[46]

For the first few months, Freneau confined his paper to purely literary or only obliquely political matter. This reflected the reticence that the editors and his patrons still felt about actively denouncing the government. Things began to change in the early spring of 1792, when the first of a stream of more stridently partisan material appeared, penned by Freneau and some of the capital's less eminent oppositionists, such as John Beckley. The two primary targets were the monarchical trappings that had been set up around President Washington and the inequalities of wealth and power being fostered by Alexander Hamilton's financial system.[47]

While carrying a full line of the serialized essays that had long been the staple of American political debate, the most striking and significant aspect of Freneau's paper was its effort to fashion and project the image of a coherent opposition party. Battle lines had appeared in congressional voting and cabinet infighting over a number of issues, but the dissidents as yet had no common basis for identifying themselves and communicating their ideas to voters. A string of items in the *National Gazette* boiled down the welter of arguments, preferences, and fears that government opponents had expressed to a few crisp points and gave a collective name to the politicians and citizens who held them. Though electoral organizing was at a very nascent stage of development, Freneau's newspaper provided the critical service of creating at least an imaginary body for readers to identify with and join.

James Madison himself began the process with a 2 April 1792 essay entitled "The Union: Who are its real Friends?" Madison's writing for the journal thus far had been aphoristic and only vaguely partisan, and he would contribute only rarely after this point, but here he set an important precedent.[48] Covering only half a column, the piece succinctly laid out some key differences between supporters and opponents of the administration, working to establish the idea that opposition to present government policies was not the same as opposition to the government itself. Madison used the format of answers to the question asked in the title: "Not those who promote unnecessary accumulations of the debt ... Not those who study, by arbitrary interpretations and insidious precedents, to pervert the limited government of the Union, into a government of unlimited discretion, contrary to the will and subversive of the authority of the people.... *The real* FRIENDS *to the Union are those,* ... Who are friends to the limited and republican system of government, ... Who considering a public debt as injurious to the interests of the people ... are enemies to every contrivance for *unnecessarily* increasing its amount."

Having thus covered public finance and constitutional interpretation, Madison threw in other paired "Not . . . Who" statements expressing opposition fears that Hamilton's policies were smoothing the way for the development of an American aristocracy and monarchy.[49]

A few weeks later, Freneau gave the "real friends" the name they would use in the party battles of the 1790s, in a sketch called "Sentiments of a Republican." Here Freneau offered both a particular analysis of current public affairs and a label that those who shared this analysis could adopt. The piece encompassed Madison's themes of increased public debt, loose constitutional interpretation, and creeping monarchy, but it put more emphasis on feelings—the reader and potential opposition supporter's feelings—about what Hamilton's policies were doing to the country. The Republican's sentiments about rising corruption, social inequality, and the betrayal of Revolutionary ideals provided a taste of the hyperbolic, Manichean rhetoric that would become common in the partisan press of the 1790s. "It would seem as if some demon . . . had whispered in the ears of the first Congress . . . the most speedy and effectual method of destroying the liberties of the United States. . . . The most barefaced efforts have been made to substitute, in the room of our equal republic, a baneful monarchy in our country; . . . Let the United States disgorge such beasts of plunder and prey" as "our wealthy speculators."[50]

Madison and Freneau used the term "republican" for themselves as a way of claiming that only the opposition fundamentally supported republican government, but it was also clear that they meant to use it as a partisan political label.[51] A few day after "Sentiments of a Republican," the *National Gazette* observed that "two parties . . . have shown themselves in the doings of the new government," the first time that his paper had used that term to describe the divisions that had emerged. He went on to outline the differences between the two parties, covering the same issues Madison had, but in his own harsher and more emotional language.[52]

Calls to political action and further catechisms for identifying political allies and enemies issued regularly through the rest of 1792. "Useful Animadversions" on the May adjournment of Congress declared that "the time has now come, that proper distinctions should be made on important political subjects." On the Fourth of July, Freneau inserted a plan for an organization called "The Friends of the People" from a London newspaper, with a correspondent's call that such "societies should be formed in every county of the United States upon similar plans." The suggestion was not taken up, but for a few weeks Freneau's writers toyed with adopting "Friends of the People" as their title, emphasizing democracy and equal rights as the essential meaning of the Revolution and the Constitution (or at least its preamble). In the meantime, further efforts were made to organize the opposition's creed, including another series of questions like Madison's.[53]

Before the end of 1792, Madison himself made two final contributions to Freneau's paper that helped fully shape the still mostly imagined opposition party. In September "A Candid State of Parties" provided a brief history of American politics. Looking to rescue his own political consistency, as a supporter of the Constitution turned opponent of the first administration under it, Madison tried to more or less officially name the new parties and distinguish the present party conflict from the earlier ones, Whig versus Tory and federalist versus antifederalist. The current division, "likely to be of some duration," was between two new groups: an "anti republican party" who "are more partial to the opulent than to the other classes of society; and having . . . a persuasion that mankind are incapable of governing themselves, it follows with them . . . that government can be carried on only by pageantry of rank, the influence of money . . . , and the terror of military force"; and a "republican party" who "believing . . . mankind are capable of governing themselves, and hating hereditary power as . . . an outrage to the rights of man, are naturally offended at every public measure that does not appeal to the understanding . . . of the community, or that is not strictly conformable to the principles . . . of republican government."[54]

In December Madison returned to the question format he had used in "The Union" but now framed the answers explicitly as the dueling creeds of opposed parties; he also adopted more of the strident, populist tone that Freneau and his paper's other writers had been using. No longer the "contemplative statesman" who had examined the state of parties in the previous essay, Madison now asked "Who are the best keepers of the people's liberties?" and answered through a scathing dialogue between a "Republican" and an "Anti-republican." In this presentation, the party difference was boiled down to the single, fundamental issue of democracy: how much of it could a republic allow and survive? Madison's earlier and later views on this question were sometimes highly equivocal, but here his party archetypes expressed blunt, starkly opposed views. They began:

WHO ARE THE BEST KEEPERS OF THE PEOPLE'S LIBERTIES?
  Republican.—The people themselves.—The sacred trust can be no where so safe as in the hands most interested in preserving it.

> *Anti-republican.*—The people are stupid, suspicious, licentious. They cannot safely trust themselves. When they have established government, they should think of nothing but obedience, leaving the care of their liberties to their wiser rulers.

By the end of the piece, the mild-mannered Virginian had the two parties calling each other names. The Anti-republican pronounced the Republican "an accomplice of atheism and anarchy," while the Republican shot back, getting the last word, that his opponent was "a blasphemer of [the people's] rights and an idolater of tyranny." Here Madison imaginatively constructed the barely emergent party conflict in much the terms that it would rage for the next two decades.[55]

While they did much with the *National Gazette* to foster the idea that an opposition party existed, Madison and Freneau were less certain about how or whether to connect their newspaper Republicans to the world of legislative and electoral politics. As the fall congressional campaigns were beginning, Freneau actually complained about the number of "electioneering pieces" in other papers.[56] Opposition activists in Philadelphia and a few other places were organizing themselves to run candidates, however, and they began to use the *National Gazette* despite its editor's apparent unease with electioneering. In August a stream of inserted articles began publicizing a ticket of congressional candidates cooked up by a conclave of Philadelphia and western Pennsylvania oppositionists the previous spring. The nominees were not all opponents of the government, and much of the campaign revolved around a complex dispute over nomination procedures, but it amounted to an effort to bring national party divisions to bear in state politics.

In late September, Freneau allowed his editorial column to be the medium through which a body calling itself the Philadelphia Committee of Correspondence announced an even larger slate, including candidates for all congressional seats and for presidential electors. It was followed one week later by a remarkable full-page article that picked out a selection of the candidates, reviewed their records, and showed that they held "principles ... forever dear to the whigs and republicans of Pennsylvania."[57] Here a definite and operational connection was being made between the imagined party of principles and values defined in the newspaper's pages and the potentially real one of voters and candidates that might actually change the objectionable policies. Newspaper politics would only succeed in the end by constantly maintaining this connection.

The nation's first presidential election campaign occurred in the same period, but here Freneau got little help and the *National Gazette*'s efforts were weak. No one yet dared oppose Washington himself, but there was a hesitant effort to prevent John Adams from being reelected as vice president. Beginning in early September, Freneau began publishing some articles against Adams, but mostly they were reprints from old antifederalist papers such as the *New-York Journal* and the Boston *Independent Chronicle*.

Freneau's first and almost only direct assault on the subject (though hardly his only criticism of Adams) did not come until 24 November, with a straightforward column headed "PRO and CON: Arguments against the re election of Mr. Adams." His handling of the actual voting was low-key to say the least, mostly one-sentence reports of state results as they arrived in Philadelphia. He never promoted the major alternative candidate, New York Governor George Clinton, nor made any effort to ensure a large turnout or generate emotional involvement in the outcome. Freneau grumbled in one of his December result reports that the people did not seem to care about the vice presidential race, based on the low number of votes for electors, but his own well-positioned newspaper had done little to prevent that outcome.[58]

If Freneau did not quite grasp how to convert the imagined party to reality, the sarcastic verse and sketches he produced for the paper inculcated a sense of party in readers by other means, expressing more compactly the political values and antipathies outlined in the journal's expository pieces. Sarcasm was uniquely suited to party building, because it invited readers to feel a shared sense of moral superiority to the ideas and people being ridiculed.

Examples included a list of "RULES: *For changing a limited Republican government into an unlimited hereditary one,*" and a spurious endorsement of pro-administration candidates (mostly wealthy merchants) for the House of Representatives on the grounds that "*understanding and property are in a direct ratio with each other,* and that [a] man of small fortune is absolutely incapable of state affairs, for he is little better than a fool." Nor did Freneau lose any opportunity to mock "courtiers" like John Fenno. In early 1793 the *National Gazette* advertised for a poet laureate, someone "with dexterity in composing *birth-day odes,* soaring above this clod for models for the characters laureated. To compare an officer of this government to any thing on this earth, would be . . . unsuited to the *majesty* of the subject."[59]

In fact, goading Fenno was one of Freneau's greatest contributions to the development of the opposition party. The *Gazette of the United States* responded with displays of intolerance and pseudoaristocratic hauteur that seemed to confirm Freneau's characterization of the government and its supporters. Conceiving his paper as an arm of the state and possessing neither the stomach nor the talent to return Freneau's fire in kind, Fenno sanctimoniously affirmed the status quo and questioned the motives of anyone who would criticize it. Often, this amounted to simply calling the Republicans names. Fenno petulantly labeled the administration's critics "dismal cacklers," "out of their wits," "propagators of calumny," "villains," "brawlers," "enemies of freedom," and "the worst and basest of men," and condemned their "malignant effrontery."[60] Fenno's reasoning was that, while it may have once been "worthy and laudable to inveigh against despotism" when it was imposed by the English, "when the people set up government with their own hands," it was "absurd to attempt uniting" them against it. In a republic, all public commentators had a "duty . . . to buoy up the government." Here Fenno was presenting a view of politics as the sole preserve of authority, a conception that was antediluvian even in the 1790s and contradicted the very notion of "public opinion" that American thinkers and politicians constantly invoked.[61]

Fenno tried to boil the party conflict down to a contrast of personal qualities between the administration leaders and their critics, a contest the administration won handily in his mind. Opposition such as appeared in the *National Gazette* could come only from vicious mediocrities, jealous of men more talented, successful, and deserving than themselves:

> Virtue, worth and talents, or any clean wholesome subject of praise, disgust these Hottentots in morals. . . . No occupation requires less talent and merit of any kind than railing and finding fault. It is the opinion of many who know the authors of newspaper calumnies, that those succeed best in this way, who are totally unqualified to act in any other.[62]

Though legal action against the opposition was years away, the administration editor called for it early on. Fenno quickly applied the word "sedition" to Republican newspaper criticisms and predicted that opposition criticism would inevitably lead to anarchy and civil war if left unchecked.[63] Jefferson and Madison, however, were immensely pleased with their journalistic champion. "[Freneau's] paper has saved our constitution," Jefferson wrote when President Washington pressured him to remove the editor as translating clerk. The secretary of state firmly believed that the drive to monarchize and Anglicize the new government had been "checked by no one means so powerfully as by that paper."[64]

A PATH NOT TAKEN: THE FALL OF THE *NATIONAL GAZETTE* AND THE FAILURE OF CENTRALIZED NEWSPAPER POLITICS

When the arrangements that had brought Freneau to Philadelphia were made public, the *National Gazette* turned into a terrible political liability for the Virginia leaders. Alexander Hamilton had been convinced for some time that Madison and Jefferson were heads of *"a faction decidedly hostile to me and my administration."* When Freneau's paper began to exhibit "the same malignant and unfriendly aspect," Hamilton immediately suspected its true provenance. The treasury secretary first used the information to turn some of the Virginians' former allies against them, and then in July 1792 launched a public assault on Jefferson's relationship with the *National Gazette*.[65]

Up until this time, Hamilton had shown comparatively little interest in newspapers as a political tool. He never celebrated the medium as Jefferson did, despite being more comfortable about writing newspaper essays himself than Jefferson was. Hamilton wrote for the press often throughout his career, while Jefferson did so rarely, or, if his own statements are to be believed, never. Hamilton stayed relatively uninvolved with the *Gazette of the United States* in its early years. Yet one of Hamilton's major concerns was maintaining the people's deference to the new government. This was crucial if republican government was to prove "by experience . . . consistent with that *stability* and *order* in Government which are essential to public strength & private security and happiness." He feared it would be difficult to keep order in a system based on the people's consent, particularly if oppositionists actively tried to estrange the government from the people's "affections" by means of the press. Jefferson and Madison's efforts to turn public opinion against the government threatened to unleash a democratic monster that would destroy both the national state and the local elite who had founded it:

> These Gentlemen are prepared to hazard a great deal to effect a change . . . not appreciating as they ought to do the natural resistance to Government which in every community results from the human passions . . . & the infinite danger that the National Government once rendered odious will be kept so. . . .
>
> They forget an old but a very just, though a coarse saying—That it is much easier to raise the Devil than to lay him.[66]

The *National Gazette* forced Hamilton to turn his own attention to the battle for public opinion. His first act was to neutralize the weapons of his opponents.

Hamilton began by inserting a short, pseudonymous notice in the *Gazette of the United States*. It announced that the editor of the *National Gazette* received a government salary and asked a rhetorical question: "Whether this salary is paid him for *translations;* or for *publications,* the design of which is to vilify those to whom the voice of the people has committed . . . public affairs—to oppose measures of government, and by false insinuations, to disturb the public peace?"[67] Freneau retorted that his "small stipend" proved only that his criticisms of the administration as "editor of a free newspaper" were that much more "honest and disinterested." Certainly, Freneau contended, his relationship to the government was much more praiseworthy than that of a "vile sycophant" like Fenno, who licked his paymaster's boots. Hamilton shot back that the only thing "free" about the *National Gazette* was that it was "Free to defame, but never free to praise."[68] A few days later, Hamilton greatly expanded on the same charges, under a second pseudonym. The *National Gazette* was "a news paper instituted by a public officer, and the Editor of it regularly pensioned with the public money." Rather than the courageous, independent political actor he pretended to be, Freneau was "the faithful and devoted servant of the head of a party."[69]

Jefferson's, Madison's, and Freneau's attempts to explain their actions in the episode led them into confusion, obfuscation, and outright lying, because Hamilton's central accusations—that the Virginians had caused the establishment of the *National Gazette* and that in doing so they were in effect acting as a party opposed to the administration—were utterly true. Jefferson and Madison insisted that there was no direct link between the translating clerkship and the newspaper. They had only intended to "patronize merit" and help a deserving Revolutionary veteran. Madison admitted that he had advised Freneau to start a newspaper in Philadelphia as opposed to New Jersey, but he disavowed any "illicit or improper connection" between the office and the newspaper, a plain lie if Madison was trying to say that no political motives were involved.[70]

On the issue of editorial control of the *National Gazette,* as opposed to the circumstances of its founding, Freneau and the Virginians made claims that were nearer the truth, though no more convincing to their detractors. The editor strenuously denied that Jefferson exerted any power over the content of his paper; Freneau even swore out an affidavit before the mayor of Philadelphia to this effect, adding that "nor was a line ever, directly or indirectly, dictated, or composed" for the paper by the secretary of state.[71] Freneau seems to have been telling the truth. Though Freneau was a hireling, he was far too much the prima donna to accept direction, nor does Jefferson seem to have tried to give any. Freneau demonstrated Jefferson's lack of control when the two disagreed over the controversial French minister Edmond Genet's high-handed tactics in 1793. The *National Gazette* maintained its vociferous support even after Genet's persistent attempts to involve the United States in the European war had estranged him from Jefferson and many other sympathizers.[72]

However, the fundamental independence of the *National Gazette* did little to alleviate Jefferson and Madison's predicament: they had opened themselves to the charge that they were "selfish, partial politicians" and thus unfit leaders according to the political culture of the time.[73] Conducting their political battle by means of a newspaper was meant to be a way out of this problem, but the strategy had backfired. If anything, the act of hiring a newspaper editor raised even deeper ideological fears. The standard scenario in which Americans imagined liberty being destroyed called for an ambitious leader or "junto" of leaders to recruit a loyal corps of helpers, men whose loyalties were to their leader rather than the community as a whole, whose political free will had been taken away by their financial dependence on salaries their leader controlled. These subverters of liberty could come in many forms: a warlord's private army, a classical dictator's Praetorian Guard, or the parliamentary pensioners and hireling newspaper editors of Britain.[74]

This was the specter Hamilton tried to raise by calling Freneau Jefferson's political "servant," and a "fit instrument" for Jefferson's subversive designs.[75] Of course, thanks to the remarkable flexibility of the classical republican ideas and rhetoric espoused by all leaders during the 1790s (and freely mixed with other intellectual traditions), Jefferson, Madison, and Freneau feared and denounced Hamilton and Fenno in exactly the same terms. Freneau's satirical definitions included one meant to describe Fenno: "*Printer*—A mere machine for public convenience. One who is understood to give up the rights of private as well as of public opinion, the moment he becomes connected with a press."[76]

In the end, much of the *National Gazette* controversy revolved around the question of which cabinet officer had committed the more heinous act of partisanship. In a move that indicated the disdain for newspaper politics always lurking beneath the surface of his paeans, Jefferson argued that Hamilton was worse because he actually wrote for a newspaper, rather than merely starting one. "Is not the dignity, and even decency of government committed," he asked Washington, "when one of its principal ministers enlists . . . as an anonymous writer or paragraphist?"[77]

Few contemporaries or historians have accepted this argument. As Stanley Elkins and Eric McKitrick have written, it was Jefferson and Madison who had first unleashed "the demon of partisanship," and Freneau's State Department job proved impossible to adequately explain. For Jefferson personally, the whole project was a costly mistake. The controversy contributed to his estrangement from George Washington and cast a pall of scandal over his resignation as secretary of state in December 1793. In the future, Jefferson and Madison would be more cautious in their dealings with newspapers and newspaper editors. Though Jefferson would remain supportive of friendly editors and get into trouble again over his dealings with James Callender, he was never again so closely involved with a partisan newspaper, possibly excepting his later administration organ, the *National Intelligencer*. Madison would keep even further away from the press, curtailing and then stopping completely his once-frequent contributions. Most revealing of their changed attitudes were the actions they took once the *National Gazette* failed. Unlike Alexander Hamilton, who swung into action when Fenno faltered, Jefferson and Madison did nothing to save or replace Freneau.[78]

The first party newspaper in American history did not actually live to see parties develop very fully, and it spawned few immediate imitators across the country. Freneau limited the *National Gazette*'s political effectiveness by paying little attention to elections, as we have seen, but the death of the paper can more accurately be blamed on the flawed strategy that Jefferson and Madison had used to create it, the recruitment of a prestigious editor with no financial stake.

With little incentive to care, Freneau displayed something approaching contempt for the practical aspects of managing his newspaper. Almost from the beginning, subscribers complained about the irregularity with which the *National Gazette* reached them. Daniel Carroll in Maryland requested that the papers be packaged differently, saying readers in his area got perhaps one out of ten. Madison relayed the complaints to Freneau, but the editor was slow to make improvements. Of course, any national newspaper faced an extraordinarily difficult task given the primitive state of the nation's transportation facilities. "This precariousness in the reception of his paper will cramp the circulation of it," warned Virginia Governor Henry Lee. "For which I am exceedingly sorry as it is rising fast into reputation." Not surprisingly, circulation flagged and many far-flung subscribers refused to pay their bills.[79]

Many readers must also have asked themselves why they needed to subscribe. Readers could often find Freneau's essays in their own local newspaper, copied there from the local printer's exchange papers, without the trouble or expense of a subscription.[80] The quick and easy dissemination of material from the "national" press under existing laws and customs formed a serious impediment to the top-down, nationally integrated system of political communication that both Thomas Jefferson and John Fenno had envisioned, in their different ways.

By the fall of 1793, Francis Childs had become impatient with the *National Gazette*'s continual losses, and in September he threatened to withdraw his backing if Freneau could not produce some profits. This was unlikely. Since the paper was already printed out of house, Freneau could not execute job-printing contracts to supplement his income, and even the limited advertising patronage he sought had failed to materialize. Freneau was complaining about the lot of an editor by this time anyway, especially about the pressure of having to discourse on public affairs twice a week whether or not there was anything new to say. Like Fenno, Freneau suspended his paper when the 1793 yellow fever epidemic struck. Unlike Fenno, he never resumed it.[81]

Many of the precedents set by the *National Gazette* were negative ones. In few cases would future partisan editors (on the Democratic Republican side, at any rate) be renowned authors recruited by national leaders, given unsolicited stipendiary employment, and completely shielded from financial risk. More often than not, future editors (up through the 1820s) would be printers by occupation (or like Fenno, learn to live and work like one), would own and manage their newspapers, and would be liable for all the personal and financial risks associated with the enterprise. While sometimes encouraged or flattered or helped by high-level leaders, partisan newspaper publishers would be independent entrepreneurs, fundamentally on their own.

Yet at the same time, the *National Gazette* defined the direction of American political development over the next fifty years. There had been pitched battles in Congress and the administration over various issues, but the *National Gazette* gave the emerging opposition its first semblance of institutional form and first authoritative, self-admitted voice. The creation of a newspaper was the first overtly partisan act by a United States government official, and the first concrete act of party building. Rather than forming a later association or even merging, the partisan press and American political parties began life as one.

4

Benjamin Franklin Bache and the
Price of Partisanship

❦

T*he early death* of Philip Freneau's *National Gazette* ended Jefferson's dream of a truly national Republican organ, but not the need for it. The emerging party still needed a voice that would bring the concerns of the leaders and activists in the capital to allies and potential supporters in other parts of the nation. The place was filled almost immediately by the Philadelphia *General Advertiser*, edited by Benjamin Franklin Bache, favorite grandson of his namesake. Founded in 1790, Bache's paper was initially a typical urban newspaper of the period. As the title suggested, it was stuffed with local advertising, with even the front page covered with ads and notices. Nevertheless, it became the most important political journal in the nation and remained so throughout the 1790s.

The *General Advertiser* (known as the *Aurora General Advertiser* after 1794) both represented and led the larger transformation of American printing and journalism that occurred as the Republican and Federalist parties coalesced. By the time of his death in 1798, the commercial printer Bache had changed his trade to that of Republican printer, meaning a full-time party spokesman and activist. Though political printing was a golden opportunity for many of his fellow travelers, who could never have risen to political consequence without it, for Bache partisanship was a costly act of conviction that required great courage. In becoming a political professional, Bache would lose both the prosperity and the social position his grandfather had labored hard to bequeath him. Bache's story makes up an important early phase in the rise of newspaper politics in itself, but it also reveals that there was more to partisanship than the self-interested ambition and greed for spoils that we typically attribute to party politicians. Party politics was a new mode of public life that involved abandoning the traditionally personal measures of fitness for political leadership, measures that even most Republican members of the Revolutionary elite embraced: respectability, character, talent, and "services" (especially military ones) to the republic.[1] By contrast, Bache came to judge all political men on the basis of their political principles, especially in terms of their commitment to democracy. Choosing his own course by the same ideological standards, Bache became a ground-level political activist and set himself on a steep path of downward mobility by leaving behind the genteel political values to which he had been born.

CELEBRITY GRANDSON AND YOUNG SOCIALITE

Bache may have had the most extensive education of any man to edit a political newspaper before the Civil War. In terms of formal schooling, he even surpassed many of the high officeholders defended or attacked in his newspaper. Most of his childhood was spent in Europe, where Benjamin Franklin had him educated in the best schools Paris and Geneva had to offer. When the two returned to Philadelphia, young Benjamin acted as his grandfather's secretary and earned a degree from the University of Pennsylvania. One of two people present when his grandfather died, Bache was considered his right-hand man and the most promising member of his illustrious family's younger generation.[2]

Unlike Fenno or Freneau, Bache was a printer and typefounder by training. Feeling he had ruined his dissolute older grandson, William Temple Franklin, by raising him to be a gentleman officeholder, Benjamin Franklin "determin'd to give [young Benjamin] a Trade that he may have something to depend on, and not be oblig'd to ask Favours or Offices of anybody."[3] But Franklin had no intention of making his favorite grandchild a simple tradesman. Rather than apprenticing the boy to a printer and letting him work his way up through the trade, Franklin arranged for "Benny" Bache to start at the top. Franklin brought in leading French printers to train the boy on Franklin's own state-of-the-art press at his estate in Passy. Then Bache was sent to study with François Didot, an eminent typefounder and "the best Printer that now exists & maybe that has ever existed."[4]

Franklin's long-range intentions for the boy were not entirely clear, but they seem to have been for the grandson to follow the grandfather's career path: make his fortune in the printing business before retiring to a life of public affairs. As author of the "Apology for Printers" and a politician who had survived a lifetime of political turmoil through conciliation and finesse rather than partisan ardor, Franklin did not set out to make his grandson a pugnacious partisan journalist. Upon returning to Philadelphia, Franklin steered Benjamin into printing but away from politics. The grandfather built a lavish new printing office and type foundry largely for his grandson's use, and together they went into the typefounding and publishing business. Their first publication ventures were a series of children's books based on the latest Enlightenment educational theories.[5]

Yet Bache's upbringing hardly disposed him to enjoy a quiet life of money making. The education Franklin obtained for his grandson was far from vocational. The French and Genevan schools had prepared him only to be a European gentleman, and he had learned printing more as an art than a trade. In later years, Bache remarked that he had not "been brought up as a man of business," a deficiency, he regretted saying, that had "proved a considerable disadvantage" in making a living from his newspaper.[6]

Bache's adolescence in prerevolutionary France gave him a much firmer grounding, and greater ambitions, in philosophy, politics, and journalism. He grew up under the shadow of a grandfather who had not been a businessman for years but was one of the most famous and popular journalists and politicians of his age. Even as a boy, Bache had felt the need to live up to the great name he bore. He had written to his grandfather from school in Geneva, "I feel how I am responsible to you and how I must do things on my part to make me worthy of the attentions you have given me." While living at Passy, Bache was allowed to share in Franklin's activities and meet many of literary and political dignitaries who constantly surrounded the American envoy. Voltaire had said the blessing "God and Liberty" over him as a small child, with Condorcet in attendance; during his teenage years, Prince Henry of Prussia burst into a private room and eagerly peppered the great Franklin's grandson with questions.[7]

More relevant to Bache's future career, Franklin numbered among his French acquaintances several journalist-politicians who became prominent leaders of the French Revolution, including Mirabeau, Desmoulins, Brissot de Warville, Danton, Marat, and the Abbé Sieyès. Most of them were members of a constitutionalist Masonic lodge that elected Franklin grand master; at around the time Bache was learning to print, his grandfather supplied some ideas and helped find a publisher for Mirabeau's first signed political pamphlet.[8] Some of Franklin's friends were participants in the Old Regime's scabrous and burgeoning clandestine publishing industry, before which France's elaborate censorship apparatus was beginning to give way in the 1780s. Though it is more than the sources prove, it seems likely that Bache, who was so immersed in French culture that he literally forgot English for a long period of his childhood, was familiar with his adopted country's outlawed popular political culture. He might thus be considered one of the numerous young French literati of the period who set out to be *philosophes* but were deflected into subversive journalism instead.[9]

After returning to Philadelphia, Bache led the life of a young socialite—"a young Man of no pressing business," as he put it: "frequenting good Company," attending society dances, and romancing his future wife, Margaret Hartman Markoe, daughter of a St. Croix sugar planter and stepdaughter of Dr. Adam Kuhn, Philadelphia's leading physician after Benjamin Rush. Bache's aristocratic lifestyle and status as Franklin's favorite grandson convinced Philadelphia's young gentlewomen that he was a "Man of Fortune." Though he protested to Margaret that his parents would get most of his grandfather's money and that he would have to earn his own by "*steady Industry,*" there is no doubt that Bache was one of the better-placed young men in the city.[10]

When Franklin died in April 1790, Benjamin Bache's inheritance was all of his grandfather's printing and typefounding equipment. Lost without Franklin's advice, Bache wrote immediately to his French teachers, the Didots, for technical help and made plans to publish a newspaper instead of books. This decision shocked and disappointed many of Bache's acquaintances in the Philadelphia upper crust. They found the newspaper business economically unpromising and generally inappropriate for a young man of Bache's station. Specifically, they worried that running a newspaper might lead the young man into partisanship that might dishonor his name. When Bache wrote to the Philadelphia financier and senator Robert Morris for help in securing government printing contracts, Morris responded with a warning:

> Some of your friends here are rather sorry for your intention of Printing a News Paper. There are already too many of them Published in Philadelphia, and in these days . . . it is difficult for a Press of such Reputation as you would choose yours to be, to maintain the Character of Freedom & impartiality, connected with Purity. They seem to entertain the opinion that you might be more honorably & more lucratively employed by the Printing of Books.[11]

Nevertheless, within six months of Franklin's death, the *General Advertiser* began to issue from Bache's palatial new printing office. At first, Bache stuck close to policies his grandfather had laid down in the "Apology for Printers," promising in the inaugural issue that his paper would be impartial. For the first few years, he restricted himself to the standard repertoire of the commercial newspaper business, filling his pages with advertising, mercantile information, and foreign news. The *General Advertiser* was bland but well executed and respectable. Through his and his grandfather's friends abroad, Bache had more and better sources of European news than most American printers, and this made his paper unusually accurate and informative for the time, especially on continental affairs.[12]

Yet almost from the beginning, impartial, apolitical journalism bored the young editor. The *General Advertiser* was only three weeks old when Bache first expressed dissatisfaction with his work, semifacetiously lamenting the lack of "party disputes" or "private abuse" to "raise the printer's drooping spirits." He wrote dejectedly to Margaret about the monotony and mundaneness of his daily routine as a commercial printer: scurrying around the city for information, scribbling copy, reading the foreign newspapers, and wrangling with newsboys and compositors "thro' out the week . . . thro' out the month, thro' out the year, & probably from year to year—for years to come."[13]

TURNING PARTISAN

Bache was primed for some more exciting and intellectually challenging endeavor. Two months after the *Advertiser*'s debut, Alexander Hamilton gave Bache his chance by introducing his financial program and inspiring the beginnings of opposition to the national administration. From that point on, Bache slowly gravitated toward the example of Franklin's French acquaintances, who were by now unabashedly partisan in their journalism and leading political actors in their own right.

Before 1792 the domestic political content of the *General Advertiser* was quite mild, but according to Jefferson its "principles . . . were always republican," a fact that showed particularly in the foreign news, which was derived from sources less hostile to the French than was usual for American papers. As Freneau's *National Gazette* began its assaults on the administration during 1792, Bache's paper followed a few steps behind. Then, in the first week of December, a rather sudden change came over the paper, as Bache began to associate himself openly with the emerging Republican party. Significantly, he did so in conjunction with a major election. A series of fierce articles appeared supporting George Clinton against Vice President Adams, including one by "Portius," who concluded that "the fall of ADAMS" would "crush the Hydra of ARISTOCRACY."

In the same issue, Bache editorialized on the emerging party division, sketching both the nature of the division and his own conception of what the newspaper editor's role in the party would be:

> A language in praise of monarchical and aristocratical institutions, and in derogation of our republican systems, which would not have been whispered a few years past, is becoming so familiar in certain scenes as scarcely to call forth observation. In this posture and prospect of things all true friends to liberty ought to be on their constant guard against insidious attempts to divide them by abuse of names, and to unite firmly in checking the career of monarchy, by bearing testimony against its advocates, keeping continually in mind that it is not a question now between federalism and anti-federalism, but between republicanism and antirepublicanism.

As one who had much experience of high Philadelphia society, Bache was in a position to know what was being said in "certain scenes." He now resolved that his newspaper would testify to the creeping antirepublicanism of his social peers and work to unite the "friends of liberty against them." That meant not just exposing the enemies of liberty, but also using the electoral process to remove antirepublicans from power.[14]

In the days and weeks that followed, Bache and other newspaper writers assailed the administration in much the same terms as Freneau and began to build a case for the legitimacy and even necessity of popular, extragovernmental politics. "Mirabeau" listed among the "Forerunners of Monarchy and Aristocracy in the United States," the increasingly common opinion—expressed often in John Fenno's *Gazette of the United States*—that "the care of the state should be the exclusive business of the officers of the government."

Reaching back to the bitter struggle in Philadelphia over American independence, during which the old colonial assembly had been overthrown by a radical pro-independence movement drawing its main support from artisans and poor people, "Mirabeau" compared the present condemnation of popular politics with the Tory spirit that had "produced so many publications in the years 1774 and 1775 which [criticized] the *mechanics* for meddling with politics." Such attitudes had no place in post-Revolutionary America, the writer argued:

It is well enough in England to run down the rights of man, because the author of those inimitable pamphlets [referring to Thomas Paine] was a staymaker; but in the United States all such proscriptions of certain classes of citizens, or occupations, should be avoided; for liberty will never be safe or durable in a republic till every citizen thinks it as much his duty to take care of the state, as to take care of his family, and until an indifference to any public question shall be considered as a public offence.[15]

This comment introduced what would be a perennial theme of Bache's paper and, later, of the Republican press generally: the positive duty of ordinary citizens to engage in politics, express public opinion, and influence government policy from the outside. Though Bache did not initially print these remarks in the context of an organized political party, the ideas provided clear justification for such an organization. A few weeks later, another *General Advertiser* writer made a significant addendum to the argument. Newspapers played a critical role in this new popular politics, not just by providing an open forum for public debate, but also by positively defending the public's rights and interests. The press provided

a constitutional check upon the conduct of public servants . . . . In a republic of which the public opinion is the basis, it is of very peculiar importance as the organ of that opinion, and in many cases, the only organ. There are many occurrences, properly within the sphere of public investigation, on which the people cannot express their sentiments by their representatives.

Newspaper writers and other politicians outside the government had to stand in as the people's representatives when the officially appointed and elected ones refused to heed their constituents.[16]

Bache's motives for turning partisan against his revered grandfather's advice were rooted in disappointment that his native country was lagging so far behind his beloved France in implementing the ideals of the American Revolution. He had followed the progress of the French Revolution avidly since it began, and he took the French Republic's recent military victories as a call to action for fellow republicans around the world. With democratic revolution flourishing in Europe, it was particularly galling that America, the great symbol of freedom that Franklin's French friends had worshiped while nurturing their own revolutionary dreams, should be drifting back toward monarchy.[17]

Suspicious Federalists such as Timothy Pickering assumed that Bache's turn to partisanship was a sensationalistic play for popularity and increased subscriptions, but they had little insight into Benjamin Bache or

the economics of the newspaper industry.[18] The young editor had grave
reservations about joining fully in the partisan battle that was emerging. It
would have been much more comfortable to lead the sheltered life of an
apolitical or conservative Philadelphia aristocrat, but Bache hoped to resist that temptation. "When [the political line] comes to be struck
definitely," he wrote of the emerging party division, "I hope I shall be
found on the right side of it."[19]

It took a long time for the *General Advertiser* to become exclusively Republican in content, but its partisanship was quite bold from early on.
Bache has become infamous among historians as George Washington's
bitterest newspaper critic. His campaign against Washington would not
reach its highest pitch until after the president signed the Jay Treaty in
1795, but constant criticism of the neomonarchical symbolism and cere-
monials that Washington had allowed to grow up around himself began
to appear as soon as the *General Advertiser* turned toward partisanship.[20]

As late as 1793, however, Bache continued to publish occasional articles
that opposed his editorial line, while feeling increasingly disenchanted
with such a permissive policy. A turning point seems to have come in late
January 1793, when he printed a paragraph chiding the paper's attacks on
the president's regal deportment but also appended a rebuttal. Inverting
the usual reasoning, the editor argued that including criticisms of the
president was an impartial rather than partisan act, because the president
was popular and praising him would be taking the path of least resistance
from advertisers, government officials, and well-heeled readers. "Impartiality [is] a duty" for a newspaper editor, and he was "unwilling to shrink
from it, though perhaps interest might point out a safer line of conduct."[21]

The old colonial printers' conceptions of "impartiality" and "freedom of
the press"—that the press should be free to all paying customers and all
sides of a political controversy—were coming to have new meanings for
Bache. They now denoted a lack of partiality toward the government and
a determination to conduct his newspaper free and uninfluenced by personal or economic considerations that might curb its political activity.
Though still quite moderate, the *General Advertiser* was already alienating
many of its editor's former friends and peers. Bache made this quite explicit in his New Year's "address" for 1794:

> In politics, the violence of parties, and the severe duties of the Editor of a free
> press leave him to regret some friends lost and some enemies made. If these
> were for a week only conductors of a impartial paper, the friends would return

and the enmity be forgotten. The Editor, however, never will shrink from what he conceives his duty. Public men are all amenable to the tribunal of the press in a free state; the greater, indeed, their trust, the more responsible are they.[22]

The New Year's address presaged an escalation of the attacks on Washington. The strategic wisdom of this decision is open to debate, but Bache's intentions were quite high minded. He aimed to preserve a polity based on "principles, not men," in which political debate and governance could take place without reference to personal loyalties, relationships, reputations, or status. "Private persons must never be suffered to weigh an instant against the public interest," Bache wrote in a quiet moment of one attack, "but every person must judge of public affairs by public considerations."[23]

Bache's statements invoked a universalistic conception of the public sphere similar to that which undergirded many productions of the Revolutionary press. One way of stating this conception is that governments draw their legitimacy not from the participation of specific people (such as monarchs and nobles, whose power had supposedly been delegated by God), but from abstract ideas (such as natural rights) that could be impersonally defended in printed debate. Hence writers rarely used their personal names or revealed their true social or official identities. Alexander Hamilton, James Madison, and the other squabbling founders debated in the press under classical pseudonyms, often chosen to evoke a particular political stance or theoretical position, rather than as the treasury secretary, the congressman from Virginia, and so on. In theory, this depersonalized political arena allowed people with wildly different levels of status and power to encounter each other on relatively equal terms: colonial protesters could take on kings, and printers could do battle with presidents, even with George Washington himself.[24]

The reality seems to have fallen far short of the theory. Hamilton and Madison used pseudonyms partly to disguise the fact that their ideas emanated from high official stations, and Benjamin Franklin Bache's ability to serve as point man in the assault on Washington seems to have been made possible by his attributes as a private man. As the living embodiment of the great Franklin, Bache differed from other Republicans in feeling no awe of Washington's reputation and position. Thus he alone was willing to take public responsibility for a campaign of vilification against Washington that intensified from condemning elaborate social protocols and high salaries to tarring nearly every aspect of the national patriarch's career.

For a time, the attack on Washington took the intermediate position stated in Bache's "Political Creed of 1795," that "a good joiner may be a clumsy watch-maker; that an able carpenter may be a blundering taylor; and that a good General may be a most miserable politician."[25] By the end of Washington's presidency, however, Bache and his friends were willing to argue more boldly that Washington's behavior as president had abrogated his "claim . . . either to the gratitude or confidence of his country." Bache's personal efforts in the campaign culminated in a lengthy pamphlet that extended the indictment even to Washington's war record. According to Bache, the president was not only a would-be king, but a bad general as well.[26] Then there was the *Aurora*'s famous send-off to Washington, on Inauguration Day, 1797:

> If ever there was period for rejoicing, this is the moment—every heart in unison with the freedom and happiness of the people ought to beat high with exultation, that the name of WASHINGTON from this day ceases to give a currency to political iniquity; and to legalize corruption . . . this day ought to be a JUBILEE in the United States.[27]

DOWNWARD MOBILITY, RADICAL POLITICS, AND THE BIRTH OF THE *AURORA*

Bache's uncompromising partisanship was politically courageous but personally disastrous. To begin with, it severely damaged his newspaper as a business. The editor could hardly expect printing contracts from a government he criticized, nor did he long retain the advertising support of merchants, brokers, and other beneficiaries of Hamiltonian policies. Many other advertisers abandoned Bache simply to dissociate themselves from political controversy—especially if it involved tarring the name of George Washington.

Some of Bache's former colleagues in the commercial printing trade disapproved of his flagrant disregard for the bottom line. Mathew Carey, who had forsaken newspapers for more profitable and less controversial fare after getting into a duel in the 1780s, clucked at Bache in his autobiography. Bache had been "popular on account of his amiable manners and his descent from Dr. Franklin." His newspaper was "ably conducted," with "a very extensive circulation. But the attacks on General Washington blasted Bache's popularity, and almost ruined the paper. Subscribers withdrew in crowds—and the advertising custom sank to insignificance."[28] Foreclosing these sources of income was a serious matter for Bache, whose newspaper had, he admitted later, "never been a very lucrative establish-ment." This was putting it mildly. According to his successor, Bache lost almost $20,000 over his eight years as proprietor.[29]

Even worse, Bache lost the "decided station in Society" he had occu-pied by virtue of his famous family, good marriage, and European polish.[30] It was bad enough for his old friends and acquaintances that Benjamin had entered an occupation of such dubious prestige. That Bache would also assault the president—and the well-ordered society and polity that the dignity of his position represented—was too much. Moreover, most of Bache's former peers in the Philadelphia elite supported Federalist poli-cies and politics, and Bache lost caste by siding with the Republicans. Federalists considered themselves a "natural" republican aristocracy, hold-ing power because they deserved it, on the strength of their superior virtue, intelligence, education, and experience. Oppositionists declared themselves outside this natural aristocracy, or worse, renegades from it, out to serve only their own base desires and selfish designs. In any number of ways, Bache had placed himself beyond the pale of respectability as his old circles defined it.[31]

The combination of class prejudice and political opprobrium that Bache's partisanship brought down on him can be seen in two encounters with a young female socialite. One morning she came to the *General Ad-vertiser* office and tongue-lashed Bache for some impertinent article. "When she so violently attacked me she knew me only as Bache the printer, and had seen me only in my rusty breeches;—she thought surely I was nobody," the editor wrote his parents. She was surprised a few days later when making her debut at the City Dancing Assembly, which Bache had long attended. "Who should hand her out of the carriage but the same said nobody; but it is so, she doubted her eyes, what is it you Mr. Bache, I really did not know you."[32]

The girl's discomfiture amused Bache at the time. When his partisan-ship grew sharper, however, the snubs mounted, as polite Philadelphia so-ciety increasingly ostracized the Baches. He would not attend many more City Dancing Assemblies. "At the time of Dr. F's death Ben was univer-sally beloved and esteemed and now he is as much despised," reported Elizabeth Hewson, a friend of the Franklin-Bache family, who fully shared her peers' disgust with the wayward editor. He was "now consid-ered in the most despicable light by the most respectable part of his fellow citizens, and by almost everyone he might formerly have considered as his particular friends." As for Margaret, "Poor woman, her old acquaintance have almost all deserted her." Hewson evidently considered it a magnanimous gesture on her part to accept Margaret's repeated invitations to visit. Hewson wrote in disbelief that Mrs. Bache "was of the opinion that her husband was quite in the right. She does not therefore suffer the pain of entertaining a mean opinion of him which I am sorry to say most people do. What a pity a few years should make so great an alteration."[33]

As the Baches' old friends deserted them, they became increasingly enmeshed in a new and less elevated social world of Republican political activists. Much more than Freneau, Bache became deeply and personally involved in Republican efforts at organizing a party and mounting election campaigns. As with many Republican activists, Bache found in Philadelphia's Democratic Society a kind of halfway house between espousing the Republican cause as a private citizen and promoting the emerging political party. One of a national network of such groups, the Democratic Society of Pennsylvania was a political club organized in support of the French Revolution. President Washington and his supporters considered the societies subversive, re-creations of the French Jacobin clubs that were in league with revolutionary France to bring social and political anarchy to America.

Bache was elected to the society's Committee of Correspondence on 2 January 1794, the day after promising the readers of his newspaper that he would not shrink from his duty as "Editor of a free press." He quickly became one of the controversial group's three or four most active members.[34] Among his other duties, Bache was placed on a committee charged with a mission that amounted to managing the Republican campaign in the 1794 congressional elections: "calling upon the people to deliberate and decide, at the approaching elections, how far their Representatives are entitled to public confidence, by approving the good and dismissing the bad."[35]

Bache became a leader of the Democratic Society's more radical faction, along with his friends, fellow activists, and contributing editors John Smith and Michael Leib. Smith was a hatter and prominent militia officer, while Leib was a German physician who was emerging as the political tribune of Philadelphia's ethnic immigrant neighborhoods. These men's thoroughgoing commitment to Republican ideals, and "outdoor" political organization as the way to realize them, eventually caused a schism in the society over the Whiskey Rebellion. After defending the Democratic Societies in the *General Advertiser* throughout 1794 as a legitimate, constitutional, and benign means of promoting their political beliefs, Bache and his friends were thoroughly dismayed by the western tax revolt. The impending violence threatened to undermine their ideal of conducting public affairs by discussion and majority vote and to discredit their argument (disbelieved by Hamilton and the Federalists) that a popular, democratic style of politics was compatible with public order. Bache and his friends opposed Hamilton's excise tax just as the rebels did, but the means they favored to stop it was electing a new congress rather than taking up arms.

At the meeting of 11 September 1794, Leib introduced a resolution condemning "the intemperance of the Western Citizens" and asserting that "so far from entitling them to the patronage of Democrats, [violent resistance] will merit the proscription of every friend of equal liberty." Leib's resolution met opposition from society moderates allied with Secretary of the Commonwealth Alexander J. Dallas (also an important Philadelphia attorney), who believed that the existing civil authorities in the West could handle the problem on their own and wanted to avoid embarrassing leading western Republican politicians such as Albert Gallatin. In the ensuing debate, "unusual warmth took place among some of the members," after which the president of the society along with about half the members walked out of the meeting. Bache's faction felt so strongly about the matter that several of them, including Dr. Leib and his brother, volunteered for the military force that marched west to quell the insurrection.[36]

In late 1794 Bache more or less officially declared the *General Advertiser* a Republican paper when he added the word "Aurora" to the title, installing his mission to promote enlightenment and Democratic Republican principles in the journal's very name:

> The AURORA, as far as the editor's exertions extend, shall diffuse light within the sphere of its influence,—dispel the shades of ignorance, and gloom of error and thus tend to strengthen the fair fabric of freedom on its surest foundation, publicity and information.[37]

The controversy over the Jay Treaty soon demonstrated the Baches' total commitment to Republican party politics and cemented his and his family's move to a totally different sphere of life. The *Aurora* revealed the treaty's previously secret contents to the world on 29 June 1795, and the newspaper's office became the command center of a national effort to spread the news of the outrageous document and organize opposition to it. Bache immediately turned the treaty's text into a pamphlet and set out northward with thousands of copies, while another Philadelphia Republican went on a similar mission south.[38]

At the various stops along the trip, Bache's fellow Republican activists (especially other editors) treated him as a comrade in arms. He instructed Margaret to send his mail in care of the leading Republican printers in Boston and New York. In Boston, he was warmly received at the offices of the *Independent Chronicle,* the city's leading Republican newspaper, and sought out by Governor Samuel Adams, "a patriot according to my own heart." The leading spirits of the *Chronicle* were also the leaders of the Republican party in Boston. Bache met with them daily and attended a town meeting on the treaty that the Republicans were able to dominate because of the documents he had brought. (Bache hoped every city in the country would have a similar meeting, and he helped organize one in New York City on his way home.) Administration supporters in Boston took alarm at this evidence of national coordination among their journalistic antagonists. The visiting editor saw himself denounced as "the arch Jacobinical tool from Philadelphia" in the Boston newspapers. Bache knew he was no tool—he had not been lured into partisan journalism with a government appointment or any other inducement—but he gladly accepted the role of national Republican spokesman and organizer.[39]

Margaret Bache was as deeply embroiled in the Jay Treaty campaign as was her husband. Margaret was left in charge of the *Aurora* while Benjamin was away, and though Dr. Leib was assigned to help her, she shared fully in the editorial and financial management of the paper during a tumultuous period. On the first day of Benjamin's trip, the office was crowded with Philadelphians eager to obtain copies of the pamphlet and the *Aurora.* "It was more like a fair than anything else," she reported happily. The editor's sudden departure, however, prevented the paper from appearing the next day, and Margaret had to face an irate clientele. "You have no Idea how angry every body was that there was no paper of Thursday," she told her husband. She managed to mollify the *Aurora*-starved readership by telling them that an accident that had damaged the press.

Then there was another setback: Saturday was the Fourth of July, and only a few of the journeymen were willing to work. "I was mortified that the Aurora did not rise in its fullest glory on this day," Margaret wrote dejectedly, lamenting that they had been able to produce just half of the normal paper. Nevertheless, she was proud to say that the Monday edition would be a "very full issue"; it was midnight when she wrote, and she was

FIGURE 1. Philadelphia *Aurora General Advertiser*, top half of front page, 29 June 1795.
(Courtesy of American Antiquarian Society)

sitting up while one of her husband's employees read the next paper's proofs.[40]

Leib, Smith, and other Republican activists had become the Baches' circle of friends as well as their political allies. The Baches exchanged their "decided station in Society" for this political underworld of journeyman printers, newspaper writers, and street- and tavern-level activists. The Bache family home and the *Aurora* office occupied the same building on Market Street. The household became a gathering place for party leaders and the headquarters of what has been called "the Republican party's Grub Street." *Aurora* staff members were free to spend the night if the work kept them too late, and over the years numerous men who were thoroughly disreputable by the standards of the Baches' former peers found a haven under the *Aurora*'s roof. Among them were refugee radicals such as the exiled journalists James Thomson Callender and William Duane, the United Irishman and utopian socialist Dr. James Reynolds, and the United Irish leader Theobald Wolfe Tone. Several of the refugees assisted Bache with the *Aurora,* and Duane eventually became its editor.[41]

Margaret formed personal and political friendships with some of these men's wives. Matilda Tone wrote in 1798 to ask how the latest pregnancy of her "dear Friend" was progressing and to inquire after the health of her children. She also made a comment that shows how fully the women shared and were involved in their husbands' incendiary affairs: "Thank [Benjamin] very much for his Aurora. I welcome it every evening as I would a pleasant, intelligent friend. You can't think How delightful it is, in this region of Aristocracy to meet a little—I had almost said *Treason.*" The First Lady of the United Irishmen signed the letter, "Health and Frat."[42]

"SURGO UT PROSIM": BENJAMIN FRANKLIN BACHE AS PROFESSIONAL POLITICIAN

Benjamin Bache's mission against the Jay Treaty also marks the point at which he became a professional politician, a man who lived both "for" and "off of" Republican politics. He was proprietor of a business (the *Aurora*) now wholly devoted to politics, and his trip to Boston was an entrepreneurial venture in both politics and publishing. His letters to Margaret expressed concern with both the treaty pamphlet's political effect and its profitability. From New York, Bache wrote that a previous bundle of treaties sent by another messenger had "sold here like mad" but regretted that the local newspapers had already republished the pamphlet. Otherwise, he thought, four times as many could have been moved. In Boston, the pamphlet sold, but "not so well as I expected"; however, Bache exulted that, thanks to those same pamphlets, "the voice of the toad-eaters of government was drowned in the universal disapprobation of the treaty." He did sell enough of the 25- to 50-cent pamphlets to pay for the trip, and total sales were sufficient to justify a second edition. (His colleague's southern journey, however, was a money loser.) In a further effort to make the trip a paying venture, Benjamin had Margaret send him a list of delinquent *Aurora* subscribers so he could collect overdue bills along his route.[43]

Henceforward, Bache would also combine business with politics in other ways. Rather than the general-interest bookstore maintained by a typical newspaper publisher, Bache started a specifically political one. Writing to a London bookseller, Bache described his business and the kind of works he wanted to order: "I publish a newspaper and have connected with it pamphlets and books of a political cast. Any thing of merit in the line of political novelty of a republican cast will be most acceptable."[44] Bache's stock of Republican "Political Novelties," constantly advertised in the *Aurora,* included the literature produced during the recent party battles, the works of Thomas Paine and Joel Barlow, the published transcripts of several Irish and English political trials, the French Constitution in translation, a history of the French Revolution, and more outré items such as the *Calendrier Republicain* and Charles Pigott's *Political Dictionary.* (This last work was touted on the basis of its author having been prosecuted in England.)[45]

To argue that Bache attempted to make money from his political activities is not to label him cynical or venal. His ideal appeared in the *Aurora*'s masthead motto, "Surgo Ut Prosim," or "I rise to be useful," both of which might be translated as a creed of doing well, or at least making a living, by doing good. In fact, the two elements of a political business did not mix very well, with the politics tending to overwhelm the business. Bache fervently believed the American people sided with the *Aurora,* the Republicans, and the French. Thus he was convinced that Republican political works would naturally sell well. Yet he constantly lost money on his ventures, allowing his desire to get politically valuable literature into people's hands to prevail over economic realities. The Jay Treaty pamphlet was a prime example, as was an edition of Thomas Paine's *Age of Reason,* which was sold at very low cost so that more could afford to buy it. As one historian has put it, Bache was "functioning outside normal trade practices," pioneering a new, political sector of the publishing industry.[46]

After passage of the Jay Treaty, Bache and his successors ran the *Aurora* explicitly as a party paper, going a step further than Freneau by actively involving it not only in political debate, but also very directly in election campaigns and other forms of practical political organization.[47] In the fall elections of 1795, the *Aurora* campaigned vigorously for the antitreaty ticket, whereas even a year before it had been vaguely apologetic about the very practice of nominating tickets.[48] After months of hammering at Washington and the treaty, the *Aurora* applied this national party issue to the local legislative elections, urging voters, in the words of one contributor, to oust the men "who voted for the man [for example, the state's Federalist senator] who voted for the Treaty."

Aurora writers extolled antiadministration candidates, denounced their opponents, and countered each new "ELECTIONEERING LIE" that issued from the *Gazette of the United States* and the rest of the pro-administration press. Around all of this election material, Bache wove a web of issues and arguments that linked the battle in Philadelphia not only to deeper concerns than which individual won or lost the election, but also to similar battles going on around the country. Exchanges and other papers sent through the mail disseminated the capital Republicans' words and deeds to their allies and sympathizers in other cities, creating the possibility of unified national action. Bache probably engaged in more of this newspaper electioneering than any other American editor at this time, and to a certain extent he was teaching others how it could be done.[49]

Bache and the *Aurora* were quite literally constructing the Republican party during the mid-1790s, and they did it as much through the construction of the newspaper as through substantive argument. In between its advertising, European news, and political essays, the *Aurora* presented resolutions of political meetings and proceedings of banquets and reports of election results from all over Philadelphia and from other parts of Pennsylvania and the nation. In a time when the national opposition party was little more than some dispersed expressions of discontent and a group of congressmen who voted together, Bache packaged all the different forms of opposition together as a unit, creating an imagined partisan community of readers to whom to these candidates, arguments, resolutions, toasts, and election results belonged.[50]

Bache and his fellow electioneers employed the histrionic language of Revolutionary ideology in their campaigning, but their sincerely made claims of an imminent threat to liberty also had specific electoral purposes, such as encouraging a large Republican turnout and winning the election. On election day, an address "To the Freemen of the City and County of Philadelphia" presented the "No Treaty" ticket (which included sometime-*Aurora* coeditor Michael Leib running for state representative) and told voters that they were "summoned at this moment to choose between liberty or slavery." Elsewhere in that day's paper, Bache reminded readers that "no privilege [was] more sacred than that of choosing the men who are to make the laws," and entreated them not to stay home "under the plausible but fallacious idea" that their single votes would not make any difference: "Be it engraven on the mind of every man who has a real re-gard for his country, that the most important questions ever agitated have been decided by very small majorities."[51]

All of this was nothing compared to later years. In early September 1796, Bache announced publicly what had been well known in Phila-delphia political circles for months, that Thomas Jefferson would be the Republican candidate for president. The editor had just discovered the long-kept secret that President Washington would not be running for re-election, and he now opened the presidential campaign. It required "no talent at divination" to guess that John Adams would be Jefferson's oppo-nent, making the election a question of "whether we shall have at the head of our executive a steadfast friend to the Rights of the People, or an advo-cate for hereditary power and distinctions."[52] From that point, the *Aurora* was a full partner in the presidential campaign masterminded by House of Representatives clerk John Beckley. It extolled Jefferson's qualifications for the presidency and rebutted Federalist attacks, while decrying Adams for his antirepublican ideas.

The paper was just as involved in the effort to reelect Philadelphia's Republican congressman, John Swanwick. The *Aurora* publicized all Re-publican tickets and meetings and later followed the election returns closely, with a partisan eye.[53] Bache's involvement in party politics moved to yet a higher level when he ran for the Philadelphia common council on a ticket of Republicans. Like any good candidate, Bache refrained from self-promotion, not mentioning his own candidacy in the paper while boosting other Republican candidates for higher office. Perhaps a bit more self-promotion was needed, however, because he and the rest of the Republican council slate lost.[54]

It was a good thing that Bache had not turned partisan for either per-sonal preferment or financial remuneration, because he received neither after Jefferson narrowly lost the election of 1796. Politically, he and the Republicans were put in a desperate position after 1796 by the French Di-rectory's increasingly high-handed and aggressive policy toward the Unit-ed States, as manifested in the "XYZ Affair" and other incidents. As France's most vocal defender in the United States, Bache came in for a share of the public opprobrium that shifted from England to France dur-ing the Adams years. Even worse, the "quasi-war" made Bache's French background and continued support of a French alliance seem almost trea-sonous.[55]

In the crisis atmosphere, the Federalist approach to Bache moved beyond disdain to outright persecution. In the spring of 1797, he was physically assaulted and rather seriously injured by Clement Humphries, a young Federalist, while touring a ship at the Philadelphia waterfront. Though Humphries was later fined by the city court, the Adams administration seemed to endorse the assault on Bache by appointing the assailant a bearer of diplomatic dispatches to France in full knowledge of what he had done. With some justice, Bache regarded this action as tantamount to "giving direct encouragement to assassination, and setting a price upon my head."

Other incidents followed. After a salute to President Adams and a long night of banqueting in May 1798, a group of young Federalists decided to visit the editor's home. Margaret and the children cowered inside, while the patriotic drunks shouted curses and pounded on the doors and windows; with Benjamin away, the men had to be driven off by neighbors. Bache strongly suspected that the highest authorities approved of these tactics, and indeed First Lady Abigail Adams was predicting in her letters that "the wrath of an insulted people will by & by break upon him [Bache]."[56]

A few weeks later, the Federalists in Congress began to prepare a bill to punish sedition, with Benjamin Bache and the *Aurora* squarely in their sights.[57] After the attack on his house, Bache had wondered whether it "might, indeed, be a gratification to some that I should have my throat cut," and the Sedition bill seemed to hold out that prospect: in the original Senate version introduced by James Lloyd of Maryland, the measure defined the French as enemies of the United States and prescribed the death penalty for any who gave them aid and comfort.[58] Some Federalists were unwilling to wait for an act of Congress to outlaw the *Aurora*, and on 26 June a U.S. Marshal arrested Bache on a federal warrant. Bache was charged with "libelling the President & the Executive Government, in a manner tending to excite sedition, and opposition to the laws, by sundry publications and republications." Bache and two sureties were required to post $4,000 dollars in bail—all without the publications in question ever being specified.[59]

Bache needed help paying this enormous sum and received it from the staunch Republicans Thomas Leiper and Israel Israel, the former a prosperous tobacconist and the latter the keeper of a tavern popular with Republicans. Whatever share of the family fortune Bache may have had access to was used up or cut off by now. The opinion around Philadelphia was that Bache's newspaper was in decline, and the editor did only a little to deny the fact. "Combinations were tried to deprive the Editor of support," he wrote in one self-vindicatory pamphlet, "and tho' by this means the establishment of the Aurora has not been as lucrative as it might have been, it has been sufficiently so to support itself and its editor." Even this tentative affirmation was belied by other signals. In July 1798 Bache printed a "communication" that praised his own political services and suggested it was the duty of every Republican to support their editor with subscriptions:

> It is hoped that the republicans, in whose cause he has suffered the most malignant persecution, and undergone the grossest calumnies, will in every part of the union countenance his virtuous exertions. Although his paper already has a very general circulation, no republican, who can afford it, should neglect becoming a subscriber.[60]

It seems likely that the sedition prosecution left Bache nearly bankrupt. Margaret had made the financial situation sound so dire in a letter to her brother that he wrote back urging her to have Benjamin put the family property in her and the children's names and move back to St. Croix immediately.[61]

Despite repeated charges that Bache was in the pay of the French or of Thomas Jefferson, the bail money was the first political financial aid he had received in eight years of running the paper. He enjoyed no salary and had no hope of government printing contracts; nor had any national Republican leaders been particularly helpful. In October 1797 James Monroe had advanced Bache $600 for the publication of a book defending Monroe's conduct as minister to France, then peremptorily asked for the money back a few months later.[62] (Repayment was the not the custom of John Fenno regarding his loans from Hamilton.) Only when it appeared that the *Aurora* might actually collapse did Thomas Jefferson take any action in its behalf. Then he solicited subscriptions, but with nothing like the energy he had expended for Freneau. The *Aurora* and another Republican paper "totter for want of subscriptions," he wrote Madison. "We should really exert ourselves to procure them, for if these papers fall, republicanism will be entirely brow-beaten."[63]

Jefferson's and Madison's correspondence reveals little evidence that they followed up on this call to arms. Jefferson seemed more concerned with preserving his reputation from too close an association with Bache and his fellow radicals. The vice president denied at great length, even to fellow Republicans, John Fenno's charge that he had met with the *Aurora* editor and his friends Doctors Leib and Reynolds.[64]

Insult was added to Bache's physical and financial injuries by the rise of William Cobbett on the Philadelphia journalistic scene. No democratic radical in his first American phase, Cobbett belligerently opposed the Republicans and all their doings, but he supported Great Britain more than the Federalists and had little to do with party politics. A character assassin and hatemonger sui generis, his satirical pamphlets and newspaper, *Porcupine's Gazette,* served up political polemic and personal attacks in a style that was earthy and accessible enough to make them popular entertainment. As such, and in contrast to most of the other political editors and writers in Philadelphia, Cobbett seems to have actually made money on his publications.[65]

Bache and the *Aurora* provided a good deal of Cobbett's material from almost the moment *Porcupine's Gazette* began in March 1797. In terms of detailed personal vilification, Cobbett went far beyond anything Fenno, Freneau, or Bache had ever published. He began by referring to Bache as a printer "notoriously in the pay of France" and continued by berating the "treasonable career of abuse" of "this prostitute son of oil and lamp-black" and wondering why the Republican paper had not been suppressed.

For publishing the *Calendrier Republicain,* Cobbett treated Bache, in November 1797, to a remarkably inaccurate and vitriolic character sketch that conflated the editor with his office-seeking cousin Temple and insulted Benjamin Franklin to boot: "This atrocious wretch (worthy descendant of *old Ben*) knows that all men of understanding set him down as an abandoned liar, as a tool, and a hireling; . . . He spent several years in hunting offices under the Federal Government . . . when he found he could not obtain employ in one quarter, he sought it in another . . . from that time to this been as faithful to the cut-throats of Paris, as ever dog was to his master." Never one to limit himself to mere politics, Cobbett added that the overworked and undernourished Bache was "an ill-looking devil. His eyes never get above your knees. He is of a sallow complexion, hollow-cheeked, dead-eyed . . . just like . . . a fellow who has been about a week or ten days on a gibbet." Cobbett later amplified the gibbet remark with the characteristically bloody-minded suggestion that Bache be dealt with like "a TURK, A JEW, A JACOBIN, OR A DOG."[66]

The toll that such journalistic thuggery took on Bache's battered reputation and sensibilities can only be imagined. If he and Margaret had any illusions about where they stood in Philadelphia society after five years of partisanship, the fact that Cobbett could write such things and be not only approved of but also popular must have dispelled them. John Fenno and his mentor, Benjamin Russell of the Boston *Columbian Centinel,* sniggered in print at the "tradesmen" who were now Bache's friends and benefactors. In response, Bache sarcastically agreed with Fenno that his friends were "mere *simple men,* none of your high-flying *well borns,* none of your *speculators in moonshine* . . . they are only plain, simple, unaffected republicans, and this is indeed a *heinous fault.*"[67]

By the end of that difficult summer of 1798, Bache was moving toward further integration with the evolving party, taking steps to make the *Aurora* a more self-consciously national party paper than it had been. He finally carried out something like the plan Jefferson had suggested in 1791 and began a "country" edition of the paper published three times a week. Each "country" *Aurora* featured two days worth of the daily paper's political matter on the front and back of a single sheet, thereby saving postage and creating a product tailored to the distant subscriber. In announcing the new edition, Bache indicated that the *Aurora*'s financial picture was finally improving. The paper had gained two hundred subscribers since the beginning of July, when the Sedition Act had been passed. "The encrease in the circulation of this paper has been beyond the editor's most sanguine expectations," Bache enthused, and since the formal sedition proceedings against him started "it has been rapid beyond parallel. Thus the daring hand of persecution already counteracts its own designs."

Bache was even more amazed to find some of the paper's subscribers paying their overdue bills and a few actually sending in the required advance payments for the next year. Like the political professional he had become, Bache took these glimmerings of business success as vindication of his political course. He wrote proudly and almost tearfully of his realization that "the calumnies of the enemies of liberty in this country have not deprived the editor of the good opinion of a great portion of his fellow citizens." It would be criminal of him

> to shrink before the frowns of ambition . . . the malice of little men dazzled by
> the glare of power, at a time when the liberal support he receives from various
> parts of the United States, evince not only the stubborn consistency of freedom and the love of truth, but a marked approbation of his past conduct as

well as a determination to aid him in the arduous and expensive undertaking in which he is engaged.[68]

Unfortunately for Bache's rejuvenated ambitions, Philadelphia was in the midst of another yellow fever epidemic. The Baches were probably no longer among those who could afford to flee to the countryside, and at any rate the editor was determined to remain zealously at his post. On Friday, 7 September 1798, the day of a nominating meeting he had been planning for, Bache apparently fell ill. The next day, his assistant, William Duane, informed *Aurora* subscriber St. George Tucker that his employer seemed to be recovering, but Bache was dead by the following Monday night. News of the editor's demise reached Tucker while Duane's letter was still sitting on his desk. "So there is an end to all his persecutions," the Virginian scribbled sadly below the signature. Bache's rival John Fenno had made a vow similar to Bache's in August, "to continue here so long as other printers remain at their Posts," entrusting his life to the Deity he was sure took the Federalist side in the party quarrel. Fenno expired exactly one week after Bache.[69]

POST MORTEM: "MOTHER BACHE" IN
MOURNING AND IN PUBLIC

A few hours after her husband's death, Margaret Bache issued a black-bordered and sternly political notice, addressed to the "friends of civil liberty and patrons of the Aurora." She promised that the paper would resume shortly under her own direction and lamented "the loss of a man inflexible in virtue, unappalled by power or persecution—and who in dying knew no anxieties but what were excited by his apprehensions for his country—and for his young family."[70] Despite her public bravery, Margaret was devastated. She had given birth just before her husband's death, and six weeks later she was "disconsolate as ever—weeping over her babe." Determined to give Benjamin an appropriate memorial, she rebuffed several attempts to buy the *Aurora* (one by Federalists) and saw to it that the paper did reemerge, with her husband's handpicked successor, William Duane, at the editorial helm, and herself as proprietor.[71]

St. George Tucker was wrong about Bache's persecutions ending at his death. When Margaret and Duane restarted the paper in November, William Cobbett made it a point of pride to unleash his savagery on her. Writing that he held the proprietor of a paper responsible for its contents over some "vagabond journeyman newsmonger," he promised "*that person*

. . . whether bearded or not bearded, whether dressed in breeches or petti-coats, . . . shall receive no quarter from me." Cobbett reached immediately for the most vicious weapon available, sexual innuendo, and then turned threatening: "I shall look upon her as the authoress of the licentiousness, falsehood, impudence, and *bawdry*, contained in [the *Aurora*] . . . she shall disavow the *whole paper*, or decency shall disavow her." Thereafter he addressed her in the paper as "Mother Bache" or "Peg."

Cobbett's assault reached an especially low point in May 1799. He reprinted Margaret's notice of Benjamin's death and attacked her "modesty" for having "struck it off before his corpse was cold." In the next column, he reprinted a snippet from an *Aurora* piece referring to castration in Italy as an example of a barbaric Old World practice abandoned during the Age of Reason. Cobbett hooted at the "*maternal* zeal with which she falls upon the *remorseless barbers*," and compared her to "a sympathetic Sow" prone to "grunt and champ and foam and fly, 'till all the *Swinish Multitude* were in an uproar." Two days later, pleased with having conceived an even more coarse and brutal jest, Cobbett added the comment that the "fury of this she-citizen" against castration "appears very natural, when we recollect the *loss* she had recently experienced."[72]

Margaret Bache remained an outcast from respectable society for the rest of her life. She married William Duane in 1800, much to the titillation of Philadelphia's supposedly high-minded Federalists. President Adams's son Thomas wrote a friend that he was considering writing a satire based on "the scandalous stories of Duane & Madam Peggy's courtship-sham marriage." Becoming a political professional in the early republic could mean losing everything—for an editor or for the woman who shared his vocation.[73]

Cobbett's attacks also had a significance apart from the human damage they did. He was trying to drive the Baches from the field of public debate. In the eighteenth-century public sphere, political writers usually concealed their identities, trying to become merely one disembodied contributor to the abstract "public opinion" that was to be formed through printed debate. In the past, the words of kings and nobles had been obeyed because they were kings and nobles, and the words of commoners, be they shopkeepers, artisans, laborers, women, or racial others, were disregarded because of who they were. In the more mild colonial American situation, gentleman and those above them on the social scale gained automatic credence for their words, while others were dismissed automatically if they had access to print at all. In the new "republic of letters," the disembodiment of the writer and the excision of his or her personal identity focused attention on what was written rather than who wrote it and theoretically evened the political odds.

Cobbett's personal exposures and ridicule thrust his targets' private identities into the public sphere, ensuring that no one could read their words without thinking of the alleged low character and bad morals of the persons who wrote them. Thus treated, Republican editors should have been rendered ineffective, illegitimate participants in political debate. Cobbett was simply engaging in a more brutal and specific form of the name-calling practiced by less skilled Federalist writers such as John Fenno. It was the politics of exclusion, of ejecting opponents from the public sphere by reembodying them in guises that were, in Michael Warner's words, "less than public."[74]

The problem with this strategy was that it could potentially backfire, by turning editors into public figures whose lowliness and sufferings ordinary farmers, workers, and shopkeepers could identify with rather than despise. When that happened, as it would in Bache's own newspaper, printed political debate could begin to move beyond the eighteenth-century customs that had made newspapers a powerful weapon in the hands of the American gentry, but not yet against them.

5

The Background and Failure of the Sedition Act

❧

O*n at least one question* concerning the politics of the 1790s, the Federalists and Republicans were in complete agreement: a decisive factor in the outcome of their struggle was the press. In the aftermath of the "Revolution of 1800," Federalists and Republicans alike blamed or credited the nationwide network of Republican newspapers for Jefferson's triumph. Jefferson praised the "unquestionable effect" of the Philadelphia *Aurora* and the other papers "in the revolution produced on the public mind, which arrested the rapid march of our government toward monarchy." A Delaware Republican attributed the "great political change in the Union" largely to the "unremitting vigilance of Republican Printers." The arch-Federalist Fisher Ames of Massachusetts growled that "the newspapers are an overmatch for any government . . . the Jacobins owe their triumph to the unceasing use of this engine."[1]

This outcome did not occur automatically or inevitably. The printing trade's habitual commercialism changed only slowly, and the bitter experiences of prominent partisan editors such as Bache did not recommend partisanship to the typical printer, who was mostly out to make a living. For much of the decade, there was little indication that anything like a Republican journalistic "engine" might develop. When John Adams took office in early 1797, the few thoroughly politicized opposition journals were scattered and completely outnumbered; even a year later, the Federalists still possessed overwhelming newspaper superiority.

The irony of this situation is that it began to change only after the Federalists had determined to tolerate the opposition press no more, weak as it was, and fashioned legislation to suppress it during the French war scare of 1798. The resulting Sedition Act was not only a political disaster that severely undermined the Adams administration's standing with the voters, but also had the opposite of its intended effect, leading to the creation of the newspaper network that the Federalists blamed for their undoing. The Alien and Sedition Acts mark the U.S. government's last attempt to punish political criticism through national legislation in peacetime. A major goal of the next few chapters is to present a possible explanation for why this experiment was never tried again. The first step in this process is to consider the paradoxically unprepossessing nature of the opposition press that inspired the Sedition Act in the first place.

SLOUCHING TOWARDS PARTISANSHIP: THE REPUBLICAN PRESS BEFORE THE SEDITION ACT

Though they self-consciously emulated British models in other areas, the Federalists attempted no massive bribery to keep the mainstream press on their side. It was not necessary. As party divisions developed, it became apparent that most newspapers, being run by traditional, trade-oriented printers, would continue in their habit of supporting the constituted authorities or shying away from politics altogether. The Federalists saw themselves as the legitimate governing class rather than as a party, and most printers agreed. Moreover, the merchants and financiers who liked Hamilton's program were major sources of advertising in the large cities. It was only prudent for profit-minded printers not to offend their major customers' sensibilities. Thomas Jefferson cited this phenomenon in explaining to a foreign observer the preponderance of Federalist journals: "the Anti-republican party . . . give chief employment to the newspapers, & therefore have most of them under their command."[2] When Jefferson made these comments in 1795, three-quarters of the nation's newspapers either favored the administration or avoided politics. There were perhaps eighteen Republican newspapers in the entire country, and they were concentrated in the large cities (the few that could support more than one newspaper) and in scattered pockets of Republican strength. (See map 1.)[3]

Whatever Jefferson's concern over this lopsided balance of journalistic power, he did little to change it. The former secretary of state lived in retirement at Monticello from 1794 to 1797 and was in no mood for new newspaper schemes. The conservatism of printers and inattention of political leaders thus combined to stunt the growth of a partisan Republican press outside the cities. The Jay Treaty year of 1795 set a record (up to that

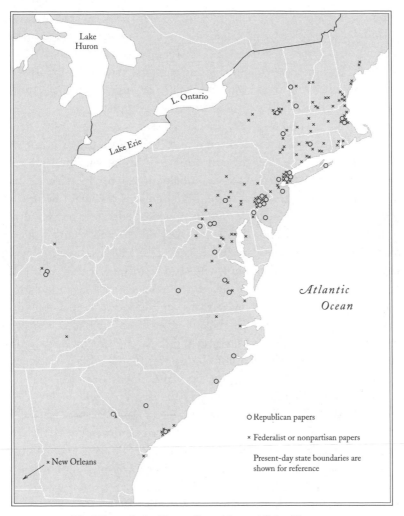

MAP 1. The War on the Jay Treaty: Opposition and Other Newspapers, 1795

time) for the founding of American newspapers, with fifty-three new journals established, but only three were strongly and actively Republican. Two of these would be extinct within a year.[4]

Beyond Bache's *Aurora*, the Republicans of 1795 were sustained chiefly by a few long-established urban newspapers that had gravitated into the Republican camp. Several had been among the handful of newspapers to print the writings of the antifederalists, including Thomas Greenleaf's

New York Journal, the Philadelphia *Independent Gazetteer,* and in Boston, the *Independent Chronicle* and *Boston Gazette.* These were joined by the Bennington *Vermont Gazette,* the Hartford *American Mercury,* and the Elizabeth Town *New-Jersey Journal,* newspapers that had supported the Constitution but that were now tending, at varying rates of speed, toward opposition to the men in control of the new government.

On the whole, this early Republican press was not especially effective or committed to partisanship. Several were decades past their prime or in severe decline, and most of the rest remained throughout their life spans substantially commercial and conventional journals, run by printer-editors who would abandon the trade's traditional policies only with the greatest reluctance.[5] In many cases, it was only after the Federalists proved unwilling to tolerate the traditional practice of printing on all sides of political controversies that these older Republican editors allowed their papers to become partisan. Even then, they tended to be inconsistent in their political activity and almost always relied on better-educated gentleman Republicans for their original matter and political direction. Possibly the strongest Republican paper of the mid-1790s, besides the *Aurora* itself, was the Boston *Independent Chronicle.* However, the *Chronicle* was a clearcut case of printers taking political direction from others. The paper's offices were a frequent meeting place for prominent Boston Republicans and the center of Republican activity in the city, yet *Chronicle* proprietors Thomas and Abijah Adams were treated as political nonentities. For decades, the paper's chief writer and financial benefactor was Benjamin Austin Jr., a wealthy merchant and Republican politician. The memorialist of New England journalism, Joseph T. Buckingham, believed that the *Chronicle* "was indebted, mainly, to Mr. Austin for its influence and success." Austin stopped by the newspaper's office every day on his way to work, recalled Buckingham, "to have a chat with the editors, and to write a paragraph,—perhaps an essay,—for the paper." When Benjamin Franklin Bache arrived in Boston on his Jay Treaty trip, Austin and his fellow *Chronicle* haunter Dr. Charles Jarvis were the local leaders who greeted him, rather than the *Chronicle*'s nominal editor Thomas Adams.[6]

At least the Adams brothers allowed the *Independent Chronicle* to be a strongly partisan newspaper. Much more cautious (and representative of printers in the mid-1790s) was Elisha Babcock, printer-editor of the Hartford *American Mercury.* Babcock leaned Republican himself, but Connecticut Republican politicians regarded his paper as pathetically subservient to the state's Federalist establishment. This was true because Babcock depended on others to write most of his material. Originally, he had been the mechanical half of a partnership that included the poet Joel Barlow, a fellow Jeffersonian, as content supplier. When Barlow left for more lucrative ventures, a somewhat bewildered Babcock stumbled into an informal arrangement with Theodore Dwight and his fellow Connecticut Wits, prolific authors of anti-Republican satires and polemics.

Babcock began to side openly with the Republicans only when the Wits and other Federalists ostracized him in 1794 for allowing a few stray Republican pieces to appear in the *Mercury* along with their own. Babcock proclaimed his independence of the Federalists—"Their frowns I do not fear,—Their friendship I can do without"—but the Republican gentlemen who stepped in to replace the Wits were continually disappointed by their editor's timidity. The *Mercury* continued to print Federalist writings alongside Republican for years after 1794: during the bitter Jay Treaty summer of 1795, the elections of 1796, and even the French crisis of 1797-98. Babcock was hardly the stuff of which "newspaper engines" are made.[7]

PRECOCIOUS PARTISANS:
MATTHEW LYON AND JOHN ISRAEL

There were several very important exceptions to the general rule that printers in the mid-1790s Republican press always took a back seat to others or shied away from partisanship. We will consider two figures who, besides being harbingers of the kind of newspaper politicians who would become dominant later, are significant because of the influence they may have had on the coming of the Sedition Act.[8]

The most notorious such exception was Matthew Lyon in Vermont. Lyon was a former printer who had first come to the United States from Ireland as an indentured servant. He landed first in Connecticut, served in the Revolution, and by the early 1790s, had become a small-time businessman and aspiring politician on the Vermont frontier. In those roles, Lyon carried on a bitter political feud with the state's ruling Federalists. His differences with Nathaniel Chipman and other Federalist leaders began with his background and coarse personal deportment and extended to his radically democratic political ideas. Chipman and his colleagues were lawyers from Massachusetts and Connecticut who had migrated north in the not-unfounded hope of instantly becoming the new state's leading men. Lyon had led the local antifederalists in the late 1780s, and beginning with Vermont's accession to statehood in 1791, mounted a long campaign to win its western congressional seat.[9]

The would-be congressman was defeated twice before reaching for a new weapon, the creation of "a republican press." Enlisting his seventeen-year-old son James as front man and printer, Lyon launched the Rutland *Farmers' Library,* as a "means of saving the district . . . from being deluged by the overpowering flood of anti Republicanism"—and, not incidentally, as a means of improving his own chances of getting to Congress. The first issue appeared between father Lyon's initial defeat in the 1793 congressional election and a required runoff contest two months later. The paper carried Matthew Lyon's own essays, defended his character and record, and attacked his enemies, all the while vigorously indicting the national government and its local supporters.

It took three years, thousands of dollars, two new printers, and a change of locations, but Lyon finally won his place in Congress in 1796. In contrast to Republican urban dailies like the *Independent Chronicle* and *Aurora,* which tried to remain commercially viable newspapers even while conducting their political battles, the *Farmers' Library* never had any purpose or function beyond political campaigning. Lyon admitted that with the local population poor and scattered and the sources of advertising meager, his newspaper never had "the least hope of being profitable." It folded soon after he left for Washington.[10]

The bitterness and persecution with which the Federalists greeted Lyon's congressional career revealed what was potentially at stake in the rise of newspaper politics. Lyon was the first former printer who had ever been elected to Congress, and perhaps the third former artisan of any kind. Quite likely, he was also the only former indentured servant in Congress. His elevation was a major moment in the democratization of American political life, and the Federalists reacted accordingly. Federalist congressmen mocked Lyon's ethnicity and accent during House debates, and in social life treated him as "a meer beast and the fool of the play." After weeks of this, Lyon finally lost his temper and spat in the face of Connecticut's Roger Griswold after a particularly hurtful remark. For this affront to a gentleman's person, the Federalist majority sought to have the "brutal" Lyon expelled from the House, and when the need for a two-thirds majority blocked that maneuver, they looked on approvingly as Griswold accosted Lyon in front of the Speaker's chair and savagely beat him with a new hickory walking stick. Even after the second incident, it was Lyon, not his attacker, that the Federalists wanted to censure.[11]

Significantly, the conflict between Lyon and Griswold had originally begun over a question of newspaper politics. Griswold overheard Lyon boasting about the potential power of the press in elections and his own prowess as an editor. Frustrated over the hard-line attitudes of the Connecticut delegation, Lyon was theorizing to House Speaker Jonathan Dayton that the people of Connecticut, where he once lived, were misrepresented in Congress, a circumstance that he believed was only possible because of the lack of Republican journalism in the state. Lyon said he was certain that if he were to set up a newspaper there, even for a few months, he could "effect a revolution" in public opinion and turn out all the present delegation at the next election.

Roger Griswold angrily contradicted this analysis, telling Lyon he "could not change the opinion of the meanest hostler in the state," but many Federalists were beginning to fear that newspapers might really have such effects. This was what made Lyon and the Republican press so threatening. By giving nongentlemen the ability to influence public opinion and electoral politics, partisan newspapers possessed the potential to overturn social and ethnic hierarchy as the organizing principles of political life, principles the Federalists defended ever more vigorously in the late 1790s. Lyon's election to Congress was the most glaring transgression of those principles that had yet occurred, and a newspaper had been the means. This and uncouth manners made Lyon a highly offensive presence to the more self-consciously aristocratic Federalists.[12]

Lyon's remarks also included the alarming suggestion that his accomplishment was replicable and portable: that skilled newspaper editors might be able to "effect revolutions" in many different locations and transform the face of politics. In some respects, Lyon predicted what would actually take place in the next few years: the emergence of partisan newspaper editors as a class of professional influencers of public opinion, intimately tied to the new political parties. It was only logical that Matthew Lyon would be one of the very first targets of the Alien and Sedition Acts.

But we should not get ahead of the story. Despite the escalating partisanship, the years of Lyon's election and beating saw only fitful attempts to augment the national Republican press. Journalistic activity was most intense at the epicenter of national politics, Philadelphia. Four new Republican journals came and went between the beginning of 1796 and the summer of 1798 as idealistic young Philadelphians and impoverished immigrant writers rushed to join the Republican "Grub Street" surrounding Bache's *Aurora*.[13]

In fact, a glut of partisan journalists developed in the capital that provided some of the impetus and manpower for the spread of an actively partisan Republican press to other areas. An example is the *Herald of Liberty,* one of the few aggressively Republican and successful newspapers to be founded between 1795 and the spring of 1798. It first appeared in February 1798 in the remote western settlement of Washington, Pennsylvania. The new paper's masthead featured a motto designed to curdle the blood of Jacobin-fearing Federalists: "MAN IS MAN, AND WHO IS MORE?"

Having thus announced its commitment to social egalitarianism and Paineite religious skepticism, the *Herald* embarked immediately on an effort to present the national and statewide Republican party to local readers and integrate it with local battles. In striking contrast to most previous newspapers, the *Herald* carried a great deal of patently party-oriented material from its earliest issues: the proceedings of Republican meetings; a pen "Portrait of a True Republican" that obviously had the party in mind; lengthy extracts from Matthew Lyon's expulsion proceedings before the House Committee of Privileges; and a Shakespearean satire on the government's military buildup against the French, "To Arm, or not to arm,—that is the question." Election results were also printed in a more-prominent-than-usual fashion. The paper duplicated, from a slightly different angle, the *Aurora's* imaginative construction of the Republican party.[14]

The paper's editor and connection to Philadelphia was John Israel, a former sailor and veteran of Philadelphia's Democratic Society. Israel's father was tavern keeper Israel Israel, a friend and financial backer of Benjamin Franklin Bache. John Israel and his brother Samuel (who also founded western newspapers) probably learned printing and political journalism in the *Aurora* office. John conceived his "arduous undertaking" in consultation with his father's Republican activist friends and such western Pennsylvania Republican officeholders as Albert Gallatin and William Findley. The young printer became a kind of emissary of the Philadelphia Republicans and their political culture, going out to reorganize western politics along metropolitan lines.[15]

Though barely out of his teens, Israel wrote almost all the *Herald of Liberty's* extensive original matter by himself. In early issues, he devoted much space to defining the broad differences between the Republican opposition and the Federalist-controlled national government. But when election time came, Israel and the *Herald* took on very practical political functions that would become typical of partisan newspapers and their editors in the future. In particular, the editor managed Gallatin's congressional campaign in the district and acted as his link to the local Republican organization. More than a month before the election, Israel inquired whether Gallatin was willing to run for office again. Receiving an affirmative answer, Israel vowed that "now that we have it *authenticated* that you will serve if elected all the exertions which we are capable of will be used for the cause." Actually, Israel had been exerting himself already, having announced Gallatin's candidacy two weeks before receiving confirmation of it.[16]

For the next two months, the *Herald* featured item after item in favor of Gallatin's election, including a series of addresses to Gallatin from each of the district's counties and the candidate's doubtless preplanned "answers" to them. One typical article praised Gallatin's character lavishly while carefully shifting the grounds of judging character from the personal qualities to political ones: "When we make a choice of a Representative, our decision is influenced, not by a simple, but by a compound view of character. It is not only necessary that the object of our choice should be of the same political complexion of ourselves but that in addition, he should unite, *Wisdom, Integrity, and Zeal.* . . . Wherever these qualities can be found, there preference should be given—Happily for this country, they meet in one man—and he is GALLATIN."

This "compound view of character" that allowed partisan commitment or "zeal" to become marks of worthiness, departing sharply from earlier canons of leadership that valued a candidate's character precisely according to his perceived disinterestedness and aloofness from partisanship, was characteristic of the new partisan journalism that Israel and Lyon were pioneering.

The article next answered Federalist attacks on Gallatin's foreign birth and then proceeded to his record in Congress, emphasizing the parts that were most appealing to western and poorer voters. Gallatin had fought to reduce the size of the tracts in which the public lands were sold, "thereby enabling the Farmer to purchase—whereas, the former plan was calculated to exclude the poorer class of society, and the sale would then have become a mere speculating scheme." Likewise, Gallatin had seen to it that the federal land tax extended to unimproved as well as improved lands, meaning that it would fall on speculators as well as farmers. He opposed the tax on salt, which was "oppressive on the poor," and tried to repeal the

Excise, "not wishing to crush the infant manufactures" of western Pennsylvania.[17]

Israel and the *Herald* seem to have been effective: Gallatin won the election, swamping his opponent three to one in the county where the *Herald* was published, offsetting a loss in Pittsburgh. The results meant, Israel wrote, "that the PEOPLE will continue to think and act for themselves, and that they will support men who are friendly to the constitution, any tricks or artifices to deceive them . . . notwithstanding." He might more truthfully have said that his newspaper had helped the people of western Pennsylvania learn to think for themselves as *Republicans*.[18]

In essence, Israel acted as the Republican party's chief spokesman and manager in western Pennsylvania. His job was to monitor public opinion and deploy whatever information and arguments seemed necessary to influence it in a Republican direction. In time, Israel wrote as one who had developed some expertise in these matters. In urging Congressman Gallatin to write a pamphlet, the editor suggested a theme and argued that Gallatin could "render an essential service to *the Cause*" by writing it. "It should commence as soon as possible," he wrote, "because the public mind is now best fitted for the reception of it."

It is equally clear that Israel became a political professional, that politics was his trade. Political benefits were closely linked in Israel's world with financial ones. Regarding the aforementioned pamphlet, Israel was quick to point out that it would be commercially viable as well as politically beneficial. The proposed publication would "sell rapidly," the printer argued, "probably 1,000 at least."[19] Similarly, Israel and others perceived the economic health of the *Herald* as almost synonymous with (or perhaps an indicator of) Republican strength in the county. On the *Herald*'s first birthday, Israel noted that "at the expiration of each six months of our paper, the exclusive Federalists have endeavored to propagate that the Herald is fast declining, and that it can't be supported another half year." The editor countered that he printed 1,296 papers a week, a respectable circulation for any newspaper of the period, to say nothing of one in a remote rural area like Washington, Pennsylvania. The paper's success, Israel argued, was owing to the "zeal and patriotism" of the paper's readers.[20]

Israel's "exertions" on behalf on Republican gubernatorial candidate Thomas McKean, a year after Gallatin's campaign, were even more impressive and provided McKean's primary newspaper support in western Pennsylvania.[21] From late summer until October, the *Herald* editorial columns contained almost nothing but material related to the McKean campaign. There were long essays comparing and contrasting the two candidates, some intended "to aid the Republican cause by placing the character of Chief Justice McKean in an honorable and true light" and others that sought to perform the opposite operation on his opponent, James Ross. Some of these took creative forms such as "Reasons of an Old Man, in Favour of the Election of Thomas McKean," and an epic poem denouncing Ross that ended with a rhyming endorsement of the Republican candidate: "But let us change the scene again / And view his opponent MCKEAN, / Whom freedom's foes assail in vain." To give the impression of a groundswell of support for McKean, Israel published the proceedings of a series of "Republican Meetings of the Western Country." Other pieces served what the *Herald* told its readers was a particularly important function for campaigners in remote rural regions: to detect and warn the people of "Federal LIES" spread "to serve electioneering purposes."

Because he was in contact with Republican leaders all over the state, including his own father, Israel was in an excellent position to do this. One lie he quashed was that McKean had died of yellow fever! Besides the newspaper itself, the *Herald* office produced and sent out handbills, pamphlets, election tickets, and other partisan documents. Referring to a particular essay or handbill he thought especially effective, the editor promised "to do all in my power to give it currency." When McKean finally triumphed, Israel announced the event by printing the candidate's name, party, and margin of victory at the top of a page in letters that dwarfed the *Herald*'s own title.[22]

Despite its political successes, the *Herald of Liberty* developed serious cash flow problems arising from unpaid subscription bills and lack of advertising, endemic problems for all newspapers but especially for rural ones. Politics compounded these problems. There were few Republicans in western Pennsylvania with money or reason to advertise regularly (merchants being the most frequent advertisers in the North), and it was hard to collect bad subscription debts when the deadbeats were voters and politicians whose support was being sought.

The *Herald*'s stability was ensured only when, less than a month after taking office, new Governor McKean appointed Israel as register of wills and recorder of deeds for Washington County. The appointment was made, the governor said, because "Israel could not support his press without making large sacrifices."[23] Israel was allowed to continue publishing his paper while holding the offices. Elevating a printer to public office (other than to a postmastership, which printers had occasionally held since colonial times)—to say nothing of a printer who was young, of partly Jewish ancestry, and a newcomer to the area—was an unprecedented (and, at this time, relatively isolated) act, which even the Republican political gentry of Washington County did not welcome. Town founder William Hoge and state senator John Hamilton appealed the appointment to Gallatin, who claimed, with great duplicity or ingratitude considering what Israel had done for him, not to have supported it. All these reactions portended dangerous waters ahead for partisan printers. External support was usually needed to buoy up their newspapers, but the chief beneficiaries of their work seemed unwilling to acknowledge or reward them once an electoral threat had passed.[24]

The *Herald of Liberty* was a prototype of the partisan Republican papers that would soon be common all over the country, but it was the exception in the spring of 1798. Other small-town newspapers that appeared around the same time displayed Republican sympathies but can be classified as strongly Republican only by their behavior later in the decade. Among such potentially Republican journals were the Alexandria *Times,* the New London *Bee,* the Norfolk *Epitome of the Times,* and the Chambersburg *Farmer's Register,* all founded in 1797 or early 1798. The editors of the *Farmer's Register,* for example, were as much refugees from Philadelphia partisanship as emissaries of it. As "young beginners" in Philadelphia, John Snowden and William McCorkle had suffered heavy losses publishing James T. Callender's incendiary works, *History of the United States for 1796* and *Sketches of the History of America.*[25]

Starting their professional lives over in Chambersburg, a small town in south central Pennsylvania, Snowden and McCorkle announced their belief in newspapers as "essential promoters of useful knowledge" only, and abjured "the idea of a *weekly distribution of malicious invective.*" Over its first two months, the *Farmers' Register* contained only a few political items but many public documents and, true to its title, informative articles on farming. Snowden and McCorkle explicitly cast their impartiality in the deferential terms of artisan printers. Introducing one of the few political essays to appear in the early issues of the paper, they commented that the "sentiments it contains fall not to our province to appreciate."[26] New editors in other areas took a similarly retiring and impartial approach.[27]

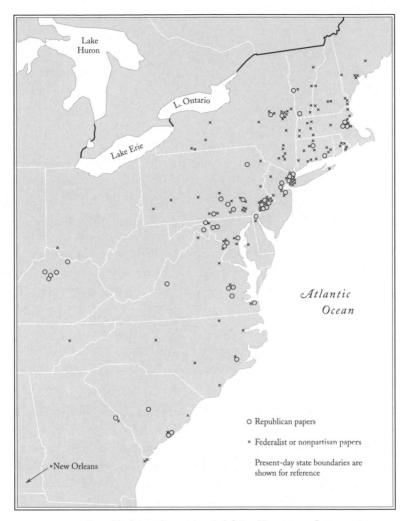

MAP 2. Eve of Sedition: Opposition and Other Newspapers, Spring 1798

Thus, as late as spring of 1798, the Republican press was relatively inconsequential: unstable, widely scattered, vastly outnumbered, and in many cases, unsure of its mission. (See map 2.) By my calculation, there were 51 Republican-leaning newspapers in the country at that point, out of a total newspaper population of 185. Yet the actual strength of opposition journalism was actually much less, since most of these journals were in the same tepid, uncertain state of partisanship as the Chambersburg

Farmer's Register. There were probably no more than ten self-consciously and aggressively partisan Republican journals in the nation.

To be sure, the Federalist-leaning majority of the country's newspapers were largely traditional, commercial, and apolitical, but the Federalists did not really need aggressive partisanship. Holding power, they controlled the flow of official information. The national government could easily disseminate its version of events through the government documents, presidential speeches, and congressional proceedings that the commercial newspapers printed in quantity, as authoritative fact. This advantage was difficult for a scattered handful of opposition editors to counter, particularly during the years of the Adams administration. With the French regularly brutalizing American commerce and insulting American diplomats, among other depredations, the news by itself was enough to push the country into an increasingly belligerent, anti-French, and pro-administration mood. The Federalists appeared to be winning the war for public opinion and seemingly had little to fear from the opposition press. Perhaps it was this very sense of strength that led to their fateful move to suppress their newspaper critics once and for all.

FASHIONING THE WEAPON: THE THINKING BEHIND THE SEDITION ACT

Federalist self-confidence probably reached a peak beginning in March 1798, when word of the so-called "XYZ Affair" reached Philadelphia. Immediately thereafter, Congress began work on a harsh program to secure the country from its enemies, both internal and external. Internally, most items on the list involved the Republican press. New England Federalists had long complained about the dangers posed by the "wild Irishmen" and other "vicious and disorganizing characters" who had fled to America after failing to overthrow their own governments at home. The first measures proposed gave the president sweeping powers to summarily imprison or deport suspicious aliens. Though rooted in a more general xenophobia, the various alien bills were aimed especially at the numerous refugees who had become newspaper editors and pamphleteers in Philadelphia and New York.[28] At the same time, congressional Federalists plotted legislation that would deal with the Republican press directly. Initially, Benjamin Bache's Philadelphia *Aurora* seems to have been almost the only specific paper that Federalist leaders had in mind. They made no secret of their intentions. "There is now only wanting . . . a sedition bill which we shall certainly soon see proposed," Vice President Jefferson wrote to James

Madison in April. "The object of that is the suppression of the whig presses. Bache's particularly has been named."[29]

In arguing for restrictions on Republican newspapers, the Federalists took an even more expansive view of the press's power than Jefferson did. The defenders of constituted authority argued that there was no government, no social bond, no religious or moral precept that could withstand assaults from the press. "Speech, writing, and printing are the great directors of public opinion, and public opinion is the great director of human action," declaimed Judge Alexander Addison before his western Pennsylvania grand jury. "Give to any set of men the command of the press, and you give them the command of the country."[30] Addison was probably the most important of several Federalist judges whose doctrines both laid the groundwork for the Sedition Act and aided in its defense. Significantly, he resided in the town of Washington, where John Israel's *Herald of Liberty* was published. Proximity to such a precociously effective and partisan journal undoubtedly sharpened and energized Addison's thinking. His grand jury charge on *Liberty of Speech, and of the Press* was made into a pamphlet and republished all over the country. In this and other works, Addison laid out a systematic case for sharply curtailing the newspaper-based popular politics that had been growing under the auspices of the *Aurora, Herald of Liberty,* and other publications.[31]

Addison's ideas about the basis of government ("the opinion of the people"), and the consequent power of the press, closely paralleled Jefferson's: "Of such force is public opinion, that, with it on its side, the worst government will support itself; and, with it against it, the best government will fall. All governments are supported by it; and, without it, can no government be supported. What is the force in the power of any government, compared to that of the people governed by it, if the people choose to resist?" Where Jefferson found in these insights the justification for a wide circulation of information, Addison and other Federalists drew an opposite but no less logical conclusion: that if public opinion was so powerful, then the means of influencing it had to be kept under strict control and in the safest possible hands. Taking the French Revolution as their text, Federalists tried to demonstrate how dangerous the press could be when put to bad purposes. Foreshadowing the arguments of modern historians on the origins of the French Revolution, Addison contended that "the seeds of insurrection [were] busily sown in the minds of the people" for years before 1789:

The printing presses were occupied. Pamphlets and books were dispersed. New principles were broached, supported, and established. Under the sanction of philosophy and reason, all prejudices in favour of religion and government were gradually sapped, to make way for liberty, equality, and the rights of man. . . . All were men; and priests and princes were no more. All respect for office ceased: and an insult to a bishop or a king was no more than an insult to an equal. Religion was but a state trick. . . . Public opinion, the great pillar of this, as of every government, being thus withdrawn, the mighty fabric of the monarchy, which . . . had stood the blasts of ages, was touched by a slight shock, and, in a moment crumbled to pieces.[32]

Congressman John Allen of Connecticut went even further with this interpretation in a furious speech leading off the House debate on the sedition bill. "At the commencement of the Revolution in France," he recounted, "those loud and enthusiastic advocates for liberty and equality took special care to occupy and command all the presses." According to Allen, the diabolical French revolutionaries understood that the press's power came especially from its sway over "the poor, the ignorant, the passionate, and the vicious; over all these classes the freedom of the press shed its baneful effects," and "the virtuous, the pacific, and the rich, were their victims." By such "arts," Allen and Addison declared, "base, factious, and wicked men" such as Robespierre had "made of France a general slaughter-house, and left of liberty nothing but a name."[33]

Now this "plague" had reached the United States. Congressman Allen expressed the determination of the majority of the Fifth Congress not to meet the same fate as the former rulers of France. He stated the Sedition Act's purpose quite plainly: "The Jacobins of our country, too, sir, are determined to preserve in their hands, the same weapon [the press]; it is our business to wrest it from them." Congress took less than a week, working over the Fourth of July holiday, to create the means of conducting their "business." The Sedition Act they passed imposed penalties of up to two thousand dollars and two years in prison on anyone who should "write, print, utter, publish, or shall cause or procure to be written, printed, uttered, or published . . . any false, scandalous and malicious writing or writings against the government of the United States . . . with intent to defame the said government . . . or the said President, or to bring them . . . into contempt or disrepute; or to excite against them . . . the hatred of the good people of the United States."

The Federalists were careful to incorporate the most progressive legal standards for seditious libel into the law, imposing no before-the-fact restraints on publication, allowing defendants to exonerate themselves if they could prove their assertions were true, and letting juries decide the law of each case—whether the statement should be considered a libel—as well as the mere fact of who published it. While the Sedition Act thus conformed to Andrew Hamilton's supposedly libertarian position in the Zenger case and was more lenient than similar laws in Europe, it nonetheless criminalized almost any criticism that might be made in protesting government policy or campaigning against an incumbent officer. It opened editors of opposition newspapers to court actions for almost any political essay or comment they might print, even a report of a public meeting, whether they wrote it or not. As Republicans soon pointed out, truth was no defense at all in matters of political interpretation and opinion.[34]

Though extremists like Allen professed to fear that the Republican press might engineer a literal revolution in the United States, Federalists also made more realistic complaints about the changes occurring in American political culture. One was a sense that Republican politics generally, and Republican newspapers in particular, were the cause and medium of widespread insubordination against the nation's self-conceived natural aristocracy. Connecticut's Uriah Tracy, a Senate supporter of the Sedition Act, blamed the problem partly on the relative prosperity of the rural population in the United States, which created a market for the press and allowed the ordinary citizen to be far too well informed. Ranting privately before a clergyman who turned out later to be a Republican, Tracy observed that far too great a proportion of the American population "are able to lay out their earnings in buying Newspapers, books, &c., and having leisure to read, they of course become mighty politicians, acquainted beforehand with all that ought to be done by government & with all that ought not to be done, are ready to pronounce what is done right & what wrong, & so will condemn public measures which happen not to comport exactly with their great knowledge, or which might cross their present interests, & will not suffer them to be carried into execution."[35]

While admitting that citizens had the right to question their rulers and the power to choose and remove them, Alexander Addison complained that the people and their self-appointed spokesmen were "too apt to confound right with capacity, and power with skill," to think themselves "qualified to do" what they were "permitted to do." The people failed to grasp that "Politics, legislation, or the art of government, is a science, and, like other sciences, to understand it, requires knowledge, study, and reflection. Respectable as this country is, we can hardly suppose, that the state of education and knowledge in it is yet such, as to enable all those who *may* judge, to judge *rightly,* of the conduct of administration." According to Addison, this problem was worsened by the tendency to let recently immigrated foreigners—meaning especially refugee radicals—who "have had little opportunity of understanding our interests" to become "the most forward to examine, and the most severe to censure, the measures of our administration."[36]

Addison believed the people had little cause to censure their government and little to fear from it as long they elected men of "understanding and knowledge" to office. Such men were inherently more qualified to hold power, because they felt a natural compulsion to do a good job and not abuse their power. This was rooted in a statesmanlike emotion only a few possessed, the love of *"station"*: "There is, in understanding and knowledge, a power, which those who possess them not, cannot feel, almost irresistibly impelling [such men] to acquire reputation by a faithful discharge of their duty. Understanding and knowledge furnish a just estimate of the importance of virtue, and inspire the mind with the desire of it."[37]

Irresponsible or ignorant criticism of the government—categories into which Addison put all of the current Republican criticism—thus imperiled good government and faithful official conduct by taking from men of understanding and knowledge the "station" or "character" they craved: "Character, reputation, or a good name, is not easily acquired, and will not less reluctantly be abandoned. It is not in the nature of man readily to give up that which we have hardly acquired, and highly value. Is it easy to conceive, that a Washington or an Adams, who have derived all their fame from their exertions in the cause of liberty, would abandon the source of their glory and pride?"[38] Indeed it was not, and under the assaults of the Republican press, the government was being removed from the hands of those best fitted to run it: "Our wisest and best public officers have had their lives embittered, and have been driven from their stations by unceasing and malignant slander."[39] Their replacements would be obscure, venal, unqualified men—those base enough to write for newspapers or benefit from newspaper writings—"without virtue or talents" who had no way "to rise into consequence, but by slander." The system of unlimited freedom of the press gave such men an advantage over gentlemen who had reputations to protect.[40]

Even more sinister than this social insubordination was the possibility that opposition printers were simply pawns in a conspiracy to overthrow the government, masterminded by unscrupulous and degenerate American gentlemen in league with the French and all the other forces of darkness. This threat, too, had its roots in the decline of virtue evident in the country's changing political culture. "To the curse and calamity of this country," Addison told a grand jury in 1795, there were "among us a set of people, known by the name of *electioneering men*, whose conduct, the whole year round, is constantly governed by prospect of influence on the day of election." To secure this influence, an electioneering man gathered "to himself others of like sentiments and views, or dupes to his art, or tools to his designs."[41] To the Federalist mind, a printer made a particularly convenient and efficacious tool.

Printers' artisanal status made the argument that they were the tools of others a convincing one. In classical republican thought, in which the Federalists were as deeply steeped as their political opponents, popular virtue was necessary for the survival of a republic. Virtue depended on a person's ability to make free, independent, and "disinterested" political decisions. For several reasons, artisans and other tradesmen were thought to lack the intellectual or material independence necessary to exercise virtue: because they came from a stratum of society that naturally deferred to gentlemen, because their lack of education left them susceptible to deceit and manipulation, and because they lived by selling goods to customers, typically well-heeled customers who would could use the artisans' or shopkeepers' need for their business to bend their political wills.[42]

Those without virtue were a potential threat to liberty because they were liable to become the "dupes" or "tools" of would-be dictators and other men intent on using government for their personal gain. Though he might have disagreed with the use that Federalists such as Addison made of it, Thomas Jefferson expressed this same fear as clearly as any thinker of the eighteenth century in his famous warnings against the dangers of a manufacturing-based economy in *Notes on the State of Virginia*. Woe betide the nation, Jefferson wrote, in which a majority of the citizens "not looking . . . to their own soil and industry, as does the husbandman, for their subsistence, depend for it on the casualties and caprice of customers. Dependence begets subservience and venality, suffocates the germ of virtue, and prepares fit tools for the designs of ambition."[43]

A like analysis informed the most frequently made argument for property requirements and other restrictions on the suffrage. According to Sir

William Blackstone (who cribbed the language from Montesquieu), political rights should be withheld from "such persons as are in so mean a situation as to be esteemed to have no will of their own."[44] If it was risky to grant the suffrage to men of questionable virtue, such as tradesmen, then how much more dangerous to turn that "great director of public opinion," the press, over to them. "To every friend of a representative democracy," Addison asserted, "it is a mortifying observation, that boys, blockheads, and ruffians, are often listened to, in preference to men of integrity, skill, and understanding."[45]

This traditional antipathy toward the inclusion of artisans in politics combined in the Federalist mind with a not-inaccurate appraisal of the self-interested approach to politics that printers had taken in the past. As Addison saw it, the recent licentiousness of the press was simply a matter of economics, of tradesmen meeting the demands of their well-heeled clients: "Newspapers are sometimes published, not that they may be useful to the readers, but to the printers; not that they may instruct, but that they may be bought; and the object of the publishers is not so much to inform the judgment by just knowledge, as to excite passion and curiosity, and support the party that will best support their custom." Happily for the Federalists, their view of the Republican printers as commercially minded tools of evil gentlemen suggested an easy means of thwarting the conspiracy. Congressman Allen predicted in his House speech that if its outside supports were removed, the Republican press would quickly collapse. Referring specifically to the *Aurora,* Allen stated flatly that the paper was "the work of a party; . . . it is assiduously disseminated through the country by a party; to that party is all the credit due; to that party it owes its existence; if they loved the peace of our Zion, if they sought the repose of our country, it would cease to admit its filth; it has flourished by their smiles; it would perish at their frowns."[46]

WHY DID THE SEDITION ACT FAIL?
ANSWERS TO AN UNASKED QUESTION

Though the Federalists speculated little on the potential effectiveness of the Sedition Act, they clearly believed that it could achieve their stated goal of "wresting" the press away from the Republicans and suppressing journals like the *Aurora.* While a sedition law could not necessarily induce Republican gentlemen to "frown" on their newspapers, it might have the capacity to rearrange the calculations of subservient, profit-minded printers by sharply raising the costs of allowing partisan Republican essays into their pages. A show of constituted authority's force would be enough to overawe printers, make partisanship unprofitable, and disperse the opposition press. The Republican gentry in Congress did not necessarily disagree. In opposing the Sedition Act, Jefferson's close friend Senator Wilson Cary Nicholas of Virginia argued that "if printers are to be subject to prosecution for every paragraph which appears in their papers . . . it cannot be expected that they will exercise that freedom and spirit which it is desirable should actuate them."[47]

With the vindictive secretary of state Timothy Pickering heading the enforcement efforts, the new law did not languish on the statute books. All three major pre-1798 Republican journals, the *Aurora*, the *Independent Chronicle*, and the *New York Journal*, were hit, along with James Callender, Matthew Lyon, and Anthony Haswell, a Vermont printer who had the temerity to print material defending Lyon in his newspaper and to reprint paragraphs from the *Aurora*. Another early victim was an exiled United Irishman, journalist, and playwright named John Daly Burk, who had the misfortune to take over the *Time Piece*, a failed try at a comeback by Philip Freneau, in mid-June 1798. Pickering had Burk arrested before Congress had even passed the Sedition Act, unsure about whether to prosecute under that prospective law or one of the Alien Acts. The spirit of reprisal that the federal laws embodied and sanctioned also opened the way for common-law seditious libel prosecutions in the state courts and other acts of vengeance and harassment against Republican newspapermen, pamphleteers, and speakers.[48]

In the short run, the Sedition Act was a great "success" for the Federalists in the sense that many of their principal newspaper targets were either suppressed or severely damaged by the prosecutions. John Daly Burk's partner and financial backer in the *Time Piece* grew nervous and abandoned the editor when Burk refused to moderate his tone in the face of prosecution. The *Time Piece* soon collapsed and Burk himself went into hiding to avoid deportation. By indicting Ann Greenleaf (widow of Thomas Greenleaf) under the Sedition Act and bringing a state-level libel action against her foreman, David Frothingham, Pickering and Alexander Hamilton also managed to shut down the venerable *New York Journal*. The Boston *Independent Chronicle* survived, but it became a largely nonpartisan paper for more than a year before the election of 1800, thanks to a fearful new owner.[49]

In the long run, however, the Sedition Act failed badly. Not only did it fail to put the partisan Republican press out of business, it seemingly called new men into the field, in greater numbers and with greater intensity than previously. The pace of newspaper creation sped up, hitting a new high of seventy-one in 1800 (see appendix 1, chart 3), on a wave of more than thirty partisan Republican sheets. In all, eighty-five strongly Republican or Republican-leaning newspapers were published in that election year, two-thirds again more than there had been before the Sedition Act was introduced. The number of heavily politicized and strongly Republican journals probably increased at several times that rate, as older papers changed character and a much higher proportion of newly founded journals embraced aggressive partisanship.

A list of the Republican papers active in 1800 by date of founding, presented in appendix 2, makes it possible to see the Republican press massing its forces as the turn of the century approached. By the time Jefferson took office, the Republican cause had a dedicated promoter of its views in every major city and in most of the principal smaller towns of every state. Map 3 shows the growth of this newspaper network. While it has long been understood that the Alien and Sedition Acts backfired on the Federalists in terms of public opinion, the expansion of the Republican press before the election of 1800 shows that they backfired on even the most basic level. The longer the persecution campaign lasted, the more Republican newspapers appeared.

This development raises a question that the vast literature on the history of press freedom has never asked, much less answered: why did the Sedition Act fail? Most accounts of the late 1790s crisis have focused on high-level politics or the evolution of legal doctrine in describing the response to the Sedition Act.[50] Thomas Jefferson and James Madison pursued the strategy of having the states declare the law unconstitutional, while Republican gentlemen in and out of Congress attacked it in speeches and pamphlets. Some of these latter productions made some genuine advances in libertarian theory, according to the much-disputed thesis of the legal historian Leonard Levy, moving beyond the "no prior restraints" and "truth as a defense" position toward the modern doctrine of absolute protection for the expression of political opinion.[51] The problem is that neither changes in legal doctrine nor high-level politics actually did much to neutralize the Sedition Act.

The ideas of the new libertarians, as stated by Levy, were not adopted by any court or legislature, either during the 1790s or for decades there-

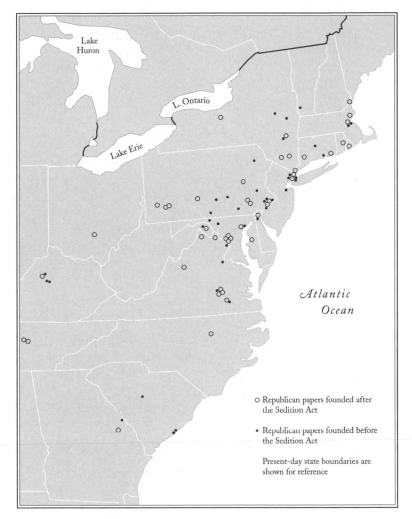

MAP 3. Editorial Revolution: Republican Newspapers Published
between June 1798 and December 1800

after, while the machinations of Jefferson and Madison fared even worse.
Their Virginia and Kentucky Resolutions were a political disaster that
came closer to justifying and saving the Alien and Sedition Acts than
stopping them. Horrified at the idea of threatening the union by pitting
the states against the federal government, no other state legislatures
passed such resolutions, and the backlash against the strategy nearly cost
Jefferson the election by severely eroding his base of support. Only some

last-minute electoral chicanery saved Virginia's electoral votes for Jefferson in 1800, and he gained only a share in the electoral votes of North Carolina, formerly one of his strongest states. Meanwhile, congressional Republicans failed repeatedly to stop or repeal the Sedition Act, succeeding only in preventing its renewal in January 1801, long after it had manifestly failed to destroy the Republican press and Jefferson and Burr had already won the election of 1800.[52]

What most accounts of the response to the Sedition Act do not deal with extensively is what the law aimed, and failed, to control: the political behavior of journalists. How can we explain the explosion of opposition journalism in the face of strong government efforts to clamp down on opposition, especially given what we know about the habitually practical approach of printers to politics? During the Revolution and the constitutional ratification debate, the commercialism of printers had allowed American leaders to stifle the development of a powerful opposition press. What was different about the late 1790s?

One hypothesis about the "failure" of the Sedition Act is that printers were simply following their old commercial instincts in new circumstances. There was more "demand" for Republican journalism, in the form of increased reader interest and especially in the form of Republican gentlemen willing to write for, subscribe to, and subsidize Republican newspapers. As they had during the Revolution, printers may simply have found partisanship suddenly profitable in highly politicized times. While perceived financial opportunities may account for some of the Republican press's expansion, the financial realities of the political newspaper business in the late eighteenth century rule out the profit motive as a very important factor in the failure of the Sedition Act. It is true that many printers followed the old trade strategies, but these habits generally drove them away from politics rather than into it. Commercially oriented practical printers were loathe to subordinate their business sense to political needs, as political publishing constantly demanded. For instance, they usually demanded that the author of a political pamphlet purchase all copies in advance. A Virginia Republican politician denounced the Richmond printers as "generally such mercenary wretches," because they stuck by this rule even in the case of a pamphlet he deemed critical to winning an election.[53]

To be sure, some of the newspapers that popped up at the end of the 1790s do look suspiciously like attempts to cash in on the rising popularity of the Republicans, and especially on their expected victory. When Oliver

Farnsworth and his brother Havila first launched the Newport *Companion and Commercial Advertiser* in May 1798, it was a slavishly conventional paper that reprinted extensively from Fenno's *Gazette* and other Federalist papers. Two years later, however, that paper disappeared and the decidedly Republican *Guardian of Liberty,* edited by Oliver Farnsworth alone, took its place. Matthias Bartgis, a longtime publisher in Fredericktown, Maryland, was even more nakedly opportunistic. Sometime between April 1800 and February 1801 (the intervening issues being lost), Bartgis changed the name of his newspaper from *Bartgis's Federal Gazette* to *Bartgis's Republican Gazette* and then applied to the new Jefferson administration for the printing of the U.S. laws.[54]

Ultimately, however, the political battles of the 1790s had much less to offer a commercially oriented printer than those of the 1760s. Revolutionary printers faced a hostile government across the water, but (once the Loyalists were expelled from an area) they enjoyed a relatively unified local elite to back their partisanship. Jeffersonian Republicans, however, faced a hostile government nearby and (outside the South) local elites that were at best divided and at worst set against them. Seditious libel prosecutions were vigorously enforced against editors all over the country, and at least fourteen Republican editors spent time in jail. It was difficult to keep money coming in while defending oneself in court or languishing in a prison cell.

Even apart from the special circumstances of the time, the profit motive makes little sense as the force behind the expansion of the partisan press in the late 1790s. For all but the lucky handful of Republican editors who obtained state printing contracts, a phenomenon limited to a few southern state capitals, the editing of Republican newspapers was more often the road to ruin than riches. The newspaper business was notoriously unprofitable, unstable, and becoming more competitive all the time, as the number of newspapers increased far more quickly than the size of the population (see appendix 1, charts 3 and 4.)

A major reason for this dismal record was the marked tendency of newspaper subscribers and advertisers not to pay their bills. Printers fell into chronic debt as unpaid invoices mounted, and they often found it impossible to collect enough money to materially alter their situation.[55] When William Duane took over the Philadelphia *Aurora* from Benjamin Franklin Bache, he was horrified to discover that the paper had $15,000 to $20,000 in receivables on its books, and those were only the debtors "south of the Delaware." A veteran newspaper publisher, Duane saw little hope of actually collecting much of this money. "Mark this plain observation of experience," he advised a wealthy Republican gentleman who was considering purchasing or investing in the paper. *"Newspaper debts are the worst of all others!"*

The problem was in the structure of newspaper debt: a large sum made up of hundreds or thousands of tiny sums due from individuals, each far too small to pay a lawyer to collect, especially if the debtor resided in a distant place. Thus a national publication like the *Aurora* was in a particularly difficult spot, thrown back on its editor's powers of persuasion alone as a tool for collecting debts. Duane and many another partisan editor could describe their financial affairs as did James Lyon, editor of many more Republican papers besides his father's. Imploring Jefferson for relief in 1800, Lyon wrote that his business was "something profitable upon paper, but the difficulty of getting my collections made, renders it rather embarrassing in practice."[56]

Even successful partisan editors could hardly look forward to a life of ease and wealth. The few early partisan newspaper printers who managed to keep their papers going for a long period of time earned at most the comfortable living of a prosperous tradesman or storekeeper. (In time, a few capital-based newspapers with fat government printing contracts would do better.)[57] The rest did much worse or found another line of work. When sixteen-year-old David Chambers was apprenticed to Benjamin Franklin Bache in 1796, he was horrified to discover the dim view the *Aurora*'s journeyman printers took of their own craft, especially its financial prospects: "They say They would give anything if they had not [become printers] . . . it is but a poor business." Chambers's father inquired of Bache whether his employees' impressions were true, and the *Aurora* editor replied with less than complete candor that the business was "lucrative, and . . . will become daily more and more extensive" (at a time when he was losing money by the bushel). Informed by his son of the penurious conditions in the *Aurora* office, the concerned parent chose not to believe Bache's assurances and allowed his son to come home from Philadelphia.[58]

In keeping with their generally low estimation of the Republican printers' capacities and morals, the Federalists routinely charged (and privately believed) that the opposition editors were in the pay of the French, Republican conspirators, or both. To the opposition editors themselves, the accusation seemed self-evidently ludicrous in view of the meager material realities of their lives. Philip Freneau wrote a poetic epitaph to this to the charge in 1797:

> Yes! they are brib'd—that's clear;
> And paid French millions by the year;
> And prov'd, most plainly, by the coats they wear:—
> They are the lads that live in houses grand,
> And own vast tracts of fertile land;
> With so much self-denial in their natures
> (They are such good, obliging creatures),
> That shunning pleasure and the glare of wealth,
> They for the public good waste time and health;
>   Sit up all night,
>   Compile and write;
> One day a shilling from Kentucky get—
> Then stay a week to starve and fret.
> Why, Mr. Fenno, if this be French gold,
> No wonder that you federalists look so bold.[59]

The real reasons for the Sedition Act's "failure" lay not in business opportunities or the activities of the Jeffersonian elite, but instead in the changes that the growth of political parties, and the Federalist repression itself, wrought on the worldviews and life goals of printers. The Sedition Act "failed" by transforming a large number of printers into something more than simple pliers of the printer's trade. The Federalist repression convinced many printers that there was no place for an honest printer who followed the traditional nonpartisan approach. Simultaneously, the growth of political parties opened new roles for printers that validated the claims that all American artisans felt they had to equal rights. Many of them became political professionals, people for whom printing was a way to make a living out of politics, rather than the other way around.

The most effective way of demonstrating and explaining these changes is a detailed study of one printer's experience, to which we now turn.

6

Charles Holt's Generation

From Commercial Printers to Political Professionals

❧

Before 1798 few printers set out with the intention of aligning themselves with a particular set of political views, much less becoming operatives of an organized political party. In addition to the trade's traditionally impartial approach to politics, printers, like most other Americans, were influenced by the classical republican ideals of the American Revolution, among other strains of thought to come out of that event. Thus they shared with most Americans a belief in independence as the primary political good, a belief that condemned anything that tended to impinge on individual political free will. Chief among the forces that tended to destroy this "freedom of elections" were organized campaigning, political parties, and the taking of money for political activity, all infamously practiced by British ministries that Americans deemed tyrannical and corrupt. Only under great pressure—or with great enticements—would most American printers modify these beliefs.[1]

CHARLES HOLT AND THE *BEE:* A CASE STUDY FROM THE LAND OF STEADY HABITS

Before the late 1790s, the state of Connecticut came closer than any other to matching the classical republican ideal: a polity in which an elite of virtuous statesmen ruled through patriotic consensus rather than self-seeking competition.[2] Leadership was remarkably stable. Though the executive officers had to be reelected yearly, in practice they usually served for life. Only seventeen different men had been governor in 150 years up to 1789. Elections were impeccably traditional and quiet. The Connecticut jurist Zephaniah Swift boasted that "no instance has ever been known where a person has appeared [in] public . . . and solicited the suffrages of

FIGURE 2. New London *Bee*, masthead, 23 August 1797.
(Courtesy of American Antiquarian Society)

the freemen." Where New York and most other states endured terrible political upheavals—including riots, bitter electoral strife, and radical reorganizations of government—during the Revolution, the well-named "Land of Steady Habits" was so little ruffled that no need was seen to even write a state constitution. The legislature simply reenacted the royal Charter of 1662, without submitting the document to a popular vote. As Swift wrote, Connecticut's "transition from . . . political subjection to Great-Britain . . . was almost imperceptible."[3]

This almost preternatural stability was made possible by an interlocking religious and political elite known colloquially as the "Standing Order." The foundation of this system was Connecticut's established Congregational Church, which retained its tax support until the state wrote its first constitution in 1818. The clergy were politically vocal, and they made sure that their pious flocks understood where the Lord stood on the issues of the day. In Connecticut, God was a Federalist, and Republicans never won a statewide election, or even a congressional seat, until after 1818.

Connecticut's political leaders conformed to a correspondingly narrow profile: they were Congregationalists, Yale graduates, lawyers, and Federalists, almost to a man. All this made Connecticut the most deferential society and polity in early America. The English diplomat Augustus John Foster felt that Connecticut was the closest thing in America to the comfortable hierarchy of the English countryside: "There is a cleanliness and an English air about everything, even to the labourers who take off their hats in passing you, which one meets with nowhere else on the American side of the Atlantic." Foster found the state refreshingly free from "the utopian nonsense of ultra-political ranters and constitution-hunters" so prevalent in the rest of the United States.[4]

Connecticut's phlegmatic political culture did not provide an environment in which the political press thrived. The colony did not get its first newspaper until the relatively late date of 1755. Those that did appear were always commercially oriented and blandly supportive of the Standing Order and its policies, favoring independence during the Revolution and strong central government during the 1780s. Wherever possible, Connecticut newspapers purveyed the usual eighteenth-century mix of foreign news, commercial information, polite literary essays, and bad poetry.[5]

The career of Charles Holt, editor of what became the Jeffersonian organ in New London, Connecticut, provides an excellent example of a traditional, commercially oriented printer who was transformed, in terms of both activities and self-image, into a nearly full-time party operative. A New London native, Holt was twenty-five years old when he established the *Bee*, his first newspaper, in 1797. The first issue of a new newspaper typically included an "address" to prospective readers explaining the editor's intentions and philosophy. Holt's was a model of submission to the wishes of the buying public:

> Do you wish to circulate political intelligence—do you wish to inculcate moral instruction—do you wish to communicate discoveries in the arts and sciences—do you wish to display the effusions of exuberant fancy—do you wish to see abstruse and philosophical questions discussed with candor and ingenuity—do you wish to exercise your talents for personal improvement and the production of literature—in fine, have you a single thought or wish that you desire to make public—the ever ready and subservient *Newspaper* stands with eager hands to accomplish all your purposes.

In another section of the front page, Holt was more specific regarding his policy on political matter: "The publisher of this paper is determined that his paper shall be, with respect to political disquisitions, in every sense of the word IMPARTIAL." Under the head "Political," Holt placed the motto "Open to all parties." The young printer kept his promise, for, in his second issue, an obviously Federalist writer replied to a Republican article that had appeared in the first issue.[6]

If Holt believed that his community's leaders expected him to literally carry out the conventional promises of impartiality, he was mistaken. For opening his pages even to a few mild pieces from the area's hopelessly outnumbered Republicans, he found himself boycotted and reviled. In response, Holt dropped the nonpartisan motto in early 1798.[7] Too young to remember what had happened to impartial printers during the Revolution, Holt expressed surprise and frustration at the Federalists' intolerance of his attempt to practice traditional neutrality: "The agitation of the public mind, during this period, has been uncommonly great . . . and the task of conducting a paper to general satisfaction rendered peculiarly arduous and difficult." For publishing "different sentiments" regarding Federalist policies, he had been "styled a *Jacobin*, a *Frenchman*, a *disorganizer*, and one who would *sell his country*." These charges of foreign sympathies were particularly galling to Holt, who was publishing in a town where he had lived his whole life. "The editor of this paper is an AMERICAN—his principles are AMERICAN—and his paper is supported by AMERICANS," he protested.[8]

Holt was lashing out at some dangerous enemies. New London's Federalists were strong and vindictive. Customs Collector Jedediah Huntington "ruled like a feudal lord over the customshouse and practically everything else" in town.[9] A young printer like Holt was particularly vulnerable to the kind of pressure Huntington and company could exert. Merchants were the primary newspaper advertisers available, and they were usually Federalists, perhaps especially in a port where an active Federalist controlled the custom house. Government was the other major advertiser, but there was no unit of government in Connecticut that the Republicans controlled. Huntington and his allies thus had little trouble choking off Holt's sources of nonsubscription revenue. They also tried to restrict the size of his subscription base and readership, declaring to New London's tradesmen and laborers that they would "employ no man that takes the Bee." Depending on wealthy customers for their livelihood, many of

Holt's potential readers seemed to have shied away from the *Bee* and the Republicans.[10]

With few allies among New London's social and political elite, Holt sought a new market in Republican gentlemen around the state who wanted to see southeastern Connecticut converted to their cause. About six months after the *Bee's* first appearance, with the paper in "an infant, humble and unprotected state," Holt wrote to the Republican leader and perennial gubernatorial candidate Ephraim Kirby seeking subscriptions and publishable material from the state Republican leadership. Holt also worried that the *Bee* was "entirely destitute of (political) literary assistance," and hoped that "with the aid of . . . men of talents, information and liberality," it would prosper.

Though he developed into a fine writer, Holt was like most printer-editors in needing help filling the columns of his paper. In the first place, the numerous manual and clerical tasks involved in putting out a newspaper left little time for writing. Equally important, Holt as yet lacked the cultural and social self-confidence to become a commentator on public affairs in his own right. Political writers were expected to display their classical erudition, and with a printer's education, Holt had little to display. "Talents, information and liberality" were qualities associated with republican gentility, replacements for the more ascriptive indices of status used in earlier times; they were the characteristics of a "natural," republican aristocracy. Lacking money, a distinguished family name, a college degree, or professional accomplishments, Charles Holt "naturally" did not qualify.[11]

Holt began to receive articles and subscriptions from Kirby and his friends. Yet on the first anniversary of the *Bee's* founding, Holt still clung to the hope that while his paper "preserves a spirit of decent freedom and manly independence consistent with a respect for truth and moderation, it will continue to merit and receive the countenance of the liberal and dispassionate of all parties." This hope was soon dashed by the Sedition Act, introduced a few weeks later. Holt editorialized against it in disbelief: "If the *constitution* of the United States was not considered by a majority of the House of Representatives as a mere *dead letter* . . . they would never have ventured to bring in a bill so directly contravening one of the most essential articles in the code of freedom, and as clearly defined as any other clause in the bill of rights, namely, *liberty of speech, printing and writing,* all of which will be not merely infringed, but wholly annihilated, should this nefarious bill pass into law."

The editor expressed confidence that "the people . . . need be under no manner of apprehensions respecting the fate of this bill" as long as the First Amendment, which he quoted at the end of his editorial, remained unchanged. With no experience of the days when government and mobs shut down newspapers at will, he mistakenly took the amendment at its word, as an absolute prohibition of any law infringing on a printer's right to political criticism.[12]

Unfortunately for him, the Federalists did remember the old days, nostalgically. As we saw in the previous chapter, they aimed the Sedition Act precisely at the Charles Holts of the political world. When the Federalist *Connecticut Courant* called the *Bee*'s editor "that lying drone from New London," it combined ridicule of his social status with a classical republican attack on the legitimacy of Holt's participation in politics. As a poor young printer, depending on customers and financial backers for his subsistence, Holt lacked the material independence that was the indispensable basis of political virtue. In a classical republican frame of reference, Holt could only be a tool of others, with no political will of his own, and thus no right to participate in public life.[13]

After midsummer 1798, more and more of the *Bee*'s political columns were devoted to attacks on the sedition law, and by November, Holt was ready to embrace partisanship explicitly for the first time. In doing so, he blamed his decision on the Federalists' violation of the printing trade's traditional nonpartisan values:

> There are generally *two sides* to every subject. To the public opinion, in a free country, there ever will and should be. And it is the duty of an impartial printer to communicate to the public on *both sides* freely. But nine tenths of the newspapers in Connecticut are decidedly partial to *one side*, and keep the *other* totally out of sight. This is not fair. . . . The public may therefore rest assured that so long as my brethren in this state print on *one side only*, so long will I print on *the other*.

Though he still felt the need to justify himself in traditional terms, Holt was moving rapidly toward a new vocation as a committed professional partisan. Economic factors helped push the printer in this direction, but political and ideological ones were even more important. As a conventionally funded commercial newspaper, the partisan *Bee* was a failure. Holt reported to Kirby that he was spending about twice as much money as he was taking in, and "suppose myself, therefore, to be insolvent." Yet the nature of Holt's commitment to running the paper had also changed:

furthering the Republican cause had become integral to it. Despite "several good offers" (most likely to work for the Republicans in another state), "my abode here, and my endeavours to gain an establishment, have confirmed me still more strongly in the principles which I profess." He wanted to stay on the job of revolutionizing his beloved native state, and asked only for subsistence in return: "If the good people of Connecticut will give me 'meat, clothes, and fire,' my best exertions are at their service. . . . By my prejudices in favor of the republicans of this state, I should esteem it my highest ambition to serve them in my professional capacity." To this end, Holt and Kirby discussed putting his relationship with the Republican party on a more regular footing. Holt offered to move the *Bee* to the larger town of New Haven and print and edit it there for a salary of twelve dollars a week.[14]

We should not infer from Holt's interest in a salary that he was a political mercenary looking to sell his services to the highest bidder. His partisanship was not based on any expectations of profit. That would have been a foolish assumption, for no one found it profitable to be a Republican in Connecticut. To accept a salary for publishing the *Bee* would not be to compromise his independence, but rather to assert it by resisting Federalist pressure; it would be a way to earn a living while furthering political goals that he fervently supported.

Holt demonstrated the genuineness of his political commitment by continuing the *Bee* even though the move to New Haven and plans for a salary fell through. Federalist ostracism had rendered even the leading Republican gentlemen little able to afford the large cash outlays that the plan required. The *Courant* lampooned Holt's efforts to make the *Bee* a going concern, predicting he would starve trying. "Holt, it will not do. . . . The Jacobins are too poor, too few, and too dishonest to support you."[15]

In fact, Holt was discovering what most party editors discovered eventually: that a political newspaper was a poor business proposition. The problem was almost inherent in the enterprise, since decisions were made on the basis of political rather than business considerations. A case in point was Holt's decision to continue publishing the *Bee* despite its lack of economic viability: the journal hemorrhaged money almost from its inception, but Holt kept it going for almost five years. "At no time has the income of the Bee been adequate to its maintenance," Holt admitted in the paper's final issue.

There were many factors involved in the *Bee*'s failure as a business.

Holt's troubles began with an editorial policy that alienated most of the advertisers in his market area, and that problem was compounded by others that all early American newspaper proprietors faced. There was, for instance, the problem of debt collection. By 1800 Holt had a seemingly healthy list of subscribers, but fledgling newspapers had to be sent out on credit, and it was almost impossible to get subscribers to actually pay for their papers. The editor estimated that one-third of debts to newspapers were "lost." Like many another printer, Holt periodically pleaded with his debtors to pay their bills, in any way they could: "Is not 'the laborer worthy of his hire'? Why then do ye not pay him? Wood, produce, or any thing (except pumpkins) to keep thanksgiving with, thankfully received, and *cash itself* will not be sent back."[16]

Charles Holt's account books have not survived, but the balance sheet of another small-town New England weekly, the Northampton, Massachusetts, *Republican Spy*, can probably be taken as representative of the situation most such journals faced. The *Spy* had 1,100 subscribers, but by the time the delivery men took their cut—newspapers were more commonly delivered to local-area readers by private post riders than through the mail—printer Andrew Wright realized only $916.67 per annum from subscriptions. Being a Republican paper in New England, the paper's advertising income was small, and Wright rounded off his total yearly income at $1,000. On the other side of ledger, paper cost $500 a year, the wages and board of two journeymen (at $6 cach pcr week) came to $624, and ink, firewood, and other necessary supplies together added another $100. In all, Wright estimated that he lost $224 a year, if all debts were paid and there was no new equipment to buy or legal judgments to pay.[17] More prominent newspapers with farther-flung constituencies were actually worse off. Long-distance (that is, beyond post rider range) subscriptions created a larger paper income but generated the ferocious debt collection problems already discussed. Charles Holt's troubles were thus compounded as his paper earned statewide and even national readership.

An editor who persevered in publishing under these circumstances became a political professional almost automatically. Something besides his nonexistent profits had to keep him going. Alexandria printer James D. Westcott and his newspaper, the *Times*, were undergoing the same evolution toward partisanship as Holt and the *Bee*, under very similar influences.[18] A rueful Westcott made his situation clear in applying for government printing contracts in 1801. Commercial prospects had brought him to Alexandria, but principle kept him there even after his hopes of business success were thoroughly blasted:

> Nothing could have justified the embarking in an undertaking of so expensive and hazardous a nature but a sanguine anticipation of the rapid increase of . . . the town of Alexandria, and of the rising importance of the metropolis of the union:—nothing could have induced a continuance, to the evident sacrifice of the interests of my family, after a prospect of a realization of my expectations had disappeared, but a conviction of duty to persevere in defence of those principles to which my paper had been devoted, in opposition to artfully-excited popular clamour.[19]

Charles Holt or almost any of the other future Republican printers of 1797 could have written such a letter themselves.

By the New London *Bee*'s second birthday, the Sedition Act was in place and Charles Holt was under the scrutiny of the Federalist authorities. For a time during the summer of 1799, his resolve wavered. In June he mournfully refused to publish pieces he had been sent that attacked "certain notorious individuals," though they "so justly meritted" such treatment. He wished to give the "men determined on the ruin of our paper . . . no pretext or opportunity for the accomplishment of their designs."[20] But the vindictive Connecticut Federalists would not be denied. On 17 September 1799, a grand jury charged Holt with seditious criticism for publishing a letter from Danbury that made (among others) the relatively commonplace, and accurate, charge that the newly expanded army, commanded by Alexander Hamilton, was intended to be the beginning of a standing army whose chief purpose was to police internal opposition. Four days later, the editor was arrested and brought to Hartford to be arraigned before the circuit court of Federalist Chief Justice Oliver Ellsworth. Tried and convicted the following April, Holt was sentenced to three months in prison, which he served immediately; he was also forced to pay court costs of $550, an enormous sum for a struggling printer.[21]

In the months between his arrest and trial, Holt turned the *Bee* into a more and more self-consciously and systematically partisan Republican journal. He began to publish a regular roster of Sedition Act defendants all over the country, pointedly appending it to a list of British journalists victimized by repression in their country. This commitment continued after Holt's release and changed the course of his life. Having been "taught the value of liberty in so exemplary a manner," he wrote upon resuming publication of the *Bee*, the editor trusted that "the sincerity of his attachment to the cause of freedom and justice will not be doubted." During the fall, he tracked and lauded Republican electoral successes and participated in the campaign himself by printing a campaign biography of Jefferson, among other material designed to alleviate pious New Englanders' fears about Jefferson's alleged atheism and libertinism.[22]

These and other publications made the *Bee* the most effective Republican paper in the state and one of the most effective and influential in the nation. Holt's geographically extensive circulation reached about 1,000, a large figure for a small-town weekly of that period, but the real source of Holt's national exposure came from the frequency with which other editors quoted and reprinted his material. After big-city papers like the *Aurora,* the *Bee* was one of the most often reprinted of all the Republican journals. An exhaustive historical survey of the Jeffersonian press rated the *Bee,* among New England Republican papers, second only to the Boston *Independent Chronicle* in its influence. Many years later, even Jefferson well remembered "the principles and intrepidity of the Bee in the gloomy days of terrorism."[23]

National prominence failed to save Holt from financial disaster. As a party editor, he occupied a uniquely exposed position in the political system. Since political commentaries in the newspapers of the day were almost invariably anonymous, the political editor alone took public responsibility for the arguments and charges made in the course of his party's campaigning. In legal proceedings, generally only the editor could be held accountable and made to suffer. Simply put, the editor's job was to be the surrogate campaigner, and, if necessary, to endure punishment in place of party leaders.

Holt's was by no means the starkest case of such surrogacy among the Republican editors. In 1802 a Massachusetts court indicted John S. Lillie, editor of the Boston *Constitutional Telegraphe,* for alleged libels in an anonymous article written by a gentleman contributor, John Vinal, "Esq." Lillie and Vinal were both tried, but while Lillie spent three months in prison, Vinal was acquitted for insufficient evidence. This was the almost certain outcome of such proceedings. The printer or editor named in the masthead could easily be linked to an article in court, but typically there was no way to legally document the identity of an anonymous contributor.[24]

Charles Holt's sedition trial brought out the full complexities of his relationship with Connecticut's Republican gentry. On the one hand, party leaders recognized an obligation to help Holt through his tribulations on their behalf. The Republican editor in Hartford visited Holt in jail to assure him that his bail money would be raised. It seems likely that Republican leaders paid Holt's legal expenses, since his defense counsel were the prestigious Federalist attorneys David Daggett and Stephen T. Hosmer. On the other hand, there was no mistaking that party leaders' ultimate loyalties were to themselves, rather than to their servant Holt. District Attorney Pierpont Edwards was the prosecutor in Holt's trial, and the fact that Edwards was one of state's preeminent Republicans did not seem to dampen the energy with which he argued the case.[25]

The editor's subordinate status became even more apparent after Thomas Jefferson finally won the presidency in 1801. The state's "persecuted" Republican leaders, including Edwards, Ephraim Kirby, and their fellow lawyers Abraham Bishop, Alexander Wolcott, and Jesse Atwater, secured from President Jefferson a sweeping purge of the state's Federalist federal offices and were appointed to those offices themselves. Another Connecticut Republican lawyer, Gideon Granger, became postmaster general.[26]

Holt expected that the "happy events" that put Jefferson in power "would restore me to the common privileges and employments of Printers, and enable me to gain an honest livelihood." Since politics and business had become one for Holt, the editor naturally thought that political success and modest commercial prosperity would go together. He was not looking for riches or honors. Like most ordinary Americans of the period, Holt's highest ambition was to gain only a "competency" for himself: the ability to live independent of debt or wage labor, in moderate comfort, and to pass those same circumstances on to his children. Instead of more typical occupations such as farming, fishing, or shoemaking, Holt wanted to earn his competency in newspaper politics.[27] But this was not to be the case.

The Republican leadership entirely overlooked Holt; the *Bee* editor did not receive an appointment or even a contract for the printing of the laws as did some other Republican printers. The former option was foreclosed to Holt because of Jefferson's insistence on education and high social status as qualifications for office. In the matter of printing the laws, Holt was apparently thwarted by a regulation stipulating that printers of the laws be located in the center of their state. The lawyers who made up the party's top leadership allowed a technicality to prevent them from aiding a political subordinate in distress.[28]

Even worse for Holt, Jedediah Huntington escaped the fate of most other federal officeholders in the state and remained in command of the New London custom house. Very early in his administration, Jefferson laid down the principle that any officer who made use of his position for partisan purposes would be considered guilty of misconduct and removed. There was ample testimony to Huntington's partisanship in government personnel files, but he was apparently still friendly with Gideon Granger and other Republicans in Washington, who remembered his antifederalism during the 1780s. The personal friendships and loyalties of gentlemen thus took precedence over the needs of a loyal Republican printer and even over administration policy itself. The administration's failure to apply its own policy in Huntington's case meant not only that Holt would have little respite from his persecution within the town, but also that he would see no financial benefits from Jefferson's victory at all, not even a share in the job printing work generated by the local federal offices.[29]

ESCAPE FROM CONNECTICUT (TO POLITICAL PROFESSIONALISM ON THE HUDSON)

The Republican leadership's utter neglect of Holt caused an already-difficult situation to deteriorate. With election year urgency fading, the *Bee's* meager income began to decrease virtually the moment Jefferson took office, as subscribers left or paid even less often than usual. By April 1802 yearly deficits of several hundred dollars had created a dangerously heavy load of debt, and Holt reduced the size of the paper to a half sheet (two instead of four pages) to save money and spend more time on collections. The *Bee's* affairs had come to a crisis. As a North Carolina congressman to whom Holt appealed for help told Jefferson, the editor was "now about to be immured in that very Prison for debt, from whence he had been so lately liberated from persecution."[30]

The solution that presented itself to Holt was to make a final, complete transition to political professionalism by taking his newly developed political skills to a different location. A group of Republicans in Hudson, New York, asked Holt to become the party's spokesman there, and apparently offered him $500 to pay for the move. The editor promptly informed Republican leader Ephraim Kirby that he had decided "to abandon Connecticut."[31] The prospectus Holt issued for the new Hudson *Bee* showed how much his sense of vocation had changed. Both the principles and the specific tasks involved in Republican party politics were now integral to it. The "ever ready and subservient Newspaper" no longer, the new *Bee's* purposes would be "to disseminate wholesome and correct ideas of government" (meaning promote Republican ideas); "to inculcate union, friendship, and liberality among all 'brethren of the same principle'" (meaning to ensure Republican party unity); and "to detect and expose falsehood and error, and defend the truth against the open or insidious attacks of its enemies" (meaning to respond to and defuse Federalist charges).[32] This statement described the job of professional campaigner.

Accordingly, Holt's career in New York, whose political culture was as freewheeling and competitive as Connecticut's was straitlaced and monolithic, would be very different. The Hudson *Bee* opened for business in August 1802 on the upper floor of the Hudson "Democratic club" in a building owned by a Republican judge. There the local Republican brain trust met around a wood stove to smoke and confer, once planning a organized brawl in retaliation for an attack on Holt. As this incident suggests, New York's frank acceptance of competitive politics did not mean that political life was easier there. On the contrary, as one veteran New York editor-politician put it, and as Holt quickly discovered, "the life of a politician" in New York was "a perpetual warfare with everything bordering on tranquility and repose."[33]

Almost the moment Holt arrived in town, the Federalist editor of the town's only newspaper began strenuous efforts to drive him out. Another Connecticut-born printer whose politics were more conventionally "steady," Harry Croswell had been publishing the decorously Federalist *Balance* in Hudson for little over a year, congratulating himself on the lack of Republican competition. Before the *Bee* had even begun publishing, Croswell rushed into print with a companion paper called the *Wasp*. Invoking the image of a larger and more vicious insect able to counteract the invasive species from New London, this was a newspaper devoted entirely to insulting Republicans, with special attention paid to Thomas Jefferson but even more to Charles Holt and other Republican editors in neighboring towns. "Jacobin printers" were being "*bought* or *hired,* and set to work in their favorite trade of detraction," Croswell wrote, and it was his job to chastise them. In the first issue, Holt read that he was "a lazy swine . . . wallowing in a puddle," and was treated to a set of perhaps mock toasts to "Republican martyrs" being hung or placed in the stocks. The fun went on from there, in twelve occasional issues published over six months.[34]

Holt chose mostly to ignore the *Wasp,* concentrating his fire on more important targets such as William Coleman's *Evening Post* in New York

City, a Federalist newspaper closely associated with Alexander Hamilton.[35] Perhaps he was even flattered by Croswell's attentions. In New London, the young printer had been hounded out of the public arena, while in Hudson he was a major figure in it. Croswell's favorite medium was the parodic song, and Holt got to be the star of such ditties as "Democratic Ding-Dong; or a Bell to Settle the Bee," "A New Yankee Doodle," and yet another version of Yankee Doodle that Croswell did not bother to title. There was relatively little about Holt to expose, so most of the abuse was fairly generic, along the lines of the following:

> There's Charley Holt is come to town,
>   A proper lad with types, sir;
> The democrats have fetch'd him here,
>   To give the federals stripes, sir.
> CHORUS.
> He prints a paper called the Bee,
>   A buzzing little thing, sir
> That from New-England lately chas'd,
>   Points here its feeble sting, sir.

Croswell may have drawn more blood when he drew attention to Holt's political professionalism, which was still beyond the pale of what even the Republicans could openly avow. "Did the contributors to the five hundred dollars purchase you, as they purchase negroes in Virginia," queried the *Wasp*, "or hire you, as they hire servants in New-England?"[36]

Croswell folded the *Wasp* in January 1803, and he and Holt settled down to five years of more routine bickering until the *Balance* moved to Albany in 1808. Holt himself left Hudson soon after Croswell. In 1809 he received a promotion of sorts: an offer to edit a paper in New York City as an organ for De Witt Clinton's wing of the Republican party. Holt's New York *Columbian* became one of the state's leading papers in the 1810s.[37] Whereas in his New London days Holt had been more strictly the party's mouthpiece, in New York he was directly involved in political management. By 1816 he was offering advice on political strategy in a tone of long experience. "I see you are endeavoring to get up Gov. Tompkins for the Presidency," he wrote, "but . . . I think you will not make out much better than we did in the last heat."[38]

In the end, Holt's political work in New York was only a little more reliable as a livelihood, and he was eventually reduced to making a formal application for relief, in the form of a political office:

After the employment of twenty years of his life as a republican editor, through all the vicissitudes of persecution, fine, imprisonment, personal contest and other events of political warfare (in behalf of his principles and his party), Your petitioner finds himself, from a series of adverse circumstances, destitute of property, with a large family (of eight young children, and, in part, two other dependents) under the necessity of applying to the honorable Council of Appointment, for the first time, for public employment in a civil office.

His moral character, he trusts, has ever been without a stain. His capacity for a humble station, the members of the Board have the means of ascertaining.

This time, Holt's wishes were granted. He was made first a ward judge, then a clerk in the New York Custom House, and he lived the rest of his working life peacefully in the bowels of the political system. He retired to the then-country town of Jersey City, New Jersey, living partly on the proceeds from his Sedition Act fine, which was finally refunded (with interest, it was rumored) when Holt was in his seventies.[39]

Charles Holt should not be seen as a mere party hack, someone interested solely in the "loaves and fishes" of political patronage. He had been genuinely radicalized by his travails with the New London *Bee*. Holt believed that, in the American republic, every citizen (meaning every white male) possessed an equal right to take part in public life and receive public honors and offices, but his editorial experiences disabused him of the assumption that this right was fully accepted by the nation's political, social, and economic elites. Though he always took a deferential attitude in his dealings with the gentleman leaders of his party, his own civic philosophy differed sharply from that of the "natural aristocracy" of either party. In an 1801 editorial, he contrasted the invidious "New Habits" of the Connecticut Federalists with the salutary "Old Habits" of earlier times. Formerly, Holt believed, ordinary people, without gentlemen's credentials, were eligible to serve in office, and serve they did, not forming any aristocracy, natural or otherwise:

> Time was, when it was conceived assuming in a republican government for an incumbent to claim a re-election merely by right of possession. . . .
>
> Time was, when the possession of an office for a year did not make a man more wise, more just, and more meritorious than all his neighbors, and when public offices were considered as belonging to the public and not to any particular individual, family, or class of men.
>
> Time was, when common sense, integrity, and capacity to make laws for

the community were obtained outside the walls of a college, and without the assistance of a diploma or licence to practise at the bar or pulpit.[40]

Of course, Holt was completely wrong about this. What he described as "New Habits" were, in fact, the traditional approach to officeholding, as the province of the economic, social, and cultural elite. Holt and many other Republican campaigners learned firsthand that Thomas Jefferson hewed almost as closely to these habits as George Washington or John Adams. The so-called "Old Habits" Holt favored came much closer to the doctrine of "rotation in office" as Andrew Jackson would express it almost thirty years later. The beginnings of this philosophy's journey to enshrinement at the core of national policy can be found in the experience of Charles Holt and his generation of Republican editors.

FEDERALIST REPRESSION, POPULAR RIGHTS-CONSCIOUSNESS, AND THE RADICALIZATION OF YOUNG PRINTERS

The much-abused term "generation" applies to this group in a strict sense. Charles Holt and the other young men who flocked into the ranks of partisan journalism in the late 1790s—and stayed there even in face of Federalist repression—formed a very clear generational cohort. They were divided from enemies and allies alike by the experience of coming to manhood *after* the Revolution and by their lack of exposure to the constrained conditions under which colonial printers had operated. The average year of birth for Republican editors who began their careers when Charles Holt did, between 1797 and 1800, was 1772. The Republican editors who were active in the same period, but started their newspaper careers before 1797, were disproportionately older men, with an average birth year of 1759. The members of the Congress that passed the Sedition Act were older still, born on average in 1753.[41]

Holt and the younger editors were at most teenagers when the Constitution was written. Unlike the leading politicians of both parties and the older generation of printers, they had grown up with such documents as the First Amendment and the Declaration of Independence and took their meaning literally. While not necessarily expecting to become political leaders or even active participants themselves, Charles Holt and the rest began their careers believing that printers and other nongentlemen enjoyed at least an equal *right* to participate in politics, to be treated with respect, and to criticize the government without fear of reprisal. During the 1790s and after, they discovered that the gentlemen in power—including some of the Republicans in power after 1800—did not share those beliefs. Phinehas Allen of the Pittsfield, Massachusetts, *Sun,* born 1776, expressed shock that the principle that "'All men are born *free* and *equal*'" could go "out of fashion in America." Yet "for several years past, *Liberty* and *Equality* have been standing themes of popular ridicule and reproach."[42]

These kinds of realizations led many young printers (along with numerous other Americans) to recognize what their political values really were. Gravitating to the Republican opposition, they began to emphasize the egalitarian ideals of the early part of Revolution and to see and present those ideals as yet unconsummated. Beginning in the late 1790s, quotations and citations from the opening paragraphs of the Declaration of Independence became a staple of the Republican press, especially around the Fourth of July. Republican newspapers often published the entire text of the document in the issue closest to the day, sometimes to let the editor participate in—or sleep off—the festivities. Republicans began holding their own holiday celebrations, usually publishing the proceedings in the newspapers, and such celebrations always featured a reading of the Declaration by some local Republican activist.[43]

The Federalists were on solid legal ground in claiming that the Sedition Act did not abridge the First Amendment, since the leading jurists of the time defined freedom of the press as freedom from prior restraint. Animated by what might be termed an alternative, popular constitutionalism, young printers clung to their own vision of the First Amendment as absolutely protective of political publishing. So armed, they fought the Sedition Act and other Federalist efforts to quash their participation in politics with increasing outrage and skill.[44]

Charles Holt was only one among many Republican-sympathizing but commercially minded printers driven into active campaigning by Federalist repression and ridicule. Previously, we saw how John Snowden (born 1776) and William McCorkle (born around 1776), former publishers of James T. Callender's pamphlets, had moved from Philadelphia to Chambersburg, Pennsylvania, in April 1798, hoping to get away from politics and publish a quiet, commercial paper devoted to farming and news. Like Charles Holt, they tried to be genuinely impartial, accepting essays and copying news that reflected both the Republican and Federalist points of view. Yet the mere appearance of a competing newspaper, along with the printers' reputations and their willingness to admit *some* Republicanism into their columns, sent the local Federalists into a frenzy.

The overreaction began with Robert Harper, printer of the town's existing newspaper, the *Franklin Repository*. Never very political, Harper was suddenly galvanized into action by the threat to his longtime monopoly in the county. Soon various members of the county's old, elite families, led by John Shippen (the county's other major town was called Shippensburg), got into the act. Shippen organized a subscription boycott intended to suborn Snowden and McCorkle to Federalism: a petition was sent suggesting that the boycotters might renew their subscriptions if the printers would become "friends to Government and the happiness of the Citizens." Snowden and McCorkle took offense at the petition's assumption that they could be brought to heel so easily and its disrespect for the traditional, impartial trade mores that they had conscientiously tried to follow. "Looking over the pages of the Register, we find that we have never indulged ourselves even in a conjecture upon any subject," the editors wrote, "but have uniformly adhered to a simple publication of facts."

So they struck back, filling the front page of the 13 June issue with attacks on John Shippen, followed by more in subsequent weeks. Decisively changing their earlier deferential posture, Snowden and McCorkle thumbed their rhetorical noses at the Federalist elite, labeling Shippen a "little" but "pompous" man who no one "ever dreamt . . . possessed sufficient abilities to *influence* any man," despite his pretensions to being a local baron. Things hit bottom in February 1799, when two Federalists came into the *Farmers' Register* office asking for a Latin text by Seneca and then jumped McCorkle with a cowhide whip when he turned to get the book.[45]

Federalist harassment thus inspired Snowden and McCorkle to return to their Philadelphia ways. They never utterly abandoned their commitment to news and impartiality, but they did turn the *Farmers' Register* into more the partisan Republican sheet the Federalists had feared in the first place. They justified themselves in the universalist terms of the public sphere, addressing their paper to a disembodied, disinterested readership that cared only for ideas and information, without reference to whose authority sanctioned them. "We acknowledge . . . that there are particular men whom the Register is not calculated to please—men, whom nothing could please but the repetition of their own sentiments. . . . But the Register is not designed for particular men; it looks up to a liberal public for support," and this public would not be served or satisfied by the government-parroting press the Federalists demanded. Their self-respect as impartial printers and independent citizens demanded a certain amount of partisanship.

So, beginning at the time of the boycott, which coincided with the congressional debates on the Sedition Act, Snowden and McCorkle gradually began filling their columns with very different material than they had in the past: attacks on Harper and the *Franklin Repository;* complaints against the Sedition Act; defenses and praise of David and Robert Bard, local Republican leaders; proceedings and accounts of Republican meetings; Irish news that cast Great Britain (and thus the Federalists) in a bad light; accounts of Matthew Lyon's trial; documents and reports on Elbridge Gerry and George Logan's efforts to conciliate France in defiance of Federalist wishes; and reprints from the *Aurora* and other Republican papers, though not the harshest material those journals had to offer.[46]

In the end, however, John Shippen and his minions must have gotten the best of Snowden and McCorkle. Complaining that many of their subscribers "have never . . . contributed one cent" of what they owed—probably many of these had signed up for the paper when it was proposed and then been scared off by the boycott—the editors decamped in April 1799 for the more Republican clime of Greensburg in the far western part of the state. If they came to Chambersburg as tradesmen, they left as politicians. This was especially true of John Snowden, evidently the brains of the team. After nearly a decade in Greensburg, he moved up the political ladder to Pittsburgh, where he founded a much more elaborate Democratic organ called the *Mercury* that also doubled as very informative commercial newspaper. Over his twenty-three years of running the *Mercury,* Snowden became one of the city's leading local politicians, serving as mayor, recorder of deeds (a lucrative political plum), and finally, after his retirement from printing, as an Allegheny County judge. Snowden obtained these offices in a later and very different era, of course, but they show the new course his life took in 1798.[47]

Other printers reacted to Federalist persecution on an even more visceral level than Holt and Snowden and McCorkle did. Augustus C. Jordan began to fill his Norfolk *Epitome of the Times* with strongly Republican political material only after a Federalist insult. A writer in the rival *Virginia Herald* advised a local artisan who had criticized the Federalist administration to "stick by your last"—a stock phrase meaning that artisans should mind their own business and not meddle in public affairs. In their responses, Jordan and his writers displayed Holt's sense that such remarks were part of a shocking effort by Federalists to roll back the gains artisans and other ordinary men had made during the Revolution. "Sheers" in the *Epitome* demanded to know what the *Herald* had meant by the remark: "Do you wish to insinuate that private characters and tradesmen have no business to meddle with government? If so, it is a bold, false and dishonest insinuation. . . . It is a cant now almost forgotten in the world."

A week later, a long and bitter piece by "A MECHANIC" denounced Federalist presumptions and forcefully argued for the right of artisans to participate in political debate, articulating a kind of labor theory of political participation. Those who contributed to the common good deserved to participate in making the community's decisions:

> Those contemptible wretches who boast that they are gentlemen because they do nothing for their living are perpetually insulting those ingenious and industrious citizens whose skilled labor contributes so essentially to the support and comfort of human life. To those well born (tho' far from well bred) gentry, the very name of handcraft man is an abomination, and if one of those aproned fellows should presume to open his mouth on what concerns his dearest rights and interests, with what contempt they affect to treat him and all that he says.

The writer regarded these gentry attitudes as the kind of outmoded nonsense that the Revolution had been fought to stamp out. The *Herald* remarks brought to mind "the wickedest and most stupid sentiments that ever disgraced a British tory." They were an insult not only to "every artificer and tradesman, but even to the spirit of the Constitution itself."[48] (This was another youthful misapprehension, since the Constitution was notably less democratic than many of the early state constitutions and had been written with the intention of restraining state-level populist demagogues.)[49] The *Epitome* then lampooned the Federalist attitude:

> "Depart ye wretches! Ye Swinish multitude! . . . You are convicted of being TRADESMEN! What rights can you pretend to who have not a dollar in your pockets. . . . Get away to your workshops: put on your aprons: go work, and be contented; and leave your rights to me, who know how to govern you."
>
> If [the *Herald* writer] were obliged to go barefoot until his genius was so highly improved that he could make a pair of shoes, or were he able to learn some useful business whereby he might honestly earn the price of them, he would perhaps by that time learn to also respect
>
> A MECHANIC[50]

Jordan's reaction, along with those of other printers to Federalist snubs and persecutions, was rooted not so much in a class consciousness as in what Joyce Appleby has called the "vision of classlessness" held by many rank-and-file Republicans. They were proud of their crafts and aware of the hierarchies still abroad in their society, but they found them old-fash-ioned, baseless, and offensive, especially when applied to politics. It was Federalist attempts to express and enforce these hierarchies that bothered young printers of Charles Holt's generation.[51]

Often in the late 1790s these conflicts over printers' participation in politics could become more than verbal. One of the more disturbing cases involved Jacob Schneider, the printer-editor of the *Readinger Adler,* a Ger-man-language Republican paper published in Reading, Pennsylvania. Schneider made the mistake of criticizing the Federalist volunteer soldiers involved in the expedition against Fries's Rebellion. By all accounts, these troops had terrorized the countryside, summarily arresting or abusing sus-pected rebels on little or no evidence and treating the German population of the area with open disdain.

A cavalry unit from Lancaster took particular umbrage at Schneider's comments, and they made a point of passing through Reading on the trip home. Schneider was seized in his office by a detachment of the Lancaster unit and hauled before its commander, a Captain Montgomery. "This *self-appointed Dictator,*" as the Philadelphia *Aurora* described Montgomery, questioned the editor briefly and summarily sentenced him to twenty-five lashes, to be administered in public at the town's market house. Schneider was stripped and had been whipped five times before another passing militia unit, a group of Philadelphia Republicans led by *Aurora* benefactor Thomas Leiper, stopped the proceeding. The Reading authorities refused to issue warrants for the assailants' arrest until after they had left the town.[52]

These kinds of challenges to the political participation of printers made campaigning for the Republicans into a noble and classically virtu-ous calling. For an artisan to be a prominent participant in the Republican opposition was to strike a blow for liberty and prove his own independ-ence. In the face of Federalist repression and reprisals, partisanship be-came a matter of self-respect and political professionalism a matter of ne-cessity. Intending to cow printers who even sympathized with the Republicans, the Federalists produced a small army of inveterate Republi-can party politicians.

7

The Expansion of the Republican
Newspaper Network, 1798–1800

❧

The *previous chapter* dealt with printers who were already publishing when the Sedition Act was imposed and who were radicalized by the experience of Federalist repression. This explains why so many beleaguered Republican newspapers stayed in business through the "reign of terror," but as we have seen, the Sedition Act went far beyond merely failing to destroy the existing opposition press. It also touched off a major expansion that transformed American journalism and created a new, politicized sector of the publishing industry. The sources of that expansion are the focus of the present chapter.

New Republican newspapers began appearing everywhere in the wake of the Sedition Act, bringing newspaper politics into interior regions for the first time and intensifying it in many larger cities and towns (see map 3, page 127). The existing Republican forces were augmented by a large number of new journals that, unlike their predecessors, avowed their partisanship and political intentions from the beginning. Rather than slowly gravitating into the orbit of the emerging Republican party, these papers were established to be part of it. The titles alone tell the story. Where the older newspapers were mostly "Gazettes" and "Chronicles" and "Registers," those founded between the summer of 1798 and the end of 1800 had names that immediately called attention to their highly charged political nature. To the earlier *Herald of Liberty* and *Genius of Liberty* were added a *Sun of,* a *Tree of,* a *Guardian of,* and finally, even a *Triumph of Liberty.* Two papers upheld the *Rights of Man.* One avowed itself a *Friend of the People.* Six new papers included the word "Republican" in the title, clearly meant in the partisan sense. These ranged from a *Republican Ledger* for the sober

Yankees of New Hampshire to a *Republican Atlas* for the presumably brawny mountaineers of western Virginia. A full list of titles published in 1800 can be found in appendix 2.[1] Even the most hard-bitten Federalists began to realize that their strategy of repression had failed. Connecticut Senator Uriah Tracy toured the backcountry in August 1800 and reported dolefully that the administration's opponents were "establishing Democratic presses and newspapers in almost every town and county of the country." The accuracy of Tracy's impression can be seen in map 3.[2]

THE LIMITS OF ELITE SPONSORSHIP

The explanation that historians have usually given of this expansion is that it was a top-down affair, the result of feverish efforts by Thomas Jefferson and other high Republican leaders to start newspapers and recruit editors.[3] In fact, the expansion was largely the doing of the Republican printers themselves. Republican leaders bought subscriptions and supplied partial financial backing for some of the new ventures, but printers provided the impetus for many others, and in any case, it was the printers who assumed the risks and burdens involved in the new partisan presses. The Republican gentry certainly knew that the press would be a potent weapon against the Federalists, and many worked to make it so. However, they achieved generally unimpressive results from their own efforts to create newspapers, and many of their successes owed more to the abilities of editors than to the influence or money of sponsors.

We can begin to see this by starting at the top, with the activities of the Republicans' standard-bearer and chief newspaper enthusiast, Vice President Thomas Jefferson. As he had while secretary of state, Jefferson repeatedly urged *other* Republican leaders to contribute editorially and financially to the party press. The most famous example is an often-quoted letter he wrote to James Madison from Philadelphia in early 1799: "A piece in Bache's paper . . . has had the greatest currency and effect. . . . It is such things as these that the public want. They say so from all quarters, and that they wish to hear *reason* instead of *disgusting blackguardism*. The public sentiment being now on the creen, and many heavy circumstances about to fall into the Republican scale, we are sensible that this summer is the season for systematic energies and sacrifices. The engine is the press. Every man must lay his purse and his pen under contribution."[4]

Jefferson applied this preachment to himself only selectively. He continued to refuse to write for the newspapers, but he did subscribe to Republican journals across the country. Doubtless the knowledge that the great Jefferson read and applauded their efforts helped struggling printers more than the two-, four-, or six-dollar subscription price. The vice president also gave money and other forms of aid to a few individual journalists, especially (much to his later chagrin) James Callender.[5]

Jefferson tried to take some broader measures while serving in Philadelphia under Adams but met with little success. Most significant were his efforts to create yet another *National Gazette,* ignoring the fact that the Philadelphia *Aurora* had already more than replaced Freneau's paper. The plan called for Jefferson and several other national Republican officeholders to raise $500 apiece for a new Republican paper to be published at the capital and to circulate nationwide. Though Jefferson pulled out many stops, even promising contributions from James Madison and James Monroe without asking their permission, the project fell through. Not enough money could be found among Jefferson's various acquaintances. This and several similar Republican newspaper schemes were doomed partly by the fact that many of the party's leaders were high-living but cash-poor planters like Jefferson and his two neighbors. Jefferson eventually succeeded in obtaining a new national newspaper, the Washington *National Intelligencer,* but not until it was too late to help with the election of 1800.[6]

Emulating their leader, wealthy and influential Republicans in many parts of the country made efforts to establish new papers in their local areas, with varying degrees of success. Nathaniel Macon and other North Carolina Republicans attributed the shocking Federalist resurgence in their 1798 state elections to the lack of a strong Republican newspaper in the state, so they recruited Joseph Gales, another refugee radical who had ended up in the Philadelphia newspaper business, to move south and establish one.

Gales launched the *Raleigh Register* in October 1799, but while generally regarded as effective, the paper contained only a smattering of original material, relying mostly on reprints from the rest of the Republican press. Then, in the fall of 1800, Gales fell severely ill, and while his wife and assistant carried on as best they could, the *Register* largely sat out the campaign. The electoral results in November did not match what Gales's sponsors must have hoped: Jefferson lost four of North Carolina's electoral votes, after winning them all in 1796, and his elector barely triumphed even in the *Raleigh Register*'s home county. Despite this disappointment, the newly Republican legislature of 1801 made Gales the state's official printer, and from that start, the editor swiftly became one of North Carolina's major political and business leaders.[7]

The starkest late 1790s example of a Republican gentleman procuring a press "engine" occurred in western Pennsylvania. The Pittsburgh lawyer, judge, and erstwhile novelist Hugh Henry Brackenridge had aided the establishment of the Pittsburgh *Gazette* in earlier times, but that paper came to lean Federalist while Brackenridge went over to the Republicans. With 1800 approaching, the judge felt the need of an opposition press.[8] Launching the project in earnest as the *Gazette* took a more partisan tone in late 1799, Brackenridge asked the Philadelphia Republican Tench Coxe to suggest an editor. Coxe recommended his unemployed ex-clerk Ezekiel Forman, formerly the prospective editor of the abortive second *National Gazette*, but after an exchange of letters with Forman, Brackenridge found him incompetent for the task. The judge sought a "young man of taste, information, & judgement," but

> from [Forman's] letters to me, it is evident that his Education has been extremely imperfect, And that his mind has received little cultivation. I saw at once that he was totally incapable of the independent conduct of a paper, & cast about in my own mind what might be done with him, under my superintendance. But . . . he talks of ideas grating to an independent mind & that he cannot descend to the humble station of an apprentice &c. I discover in all this a state of mind that will not suit that subordination & absolute scholarship, which would be necessary should I undertake his instruction.

Brackenridge wondered whether he might not be better off taking "a lad from the woods," or better yet if "some compositors of types . . . may be found, & in that case the labour & expence of an Editor may be saved." In the end, a typesetter may have been more what Brackenridge had in mind. If he were going to write anything for the paper, Brackenridge added, "the Editor must be a ready amanuensis, for I dictate all." Judge Brackenridge was an uncommonly egotistical man, but his attitudes are revealing of the Republican gentry's contradictory attitude toward their own press. They wanted to avoid putting their own reputations on the line, so they procured others to edit and take responsibility for their newspapers. These editors needed to write and select with the cultivated taste and style of a gentleman, yet they also needed to faithfully and uncomplainingly take direction.[9]

Eventually, Brackenridge dropped the idea of starting his own newspaper and instead coaxed John Israel into starting a "Branch Press" of the *Herald of Liberty* in Pittsburgh. The judge had an outbuilding constructed on his own lot to house the journal. Though Brackenridge denied "being the Editor either actual or avowed" of the new *Tree of Liberty*, his enemies and his own son believed that he was the real editor, and owner of new paper's type and press as well. Yet Brackenridge's apparent influence over the new paper was deceptive. Israel had already established himself as an independent political force in Washington County, and Brackenridge soon received a high judicial appointment and left Pittsburgh. Israel was a credible enough politician on his own to be an early (though ultimately unsuccessful) contender for Congress in the 1804 elections. In the end, Brackenridge's sponsorship was only the occasion, not the cause, of Israel becoming a political leader in Pittsburgh. Rebutting the charge that he was Brackenridge's tool, Israel wrote that it required "no *stimulus* to urge [him] after" the Federalists; he had strong personal reasons for being a partisan Republican. Israel and the rest of the printer-editors were fighting not only for Jefferson and other high Republican leaders, but also to save the American republic as they understood it and secure their own right to participate in public life.[10]

The relative successes of Nathaniel Macon and Hugh Henry Brackenridge in fostering effective newspapers were isolated cases. Many more top-down newspaper schemes were hatched than came to fruition, and many that did fared badly as the result of half-hearted or underfunded support. For instance, a group of Richmond gentlemen formed a corporation to publish yet another national Republican newspaper and even sold shares in it, only to have the publication itself expire after two issues.[11] That level of industry among encouragers of Republican presses was unusual.

More typical was Albert Gallatin's attempt to have a German-language Republican newspaper established in his western Pennsylvania congressional district. Gallatin urged his idea on Solomon Myer, printer of a German Republican paper in the town of York. Myer demurred, but suggested that if sixty to eighty pounds in subscriptions or other funds could be drummed up, he knew a young man "of the first talents and republican principles" who might be willing to undertake the project. At the mention of money, Gallatin seems to have dropped the idea. A year later, the printers John Snowden and William McCorkle carried out Gallatin's plan on their own initiative, establishing a German translation of their Republican *Farmer's Register* at Greensburg.[12]

An alternative to sponsoring newspapers was for members of the Republican gentry simply to enter the newspaper business themselves, but few Republican lawyers, planters, or merchants chose to do so. More than 80 percent of the Republican editors active between 1797 and 1800 were printers by occupation.[13] Most of the rare cases in which nonprinters became Republican newspapermen occurred in the South, which early on developed its own distinctive pattern of newspaper politics.

In the eighteenth-century North, few nonprinters chose newspaper work as a career if they had other options, but in the South, educated and professional men found political publishing much more attractive. The reasons for this difference can perhaps be traced to the political economy of the region. The lack of great cities or extensive commerce left many educated professional men underemployed in the South and thus more open to different kinds of opportunities. What was more, the financial prospects of southern political newspapers were not as bleak as they were in the North. This may seem paradoxical because the pool of potential newspaper subscribers (free, white males prosperous enough to afford a subscription) was actually smaller there. However, the paucity of newspapers and the relative unity of the political elite in many southern states made it much more feasible to bestow the state printing on a newly created journal, lessening the risk and increasing the profitability of political publishing.

Then there was the question of advertising. There were not as many advertisers in the South, but Republican politics did not alienate the ones there were in the way it did most northern merchants. Many ads in southern newspapers did not come from the merchants and storekeepers who patronized northern journals, but instead from slaveholders looking for runaways. (Runaway slave ads had been a staple of colonial newspapers everywhere in America, but seem to have faded from the northern press as slavery was phased out after the Revolution.) In addition, one of the "commodities" that southern merchant advertisers dealt in was slaves. Slaveholding advertisers could be comfortable with a party whose standard-bearer, Jefferson, was one of their own and whose electoral strength was concentrated in the South. Hence they had few objections to patronizing Jeffersonian newspapers.

The former English radical Joseph Gales's *Raleigh Register* ran nearly two hundred runaway slave advertisements between 1799 and 1820, for an average of between eight and nine a year, a large number for a four-page weekly that repeated its ads week after week. It should not be inferred that supporting the Republican press was the runaway slave advertisers' primary purpose, or that there was a unique connection between Jeffersonian Republicanism newspapers and slavery. The advertisements were also common in Federalist and apolitically commercial southern newspapers.[14]

At any rate, a few of the new southern newspapers of the late 1790s were edited by educated gentlemen rather than printers. Later this would become the norm, but early on there were many difficulties with this southern variant of newspaper politics. These can be seen in the careers of two editors from Virginia, Robert Mercer and Meriwether Jones. Though both men were members of the planter aristocracy, they were not among its most distinguished members. Robert Mercer of Fredericksburg was the eighteenth of the wealthy lawyer and planter John Mercer's nineteen children. John Mercer died when Robert, his youngest son, was a toddler, leaving an estate weighed down by debt and soon to be under siege from the boy's oldest half-brother, George, an exile in England after his unfortunate acceptance of a stamp distributor's commission in 1765. In need of other means of support, Robert Mercer became a lawyer, married into the Carter family, and, at least for a time, served as commonwealth's attorney for Fredericksburg.[15]

In late summer 1798, he found a new niche for himself and went into the partisan newspaper business, revamping and enlarging a paper called the *Genius of Liberty; and Fredericksburg and Falmouth Advertiser.* In his proposals for the new paper, Mercer avowed that in "an age of Science, when force and prescription have yielded to public opinion, the Press must be regarded as a most important engine of good or evil to a community," and he rededicated the paper to "Public Liberty and the Rights of Man." The paper also dealt with such less-elevated matters as quashing a rumor that one of Mercer's relatives had withdrawn from the race for Congress. Mercer recruited hands from Philadelphia and Baltimore to print the paper and procured loans to pay them from his father-in-law, Landon Carter of Cleves.[16]

Meriwether Jones was a Richmond attorney who had served in the House of Delegates and on the Executive Council before securing an appointment as state printer in 1798. He was also an inveterate duelist and aficionado of the mixed-race popular culture that flourished around Richmond in the 1790s. It was charged in the Richmond newspapers, and not denied by Jones, that he had installed a slave mistress in an apartment and moved her into his own bedroom when his wife was out of town.[17] Jones was given the state's printing contracts so that he could provide Virginia with its first hard-hitting Republican newspaper. The new journal first appeared on a Monday in early December 1798, and the legislature named him public printer on the following Thursday. The actual printing of the newspaper and public documents was subcontracted by Jones to John Dixon Jr., scion of one the state's old colonial printing families.[18]

Jones changed Dixon's former newspaper, the *Observatory*, into the Richmond *Examiner*, and greatly radicalized its political tone. The partnership with Dixon soon collapsed, and when the ubiquitous James T. Callender was forced to flee prosecution in Philadelphia, Jones invited him to Richmond to write for the *Examiner*, even providing the editor with room and board for a time.[19]

Jones and his newspaper became a hub of the state Republican party. To Republican officeholders at the national capital, Jones offered information on local developments in Virginia. At home, Jones clearly conceived of himself as a party strategist and of the *Examiner* as the means of implementing that strategy. Writing in April 1799, Jones outlined his plan for the coming election campaigns, suggesting the most effective themes for Republicans to put forth. According to Jones, party activists should

> frequently recur to governmental expenses:—it is an ample field, and one on which the people ought to be well informed.—'Tis in vain in the present temper of the United States to talk of *principle;* from that there has been considerable defection: we ought therefore to bring our arguments home to their feelings.—I am sorry to speak thus ill of the *sovereign people,* but they really have become very mercenary, and of consequence, opposed to war expenses.—Let peace & oeconomy then be our constant theme.[20]

Jones and a more moderate Richmond editor, Samuel Pleasants Jr., established a tradition in Virginia of state-supported Republican editors who were simultaneously leading members of the party's official high command. Beginning in 1800, the Virginia Republicans had a Richmond-based General Committee of Correspondence, in effect a central committee charged with the statewide superintendence of nominations and election campaigns. Jones and Pleasants were virtually permanent (one might even say ex officio) members of this five- to six-man committee, and after Jones finally died in one of his duels in 1806, Thomas Ritchie, the editor of the *Examiner*'s successor, the *Richmond Enquirer,* took over his seat on the committee and (in time) the state printing, too. The General Committee and its newspaper connections formed the basis of the so-called Richmond Junto that would dominate Virginia politics for decades to come.[21]

During the 1790s, however, southern gentlemen experienced enough difficulties publishing newspapers to prevent the pattern from becoming very common. Though nonartisan status gave them a political legitimacy that printers lacked, men like Jones and Mercer found printers irksome to work with and their own lack of printing experience a handicap in the management of their businesses. The editors often found themselves at the mercy of the practical printers in their employ. Robert Mercer had difficulty finding and keeping journeymen, and when he died suddenly just before the election of 1800, he left a mass of unpaid debts. Meriwether Jones complained incessantly of the treachery of his printer employees. "Various impositions are practiced upon me," he wrote James Madison in applying for a federal printing contract, "and I find it . . . impracticable to become well enough acquainted with the mechanical arrangements of an office, to make my profits commensurable to the labor & expense."[22]

PRINTERS OF THE REPUBLIC: THE NEW PARTISAN PRESS OF THE LATE 1790S

On the whole, then, the phenomenal growth of the Republican press cannot be attributed to the scattered, episodic efforts of the officeholding gentry, whether in person or by proxy. At the heart of it was a new breed of printer, a group of artisan politicians who dispensed almost entirely with the standard commercial ideology of the printing trade, beginning at the point to which Charles Holt had to be forced. All the new papers announced their partisanship in one way or another in their earliest issues. Many were shockingly frank, openly deriding impartiality as a pernicious fiction. In the first issue of his Baltimore *American*, Alexander Martin explained that he "feels himself superior to adopting the hackneied, hypocritical protestations of those editors, who *at first*, avow a rigid *impartiality*, and as soon as their papers have gained a circulation, prostitute them to the service of any party which distributes the '*loaves* and *fishes*' with the greatest liberality." Pushing further an argument that Charles Holt and other converts to partisan printing hinted at, Martin argued against impartiality in terms of republican virtue. In classical republican discourse, virtue was the ability to exercise one's political will independently; traditionally that had meant rising above partisanship and seeking the common good. Applying the concept of republican virtue to the situation that Republican printers faced in 1798, Martin drew the opposite conclusion. The Federalist repression rendered partisanship virtuous, Martin argued. Any printer who was too cowardly or avaricious to actively and openly join the Republican opposition proved himself a slave to power and not a virtuous republican citizen at all: "American people have long enough been imposed upon by the pretended impartiality of printers; it is all delusion; every party will have its *printer,* as well as every sect its *preacher.* . . . Every Editor who is capable of soaring above the flattery of villainy, and the adulation of power, has too much at stake, in the contest of liberty against slavery . . . to admit of more than a *limited impartiality.*"[23]

John Israel sounded the same theme in the first issue of his Pittsburgh *Tree of Liberty,* founded in August 1800, suggesting that any editor who claimed impartiality could not be trusted: "When the political ship is tossed by the jarring of contending opinions, we believe with Solon that the individual who does not take part, is unworthy of confidence, and merits exemplary punishment."[24] Launching a new paper in New York called the *American Citizen,* David Denniston admitted, "Professions of impartiality in cases of this kind are generally expected." If impartiality meant accurately reporting on current events, Denniston promised to practice it. "But if by impartiality, it is intended to convey an idea of equal attachment to aristocracy as to republicanism, then this paper necessarily rejects . . . an impartiality so ruinous to the best interests of mankind."[25] There was a sense of release in their violent opening salvos, as though they were throwing off a mantle of printerly neutrality that they found increasingly restrictive, hypocritical, and even demeaning.

The new partisan press attracted young printers and other undistinguished men in the North, because it gave them an outlet for the expression of their personal virtue and independence, an outlet that was denied in the consensual, elite-dominated politics favored by the Federalists. A voluble example of this phenomenon was Samuel Morse of Danbury, Connecticut (no relation to the famous inventor), one of the new Republican editors who corresponded frequently with various Republican leaders. Before taking up the pen, Morse was an ordinary laborer who had studied medicine through the kindness of a local country physician but lacked the money to get the more extensive training he needed. He also made himself unpopular in town with his tendency to speak out against orthodox Connecticut opinions, especially when they were supported merely "by the positive proof that a great man said so, or a servile repetition of another man's words." Morse had "too much pride to flatter the great or hold myself in a rank below them," and as a result found himself the recipient of much "illiberal abuse, poured in copious draughts upon me, because I dare to think for myself, and speak what I think."[26]

In 1800 Morse went a step beyond merely speaking his mind, buying out a misnamed local newspaper called the *Republican Journal* and transforming it into the *Sun of Liberty*, a paper "dedicated to . . . the cause of Republicanism." He then promptly wrote Jefferson a long, confessional letter to announce the fact, revealing one way in which Republican newspaper politics was contributing to the psychological democratization of public life.

Like other Republican editors, Morse was an idealistic young man who had large ambitions but not the money, education, or social position to realize them very easily. Outraged by the Federalist elite's unwillingness to allow relatively plebeian young men like himself to participate independently in public life, Morse believed that Jefferson and the other Republican gentlemen were different. They would accept men of humbler origins as colleagues in their political struggle and fellow contributors to the common good. Sending one's innermost thoughts to a stranger—and exalted national leader—would normally be a gross breach of decorum, Morse reasoned, but he knew "that Thomas Jefferson, the people's friend, will not be offended with the plainness and sincerity of an American youth." Morse explained to Jefferson exactly how newspaper politics would help plain American youths fit into political life. Their role would be campaigning. His major function as a newspaper editor, Morse told Jefferson, would be to "endeavor to promote your election to the next presidency [so that] if possible . . . you may have some of the votes from this State."[27]

In introducing the *Sun of Liberty* to readers, Morse rejected impartiality more flatly than any editor yet. "A despicable impartiality I disclaim," Morse wrote in an opening address that the *Aurora* praised and reprinted in full. "I have a heart and I have a country—to the last I shall ever dedicate the first, nor will I receive, with equal approbation, the productions of the friends of slavery and the sons of freedom." The *Sun of Liberty* was completely a product of political commitment, rather than any kind of economic calculation or outside financial encouragement. "The prospect for this paper is not bright, and the opposition is very great . . . there not being one influential character on my side," Morse confessed. He had only five subscribers in Danbury. He told Ephraim Kirby that "If I can have done good to my country, if I can have extended the influence of freedom . . . whatever I may suffer in the cause I shall be abundantly repaid for it." It was a good thing, for clearly such psychic currency was the only form in which Samuel Morse would ever be repaid.[28]

Other of the new editors, facing somewhat less formidable odds, took a more subtle approach than Samuel Morse. In launching his Lancaster, Pennsylvania, *Intelligencer,* the printer William Dickson gave the old trade ideology a subtle twist that changed its meaning entirely. Making the standard statement about the need for the press to be a "pure" and unadulterated source of information, Dickson held that newspapers were also responsible for the purity of the political principles they taught: "The Liberty and Independence of the Press were intended to be exercised, or they were guaranteed to no purpose. . . . Men conducting a newspaper, sensible to their own interests, will always preserve it pure; . . . It is therefore incumbent upon us to avoid, as much as possible, the dissemination of errors, either in news *or policy* [emphasis mine]."[29]

Phinehas Allen of the Pittsfield *Sun* was similarly wary but firm in announcing his partisanship. Allen's opening address disclaimed "the use of calumny, slander, and falsehood, as weapons fit only for the *Coward* and the *Assassin,*" and even avowed a duty to "aid and support" the government. But Allen added a critically important proviso that had the effect of justifying opposition newspapers and announcing his as one. The editor meant "not to pledge himself to applaud every measure of every administration. So far from this, he holds it a most sacred right and duty in every Man, in the mode pointed out by the Constitution [that is, elections], to endeavor to effect an alteration in any measure, which he may view as unfriendly to the peace, prosperity, and happiness of our Country."[30]

Here Allen added a critically important element to the political editor's portfolio of tasks, or rather, he codified a task that the most effective Republican editors had been assuming since Benjamin Bache changed the name of his newspaper. An editor should not only disseminate truth, but also work in politics to see that the truth was properly acted upon. Rather than the traditional (and the twentieth-century) press mission of merely putting ideas and information before the "public" and letting the chips fall where they might, the new partisan press would take responsibility for its ideas and act purposefully to promote and enact them.

The Republican editors conceived partisan newspapers and partisan organization as integral parts of the electoral process, "the mode pointed out by the Constitution" by which people could influence their government. They rejected the Federalist doctrine that "outdoor" political organization and newspaper criticism of officeholders were unnecessary in an elective government and that public political opinion could be adequately expressed in the mere solitary act of voting and needed no other outlet. Far from obviating the need for criticism, the people's electoral power over their representatives made it a necessity that the political press "minutely examine their proceedings" and make public opinion into a real, directed force.[31]

In the nascent political parties, printers and other editors found a new and more meaningful civic role for themselves. The classical republican elements of American political culture—which coexisted uneasily with many others—emphasized the fragility of republics, pointing to their vulnerability in the face of the "aggressiveness" of power and "its endlessly propulsive tendency to expand itself beyond legitimate boundaries." Republics needed vigilant watchmen to alert the virtuous to the encroachments of power before it was too late. As John B. Hench has shown, this was what American printers conceived to be the role of "the newspaper in a republic." Printers had long seen their newspapers as, in the words of the Boston *Independent Chronicle*, "centinels placed upon the out-posts of the constitution." Hench argues that the newspaper role thus conceived "was essentially negative rather than positive." The press could destroy the republic's enemies but provide little constructive direction.[32]

In the context of developing political parties and the explicitly antidemocratic rhetoric of the Federalists, however, the "watchman" role became a more active and constructive one. Samuel Morse provided a textbook formulation of the newspaper editor's version of republicanism in his opening address: "That a fondness for power is inherent in the human mind, I believe an incontrovertible axiom, that this fondness would lead many to practise any baseness to acquire their favorite object; and that the liberties of a nation might in this way be overthrown unless their machinations were timely discovered and prevented, I think equally indisputable. It is the press that must discover to the public a detection of such machinations." Note that for Morse the newspaper's role was not only to

FIGURE 3. Goshen, N.Y., *Orange Patrol*, masthead, 13 May 1800.
(Courtesy of American Antiquarian Society)

detect, but also to prevent, antirepublican machinations, apparently by any means necessary.[33]

The most graphic expression of the watchman theme in the Republican partisan press of this period appeared in the name and masthead of the Goshen, New York, *Orange Patrol,* published in rural Orange County near the Pennsylvania border. The "patrol" referred to was literally a patrol on the frontiers of the republic. The masthead featured a drawing of a sentry between the words of the title, strikingly rendered in large, slanting typography of the kind now used to denote speed or dynamism. A word balloon rising from the sentry's mouth contained the words "All is well." The printer John G. Hurtin had established the paper just in time for the critical New York state legislative campaign of 1800, and in content the paper was the Orange County arm of the Republican campaign. The *Orange Patrol* may even have been an early example of a common nineteenth-century phenomenon, the campaign newspaper. Most of the second page of one issue was taken up by a minutely detailed "Statement of the Canvass in Orange"; when the results were in, Hurtin published a list of Assembly winners by party and editorialized, "HUZZA FOR JEFFERSON AND LIBERTY!"[34]

Regardless of how they broke with trade traditions, almost all of the post–Sedition Act papers were working parts of the Republican party from their inception. The editors of the 1798–1800 period were in fact not just manning the "outposts" of the republic; they were becoming actual agents of new organizations—the political parties—that could translate the "detections" of newspapers into an actual change of rulers. Perhaps the clearest indication of this to appear in any newspaper anywhere was the letter of a correspondent to the Portsmouth, New Hampshire, *Republican Ledger*. Addressing himself to "Mr. Printer," the writer mentioned how pleased people in his neighborhood were with "Your nomination of members to be chosen for the next Congress."[35]

The intimate relationship between party and press assumed by the *Republican Ledger*'s correspondent could be found all over the country. Belying the mild tone of William Dickson's opening address, the Lancaster *Intelligencer* contained few ads but column after column of closely spaced political matter, and it plunged immediately into the 1799 Thomas McKean gubernatorial campaign. There were ideological essays in the paper, but much attention was also given to the practicalities of electoral politics. Dickson devoted the front page of one early September issue to a chart detailing the requirements of the state election law, which changed radically in Pennsylvania from year to year. A few weeks after the *Intelligencer*'s appearance, Lancaster Republicans held the usual public meeting to organize themselves for the campaign, and William Dickson was placed on the committee of correspondence. The editor remained a functionary of the party in Lancaster for years, eventually becoming treasurer of Lancaster and then a member of the town's first elected city council.[36]

Politics became the real vocation of many of these Republican editors, and (they hoped) the source of their livelihoods as well. They acknowledged in their papers that their personal fortunes depended on their ideological and political success, often making explicit statements to that effect. These statements rested on two basic premises: first, that a newspaper espousing a popular cause would naturally gain a wide circulation, and, second, that promoting the cause was a Republican newspaper's fundamental vocation. The New York *American Citizen*'s editor believed that his paper would naturally be popular because its political principles were sound. It would not be unpopular "because every American citizen is essentially interested in the establishment of the universal and equal Rights of Man."

In the first issue of the Boston *Constitutional Telegraph,* a new paper that appeared to replace the temporarily quieted *Independent Chronicle,* a column appeared "On the Duties of the Republican Editor." In this piece, "Democritus" advised editors on the best methods of making their papers both politically effective and financially profitable. They should refrain from gratuitous or mean-spirited partisanship so as to maintain credibility with the casual reader, and avoid the inflated and complex language of the Federalist papers so as to be better understood by the common people. Democritus jibed that in the papers favored by "gaudy partisans of despotism . . . a *sloop of war,* for instance, cannot be launched, but it must *glide down majestically to its defined element.*" However, they should also express themselves forcefully enough to command attention and allow no mistake about what they supported. "These qualities," Democritus assured the editors, "will ensure patronage and confidence, the want of them will be attended with contempt and ill-success."[37]

Perhaps the strongest evidence of the Republican editors' vocational commitment to politics can be found in the fact that many of them went on to hold public office or to seek conventional political careers. At least thirty-three of the Republican editors active in 1797–1800, twenty-four of them printers, held public office at some time during their lives. Some became elected officials: twelve served in state legislatures, four became mayors, and two even made it into Congress. The majority of the editor-officeholders were appointed to office. Five received various kinds of low-level judgeships, and six obtained what was once the traditional printer's office of postmaster. These statistics do not include nongovernment offices held by editors in bodies such as Virginia's General Committee of Republicans and the New York Tammany Society. Editorial officeholding was a controversial development, and many of the Republican editors of the late 1790s did not receive their offices until years later. Still, the number of future public officials in their ranks provides a practical demonstration of the changing vocations of Republican printers.[38]

The contrasting officeholding pattern of the Federalist editors is striking. There were only twenty-two public officials among the much larger

FIGURE 4. Pittsburgh *Tree of Liberty*, masthead, 13 June 1801.
(Courtesy of American Antiquarian Society)

pool of Federalists, and thirteen of them held the traditional printer's office of postmaster. Though the Federalist editors' postmasterships undoubtedly helped support the Federalist press, most were not held as political offices, and many dated to before the party conflict erupted. The Federalist editor-postmasters were not party "cadres," as one historian has put it, but were merely junior partners in constituted authority, upholding (often with no great skill or energy) a social and political order in which they were comfortable subordinates.[39]

FEDERALIST REPRESSION AND THE FORGING
OF THE REPUBLICAN NETWORK

As Republican editors became incipient political professionals, they also became nearly impervious to Federalist persecution. Though many suffered greatly at the Federalists' hands, few were silenced by such harassment, and most saw each new act of Federalist repression as a political opportunity, a gaffe that could be used to embarrass the men in power and reduce their standing with the voters. We can see how this worked by returning to the case of John Israel, who endured nearly every form of torment that Federalist ingenuity could devise, yet remained an imperturbable force in western Pennsylvania politics. Israel's perceived Jewishness (he was actually an Episcopalian with a Jewish paternal grandfather) made him especially vulnerable to attack, and his Federalist opponents did not fail to avail themselves of the opening. Besides exploiting whatever anti-Semitism existed among the voters and readers of western Pennsylvania, the attacks dovetailed nicely with the larger Federalist theme that Jefferson and the Republicans were trying to sully the American polity with alien, anti-Christian ideas.[40]

When Israel had worked in the town of Washington, an issue had been made of his plan to publish the paper on Mondays, requiring the office to work on the Christian Sabbath. Upon his arrival in Pittsburgh, Federalists turned up the volume considerably. One week after the *Tree of Liberty* made its debut, John Scull's Pittsburgh *Gazette* treated Israel to virtually an entire issue of crude anti-Semitic remarks and allusions. Scull frequently referred to Israel and his sponsor Hugh Henry Brackenridge as "the Judge and the Jew." Brackenridge (whose irreligiousness was proverbial in the *Gazette*) was said to have developed a "hankering after the Jews" in old age. Because the *Tree of Liberty* office was located on Brackenridge's property, the Judge was facetiously accused of building a "*synagogue* on his own ground." Scull and his writers also dilated on the subject of circumcision: "If in one of his crack-brained *vagaries* Hugh has submitted to the *knife* of his High Priest, is it expected that man, woman, and child will do the same? Are we all to be circumcised?" In the next issue, *Gazette* writers moved on to more substantive anti-Semitism, expounding on the assumed shiftiness of the Jews and applying the classic racist formula, "Can the Ethiopian change his skin or the leopard his spots?"[41]

Israel's antagonists employed legal reprisals as well as ethnic slurs. These emanated particularly (and unsurprisingly) from Judge Alexander Addison, the archnemesis of Republican printers and one of western Pennsylvania's leading Federalist politicians. Addison denounced the *Herald of Liberty* before it even appeared and repeatedly tried to assault it from the bench. Addison preferred three bills of indictment against Israel in two years, two of which the grand jury rejected and the third of which resulted in an acquittal.

Unable to stop the editor in the courts, Addison mounted a furious campaign against his subscription list, sending out circular letters attacking Israel to *Herald* subscribers, denouncing individual subscribers in court, and suggesting in orations that readers were as guilty of sedition for reading the paper as Israel was for printing it. In 1799, doubtless thanks to Addison, Israel and many other young Republicans were stripped of their voting rights when the county election commissioners made up the list of qualified voters from the tax list of 1797, the year before he had moved there. Israel's move to Pittsburgh afforded no respite from Addison's vigilance. Soon after the *Tree of Liberty* began publishing, Addison and two other Federalists sued Israel for libel.[42]

None of these harassments came close to intimidating Israel. He inaugurated the *Tree* by vowing to do what the Sedition Act outlawed, exciting "the hatred of the good people of the United States" against the authorities as presently constituted:

> At this period . . . when the strong and tyrannic arm of Power has been raised to awe into silence and servility the independent presses of the Union, . . . we should be wanting in that respect we owe to the Public, if when gross or daring innovations are . . . attempted by any man, or set of men, we did not expose the facts and characters to the execration of the *Sovereign of America*—THE PEOPLE.[43]

Addison's behavior and ideas were personally repugnant to Israel because they aimed to eliminate his kind—whether he chose to identify himself as an artisan or a Republican or to avow his Jewish ancestry—from public life. Yet Addison also supplied Israel with a wonderful opportunity; after all, here was living, breathing, ranting proof of all the Republicans' arguments against the present regime. Hence Israel refused to stop fighting. "With the malignity of a fiend, he has attempted to awe me into silence, or hunt me out of the country," Israel declared of Addison in the second issue of the *Tree,* but the editor vowed that the newspaper would be "a rod of chastisement for [Addison's] indelicacies, as well as a check to his ambitions."[44]

Such was the self-defeating nature of the Federalist repression: it transformed printers into Republican politicians, or gave them the chance to become Republican politicians, then handed them an extremely effective issue to use. The best and most devastating way to respond to a Federalist threat was to print it. When the federal marshal in Wilmington threatened to beat the editor of the *Mirror of the Times "till he should not be able to rise from his bed—or shoot at him through the third story window,"* James Wilson merely inserted a report of the incident in his paper as the latest example of Federalist bigotry and violence against their critics. He had been running a series of such items, once under the ironic headline "GOOD ENCOURAGEMENT FOR REPUBLICAN PRINTERS!" The real irony was that, politically speaking, such imprudence and desperation really were encouraging.[45]

In fact, the ironies of the Federalist repression and the political campaign in response to it went far beyond emboldening individual Republican printers. The pressures not only increased the number of Republican newspapers, but also led the editors of those journals to cooperate ever more closely with one another, forming a loose nationwide Republican communications network. This development was so obvious and so beneficial to the Republicans that efforts were made to consolidate the network into a formal national organization.[46] Matthew Lyon's son James was the most visionary editor in this regard. Possibly he was too visionary for his own good. During his lifetime, James Lyon took part in the founding or editing of at least sixteen different newspapers and one magazine, including seven in 1800 alone. However, until he established the *Pee Dee Gazette* in Cheraw, South Carolina, late in life, he never managed to keep a journal going longer than three years.

Despite the lack of success of Lyon's plans in 1800, they were quite brilliantly conceived. He wanted to create a single publication, or a chain of them, that would act explicitly as a national medium of political communication for the Republicans. With such a structure in place, the Republicans would be able to disseminate useful information and material more efficiently and to control and standardize what was being done and said on the party's behalf everywhere in the country. The editor summarized his plan in the prospectus of his projected national newspaper:

> This paper is calculated for general circulation and equal usefulness throughout the union. . . . The motives which have induced me to commence this publication . . . are the most pure and patriotic. In every state of the union, be it said that there are a number of uncorrupted and firm republicans. In most instances, their exertions are seconded by the aid of a Press. But this is too frequently so involved in a certain circle of local politics and personal affairs that

it often forms an imperfect link in the shattered chain of political intelligence. [Lyon's goal was to] render this chain more complete in the United States, to rally, concentrate and nationalize the efforts and opinions of those unorganized, persecuted and worthy republicans.

At least a few of the editors did work with Lyon. For instance, Lyon sold subscriptions for northern Republican papers in Virginia, and in return they inserted advertisements for his national publications.[47]

Ultimately, Lyon's projects may have failed because they were unnecessary. The government postal and printing policies described earlier had already created the conditions for a national newspaper network. Free exchanges, cheap postage, and an expansive postal system made newspapers from every region of the country widely available in the other regions, especially to printers. Reprinted articles obtained through exchanges had long been the source of most American newspaper content, and editors were always searching among their exchanges for a particular writer or paper that consistently provided good material. At the same time, free exchanges doomed any efforts to make money out of producing or distributing national political journalism, because no sensible newspaper publisher was "willing to pay money for information, which they receive in their exchange papers."[48]

Free exchanges were initially a nationalizing force, as the colonial custom of free exchanges had been an imperializing one, binding together distant parts of the nation and world through information. With the rise of political divisions in the 1790s, that force began to work very differently, binding together like-minded partisans across space and fostering the growth of partisan newspaper networks. Each editor began to focus on selecting materials that expressed his own views and helped promote his own political goals, arranging the newspapers he received along a political spectrum into which he could also insert himself. Having identified some journals as political opponents, editors looked through them for outrageous remarks to score points against, arguments to answer, and misinformation to correct. An especially powerful political essay or paragraph could spread through the country in a matter of weeks, and an especially well-executed newspaper could gain national, targeted exposure far beyond its own direct circulation.

To all these factors fostering the emergence of a nascent Republican newspaper network were added more direct pressures that helped to forge a real one. The Federalist "reign of terror" forced Republican editors to follow and report on each other's activities even more closely than usual, and in the process they learned to see themselves as a coherent unit. This was reflected in a toast after Jefferson's final victory in 1801: "Republican Printers—of all men the most hated, and persecuted, because of all men the most dangerous to Tyrants."[49]

The campaign to elect Thomas Jefferson and men allied with him became a common goal. By 1800 Republican editors were acting fairly self-consciously as a group, copying from each other frequently and focusing on a consonant, but not identical, range of themes everywhere. Thus the collectivity of Republican papers became a modified version of the national republican vehicle that Jefferson had wanted since 1791. No single national newspaper existed, but there was a kind of confederation of newspapers that served much the same purpose. Possibly the confederation model worked better than a national newspaper would have. In a diverse and still heavily localized society, decentralization was an advantage. Printed in the local newspaper, even national party messages seemed to emanate from a local source. If necessary, they could also be filtered. Local editors could choose only those aspects of the national campaign that best suited their local community's culture, interests, and political situation. Standardization of the message might have been disastrous.

Had he succeeded, James Lyon's major contribution would have been to give the body of Republican newspapers a head, but in fact they already had an informal kind of central direction. In the Philadelphia *Aurora*, which the exiled Irish radical William Duane had taken over after Benjamin Bache's death in 1798, Republican editors had a source of information on Federalist doings at the capital, cues on the most appropriate responses to particular issues and developments, and a clearinghouse for the best essays and arguments from around the nation. As the 1800 campaign heated up, they copied from the *Aurora* more than any other journal, making it if not the head, then certainly the heart of the Republican newspaper network.[50] According to an admiring New Jersey editor, the *Aurora*'s columns served as "a common reservoir, from which many aqueducts [were] continually replenished."[51]

The *Aurora* owed its preeminence partly to geography. While Philadelphia was still the capital, the *Aurora* had access to more, and more accurate, information on national government than most other journals. It could also benefit from the collusion of influential Republicans. Bache received a copy of the secret Jay Treaty from a Republican senator back in

1795, and Duane received similarly explosive information in early 1800, when another senator warned him about the Ross election bill, which would have changed the procedures for counting electoral votes in Congress so as to greatly reduce Jefferson's chances.[52]

However, the most important reasons for the *Aurora*'s preeminence in the 1800 campaign were the powerful writing, political expertise, and editorial "presence" of William Duane himself. The next chapter turns to a more detailed study of Duane and his role in Republican newspaper politics and the election of Thomas Jefferson.

8

A Presence in the Public Sphere

William Duane and the Triumph of Newspaper Politics

❧

W*illiam Duane* provides the ultimate example of an editor whose presence helped transform the early American public sphere. Though little known among nonhistorians, Duane was, by the end of 1800, one of the most prominent political figures in the country.[1] More than that, he was a shockingly new type of political figure, one whose plebeian, radical, cantankerously partisan image was far from that of the statesmen and generals who had been the only real presences, other than Thomas Paine, in the American public sphere up to that time.

Unable and unwilling to conceal himself using the standard eighteenth-century conventions, Duane battled all comers in his own name, turning every Federalist exposure of his tumultuous past, every effort to embarrass or intimidate him out of the political arena, into an object lesson in the current regime's betrayal of the nation's Revolutionary ideals and its intolerance toward common Americans who dared to exercise their own liberties. In the process—one in which the other editors shared to different degrees—the newspaper arena of political debate changed from a marketplace of disembodied ideas to a battleground for committed political warriors. At the same time, a more emotional and less genteel political voice and style was allowed to enter public life and actually direct affairs in a way that had happened only briefly and sporadically in the past.

THE MAKING OF A TRANSOCEANIC RADICAL

Though he topped the Federalist hit list of undesirable aliens, Duane was born in America, in 1760, to an Irish couple that had recently immi-

FIGURE 5. William Duane, 1802 engraving by Charles B. J. F. de Saint-Mémin.
(Courtesy of National Portrait Gallery, Smithsonian Institution; gift of Mr. and Mrs. Paul Mellon)

grated to upstate New York. His father, John, was a distant relative of the New York manor lord James Duane. John Duane was also his kinsman's tenant and probable agent on the Duane lands near Lake Champlain. When William Duane returned to the United States after decades abroad in 1796, he was asked whether he was of the New York family. Duane replied that he was "not sufficiently opulent . . . to be acknowledged, but that I was of that blood." The New York Duanes were Federalists of a high-toned variety, and they refused to help when the editor's American citizenship was threatened by a politically inspired lawsuit.[2]

Like many other aspects of William Duane's life, his parents' emigration did not work out as planned. John Duane died in 1765, and his wife, Anastasia, took her young son back home to Clonmel, Ireland, to live among her apparently wealthy relations. "Being in comfortable circumstances," wrote Duane's grandson of his great-grandmother, "she did not bring her son up to any occupation." Mrs. Duane sent her son to a Franciscan school, according to another story, to be "bred for a Roman Catholic priest." Whether or not he trained for the clergy, Duane rebelled against his proper Catholic education at age nineteen by impregnating and then marrying a seventeen-year-old Protestant girl named Catherine Corcoran.[3]

Disowned by his mother for this deed, Duane was forced to learn a trade to support himself, and he chose printing as one of the few trades in which a literary education was of any use. Probably he intended a career in journalism, rather than printing per se, from the beginning. The young ex-gentleman served an apprenticeship with a Clonmel printer, then moved to London, where he reported parliamentary debates for a Foxite newspaper, the *General Advertiser*. This was Duane's first direct exposure to the world of reformist politics, but he showed little interest in a political career as yet. In 1786, dissatisfied with his financial prospects in London, his abruptly chosen marriage, or both, Duane sent his family back to Ireland and set off for India as a private in the East India Company's army.[4]

In India Duane gained some firsthand experience with arbitrary power of the type he would rail against in many an issue of the *Aurora*. Dismissed from the company's military service, Duane became a junior partner in the *Bengal Journal*, an English-language Calcutta newspaper owned by two lawyers in need of an experienced practical printer. The paper apparently prospered under Duane's guidance until a stray reference to the "renigade French" living in India, whom Duane found distasteful because they did not support their country's revolution, angered the local French commander. To the editor's surprise, the British authorities took the Frenchman's side, summarily clapping Duane in jail until he could be deported. Then his partners decided to protect their investment rather than their editor, refusing to pay his bail and taking everything they could claim as newspaper property from the editor's home, office, and prison cell. Duane was saved from deportation and ruin only by the arrival of a new French commander sent by the revolutionary government. This incident confirmed Duane's growing admiration for the revolutionary French, as well his budding hatred for the British and the legal profession.[5]

Yet, for the time being, the young printer refrained from politics and carried on as a doughty entrepreneur. With money from an "unknown benefactor"—perhaps the revolutionary French commander—he started over, founding a new newspaper called the Calcutta *World*. This he tried to conduct in a careful, apolitical, and impartial fashion, relying especially on sophisticated summaries of the news from Europe. The *World* attracted a wide readership, and Duane enjoyed one of the few prosperous periods of his life. However, his fortunes took a turn for the worse, as they always did, in 1794, when the *World*'s studiously impartial European news summaries began to strike the local British as too warmly sympathetic with the French Revolution, and some disgruntled army officers were allowed to complain against the East India Company in his pages. Duane soon found circulation flagging and himself cast out of the British colonial community. At length, the governor general, Sir John Shore, decided that Duane was a dangerous subversive, and in May 1794, he suddenly ordered the editor out of the colony for "advocating the cause of France, and attempting to disseminate the democratic principles of Tom Paine."[6]

Unable to sell his business because of his debts and the legal machinations of his former partners, Duane faced losing everything if he left India and stalled for months. Still considering himself a commercial printer rather than a promoter of political ideals, he offered to avoid whatever subjects the governor general wished and sought a personal audience that he was sure would resolve the matter.

Finally, in December 1794, Duane committed a grave tactical error: he informed Shore in a letter that an account of his troubles with the government had been printed and would be distributed the next day unless the governor-general agreed to personally hear his case. Duane's sense of self-respect made threats more comfortable for him than begging. Shore sent word back that same evening that he would receive Duane at the Government House at ten o'clock the next morning. Duane was confident his plan had worked, but he was in for a rude surprise. Shore's private secretary met the editor in the governor's anteroom and bluntly informed him that he was a prisoner. The secretary stamped on the floor, and "about thirty sepoys sprang instantly from an inner apartment, and presented their bayonets to my breast." Duane could see Shore and a colleague watching from an adjoining room and shouted that they knew nothing of the British constitution if they thought he could be treated so. The guards immediately hustled the editor off to a cell in Fort William, where he was kept for three days until he and three adopted children were put aboard the *William Pitt*, bound for England. Here they spent six unbroken months, treated as dangerous criminals and confined to the ship even during a month spent anchored at St. Helena.

Shore's government issued a formal warning to the other Calcutta printers "not to insert a syllable against the Constitution of England, otherwise they should positively experience the fate of Duane." This was only the first instance in which a government would attempt use Duane to teach other printers a lesson.[7]

Duane never quite recovered from this incident. His mistreatment in India shattered his faith in the British constitution, which he had once admired even if it needed reform. It also filled him with loathing for colonialism and the arbitrary power required to enforce it. Despite the vaunted rights of Englishmen, it appeared to Duane that ordinary British citizens in fact had no more liberty than the subjects of Asian despots as portrayed in European popular culture. "I never expected to have seen Constantinople epitomized but on the Theatre," Duane wrote in one of his many appeals for clemency, "it wanted but the Bowstring or the poisoned bowl to complete the Asiatic Costume Completely."[8]

In India, Duane was merely an idealistic young printer who inadvertently overstepped his bounds. Six months on the *William Pitt* spent contemplating his fate transformed the young editor. According to Duane's biographer, "The Whiggish loyalist from County Tipperary, with his faith in British liberties and justice and his confidence in the future reform of . . . Parliament, had disappeared, and had been replaced by an embittered radical."[9] To the commander at St. Helena, who would not let him or his children ashore, Duane was defiant: "Ignorant of crimes or Vices, and boldly confident that the most odious and depraved of Characters could not charge me with an action deserving of reproach . . . only teaches me to value myself the more." Duane would strike this note often during his editorial career in America. His outrage against unjust and unfounded assertions of power or superiority fueled a determination not to allow them to stand.[10]

Back in London, reunited with his original family but destitute, the suspected political agitator became a real one. Duane's repeated attempts to get government compensation for the property he had lost in India were rebuffed, and an attorney advised him not to waste what little money he had left in a hopeless legal battle with the well-connected East India Company. In the meantime, he became involved in the London Corresponding Society (LCS), a working-class political club of the Paineite radical persuasion that favored parliamentary reform and opposed the war with revolutionary France. The group provided Duane with his first foray into political professionalism: he found work editing the *Telegraph*, a small-circulation newspaper that was the only London journal supporting the LCS. The paper's office doubled (like many American Republican newspaper offices) as a meeting place for the group's leadership.

Unfortunately, Duane's association with the LCS began only a few months before the Pitt government ruthlessly suppressed the group with the so-called "Two Acts," introduced in November 1795. The high point of Duane's LCS career came on 12 November, when he was named chairman of a huge outdoor meeting held to protest the acts. Standing before some 300,000 people, Duane opened the meeting on a mild but threatening note, recommending "measures of peace and firmness" but also warning that "it would remain with the people of this country to determine, how long they would bear innovation on their liberties, an unnatural war, and the invasion of their domestic rights." The addresses adopted by the meeting, and signed by Duane as chairman, suggested that the king would be deposed in a second Glorious Revolution if the repression of the LCS was carried through and Parliament failed to reform itself.

Though the LCS was far from able to carry out these threats, such statements stoked the high-strung Pitt ministry's fears about the group and its new editor, who seemed to be proving the truth of the accusations that had followed him from India. The Two Acts went swiftly into effect, and William Duane suddenly needed to absent himself from yet another country. In early 1796 he and his family set out for the United States, their passage funded by a more prosperous fellow refugee.[11]

EXILE ON MARKET STREET: DUANE AND THE *AURORA*

By the time he returned to America, then, Duane was a seasoned veteran of political repression, determined not to be driven from a third country for political honesty. He did some literary hackwork in New York but ended up in Philadelphia, the whole family living in a one-room apartment the landlady of which harassed them because they were rarely able to pay the rent. Nevertheless, as he had in London, the already "wretchedly poor and friendless" Duane made himself politically controversial almost from the moment of his arrival.[12]

The Duanes' arrival in Philadelphia happened to coincide with George Washington's farewell address. Struck by the similarity between Washington's views on the illegitimacy of the Democratic Societies and the British government's attitudes toward opposition political clubs like the LCS, Duane published a "Letter to George Washington," under the pseudonym

Jasper Dwight, that made the comparison publicly. Duane pointed out the hypocrisy of Washington's complaining about party spirit when his speech had so manifestly reflected partisan Federalist views. He vigorously defended the organized expression of political opinions outside of government:

> It is evident that in this part of the address you were governed by feelings very separate from those of . . . benevolent patriotism; and this regard for the constitution . . . appears awkward when engaged in stimulating one side and depressing the other, and still condemning party; . . . your judgment must have been under the domination of a most domineering prejudice when you pronounced an anathema against all combination and association, because a few popular societies of your countrymen *dared to assert their opinions* in opposition *to yours*—because they differed from you on a question which every day's experience since . . . tend to display your error and their propriety.

Duane made an analogy, which would become common in the *Aurora,* between the political agitations of the 1790s and those that had preceded the American Revolution: "You forgot that it is to association, to secret meetings . . . the United States owe this day the blessings of Independence; you forgot that whatever may have been the pernicious consequences of some associations . . . that still the sum of good has been greater than the evil; you forgot that it is the indifference of a people towards their governors, and the measures they pursue, enables tyranny always to obtain an establishment on the ruins of freedom." Duane went on to echo all the standard Republican criticisms of Washington's policies. Even more boldly, he joined the Republican radicals' recently begun and highly controversial assault on the outgoing president's character and record. Washington was never a sincere supporter of American Revolutionary ideals, Duane argued. Had the British proffered the officer's commission he expected after his heroism at Braddock's defeat in 1754, Washington's "sword would have been drawn against [his] country." The point was proven by the fact that, "twenty years after the establishment of the Republic" and the proclamation of Declaration of Independence, Washington still "possessed of FIVE HUNDRED of the HUMAN SPECIES IN SLAVERY."[13]

The identity of the pamphlet's author became known immediately in the Philadelphia publishing industry, bringing the new arrival to the attention of Benjamin Franklin Bache and the other Republican radicals. Bache's recommendation soon secured work for Duane on two relatively nonpartisan newspapers. By the end of spring 1798, he no longer held either job and had not been paid for his New York hackwork. In June his landlady confiscated the family's possessions for unpaid rent and Duane had to beg James Thackara—an engraver and bookseller who was also a committed Republican—for relief.

Within a month, Duane's long-suffering wife was dead. It was sometime in this horrifying period that Bache, though ailing financially himself, took on Duane as his assistant. In September 1798, probably only a few weeks after Duane was hired, Bache contracted yellow fever, dictated a will to his new assistant, and died within a few days. Bache had named Duane as his successor, and although the *Aurora's* new editor found the "affairs of the office in distressing disorder," he promised the other Philadelphia Republicans that their organ would carry on. "I trust though the loss [of Bache] is irretrievable," he promised Tench Coxe, "that the shock will not be fatal to *principles.*" Unfortunately, Duane and his teenage son William J. Duane, also a printer and by now his father's editorial sidekick, immediately took ill themselves. The son was given up for dead, and though both managed to survive, the *Aurora* was forced to shut down for a time.[14]

With much financial assistance from Coxe and other relatively wealthy Republicans, Duane recovered and began working with Margaret Bache to reestablish the newspaper. Their efforts came to fruition by the end of October, and the *Aurora* began publishing again on 1 November. To battered Republican activists, the resurrection of their favorite newspaper was a cause for celebration. "I perceive that the Aurora has arisen," wrote John Beckley from New York, "with poison (to Aristocracy) under its wings."[15]

The *Aurora* under William Duane was even more thoroughly political than it had been under Bache. While Bache often focused rather narrowly on Federalist monarchism and on the British-French foreign policy crisis, Duane sought and wrung all the political benefit he could from a wide range of material. He had a particular talent for sensing the political possibilities of whatever documents or incidents came to his attention and then exploiting them for Republican advantage. Besides carrying out the party newspaper's more directly electoral functions—broadcasting party addresses, tickets, and toasts—on a national scale, Duane's efforts maintained the political pressure on the Federalists year round, constantly adding to the evidence against them and keeping their spokesmen on the defensive. The *Aurora* trained a constant Republican spotlight on world and national politics, under which the Federalists could not help but appear perfidious and unworthy of the offices they held.

Among many such issues, Duane led the way (and other Republican editors followed) in exploiting the case of British seaman Thomas Nash, also known as Jonathan Robbins, a suspected mutineer who claimed to be an American from Danbury, Connecticut. The Adams administration refused to accept Robbins (who eventually admitted to being Nash, an Irishman) as an American citizen and turned him over to the British. Once in custody, "Robbins" was swiftly tried and executed. Already angry about the Royal Navy's habit of impressing American seamen and the apparent lack of Federalist interest in curtailing the practice, Duane accepted Nash's story, which was perfectly plausible in the context of known British naval practices. It was also easy for Duane to believe and empathize with "Robbins's" difficulties in proving his American citizenship. As a native-born American without documentation, the editor faced similar problems himself when the Federalists tried to use the new Alien Laws against him. Even more important was the enormous political potential he saw in the Robbins case, which encapsulated many of the Republican party's perennial themes.

In the version of the story the *Aurora* told again and again, the Federalists were mere British cat's-paws, who cared more about pleasing their masters and lining their pockets than protecting the rights of common Americans. The British appeared as cruel tyrants who would hunt down to death any who dared defy them. The revelation that Robbins was really a fellow Irishman abashed Duane not at all; it merely suggested to him that in Federalist and British eyes, it was no crime to kill an Irishman.

The *Aurora* highlighted the case for months, in the most heart-wrenching terms Duane and his writers could manage. The editor suggested to Republicans in Robbins's alleged native state of Connecticut that they make more active use of the case themselves. The publicity caused Congress to devote weeks of debate to the Robbins issue, forcing President Adams and other administration officials to expend much time and effort defending themselves, and this was only one of many British depredations reported and enlarged upon in the *Aurora*.[16]

Federalist malfeasance in office was another favorite topic. Combining the role of investigator and party spokesman, Duane dug incessantly for evidence of corruption and trumpeted whatever he found in the *Aurora*. In cases where the details of the alleged corruption were highly technical, he found an expert who could handle the subject. In July 1800 Duane obtained copies of several letters written by Speaker of the House Jonathan Dayton, a Federalist, documenting Dayton's use of "his official influence as Speaker" to further his land speculations. "These may be made great use of," Duane was sure, but admitted he was "not so much the master of the Subject of Land Affairs" and feared "not doing that justice to the subject which it requires." So he sent the papers to Tench Coxe, Pennsylvania Land Office commissioner and big-time land speculator, asking him to write the *Aurora*'s pieces on the subject.[17]

Even more extensive was the *Aurora*'s exposé of what a later political generation would call waste, fraud, and mismanagement in the U.S. Treasury. This series ran throughout the summer of 1800. Two Republican-sympathizing Treasury clerks came to Duane in June with their suspicions that the public funds were being mishandled on a wide scale. One of the clerks removed the actual Treasury account books from the office for a day, while Duane, John Beckley, Israel Israel, and Samuel Israel combed through them and copied down details for publication in the *Aurora*. While there was little evidence of outright theft in the books, it was apparent from them that various officials, including former secretary of state Timothy Pickering, Speaker Dayton, and many lower officials, had failed to account promptly or adequately for unusually large sums of public money disbursed to them for official purposes. At the very least, Republicans argued, Secretary of the Treasury Oliver Wolcott had been excessively lenient with his fellow Federalists, allowing a substantial amount of Treasury funds to remain unmonitored and unprotected for months and years at a time.

Republicans suspected (probably with justice, since public monies were typically paid into the personal funds of the officers involved) that some of these officials used the funds for speculative investments, hoping to make a profit and then pay the Treasury back later.[18] All of this was perfectly acceptable under eighteenth-century canons of officeholding, which were predicated on the notion that government officers were gentlemen responsible to their own honor and the good opinion of the community, in need of no more oversight than a yearly settling of accounts. Yet the practice looked rather sinister to a struggling editor (and presumably to many of his readers) who had never enjoyed such moral, not to mention fiscal, carte blanche.[19]

The material thus collected, Duane announced on 17 June under the head "PUBLIC PLUNDER," formed a "long and black series of *abuses* and *waste* of the public money." The editor promised "from day to day [to] lay before our readers the particulars—and we shall not go upon the vague ground of supposition or of surmise." Duane and his friends reckoned the total unaccounted for at eight million dollars and bid readers to ponder "how their money has been employed—how the administration had discharged its trust," especially in light of the new taxes the Federalists had levied along with their military buildup. In the next installment, Duane laid out the conclusion the voters were to draw from the series, casting it specifically as a partisan electoral question:

> If it shall appear that the public money has been withheld from the public coffers, while immense sums have been borrowed at enormous interest—if it shall appear that those who have held those public monies have been speculating in princely estates while they possessed those public monies, then if they can say; these things ought to be so . . . then we shall confess that we have mistaken the true meaning of *oaths,* of *public obligations,* of the *intent of laws;* of the nature of our republican government.
>
> On the other hand, if it shall appear that the very men who have held these public monies are the *authors* and *supporters* of the most violent measures of every species which the country has witnessed and deplored for years past . . . then we shall submit it to honest men, real Americans, devoted to liberty, virtue, and national independence, and whether any confidence can be placed in such men, their adherents, or supporters.

Duane spent the rest of the summer filling the *Aurora*'s columns with annotated extracts from the government accounts. Moving beyond simply exposing government corruption, Duane also made sure that his exposés were actually deployed in political combat. Writing to the Connecticut Republican leader Ephraim Kirby, he pledged that all the damning figures were "impartially and strictly copied from the books of the Treasury" and encouraged Kirby to use them "in any forum you chuse in the market place or from the pulpit—in the Senate or in the newspapers."[20]

THE EDITOR AS LEADER AND LIGHTNING ROD

Duane's efforts brought admiring notice from his brother Republican editors. The Baltimore *American* praised the *Aurora* editor's exposures in a satirical nursery rhyme:

> *The Treasury.*—This is the house that Jack built.
> *8,000,000.*—This is the malt that lay in the house that Jack built.
> *Tim. Pickering.*—This is the rat that eat the malt that lay in the house that Jack built.

> *Billy Duane.*—This is the cat that catch'd the rat that eat the malt that lay in the house that Jack built.
>
> *Sedition Law.*—This is the dog that snarl'd at the cat that catch'd the rat that eat the malt that lay in the house that Jack built.[21]

The Baltimore printer took the term *rat* from the traditional lexicon of the printing craft. Among printers, *rat* denoted a traitor to the trade, such as one who accepted lower-than-prevailing wages or refused to honor a work stoppage.[22] Duane adopted the term as his own, labeling any item that exposed a Federalist misdeed with a title like "ANOTHER OF THE RATS."[23]

Duane's influence also grew for reasons in addition to the skill with which he used the *Aurora* in partisan battles. Republicans came to recognize the well-traveled editor as an astute and knowledgeable commentator on international affairs. Readers eagerly awaited his interpretations of events in Europe. A southern planter dumbfounded by the latest permutation of the French Revolution pestered a relative for his copy of the *Aurora:* "This last Revolution *stuns me.* I cannot yet tell whether it will serve the cause of liberty. . . . The Universal Gazette has simply given us facts. I want to see Mr. Duane's observations on the Event."[24]

The *Aurora* itself was only one of the many political activities that brought Duane notice. He frequented Republican party meetings and mounted a petition drive against the Alien Law in Philadelphia's Irish community. To counterbalance Federalist domination of the city's elite militia companies, which had been openly trying to intimidate the opposition since the French war scare began, Duane organized a "Militia Legion" that would be controlled and manned by Republicans. The soldiers in the Legion were artisans and laborers from working-class and immigrant Philadelphia wards, and their mobilization helped make inner-city Philadelphia the backbone of the Republican party in southeastern Pennsylvania. Party activists such as "Colonel" Duane became officers and thus gained some needed social standing (which they did not have from their backgrounds as printers, hatters, and tobacconists) for political dealings and runs for office.

The Legion also served multiple other political purposes: it protected Republicans—especially Republican editors—from Federalist soldiers, represented the Republican party at public events, and made a convenient source of political workers at election time. By the Fourth of July 1800, Duane's Legion had enabled the Republicans to virtually usurp the city's ceremonial public life from the Federalists, at least for one year. The Legion was the only militia company in Philadelphia to hold exercises on the big martial holiday, as Federalists desponded over the Republican tide they sensed rising under the *Aurora's* gravitational pull.[25]

By the end of the 1800 campaign, then, William Duane was literally the toast of Republican America and a man of national influence. In early August Philadelphia Republicans held a dinner at Lovett's Hotel in the editor's honor. The affair was probably the first such honor ever bestowed on a working American newspaper editor. At the end of the dinner, the company lifted their glasses to "William Duane—The firm and enlightened Editor of the Aurora; virtuous and undaunted in the worst of times, the friend of his country, and the scourge of her enemies." Duane eagerly embraced this heroic image of himself. When Federalists in the Pennsylvania Senate took the state's electoral votes hostage by blocking an election law, Duane rushed to the state capital to deal with the crisis personally. He would report the debate for the *Aurora* "if necessary," he told Tench Coxe, but mostly counted on the mere presence of the famed "rat-catcher" to keep the Federalists in check: "The effect at least will be to keep them from indecency and violence, from a conviction that I will not spare them where they are vulnerable."[26]

Duane was more than capable of egotism, but the Federalists readily agreed with his own and his Republican friends' estimation of his importance. By the time of Duane's dinner, the Federalists knew they were being beaten, and some of them had begun to see how. Secretary of War James McHenry complained bitterly but tellingly about "Duane and his party" in a letter about the campaign in September 1800. A few weeks earlier, a *Connecticut Courant* writer had outlined what to him was a sinister (but highly effective) Jacobin conspiracy, led by Duane:

> Whatever appeared in [the *Aurora*] was faithfully copied into the others. . . . They were read by [a few], the main sentiments were repeated to others, and in this way the sentiments were not only scattered, but a perfect union of opinion was established . . . on every important subject, the sentiments to be inculcated among the democrats, has been first put into the Aurora. This was the heart, the seat of life. From thence the blood has flowed to the extremities by a sure and rapid circulation. . . . It is astonishing to remark, with how much punctuality, and rapidity, *the same opinion* has been circulated and repeated by these people from the highest to lowest.

While this writer exaggerated in the manner of most conspiracy theorists, this was in fact not a bad description of the way the Republican newspaper network worked.[27]

Duane's rise to prominence constituted an unintentional but significant modification of the young nation's public sphere. Typically only certain official persons were permitted to be "present" in the public sphere, where their authority could be opposed and criticized by a disembodied public opinion that supposedly emerged from rational debate. "Public opinion" produced in this way could counterbalance the state precisely because it was disembodied.

Duane and the *Aurora* represented a significantly different approach. The *Aurora* still carried mostly anonymous or pseudonymous essays and reports, but Duane's own personality, rhetorical style, and ideological predilections dominated the proceedings. The journal was unmistakably authored, conveying to readers a strong sense of the editor's identity, which was distinctly not a genteel or polite one. This impression was increased by Duane's habits of responding virulently to attacks on the *Aurora* or himself and reporting at length on the various persecutions and difficulties he endured. Duane was not the first American editor to infuse his own personality into his newspaper or to make himself the hero of his own narrative, but he sustained his personal journalism much longer and achieved greater political significance than any previous editor. Through his newspaper, Duane had made himself a definite presence in the public sphere. What was more, he connected his efforts to the building of a separate institution (the Republican party) that proposed not just to criticize the authority of the state, but actually to exercise some control over it via the electoral process. Duane showed how a partisan editor and his newspaper could embody his party and the collective public opinion it hoped to represent.

It was logical for the Federalists to make Duane their chief target of persecution, but politically and rhetorically they played into his hands. Between 1798 and 1801, he was tried in state court for "riot and assault," indicted under the Sedition Act, prosecuted and forced into hiding for breaching the legislative privileges of the U.S. Senate, sued several times for libel, and brutally beaten by a gang of Federalist soldiers, among other tribulations. Yet the *Aurora* continued to appear and hammer at the Federalists, its arguments made all the stronger by the Federalists' actions. "The AURORA stood alone," Duane wrote much later in a characteristi-

cally self-dramatizing tone, while "the Democratic papers in Massachusetts, Connecticut, and New York were prostrated by the imprisonment
and ruin of the editors."[28]

The most horrific attack was the assault by the soldiers. Like the whipping of Jacob Schneider, Duane's beating was administered by the troops
returning from the expedition against the so-called "Fries Rebellion" in
Northampton County. Irritated by the *Aurora*'s comments on their misbehavior during the march, some thirty members of the city's volunteer cavalry marched into the *Aurora* office on 15 May 1799, led by Republican gubernatorial candidate Thomas McKean's wayward son Joseph. Part of the
group kept the newspaper's staff at bay with pistols, while the rest surrounded Duane at his desk. Duane chided McKean for acting against his
father's election, arguing that the attack was "an *election trick*, in which you
are made a dupe." He offered to fight any one of them "singly," according
to the "resort of men of honor" (meaning a duel), but was refused. Duane
was no gentleman as far as these angry young blue bloods were concerned.

Convinced he was about to be beaten, the editor affected to ignore the
angry soldiers and calmly put away the papers on his desk. Duane had begun to write a letter, when the infuriated McKean, egged on by his companions, finally punched the insolent editor in the mouth; Duane lunged,
but was overpowered by the group and dragged outside by his collar. In
Franklin Court outside the office, the soldiers formed a circle around Duane and took turns striking him, their largest man more often than the
others. Duane got back to his feet after each blow, until stunned by one to
the back of his head. Duane's eldest son, William J. Duane, escaped from
the guard in the office and forced his way into the ring to protect his father, only to be beaten away. When the editor finally stopped getting up,
the soldiers whipped him for good measure. Duane rewarded the irate
soldiers with a long article recounting the incident in the next day's *Aurora*
under the heading, "MORE OF GOOD ORDER AND REGULAR GOV-
ERNMENT!", and following it up with an even more detailed account a
few days later. The second article named the "heroic commanders" involved.[29]

This was a typical result of Federalist attempts to persecute or intimidate Duane. The later Senate prosecution forced the editor into hiding
temporarily but also produced yet another series of embarrassing *Aurora*
articles.[30] To the Republican editors who copied from the *Aurora*, these
exploits made Duane a kind of folk hero and symbol of their cause. They
dutifully reported on his troubles and reprinted his salvos against the Fed-

eralist authorities. Duane thus became the more or less acknowledged leader of the informal but tight-knit Republican press organization.

When Duane began to edit the *Aurora* under his own name (as opposed to Margaret Bache's) in the spring of 1800, Charles Holt published an encomium that well expressed both Duane's role in the 1800 campaign and the way his fellow editors felt about it: "The genius, the talents, and the extensive political information ... exhibited by the present editor and proprietor of the Aurora, are circumstances to which the American mind may advert with confidence, and the future development of Republican principles may be anticipated with equal confidence. The Aurora has been a correct channel through which vast political information has been diffused through every part of the country."[31]

Duane accepted and relished his leadership of the Republican journals during the campaign and also afterwards, when the editors began to face the issue of their place in the new Republican order. During the transition period, Duane took it upon himself to look after the welfare of his brother editors and often tried to represent their interests to Jefferson, Madison, and the other high Republican officeholders. After the "Revolution of 1800," Duane suggested to Attorney General Levi Lincoln that government printing contracts be given only to Republican papers that had fought in the recent campaign. Reporting on his request to Lincoln, Duane wrote to Secretary of State James Madison that he had

> urged that it would be rendering an useful service to the public, and to the republican printers, if the latter were authorized to publish the laws of the Union ... That such papers only should be authorised to print them. ... This step would contribute to the circulation of the laws themselves, and of the Republican newspapers, and it would counteract to a degree the artful stroke of the late administration in pensioning papers in advance to oppose the present administration. If it were necessary, I could a furnish a list of all the papers which have been so active and useful as to lay claim to the attention of the administration.[32]

Here Duane indicated that he was keeping tabs on his fellow editors as they were on him. The *Aurora* editor was once again leading the Republican journalists, now into the less glorious but no less necessary area of remuneration for their political work.

WILLIAM DUANE'S AMERICAN DREAM

As we have already seen in the case of Charles Holt, some form of remuneration was a matter of survival rather than greed for the Republican editors. Working in a difficult industry to begin with, they labored under a number of unique disadvantages stemming from the basically political rather than commercial purposes of their enterprises. They had few paying advertisers, no government printing contracts, and numerous projects (pamphlets, handbills, even the newspapers themselves) that had to go forward for the good of the cause no matter how much money they lost. The *Aurora* was no different from the rest. Even with a circulation that was national in scope and almost certainly the largest of any Republican paper, it barely stayed afloat.

Duane made enough from the paper to support his large, compound family, but not enough "to disencumber myself from the debts with which [the *Aurora*] was incumbered during the unexampled struggles and sacrifices of my predecessor." Duane rued the deceptiveness of his business affairs. "The world think me making a fortune . . . ! The best paper in the United States must of course be the most profitable!" In truth, profit was in no way proportional to the influence or quality of a political newspaper. The extensive nature of Duane's circulation only made it that much more difficult to get his subscription bills paid. "Had the Aurora produced as much profit as reputation," Duane said, he wouldn't need help, but the paper generated no windfalls besides the nonnegotiable "*credit* attached to the services it is said to have rendered the public."[33]

By early 1801 Duane and most other Republican editors were in critical need of outside aid. The problem they faced in asking for it was, how could such aid be distinguished from British-style corruption of the press, in which the services of opportunistic hacks were simply bought? In the matter of printing contracts, at least, Duane suggested that since "these favors . . . are professional" and since he would "be able to execute [the government printing] as well and on as reasonable terms as any other person," his solicitations could not be considered as improper. Indeed, he went even further and tried to justify editors' making money from their partisan activities on the basis of merit. The editors were faithful political operatives who had performed legitimate, praiseworthy services to the republic when they helped oust John Adams from power. As Duane proudly stated his case to Madison: "I have not hitherto asked any favor of the administration, tho' honored by the confidence and good opinion I believe of the majority of the People of America—and I seek no other favor than such as may be given and received with honor and independence to the Administration and to me."[34] Duane often waxed histrionic about the rewards he deserved for what he had done, typically working in the fact he was now (since marrying Margaret Bache in 1800) custodian of the Franklin legacy.[35]

To be sure, Duane had a strong vested interest in the policy he was urging on the administration, and he clearly planned something more grandiose for himself than Charles Holt's simple request for restoration to the "common privileges and employments of Printers." He was busy in the spring of 1801 preparing to open a new printing office and stationery store in Washington City, in expectation of large-scale government business. He had originally planned to move the *Aurora* to Washington outright but had been asked (probably by Jefferson himself) to "sustain the Aurora at Philadelphia." Speaker Nathaniel Macon promised him the printing of the House journals instead, so Duane decided to become the government's major supplier of printing, stationery, and books. He hoped that this new status would increase his stature in the book trade generally and make even his nonpolitical operations more profitable. He touted his new connections to Boston bookseller Joseph Nancrede, asking for help in establishing business contacts with the leading booksellers of Europe: "You know very well my present standing . . . ; there can be no doubt of my arriving at such a rank in the book-selling and stationery business as must render my correspondence a very eligible one to any man in trade in London."[36]

Duane has been judged harshly, in his time and by later historians, for the avidity and frequency of his attempts to reap material benefit from the victory he helped engineer. John Quincy Adams, who nursed his parents' loathing for Duane for decades despite turning Republican himself, believed the editor's "only object is to sell himself for as much as he can get."[37] But there is another way to look at Duane's brand of spoilsmanship. He and the other editors had performed an indispensable and unprecedented service for the Republicans and, they believed, for the republic itself. If the work they did was truly worthwhile, then they deserved to be paid. Duane was groping toward a political system under which political operatives might legitimately and honorably make their living from politics.

This was a distinctly more plebeian approach to public life than the one practiced by most of the men we now know as the founders. Unlike the patriot kings or disinterested statesmen of classical republican theory, Republican editors were people who worked for a living and could not dispense with their daily earnings as a condition of their participation in politics. Yet they still wished to participate, and the rise of the Republican press had provided them with a critical role to play. The natural next step was to sustain the editors in that role by enabling them to earn an income from their political work. This would institutionalize the new newspaper politics and, with it, a very direct way that men from the lower ranks of American society could contribute to public life. At the very least, such institutionalization would require that government printing contracts be redirected to partisan printers exclusively. Eventually, it would mean appointing them to office as well.

In Duane's mind, there was much more to his political professionalism than the opportunity to make a living. It was the realization and ratification of his ideal of republican citizenship, in which men from relatively humble backgrounds could become full actors in the public affairs of their community, deferring or bowing to no man. The leading role that he and his fellow Republican editors played in the 1800 campaign probably represented the most direct and responsible part ever taken by working-class people in the selection of a national leader. It filled Duane with emotion that someone like himself—an artisan, a recent immigrant, a member of a despised minority group (Irish Catholics), and a holder of political opinions persecuted the world over—could be the close ally, correspondent, and (as Duane saw it) colleague of a great statesman like Thomas Jefferson. For Duane, it was the great glory of America (along with its Republican party) that it allowed him to be a national leader, when Europe had tormented and expelled him for much less. Thus, when a hostile editor tried to belittle Duane by mentioning that he had been a journeyman printer, the *Aurora* editor thundered back:

> Perhaps it was from a supposition that my excessive vanity would be extremely mortified that you have informed the world that I was a *journeyman printer.* What an abominable thing, that a journeyman printer should have the ambitious temerity to become an organ of public opinion in America! That a man who had been a journeyman printer should dare to become a writer on American affairs, a politician . . . or be deemed worthy of the regards of men distinguished by their talents and their virtues in an age like this![38]

There could be nothing wrong with both the recognition and the financial subsistence conferred on printers by public offices and printing contracts. Political professionalism was for Duane a natural and noble outgrowth of his status as a printer, a free man, and a republican citizen. It was the fulfillment of a particular kind of American dream.

By the time Jefferson took office, William Duane was the nation's most prominent political professional and a national leader of the Republican party in his own right. "While gratitude continues to characterize Republicans," wrote a wishful brother editor, Duane's name would "be gratefully remembered . . . for what he has done and suffered in their support." Even John Quincy Adams admitted that Duane "had much influence" because of his "considerable talents" and "indefatigable, unremitting industry." The network of editors Duane led gave the Republicans a national means of political communication and the only meaningful national organization the party had. No modern Democrat has ever attended a William Duane Day dinner, but they probably should have. The *Aurora* editor was at least as much a founder of the party as any president.[39]

9

The New Conventional Wisdom

*Consolidating and Expanding a
Newspaper–Based Political System*

✍

In the aftermath of the Jeffersonian victory in 1800, it was clear to many observers that a new political epoch had arrived. One of the more substantial—and most conflicted—commentaries on the new political dispensation appeared in 1803, when the Rev. Samuel Miller included a chapter on "Political Journals" in his misnamed *Brief Retrospect of the Eighteenth Century,* a sweeping, worldwide catalog of the previous century's many developments in culture, science, and philosophy. Newspapers, Miller believed, had "entirely changed their form and character" during the eighteenth century:

> They have become the vehicles of discussion in which the principles of government, the interests of nations, the spirit and tendency of public measures . . . are all arraigned, tried, and decided. Instead, therefore, of being considered of small moment in society, they have become immense moral and political engines closely connected with the welfare of the state, and deeply involving both its peace and prosperity.[1]

While this observation held true in Europe to some degree, it applied particularly to the United States. Indeed, Miller reflected somewhat mournfully that the political newspaper probably constituted his country's primary contribution to world literature. "Perhaps in no respect, and certainly in no other enterprizes of a literary kind," he wrote, "have the United States made such rapid progress as in the establishment of political journals."[2] Here, these "immense engines" had achieved unprecedented scope. Never before, anywhere, "was the number of political journals so

great in proportion to the population of a country as at present in ours";
moreover, nowhere else were newspapers "so cheap, so universally diffused, and so easy of access." This wide distribution had greatly enlarged
the number of people who could be informed about and participate intelligently in the political life of the community, opening these opportunities
to many who had never been part of the political class in any previous society. The United States, Miller wrote,

> especially in the last twelve or fifteen years, has exhibited a spectacle never be-
> fore displayed among men, even yet without parallel on the earth. It is the
> spectacle, not of the learned and the wealthy only, but of the great body of the
> people; even a large portion of that class of the community which is des-
> tined to daily labour, having free and constant access to public prints, receiving
> regular information of every occurrence, attending to the course of political
> affairs, discussing public measures, and having thus presented to them constant
> excitements to the acquisition of knowledge, and continual means of obtain-
> ing it.[3]

By providing an effective means of communicating with such a wide
political public, newspapers had revolutionized the arts of political persuasion and organization. Before printing, "to sow the seeds of civil discord, or to produce a spirit of union and co-operation through an extensive community, required time, patience, and a constant series of
exertions." The advent of "the general circulation of *Gazettes*" ushered in a
new political era, in which "impressions" could be made "on the public
mind . . . with a celerity, and to an extent of which our remote ancestors
had no conception." Among the many effects of this new form of political
communication were "to keep the public mind awake and active; to
confirm and extend the love of freedom; to correct the mistakes of the ignorant, and the impositions of the crafty; to tear off the mask from corrupt and designing politicians; and, finally, to promote union of spirit and
of action among the most distant members of an extended community."[4]

When Miller turned from discussing the abstract power of the press to
a consideration of the men who actually controlled it, his mood darkened.
If "the conductors of public prints" were uniformly "men of talents, learning, and virtue," Miller opined, then newspapers "would be a source of
moral and political instruction, and, of course, a public blessing." In the
United States, however, this was not the case. Miller claimed that "talents
and learning, at least" had once been "thought necessary in the conductors
of political journals." Here Miller referred to the gentlemen who had done

the writing for colonial and revolutionary printers. "Few ventured to intrude into this arduous office, but those who had some claims to literature." But during the past few years, "persons of less character, and of humbler qualifications, began, without scruple, to undertake the high task of enlightening the public mind." This trend had proceeded apace in the recent politically driven expansion of the newspaper press, until any "judicious observer" had to agree that "that too many of our Gazettes are in the hands of persons destitute at once of the urbanity of gentlemen, the information of scholars, and the principles of virtue."

There was no mistaking which "Gazettes" Miller was referring to: he meant the press that had fought the recent presidential campaign, especially on the Republican side. As we have seen, Miller was largely correct if we ignore his pejorative tone. American political journals were managed largely by men from humble backgrounds, who possessed no great degree of formal education, and who had few claims to "virtue" or "literature" as the eighteenth century understood those terms. The consequences of leaving the press in such hands were dire indeed:

> When an instrument so potent is committed to the weak, the ignorant, and the vicious, the most baneful consequences must be anticipated. When men of small talents, of little information, and of less virtue, undertake to be . . . directors of public opinion, what must be the result? We may expect to see the frivolity of weakness, the errors and malignity of prejudice, the misrepresentations of party zeal, the most corrupt doctrines in politics and morals, the lacerations of private character, and the polluting language of obscenity and impiety, daily issuing from the press, poisoning the principles, and disturbing the repose of society; giving to the natural and salutary collisions of parties the most brutal violence and ferocity; and, at length, consuming the best feelings and noblest charities of life, in the flame of civil discord.

Miller was unusual in upholding party divisions as "natural and salutary," but he agreed with many of his peers that parties as they presently operated—under the supervision of editors who were usually artisan printers by training—were distasteful and potentially calamitous. The frequency of elections meant "a corresponding frequency of struggle between political parties," and these struggles naturally generated "mischievous passions, and every species of coarse invective." If newspaper editors had "more diligence, or greater talents," these unfortunate by-products of party could be kept from dominating public life, but "unhappily, too many of the conductors of our public prints have neither the discernment, the firmness, nor the virtue to reject from their pages the foul ebullitions of prejudice and malice."

Since it was not in such qualified hands, the political press that had emerged from the election of 1800 seemed to Miller a grave social problem. "The friend of rational freedom, and of social happiness, cannot but contemplate with the utmost solicitude, the future influence of political journals on the welfare of society," he wrote. "As they form one of the great safeguards of free government, so they also form one of its most threatening assailants." Unless the "growing evil" were corrected somehow, Miller could only foresee "the arrival of that crisis in which we must yield either to an abridgement of the liberty of the press, or to a disruption of every social bond."[5]

Miller's essay reflected well the mixed feelings harbored by many Americans concerning the role that newspapers and newspaper editors had assumed during the political battles of the 1790s. Most confused of all were the old trade-oriented printers. Though in many cases they participated in the new system themselves, they were suspicious of the new printer-politicians, who seemed to have completely abandoned the trade's most basic values. The perceived scurrilousness of political papers such as the *Aurora,* and their role in spreading the baneful influence of party throughout the society, cast opprobrium on the whole fraternity of printers. It pained the orthodox printers to read such scathing remarks on the trade from the pen of a learned gentleman like Miller.

The old-time printer and Federalist Isaiah Thomas printed a long excerpt from Miller's remarks in his 1810 *History of Printing.* Thomas noted that he himself differed from Miller only in having a higher opinion of the "literary acquirements" of "many" (he was unwilling to say all or most) American editors. For Thomas, "the great difficulty" for the printing trade was "the frequency of elections," which fostered party spirit and constantly tempted "the conductors of newspapers" to enlist "as partizans."[6]

For traditional political leaders, meaning those who were not editors, the post-1800 dilemma was better defined. On the one hand, the apparently decisive impact of the Republican press in the 1800 campaign transformed Jefferson's instincts about the political efficacy of newspapers into the central axiom of American politics. The new role for newspaper editors that emerged in the 1800 campaign became ever more firmly established, with the active connivance of the gentlemen at the top of hierarchy. On the other hand, the cession of such an important political role—and the potential it held for independent political power—to men outside the gentry class became increasingly intolerable to the nation's "natural aristocracy." The first two decades of the nineteenth century saw both the consolidation of the new system of newspaper politics and a sub-terranean conflict between the lawyers, merchants, planters, and other gentlemen who composed the American political elite and the newspaper editors who had become the new parties' indispensable public spokesmen and managers.

THE LESSONS OF 1800

Though many shared Samuel Miller's misgivings about the new dis-pensation, political leaders of all stripes and levels and regions joined in expanding the newspaper-based political system that was born in the late 1790s. Indeed, they made this a leading political trend of the early nine-teenth century, one that moved forward even while the Republican versus Federalist party division was decaying. The trend was the product of a de-cisive shift in strategic thinking and even of political perceptions that affected every politically active American. The election of 1800 was what some political scientists have called a "critical" election, an extraordinary, pattern-setting contest that changed not only the party in power but, more important, the underlying political culture. By confirming the strategic insights of a victorious group of insurgents, critical elections shock the political world at large into a new sense of what it takes to win power. From such a shock, a new pattern of public policies, ongoing is-sues, and geographic coalitions emerge, as well as a new set of rules for how the game of politics should be played.[7]

Thomas Jefferson's victory taught all politicians several related lessons. Most basic was the feasibility of organizing a peaceful opposition to na-tional government policies and appealing for mass support outside official channels. The Jeffersonians' success in that appeal demonstrated that anti-democratic rhetoric and ruling-class pretensions, such as the Federalists had increasingly flaunted during the late 1790s, were losing propositions in the American republic. After 1800, even the most sincerely blue-blood-ed politicians usually took care to hide their antidemocratic views, and of-ten they tried to obfuscate their social identity as well. As Alan Taylor has put it, gentleman candidates began to pose as friends of the people, rather than authoritarian fathers, as colonial and Federalist politicians had.[8]

The best-learned lesson of 1800 was tactical in nature: if you wanted to win a political battle in this ever more public opinion–based polity, you needed actively partisan newspapers, and lots of them. Within a few short years of its emergence, newspaper-centered politics achieved the ultimate victory for any new idea—enshrinement in the conventional wisdom. Politicians now routinely judged their party's or faction's strength in a given locality by the number of allied newspapers there and considered the founding of a newspaper the single most crucial step in winning an area. As elections approached and factional disputes broke out, leaders worked (and often spent) to see that newspaper artillery was in place, especially in areas where their viewpoint was weak or threatened. All the activity created many opportunities for young editors and printers (many combining or moving between the roles) to make their careers in political work. At the same time, the possibility of an entree into politics proved so tantalizing to ambitious, intelligent, but impoverished young men that many set up partisan newspapers even without high-level encouragement.[9]

The result of this process was that partisan newspapers multiplied across the land, bearing newspaper politics with them. While the growth rate in the total number of newspapers publishing declined from the explosive levels of the 1780s and 1790s, the absolute number of newspapers skyrocketed, climbing from 260 in 1800, to 396 in 1810, all the way to 582 in 1820, unaided by innovations in technology, circulation methods, or physical form. (See appendix 1, chart 2.) The Scottish cartographer John Melish concluded in 1818 that "more newspapers are circulated in the United States than in any other country in the world." While population growth and westward migration drove some of this expansion, political factors were also heavily involved. The newspaper press continued to grow far faster than the market for it, as measured by population. (See appendix 1, chart 4.) More significantly, the new growth consisted mostly of journals that were intended to play a role in party politics. For his 1810 *History of Printing,* Isaiah Thomas compiled a list of all the newspapers then publishing in the nation, along with the political party, if any, they supported. Out of the 359 papers Thomas listed for 1810, there were only 33 to which he could assign no party affiliation.[10]

To a certain extent, Thomas's assignments may have exaggerated the disappearance of traditional commercial journalism. Many printers, even some who were publishing nominally Federalist or, less commonly, Republican journals, favored foreign news, reprinted documents, business notices, and advertising over politics in the tried-and-true manner of the

colonial printers. Press partisanship also remained nominal in newly settled or extremely rural areas, and in areas where politics was relatively un-
competitive. Yet for Thomas, Samuel Miller, and most other observers,
the most prominent feature of the American journalistic scene in the years
after 1800 was the abundance of politically active newspapers. The changing rate at which new newspapers were established clearly shows the gravitational influence of party politics. Newspaper publishers caught their
breath in 1801 after their record-setting year in 1800 (seventy-one journals
founded), but the yearly total had climbed back to late 1790s levels (fifty
or so per year) by 1803 and 1804, in time for Jefferson's reelection campaign. (See appendix 1, chart 3.)

A small army of British travelers (along with a few locals) were publishing assessments of the national character in this period, and they seldom failed to mention the political newspaper phenomenon. Though a
bitter detractor of them, John Lambert was so impressed with the central-
ity of newspapers in American political life that he included a (highly inaccurate) sketch of William Duane in his appendix of "Biographical Notices . . . of some of the most eminent Public Characters in the United
States, and of those who have . . . borne a conspicuous part in the politics
of that country." Strikingly, the commentaries emphasized not just the
partisan newspapers' ubiquity, but also their apparent popularity with
common people. "Everybody reads newspapers," exclaimed the Boston
merchant and belletrist William Tudor, "the market-man, riding home in
his cart, will be often seen poring over their pages;—they are found, not
only in every inn, as in England, but in almost every farmer's house."
Censorious British commentators added this enthusiasm for newspapers
to their lists of American demerits. John Bristed blamed the country's literary underdevelopment on "the propensity to consume the talent of the
country in the effusion of newspaper essays, and political pamphlets." The
origins of this terrible waste lay in the vulgar, hyperpoliticized tastes of
American readers:

> For the literary, like every other marketplace, must always be supplied with
> commodities in quality and quantity proportioned to its demand for mer-
> chantable wares. If the purchasers insist upon being provided with nonsense,
> there will always be a sufficient supply of that article forthcoming for the use
> of the home consumption trade. Hence . . . the press teems with . . . mush-
> room productions of folly . . . engendered by the conjunction of ignorance
> with impertinence.

Many partisan newspaper publishers discovered a less reliable demand for their product than Bristed's analysis predicted, but it was widely believed that the productions of the newspaper politicians were very widely read and enjoyed. Certainly such a conviction, whether true or not, guided the actions of most American politicians after 1800.[11]

INVADING THE FEDERALIST HOMELAND

The Republicans had been most successful and creative with the newspaper weapon up through 1800, and so naturally they were the leaders in expanding and consolidating its use after 1800. The new administration began the process of institutionalizing newspaper partisanship when Secretary of State James Madison transferred some contracts for the printing of the laws to Republican newspapers after he took office. Though Madison's efforts were hesitant and limited, they set an important precedent for the future.[12]

A more significant force for consolidation and expansion was the larger campaign to carry the "Revolution of 1800" into the surviving Federalist strongholds. Heavily involved in this campaign were two New Englanders in Jefferson's cabinet, Attorney General Levi Lincoln of Massachusetts and Postmaster General Gideon Granger of Connecticut. While both were eminent attorneys and capable officials, Lincoln and Granger were also energetic Republican party activists, with an affinity for practical political work and bitter views of the Federalist elite that dominated their home region. While not neglecting their duties, the two cabinet officers apparently became frequent contributors to the administration-dominated *National Intelligencer.* They also became embroiled, probably by Jefferson's design, in the efforts to win New England over to the Republican cause. They reported back to Jefferson on political conditions at home, successfully urged (and then guided) his extensive removals of Federalist officeholders in the region, and took more active steps as well.[13]

One of Lincoln and Granger's highest priorities was the creation of many more Republican newspapers in New England and other pro-Federalist areas. They equated Republican political strength with Republican newspaper circulation. The Hartford *American Mercury*'s reaching 4,000 copies a week was reported as a cause for optimism about the fortunes of Republicanism in Connecticut. Conversely, Granger worried about the "very general circulation of federal papers" he found along the road in rural Pennsylvania and Maryland: "They were to be seen at most of the public houses while on the whole road, say 190 miles. Through the best farming country, I saw but one republican Paper. This was not altogether pleasing to one who believes that public opinion will in a great measure be governed by that Vehicle of Intelligence."

Granger's comments reflected at least two working assumptions of the Republican leadership. The first assumption was that common American farmers could not really be Federalists at heart, even if they regularly voted that way. The second assumption, built on the first, was that unfair tactics were the only way the Federalists could win an election. The beleaguered and outnumbered New England Republicans clung to this belief especially tightly. Lincoln assured Jefferson from his hometown of Worcester that "the body of the people" where he lived "have been federalists from deception, and imitation" only.

In darker moods, the New Englanders added indoctrination and intimidation to the list: the common people were cowed by their social betters in town meetings and browbeaten in church by a politicized clergy. The root of all these evils, however, was misinformation. The Federalists had built their New England majorities on "falsehood and violence," and their power would evaporate "the moment [the voters] can be made to understand the principles & the measures of the past & present administration. . . . They are republicans, in their sentiments, & habits—they reason right on their principles, were these corrected, they would get right— the misfortune is, they have had imposed on them errors of fact."[14]

Newspapers, of course, were seen as the panacea for this problem. Lincoln was optimistic that even a small additional infusion of Republican journalism, concentrated at strategic points, would turn New England around. By the summer of 1801, there were only four strongly Republican newspapers in the state, and perhaps ten in all New England. "If Massachusetts gets right, all will be right; the other eastern states will be with her," he wrote in July 1801. "A few more republican newspapers and the thing is accomplished."[15]

The deeper motivations behind Lincoln and Granger's drive for newspaper creation were fraught with irony in view of its long-term effects. Like most of his peers among the old leaders of the Revolution, President Thomas Jefferson was, philosophically and rhetorically at any rate, a detractor of party politics. "Such an addiction is the last degradation of a free and moral agent," he had once declared. "If I could not go to heaven but with a party, I would not go there at all." Approving the organized Republican party only as a temporary measure in time of constitutional emergency, Jefferson had no interest in a continuing party system. His inaugural address held out an olive branch to the Federalists, and he promised old revolutionary colleagues "a perfect consolidation [of parties], to effect which, nothing shall be spared on my part." Through moderation in policies and personnel decisions, Jefferson planned to win the more reasonable and ambitious Federalist leaders over to supporting his administration.

Coupled with the inevitable "return" of common New England voters to the Republican fold, this course would isolate Federalist extremists, destroy their party as a national force, and eliminate the basis of the party conflict. Granger and Lincoln endorsed this plan and shared their chief's antiparty partisanship. Lincoln made the argument to Federalists back home that "every good Citizen" should promote Jefferson's reelection because "a government of the people not of a party was necessary to the prosperity and happiness of the Country."[16]

The practical conclusions that Republican statesmen drew from their somewhat confused premises shaped the role they envisioned for political newspapers. The interaction of party conflict and a national, postally networked political arena had produced a situation in which local politicians had to answer personally for the policies and actions of national leaders. This was especially complicated in New England after 1800, where Republicans found themselves with the worst of both worlds: shut out of power at home and yet vulnerable to all the criticism arising from the Jefferson administration's decisions. With Federalist ministers and officials constantly dilating on Jefferson's crimes against religion, good government, and New England, the region's Republicans desperately needed lines of communications from the seat of government that could provide information and arguments to combat Federalist "imposition" and "refute effectually the suggestions of prejudice and party."[17]

The national administration's political standing, and the larger goals of reelecting Jefferson and wiping out the party conflict, depended heavily on how effective these local refutations could be. "The Federalists have associated in an organized body to destroy the reputation of the present administration by the propagation of every species of slander and calumny which they have the ingenuity to invent," Gideon Granger wrote to Ephraim Kirby, one of several newly appointed Jeffersonian officeholders in Connecticut. Granger urgently solicited Republicans away from the capital to "repel every attack from time to time as they appear . . . instant in season and out of season . . . by counter Publications in the Republican newspapers."

Newspapers seemed the only means by which such regular responses could be delivered, on practical but also on more substantive grounds. National officeholders were too busy and too far away to respond to local critics, but they were bound, by the classical republican political morality that was very much still in force, to act the part of self-abnegating patriotic statesmen. "Both our situation and our duties . . . render it impossible to perform this service," Granger wrote. Jefferson's reputation would suffer terribly if he or his cabinet ministers openly shilled for themselves in the newspapers. The need for surrogate campaigners that Jefferson had felt when he hired Philip Freneau back in 1791 applied doubly now that he was president.[18]

Not surprisingly, some of the strongest and earliest efforts to put additional Republican newspapers into New England occurred in Levi Lincoln's hometown of Worcester. Isaiah Thomas's once-retiring *Massachusetts Spy* had begun to turn more vociferously Federalist, so in the fall of 1801, the attorney general traveled the state raising money and recruiting personnel for Worcester's first openly Republican journal, which would be the only one between Boston and the Berkshires. Lincoln kicked in $100 himself, and several other leading Massachusetts Republicans contributed similar sums. "We promise ourselves pleasing effects," Lincoln told Jefferson in midst of the project. The results of his efforts, the Worcester *National Aegis,* appeared in early December 1801 and would remain one of the town's primary political newspapers for the most of the nineteenth century.[19]

In form and content, the *National Aegis* took the newspaper politicization trend to the furthest extent yet seen. Editor Francis Blake, a young lawyer recruited by Lincoln, wrote that his journal would be "consecrated to a republican administration, and an unceasing opposition to its enemies." The very name *Aegis* connoted this purpose: the journal was to be "interposed as a shield [for the new government] against the envenomed arrows of slander." The first regular issue contained no advertising whatsoever in four closely spaced pages of political matter. (The *Aegis* still had only two columns of advertising years later.) Reportage of current events was confined to a brief "epitome"; documentary reprints concerning current events were much fewer than in most papers and obviously were se-

FIGURE 6. Worcester *National Aegis*, masthead, 10 Nov. 1802.
(Courtesy of American Antiquarian Society)

lected with politics in mind. Blake also managed to politicize the obliga-tory literary page on the back of the journal.[20]

Even more interesting was the quite systematic manner in which Blake and his successors used the *National Aegis* to strengthen Worcester's strug-gling local contingent of Republicans by integrating their efforts with na-tional issues and a broader Republican party ideology. In the congression-al campaign of 1802, for instance, the *Aegis* defined what the Republicans stood for and applied that standard to the candidates for Worcester's seat, the Federalist incumbent Seth Hastings and his Republican challenger Edward Bangs. The paper set the dividing line between the parties squarely on the issue of democracy:

> By Republican, then, is meant a sincere and hearty believer in the "SOVER-EIGNTY OF THE PEOPLE"—one, who contends, not that *"an essential share,"*

but that the entire control of their Governmental concerns, should, *ultimately*, rest with the citizens;—in short, in theory, an advocate of a *Representative Democracy;* and, in practice, a friend to public justice, order, and economy.— Such a Republican, Citizen Electors, is EDWARD BANGS.

In making such a clearly partisan case, the *Aegis* pushed against New England's traditional political culture, which upheld personal over political characteristics as qualifications for office and usually prescribed the automatic reelection of any incumbent whose character remained unblemished. "An open libertine" should not be elected, editor Blake admitted, but otherwise "the first and most momentous qualification" should now be "correct political principles." Elections conducted in New England's traditionally nonpartisan, character-focused manner left voters to seek for a candidate's principles "by the aid of indirect construction or fallacious surmise." It was far better to openly state a candidate's principles, as the *Aegis* was doing. Partisan campaigning awakened voters to the larger implications of their choices, which Blake tried to relate directly to the well-being of individual readers and their families: "The people are not then to chuse merely between BANGS and HASTINGS . . . ; [but] between *Republicanism* and *Monarchy; peace* and *war,* . . . *plenty* and *poverty, property* and *ruin.*"[21]

Here we can see that local partisan newspapers such as the *Aegis* did not simply pump out a national party line set at the capital. They had national papers from which to reprint and take cues, but they were also able to tailor party messages to suit local audiences. The *Aegis* used relatively few essays from other newspapers, as its editors exploited the decentralization of the Republican newspaper network to present the party in a form that was far more acceptable to New England sensibilities than the one appearing in the *Aurora* or even Jefferson's Washington mouthpiece, the *National Intelligencer.* This capacity to filter national political messages for local consumption was a major advantage of a political communication system based on large numbers of local, small-circulation outlets rather than a small number of national, large-circulation outlets. In the early 1800s, technological limitations rendered this the only feasible system, but the combination of government policies encouraging decentralization and the system's manifest utility in a regionalized, federated political arena would keep it in place long after the technical limitations had disappeared.

Extensive tailoring can be seen in the columns of Worcester's *National Aegis.* Essays on Jefferson praised his democratic beliefs, yet also depicted him as a learned, sober, and economical magistrate, just like the leaders preferred in New England. The Republican cause more generally was cast in as conservative a light as possible, with much emphasis given to the fact that it was Jefferson who now represented established authority. Another frequent theme was that the Federalist clergy's lurid predictions about the results of a Jefferson victory had not come to pass. The "kingdom of Satan" had not been erected on the ruins of the Christian religion, no ministers had been butchered or churches burnt. Indeed, Christianity was flourishing as never before, as indicated by the enthusiastic religious revivals then sweeping the South. Moreover, Jefferson had made none of the feared "innovations" in government, but largely adopted "the same system pursued by Washington." The Republican slate of candidates was dubbed the "Washington and Jefferson Ticket."[22]

More examples can been seen in the *Aegis's* careful manner of dealing with issues that were especially damaging for the Republicans in New England. Jefferson had allowed Thomas Paine to return to the United States, at a time when his recent writings against George Washington and organized religion had made him persona non grata in New England and much of the rest of the country. The *Aegis* defended Jefferson's actions while nearly disavowing Paine himself. The United States owed Paine for his services in the Revolution—thus Jefferson had acted rightly in giving him refuge in his old age—but the author of the *Age of Reason* was not "the *Mentor* of Mr. Jefferson," as the Federalists had charged, nor did he even have the confidence of the administration. Editorially, the *Aegis* could not "acquiesce in *all* of his opinions, or approve of *all* his language." Even so, other essays in the paper characterized Paine as little more than a slightly free-thinking Federalist, who "inculcates, with energy and eloquence, . . . the existence of a God;—and . . . recommends *government*, though not a *despotic* one—*order*, though not *slavery.*"

Like virtually every Republican paper, the *Aegis* also spent some of 1802 responding to James Thomson Callender's revelations regarding Jefferson and his slave Sally Hemings. This scandal was particularly harmful in New England, because it reminded moralizing Yankee voters both of Jefferson's alleged libertinism and his status as a slaveholder. *Aegis* writers tried to counter this problem by installing Callender in New England's pantheon of diabolical liars and tricksters, comparing him to the New England celebrity criminals Stephen Burroughs, George Barrington, and Beelzebub himself.[23]

Where it was not possible to create a *National Aegis,* Republican strength in New England was augmented by renovating existing journals. Northern New England's oldest and most widely circulated newspaper, the commercial but Federalist *New Hampshire Gazette* of Portsmouth, was sold in February 1802. Fortified with a brand-new federal law-printing contract, new proprietors Nathaniel S. and Washington Peirce proclaimed themselves "pure AMERICANS at heart" and firm friends of the Republican-controlled national government. While it never became a fount of original partisan material, the journal's front page in one year went from reprinting Alexander Hamilton's New York *Evening Post* to copying from the *National Aegis* and other ultra-Republican papers. The Peirces kept up some pretenses to impartiality for a while, but in January 1803, they placed a motto on their banner declaring Republicanism to be their "polar star."[24]

Another renovation occurred in Salem, Massachusetts, hometown of Timothy Pickering and his so-called "Essex Junto." There had been a nominal "opposition" paper in Salem since May 1800, when the printer William Carlton (cashiered from the established *Salem Gazette* two years earlier for Republican sympathies) began printing the *Impartial Register.* But as the name would suggest, it was not strongly political. Carlton acted the partisan mostly by allowing a few essays departing from the town's extreme Federalist line into the paper, especially from the pen of the Rev. William Bentley, a pioneer Unitarian and a rare Jefferson sympathizer among the Massachusetts Congregational clergy. Bentley and the *Impartial Register*'s most loyal advertisers, the Crowninshield family of merchants, would later become very prominent state Republicans. (Bentley served as chaplain of Congress and two Crowninshield brothers as cabinet members during the Jefferson and Madison administrations.) The Crowninshields had also financed Carlton's purchase of the press he used to print the *Impartial Register.* Yet they all had qualms about openly embracing the Jeffersonian cause. Carlton affixed a nonpartisan motto to his political section ("Uninfluenced by party, we aim to be just"), and the paper favored John Adams in the election of 1800, attacking the local Federalists for not supporting the president strongly enough.[25]

After Jefferson was elected, Carlton, Bentley, and the Crowninshields (with whose aunt the editor and minister both boarded) came out of the political closet, with the strong encouragement of Levi Lincoln and the Jefferson administration. With the first issue of 1802, Carlton dropped "Impartial" from the title of newspaper, and during the summer, he placed a new motto in the banner, beginning with the more pugnacious line, "Here shall the PRESS the PEOPLE'S RIGHTS maintain."

The motto change appeared to signal the opening of the fall campaign, as the no longer impartial *Register* soon began a vigorous crusade to wrest Salem's congressional seat away from the Federalists. Jacob Crowninshield ran against none other than Timothy Pickering, who had returned to re-assume his leadership in Salem at the urgent request (and with the financial help) of the local Federalists. It was truly a no-holds-barred contest, making 1802 Salem's bitterest year since the witch trials. Carlton would serve time in jail for what he printed, and his Federalist counterpart's life would be threatened. With Crowninshield money (but little profit to the printer), special stripped-down editions of the *Register* were printed and sent to every town in the district free of charge. As many papers were handed out, Lincoln reported to Jefferson, "as there were individuals who could be induced to take & read them." When Jacob Crowninshield won the election, inflicting a wound in the very "headquarters of opposition principles," it struck Lincoln as a test case for what newspapers could and would do everywhere.[26]

Thus inspired, Republicans in Federalist strongholds began to heed Lincoln's call for more newspapers in earnest as the 1804 presidential election and key state contests approached. In October 1803, William Bentley commented that "Gazettes" were appearing and changing places so quickly he could no longer keep track of them.[27] In the year and a half before the electors were chosen, new Republican papers materialized at New-buryport, Northampton, and Portland (District of Maine) in Massachusetts; Danbury, Bridgeport, and Norwich in Connecticut; and Walpole in New Hampshire. Outposts were thus established in areas where the Federalists had formerly been overwhelmingly dominant, such as the coastal area north of Boston, the Connecticut River Valley, and Fairfield County, Connecticut. (See map 4.) At least some of these new journals had high-level backers like the *National Aegis*. Vermont Senator Stephen R. Bradley lent his patronage to the Walpole *Political Observatory* and to its editor, imported from Connecticut. In Maine, embattled Republican Congressman Richard Cutts recruited an editor and helped establish the Portland *Eastern Argus*.[28]

Jefferson had also been weak in parts of the middle states, losing Delaware and New Jersey outright in 1800 while dividing the electoral vote in Maryland and Pennsylvania. Journalistic reinforcements appeared

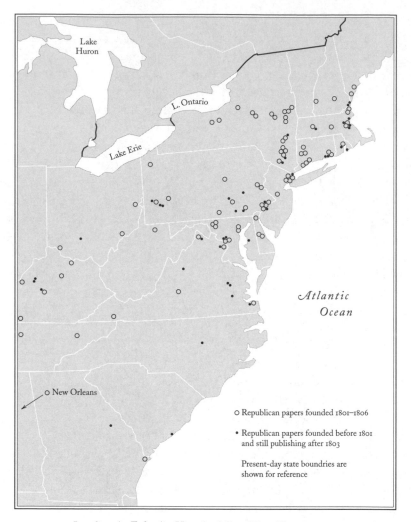

M A P 4. Invading the Federalist Homeland: Republican Newspapers, 1801–1806.

in key areas here as well. (See map 4.) Republican printers set up shop at Norristown and Easton in traditionally Federalist areas of rural eastern Pennsylvania and also established outposts at Northumberland, Meadville, and Gettysburg in the still-settling interior. New Republican journals even appeared in the interior of Delaware, where newspapers had rarely been printed at all. New Jersey was an especially puzzling case for Republican leaders, a predominantly agricultural (and thus, in Republican minds, naturally Jeffersonian) state without a merchant elite that nevertheless voted stoutly Federalist. The problem, they thought, must be a lack of Republican newspapers. Party leaders credited their relative strength in northeastern New Jersey to the presence of several Republican journals there, but there were none in the more rural areas to the south and west. Hence, the very week of Jefferson's inauguration, Gen. Joseph Bloomfield and other Republican leaders helped establish a journalistic beachhead in mid-Jersey, the Trenton *True American*. Jacob Mann, printer of the Morristown *Genius of Liberty*, moved south to run the new journal.[29]

As in the 1790s, the actual extent of the aid that Republican editors received from gentleman Republican politicians should not be overestimated. There were only a few cases of regular, long-term financial assistance or formal "subsidies." Leaders trying to get a new journal started often provided or arranged start-up loans and helped assemble an initial subscription list. Following Jefferson and Madison's example, some especially broad-minded or ambitious leaders tried to boost the party's national strength by subscribing to Republican papers in distant locations.[30] All these forms of aid were limited and sometimes even counterproductive. Friendly sponsors often turned into vengeful creditors in the event of political differences or financial exigencies, and distant subscriptions often became bad debts too costly to collect. The proprietors of the *Political Observatory* were on such a tight budget that their hired editor was allowed only three copies of each issue for his own use. The *National Aegis's* galaxy of patrons could not prevent $2,000 in delinquent subscriptions from building up by June 1804, for a publication that only cost $2 per annum in the first place![31]

Even after all the activity, Republican newspapers were far outnumbered in New England during the 1804 election. Nevertheless, the Federalists proved highly vulnerable. Defensive about the recent inroads, Federalist-controlled legislatures in Massachusetts and New Hampshire allowed the voters rather than the legislature to choose presidential electors. Far from staving off defeat, the move created an opportunity for the Republicans to campaign on the national issues where they were strongest: Jefferson's rising popularity, the Louisiana Purchase, the successful Tripolitan War, the prevailing economic prosperity, and the legitimacy of democracy itself.[32]

Once again, the *National Aegis* provides a good example. Launching

Worcester's formal Jefferson reelection campaign in early September 1804, new editor Edward Bangs framed the contest around an issue that neatly connected local concerns with national politics. Alarmed at their declining popularity and heavily out-migrating population, the New England Federalists were mounting a hysterical opposition to the Louisiana Purchase: some hinted at secession in response, a few actually plotted, and many more secretly desired it. In public politics, these sentiments manifested themselves as appeals to New England sectional pride against overweening "VIRGINIAN INFLUENCE."

In the spring of 1804, the Massachusetts legislature called for a constitutional amendment to repeal the framers' compromise on slavery and base the apportionment of taxes and representation on free white population only. Bangs and other Republican editors correctly sensed an opportunity for their side. Convinced that the Louisiana Purchase was as popular with the common voter in New England as it was elsewhere, they openly celebrated the event. During the fall campaign, they portrayed the election as a choice between a responsible Republican government, the true heir to the mantle of Washington, and desperate Federalist conspirators who would rather destroy the union than lose power: "They join cordially in the sentiments of Milton's Satan, *'Better to reign in Hell, than serve in Heaven.'*" Bangs stuck relentlessly to this theme throughout the fall and incorporated it into a splashy electioneering section of the paper issued just before the election. Taking up a full page, divided into two columns rather than the usual four, the section was headed with the "Republican Electoral Ticket" and included a lengthy address to the voters that explained (in Bangs's terms) the national choice that voters were making: "Decide, then, between the respective Electoral Candidates;—and RE-MEMBER that in deciding between them, You may GUARD THE SAFETY; OR SEAL THE DEATH WARRANT OF THE NATIONAL UNION!"[33]

The result was a shattering, near-fatal defeat for the Federalists and another leap forward in the press's reputation for political efficacy. Jefferson carried every New England state except hard-bitten, constitution-less Connecticut, where Federalists survived only by extreme measures. (Their most notorious step was the "Stand-Up Law," a draconian form of viva voce voting in which voters had to stand up and identify themselves before vengeful town fathers.) Outside of New England, only Delaware resisted Jefferson's charms. Yet even Connecticut and Delaware had acquired a complement of political newspapers that would remain on a permanent basis. The infrastructure of party conflict had been expanded, permanently, into formerly somnolent or monolithic regions, and patterns were ingrained that would sustain it in one form or another for decades. The changes occurred not just in presidential but in local voting as well. All of the New England states except Connecticut elected Republican legislatures and governors before Jefferson left office, and everywhere the total number of Republican votes (and the level of voting per se) increased greatly.[34]

Editors were typically modest about their role in these changes, but occasionally they could not help noticing the seemingly close relationship between Republican newspaper circulation and Republican electoral victories. Nathaniel Willis Jr. of the Portland *Eastern Argus* reported frequently on the rapid expansion of his subscription list, partly because he regarded it as "undeniable proof of the increase of friends to . . . Republican Principles." Willis had 800 subscribers by the end of his first four months in operation, without any of the "public emoluments, private funds, or auxiliary exertions" that the Federalists imagined he had. During 1804 alone, he acquired 786 more. When a Federalist newspaper suggested that a partner of Willis's had quit because the business was failing, Willis treated it as a campaign issue, an aspersion on the Republican cause. He retorted that the *Argus* had gained sixty-five new subscribers since the partner had left and lost only one! After an unnamed Federalist tried to organize a boycott of the paper in York County, Willis detailed the number of papers still going to each town there. Just after Jefferson's reelection, the editor rhapsodized about the glorious state of the country's political affairs, and while he could not give himself all the credit, he was pleased to reflect "that his efforts have not been ineffectual." Willis underlined this conclusion after the spring state elections of 1805 by printing a chart showing the Republicans' changing fortunes over the two years that he had been in business:

> *Federal Majority, in* 1803,   4881
> *Republican Majority, in* 1804,   64
> *Republican Majority, in* 1805,   1905

The editor attributed both this stunning electoral turnaround and his own business success to the "powerful effect of *correct politics.*" To Willis and many other American politicians, the two now went hand in hand.[35]

TRAMP POLITICIANS: THE EMERGENCE OF
POLITICAL EDITING AS AN OCCUPATION

Jefferson's reelection signaled only the slightest letup in the growth of newspaper politics. There was seemingly less need to push Republican politics into new areas after Jefferson's landslide, but other forces generated demand for new political journals. The Federalists were trying to improve their own press (as we will see later), and the victorious Republicans were becoming increasingly factionalized. According to the emerging custom, each wing of a local party required its own organ to have any chance of winning control or even being taken seriously.

The decade's nastiest intraparty squabble, between Vice President Aaron Burr and the Clinton and Livingston families in New York, provides an example. With Jefferson openly snubbing his understudy for suspected intrigues during the Electoral College deadlock of 1801, Burr's rivals sensed his vulnerability and launched a concerted pamphlet and newspaper assault on his reputation beginning in the late spring of 1802. Desperate to respond, the Burrites found themselves frozen out of New York's only Republican daily, the *American Citizen*. Editor James Cheetham, a gone-to-seed refugee radical, had requested a $2,000 bribe if he was to defend Burr, and when refused, became instead his primary attacker. The Federalist papers were only too happy to open their columns to Burr supporters, but the fact that pro-Burr pieces appeared there only lent credence to the charge that Burr was an unreliable Republican.

The New York City Burrites therefore needed a journalistic outlet of their own, and they established the *Morning Chronicle* in the fall of 1802. The ringleader was the former partisan printer Matthew Livingston Davis, Philip Freneau's one-time partner on the New York *Time Piece* and now Aaron Burr's chief henchman. The Burrites and their enemies virtually equated the *Morning Chronicle*'s publishing fortunes with the faction's political prospects. Both newspaper and faction went into decline after Burr killed Alexander Hamilton and fled to the West. By August 1805 the *Morning Chronicle* was bleeding money at the rate of $2,000 a year, but Matthew Davis argued that the publication had to be kept alive at all costs. He saw the newspaper as the key to the faction's very survival: "The instant the Chronicle ceased to exist, *the Burrites would become 'uninfluential atoms,'* there would be *no rallying point*," and, even worse, their popularity and organizational vigor would be judged so weak as to be "*incapable any longer of supporting a press.*" That perception amounted to a political death certificate. Open Burrism and the *Chronicle* finally expired together in 1807.[36]

Maintaining a newspaper had become the sine qua non of existence for any serious political group. Any roiling of the political waters produced more newspapers. By 1807 local infighting had begat three different Republican organs in Philadelphia, two each in Baltimore and Pittsburgh, and the phenomenon was spreading to smaller towns apace. Hence the tide of newspaper politics continued to rise even after the party conflict that had spawned it was apparently won.

Even more than this editorial revolution of 1800, it was the process of consolidation and expansion that led to the emergence of political editing as a definable occupation. The upward-spiraling demand for more newspapers created a demand for more editors, and as Levi Lincoln admitted to Jefferson, finding an appropriate editor was the most crucial and difficult aspect of creating an effective political newspaper. A question with no obvious answers for Republican statesmen was, where could platoons of young men be found who were willing to face maximum exposure to character assassination with minimum opportunity for substantial money making?

In the past, editors had usually come from the ranks of printers, but many Republican leaders were dissatisfied with the results of this approach and mistrustful of tradesman as mere mercenaries in any case. They sometimes found a printer to be nominal editor, a front for a clique of gentleman who really wrote and controlled the paper. Theoretically, this arrangement offered the best of both worlds, protecting statesmen and prominent professional men from the stigma of campaigning, while still granting them control of their party's message.[37]

Yet few such arrangements remained stable for long or even served their intended purpose. Though Benjamin Austin of the *Independent Chronicle* did it for years, most human beings could not withstand the strain of pursuing a professional career and running a newspaper on the side. Even if they could manage it, other problems developed. The division of legal responsibility and editorial control could engender recklessness that was dangerous to the health of both newspapers and printers. Charles Shepherd, a Republican lawyer in Northampton, Massachusetts, who "furnished, or inspected every original piece" published in the *Republican Spy,* burned up four printers in four years, eventually destroying the paper, because of his own wild rhetoric. The first printer left the state after an indictment, and the second spent six months in prison.[38]

An additional problem was that a shadow editor's cover rarely held. Editors hurled charges of outside control at each other with abandon and regularly named suspected shadow editors. The *Salem Gazette* frequently referred to the "Reverend Editor" when attacking the *Salem Register,* because the Federalists firmly believed that the Rev. William Bentley rather than printer William Carlton controlled the paper. Carlton denied this charge furiously and with much justice. Being a mere "tool" in the hands of another was one of the most damning accusations in the American political lexicon, especially for a printer. Bentley edited the paper for real only after the hard-drinking Carlton died in 1805, learning in the process why printer-editors were necessary in the first place. The arrangement was supposed to be temporary, but the search for a new editor dragged on for two years, crushing the preacher under the workload and giving him a new and (negative) perspective on an editor's lot. "I have all the labour and none of the profit," Bentley fumed.[39]

Another, more attractive method for gentlemen wanting to create a front was to recruit younger versions of themselves as full-time editors and set them up in partnership with a printer. Just beginning their careers, rising young professionals had plenty of energy, as well as taste and learning, that would provide (as many Republican gentlemen saw it) some much-needed elevation to Republican party politics. A stint editing a newspaper could also serve as a kind of political apprenticeship for a young man just reading law. The Natchez printer Andrew Marschalk's newspapers, for instance, were edited by a series of budding gentleman politicians, most notably the future historian John F. H. Claiborne, who was studying with the Natchez law firm of Griffith and Quitman at the time.[40]

The problem was that, while bright young college men suited the tastes of recruiters, they proved to be highly unreliable journalistic talent in the long term, as Levi Lincoln discovered in trying to staff the *National Aegis* with rising local lawyers. The first editor, Francis Blake, was restive from the outset of his tenure. He never intended to give up the law even temporarily, and, in an early issue of the paper, inserted a front-page announcement that "Francis Blake, Attorney at Law" (the newspaper being edited by the fictitious "Hector Ironside, Esq.") had opened a law office in Worcester. Blake then grew increasingly irritable on the numerous occasions when he was forced to slight his promising legal career in order to deal with the penny-ante frustrations of the small-town newspaper business. Suffering the usual troubles with delinquent subscribers, Blake took the occasion of the paper's first anniversary to issue a petulant statement of his priorities: "The Editor wishes it may be explicitly understood, that his concern in the Aegis is with him a secondary object, and that the engagements of a laborious profession will at all times command his *primary* attention."

Blake finally walked off the job in March 1804, just before the state elections when he was most needed. Soon after, his only connection with newspapers was filing debt suits for the *Aegis's* Federalist rival, the *Massachusetts Spy*. The *Aegis* editorship became a revolving door through which nearly every Republican lawyer in Worcester eventually passed, including three of Levi Lincoln's sons, two of his law students, and several close associates. (It was a very successful political apprenticeship, however, producing two governors and numerous legislators.) The journal seemingly survived only as a permanent Lincoln family appendage.[41]

Money was the principal factor that made a political editor's chair uncomfortable for a well-trained professional man. We can see this in the case of the Jefferson administration's most distinguished editorial supporter, Stanley Griswold of the Walpole *Political Observatory*. Educated at Yale alongside the future leaders of Connecticut's "Standing Order," Griswold became one of that state's most eminent clergymen, a legendary preacher and intellectual who rejuvenated a moribund church in New Milford; unfortunately, he also stood out among Connecticut divines as an articulate Unitarian (the state's first, apparently) and a supporter of Thomas Jefferson.

After years of harassment from his clerical colleagues, including an ecclesiastical prosecution for his political views, a disgusted Griswold decided to quit the ministry in 1802. Casting about for a new line of work, he entreated Jeffersonian friends for a government job, with no results for nearly a year and a half. Finally oppressed to the point that "almost *any* other business" seemed preferable to the cloth, in the fall of 1803 he accepted a position as editor of a fledgling Republican weekly at Walpole far up on the Vermont-New Hampshire border.[42]

Though it was hardly his first choice of new occupations, Griswold made an excellent editor. He enjoyed hurling thunderbolts down the Connecticut at his old antagonists, and the *Political Observatory* became one of the best-written and most reprinted journals in New England during Jefferson's reelection year. However, the ex-minister and his printer-employers quickly discovered that they could not afford each other. Griswold's editorial salary could not begin to meet his family's expenses, and even then his employers were losing money by the week. Once Jefferson had safely carried Vermont and New Hampshire, the owners decided to sell. Griswold renewed his pleas for government employment in even more piteous terms than before, and a phalanx of prominent supporters soon won him a job as secretary (second-in-command) of the new Michigan Territory.[43]

If low pay often disenchanted gentleman editors with the newspaper business, unpaid bills and unmet commitments could embitter commercial printers against editors and their sponsors. The *National Aegis* went through nearly as many printers as it did editors, and in 1805-1806, long-simmering disputes among its printers, editors, and sponsors nearly killed the paper. In October 1805, debt-ridden printer Sewall Goodridge sold the office to a fellow printer named Samuel Cotting. Goodridge made the sale, however, without the permission of former editor Francis Blake, who claimed to own some of the establishment himself on the basis of money he had advanced (or been owed by) the printer. As a good attorney, Blake promptly filed a writ of replevin against Cotting and claimed the paper for his own.

In mid-December, the *Aegis's* printing press and office furniture were seized and the paper itself shut down. The local Republicans (no longer including Blake, apparently) raised money all over again, found some new printing equipment, and brought out a new *Aegis* in February 1806. The new publishers were a committee of Republican trustees headed by Levi Lincoln's brother, Abraham. They offered Samuel Cotting a contract to print the new paper, but Cotting, outraged at their presumption and believing himself the rightful owner, plotted revenge. On Sunday morning, 6 July, while the rest of Worcester was in church, Cotting broke into the *Aegis* office and stole some of its type and the half-printed sheets of that week's newspaper. Allowed to use the *Massachusetts Spy's* printing press, he then proceeded to publish the paper on his own beginning the following week and continued to do so for the next five months.

Cotting's stroke threw the Worcester Republican party into a bizarre existential crisis. Their only public face had been stolen by an imposter, but without type, they were unable to even tell outsiders what had happened. The trustees scrambled for more type and soon were publishing again, but Worcester now had two papers publishing on the same day with the same name that claimed to speak for the same party. The "Trustees' Aegis" furiously asserted that Cotting's actions were a Federalist plot and that all of his subscribers and writers would be Federalists. Yet Cotting maintained the paper's Republican identity and sent it to the old subscription list. Most outrageously, from the trustees' perspective, he attacked the Lincoln family's habit of treating of the paper and the local party almost as their own private property. Cotting must have carried at least some readers with him, because the trustees took the extraordinary step of calling a county Republican meeting to certify their paper as the one, true *National Aegis,* organ of the Worcester Republicans. There was no official body to bring together, of course, merely a community of readers who physically assembled during the September county court week and agreed to "discountenance" Cotting's paper. Three months later, the aggrieved printer finally gave up.[44]

This was the all-time worst case of bad printer-party relations, but it reflected the tensions and misunderstandings that often arose when printers worked for politicians rather than being politicians themselves. Over time, it seems to have become apparent that to be stable and consistently effective, a partisan newspaper needed to be under the guidance of someone who would take full responsibility for the enterprise and give it his full time and attention. That meant someone whose background was sufficiently plebeian (or at least checkered) that he could not expect to follow a lucrative profession.

The Walpole *Political Observatory*'s owners gave Stanley Griswold his notice in revealing terms. "The establishment must be committed," they told him, "to the sole management of an able printer." Likewise, the *Salem Register*'s long search for someone to replace William Carlton and relieve William Bentley ended with a young journeyman in their own office, Warwick Palfray Jr., a bright young boy whose prospects in life had been blighted by his father's improvidence. Palfray exemplifies another feature of the emerging occupation of political editor. A partisan newspaper needed a conductor who not only worked at it full time, but who also had political interests, knowledge, and ambitions of his own. Beginning as William Bentley's teenaged journeyman, Palfray would edit the paper until his death in 1838, becoming a founding member of the Salem town council and a multiterm state representative. His colleagues at the *Register* eulogized him primarily as a "firm, unwavering, and consistent politician."[45]

Hence as political editing became an occupation, it remained largely the province of artisans and other persons of lower middling status who were essentially their peers. Building on the changes of the late 1790s, the scramble for editors after 1800 created numerous opportunities and, in time, a reasonably well-marked career path for printers who wanted to work in electoral politics for a living. Printers were sometimes recruited, as in the Worcester and Salem cases, but in other cases they sought the opportunities out for themselves.

The best-qualified candidates available were the hardened veterans of the 1790s political wars. Beleaguered and nearly bankrupt, many of them were more than ready to evacuate the scene of their first political labors and escape old enemies and creditors. Charles Holt and several others found somewhat greener pastures in other towns or states, and they were not alone. Editorial migrations became even more common after 1800.

There were also yet more refugee radicals available, some with long experience in political professionalism. The most significant late arrival was John Binns, a United Irishman who had also been a paid organizer ("delegate") for the London Corresponding Society. Binns survived numerous imprisonments and twice was nearly tried for high treason. "For an active politician," Binns remembered, the worst aspect of prison was his "total privation" of newspapers or any other information on public affairs, which "he had heretofore regarded as absolute necessaries of life." Released from prison, Binns left Great Britain in 1802 and went to join his friends and fellow radical exiles Thomas Cooper and Joseph Priestley in the remote village of Northumberland, Pennsylvania.

The appearance of a professional radical on the upper Susquehanna, a hitherto Federalist-dominated area, delivered an immediate political shock. A practiced speaker, Binns gave a Fourth of July oration not long after his arrival and had it printed in the local newspaper, the *Sunbury and Northumberland Gazette*. This was a largely commercial paper, but pressure from the local Federalists over Binns's address got him banned from the journal's pages. Outraged but also sensing an opportunity, Binns followed in the footsteps of many fellow refugees and issued proposals for a newspaper of his own, the *Republican Argus*. After a few months of publishing this journal, Binns had become one of the region's leading political figures. He and his newspaper helped convert the Northumberland area to Republicanism and set a local politician named Simon Snyder on the road to becoming one of the state's most popular governors.[46]

Though exact numbers are difficult to document, it seems likely that the most prolific source of candidates for the new editorial positions were apprentice and journeyman printers working in the established partisan newspaper offices, whose experiences made them almost political activists by training. During the intense politicking of the 1790s, one Boston *Independent Chronicle* apprentice remembered, the newspaper office became "a political school" in which young printers could not help but imbibe knowledge of political events, personnel, and methods. Thus educated, graduates of the *Aurora, Chronicle*, and other older Republican shops fanned out across the countryside to seek their fortunes by emulating their former employers.

Sometimes this was a matter of a master printer-politician extending his influence. For instance, when the Pittsburgh *Tree of Liberty* fell into the hands of a rival Republican faction, William Duane sent his employee (and fellow Irishman) Ephraim Pentland to start a competing Republican journal called the *Commonwealth*. In other cases, local leaders looking for an editor just naturally turned to an established journal they read and trusted for a likely candidate. When District of Maine Republicans needed an editor for their new paper, Boston Republican leader Benjamin Austin recommended Nathaniel Willis Jr., an *Independent Chronicle* journeyman who had also served his apprenticeship there, as "reliable for my politics and industry." Willis was soon proprietor of the Portland *Eastern Argus* and a major political force to boot.[47]

The possibilities were exciting enough for ambitious young journeyman that some sought out locations for new political journals themselves without being recruited or enticed. Eighteen-year-old Selleck Osborn, a journeyman in the New York *American Citizen* office, began sending out letters soon after the election of 1800. He eventually made contact with Henry Dering, the collector of the port at Sag Harbor, Long Island, where the only newspaper was three years deceased. Dering helped Osborn found the *Suffolk County Herald*. This journal lasted only a few months, but it led to a long string of Republican editorships that would take Osborn back to his native Connecticut, then to Boston, Philadelphia, Wilmington, and finally, back to New York again.[48]

These Republican journeymen were following some of the printing trade's traditional patterns. Successful printing offices had often spawned others as apprentices came of age and journeymen acquired the means to become masters of their own shops. A large number of the colonial-era newspapers were founded by Benjamin Franklin's former assistants. An even more common pattern was "tramping," the practice of journeyman printers' moving frequently between towns and printing offices in search of work, better wages, or simply a change of scene. This was an expected phase of a printer's early manhood that would ideally end in his acquiring a shop of his own. "An assertion of personal independence, a source of experience and worldly knowledge, and a rite of initiation," according to its most perceptive historian, tramping spread both technical knowledge of printing and its rich work culture across the continent.[49]

The printing trade traditionally offered the likelihood of modest social and economic mobility over a worker's lifetime, along with the self-respect and sense of identity that came with membership in a proud craft of demonstrated usefulness to the community. The rise of newspaper politics preserved some of the old patterns, while adding new opportunities and subtly modifying the trade as a whole.

Most fundamentally, some printers' opportunities for social mobility may have been preserved by the partisan press. As the nineteenth century wore on, the old system of progressing from apprentice to journeyman to master over the life cycle broke down. Fewer and fewer journeymen were able to become masters, and tramp printers turned into an underclass of permanent nomads. The pinch was felt first in the large cities and major towns, where publishers increasingly turned to industrial methods.[50]

Newspaper politics provided a way out of this trap for printers of sufficient ability. Newspaper-based parties required networks of newspapers scattered across the nation, and most of these four-page journals with circulations of 500 to 2,000 were best produced by traditional methods. Political needs inspired the creation of many more small newspapers than economics alone would have dictated and opened sources of credit and income for these small community journals that would never have been available otherwise. Precisely because the economics of partisan printing were so difficult, these new establishments were available to very young and marginal members of the trade. A fast track to master or some equivalent status was thus opened for many printers who otherwise might not have achieved that goal at all.

At the same time, partisan printing held out rewards that traditional printing never had. Partisan editors became public figures in ways that the old printers who cut and pasted from European newspapers and set the local lawyers' essays in type never had. As working politicians, they could achieve greater notoriety and a fuller, more constant sense of republican citizenship than a traditional craftsman could. Partisan editors had access to an arena for literary expression, one in which the standards were based more on political results than literary skill, academic learning, or intellectual sophistication. National readership awaited any half-educated boy who was willing to come out pens blazing. Moreover, even if their newspapers never became profitable, political involvements held out the possibility (though often only that, in this early period) of the income and honor of public office.

If political editing felt like a trap for professionals like Blake, Bentley, and Griswold, it opened broad new horizons for less fortunate young men. Budding political editors were full of idealism about the seriousness of their calling and its utility to the republic. In 1807 President Jefferson received a letter from John Norvell, a teenage printer who was working in a rural Kentucky town and planning to strike out on his own in the political newspaper business. Norvell addressed the "Venerable Republican" Jefferson for some last-minute help preparing for his new career, most notably "the proper method to be pursued in the acquisition of sound political knowledge." At the end of a series of specific questions, Norvell turned to the specific application he intended to make of his political knowledge. How, he asked, should a "a newspaper, to be most extensively beneficial . . . be conducted"? Norvell's own answer to this question seems to have revolved around political effectiveness. He went on to edit party newspapers in Lexington, Baltimore, and Philadelphia (where he founded the *Inquirer*), and eventually parlayed his work into a number of important offices, including one of Michigan's first two U.S. Senate seats.[51]

At some point in the years after Jefferson took office, a moment arrived when many prospective printers expected to enter politics and regarded that as a chief attraction of the trade. Those who came into the partisan newspaper business from the 1790s on were too young to remember the Revolution or to have any feeling for the impartial, commercial traditions of the colonial printers. They had grown up instead with incessant political warfare and simply expected that their newspapers and printing offices would be vehicles of party combat. For instance, when seventeen-year-old journeyman Thurlow Weed was working for the Federalist Herkimer *American,* he was already a sufficiently active and well-known Republican that the local Republicans (having no newspaper of their own) commissioned him to print their campaign handbills. Weed locked his employer out of the office to do the job, and for his trouble earned a five-dollar bonus from the Republicans.[52] When printers like Weed (future architect of three major national political parties) tramped from town to town, they carried not only the craft culture of printing, but also the new traditions of newspaper politics.

The utility of these new traditions in a trade where the cutomary avenues of social mobility were closing showed in the course of Weed's life just after Herkimer, when politics would quite literally become his exit from a crisis that was enveloping many fellow journeymen printers. Between 1816 and 1818, Weed drifted from shop to shop in Albany and New York City. The industrialization of printing was just beginning: rollers were introduced to replace the balls used to beat ink onto the type, allowing a boy apprentice to do much more cheaply a job that once required the strength and skill of an adult journeyman. At the same time, some printing offices were purchasing the new stereotype plates for their larger jobs, further reducing the need to employ journeymen. The impact on journeyman printers was immediate: some lost their jobs, some saw their wages cut, and many tried to fight back by organizing and sometimes striking.[53]

Weed's correspondence during this period is dominated by letters from brother printers who were struggling through the crisis, and whose sentiments he seems to have shared. While he was in New York in 1816, one of his former coworkers in Albany described the aftermath of an unsuccessful strike: one of their friends had fled to Boston, another had just been released from jail, another had just been sent to jail for debt, and still another had left printing to become a teamster hauling freight in wagons—not an upward career move. After Weed went back to Albany to become foreman of the *Register* there in 1817, his New York friend Samuel Moore reported losing his job in the *Columbian* newspaper office: a new owner, needing to cut expenses, had bought rollers and hired boys as compositors. Moore was trying to raise "a company of ten young fellows" to emigrate west, but died before he got the chance. In the meantime, the city's master and journeyman printers were at odds over stereotyping. The journeymen spread the word that three stereotype-using master printers were "RATS"—traitors to the trade—and tried to force in a higher and more firmly set scale of prices for stereotype work. Eventually, in early 1818, the leaders of the New York Typographical Society, an organization of journeyman printers thatWeed belonged to and on whose board of directors he had once sat, asked their Albany-based friend to help them get a corporate charter for the society approved by the state legislature.[54]

Weed succeeded in this mission, his first in a long career of such lobbying assignments, but not without meeting resistance that must have influenced his estimation of the prospects ahead for journeyman printers. The man who would come to be known as the dictator of New York state politics remembered "with what deference I then ventured into the presence of distinguished members of the legislature." The feeling that the young printer did not belong there was mutual: two members "sharply . . . rebuked" Weed, "quite shocked at the idea of incorporating journeyman printers." The New York Typographical Society charter only passed the legislature once an amendment was added barring the organization from engaging in any efforts to regulate the price of printers' labor. This effectively converted it from an incipient trade union to a mere benevolent society.[55]

Weed left the latter humiliation out of his autobiography, but his letters and actions suggest an immediate conclusion that politics rather than printing on its own would have to be his means of moving forward in the traditional printer's life cycle. At the *Register,* Weed learned to write copy, without a manuscript, as he stood at the case and composed type. Beginning with paragraphs of simple news, he soon graduated to short political essays and then longer articles. Having mastered this skill of opining while printing, and with journeymen fleeing depressed conditions and greedy employers in Albany, Weed was ready to leap when the chance came to purchase a newspaper office in tiny Norwich, New York, on credit from several local supporters of De Witt Clinton.[56]

Weed's Norwich *Republican Agriculturalist* was not a great success financially, but it changed Weed's life forever. From then on, his correspondents and contacts were no longer struggling journeymen but other editors and major political leaders. Governor Clinton himself was a subscriber and thought highly enough of the young printer-editor's work to have him appointed a commissioner of deeds. Offers to buy or work on other newspapers came in regularly, and by the time Weed established himself in the growing town of Rochester a few years later, he was both a rising politician and a leading member of his community.[57] In 1824, after he secured a legislative charter for a bank in Rochester, the grateful town sent him back to Albany as a member of the legislature he had once been reprimanded for approaching. (Weed later decided that he could wield even more power by staying out of office.)[58]

Weed was an unusually successful printer-editor, but his emphasis on politics was not unusual at all. The generally political orientation of print-

ers after 1800 can be seen in the fact that at least fifty-four of the Republican editors named on Isaiah Thomas's list of American newspapers published in 1810 held political offices at some time during their careers
(though in many cases well after 1810). More than 80 percent of these editor-officeholders began their working lives as apprentice printers. The
offices they held were mostly of the local or low-level appointive variety—
town council slots, county offices, postmasterships, state legislative seats—
but these often carried great influence. Some printers who were particularly adept at exploiting their position in the system even managed to be
elected to the national Congress, which thus far only Matthew Lyon had
done. Rather inadvertently, newspaper politics had created a significant
opening for the democratization of active political life.[59]

As the case of labor-leader-turned-bank-lobbyist Thurlow Weed suggests, however, these serious inroads by artisans into the ranks of the political elite were hardly an unmitigated triumph for printers or artisans
generally. The process of making the leap from mechanic to politician sent
ambitious partisan printers on a trajectory that took their values and
lifestyles outside the culture of the trade. While some printer-politicians
continued, throughout their lives, to identify themselves as artisans and to
lack much in the way of gentility and sophistication, many tried to shed
their working-class heritage after taking up the editorial pen. They
worked to be accepted as gentlemen, and it was quite common for printer-editors to become lawyers later to further enhance their status. A few
became wealthy from their political connections and printing contracts,
and most others fully embraced the individualistic, entrepreneurial values
of other nineteenth-century businessmen.

However, many factors prevented political editors from getting too
firm a hold on middle-class prosperity and complacency. Their rise to
public stature was stiffly resisted, and as often-embattled public figures,
their less-than-elite, and sometimes less-than-respectable, backgrounds
were constantly exposed by enemies. Then too, the generally unprofitable
nature of the political publishing business, and the susceptibility of what
profits there were to momentary political shifts, left editors vulnerable to
sudden reversals of fortune. Master status, property ownership, and public
stature were easily gained through newspaper politics, but just as easily
lost. Despite all that, there seems to have been no shortage of young
printers willing to try their hands at the trade.[60]

10

The Federalists Strike Back

❧

For *several reasons,* this work emphasizes Republicans over Federalists as the exemplars of newspaper politics. Administration editor John Fenno played a role in the genesis of the phenomenon, but it was opposition statesmen and opposition printers who first conjoined newspapers and party politics. It was the Republican newspaper network that proved itself by unseating John Adams, inspiring a flurry of pattern-setting imitation and expansion. Finally, it was Republican editors and newspapers that formed the background for the mid-nineteenth-century heyday of newspaper politics. The Federalist party had virtually ceased to exist by the 1820s, so it was the Republican party from which both of the Jacksonian-era parties developed.

Nevertheless, it seems important to acknowledge that newspaper politics was not an exclusively Republican phenomenon. A brief discussion of Federalist newspaper politics will help illuminate the internal differences between the two parties and add another dimension to the traditional explanation for the Federalists' demise as an opposition party. It also forms a logical starting point for a major theme of the next few chapters, the bipartisan but largely failed efforts to gentrify the political press by reclaiming it from printers.

RENOVATING THE FEDERALIST PRESS

After trying to destroy it during their "reign of terror," Federalist leaders embraced newspaper politics in the aftermath of their defeat. They well understood that Republican newspapers had been a crucial factor in the Federalists having lost both the presidency and their congressional majority. Having wrung their hands so often over the dangerous sway that newspapers held over the republic and imputed to them the most frightfully destructive capacities, the Federalists had worked themselves up to the point of outdoing the Republicans in their estimate of this "ready and powerful instrument." According to one Federalist editor, the Republican journals had wrought "A general corruption of manners—decay of morality—vitiation of taste—a disrelish of literature— . . . bankruptcy in virtue, and *national* degradation!"[1]

The press even became a kind of excuse, allowing Federalists to believe that it was not their personnel or ideology that had been rejected. Regarding the influence of newspapers as a testament to the citizenry's ignorance and weak-mindedness, they believed the press might be used to carry people as easily one way as another. Damning the press and plotting to exploit it were almost two sides of the same coin. Fisher Ames of Massachusetts took a back seat to no one in lurid fears of Republican journalism. Because "the majority of citizens form their ideas of men and measures almost solely from the light that reaches them through the magic-lantern of the press," Ames wrote in "The Dangers of American Liberty," it could become the "base and venal instrument of the very men it ought to gibbet to universal abhorrence." So Jefferson, Duane, and company had done: "While they were climbing to power it aided their ascent; and now that they have reached it, does it not conceal or justify their abominations?" In a different mood, however, the same basic analysis drove Ames to be a leader in building up the Federalist press: "As the newspapers greatly influence public opinion, and that controls everything else," he wrote to an ally in 1801, "it is not only important but absolutely essential, that these should be used with more effect than ever."[2]

By the admission of Federalist leaders, the Federalist press had been no match for the opposition during the 1790s, despite its larger numbers. Several reasons were suggested for this deficiency. With the notable exception of Alexander Hamilton, Federalist leaders had taken printers' support as their due, doing relatively little to sustain, improve, or expand their partisan press. Virginia Federalist John Nicholas argued that the Republicans had been successful only because of

> their incessant industry & application to these objects, & our supineness and want of exertion. One of their main plans has ever been, to support with their best *energies,* both Mentally and pecuniarily, their best printers; & with the utmost industry, care & activity, to disseminate their papers and pamphlets: While the Federalists leave their printers to scuffle on the support of their *subscribers* . . . a very *flimsy & uncertain daily sustenance,* and to scribble out their own way to conquest!

Nicholas exaggerated the extent of Republican leaders' support and shed unnecessary tears for the majority of Federalist printers, whose papers were generally profitable enterprises well sustained by business advertisers. Yet clearly the Federalist press needed help, if only in the form of prodding to be more political and advice on how to do it.

The majority of printers who had supported the Federalists did so out of social traditionalism and conservatism of temperament. They rather agreed with the Federalist gentry that artisans were to be employed and not heard, and in any case they felt content to earn their livings while leaving the direction of community affairs to others. With a few exceptions, Federalist printers were as suspicious of electioneering as their leaders were; they were loathe to become wholly partisan or to get deeply involved in election campaigns. Usually, their political exertions were sporadic, inconsistent, and overly decorous.

A particularly glaring fault, explained Nicholas, was the Federalist newspapers' failure to take advantage of postal policies and act as a network, as the Republicans did: "They seldom republish from each other; while on the other hand, their antagonists never get hold of any thing, however trivial in reality, but they make it ring thro' *all their papers* from one end of the Continent to the other." When Federalist printers did become partisan, they tended to take John Fenno's route of socially belittling the opposition and histrionically denouncing its leaders as atheists, libertines, anarchists, and agents of France. Their basic message had been that opposition itself should cease, for only the evil-minded and poorly bred would cavil at the policies of the sainted George Washington and his disciples.[3]

A good example of the political limitations of the Federalist press before 1800 can be found in the Keene *New Hampshire Sentinel,* established in early 1799 just as hyperpolitical Republican journals were spreading across the country. In sharp contrast to its Republican contemporaries, the *Sentinel* approached the building "political tempest" gingerly, restricting the amount of political material and limiting what there was to allusive, literary matter unlikely to have much political impact, such as a strained "Dialogue between GALLATIN and RANA the frog."

While printer John Prentiss seemed to recognize some need to campaign at election time, his newspaper's efforts in that line were almost comically reticent: two short notices inserted by readers for the fall 1799 elections, one "Electioneering" column in one issue during the spring of 1800, and only reports of the voting in fall of 1800. The tone of this material is captured by the hard-hitting remarks of one of the 1799 notices: "In many respectable circles, it is thought . . . that in doing the most good in Congress, no one would better fill the vacancy than the Hon. DANIEL NEWCOMB, Esq." In between elections, the *Sentinel* occasionally mixed its political message by printing pro-Republican items, including some harsh criticism of William Cobbett and an account of William Duane's beating that was sympathetic to the editor.[4]

As with many Federalist newspapers, the *Sentinel*'s relative nonpartisanship was driven at least partly by Federalist philosophy, which saw political agitation itself (while wise and good men ruled) as a primary cause of the nation's distress. Its first issue featured a long congressional defense of the Alien and Sedition Acts (exempt from qualms about campaigning because it was an official document) on the front page, and, on the back page, a poem, "Extracts from a Town Meeting," that portrayed the outbreak of partisan debate in New England's most cherished political institution as literally the work of Satan, that "great Jacobin of yore" who was thrown out of heaven for "Sedition." Speaking volumes about New England Federalist distrust of popular, competitive politics, the poem pictured a Republican politician bringing a raucous crowd into the meeting, "To banish order, stir up evil, / And serve their lord and master Devil."[5]

This kind of crabbed, conflicted political journalism had proven ineffective, and, what was worse, many of its basic elements became obsolescent after 1800. It was manifestly self-defeating for Federalists to argue the illegitimacy of opposition politics when they were themselves in opposition, and with their predictions of anarchy, rapine, and pillage under Republican rule failing to materialize, election campaigns, like them or not, began to seem the only safe route back to national power. Some Federalists became so disaffected as to venture down more dangerous avenues, such as plotting to make Aaron Burr president or seceding from the union, but the wisest of the self-styled wise and good gradually and grudgingly turned their attention to beating the Republicans with their own methods. That meant conducting themselves more like a party, organizing for elections in a way they never had before, and working to match Duane and the Republican newspaper network.[6]

The vast majority of newspapers supported the government when the Sedition Act was passed, but only a handful of these were politically active and even fewer were run by serious newspaper politicians in the manner of William Duane. Probably the closest to this model that the Federalist press came was Benjamin Russell and his Boston *Columbian Centinel,* which had been vituperating against the Boston elite's enemies since the 1780s and which came to serve as the chief article supplier for many other New England newspapers. By the 1790s Russell himself had become an energetic if junior member of Boston Federalist political councils and an important street-level leader. John Prentiss, an apprentice for the Republican *Chronicle* who followed Russell's Federalist line in his own editorial career, remembered often seeing "Maj. Russell . . . in State Street, surrounded by his political friends," where he "administered political party law!" Unlike most Federalist printers, Russell pursued a political career in his own right, becoming a prominent local officeholder beginning in 1805. Besides positions on the Boston School Committee, Board of Health, and as a city alderman, he represented Boston in the state legislature from 1805 to 1835 continuously, capping his career with a term on the Executive Council.

However, Russell rarely strayed from his role as a loyal auxiliary, and he was certainly no peer, competitor, or even kingmaker to the Adamses, Quincys, Otises, and such who were the leading lights of Massachusetts Federalism. A stonemason's son and a semieducated artisan printer himself, Russell "never forgot that he was a mechanic," according to his friend Joseph T. Buckingham, and always punctiliously observed all social distinctions and honorary titles.[7]

The only other notable and actively partisan early Federalist journals were the *Centinel*'s spin-off, the *Gazette of the United States;* the Hartford *Connecticut Courant,* organ of the Standing Order; and perhaps the Baltimore *Federal Gazette.* Others grew more partisan when a Republican printer set up shop in their town, as in the case of John Scull's *Pittsburgh Gazette.* In the hinterlands and in the South, there were a great many cautious, conservative printers, but almost no partisan Federalist sheets.

The first glimmerings of a change came appropriately enough in July 1798, with the appearance of the Trenton *Federalist,* the first partisan newspaper to take that appellation. Trenton hardly opened the floodgates, however. Of forty-two Federalist-leaning newspapers founded in 1798 and 1799, at least seventeen must be classified as apolitical, moderate, or independent, including the previously discussed *New Hampshire Sentinel.* Salted here and there were more avowedly partisan journals such as the Richmond *Virginia Federalist* (May 1799), the Charleston *Federal Carolina Gazette* (January 1800), and the *Washington Federalist* (September 1800).[8]

In their more prolix and self-consciously dignified fashion, some of these new Federalist papers echoed their newly founded Republican contemporaries in avowing their partisanship, at least backhandedly. "At a time when . . . the enemies of the General Government are laboring . . . to rob it of public confidence and affection," announced the *Washington Federalist,* "we should hold a promise of absolute indifference between parties . . . to be merely an ill-timed sacrifice of our political sentiments—a cold apathy to the interests of our country—and a base renunciation of editorial independence."[9]

It was after 1800 that more serious efforts began. (See map 5.) The new opposition party gained a flagship of sorts in the fall of 1801, when Alexander Hamilton raised thousands of dollars and organized the founding of the New York *Evening Post.* Hamilton hoped the paper would help recoup the political standing he had lost by backstabbing John Adams in 1800. That same year, the westward migration from New England produced two well-regarded local Federalist partisans. The sometime printer and clergyman Harry Croswell, originally from West Hartford, Connecticut, moved to Hudson and set up the *Balance,* which soon would spar with Charles Holt's *Bee.* Meanwhile, the printer Asher Miner of Norwich, Connecticut (soon joined by his more talented brother and fellow printer Charles) chose political journalism over pioneer farming and started the *Luzerne County Federalist* at Wilkes-Barre, Pennsylvania. Croswell's *Balance* would later become the state capital Federalist paper, while Charles Miner would achieve national recognition as an editor and writer, most notably for coining the phrase "he has an ax to grind" in a satire on Republican officeseekers.[10]

Such newspaper propagation by independent entrepreneurship would always be rarer among the Federalists than the Republicans. Heroic top-down efforts like Hamilton's were usually required. With many leaders in Federalism's New England heartland preoccupied with secessionist conspiracies, the Federalist press grew rather slowly during most of Jefferson's two presidential terms. As shown in appendix 1, chart 5, the Federalists matched the Republicans from 1801 to 1803, when the Republican effort had slowed down, but fell far behind for most of the rest of Jefferson's presidency, as new Republican papers popped up all over New England and the West. (See map 4, page 212) Still, when new Federalist journals did appear they were almost always decidedly partisan, or gradually became so (as the aforementioned *New Hampshire Sentinel* did by 1802). In

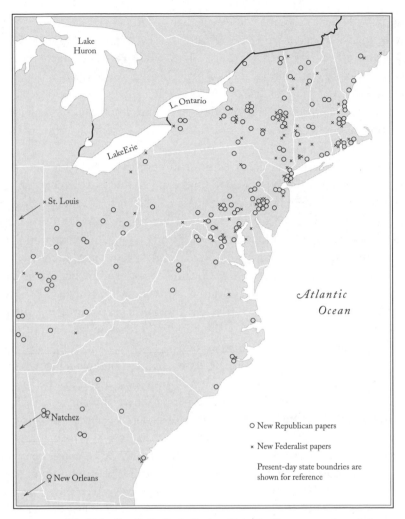

MAP 5. The Federalists Strike Back: Partisan Federalist Newspapers, 1800–1806.

addition, many an old, established *Gazette*—the colonial-vintage title that staid, commercial, Federalist-leaning monopoly newspapers usually pre-ferred—was renovated in this period. Newspaper politics was taking hold among its former victims, especially as a younger, less despondent genera-tion of Federalist gentlemen came to the fore.[11]

The most powerful burst of Federalist newspaper energy came in the wake of Jefferson's embargo in 1807. With their first chance to make serious inroads since 1800, the younger Federalists took over and tried hard to make their party competitive, especially in New England. Harrison Gray Otis and others had been building a tight-wired Federalist party organization to carry state and local elections. This did not mean they had reconciled themselves to democracy or continuing party competition: the organization was strictly secret and designed more to efficiently implement the Boston elite's decisions rather than move the Federalists into any truly democratic style of politics.

Following the conventional elite assumption that the common voter was hopelessly localistic in outlook (and expecting to out-demagogue the Republicans), Federalist speakers and writers focused on appealing to Yankee sectional prejudices in their criticisms of Jefferson, emphasizing the distasteful aspects of southern culture and casting administration policies as indifferent or hostile to New England's economic interests. The embargo was a jackpot in this regard, and the younger Federalists made a strong push to get their message out. A network of Washington Benevolent Societies was created to soften the Federalists' elitist image by giving money to the poor and allowing the middling classes to bask in the glow of banqueting with the local aristocrats.[12]

At the same time, a new wave of extremely partisan Federalist newspapers appeared, surpassing in number and bitterness anything the friends of order had done before. This was apparently part of a concerted effort. In Massachusetts, Otis drew up a survey of Federalist presses in New England, noting how politically effective they were, how well they were subsidized by Federalist leaders, and where further subsidies and literary assistance were needed. The purpose of the subsidies was not only to keep Federalist newspapers afloat, but also to enable free or very low-cost distribution to voters before elections, something the Federalists believed the Republicans had done regularly. As a result of Otis's plan and similar efforts in other areas, more than forty new Federalist journals were created during 1808 and 1809 alone, igniting a journalistic arms race with the Republicans. (See map 5 and appendix 1, charts 3 and 5.) Among these journals were the disingenuously titled *Impartial Observer*, founded by Judge William Cooper at Cooperstown, New York, to smite his local enemies (he was shortly forced to rename it the *Cooperstown Federalist*); and the soon-to-be-infamous Baltimore *Federal Republican*, created by a coterie of wealthy young Federalists.[13]

TALENTS, VIRTUE, AND WEALTH: REAL AND
IMAGINED FEDERALIST ADVANTAGES IN
THE JOURNALISTIC ARMS RACE

One distinct advantage the Federalists enjoyed in this race was money. As we have seen, Federalist newspapers were sounder financially than their Republican counterparts, because they were more commercially oriented and benefited from having a major political constituency (merchants) that bought advertising and needed newspaper subscriptions for year-round, other-than-political purposes. The advantages became potentially greater in times of political crisis when large numbers of new papers were needed. Republican gentlemen tended to be upwardly mobile lawyers or cash-poor planters, and they often disappointed the legions of printers who sought or were offered their aid. As the party of the nation's wealthiest and most liquid citizens, the Federalists were better able to supplement their verbal encouragement of printers with the more material kind. Jefferson had written letters urging Republican leaders to contribute money to newspapers, but Harrison Gray Otis was able to draw up a list with specific figures. Concerned that the *Washington Federalist* was faltering for lack of operating funds, Benjamin Russell advised the journal's editor that all he need do was bring up the subject with Massachusetts congressman Josiah Quincy.[14]

Financial advantages translated into technical advantages, and Federalist newspapers generally looked better, in terms of paper quality and type clarity, than Republican journals. Indeed, Federalist leaders believed that Federalist readers, presumed to be more discerning than the earthy Republican variety, would not subscribe to or follow the political guidance of a newspaper that did not "look respectable." Thus even Federalist start-up newspapers came out in style, sometimes capitalized in the tens of thousands of dollars, while Republican journals were more likely to begin publishing on a used or borrowed press with worn-out type.[15]

The New York *Evening Post* was the ultimate example. Raising more than $10,000 in a few weeks, Hamilton was able to pay his chosen editor, the attorney William Coleman, a $2,000 salary and set him up with a printer, a brick building, four fonts of brand-new type, and a large supply of high-grade white paper. From the outset, the *Post* carried fourteen or fifteen (out of twenty) columns of Federalist merchant advertising in every issue. (To put Coleman's salary in perspective, compare it to one of the few other editorial salary figures that appears in the record: the editor of the Republican Worcester *National Aegis* made only $150 per annum, thirteen years after Coleman was hired.) Coleman made much of his paper's dignified appearance, and even a Republican writer remarked that it was "beyond all comparison, the most elegant piece of workmanship . . . seen either in Europe or America."[16]

Federalist wealth also allowed the development of one of the unique features of the Federalist press, the use of short-term satirical newspapers devoted exclusively to grinding down Republican reputations. Usually published without advertising, they were presumably bankrolled by Federalist leaders and distributed free or at very low cost. Harry Croswell's *Wasp* seems to have been the first, and its fame spawned at least seven imitators up through 1811, most with similarly self-explanatory titles: a *Porcupine* in Baltimore, a *Scorpion* in Worcester, a *Switch* in Cooperstown, and a *Scourge* at various times in Boston, Providence, and Baltimore. If the giant woodcut of a vengeful insect on Croswell's banner did not announce his publication's intentions clearly enough, his motto, "To lash the Rascals naked through the world," certainly did.[17]

An advantage that the Federalists *felt* they had over the Republicans was talent. Firmly believing in their own social, intellectual, and moral superiority, many Federalists were convinced that if only their forces could be properly marshaled, they could easily overwhelm the Republicans with their own weapons. According to John Nicholas, with "the talents, the virtue, the wealth" of the country lay "expressly against" Jefferson and his followers. There was no reason that such "*whimsical* and *theoretical* visionaries" should be suffered to "sway the public opinion & hold the rod of popular despotism" when so many writers and speakers of "better qualifications and more useful powers" could be arrayed against them.

Thus Federalists did not seek to just copy the Republican press; they wanted to improve upon it. Fisher Ames complained that the recent Republican campaign had made "uneducated printers, shop-boys, and raw school-masters . . . the chief instructors in politics." New Federalist political journals ought to try to remedy this and make newspapers the speaking trumpets of the natural aristocracy once more: "Let the interests of the country be explained and asserted by the able men, who have had concern in the transaction of affairs, who understand those interests, and who will, and ever will, when they try, produce a deep national impression." Moreover, the new Federalist editors would not lower themselves to the level of

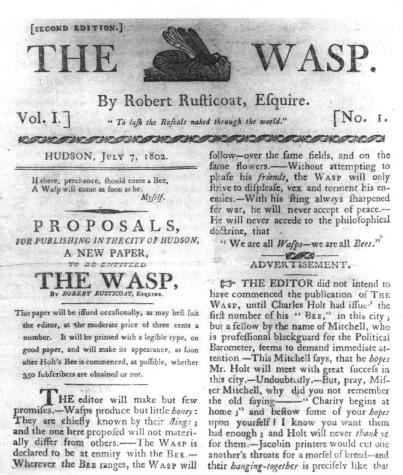

[SECOND EDITION.]

THE WASP.

By Robert Rusticoat, Efquire.

Vol. I.]   " To lafh the Rafcals naked through the world."   [No. 1.

HUDSON, JULY 7, 1802.

If there, perchance, fhould come a Bee,
A Wafp will come as foon as he.
Myfelf.

PROPOSALS,

FOR PUBLISHING IN THE CITY OF HUDSON,

A NEW PAPER,

TO BE ENTITLED

THE WASP,

By *ROBERT RUSTICOAT,* Esquire.

This paper will be iffued occafionally, as may beft fuit the editor, at the moderate price of three cents a number. It will be printed with a legible type, on good paper, and will make its appearance, as foon after Holt's Bee is commenced, as poffible, whether 350 fubfcribers are obtained or not.

THE editor will make but few promifes.—Wafps produce but little *honey*: They are chiefly known by their *ftings*; and the one here propofed will not materially differ from others.——The WASP is declared to be at enmity with the BEE.— Wherever the BEE ranges, the WASP will follow—over the fame fields, and on the fame flowers.——Without attempting to pleafe his *friends*, the WASP will only ftrive to difpleafe, vex and torment his enemies.—With his fting always fharpened for war, he will never accept of peace.— He will never accede to the philofophical doctrine, that

"We are all *Wafps*—we are all *Bees.*"

ADVERTISEMENT.

☞ THE EDITOR did not intend to have commenced the publication of THE WASP, until Charles Holt had iffued the firft number of his " BEE," in this city; but a fellow by the name of Mitchell, who is profeffional blackguard for the Political Barometer, feems to demand immediate attention.—This Mitchell fays, that he *hopes* Mr. Holt will meet with great fuccefs in this city.—Undoubtedly.—But, pray, Mifter Mitchell, why did you not remember the old faying——" Charity begins at home;" and beftow fome of your *hopes* upon yourfelf! I know you want them bad enough; and Holt will never *thank ye* for them.—Jacobin printers would cut one another's throats for a morfel of bread—and their *hanging-together* is precifely like that

FIGURE 7. Hudson, N.Y., *Wasp*, front page, 7 July 1802. *(Courtesy of American Antiquarian Society)*

---

the Jacobin printers but would conduct their operations in a more refined manner. The Boston paper Ames was planning would be "fastidiously polite and well-bred. It should whip Jacobins as a gentleman would a chimney sweeper, at arm's length, and keeping aloof from his soot."

The Federalist indictment of political newspapers run by printers and their ilk included many of their own journals as well as the Republican ones. For too long "newspapers have been left to the lazy or the ill-informed," Ames thought, but they were "an engine that wit and good sense would make powerful." The wealth of the country might be in danger from the Republicans' "wild destroying rage," but if its "defense was committed to the wit, learning and talent of a few, then it will be safer than armies could make it."[18]

Thus when Ames, Hamilton, and other Federalist gentlemen set about improving or establishing newspapers, they took pains to place them under the management of men of education, good breeding, and demonstrated facility in the field of polite letters. These new editors were rarely printers by training. They often remained officially anonymous and were typically charged only with overseeing the paper's editorial content, the financial and mechanical aspects of the concern being left with a practical printer or business manager.

In Boston, Fisher Ames and his friends organized some additional financial support for the *Massachusetts Mercury,* a commercial paper published by the printers Alexander Young and John Minns. (Most notably, they bought a prepaid subscription for every clergyman in New England.) While Federalist-leaning like all prudent Boston tradesmen, Young and Minns had been relatively impartial in the past, even allowing William Bentley space to contest the anti-Jeffersonian, anti-Masonic conspiracy theories of the Rev. Jedidiah Morse. Fortified with Federalist money, the printers increased the journal's size, upgraded its paper, added *New England Palladium* to the title, and, most important of all, hired the New Haven lawyer and Yale graduate Warren Dutton, "a gentleman of fine talents, and a scholar of high reputation," to take over the editorial duties.[19]

Alexander Hamilton's hand-picked editor William Coleman also fit Ames's specifications. Born in Massachusetts, Coleman came from humble origins but rose in the world (like Hamilton himself) through upper-class patronage and came to identify heavily with his benefactors. "Discovered" as a child by an unidentified Boston gentleman and sent to Andover Academy, he afterwards practiced law in Greenfield, Massachusetts, enjoying some success in politics as well as law. A frequent political writer in the *Greenfield Gazette,* Coleman represented the town in the state legislature and was building a mansion when the collapse of the Yazoo land speculation suddenly bankrupted him. He moved to New York to begin life anew and attracted the attention of Hamilton, who had him appointed to a court clerkship. When the plan to create the *Evening Post* was hatched, Coleman's newspaper experience, legal credentials, and dependence on Hamilton made him a logical choice to edit the paper.[20]

Other Federalist leaders found other William Colemans. Federalists in and around the District of Columbia engaged local printer William A.

Rind (son of the man Thomas Jefferson had recruited to print his "free" *Virginia Gazette* before the Revolution) to publish the *Washington Federalist*, edited by a string of young gentlemen, including Elias Boudinot Caldwell, the Princeton-educated clerk of the Supreme Court, and Charles Prentiss, a highly regarded Harvard graduate, who bypassed the law to pursue his dream of working as a professional writer. In Philadelphia, John Ward Fenno (the original editor's son) was succeeded at the helm of the *Gazette of the United States* by Enos Bronson, a young attorney and Yale graduate. Another Philadelphia Federalist paper was edited by the revolutionary veteran and lawyer William Jackson, secretary of the 1787 Constitutional Convention, former close aide to George Washington, and son-in-law of Thomas Willing, one of the city's wealthiest merchants.[21]

ALEXANDER CONTEE HANSON VERSUS THE "RULES OF ARITHMETICK"

The most extreme Federalist newspaper of all, the Baltimore *Federal Republican* (founded 1808), also had the most aristocratic of the Federalist editors. This was the planter and attorney Alexander Contee Hanson Jr., a graduate of St. John's College and scion of one the state's most influential old families. Hanson's grandfather and father before him had been important political leaders and serial officeholders. The former's career peaked with his service as the first president of Congress under the Articles of Confederation, while the latter enjoyed a sixteen-year run as chancellor of Maryland. From this illustrious lineage (and the estates that went with them), young Hanson the editor inherited a strong sense of entitlement to public leadership and a total unwillingness to suffer political errors in silence. These traits gave Hanson's journalism, speeches, and letters an ideological hauteur and aggressiveness that some historians have found almost pathological.[22]

Under Hanson's direction, the *Federal Republican* was an extreme Federalist journal on almost every count. On the one hand, its distaste for democracy and enthusiasm for the British cause in the Napoleonic Wars rivaled anything found in Hartford or Boston. "THE RABBLE," one early item was headed, more or less summarizing Hanson's feelings toward the mass of voters who were providing Republican majorities in Maryland, and especially in Baltimore. These rabble were not only stupid but vicious and violent, and granting them political influence would inevitably lead to chaos and mass murder. Hanson sometimes argued that

the people of Maryland were merely being misled by Republican demagogues, but in the same breath deplored the "tame and submissive spirit"
they showed for following such leaders and thus coupling themselves with
the "scum of society."

While other Federalists were learning to tone down their antidemocratic rhetoric, Hanson wrote as though guillotines were operating in the
streets of Baltimore. An item entitled "Democracy delights in blood"
managed to get, in less than one-third of a column, from condemning a
Republican reference to Timothy Pickering, John Marshall, and Aaron
Burr as traitors to warning that the "germ of French democracy, more ferocious than the tyger, more desolating than the pestilence" was abroad in
the country. "Are we in Turkey, the slaves of a tyrant . . . do we live under
Robespierre?"[23]

Hanson recognized few limits on his partisan rhetoric or behavior. Jefferson and Madison were depicted as despotic, pusillanimous, and incompetent all at once, most infamously with the remark that in the areas of
"tyranny and oppression," George III had nearly been matched by "Jefferson and his political pimp . . . whiffling Jemmy."[24] Though several years
after the fact, Hanson's retrospective attacks on the cowardice of the
American officers involved in the *Chesapeake* affair were so harsh that one
of them, Capt. Charles Gordon, challenged the editor to a duel. As a
plantation-owning southern gentleman, Hanson was better trained for
this kind of thing than most editors; "a crack shot," he wounded Gordon
in the abdomen and left him crippled.[25]

Even more troubling was Hanson's advocacy for the British, which at
times involved not just defending the once-and-future enemy government, but turning the *Federal Republican* into a direct conduit for British
diplomatic propaganda. For instance, when the Madison administration
asked for the recall of British minister Francis James Jackson in the wake
of the "Erskine letter" fiasco, Hanson published a long, detailed essay series defending Jackson, essays which were written by Jackson or based on
documents he supplied. (The editor carried on an extensive correspondence with the British minister under an assumed name.) Then Hanson
arranged to have the essays published in pamphlet form, apparently at
British government expense! In the context of this direct collusion, it is
not surprising that when it came to United States efforts to punish the
British through trade sanctions or raise troops in preparation for war with
them, Hanson went beyond merely opposing the policies and urged the

people of Maryland to ignore or disobey the government's requests and orders.[26]

The *Federal Republican* bristled with prejudices of a more personal sort as well, against immigrants, Republicans, merchants, the working people of Baltimore, indeed virtually everyone who was not a rural landowning Federalist like Hanson himself. When an immigrant Republican editor offered a relatively innocuous plan "to unite the democratick party from Maine to Mississippi," the *Federal Republican* responded with a startling sneer that used special symbols and extra-large type for emphasis:

☞*Here is our plan.*

Let every officious foreigner, who presumes to interfere in the great concerns of the country, who dares to dictate to our national representatives . . . who has the audacity to slander native virtue and patriotism, be branded with scorn and sent back to the country, which first cast him out.[27]

Republican candidates and editors were lampooned for foreign accents, bad grammar, and poor educations. "This new *made* politician rose to 'spake of the Ambargo,'" began one account of a speech by congressional candidate Alexander McKim. It went on to heap scorn on the candidate's mercantile background ("his great commercial acquirements") and the "bullies and babblers" from the city who came out to see him speak.[28]

Conversely, while never able to suppress his prejudices or limit his forays into disloyal opposition, Hanson was a defender of party politics who genuinely believed that Federalists could win back power through the electoral process. The *Federal Republican* argued that too many Federalist gentlemen "injure our cause with their timidity and want of zeal," based on a "false calculation of strength in the democratick party." By failing to act as zealous partisans, these Federalists had "contributed more to fasten democracy upon us than either the influence, exertion, or numbers of our opponents."[29]

Working to reenergize the Federalist party, Hanson was heavily involved in organizing electioneering committees and the Washington Benevolent Societies that younger Federalists had devised to counter Republican fraternities, such as the Tammany Societies.[30] More important for present purposes, he tried hard to make his newspaper a politically potent one. Somewhat obsessed with William Duane, "the source of all the polluted streams of democracy with which this country is poisoned," he morbidly admired the *Aurora* editor's influence and techniques, once remarking of a rival editor trained by Duane that with such a political education "not even Moloch himself was better qualified for . . . mighty revolutionary purposes." Hanson wanted the *Federal Republican* to match or surpass for the Federalist cause what the *Aurora* had been able to do for democracy.[31]

With that inspiration, the *Federal Republican* was often a very effective and resourceful partisan newspaper. Hanson and coeditor Jacob Wagner frequently used headlines and titles ("How to Carry an Election by Storm"), and created several short comparative items that tried to define party differences in a succinct, slogan-like fashion. For instance, one item summarized Federalist versus Republican foreign policies when faced with a European war, namely Adams's military buildup versus Jefferson's trade embargo: "FEDERAL DOCTRINE. 'Millions for defence, not a cent for tribute!' . . . DEMOCRATICK DOCTRINE. 'Millions for tribute, not a cent for defence.'" (An earlier version had quoted secretary of state James Madison under the "Democratic" head: "France wants money, we must give it to her.")

The *Federal Republican* also closely linked its political material with Federalist candidates and election campaigns. Hanson and Wagner printed Federalist election slates under headings designed to put the Federalist cause in the best light, such as ANTI-FRENCH TICKET and ANTI-EMBARGO TICKET. They addressed various essays to the common voter, focusing on the "honest yeomen" of Baltimore county rather than the city Republicans. At least one campaign article, signed "AN ENEMY TO POLL TAXES," tried to outdo the Republicans in terms of sympathy for ordinary voters, decrying taxes and militia laws that required the poor to pay the same amount of money as the rich. Giving extensive coverage to live campaign events held in the area, they upheld local Federalist candidates and belittled their opponents.[32]

This side of Hanson revealed him as a product of Maryland's uniquely sophisticated political culture, which combined the Chesapeake tradition of barbecues and stump-speaking in the rural areas with Pennsylvania-style partisanship emanating from Baltimore. Building on these traditions, and fueled by great economic diversity and deep political divisions, Maryland became one of the earliest states to display many features of nineteenth-century mass party politics, including extensive public campaigning (such as issue-oriented debates between candidates) and stable partisan voting. Thus it was no accident that Maryland produced one of the first Republican newspapers to declare itself a party organ from its birth (the Baltimore *American*) and one of the most uncompromisingly and self-consciously partisan Federalist journals in the *Federal Republican*.[33]

Hanson's extremism and erratic behavior have led many historians of the Federalists to treat him as a marginal or unusual figure. Yet there was probably no Federalist politician who more clearly embodied the contradictions of the Federalist political project after 1800, which was to conduct vigorous popular political campaigns in support of ideals and men sincerely opposed to, or extremely doubtful about, the democratic principles on which popular campaigns were based.[34]

For many Federalist leaders, even so basic a democratic proposition as heeding the wishes of the majority of citizens was deeply troubling. To bow to mere numbers, in Hanson's view, was deeply wounding to the high feelings of any gentleman who was fit to make or execute the laws. "A thousand puny politicians in this country" based their "political calculations . . . solely upon the rules of arithmetick," not understanding that "the unconquerable mind, the determined spirit, and the heart warmed with the love of honor" were far more powerful than mere numbers or physical force. This thinking authorized Hanson's all-out rhetoric and tactics, but while it may have made a satisfying personal psychodrama for him, it ranged from ineffective to dangerous as a political strategy, looking as it did for enemies and opponents to suddenly realize their errors and bow before superior honor and virtue.[35]

Of course, this is not what happened in Baltimore. The *Federal Republican* became the nation's most virulent detractor of Jefferson and Madison's anti-British foreign policy and the resulting War of 1812, despite being published in the nation's most exposed, anti-British, and pro-war city. The Republican administrations were supported by a well-organized and increasingly politicized artisan community that did not appreciate Hanson's assertions that they were cowards, dupes, and thugs for making the political choices they had. The mechanics' local political hero was merchant-politician Gen. Samuel Smith, who had long crusaded against any form of submission to the British and helped forge a strong link in his followers' minds between American independence from Great Britain and their own aspirations for independence and equal rights. Much of the population of Baltimore came to loathe Hanson's newspaper, not least because it was published insolently in their midst.[36]

Thus the extremist *Federal Republican* eventually called forth the most extreme violence ever visited on a partisan newspaper office. Just after war was finally declared in June 1812, Hanson published his editorial response under the title "Thou hast done a deed whereat valour will weep." Beginning with some pertinent remarks about the nation's unpreparedness for war, he then sailed off into the ether, charging the declaration was opposed by the "vast majority of the nation," that the motivations for it bore "marks of undisguised foreign influence," and that the real aims of the war were to offer a pretext for repressing the administration's enemies and to place the United States in the power of Napoleon Bonaparte.

Hanson committed the *Federal Republican* to an aggressive campaign of what the Federalists had once defined as sedition: "We mean to use every constitutional argument and every legal means to render as odious and suspicious to the American people . . . the patrons and contrivers of this highly impolitic and destructive war." But Hanson could not stop himself even there, at mere criticism and exposure, and ended by vowing rebellion if necessary: "We are avowedly hostile to the administration of James Madison, and we never will breathe under the dominion, direct or derivative, of Bonaparte, let it be acknowledged when it may." He challenged all patriots to "adopt this confession."[37]

As Baltimore Republicans saw it, Hanson had revealed himself as a traitor, siding with the enemy and accusing the president of treason while planning further treason of his own. With some encouragement from the Republican press, a crowd of artisans and other street Republicans attacked and destroyed the *Federal Republican* office a few days later. This was a classic example of what John Nerone has labeled "majoritarian" violence against the press, a rough but semiorganized means of expressing (and enforcing) prevailing community opinion akin to what had been used against Loyalist newspapers during the Revolution. Unfortunately, Hanson refused to stop once the community had rejected him. A few weeks after the riot, he procured a fortresslike, three-story brick mansion to be the new *Federal Republican* office, gathered friends from the Federalist countryside along with enough weapons to mount a minor military campaign, and went back to Baltimore looking for a glorious showdown with the forces of anarchy.

Many Maryland Federalists did not especially approve of Hanson's course, and their reaction formed the beginning of a serious rift in the party. A substantial group of more moderate Federalists opposed the declaration of war but felt they had to nominally support the government now that war had begun. Further provocations of the type that Hanson was bent on were out of the question. Rising Federalist leader Roger B. Taney argued that returning to Baltimore armed was an invitation to further violence and that this time the Federalists would be just as responsible for it as the Republicans. Fearing serious consequences, Taney advised his younger brother not to go with Hanson. Taney's fears turned out to be more accurate than he knew. A Republican crowd besieged the house as expected, but things spun out of control after Federalist shots killed a leader of the mob and an innocent bystander. The rioting crescendoed with a group of angry artisans pulling ten of Hanson's men from jail—where they had been placed for their own protection—beating most of them senseless, killing one, and setting fire to another, some of this while serenading the victims with revolutionary-era chants and songs.[38]

The *Federal Republican* was sustained through these travails, and the years of mere unpopularity that preceded and followed them, by massive infusions of cash from the "association" that printed it, including the Hanson family and other wealthy Maryland Federalists. The total came to at least $40,000 during the war years alone. The heavy financial backing showed at every point in the newspaper's career. Early on, Hanson freely admitted that the paper was being given away to the "honest poor," to further the journal's "useful and patriotick work" of instructing "those willing to be instructed who have not . . . means of acquiring information." The proprietors were able to resume publication in Georgetown only five days after the first riot, and then to arrange immediately for expensive new facilities. These too were destroyed, but the publishers' bodies were in far greater jeopardy than their newspaper. After the second riot, they went back to publishing in Georgetown for the rest of the war, then returned to Baltimore once more and continued publishing until Hanson's death in 1819.[39]

Near martyrdom made Hanson a hero among a certain set of Maryland Federalists. In the fall elections following the riots, Hanson was put up for Congress from the safely Federalist district comprising rural Montgomery and Frederick Counties, as a stick jabbed in the eye of Republican Baltimore. Later, when the Federalists gained control of the state House of Delegates, the editor was elevated to the national Senate. He kept charge of the *Federal Republican* all the while, making him one of the few members of Congress to actively run a newspaper while in office. The journal did double duty by publishing Hanson's speeches.[40]

Despite his seeming political success, the years after the riots were frustrating for Hanson. He never forgave the Taney wing of the party for failing to support him, and they in turn prevented the *Federal Republican* from being recognized as the Maryland Federalists' premier organ, a distinction that went to other more staid journals. Detesting the "mean, servile, temporizing spirit" he saw growing among his fellow Federalists after the end of the war, Hanson stuck ferociously to his guns and found himself in the kind of money trouble with which radical Republican editors were familiar, but with a peculiarly Hansonian spin: he was too proud to focus on collecting his back subscription bills, and so expended most of the family fortune making up the *Federal Republican*'s losses.

In Congress, Hanson spoke in the same enraged vein in which his newspaper articles were written, nearly causing several duels with various Republicans and alienating many of the Federalists as well. Fellow young Federalist congressman Daniel Webster admired Hanson as a hero when the two first met, but two years later, after getting to know the editor better, Webster and other Federalist leaders saw to it that Hanson was the only congressman of their party not invited to a meeting to plan for the next election. His last years were spent waging a factional war for control of the Maryland Federalist party that helped usher it out of existence. Still failing to recognize the rules of political arithmetic that doomed his cause, Hanson traveled the road from martyr to embarrassment in record time.[41]

THE LIMITS OF FEDERALIST NEWSPAPER POLITICS

Most Federalist editors were not reactionary firebrands like Alexander Contee Hanson. The largest group of them would probably be best classified as young lawyer-literati. Most of the self-consciously "literary" writings of the period were produced by men who were some combination of lawyer, college graduate, and Federalist, and many of them were persuaded to lend their talents to political newspapers.[42] The essayist, attorney, and Harvard graduate Joseph Dennie, named by some sources as the country's first professional author, ran a Federalist newspaper at Walpole, New Hampshire, in the mid-1790s and then was hired to help John Fenno's son edit the *Gazette of the United States*. In 1801 he founded a literary weekly called *The Port Folio*, which in addition to becoming one of the nation's foremost outlets for polite literature, doubled as a partisan Federalist journal of opinion.[43]

The most prominent Federalist author-lawyer to turn editor and political professional was Theodore Dwight, brother of Yale president Timothy

Dwight and a graduate of the college himself. Though largely forgotten now, in his own time Theodore Dwight was, as a leading Connecticut Wit, one of the nation's best-known writers. He produced many of the group's most bitterly political satires, including *The Political Greenhouse for 1798* and the "Echo" series. Some time around 1800, Dwight began aiding the printer George Goodwin with the political direction of the Hartford *Connecticut Courant*. While filling the *Courant*'s columns, Dwight continued to practice law and also acted as the Connecticut Federalists' primary party manager. He served a term in Congress during Jefferson's second administration but apparently found more fulfillment in winning elections and writing newspaper polemics than in debating legislation. (He may have been influenced by the fact that congressional Federalists were now typically defeated by margins as overwhelming as those by which the Connecticut Federalists usually won at home.) Soon after leaving Congress, Dwight became a party editor. In 1809 he founded the Hartford *Connecticut Mirror*, an elegantly written paper that viciously attacked all Republicans and became (along with Hanson's *Federal Republican* and the Boston *Columbian Centinel*), the War of 1812's nastiest critic. Dwight himself was a leading spirit (and in later years, a leading defender) of the Hartford Convention, in which he served as secretary. Soon after that body's disgrace, Dwight moved to New York, where over the next two decades he edited a series of diehard Federalist papers in Albany and then New York City.[44]

Following Fisher Ames's formula for gentrifying the partisan press, printers played a strictly subordinate role in most Federalist newspapers. Whereas the political role of Republican printers such as Charles Holt and William Duane represented democratization in action, the internal structure of the Federalist press amounted to democratization forestalled. Reminiscing about his early days in the printing trade, the Republican editor Isaac Hill recalled that the Federalist paper in Concord, New Hampshire, though printed by his friend Jesse C. Tuttle, "generally was conducted by a hired editor of liberal education" whose name was not on the masthead. Thomas Dickman, editor of the Greenfield *Gazette*, was in fact a Republican himself, having been an apprentice of Benjamin Edes. Yet Dickman "never undertook to write for his paper any article of greater length than the statement of an ordinary occurrence" and allowed his predominantly Federalist writers and subscribers to determine the political character of the paper.

These kinds of arrangements were typical. With a few notable exceptions, Federalist printers, rather than taking any active or leading role in
politics themselves, provided strictly mechanical services to Federalist political leaders. The most a Federalist printer could usually hope for was to
be the business manager of the operation, overseeing finances and production, as William Coleman's "partner and printer" Michael Burnham did at
the New York *Evening Post.* Even then, he could expect to be sniffed at, as
Burnham was by Coleman, as a vulgarian who could not possibly fathom
the literary and philosophical concerns of an educated gentleman.[45] In
Federalist politics, the class distinctions were even sharper. Printers of
Federalist newspapers were much less likely to hold office than their Republican counterparts, and few Federalist printers can be considered political professionals or even politicians.[46]

There was a great irony in this for the Federalist leadership, so self-
consciously committed to the idea of themselves as the virtuous few.
Though they wanted to destroy the politics that those sleazy Republican
editors had helped create, many Federalist gentlemen ended up engaging
much more directly in newspaper politics than their Republican counterparts did. There is virtually no example of a prominent Republican statesman who became a newspaper editor. There were too many artisans and
clerks eager for the job. Republican editors were typically people who entered politics through newspapers, not the other way around. Most of the
many Republican editors who won election to Congress, for instance, did
so after their newspaper service.[47]

The Federalists reversed these patterns almost exactly. Some of the
most illustrious Federalist statesmen—Hamilton, Fisher Ames, and John
Quincy Adams among them—wrote incessantly for newspapers, and
countless prominent or rising Federalist politicians became editors or
shadow editors.[48] Hamilton never actually edited the *Evening Post,* the
newspaper that still boasts of being founded by him, but he was deeply involved in its daily affairs. William Coleman proudly admitted to friends
that whenever there was a tough editorial to write, he made an appointment with Hamilton: "As soon as I see him, he begins in a deliberate
manner to dictate and I to note down in short-hand . . . ; when he stops,
my article is completed."[49] Like Theodore Dwight, the typical Federalist
editor-congressman took up the newspaper business after leaving Congress. In short, the Federalists diverted what they believed to be the nation's greatest literary and intellectual talents into the newspaper politics
they deplored.

Some Republican gentlemen were jealous of the Federalists' more respectable press. "Federal papers are conducted by gentlemen of education, talents, and respectability," fumed one Maryland Republican officeholder, to the *Federal Republican*'s delight, "while the democratick prints are in the hands of men of no talents, learning, or character, the mere scum of the party." By standards of polite society, this was true enough, but how much political difference would it make?[50]

Though Federalist leaders successfully gentrified their press, their high political expectations for it were not met. Though Ames had advised that "truth ought to be made popular," the poets and belletrists who tended to become Federalist editors found this difficult, uncongenial work. Their genteel habits and tastes turned out to be poorly suited to the political tasks they were given. More concerned with crafting their prose or honing their literary personae than effective campaigning, Federalist editors tended to be reticent about promoting candidates and to dislike devoting space to electioneering.[51] Examples abound, even in the newer Federalist journals. Harry Croswell's Hudson *Balance* ran a twenty-part series on education and an eleven-part rebuttal to Jefferson's annual message, but its response to the state elections of 1802 consisted of an inserted nomination notice, a stray essay or two, and brief reports of the results. Though full of criticism of Thomas Jefferson's administration, the *Washington Federalist* made no mention of the presidential election contest during the fall of 1804, nor any notable reference to the existence, much less the merits, of Federalist candidate Charles C. Pinckney.[52]

Many well-bred Federalist editors simply lacked the appropriate temperament for political combat. In this category fell the shy, sensitive, Yale-educated lawyer John G. C. Brainard, who was one of Theodore Dwight's successors on the *Connecticut Mirror*. "Of child-like disposition," Brainard's real love was sentimental poetry, and while he controlled the *Mirror*, the paper contained many verses on such subjects as the sublime beauty of Niagara Falls, but had little political impact.[53]

Joseph Dennie was less retiring than Brainard, but he shared a preference for literature over politics. The *Port Folio* would probably be slighted by "grave politicians," Dennie poetized, but he would esteem himself fortunate if it pleased the "sprightly nymph who . . . / *Finds*, BROILS, and BATTLES, but neglects them all, / For SONGS, and SUITS, a birthday and a ball."[54] When Dennie and his contributors did write about politics, they were unwilling to deal with elections and candidates, or even to try to influence popular opinion. Dennie was "contemptuously careless of vulgar popularity, but anxiously ambitious of a nobler approbation," and cited with approval a British aristocrat's statement that there was "not a *single* action of my life, where the *popularity of the times* ever had the *smallest influence on my determinations.*"[55]

Dennie evidently meant all this, for his newspaper was filled with material that, far from being calculated to advance the Federalist cause, seemed ready-made Republican campaign fodder. Editing the journal under the pseudonym "Oliver Oldschool, Esq.," the young attorney adopted the contrived stance of a haughty old aristocrat preserving the remnants of a noble ancien régime against the vulgar masses and their mistaken notions of progress. Thus, while supposedly engaged in trying to beat the Republicans with their own methods, he devoted much space to long disquisitions and intemperate paragraphs against the relative political equality and democracy enjoyed by American voters. Some early issues of the *Port Folio* contained a pedantic series of articles condemning the compositional style of the Declaration of Independence.

In late 1802 a series on equality ran, beating the long-dead horse of the radical phase of the French Revolution and lambasting the "extravagant" notion "that man could exist . . . without those shades of rank and dependence . . . hitherto . . . thought to constitute the *organization* of civil society." (Of course, this was a notion that many ordinary Americans believed to have been the whole point of their own revolution.) "Aurelius" discoursed on what a "wild project" it was to create a polity in which "the rich and the poor, the high and the low, have equally a constitutional privilege, to direct the machine of government."

A few months later, Dennie himself contributed the bon mot that democracy, said to be "on trial" in the Jefferson-ruled United States, was a "radically contemptible and vicious" system attributable to the "villainy of some men" and "the folly of others." It "was weak and wicked in Athens . . . bad in Sparta, and worse in Rome." England had justly rejected it and restored its monarchy. "No wise man but discerns its imperfections, no good man but shudders at its miseries, no honest man but proclaims its fraud, and no brave man but draws his sword against its force." Not all Federalist journals were as high-toned as the *Port Folio*, but most of them shared a similar outlook. Fisher Ames's *New England Palladium*, supposedly a model for the new, more effective Federalist press, ran a series by Ames himself that condemned voters in the South and the mid-Atlantic cities, who presumably needed to be won over, as "the squalid tribe of vice and want, and ignorance" and a "rabble, unfit for liberty."[56]

The contradictions between the mission of the new Federalist press and its rhetoric revealed the Federalist editors' profound confusion about who their audience actually was. While Federalists boasted to each other about how the press could be used to turn back the Republican tide, much of their newspaper output appealed only to people like themselves—self-styled aristocrats, Anglophiles, chauvinistic New Englanders—while repelling or insulting nearly everyone else. Joseph Dennie was more clearheaded than many Federalist editors when he announced that the *Port Folio*'s prospectus was submitted to "men of affluence" and "men of letters."[57]

Federalist journalism was typically addressed not to the republic of voting United States citizens, but to the older and socially much more restricted republic of polite letters. This was a severe political handicap, putting the style and concerns of the Federalist press at a severe variance with its purposes. The Federalist lawyer-literati were great admirers of the early eighteenth-century English "Augustan" writers, especially Jonathan Swift and Alexander Pope, also conservatives who saw themselves battling the forces of vulgarity, stupidity, corruption, and misguided innovation. The Federalists were drawn to the Augustans' bitter, derisive tone and their signature genre, satire. In particular, they liked long, long poems, modeled on Pope's *Dunciad* and Samuel Butler's *Hudibras*. Under titles like *Democracy Unveiled*, "The Triumph of Democracy," and most memorably, *Sunbeams May Be Extracted from Cucumbers, but the Process Is Tedious*, Federalist wits filled pamphlets, books, and newspaper back pages with poetry and sketches stuffed with literary allusions and current political references, often so stuffed that they had to be footnoted. While sometimes amusing to the expert reader, these works were like most polite literature in being written for insiders, people who shared the same reference points and would grasp the allusions, puns, and allegories. Young Federalists can be imagined chortling over such material on a slow day at the law office, reaffirming their feelings of superiority, but it is difficult to see how even they could have expected it to change their political fortunes.[58]

Even some of the Federalists' seemingly most aggressive and political uses of newspapers were deeply entangled in polite literary conventions. Harry Croswell's Hudson *Wasp* and its fellow temporary smear publications have been labeled "Federalist electioneering newspapers" and interpreted as a sign of the Federalists' embrace of modern political methods.[59] In fact, these satirical journals bore only superficial similarities to the "campaign newspapers" of later decades, and are better understood as particularly elaborate examples of Federalist journalism's Augustan and traditionalist tendencies. One of Harry Croswell's stated motives for starting the *Wasp* was his desire to minimize the partisan politics in his main newspaper, the *Balance*, which he declared "will not be soiled with a *personal* contest." In the first *Wasp*, he explained that "respectable federal papers" should not try to engage with the "swine" and "unprincipled adventurers" who ran the "democratic presses." Therefore, he had set up the *Wasp* "for the purpose of meeting my democratic neighbors on an equal footing."[60]

The very names of several other Federalist attack papers suggested that their goal was not so much electoral victory as vengeance and social discipline. Names like *Switch* and *Scourge* carried an unmistakable note of beating rebellious children, appropriate to the Federalist self-image as "fathers of the people." (Republican editors never invoked such images in their titles, except for an occasional *Scourge of Aristocracy*.) While less coherently named, the Worcester *Scorpion* was no less paternalistic in its outlook, correcting the grammar of Republican toasts and the translation of Latin phrases used in the *National Aegis* while belittling the social status of local Republican leaders. The *Scorpion* labeled the *Aegis* editors "an apothecary, a Cobler and a Stage-Man," and made the supposedly damning allegation that Levi Lincoln was once an apprentice blacksmith.[61]

Rather than electioneering or even smearing political candidates, the *Wasp* concentrated on insulting Charles Holt and other neighboring Republican editors, usually in rather generic, stylized terms. Croswell also ran plenty of the usual "Augustan" literary fare, including "hudibrastic" poetry and allegorical sketches written in such characters as "Bumbasticus Bumbernickle, Esq.," "Simon Sleekjacket," and "Philo Parodisticus." Meanwhile, the *Balance* remained resolutely highbrow, as planned. Croswell later affirmed his allegiance to genteel culture by becoming an Episcopal priest and making a name for himself as rector of an upper-class New Haven parish.[62]

Misapplied literary conventions may have been only a manifestation of a deeper problem for the Federalist press, namely, the basic contradiction between newspaper politics and the Federalists' most basic values, especially in New England. Disapproving of democracy and political competition, pessimistic about the mental and moral capacities of the common voter, deep down they saw no road to political victory that did not involve demagoguery, a game they could not and did not want to win. New England Federalists were plagued by old Calvinist fears that, given mankind's inherently sinful nature, allowing ordinary people free rein in their political choices could lead to nothing but the reign of sin. Still calling for the outright suppression of Republican newspapers in 1801, an unusually frank piece signed "Novanglus" argued that boycotts and other economic pressures would never eliminate the offending journals because they were truly popular with the people. The source of that popularity was the intrinsic appeal of sin to the common person. Thus it was useless for the wise and good to respond in kind, with wise and good newspapers. Democratic newspapers would "be read and approved by multitudes, as long as there are base and unhallowed passions in human nature to be gratified by them."[63]

Because of this attitude, Fisher Ames found that his calls "to form a phalanx to write . . . produced some ridicule, more disgust, no cooperation." But Ames himself was unsure of what he wanted. He grew disenchanted when Warren Dutton's *Palladium* became slightly less elevated, meaning more attuned to partisan and electoral politics. Favoring aggressive action, but wedded to the notion that the public sphere should be an abstract arena in which only arguments fought, Ames withdrew his patronage and began organizing another journal that would be more purely literary and philosophical.[64]

When Federalist editors did try to play to the loose and unhallowed passions that they imagined roiling in the people's hearts, it made for some of the party's darkest hours. Despairing of regaining national power, editors joined many Federalist statesmen in trying to hold New England at any cost, whipping up sectional hostility, especially toward Virginia. In many cases, Federalist editors were quite consciously preparing the ground for New England's secession from the union, probably in full knowledge of the plots being hatched by extremists such as Timothy Pickering. Before and during the War of 1812, it was not only the wild *Federal Republican* that actively hampered the war effort, discouraging army enlistments and subscriptions to federal loans when troops and money were badly needed, but also the most prominent and establishment-oriented Federalist newspapers, including the *Evening Post, Connecticut Courant,* and *Columbian Centinel.*[65]

Gentility notwithstanding, Federalists editors and writers also far outdid their Republican opponents in scurrilous and viciously personal defamation, though neither side ever matched the now-departed William

Cobbett. Benjamin Bache and William Duane had often accused Washington and Adams of holding monarchical views and running corrupt, repressive administrations, but they almost never descended to sexual or
strictly personal innuendo. For Federalists, however, the personal im-
morality of Republican leaders and journalists was an unshakable core belief and (they hoped) a strong issue with the voters. Federalist editors also
tended to believe they were slumming in taking up the editorial pen, both
in the sense of pursuing an occupation beneath their station and in the
sense of pitting themselves against vulgar, degraded characters like the
Republican editors. In this frame of mind, Federalist editors tended to
forget their well-bred inhibitions. Thus priest-in-training Harry Croswell
could remark that, since he had "undertaken the chastisement of a set of
fellows who are intrenched in filth," he was resolved to "wade knee-deep
in smut" that he might "meet his enemies on *their own ground*."[66]

This penchant for righteous prurience showed up most clearly (though
not solely) in Federalist press commentary on Thomas Jefferson. Though
Federalist editors had long derided James T. Callender as a "common
drunkard" and "a bloated lump of corruption," they eagerly disseminated
and embellished Callender's various aspersions on President Jefferson's
personal and political morality: that the president kept a slave mistress
named Sally Hemings and had fathered children by her, that he had once
tried to seduce the wife of a close friend, that he had paid Callender himself to smear Washington and Adams. Despite their almost militant
refinement, Federalist literati particularly enjoyed working sexy references
to "*sooty* Sal" into their sketches and poetry. Joseph Dennie envisioned a
scene in which Jefferson orders "Black Sall . . . to display all her charms,"
all her charms, for Tom Paine on a visit to Monticello.

John Quincy Adams and many other Federalist luminaries also poetized on the subject. Though northern Federalists made much of Jefferson's
hypocrisy as a slaveholding apostle of freedom and usually professed opposition to slavery, their satirical uses of the Hemings controversy were
palpably racist. They lampooned Jefferson more for having sex with a
black woman than for taking advantage of a slave. The message seemed to
be that, having abandoned their gentlemanly commitments to decency
and order, there were no limits to the depths that democratic demagogues
like Jefferson would lower themselves to, politically or personally. Another
interpretation of the racist satires is simply that Federalists wanted to
equate Republicans with what they imagined to be the lowest order of hu-

manity. Hence one issue of the Worcester *Scorpion* featured a sort of blackface parody of a Republican meeting, in which dialect-speaking members of the "Black Brethern of the Tammany Society" toasted *"Old Massa Tammany"* and leered over African American poet Phyllis Wheatley.[67]

Amidst and often obscured by the Augustan stylings of the more prominent Federalist editors, there were a modest number of Federalist newspaper politicians who were much like their Republican counterparts: printers who edited their newspapers, got involved in politics through journalism, and built careers as political professionals and, sometimes, officeholders. Good examples can be found in the three Federalist printers who ended up as congressmen later in their lives: John Holmes Prentiss of New York, John Crafts Wright of Ohio, and Charles Miner of Pennsylvania. Wright and Miner went to Congress as Adams-Clay supporters in the 1820s, Prentiss as part of a wave of Jacksonian editors elected to Congress in the 1830s. In their Federalist days, none of these editors were secessionists or violent antidemocrats, and they easily embraced competitive electoral politics. All were transplanted Yankees who came into the printing business after 1800 and ran their own papers without overbearing sponsors. Prentiss was a journeyman printer and foreman at Coleman's *Evening Post* who was tapped by Judge William Cooper to edit the *Cooperstown Federalist*. Cooper soon died, however, and Prentiss became a locally prominent Federalist leader in his own right.

Prentiss, Miner, and Wright had plenty of differences with the Republican editors on policy matters such as the embargo and the war, but in terms of political style and the shape of their careers, the distinctions were incremental. These Federalist editors were more deferential to their party superiors than Republicans typically were, less strident in their campaigning, more self-consciously genteel in their own values and deportment, and quite a bit more commercially oriented: Wright became a railroad director and a prominent attorney, Prentiss a bank director, and Miner a major developer of anthracite coal mining. They all achieved their later eminence, however, by following the Republican model of newspaper politics. That was doubtless a key factor in their politically outliving the party of their youth.[68]

Improving on the Sedition Act

Press Freedom and Political Culture after 1800

∽

Despite, *or perhaps because of,* their role in the rise of newspaper politics, Republican gentlemen typically held many attitudes toward
printers, editors, and political newspapers that were similar to those of the
Federalists. Though sympathetic to their own personal journalistic supporters, many Republican leaders allowed their irritation at Federalist
slanders to mature into general principles, lumping all newspaper editors
into a single licentious mass. This was especially true for the highest Republican leader of all. When the young printer and budding editor John
Norvell wrote to Thomas Jefferson for advice on running a newspaper, the
president replied with a screed blasting his correspondent's choice of careers. "It is a melancholy truth," Jefferson sighed bitterly, "that a suppression of the press could not more compleatly deprive the nation of its
benefits, than is done by its abandoned prostitution to falsehood." He
elaborated:

> Nothing can now be believed which is seen in a newspaper. Truth itself be-
> comes suspicious by being put in that polluted vehicle. . . . I really look with
> commiseration over my fellow citizens, who, reading newspapers, live & die in
> the belief that they have known something of what has been passing in the
> world. . . . I will add that the man who never looks into a newspaper is better
> informed than he who reads them; inasmuch as he who knows nothing is
> nearer to truth than he whose mind is filled with falsehoods & errors.[1]

Many of Jefferson's lesser colleagues agreed. Republican Congressman
George W. Campbell asked his Tennessee constituents to disregard (without party specification) "*the slanderous publications of party, hireling, and
petty newspapers,* calculated only to sow dissensions, excite distrusts, and
disturb the public mind."[2]

Republican leaders did not usually practice the open, ham-fisted social prejudice of the Federalists, but they shared the Federalist desire for a gentrified press. The perceived personal and rhetorical vulgarity of printer-editors was distasteful enough, but beyond that statesmen simply did not trust printers and other relatively plebeian types (such as the refugee radicals) to take the calm, rational view of public affairs that educated gentlemen supposedly did. They preferred editors whose backgrounds and likely reactions were closer to their own, or who could be easily controlled, as they found that refugee radicals and printer-politicians often could not be. Even while encouraging the spread of newspaper politics, Republican leaders avoided too close an embrace of the new political professionals, especially those who lacked gentility, and eagerly sought for more palatable alternatives.[3]

Hence Jefferson had chosen a young Philadelphia gentleman over more experienced printer-editors to manage his administration organ, the *National Intelligencer*. Besides his impeccable family background, Samuel Harrison Smith had multiple degrees from the University of Pennsylvania and a membership in the American Philosophical Society, attributes that strongly recommended him to Jefferson despite his mediocre track record as a publisher of largely apolitical Philadelphia newspapers. No troublesome radical, Smith proved an utterly reliable mouthpiece. Refusing to seek any political role or glory for himself, he allowed administration members to insert articles at will and set the *Intelligencer*'s political line. Smith's handpicked successor, Joseph Gales Jr., admitted that his onetime mentor was "so bound to follow the directions of others that he would march directly into a brick wall if ordered to do so by a superior." According to the *National Intelligencer*'s biographer, "Smith's deficiency of creative power . . . blind subservience . . . mild manner and moderation produced a newspaper with these same characteristics." That was just how Jefferson liked it. Given his lack of political fire, it is not surprising that Smith tired of politics relatively early, retiring to banking, real estate, and country life in 1810 at the urging of his Federalist socialite wife. In fact, Margaret Bayard Smith, a novelist and popular Washington hostess, was a far more respected and influential political figure than her milquetoast husband.[4]

THE GENTRIFICATION OF THE SOUTHERN PARTISAN PRESS

Jefferson's preference for the pliable, genteel Smith over a more difficult character such as William Duane, who expected to edit the administration organ himself, was rooted partly in the larger southern aversion to printer-editors. This first showed itself in the 1790s but intensified later, as native-born southern gentlemen learned to be successful newspaper proprietors. An important factor in this was heavy state government support for certain favored newspapers whose editors were well integrated into the state's political elite. Eventually, the aversion extended beyond printers to editors who were aliens of any kind (social, ethnic, regional, or ideological) to the southern gentry. These trends show clearly in the history of the last newspaper with which Jefferson was involved, the Richmond *Enquirer.*

Virginia's experience with outsider journalists was notoriously terrible. James Thomson Callender had been brought in to edit the *Enquirer's* predecessor, the *Examiner,* in the late 1790s, but after Jefferson's victory, he turned against the Republican establishment for failing to support him adequately. He wanted to be postmaster of Richmond, but the capital of the president's beloved home state (to which Jefferson always applied very different standards than the rest of the country) was the last place on earth where this particular president would ever appoint a common, hard-drinking, foreign radical like Callender. The Richmond postmastership was reserved for a man of "respectable standing in society," Jefferson wrote. A stern moralist in spite of his bibulous habits, Callender also became disgusted by Virginia culture: the dueling, the pretensions to aristocracy, and, most of all, slavery and the sexual hypocrisy surrounding it. Callender vented his feelings by leaving the *Examiner,* starting a rival newspaper called the *Recorder,* and publicizing the alleged affair between Jefferson and Sally Hemings, to which he added similar innuendoes about other leading Virginia Republicans.[5]

After Callender's defection, the *Examiner* sagged and eventually collapsed under the mismanagement of the dissolute gentleman-duelist Meriwether Jones. Then, with Jefferson's encouragement, a scholarly young dilettante named Thomas Ritchie purchased the paper and renamed it the *Enquirer* in 1804. One sign of Jefferson's countenance was that Ritchie's paper had the local contract for publishing the U.S. laws from its very first issue, a highly unusual honor for a new newspaper.[6]

Unlike Callender, the *Enquirer's* editor was a thoroughly safe man. The younger son of a wealthy merchant who had made himself a substantial planter, Thomas Ritchie had flitted from career to career, reading law briefly with his mother's relative Spencer Roane, the eminent Virginia jurist, then moving on to studying medicine in Philadelphia. When

Ritchie's "tender sympathy with human suffering" cut that educational plan short, he followed his literary tastes into stints as a teacher and a bookseller, before finally determining "to take up the editorial pen."[7]

Connected by parentage and marriage to numerous aristocratic Virginia families, Ritchie was a different kind of political professional from his northern counterparts, a full social equal of the political leaders he dealt with and a man of eminently genteel values and sensibilities. While reigning for decades as Virginia's leading political editor, Ritchie was also Richmond's leading society toastmaster: managing balls, joining clubs, receiving dignitaries, and being "the perfect gentleman in his attentions to the ladies." These were not roles that James Callender or William Duane could have managed.[8]

Ritchie's paper was as thoroughly refined as its editor. Its rhetoric was florid and formal, its tone ostentatiously high-minded. In an early issue, the editor ended a lengthy statement of his theories on "The Press" with a typical gentleman's declamation against "licentiousness" in the press. Using much the same language as Jefferson's letter to Norvell, Ritchie declared a licentious press "almost as useless as no press at all." What value could be derived from writings "which contain not the luminous opinions of a candid judgment, but the suggestions of party spirit"?[9]

On a more practical level, Ritchie had no intention of eschewing party spirit: he was installed on the state Republican General Committee within two years of the paper's founding and remained one of the state and national party's most influential figures into the 1840s.[10] He was also a professional rather than an amateur politician, applying for the office of public printer even before his newspaper began publishing. Still, even in his most narrowly pecuniary political dealings, Ritchie always maintained a gentleman's decorum and dignity. He managed to sound like a statesman even when he was soliciting printing patronage, displaying elaborate indifference to the favor he was seeking. Take, for instance, his initial application to the governor for the post of Virginia public printer, which he was to hold for decades:

> T. Ritchie offers his . . . services to the Executive for the office of Public Printer. In bringing himself forward as a candidate for this appointment, he does not pretend to decide on his own qualifications or those of his competitors or on the interests of the State. He merely wishes to express to the Council his willingness to discharge the duties of this office, and his decided belief that they will not be neglected should they devolve on him.[11]

Ritchie engaged in political combat, but he did so in the "fastidiously polite and well-bred" manner that Fisher Ames had prescribed for the Federalist press. He promised that there would be only so much of party in the paper "as may be necessary for the elucidation of unsettled truths, without mixing up with it any of the grossness of vulgar or personal abuse." By all accounts, he largely kept this promise throughout a long career. It was backed by his desire that the *Enquirer* do nothing to besmirch "his own personal honour" as a gentleman, language foreign to many northern political professionals.[12]

Ritchie proved to be exactly the sort of urbane, elevated, prudent man that Thomas Jefferson had always wanted in an editor. Pleading a need for "tranquility and a retirement from the passions which disturb it," Jefferson claimed not to read or subscribe to newspapers after his presidency, making a single exception for the *Enquirer*. The former president repeatedly boasted to correspondents that he read "no newspaper . . . but Ritchie's." Writing to John Adams, he offered an unsolicited testimonial. Ritchie, Jefferson wrote, "culls what is good from every paper, as the bee from every flower."[13] The man whom Duane and Callender had helped raise to the presidency preferred a sweeter-smelling journalism and politics than they had practiced.

This pattern of newspaper politics falling under the control of bona fide southern gentlemen (in terms of both social and geographic origins) held true throughout the Old South. Of more than 110 editors who served in Congress up to 1850, only one of the southerners, Seaton Grantland of Georgia, was a printer by training, and later even he became a lawyer and bought a plantation.[14]

In class-conscious South Carolina, for instance, the roster of men who edited the leading Republican and Democratic papers, the *City Gazette* and *Mercury,* was a long parade of highly educated and distinguished personages, getting more so, and more insularly South Carolinian, over time. The list of distinguished Charleston editors begins in the 1780s with Philip Freneau's calmer brother and fellow Princeton graduate Peter, a migrant from New Jersey but a longtime resident who also served as South Carolina secretary of state.

Freneau was joined in 1801 by David Rogerson Williams, educated at the future Brown University until "the remittances from his plantation . . . failed him" and he had to come home and restore the family fortune. This Williams did by converting his plantation to cotton and then opening one of the South's first textile mills. After editing the *City Gazette* for three years, Williams served successively as an important member of Congress, brigadier general in the U.S. Army, governor of South Carolina, and state senator. As an editor, Williams employed an interesting method of neutralizing some of the editor-printer friction that had plagued earlier southern political journals: he joined the Charleston Mechanic Society.

After Freneau and Williams came the novelist William Gilmore Simms and then Henry Laurens Pinckney, a scion of the state's great founding family and a South Carolina College graduate. The longtime editor of the Charleston *Mercury* and a staunch Nullifier, Pinckney served two terms in Congress, as speaker of the state House of Representatives, and as mayor of Charleston. Like many elite Carolinians, he seems to have worn his lineage on his sleeve. Later it was written that no one who knew Henry Pinckney ever forgot his "marked bearing." Another specimen of swaggering southern manhood among the Charleston editorial corps was John Lyde Wilson, a lawyer who edited the Charleston *Investigator* during the 1810s and soon after was elected governor. Wilson became best known, however, as the Old South's leading authority on dueling, by virtue of authoring *The Code of Honor,* a popular handbook on the subject.[15]

Southern editors were not always as blue-blooded and self-consciously southern as these South Carolinians, but an exception from North Carolina will demonstrate the rule that seemed to exist almost everywhere in the region. Growing wealthy off state printing contracts, the radical exile Joseph Gales moderated his political beliefs and settled in for decades of comfort, editing the *Raleigh Register* as the organ of the North Carolina Republican establishment. His college-educated son and assistant, Joseph Gales Jr., later proved an ideal choice, in terms of reliability and predictability, to take over the *National Intelligencer* after Samuel H. Smith's retirement.[16] The experiences of other editorial migrants to the South tended to be more like those of Callender: short, stormy, or both. In Georgia, for instance, several editors of foreign or northern extraction, including the refugee radical Denis Driscol and the exiled Connecticut editor Samuel Morse, arrived shortly after 1800, only to meet failure or early death.[17]

After the time of Callender, precious few Yankees, foreigners, radicals, or even printers would be allowed to guide southern public opinion again, a task rendered highly sensitive not only by the oligarchic nature of southern politics but also by the need to protect the institution of slavery from criticism and political action. As the southern elite's commitment to slavery hardened and its retreat from the relative freethinking of the late eighteenth-century hastened, the peculiar institution would rarely be challenged by the region's thoroughly gentrified press. The South became a place where political dissent or even debate (at least on fundamental issues such as slavery) was increasingly unwelcome, and the southern party press was fully complicit in this process.[18]

EDITORS AND OTHER POLITICIANS:
EMERGING TENSIONS AND DIFFERING PERSPECTIVES

The South developed its own uniquely genteel tradition of newspaper politics, but elite desires for gentrification and second thoughts about newspaper partisanship and printer-politicians were by no means strictly southern phenomena. The impulses appeared everywhere as the lawyers, planters, and merchants who made up the nation's traditional political class considered the implications of the new politics and pondered the wisdom of abandoning their privileged position in public life and ceding away control of the printed public sphere. Gentleman politicians of both parties generally decided in the negative, and in no area was this clearer than in their course on the question of press freedom.

If, as the leading scholar of American press freedom has argued, a "new libertarianism" emerged among Republicans in the wake of the Sedition Act, it was not unanimously or consistently espoused. The most radical tracts of the late 1790s were written by young firebrands such as Virginia's George Hay and New York's Tunis Wortman and John Thomson, men whose leadership status in the party was marginal at the time they wrote. Numerous Republicans of greater stature never abandoned older, more restrictive notions of press freedom, and even some promoters of the new approach rethought their positions later.[19]

At any rate, serious reservations about a completely unrestrained press overtook Republican gentlemen almost as soon as they became office-holders themselves and began receiving blasts from the newly energized Federalist press. As the primary target of these attacks, Thomas Jefferson was foremost among those who concluded that some form of check on the press might be necessary after all. When Pennsylvania Governor Thomas McKean, himself a past master at suing and prosecuting editors, suggested legal action against some of the Philadelphia Federalist editors in early 1803, Jefferson responded with cautious but distinct enthusiasm, rationalizing that some purgation would purify and actually strengthen the press. "Having failed in destroying the freedom of the press by their gag-law," Jefferson argued, the Federalists now sought to undermine it with an opposite strategy, "that is by pushing its licentiousness & its lying to such a degree of prostitution . . . that even the least informed of the people have learnt that nothing in a newspaper is to be believed. This is a dangerous state of things, and the press ought to be restored to its credibility if possible." Jefferson still believed that the First Amendment barred any federal action against the press, but he now took the position that states could and should punish sedition when necessary. "I have therefore long thought," he concluded, "that a few prosecutions of the most prominent offenders would have a wholesome effect."[20]

McKean heeded this advice and more, not only launching a prosecution against Federalist editor Joseph Dennie, but also proposing a tightening of the state libel laws. Dennie was prosecuted for his undeniably rather seditious-sounding remark, quoted earlier, that any "brave man" would "draw his sword" against democracy. It was urgent, the governor argued in his opening address to the state assembly in 1802, that the press's "unparalleled licentiousness in publishing seditious and infamous libels," which was threatening "finally to annihilate every benefit of this boasted medium of public information," be "controuled and corrected." Though McKean's comments referred mostly to Dennie and other Federalist journalists, they glanced at a deeper problem that was equally traceable to the Republican editors. Echoing Alexander Addison's grand jury charges of a few years past, McKean raised the specter of newspaper editors, persons with few "natural" claims to leadership who nevertheless controlled access to print, ruling the community solely through their power over the precious reputations of gentleman politicians. Present conditions amounted, McKean complained, to "a tyranny, by which the weak, the wicked, and the obscure are enabled to prey upon the fame, the feelings and the fortunes of every conspicuous member of the community."[21]

Though the 1802 Pennsylvania legislature declined to carry out Governor McKean's suggestion, Republican officials in New York and Connecticut did follow his example, hauling Federalist editors (and in the latter state, even some clergymen who had attacked Jefferson from the pulpit) before the courts.[22] In Virginia, lawyer George Hay resorted to lawsuits and violence against the press, in the form of James Callender, a few years after penning one of the major "new libertarian" tracts. Hay found it necessary to write a second pamphlet reconciling his actions with his earlier theories and significantly qualifying his libertarianism.[23]

Massachusetts attorney general and Republican leader James Sullivan perhaps best expressed the new Republican establishment's sense that the more extravagantly permissive doctrines put forth in the 1798-1800 period needed to be tempered. In 1801 Sullivan published a pamphlet on political libels, attempting to set down sober legal doctrines on the issue as opposed to the impassioned political statements of Hay, Wortman, and Thomson. He condemned the Sedition Act not so much for its legal principles, which he deemed sound, but because it was not "executed with that discretion which might procure the confidence . . . of the people." The government still needed protection from sedition, he believed, and could secure it under a rejuvenated federal common law. Sullivan was willing to tolerate criticism of the government's acts and policies but not attacks on government officials themselves. Moreover, even ostensibly protected commentaries on government policies could be subject to sedition proceedings if their words had "an intent to subvert the government . . . , to bring it into hatred or contempt, or . . . to alarm the people or to cause them to withdraw their love and support," statements remarkably reminiscent of the Sedition Act itself.[24]

Indeed, the legal standards for criminal libel that Republican jurists employed in the early nineteenth-century cases were actually somewhat more restrictive than were the Zengerian principles embodied in the Sedition Act: truth was allowed as a defense only if the libel was not maliciously intended and only if it directly involved an official's public conduct in office. New York's Republican attorney general Ambrose Spencer put this standard into action in 1802, when he prosecuted Harry Croswell, editor of the Hudson *Balance* and *Wasp,* for criticizing Thomas Jefferson.

Spencer admitted that "in a government fixed on the basis of liberty, it is important that citizens should know the conduct of their rulers." But if the facts threatened to "loosen the bands of society" by destroying a gentleman's hard-won reputation and bringing on a duel or some other disruption of sociability, then even factual statements could be criminal, "especially if they are such, with which the public have nothing to do; if they merely touch the private deportment and morals of the man." In practice, Spencer did not follow his own standard, harassing Croswell not for remarks on Jefferson's sexual relationships, which the budding clergyman had avoided, but instead for charging Jefferson with the far more "hellish" infraction of paying Philip Freneau and James Callender to write newspaper articles and books. The real standard seemed to be that only the most politically embarrassing charges would be prosecuted, and evidently the new Republican establishment felt especially embarrassed about their role in the rise of newspaper politics.[25]

THE VIEW FROM THE PRINTING OFFICE

The surprisingly limited conceptions of press freedom and increasingly negative view of newspaper politicians evinced by Republican officeholders brought a complex reaction from the Republican editors. As committed party zealots, they usually tried (if no factional dispute interposed itself) to support whatever actions national, state, and local Republican officials took, including the occasional legal proceedings against their Federalist counterparts. They did so, however, with some reluctance and an uncomfortable awareness of the ironies involved.

In response to Governor McKean's libel proposals of 1802, William Duane agreed that newspapers given to "indiscriminate abuse" of public men ought to be "discountenanced." He thought the *Gazette of the United States* particularly well suited for this treatment. Still, the *Aurora* editor pointedly omitted any words of approval for the suggested tightening of the libel laws. He endorsed only the idea that the libelous papers should not be "supported by the patronage of men friendly to the constitution." In other words, no one should subscribe to Federalist newspapers or give printing contracts to their proprietors, limiting the coercion used to that which could be exerted through the marketplace. In a similar vein, the Danbury *Republican Farmer* declared that while it was clearly time that many "disgraceful" Federalist publications be "checked," this should be done "not by legal shackles, or legislative provision, but by the neglect of the people," which would force "these wrong-headed editors . . . to seek some other means of living, than ravaging their country with political pestilence."[26]

Duane particularly objected to the prosecution and continuing harassment of the turncoat Callender in Virginia. Though the *Aurora* had spent much of the previous year eviscerating Callender, Duane spoke from his own experience in making political hay out of martyrdom when he questioned "whether the method taken . . . will have any effect other than the contrary of what was intended." No one believed Callender's tales, Duane argued; persecution would only give him notoriety and credibility that he otherwise lacked. Moreover, freedom of the press seemed "much endangered" by the precedent of Republicans prosecuting an editor.[27]

Charles Holt reacted with cagey ambivalence to the troubles of his crosstown rival Harry Croswell. Though still deeply bitter about his own troubles under the Sedition Act, Holt refrained from calling for Croswell's prosecution and focused instead on the hypocrisy of the Federalists regarding the press, calumniating government leaders when they had once wrung their hands over the dangers of any political criticism and crying out for the same liberties they had recently tried to suppress. He marveled at such "low and venomous slander" coming from "men who but a few months since were harping upon the respect due to constituted authorities, and the sacredness of private character." The Republicans' renunciation of sedition prosecutions was one of the qualities that made them superior to the Federalists. "If republicans made use of *sedition laws* or the *good old common law* to protect their rulers from these unprincipled vipers," Holt suggested in September 1802, before any of the actions against Federalist printers had been commenced, "alas! every gaol would be a federal printer's office."[28]

When the proceedings against Croswell began, Holt had to adjust his course. Commenting on a call by William Coleman for private suits against Republican editors, Holt allowed himself to vent an entirely natural desire for Federalists to suffer as he had while still making his own disapproval of the prosecution clear. "We shall see how long [Coleman] will hold his high opinion of prosecutions," Holt wrote in June 1803, "for he may shortly, from bitter experience, deprecate their effects." Once Croswell was convicted in July, the Hudson *Bee* printed only a "communication" from one of the participants defending the fairness of the trial, rather than editorializing.[29]

When the conviction was upheld by the Republican members of the state supreme court in August, the Republican party's spokesman in Hudson could avoid the subject no longer. Holt did not condemn the trial outright, but he did attack the Federalists' objections to it. He recalled the sad case of David Frothingham, a journeyman printer who assisted Thomas Greenleaf's widow Anne in the management of the *New York Journal*. Frothingham was hauled into court, under the common law of seditious libel, for republishing a piece against Alexander Hamilton. Denied the use of truth as a defense, the printer was swiftly condemned to a

$100 fine (the equivalent of three months wages) and four months in Bridewell prison; once released, he had to pay an additional $2,000 bond for his "good behavior." The *Journal* folded, and Frothingham, his printing career cut short, apparently went to sea, dying penniless years later.[30]

The case paralleled Croswell's well, except for the more severe punishments and more ignominious fate meted out to the Republican Frothingham. If Blackstonian libel rules had been "rigorously enforced against a republican printer" by Federalist authorities, Holt asked, "with what propriety can the federalists . . . now clamor" when the same rules were used "to punish one of the most systematic and execrable libelers in the United States?" He answered that "their lips ought to be sealed on the subject." The Croswell case was simply a matter of the Federalists being hoist by their own pernicious doctrines:

> If the law on which Croswell's conviction took place is hostile to freedom and a republican government, why did they not, after the trial and conviction of Frothingham, manfully step forth and correct it? No, the common law of England was then right, it was the stupendous fabric of wisdom which they revered; but now the tables are turned, its lash impends over one of the brotherhood, and it is all that is vile and detestable.[31]

All in all, it was a splendid performance: Holt managed to keep a consistent Republican line—attacking the common law and expressing distaste for seditious libel prosecutions—while appearing to support the party leadership. However, Holt obviously hoped that the Republican crackdown would end soon. Two weeks later, when the state supreme court charged a Federalist printer in Ulster, New York, with contempt of court for criticizing the Croswell decision, a disappointed Holt announced that he would "forbear any animadversions" for the present and trust that the "rights of editors" would be properly upheld when the case was actually tried.[32]

Other Republican editors shared Holt's attitude. Reprinting one of the *Bee's* articles on the Croswell case, Samuel Morse, a former Connecticut Republican editor now running the Savannah *Georgia Republican,* chuckled that the Federalist papers were suddenly "in flaming zeal for the protection of the liberty of the press," but for once, he quickly added, the Federalists were in the right. It was all well and good to shield private individuals from newspaper attacks, but since governments and legislatures were made up of private individuals, "unless a very considerable latitude is given in discussion, liberty may be endangered."[33]

At least a few Republican printers came to agree with the Federalists that Republican leaders were merely demagogic hypocrites, on libel as well as other subjects. To some Republican gentlemen, it seems, printers were mere tools who could be flattered, ignored, or prosecuted as the situation demanded. Both Nathaniel Willis Jr. and Andrew Wright, printers jailed during the Republican newspaper invasion of New England, had the experience of being financially betrayed by sponsors when they got in trouble. Both printers were asked to print what seemed to them dangerously personal attacks and, when they expressed doubts, were promised that they would be fully protected from the consequences.

Trying to reelect a friend and destroy a local ally who had switched parties, Portland Republican leader Dr. Thomas G. Thornton assured Willis, editor of the *Eastern Argus,* that he "would not be hurt a hair of my head" by publishing Thornton's intemperate exposures of the renegade. Yet when Willis had been sued and jailed and faced a $4,000 judgment, Thornton decided that the money was the printer's responsibility. Willis successfully appealed to other, more honorable Republicans, who took over Thornton's obligation and paid Willis for past-due subscriptions, allowing him to both satisfy the judgment and pay back $1,300 he had originally borrowed to buy the paper. Nevertheless, Willis learned a lesson that soon drove him out of political publishing: "I learned that politicians are not only ungrateful, but supremely selfish. They used me as the cat's-paw, but took good care to keep all the chestnuts for their own eating." Willis was converted at a local revival shortly thereafter and became a great success as editor of the *Boston Recorder,* one of the country's first religious newspapers.[34]

The Northampton, Massachusetts, printer Andrew Wright's experience with political publishing was even worse. Despite repeated promises of "indemnification" for printing Republican attorney Charles Shepherd's rather scurrilous articles against Governor Caleb Strong, the only concrete aid Shepherd ever gave Wright was the income from a published report of his own libel trial. Wright himself had to fold and stitch 1,100 copies of this report in his prison cell, but only twenty-odd copies were sold. Promises to raise a subscription, appeal for help in the columns of the newspaper, or find Wright an office were all conveniently forgotten, leaving the printer to spend many years in and out of court and prison dealing with the financial aftermath of his prosecution.

Five years after the trial, Wright went to the trouble of publishing a pamphlet about his dealings with Shepherd. "My object in this publication is . . . *Revenge!*," Wright admitted, but he also had a serious point to make about the inconsistency of self-styled democrats mistreating and lording it over the artisans they asked to be their allies: "Fellow citizens, weigh these things, and then say what you can think of . . . a man who is bawling 'Liberty and Equality,' in every public place, who is himself wallowing in wealth, and rolling in luxury, who could suffer one of his own species to become a victim to his too great confidence in him?"[35]

Sedition prosecutions and money were only two issues over which the partnership of Republican gentlemen and Republican printers could go astray. In fact, it was a relationship fraught with tensions, generated not only by financial practicalities but also by the two groups' very different perspectives on political life. The differences were partly rooted in class. Gentlemen could not tolerate having their hard-earned "characters" taken away by a mere printer. A primary object of political libel law had always been the prevention of such occurrences.[36] As Alexander Hamilton argued at Harry Croswell's trial, complete autonomy for newspaper editors "would put the best and the worst on the same level." But editors did not agree that their own entrance into public life constituted, as Thomas McKean put it, "a tyranny" of "the weak, the wicked and the obscure" over their betters, and they fought for their own right to participate.[37]

Overlapping the class divide but also creating a distinct set of issues was occupational competition. Simply put, editor-politicians offered a challenge to the supremacy of the legal profession over American politics and government. "The United States are ruled by lawyers," observed one of Alexis de Tocqueville's informants, exaggerating only slightly. In every period of American history, lawyers have held political office at rates far outstripping their proportion of the population. This state of affairs was established at the very dawn of the United States. Ambitious but politically frustrated colonial attorneys such as John Adams were major leaders of the American resistance movement during the 1760s, and once the resulting revolution broke out, American lawyers seized power and never looked back. They made up almost half the men who signed the Declaration of Independence, more than half of those who attended the Constitutional Convention, and at least 48 percent of the House of Representatives membership up to 1820. Between 1789 and 1952, the legal profession supplied 75 percent of all presidents, vice presidents, cabinet members, Supreme Court justices, and Speakers of the House.[38]

The rise of lawyers to political prominence at the time of Revolution was noticed and resented by many contemporaries. Ordinary citizens buffeted by the economic upheavals of the revolutionary years perceived, correctly, that the legal profession had benefited from turmoil that had threatened everyone else. For many, lawyers were active agents in maintaining the economic inequities within American society, swarming in to defend the property and privileges of the wealthy or to take away the small holdings of the poor and debt ridden. Moreover, the complexities of the law, especially the unwritten English common law, seemed designed to mystify ordinary men and obfuscate justice.[39]

In the late 1780s, growing popular antipathy toward the bar inspired a major movement to reform the legal system and restrain the power of lawyers, with the Boston *Independent Chronicle*'s Benjamin Austin as one of its major spokesmen. Some reformers aimed at nothing less than the destruction of the profession, but lesser goals included prohibition of English precedents, appointment of nonlawyers to the judiciary, and the defeat of lawyer-candidates for office. The most innovative proposal was a new court system that would transfer much adjudication from judges to arbitrators who were social and occupational peers of those they judged. This radical reform movement largely failed. Lawyers turned back efforts to regulate or restrict the profession and spearheaded new state and national constitutions that scaled back the democratic features of the revolutionary state governments and established a potent source of power for the legal profession, in the form of the "independent judiciary," a separate, unelected branch of government.[40] During the 1790s, the conflict over the legal profession and legal system was supplanted by other issues, but it became an important source of the rift that took place in the Republican party after 1800.[41]

Printer-editors had their own particular reasons for disliking the legal profession, reasons that lay at the heart of the difficulties in intraparty relations. Burdened by chronic debts and constantly under the gun of libel law and contempt of court citations, editors found themselves more often victimized than protected by the legal system. William Duane and others had long crusaded against the common law as repressive and un-American, and for them it was discredited once and for all by the Federalists' abuse of it during the crisis of 1798–1800. The "reign of terror" had also cast much unfavorable light on the independent judiciary. The open partisanship of judges such as Alexander Addison and Samuel Chase in the sedition cases, and President Adams's attempt to fill a newly expanded federal bench with Federalists in the waning hours of his administration, convinced many Republican editors that the "independent judiciary" was merely a cant phrase for the institutionalization of arbitrary power in flagrant defiance of the people's wishes.

Some Republican printers seriously doubted whether any lawyer would or could be a sincere democrat. "Farmers, Mechanics, and Laborers are generally . . . attached to equal rights and rational liberty," wrote James J. Wilson of the Trenton *True American,* but lawyers were naturally disposed to "bend at the throne of Power" or "worship at the shrine of Wealth." Though there were lawyers in both parties, Wilson regarded the whole profession with a skeptical eye. On a day when the state supreme court was sitting in 1802, he wrote to a friend that he:

> could count as I sit at my window not less than an hundred Lawyers, passing and repassing. . . . Is it any wonder there are so many poor people, when it is considered what swarms of locusts infest the land and devour their substance? What a pity a general combination were not formed to starve . . . them to death or to work, "as the case may be." Yet if such a plan were adopted general-ly, we should lose [some] good *Demos,* tho' a much greater number of evil *demons.*

It was much easier for Republican printers to believe that all lawyers were actual, latent, or hidden Federalists and elitists.[42]

Knowing that ordinary voters shared their hard feelings, printers were not above turning lawyer domination into a campaign issue. During the 1808 campaign, the Easton, Pennsylvania, printer Thomas J. Rogers asked voters which they preferred for public servants, "*lawyers,* who invariably treat you with contumely and contempt, or honest & well meaning *farmers,* who will always treat you with kindness and attention? If you prefer honest farmers to haughty and overbearing lawyers, then to the poll and vote for the Republican ticket." To underline the point, he printed the opposing candidate slates as the "Republican Farmers' Ticket" and the "Federal Lawyers Ticket." Years later, as a congressman fighting for reelection, Rogers would use the same ploy. He was victorious in both cases.[43]

These two groups—lawyers and printer-editors, with different relationships to the society, the economy, and the legal order—were thrown together after 1800 as co-custodians of the Republican party. Though not monolithic on either side, the contrasting points of view generated contrasting ideas. In the area of libel law, many of the Republican party's lawyers were loathe to destroy the infrastructure of legal doctrine that had always served to check potential social insurgents, while editors saw it only as a cudgel with which they would eventually be beaten.[44]

Perhaps the sharpest contrast could be found in the two groups' approach to political life itself. Lawyers regarded the public sphere with a strong sense of both entitlement and the dignity that ought to attach to men in public stations. The vast majority of gentlemen among the lawyers were also uncomfortable with the new direction in which editors had taken the political culture in the late 1790s. They were not anxious to see such freewheeling, vituperative partisanship institutionalized. On a less conscious level, the legal fraternity was also jealous of the competition editors offered to their dominance of American politics and government.

For their part, editors were well aware—and resentful—of the way lawyers and other educated professional men dominated the nation's public life. Connecticut Republican printer Selleck Osborn described his state as "a country conquered by lawyers," who "have succeeded each other in all the offices, as sons of noblemen." When a Federalist writer expressed horror that many Americans "educated only to follow the plough consider themselves capable of guiding the helm of state," Osborn responded with an explosion of sarcasm:

> Have we indeed arrived at that period of *degradation,* when others besides *lawyers & doctors* dare to appear in our legislature? . . . Can no decisive measure be immediately adopted to keep these *ignorant* FARMERS at a distance from the helm? *Ungrateful farmers!* Was it for this that so many lawyers . . . have united in their labors, that their sons . . . endured *rigid abstinence* and intense *application* at Yale College; and afterwards "grew pale at the midnight lamp," to acquire the science of law . . . ? Must we after being *"educated"* on purpose for Governors, Councillors, Judges, and representatives, endure the mortification of seeing our *natural privileges* usurped . . . ?[45]

Printer-editors could have no such sense of entitlement about their role in politics, and they were outraged to encounter it in others.

THE FEDERALISTS AND CIVIL LIBERTIES: THE EVEN DARKER SIDE

It is significant that Selleck Osborn directed these comments to a Federalist writer. Like most Republican editors after 1800, he knew that the most dangerous threat to the democratic values, political role, and personal liberty of printers came not from Republican lawyers but from the Federalists who still controlled many state governments and dominated the courts in most places outside the South.[46]

Famously, and rather deceptively, there was a sudden awakening of libertarianism among some Federalists now that some of the weapons of state were in Republican hands. Alexander Hamilton helped defend Harry Croswell and thereby earned himself a rather ironic place in the pantheon of crusaders for press freedom.[47] In reality, the libertarian aspects of Hamilton's position were relatively few: the New York court had tried to restrict the jury to deciding the facts of publication, the traditional position of Blackstone and the English common law, but Hamilton reaffirmed the right of the jury to decide whether the publication was libelous, as stipulated in the Sedition Act. At the same time, Hamilton demolished Judge Spencer's distinction between criticism of government measures and of the men who made them. If the latter could not be discussed along with the former, it would render the people's right to change their rulers useless, Hamilton argued, and "in vain will the voice of the people be raised against the inroads of tyranny." Of course, this was a point that Republican newspapers had often made in defending their criticism of Washington, Adams, and Hamilton.[48]

Rhetoric aside, Hamilton largely concurred with the Republican lawyers on a libel standard somewhere to the right of the Sedition Act. The former treasury secretary contended for "the liberty of publishing truth . . . even though it reflect on government, magistrates, or private persons." Yet he did not argue for "unbridled licence." Indeed, Hamilton considered "the spirit of abuse and calumny as the pest of society." Even George Washington had not been exempt from attack, and "falsehood eternally repeated would have affected even his name." Complete freedom of the press "therefore cannot be endured." The press should be "under the restraint of our tribunals," which would "interpose and punish" the licentious.[49]

Therefore, truth by itself should not preclude a publication's being judged libelous. The "weapon of truth" should not be used "only to make a man disliked" or for "disturbing the peace of families" or "for relating that which does not appertain to official conduct." In legal terms, the standard Hamilton advocated was that the press could publish any statement that was true, as long it did so "with good motives and for justifiable ends." This "truth-plus" libel standard became the basis of most nineteenth-century state libel statutes. Legislatures and judges embraced it because it provided more rather than less protection for the reputations of officials, leaders, and governments than did the Zengerian standard of the Sedition Act. By giving defendants the additional burden of proving the purity of their motives, the Croswell doctrine left ample room for judges, still mostly Federalists and always gentlemen, to act on their personal and political sympathies and antipathies.[50]

In essence, the judge and jury's subjective beliefs about the character and intentions of an author or publisher became the measure of a publication's libelousness. This principle was spelled out especially clearly by Massachusetts Chief Justice Theophilus Parsons in the 1808 case *Commonwealth v. Clap*. A Bostonian named William Clap served two months in prison for posting notices along State Street asserting that auctioneer Caleb Hayward was "a liar, a scoundrel, a cheat, and a swindler," after Parsons upheld a lower court's refusal to hear evidence that the charges were true.

Parsons's decision expounded the ancient common law doctrine that negative statements about a person could be offenses against the state not because of their falsity, but because of their tendency to breach the peace by inspiring quarrels and vengeance. Thus true statements could actually be more dangerous than false ones, and "the truth of the words is no justification in a criminal prosecution for a libel." The only defense against a libel charge, in Parsons' view, was "by proving that the publication was for a justifiable purpose." Parsons allowed that truthful publications attacking public officers or candidates might sometimes be allowed, but severely restricted the possibility of this right being successfully used. Criticism "made with the honest intention of giving useful information, and not maliciously, or with intent to defame" might be lawful, but "calumny against public officers, or candidates" (as the court defined it) remained "an offence most dangerous to the people, and deserves punishment, because the people may . . . reject the best citizens, to their great injury."[51]

With judges like Parsons deciding the cases, there was little or nothing to stop state Federalist leaders from trying to punish their critics just as they had done at the national level during the 1790s. In Federalist-controlled New England, the Republican push to win over the region with newspapers brought not only a journalistic arms race, but also a new wave of persecution against Republican editors. Naturally, Massachusetts led the way. In 1802 John S. Lillie of the Boston *Constitutional Telegraphe* spent three months in prison for an oblique comment about state chief justice Parsons. Lillie lost his newspaper in the meantime, but he avoided total disaster by finding work (doubtless through political means) in the local United States Loan Office and then in the Boston branch of the national bank.[52]

William Carlton of Salem was not so lucky. Regarded as one whose "day & night, exertions to erase error & falsehood . . . defeated federalism" in the 1802 congressional election, the *Salem Register* editor was targeted by Federalists as an example, one that would "douse the ardor, & render vapid and ineffective" the other new Republican papers in the region. Carlton was indicted for a campaign paragraph opining that it was hard to believe that the British had never bribed their warm supporter Timothy Pickering, the Federalist candidate. The trial was moved to the strongly Federalist town of Ipswich, and the jury there quickly found the editor guilty, sentencing him to two months in prison and imposing bonds for his good behavior (meaning his political silence) for two years.

This was not the harshest sentence an editor ever received, but like many others in his position, Carlton was a marginal person who could not readily absorb the blow. A typically hard-drinking printer whose health had been impaired accordingly, Carlton fell seriously ill while serving his jail sentence, the stresses on him being increased by the threat of two new Federalist suits: a private libel action by Pickering and a prosecution for keeping the *Register* office open on Sunday. Carlton's friend Rev. William Bentley believed he never recovered, and two years later Carlton was dead at age thirty-four. He was quickly joined by his wife Elizabeth, a downwardly mobile local socialite who had fallen into Carlton's bibulous habits under the stresses of trying to manage as a struggling printer's wife. Salem's embittered Republicans flatly regarded the couple as casualties of Federalist persecution.[53]

The Carlton and Lillie cases inspired Massachusetts Republicans to try to reform the state libel laws in 1804, but Federalists defeated the proposal and went on as before.[54] Meanwhile, Massachusetts Federalists waged a legal war against the Republican press. The Northampton *Republican Spy,* one of the new papers founded for the election of 1804, became a particular target. In 1805 a grand jury indicted Timothy Ashley, the journal's printer, only to have him flee the state. The *Spy's* real editor, attorney Charles Shepherd, found another printer, the aforementioned Andrew Wright, to take over in 1806, but he was hit even harder than Ashley. Against his own better judgment, Wright had published some charges of Shepherd's against Governor Caleb Strong, specifically that he had speculated in government securities while sitting in Congress and that he pressured underlings to give his son a state government job. Wright was charged with seditious libel, and at his trial Chief Justice Parsons brushed aside the defense's strong evidence that the assertions were true. The distinguished Federalist jurist sentenced Wright to serve six months in prison, pay the costs of his own prosecution, and then submit a bond for three years of good behavior after he was released. Wright was ruined as a printer and later served more jail time for debts arising from his imprisonment.[55]

There was also sporadic Federalist violence against the New England Republican press. A year before the Republican mob destroyed Alexander Hanson's *Federal Republican* office in Baltimore, Federalist vigilantes calling themselves "Silver Greys" broke into the Newburyport *Independent Whig* late one night, sacking the office and melting much of the type. The local Republicans knew that the crime would have to be "redressed by subscription, not by prosecution" in Federalist-controlled courts. The fledgling *Independent Whig* proved a much more vulnerable target than the well-funded *Federal Republican*. After an abortive attempt to revive the *Whig* ended with a suspicious fire in June, Republican journalism would not show its face again in Newburyport for the rest of the decade.[56]

In areas where Federalists did not control the state and local governments, they devised more subtle means of coercion. Around the time of the Croswell case, the New York *Evening Post*, perhaps in one of its Hamilton-dictated editorials, called for Federalists to file private defamation suits whenever Republican editors criticized them. "There is no method so likely to bring them down from their daring flights of effrontery in slander," editor William Coleman opined, "as for the injured constantly to appeal to the laws of the land for redress." Given the sorry financial state of most Republican newspapers, the legal costs alone might be enough to put them out of business. Coleman speculated that if such a method had been employed earlier, the Federalists might still be in power.[57]

The *Evening Post*'s advice was followed, and private lawsuits became the approach of choice for gentlemen interested in punishing troublesome newspaper editors. In some parts of the country, editors even took to suing each other. By 1806 William Duane alone had been the defendant in sixty to seventy private libel suits and had filed at least one himself. James Cheetham of the New York *American Citizen* suffered tens of thousands of dollars in libel judgments, from suits instigated by both Federalists and the same Republican grandees who persecuted Harry Croswell.[58]

This form of harassment was in many ways more effective than criminal libel prosecutions. Private suits created less damaging publicity than sedition prosecutions, since they involved an injured individual attempting to restore his reputation rather than a despotic government trying to quash opposition. Instead of handing an editor the chance for glorious, public martyrdom, private legal harassment wore his emotions and finances down quietly over months and years and allowed the instigator of the suit to keep the moral high ground. By the end of Jefferson's administration, private lawsuits had reduced Duane to the point where he feared to travel more than two days' ride from Philadelphia, because such a trip would "carry me out of range of the courts of law, in which I am doomed I fear to linger out my life."[59]

In an age when people were imprisoned for debt, private libel suits against a impecunious printer could result in jail time even more easily than seditious libel prosecutions. In 1806 Nathaniel Willis Jr. of the Portland *Eastern Argus* lost a $2,000 private libel judgment, and because he was unable to pay, spent 100 nights in jail. Borrowing money for a $2,000 bond, Willis was allowed "liberty of the yard," meaning freedom to move about town during the day so he might find or earn money to pay his fine. However, when the editor dared to go outside the jail for water one winter evening when the pump inside had frozen, a trumped-up charge of "making an escape" was filed and upheld by the court. Forfeiting his bond, Willis found himself owing $4,000 when his business probably grossed half that much in a year.[60]

As William Coleman expected, the private libel approach was also much harder on Republicans than Federalists. Republican politicians filed private libel suits against Federalist editors but never found the method an effectual check, because Federalists typically had courts, money, and the finest available legal talent in their corner. (An exception must be made for William Cobbett, who left Philadelphia and then the country because of a $5,000 judgment in a case brought by Benjamin Rush.) Well-funded, well-connected, and an attorney himself, William Coleman never lost a lawsuit in which he was the defendant. Coleman was also highly successful as a plaintiff; in 1811 he won the largest libel judgment in New York history to that time against Solomon Southwick, a Republican editor-politician based in Albany.[61]

The most celebrated incident in the renewed Federalist repression campaign occurred in Connecticut. During Jefferson's second term, the printer Selleck Osborn came home to his native state after working as a journeyman in New York City and an editor in Sag Harbor, New York. Concentrating on editing and writing rather than printing now, he was first an assistant editor of the Danbury *Republican Farmer,* and while working in that town, gave a strongly partisan Fourth of July oration that received excellent notices from the national Republican press. That exploit probably earned Osborn the necessary backing (or perhaps just encouragement) for an even braver venture: the founding of a Republican newspaper at Litchfield, in the Federalist heartland of ultra-Federalist Connecticut.[62]

Osborn's paper, the Litchfield *Witness,* railed at the "Cloven Foot" of Federalism with a ferocity borne of an articulate printer's rage at the militant steadiness of his home state's social and political habits. Though more given to sarcasm than character assassination, Osborn vowed to give no quarter to the Federalists, who apparently had long succeeded in convincing Connecticut voters, through newspapers, sermons, and word of mouth, that Republicans were social climbers, infidels, libertines, larcenists, and worse. The new editor warned his opponents to "put up your scalping knives, and cease to mangle" Republican reputations, unless each Federalist was "willing that *every* transaction of his life should appear in public print."[63]

Osborn had not been in business two months when the Litchfield grand jury indicted him for criminal libel. For publishing a partisan but reasonable account of a recent trial in which a biased court had enabled two influential Federalists to successfully sue a Republican for allegedly fraudulent business dealings, Osborn was accused of defaming the judges and jury of the superior court. Later, the son of one of the Federalists attacked the editor with a whip. Then a local justice of the peace sued Osborn for calling him the "Crowbar Justice." The editor had issued the nickname after the justice had, during the "freemen's meeting" in which Connecticut citizens voted, openly threatened a poor debtor with reprisals if he voted Republican.[64]

In the spring of 1806, Osborn was found guilty in both cases. In the "crow-bar case," the editor and his partner, Timothy Ashley, a more conventional printer, were ordered to give bonds for their good behavior. Ashley complied, but Osborn, given the choice of having "his body or his mind in imprisonment," refused; he bought Ashley out of their business and began writing the paper from within the Litchfield jail. The Federalist authorities kept Osborn behind bars, without bail or "liberty of the yard," for the next year. Often he was not allowed visitors, and for a time his cell mate was a deranged man who had recently raped and killed a young woman. Throughout the year, however, Osborn continued to publish the *Witness,* conduct election campaigns, and excoriate his captors.[65]

In August 1806 Republicans from all over New England, including many of the state's now-Republican U.S. government officials, assembled to protest Osborn's plight. A procession marched through the streets of Litchfield and underneath the editor's cell window, and at a later banquet his supporters lifted their glasses to Osborn and "*Liberty of the Press—Litchfield Jail its Stronghold.*" Among the marchers was young John C. Calhoun, then a student at the famous Litchfield Law School and one of only two of the young attorneys to openly sympathize with the local "Jacobins."[66]

Fame did not, however, make the *Witness* into a successful business. Not surprisingly, the paper's accounts became "confused" during Osborn's stay in prison, and "the vast sums of money which have been levied upon the Editor and Printer in the shape of fines, damages, costs, &c. &c. &c" weighed heavily upon it. Despite the wide publicity that had attended the editor's case, many of the *Witness*'s Republican subscribers did not pay their bills, and the paper collapsed within a few weeks of his release. Osborn moved on to the Boston *Democrat* and a year later received a junior officer's commission in the army from President Jefferson. After the War of 1812, he returned to the political trade, editing a Delaware Republican paper that, unsurprisingly given his experiences in Connecticut, would be sharply critical of postwar efforts to minimize the differences and end the conflict between Republicans and Federalists.[67]

Those differences should not be underestimated. Though some Republican gentlemen shared their Federalist counterparts' distaste for newspaper politics and especially for newspaper politicians, even the most hardbitten Jeffersonian jurists realized at some level that seditious libel prosecutions were inconsistent with their stated creed. Thus Republican persecutors of the press often found their resolve or political support cracking. Harry Croswell's case was dropped when New York's highest court split along party lines, and the Republican-controlled state legislature followed it immediately with a guilty-minded reform of the state libel laws, endorsing the defense's position in the trial. The few Republican officeholders who made serious efforts to curb the Federalist press, or became prominently associated with seditious libel doctrines, such as Thomas McKean and Ambrose Spencer, faced strong criticism and electoral challenges from within their own parties.[68]

The Republican officeholder who tried to employ seditious libel most systematically was also the Republican most quickly repudiated for it. This was Elbridge Gerry, close friend of Sedition Act signer John Adams and Massachusetts governor on the eve of the War of 1812. Gerry ordered his attorney general and solicitor general to conduct a study of the Boston newspapers to document the extent of the libels in them. They found 236 actionable items in the Federalist journals (along with 17 in the Republican press), for which Gerry then sought indictments. Meanwhile, the governor gave and published a special message to the legislature, with the report appended, that proposed tightening the state libel laws. Mere weeks after delivering this message, however, Gerry was turned out of office by the voters, effectively ending his career as scourge of the Federalist press.[69]

Overall, the most striking aspect of this "darker side" of Republican libertarianism is its utter ineffectiveness. The 236 libels in Gerry's report produced only ten indictments and three convictions. No Federalist editor other than the grandstanding Hanson served jail time, so far as I have discovered, and the vast majority of Republican-initiated prosecutions failed far short of imposing punishment. Even Hanson went to jail largely for his own protection, and Republican irresolution allowed him to escape at least one major prosecution. In early 1809 Maryland governor Robert Wright ordered Hanson (in his capacity as a militia officer) to be tried for mutiny after the *Federal Republican* published an item urging the people of Maryland to disregard the president's recent mobilization of the state militia. Fortunately for Hanson, the Republican judge advocate in the trial was so disturbed by the questionable legality of this maneuver—Hanson had not been on active duty when the piece was published and had disobeyed no military order—that he wrote Governor Wright a lengthy letter demolishing the prosecution's case and asking for guidance. When Wright did not respond, the judge advocate simply read his letter into record and suspended the trial. "He had no idea of making himself a political prize fighter," the judge advocate said, despite his grave differences with the man before the court.[70]

Federalists, however, were hard-fisted with Republican printers when given the opportunity, with high rates of conviction and plenty of Republican printers ruined. They made a habit of giving even their libertarian actions an antilibertarian edge. Joseph Dennie was acquitted before a Federalist judge who based his jury charge on Hamilton's *People v. Croswell* arguments but, in the process, judicially diluted the Pennsylvania Constitution's press clause, which had flatly allowed truth as a defense with no stipulations as to motives or ends.[71]

The party difference over press freedom showed most clearly in the Republicans' behavior during the War of 1812. The Madison administration allowed Federalist newspapers to publish freely even when they were actively subverting the war effort, making this one of the very few American conflicts in which severe curbs on press freedom were not imposed. The defeated Elbridge Gerry became something of a hero to other Republican leaders for his crusade in Massachusetts, but they ignored his call for Federalist editors to be arrested en masse. (In some respects, Madison's greatest wartime service to press freedom may have been choosing Gerry as his second vice president, in which place his influence was effectively neutralized.) Despite the mob attacks against Hanson and a handful of other Federalist editors, then, it would be an understatement to say that their antiwar message had little trouble getting out.[72]

While Federalist control of the independent judiciary was probably the most important cause of the lopsided results of the post-1800 libel cases, another factor was the new Hamiltonian libel doctrine itself, which lent itself much more readily to use against Republicans than Federalists. Coping with a Federalist press that constantly attacked Jefferson's private moral character and religious views, Republican judges and attorneys argued that libels could only occur when criticism did not apply to public measures and official conduct. If that test was met, criticism should be largely immune to prosecution; as the Republican attorney general in *Commonwealth v. Clap* put it, the people were the only "proper and constitutional judges" of public men and measures, and the electoral process was the only remedy. This standard would have well suited most Republican editors, who frequently denounced religious intolerance and rarely dealt with private morality. The Federalist standard that won out placed much more of a burden on the good intentions of the publisher, and this allowed even the most prurient comments and imaginative speculations to be justified in the name of defending the community's faith and morals. Republican officials thus had relatively few effective legal weapons, leading to stretches like Hanson's failed court-martial.

Hence it was far from coincidental that in the year before the court-martial, Hanson had celebrated two different convictions inflicted on the most radical local Republican editor, Baptis Irvine of the Baltimore *Whig*. In March 1808 Hanson the lawyer helped put Irvine in jail for a month, having been held in contempt of court for criticizing an assault conviction against one of his journeymen. Then, in July, Irvine was sentenced to sixty days imprisonment, and fined $200, for accusing City Register Edward Coale of corruption. In response to this second verdict, the *Federal Republican* lauded the inequities of existing press freedom doctrines. "Do these noisy ignoramuses know that federal printers deal not in libels?" Hanson asked. "Tell us of an instance of a federal printer being convicted in a court of justice, if you can, and we'll answer you three to one."[73]

It was not until two decades later, when Federalism had disappeared and both party politics and Republican-style newspaper politics had achieved full legitimacy and ascendancy, that the use of criminal libel prosecutions to control political editors truly became insignificant. Even then, there were many descendants of old Federalists, such as James Fenimore Cooper and a group of Connecticut Congregationalists irritated by Jacksonian editor P. T. Barnum, who kept on trying. Federalist culture, it seems, never really came to terms with newspaper politics at all.[74]

12

The "Tyranny of Printers" in
Jeffersonian Philadelphia

ϵℐℴ

The *veiled but potentially volatile* tensions between printers and gentle-men spilled into public when Republican editors tried to assert the potential of their position for independent power or departed from the political line set by the party's increasingly conservative, lawyer-dominat-ed leadership. This happened most clearly in Philadelphia, where an all-out war broke out between newspaper editors and others for control of the Republican party and ascendancy over the style and substance of political life.

The catalyst for the Philadelphia blowup was William Duane. After 1800 the *Aurora* editor emerged as one of Pennsylvania's preeminent Re-publican leaders, backed by the influence of his newspaper and a strong party organization in inner-city Philadelphia. Aggressive and unapolo-getic about using these tools to guide the party, Duane presented to gen-tleman Republicans the unwelcome spectacle of a former henchmen tak-ing command over them. This was made especially bothersome by the fact that Duane espoused and wanted to implement a much more radical and democratic brand of republicanism than most gentlemen favored. With an exaggeration typical of elites who sense their monopoly on power eroding, many of Duane's former allies came to see the influence of news-paper editors like him as nothing less than "the tyranny of printers," an inversion of necessary and appropriate social hierarchies that was not to be tolerated. Elite Republicans banded together (and sometimes made common cause with the Federalists) to take back the party from Duane, but while they eventually succeeded in deposing him, they had little suc-cess in rolling back newspaper politics more generally.

All the problems began with the great differences, in political values and expectations, that high Republican leaders and the men who campaigned for them took into the period after 1800.

WILLIAM DUANE AND THE MORNING AFTER

Perhaps the clearest sign of the Republican elite's desire to gentrify the party was its discomfort with the prominence of its leading editor. Though Duane was the *"Sage of Clonmell"* to his fellow editors, a number of Republican gentlemen found him nearly as irritating as the Federalists did. Many resented that he presumed to speak the sense of the party, especially when the opinions he often expressed contradicted or condemned their own courses of action.

Chided in the *Aurora* for compromising too much in 1800, one peevish Republican legislator wrote back to Philadelphia that if Duane and his friends were dissatisfied, they could find someone else to serve next year. Others detested the ferocity and freedom of Duane's attacks, both intrinsically and for fear that carefully wrought private stratagems might be upset. The Virginia Republican congressman John Dawson read "with pain" the *Aurora*'s criticisms of another member he was cultivating and urged Alexander J. Dallas, Philadelphia's leading gentleman Republican, to do everything he could to rein Duane in and "prevent the danger of imprudent conduct." Yet nothing could restrain the editor from attacking someone he believed guilty of treason against the country, the people, the party, or his own friendship. He would accuse his own father, Duane responded to one critic, if his father did something to attack "the liberties of a nation."[1]

Elite politicians often expressed disgust with newspaper "abuse," but Duane regarded such attacks as a matter of high principle. In an 1807 pamphlet that was the closest he ever came to a systematic exposition of his political philosophy, Duane assigned frequent political campaigns, in which newspapers arraigned or defended the conduct of public figures, a crucial role in the functioning of a democracy. Public opinion, he argued, was the only effective check on a government officer, trumping institutions, other officers, and the "idea of virtue." Therefore, "nothing else secures the community any length of time against tyranny and corruption, but . . . a political system, which places *every officer* at certain reasonable periods . . . precisely in the same situation in which he was before he was elected or appointed, as a private citizen, to be again submitted to the ordeal of public opinion, and elected or appointed, or rejected, on the true principle of democracy—*utility to the people.*"

Political newspapers were the means by which public opinion could be brought to bear on government officers. Duane's use of the word "ordeal" was significant, for that was precisely what he believed it his duty to put public men through—an ordeal in which their characters, principles, and actions would be rigorously tested for their republicanism and "utility."[2]

The *Aurora's* publication policies were another area that sometimes put Duane at odds with other Republican leaders. While genteel Republicans such as Dallas and Dawson and Tench Coxe believed the press was or ought to be under the control of gentlemen like themselves (hence Dawson had written to Dallas to influence the *Aurora*), Duane maintained an iron grip on the content of his paper, filling much of it with his own writings and reserving the right to refuse or alter all anonymous submissions. Duane accepted his roles as surrogate campaigner for gentleman candidates and public spokesman for the party, but he would not be passive or submissive in those roles. Since he was the one who would suffer for what was published in the *Aurora,* he demanded full control over his own fate.

In one case, Duane declined to publish a piece by Coxe on land policy but used some of the facts cited in it elsewhere in the paper. When the touchy Coxe protested, Duane replied that readers had begun to complain that Coxe, a major land speculator, wrote on lands only to increase the value of his own vast holdings. In any case, Duane said, "the opinion which I have always entertained of the duties of an Editor, is, that over *every anonymous article,* he has the *absolute right* of publishing in whatever manner he may please." This was the practice of European editors, "and this is no more than reasonable, because upon [the editor] alone lies all responsibility." The anonymous author had the power to reveal his identity or conceal it, as he wished or circumstances warranted; the editor was known to all and unavoidably liable for any consequences.[3]

Duane's independence left many upper-class Republicans with no particular eagerness to defend the editor from his numerous persecutors. When the Senate tried him for contempt of its privileges during the 1800 campaign, a Virginia Federalist reported home that "not withstanding all his whining that he was about to fall victim for his steady support of liberty and republicanism, he finds but two here disposed to support him and indeed all here, even among the moderate Demos, reprobate his insolent conduct."[4]

If Duane assumed that Republican victory would put an immediate end to his persecutions, he was wrong. Congress simply allowed the sedition law to expire, leaving the proceedings already begun against Duane and the others to continue past the expiration date as stipulated by the statute. Eventually Thomas Jefferson ordered the Sedition Act prosecutions stopped, but a number of circumstances, including the hostility of the president's close advisers, combined to ensure that Duane enjoyed minimal relief. Constitutional scruples prevented Jefferson from interfering with the Senate prosecution, and Treasury Secretary Albert Gallatin successfully opposed the president's desire to explicitly condemn the act and promise reparations to the victims. Then Attorney General Levi Lincoln and his underlings took such a cautious, narrowly legalistic approach to carrying out Jefferson's instructions that several of the sedition cases went forward anyway. Lincoln diffidently instructed Alexander Dallas, previously Duane's own lawyer but recently appointed district attorney for eastern Pennsylvania, to drop the cases against Duane, but Dallas hesitated, informing Lincoln that one prosecution had been launched under the common law rather than the Sedition Act. (He did this even though the Republicans had often denounced the common law in the late campaign and had repeatedly denied that the common law even existed in the federal courts.) Lincoln decided that the case fell outside the president's order and told Dallas to continue prosecuting Duane.[5]

Meanwhile, a private suit initiated by the Federalists Levi Hollingsworth and Jared Ingersoll also proceeded in the federal courts. Though technically an action for libel, its real aim was to have Duane declared an alien, which would occur if the federal court decided it had jurisdiction over the case. The circuit court judges, all Federalists, took the sophistic route of admitting that the editor was born in New York but advising the jury to strip him of citizenship rights anyway, because he and his mother had returned to Ireland before the Declaration of Independence. When Duane pointed out the irony of a former Tory like Ingersoll having a lifelong crusader against British power declared a British subject, the same Federalists sued to have the editor declared in contempt of court. A. J. Dallas refused to defend Duane against the contempt charge (though he did offer to countersue a Federalist editor who had also commented on the case) and in fact conceded Duane's guilt before the court while arguing that there were extenuating circumstances. Thus "defended," Duane was sentenced to thirty days in prison.

President Jefferson began to think he should simply issue a pardon and put an end to the multifront vendetta being waged against Duane, but the New York jurist Robert R. Livingston convinced him otherwise. Livingston had spoken with the leading Republican attorneys in Philadelphia, and they were "unfavourable to Duane's conduct this occasion." The court's verdict had been correct and the editor's comments "gross & violent." In other words, Duane's own comrades had decided that he needed to be taught a lesson in showing proper respect for courts, judges, and lawyers.[6]

Thus it was that, though Duane had avoided prison while his enemies were still in power, he spent a month in jail during the first 100 days of an administration that was partly his own creation. The irony of this turn of events notwithstanding, Duane was convinced that "This like former Attacks upon me is likely to produce public good, and perhaps personal good to me." Not knowing that his own lawyers were responsible for his predicament, Duane thought that such a blatant "Act of Vengeance" would unify the Republican party, and he relished the many signs of popular support for himself that the incident elicited. The courtroom was "thronged" with Republicans during Duane's trial, and a "great Body" of them paraded with the editor as he was taken away to prison. The jailkeepers were by now Republicans, and they treated Duane well, giving him "the best room in the Debtor's Apartment" and allowing nearly unrestricted visits from his wife, children, and friends.[7]

The throngs at Duane's trial indicated that, despite the low esteem in which many elite Republicans held him, the editor was becoming a genuinely popular leader in the streets and taverns of Philadelphia. Unabashedly embracing the appellation "democrat" as well as "republican," Duane and his political partner, Congressman Michael Leib, were building a political organization that reached deep into Philadelphia's neighborhoods, a strong advantage in a city where the electoral rules greatly magnified the importance of ward-level elections.

Particularly strong in the crowded, ramshackle Northern Liberties and Southwark districts, home to many Irish and German immigrants, the Duane-Leib group integrated politics into neighborhood life through a network of clubs and societies. These included some overtly political groups (such as the True Republican Society and the Democratic Young Men) and some fraternal orders and benevolent societies (such as the Tammany Society, the United German Benefit Society, and the St.

Patrick's Benevolent Society) that became heavily politicized. More important than any of these was the Philadelphia Militia Legion, both a functioning militia unit and a "democratic political army" of which Duane was a high-ranking officer.

These institutions served many practical political functions, such as supplying the personnel to fill a public nominating meeting or blanket the city with tickets on election day, but more important, their activities made politics more accessible and attractive to ordinary citizens. Holding numerous public events, the clubs supplied camaraderie, conviviality, entertainment, and sometimes charity in addition to political proselytizing and involvement. For a young man, it was entirely possible to have a social life built completely if loosely around Republican party politics. Both Duane and Leib also maintained strong followings in their respective ethnic communities. They cemented the loyalty of their followers by vigorously promoting causes that concerned them, such as the relaxation of the naturalization laws, the prevention of epidemics in Philadelphia's crowded poorer neighborhoods, and reforms of the legal system designed to make it cheaper, fairer, and more accessible to ordinary citizens.[8]

The prison stay prompted Duane to some disturbing reflections on the incongruity of his situation. Despite his popularity in Philadelphia and President Jefferson's apparent good wishes, little seemed to have changed for the editor since the transfer of power. Why should he continue to be singled out for harassment? Duane poured his heart out in a letter to Jefferson from jail:

> I began to feel the injury I have sustained [at the hands of the Federalists], and to consider that it has been done, not because I was base—but because I have been formidable to oppressors. I look at my family and I see united in it those who have been long the victims of Federal persecution along with my offspring, combining the claims of eight years contest and persecution: the descendants of Franklin and the beloved wife of the amiable and good Bache. . . . When I see my countrymen at peace, and republicanism diffusing concord and harmony, under the reign of liberty and moderation, I cannot but think it hard that I alone should still remain the victim.[9]

Though presented in his overheated manner, Duane's predicament was real. To an extent of which he was not yet fully aware, his troubles continued—were allowed to continue, by fellow Republicans—because he represented political trends that gentlemen in neither party wished to see flourish, trends embodied in the *Aurora* and in his and Leib's Philadelphia organization.

ORIGINS OF THE REPUBLICAN SCHISM

Duane's biographer notes that a split in the Philadelphia Republican party along class and ethnic lines had been evident since at least 1794.[10] In that year, Michael Leib and Benjamin Bache's radical policies in directing the Democratic Society of Pennsylvania had driven out most of the group's more moderate, wealthy, and conventionally respectable members. That schism in turn had roots that went back to the bitter battles over the radically democratic, unicameral Pennsylvania Constitution of 1776.

The old Constitutionalists had formed the core of the Republican party of the 1790s, but they had been joined by other men who were less sympathetic to Constitutionalist ideals but disgusted with Federalist excesses. These included Albert Gallatin and Alexander Dallas, both politically ambitious attorneys who had become Republicans at least partly because their recent arrival in the country barred them from preferment in the Federalist party. Gallatin and Dallas's influence had significantly tempered the democratic radicalism of the Pennsylvania Republicans. Dallas had been instrumental in the 1799 nomination for governor of Thomas McKean, an autocratic judge and former Federalist who had led the successful campaign that replaced the 1776 constitution with a more conservative and conventional one in 1790. Far from democratic in his ideas, temperament, or personal ambitions, McKean had not been the first choice of Duane and Leib for governor.[11]

Adversity kept the party together in 1799 and 1800, but the latent divisions could be observed in the separate banquets held to celebrate Jefferson's inauguration in March 1801.[12] A. J. Dallas and his allies sponsored an "elegant entertainment" at Francis's Union Hotel, mounted and presented in the manner of a society ball. Meanwhile, a group of immigrant radicals held a less lavish dinner at John Cordner's tavern, Republican activist John Beckley's Republican committee hosted another one at the county courthouse, and Duane's militia company held yet another, outdoors at Bushill.[13]

The Dallas function toasted the memory of George Washington and expressed a number of other sentiments that softened the edges of the Republican creed and reflected a strong distaste for partisanship. One toast wished for the "spirit of Union [to] allay the feuds of party" and, tellingly, for the "spirit of conciliation [to] revive the harmonies of Society," by which was meant the genteel social life that had been so disrupted by the party conflict. By contrast, the other gatherings were much more pugna-

cious, expressing no desire, and holding out no prospects, for reconcilia-
tion with the Federalists. The group at Cordner's wished "a leaden weight
to the heels of sinking federalism" and for "political enemies" to be "well
treated but never trusted." And whereas the moderates at the Union Hotel had made no mention of the Pennsylvania constitution, these radicals
called for a "speedy revision" of the more conservative 1790 document.[14]

The militia meeting condemned "the authors of the Alien and Sedition
Laws" to "universal and perpetual execration" and saluted the "Duke of
Braintree" (John Adams) with three groans. John Beckley's dinner led off
with a toast to "The People—The only legitimate source of all power." The
guests then drank that the U.S. Constitution should be "faithfully supported," but they had much stronger praise for the egalitarian Declaration of
Independence: "May it become the political gospel of our country."[15]

The meetings also expressed differences on the role of the press in politics and the value of political campaigning. The Dallas group simply
praised "a free press," among a list of other items in a toast, and had little
else to say about practical politics. The radical conclaves, however, forth-
rightly endorsed the methods by which Duane and his fellow political
professionals had fought the late campaign. The Cordner's meeting pronounced the press "the torch of the world—May the reptiles of despotism
shrink from its blaze" and suggested that true Republicans should "con-
quer by the force of argument, and not by the argument of force."[16] The
dinner at the courthouse extolled "free, pure, and frequent elections." At
the militia picnic, Duane's men saluted their leader, who was in Washington City attending the inauguration, as a "man of firm and unshaken
virtue, who withstood the wickedness of federal storms, with the energy
and fortitude of a true republican."[17]

These symbolic divergences presaged the substantive disagreements
within the Republican party that swiftly followed. Duane and his fellow
Republican radicals had long assumed that, in the event of a Republican
victory, those of their Federalist antagonists who held appointive public
offices would be swept out. This belief was more than a matter of vindic-
tiveness or a desire for the spoils of office, though both of those impulses
were present. "Men like Duane," writes his biographer, "who had criticized President Washington for his seeming indifference to the social
fulfillment of the Revolution saw [the election of 1800] as a mandate" for
an approach to governing (and the staffing of government) completely
different from that of the Federalists.[18]

Duane and his friends believed that many Federalist officers had profited corruptly from their offices and used them to influence elections and persecute Republicans. More important, they were convinced that the Federalist officeholders had rejected the direct sovereignty of the people and attempted to make of themselves an exclusive officeholding class. To Duane, it was ludicrous to believe that men who professed to believe "*democracy* . . . a system of massacre and murder, rapine and desolation" could faithfully or effectively serve under a democratic regime.[19]

To facilitate the expected mass removals, Duane took it upon himself to provide Jefferson with information on Federalist depredations in the lower substrata of politics he knew best. Signing himself "Citizen W. Duane," he compiled a detailed register of the capacities and political leanings of the federal government's clerks and other subordinate officials, replete with caustic epithets, expecting that this kind of information would guide future hiring policies.[20]

So certain was Duane that the purge was coming that he acquiesced in the go-slow removal policy announced in Jefferson's inaugural address; the editor reassured his Philadelphia associates that he simply could "not be persuaded from what I know that there is any disposition to retain Persons who must be well known to be the Creatures of those who have abused the Country and the Public trust." While patiently waiting, Duane did occasionally make his views known, in an unusually soft-spoken way, in the *Aurora* and to Jefferson personally.[21]

The administration's removal policy was much more cautious than that supported by Duane. Uncomfortable with removing officials on the grounds of their political beliefs alone, President Jefferson at first decided to replace only those guilty of outright misbehavior in office or whom he considered to have been appointed illegitimately. Jefferson slowly inclined toward a more aggressive policy, but Albert Gallatin, along with many of Duane's erstwhile Pennsylvania allies, continued to urge restraint.

At around the time of Duane's incarceration, Gallatin asked his friend Alexander Dallas for advice, both on the general policy and its specific application to Pennsylvania. In his reply, Dallas offered a long statement of the "moderate," genteel Republican position on the matter. "All official arrangements must depend . . . on the principle, the policy, and the promise of the Republican party," he wrote, defining all three as "equality."[22]

Duane might well have agreed with this statement, except that Dallas was not thinking of equality in Duane's sense, as among white men from all classes and occupations. (Duane occasionally extended the term to women and nonwhites as well.)[23] Dallas instead meant equality between Republican and Federalist gentlemen! He proposed an "equilibrium," in which enough Federalists would be gradually removed so as to put half of the offices in Republican hands. The demands of people like Duane should be ignored: "Whatever the flaming zealots of party may suggest, in the moment of triumph, no good man can desire to perpetuate the feuds that have already destroyed the harmony of society, and must dissolve the unity of the nation, if not extinguished or allayed." In Dallas's view, the zealots' "clamor" for removals was rooted in nothing more than a lust for those offices themselves. Republicans of "good sense and good temper," on the other hand, "would rather reclaim . . . their [Federalist] opponents" and "divide the profits of office . . . than endanger the stability of government." Apparently a gentleman wishing to "divide the profits of office" was inherently incapable of a vulgar lust for them.[24]

Turning to the specific situation in Philadelphia, Dallas recommended that one Federalist who might be spared was customs collector George Latimer. Latimer was not accused of any financial delinquencies, Dallas said, "and I cannot discover that he has exerted his official influence for party purposes." What was more, the collector was popular with the merchants. Actually, Dallas was listening more closely to the Federalist merchants than to his own Republican comrades. As Dallas must have known, Latimer *had* exerted political influence through his office by discouraging Philadelphia businessmen from advertising in the *Aurora*. According to Duane, such advertising was "the *only profitable* part" of a partisan newspaper. Without that source of profit (or some replacement), the income from a newspaper was "too inadequate to render it a pursuit eligible for any man who has a family to provide for."[25] Nevertheless, Dallas used his influence to prevent Latimer's removal for nearly a year and a half after the inauguration, when his own political calculations finally demanded it.[26]

Dallas's pontifications were self-serving as well as misleading. Trying to establish his family in the Philadelphia elite, Dallas socialized with Federalists and was anxious to impress them with the respectability and moderation of Republican rule.[27] Though he high-mindedly deprecated the "clamor" for office, he himself had held office continuously for more than a decade. He had been appointed secretary of the commonwealth in 1791, while still a relative newcomer to the country, and had taken advantage of

Gov. Thomas Mifflin's alcoholism to make the office into a virtual cogovernorship. Holding that post until 1801, Dallas had used the contacts it conferred to build a highly remunerative law practice on the side. In 1801 President Jefferson had appointed Dallas district attorney as one of his first official acts and soon followed that with a second appointment as a bankruptcy commissioner. Governor McKean quickly added a third office to Dallas's collection, the Philadelphia city recordership.[28]

Dallas's attitude toward these offices was thoroughly mercenary. When other Republicans protested his having so many appointments, the eminent attorney declared it absolutely necessary that he hold several offices at once: the salaries attached made none of them worth holding by themselves, he argued, and at any rate he deserved to be compensated for losing out on "a share in [a] very lucrative [law] practice." His assumption that public officials should not have to sacrifice lavish incomes and aristocratic lifestyles was common among the better-placed Republicans. A friend once wrote Dallas with the wish that he would "continue to make [his official station] beneficial to yr. pocket as well as to your reputation." When William Jones, a wealthy Philadelphia merchant and sea captain, was considered by Jefferson and Madison for the post of secretary of the navy, his supporters complained that the salary of the office "would not support Capt. Jones in the mode of living he has been used to, and he cannot brook looking to a worse one." They suggested that the salary be raised so he could accept it.[29]

The Jefferson administration appointments policy, dominated nationally by Albert Gallatin and in Pennsylvania by Gallatin's friend Dallas, closely followed the double standard that Dallas's career exemplified. The spoils of victory were not considered such if the recipient happened to be a man of wealth, gentility, or what Gallatin called "superior weight and talents." Less weighty men who demanded removals or solicited offices, however, were condemned as "men under the influence of passions or governed by self-interest."[30]

Duane and his fellow editors thus fared rather poorly under the administration they helped elect. Jefferson was just as concerned as Dallas to demonstrate the falsity of Federalist claims to a monopoly on gentility and talent; he would make no appointments that would give blue-blooded Federalists cause to sneer. Moreover, it suited his own cosmopolitan tastes, high regard for formal education, and Virginia-bred respect for family pedigree to choose only learned gentlemen of certified respectability as his officeholders. Artisan printers did not meet Jefferson's educational and social requirements, and thus newspaper editors were usually not even considered for presidentially appointed offices.

Though willing to benefit from editors' help and to give them the impression of his friendship when it suited, the president made his true estimate of them brutally clear in a comment to James Monroe. Some actions of Jefferson's had been misreported in the press, potentially hampering negotiations Monroe was conducting with the British. "My confidence was firm," Jefferson wrote, "that neither yourself nor the British government . . . would believe me capable of making the editors of newspapers the confidants of my speeches or opinions." As a gentleman and a statesman, Jefferson implied, such an indiscretion would have been far beneath him.[31]

The exceptional case of one editor who was appointed to office supports the notion that Jefferson excluded them as a class. This was Stanley Griswold, the Yale-trained ex-minister who edited the Walpole *Political Observatory*. He obtained a whole series of appointments from Jefferson and then Madison, culminating in an Illinois Territory judgeship. In his first application letter, Griswold plucked Jefferson's heartstrings by telling of his "indescribably painful" sensations at trying to maintain his family on "but an inadequate support." He asked presidential help to prevent the fulfillment of Federalist taunts that he was "sacrificing once flourishing prospects and ruining myself by *democracy*." Such downward mobility in a prominent Republican was an embarrassment to the cause, and Jefferson could not help but come to the rescue.[32]

Printer-editors were another matter. Few printers even tried to angle for offices, but they failed when they did. Jailed for his campaigning in 1803, William Carlton of the Salem *Register* applied for the job of naval officer at the local custom house. No one in Salem had been "more buffeted in the political tempest than him," Carlton observed accurately, but he asked the office not so much for the money as for a mark of approval from the administration. The local Federalists were denouncing Carlton as a despicable tool, and the editor needed some sign from on high to improve his community stature. "It would be extremely agreeable to 500 citizens of this town," Carlton suggested, "that I should be noticed, particularly noticed, by the Gen. Govt. as I have been *so particularly* noticed by the rancorous enemies of that Government." Unbeknownst to Carlton, Levi Lincoln and others had already offered the position to the Harvard graduate Joseph Story, Salem's most eminent young Republican attorney and a future Supreme Court justice.[33]

In a departure from previous policy, the Jefferson administration even excluded newspaper editors from their traditional niche in the postal service. Postmaster General Gideon Granger explained in removing a Georgia Federalist printer from his office that "Printers of newspapers ought not to be employed as postmasters" because possessing the office gave them unfair advantages over their competitors and tempted them to tamper with the mail for partisan benefit. During the 1790s, Republicans had constantly complained of such interference as the opening of their letters or the theft of opposition newspapers by Federalist postal authorities. Twenty editors had held postmasterships under the Federalists, but Granger's appointments cut the number to three. The only partisan Republican editor to be named a postmaster was Thomas Perrin Smith, a nonprinter and young Virginia gentleman who published the Easton, Maryland, *Republican Star.*[34]

In the matter of printing patronage, the editors were somewhat more fortunate, but only somewhat. Secretary of State Madison was unwilling to fully link the law-printing assignments to politics and so neglected some of the most stalwart editors who had fought in the 1800 campaign. Charles Holt's New London *Bee* was passed over in favor of the old, established, moderately Federalist New Haven *Connecticut Journal,* and many other partisan sheets were also ignored, including all the German-language Republican papers. Conversely, newer journals founded through the direct efforts of high national leaders—such as Levi Lincoln's Worcester *National Aegis*—were immediately noticed.[35]

As for Duane himself, it was widely believed, in John Quincy Adams's words, "that he had obtained by extortion almost the whole of the public printing" and enjoyed a special status with the new administration. Duane's confident behavior and the opening of his new branch printing office in Washington helped foster this impression.[36] In fact, Duane had been asked to stay in Philadelphia largely so that the more respectable and tractable Samuel Harrison Smith could be installed as the Jefferson administration's leading editorial supporter.[37] In terms of job-printing contracts, Duane's Washington shop—founded with the encouragement of House Speaker Nathaniel Macon and other congressional leaders—was to receive only "such part of the printing as Mr. Smith cannot execute."[38]

Over several years of wheedling and pleading, Duane did eventually acquire a substantial amount of government business, estimated at $1,000 to $2,000 a year. But that was insufficient even to make the branch office profitable, let alone make him a leader of the book and stationery trade, as he had hoped. Those who wished the editor ill regarded his solicitations for printing contracts as evidence of his "insatiable rapacity" for "public plunder," but as Duane argued repeatedly, he was merely seeking the kind of aid without which a national political newspaper like the *Aurora* could not remain solvent.

Duane's Washington investment ultimately became a huge debt that weighed on his finances for most of the rest of his life.[39] By the end of the Jefferson administration, conflicts within the party (especially between Duane and Gallatin) had left the *Aurora* office with no federal printing patronage at all.[40] Thus Duane was forced to become more creative in his efforts to actually make money at political publishing. At Madison's suggestion, he spent years organizing the publication of an indexed edition of the U.S. statutes. He also wrote and published several military handbooks and drill manuals based primarily on his experience with the Militia Legion, hoping to have them adopted by the government for official use.[41]

None of these projects could rescue Duane from his financial quagmire. Writing to James Madison about his edition of the laws in 1808, Duane expressed his continuing frustration that doing good for the Republican cause had not resulted in doing well, or even tolerably well. "My activity in the best interests of my country," he complained, had thus far thwarted his efforts to support his family and pay his debts, "rather than promoted [them] as might in justice have been expected."[42]

Of course, Duane brought many of the problems on himself. Always overambitious and never adept at controlling costs, the editor failed in his various publishing ventures principally because of his tendency to allow the tactical, ideological, or prestige value in a project to outweigh or destroy its profitability.[43] In producing his military books, for instance, Duane became convinced that he was making a vital contribution to the republic, both strengthening its defenses and instilling a new martial spirit more republican and democratic in character. Rather than potboilers, his drill manuals were to be nothing less than "a revolution in military discipline." Sending a copy of one of these works to Jefferson, Duane proudly noted that "Such are the works that are wanted throughout the country; they disrobe military subjects of the mystery in which *ignorance* and cunning have involved them." His first military book, *The American Military Library*, was a compendium of military information compiled and abridged from a panoply of European works and intended for use by militia officers. Though now considered an important and original work by military historians, it grew too large, diffuse, and high-priced for its purpose, which Duane justified with the excuse that he had "not looked so much to profit as to public utility."[44]

Another major factor in Duane's publishing failures was the depth of hostility he inspired in some quarters. A few years after writing his *Military Library*, he produced a *Handbook for Infantry*. In a rare victory of merit over politics, the War Department adopted Duane's work as an official manual at the beginning of the War of 1812, despite the opposition of Federalist-sympathizing generals and Republican factional opponents reluctant "to give the writings of a suspected *heretic in politics* any countenance in *war*."[45]

As the official supplier of drill manuals to the U.S. Army, Duane felt that he would at last be able to provide his wife and children with a "handsome income" for the foreseeable future. As in many of Duane's ventures, this victory swiftly turned disastrous. Though three successive secretaries of war had encouraged Duane's effort to become the army's official expert on discipline and one had even appointed him a lieutenant colonel for the purpose, political enemies prevented his appointment to a board for establishing a uniform system of discipline. The board then dropped Duane's *Handbook* and refused to accept two other manuals he had been commissioned to write, transforming his prospective handsome income into another large debt and a roomful of unsalable books.[46]

If Duane had ever been inclined to become a passive apologist for the administration like Samuel Harrison Smith, his disappointments in printing patronage dissuaded him. He came to realize that he could not simply put his trust in the political gratitude of the party's officeholders. "If I depended on anything but my own activity and principles," he told the Connecticut Republican activist Abraham Bishop, a Yale graduate who, in contrast to Duane, was rewarded by Jefferson, "I should have been left in the *Slough of party*, trodden upon, and like my predecessor forgotten. My independence is my pride."[47] Thus, though always personally loyal to Jefferson, Duane resolved early on in Jefferson's administration to pursue his own political course.

EDITORS, LAWYERS, AND THE PENNSYLVANIA LEGAL REFORM MOVEMENT

Duane's resolution notwithstanding, it was Alexander Dallas and the other gentleman moderates who sparked the divisions among the Philadelphia Republicans into open conflict. They did so over radical Republican efforts to restrain the judiciary and the legal profession. Upon the Republican accession, an important item on the radical agenda was the repeal of the Judiciary Act of 1801, which had been passed in the final days of the Adams administration. Although that measure contained some needed reforms, many Republicans perceived it mainly as an attempt to vitiate their victory by ensconcing Federalism inside the impregnable fortress of a greatly expanded "independent" federal judiciary. Action on the issue was spurred by Chief Justice John Marshall's decision to hear the case of *Marbury v. Madison,* in which four of the judges appointed under the 1801 act were suing to force the administration to deliver their commissions.[48]

Duane was visiting Washington during the congressional debate on the repeal in early 1802, expecting to see the overweening ambitions of the judiciary dealt a strong blow by a righteous, united party. Public opinion on the matter seemed clear: mass meetings were convening in Philadelphia to denounce the 1801 act, and the Pennsylvania legislature had instructed the state's congressional delegation to support repeal. It was no surprise when Pennsylvania senator James Ross, a Federalist, introduced a memorial from the Philadelphia bar protesting the repeal, but Duane was appalled to find that A. J. Dallas and several other Republican lawyers had also signed the document, which cited "professional duty" as the signers' motivation. Dallas and the others had joined with several of the city's most prominent Federalists, including a plaintiff in the suit that had caused Duane to be declared an alien.[49]

Still committed to maintaining the unity of the party, Duane revealed his anger gradually. Writing daily letters back to the *Aurora,* he first merely praised the "few republican lawyers of our city who have so manfully maintained their ground" by not signing, but a day later he condemned the "extreme presumption" it took "for a few lawyers to interpose their *professional duty* as an argument for interfering with legislative provisions or constitutional principles." Duane observed that though none of the Republican signers may have intended to divide the party, Federalists were using the bar memorial that way. The editor wondered in print how Dallas and the others could have been "so blind to the secret and avowed hatreds of men, whose name in the same list with theirs was a reproach."[50]

Two days later, Duane laid out the basic issues, as he saw them, between supporters and opponents of the repeal: the independence of the judiciary and the role of lawyers in American society. The former concept, Duane argued, had been mistakenly transferred from England to America. In the mother country, the term had referred to the independence of judges from the influence of the king and his ministers; they were not at all independent of Parliament, which could remove judges by simply voting to do so. In America, the doctrine had been badly misconstrued into the notion that the judiciary was to be independent of any other power, including the people themselves. Unlike their ironically more accountable English counterparts, American judges could be dislodged only through the cumbersome process of impeachment and trial. Hence they were becoming so "independent of the original fundamental authority of the people, as to have become in a measure their masters and not their officers."[51]

Besides the injustice of giving judges and lawyers a kind of veto power over all the community's decisions, Duane condemned the present system for distorting the incentive structure of the society and diverting a disproportionate amount of talent and wealth into the parasitic legal profession. "As things are managed at present, it is the interest of every man . . . to bring up his sons . . . to the study of the law," Duane observed, and the resulting overabundance of lawyers contributed mightily to all the distresses and difficulties of American life, including a debilitating litigiousness. Echoing the antilawyer movement of the 1780s, Duane proposed that law courts be resorted to only after a mutually agreed-upon arbitrator failed to settle a dispute.[52]

The Judiciary Act was successfully repealed, and the issue died down until the next meeting of the Pennsylvania legislature, in late 1802. That body passed two legal reform measures that reflected the general viewpoint expressed in Duane's comments on the bar memorial. One bill established a permanent system of arbitration that citizens could use to resolve disputes without resort to the courts or the legal profession; the other, the so-called "Hundred Dollar Act," implemented the same principle by allowing all cases in which less than $100 was at stake to be tried, without counsel, before a justice of the peace. The bills passed by large margins and aroused little controversy—until Governor McKean abruptly vetoed them.[53]

McKean had already made himself unpopular by appointing too many relatives and personal retainers and too few loyal Republicans to state offices. This new act of apostasy aroused the fury of rural legislators and Philadelphia radicals alike. Though he shifted with the slightest political breeze on most other issues, McKean was immovable when it came to protecting the prerogatives of the legal profession. The governor refused, he wrote contemptuously in one of the veto messages, to see Pennsylvania "imitate the practices of rude inceptive governments subsisting in rude and unlettered times" before lawyers stalked the earth.[54]

Even more explosive was the case of Thomas Passmore, a Philadelphia merchant who, like Duane and many others, had been jailed for contempt of a state court. When one of Passmore's ships sank, he had filed a claim against his insurers and received an arbitrators' judgment in his favor. Instead of paying, the insurers appealed the decision to the state supreme court, leading a furious Passmore to post an insulting notice (about the insurers) on the bulletin board of the City Tavern. The insurers' attorney, none other than A. J. Dallas, filed a motion for contempt, and after lengthy proceedings, the court ordered Passmore to apologize for the insult. Refusing, the embittered merchant was fined and sentenced to a month in jail. Passmore sent a memorial protesting his treatment to the legislature, which ordered an investigation of the judges in the case. In addition, a bill was introduced to severely restrict the power of judges to punish for contempt of court. The investigation was popular, but opposition to the contempt bill was strong among the lawyers and other moderates in the legislature, and it failed in a tie vote.[55]

The Passmore case, with its obvious analogies to newspaper editors' encounters with the legal system, provoked Duane into making radical judicial reform the defining item on the state Republican agenda. He lashed the state legislators who had balked at the contempts bill and foresaw that "a total revision of the received maxims concerning the tenure of judicial office" would soon be necessary.[56]

Meanwhile, in Philadelphia, open fighting erupted along the party's historic fault lines. In September 1802 moderates in Philadelphia County (the area outside present-day Center City Philadelphia), meeting at a tavern called the Rising Sun, nearly blocked Michael Leib's renomination to Congress. The attempt was made at the instigation of Senator George Logan. Living at a palatial country estate called "Stenton," Logan had always regarded himself as the area's political squire and decided that the flamboyant populist Leib was an "improper character" to represent his district.[57]

Duane and the *Aurora* came immediately to Leib's rescue, condemning the insurgents and demanding that they honor the regularly nominated ticket. After the *Aurora's* attacks, a second Rising Sun meeting, with Duane and Leib's supporters in attendance, faithfully carried out the editor's instructions. Having survived this initial plot, Leib and Duane were determined to make a stand for their own position in the party. Apparently, the moderates were no longer willing to tolerate the leadership of real democrats.[58]

In March 1803 Leib and Duane's neighborhood organization orchestrated a series of ward-level public meetings to protest the continued retention of Federalist officeholders, culminating in a memorial to President Jefferson. As intended, the protest campaign drove the moderates from cover. Merchant-congressman William Jones, along with several of his colleagues in the Pennsylvania delegation, drafted a letter to Jefferson expressing complete satisfaction with the administration's removal policy and denouncing "indiscriminate intolerance" in appointments. Duane caught wind of this while visiting Washington and wrote back to Philadelphia with an order "for the Ward Committees to take up this subject." Here was not only a political opportunity but another proof of the moderates' disloyalty to their erstwhile comrades: "the tendency of [Jones's] letter is to break us all to pieces, and to depress men who have stood the brunt of the battle, while those who have come in after the danger are seeking not only the honors of the triumph but to rob the victors of their laurels and their reputation."[59]

William Jones and his friends greeted the news of popular outrage back in Philadelphia with disgust, for both the Leib-Duane group and the common people who followed them. "We are told that the Knowledge of our Conduct . . . has excited their Contempt and Indignation against us," wrote one member of the congressional delegation. "My God! are the People of Philadelphia composed of such Materials?" Revealing his utter disdain for Leib, Duane, and their democratic form of politics, Alexander Dallas reported to Gallatin that the protest meetings were merely a "nuisance" that would "bring the Republican interest into some discredit" in respectable circles. "There is not . . . any man of character disposed to countenance their proceedings." Gallatin bluntly described the emerging schism to Jefferson as one between the "thinking party of the community," who would "not submit to the decrees of partial ward or township meetings" (of course, the meetings were only "partial" in the sense that Leib and Duane had organized them), and a "violent party" who unjustly enjoyed "a strong hold on public opinion." When Jefferson wrote a reply to the Philadelphia ward meetings' memorial in the form of a private letter to Duane, Gallatin dissuaded him from sending it, because it would have given the *Aurora* editor and his "malcontents" a sign of the president's respect and confidence.[60]

The political strife of 1803 launched an increasingly intense battle over the rights to the party label "Republican" in Pennsylvania and the concomitant right to public affiliation with President Jefferson. The *Aurora's* role in the campaign of 1800 gave it strong advantages in this struggle, as did its longstanding opposition to lenience toward Federalists or any reduction in party consciousness. In June 1803 the paper coined one of the seminal political terms of the Jeffersonian era when it castigated moderation as practiced by its opponents within the party as "a *half-way house* between virtue and vice, between truth and falsehood, where souls devoid of energy, and minds twisted by corruption may repose. . . . What an hermaphrodite thing, partaking of two characters, and yet having neither! A *tertium quid* from the combination of good and evil, of the *mule kind*, incapable of propagating itself."[61]

The label "Quid" eventually stuck fast to Republican schismatics around the nation.[62] This was a good example of Duane's (and many another editor's) basic strategy in party disputes. Casting his paper as the one true voice of the party, he methodically labeled his opponents in ways that placed them outside acceptable party norms. Detractors of Duane and Leib and the *Aurora* found themselves "traduced as *traitors,* apostate whigs, hypocritical wretches, VILLAINS, MONSTERS" for week after week and month after month in its pages.[63]

The moderates' maneuvers failed badly in 1803, as the next legislative elections went heavily for the Republican radicals. The resulting legislature repassed the vetoed judicial reform bills by veto-proof majorities and impeached the supreme court judges who had jailed Passmore. Hostility to McKean reached new heights, and the battle lines came more clearly into focus when Hugh Henry Brackenridge, the lone Republican on the supreme court, sided with his profession over his party and asked to be impeached along with the other judges even though he had not even participated in the Passmore case. A. J. Dallas followed suit, refusing an offer to act as prosecutor at the coming impeachment trial. The legislature passed an address demanding Brackenridge's removal, but to no one's surprise, McKean ignored it.[64]

As late as February 1804, Gallatin and Dallas believed a political civil war could yet be averted, but that hope was premised on their refusal, against all the evidence, to take William Duane seriously as an independent political actor. They assumed that the *Aurora* was under the control of Michael Leib, who was, after all, a liberally educated man despite his despicable slumming. Duane, however, might be pressed into their own service by threats or enticements. The editor was summoned into Albert Gallatin's office and made "a formal overture . . . to abandon Leib, or I should be destroyed politically myself." Duane exploded with rage at the suggestion and "threatened to denounce the secretary, in the Aurora, if he would talk in a such a manner."[65] A few weeks later, Gallatin's friend Dallas tried again. On the morning before an important political meeting, he sent Duane a note, offering a $1,000 contract to print a series of law reports Dallas had compiled. Duane correctly interpreted this offer as an attempt at seduction by "pecuniary temptation."[66]

Though rooted in longstanding elite beliefs about the mercenary nature of printers and other artisans, it is difficult to imagine a more erroneous assessment of character than Gallatin and Dallas made in these cases. The independence of his political judgments and loyalty to his political friends were the two qualities in which Duane most fundamentally grounded his self-respect. Gallatin and Dallas asked him to betray both. Duane was appalled to discover just how low an estimate his former allies held of him. Gallatin and Dallas's proposals inspired not a sense of "personal danger to myself but the infamy of the proposers."[67]

Almost simultaneously with the attempt to seduce Duane, the Quid insurgency took on its most tangible form yet, with the appearance of the *Philadelphia Evening Post* on 20 February 1804. In founding the paper, the Quids were acting on the recently established axiom that no political movement could succeed without a newspaper. The printer they selected, William McCorkle, had strong credentials in Republican journalism. With his former partner John M. Snowden, McCorkle had published James Thomson Callender's books and later the *Farmers' Register* at Chambersburg and Greensburg, Pennsylvania. McCorkle must have been the mechanical half of that partnership, however, because his role on the *Evening Post* was limited to printing.[68]

The new paper was intended to be the kind of journal that the moderates wished the *Aurora* was, firmly under the control of gentlemen. The *Post*'s real editor and political director was none other than Tench Coxe, Duane's longtime ally and benefactor and a frequent contributor to the *Aurora*.[69] This was only the latest of many turnabouts in Coxe's serpentine political career (he had been a Tory, a Whig, a Federalist, and then the most violent of Republicans), but his motives in this case are especially hard to discern. Though a man of aristocratic lineage, much learning, and great personal refinement, Coxe had been an unusually aggressive office-seeker after the 1800 election and a bitter proponent of removals. In Duane's mind, he and Coxe were close friends; the editor had gone to some lengths to help Coxe secure his appointment as federal purveyor of public supplies.[70]

Though it claimed to lean toward neither party, the *Evening Post*'s political affiliation was encapsulated in its motto, "Pledged to Religion, Liberty, and Law." The mention of religion echoed Federalist papers more than Republican, and the reference to law clearly associated the *Post* with the legal profession's side of the judicial reform debate.[71] The paper mostly avoided politics in its first few weeks but then became increasingly open in its advocacy of the Republican moderates. In April the editorial column proclaimed a crusade to redeem the party from "the disgrace which has encircled it." It should "not be supposed that republicans, generally, are enemies to the judiciary—NO," Coxe wrote, "There are thousands of republicans who will not stand by as tame spectators of the present scenes." What was more, they would "stretch forth their hands to their brothers"—meaning the "honest" Federalists—"for help."[72]

Besides promoting the Quids, the *Evening Post*'s other major aim was deposing William Duane as leader-spokesman of the Philadelphia Republicans. The attacks began obliquely. In the paper's opening address, Coxe suggested that one of the most serious problems facing the country was the threat that present political conditions posed to the rights of free expression. Without naming the source of the threat more specifically, Coxe argued that it should be condemned and resisted: "All attempts to frustrate these rights, whether in a public or a private station, by directly or indirectly working upon the fears for character, interest, or life, with a view of forcibly subjugating the will, and enslaving the free agency of man, must not only be considered as anti-republican and unconstitutional, but as being wicked and tyrannical in the extreme."[73]

Coxe was thinking not of a government threatening political writers but of political writers threatening other politicians. Making an argument that would become common in Philadelphia and other places over the next few years, Coxe implicitly condemned the role that party editors like Duane had fashioned for themselves, acting as arbiters of party policy and enforcers of party discipline.

In late spring, Coxe began to lay the groundwork for the year's legislative and congressional elections, when the battle over Michael Leib would be taken up again and the outcome of the coming impeachment trials might be determined. Coxe's strategy was to turn the campaign into a referendum on Duane, Leib, and the new political culture they represented. Thematically, Coxe grounded his arguments in the loathing of strong party organization that still lingered among the political gentry and extended them into a condemnation of the social (and to a lesser extent, ethnic) insubordination that the power of newspaper editors embodied. Coxe revealed his strategy in a formal statement of the *Post*'s "political creed": The editors and supporters of the *Evening Post* "believe that the people have placed, as it were by tacit consent, too much power in the hands of newspaper editors, . . . [who] arc, of all persons, the most improper to become leaders of parties."[74]

If allowing newspaper editors themselves to become leaders was bad, the type of men they would raise to office was even worse. The *Evening Post* creed reprobated "that systematized intrigue," meaning political organizations like Duane and Leib's, "which endeavors, by every mean art, trampling upon the rights of the people, to force persons into office who are neither fitted for it by talents, character, nor standing in society, and of whom the only fitness required is, *'will you do as you are bid?'*" Coxe made the social dimension of his attack on Duane and Leib perfectly clear when, on another occasion, he enjoined the *Aurora* never to mention the name of Duane's predecessor: "*Benjamin Franklin Bache* was a GENTLE-MAN, and the world acknowledged him as such. He would not have turned out to be a tyrant and a dictator."[75]

This last charge, of "editorial dictation" as it was sometimes termed, became a constant litany of those locked in political battles with newspaper editors. Struggling editors found the idea of themselves as "dictators" ridiculous, but like many another elite faced with having to share or give up some power, their opponents took it quite seriously. Coxe compared Duane to Robespierre, an attack that hearkened back to Federalist charges of the 1790s and captured the key elements of the moderates' antipathy to Duane. They saw in his attempts to keep the party in line behind particular candidates and opinions an invasion of their political free will, and in his policies a vision of democracy run amok, moving from limited, salutary reforms to a wholesale demolition of conventional morality, social order, and good government.[76]

Coxe's strategy failed badly. Fueled with rage at his erstwhile friend's duplicity and disloyalty, Duane was able to turn the 1804 campaign around, making it, in the words of Coxe's biographer, "a referendum on Coxe" instead of on Duane and Leib. By using Coxe as the prime example, Duane could argue persuasively that the moderates were merely Federalists or even Tories in disguise. Tirades and jibes against Coxe, or "Janus," filled the *Aurora*'s pages for weeks as Duane rehearsed, with information accumulated from years of close association, every sordid incident and little hypocrisy of his former friend's frequently wayward life and career, including his Toryism, his compulsive office seeking, and the undeniable fact that he had "espoused and betrayed every cause in succession."

Duane largely spared William McCorkle, or "poor Numps," the *Post*'s nominal editor, except to tweak him for not being a politician in his own right, as a proper editor should be. McCorkle was "indeed *innocent*—and ought to be pitied" for being "too much under the necessity of using others through want of any judgment of his own." In the fall election, Leib was reelected to Congress yet again; in the races for state legislature, the radicals ran even more strongly than Leib. As for Coxe, the campaign obliterated whatever political prospects he may have had and forced him into political retirement.[77]

Having no particular love for Tench Coxe himself, the busy lawyer and officeholder A. J. Dallas was publicly inactive during the 1804 election season.[78] In August, however, he had finally canceled his *Aurora* subscription, and upon seeing the results of the fall election, he became dismayed enough to consider taking up the fight against editorial dictatorship where Coxe left off. "The violence of Duane has produced a fatal division," Dallas reported to Gallatin, with either great disingenuousness or monumental self-deception, considering the origin of the recent troubles. "He seems determined to destroy the republican standing and usefulness of every man, who does not bend to his will."[79] Other gentleman moderates were moved beyond dismay to near hysteria. "The weight, power, and influence of Mr. Duane are at this time much greater than that of any other individual in the nation," wrote Andrew Ellicott, a McKean appointee and charter-member Quid. Ellicott was convinced that unless drastic measures were taken to "lessen the dangerous influence [Duane] is now exerting . . . *liberty must expire.*"[80]

The impeachment of the judges in the Passmore case was the most important task at hand when the new legislature met in December 1804. Dallas joined with the eminent Federalist attorney Jared Ingersoll to defend the judges. The legislature was unable to find any sufficiently distinguished Republican attorney in the state who would take the case, so the assignment went to the relatively young Caesar A. Rodney of Delaware. Rodney was no match for the combined legal might of Dallas and Ingersoll, but the case seemed so clear-cut to most radical Republican legislators that the majority of the Senate voted for conviction. There were, however, just enough lawyers in the Senate to prevent the necessary two-thirds majority.[81] "All is well," exulted one Quid state officeholder after the verdict. "Law, (nay, even the *Common* Law) with common Sense (tho' not Tom Payne's), and common Honesty, have triumphed over Anarchy, Folly, and Rascality. The Judges are safe. The arch-fiend, Duane, is *done.*"[82]

A. J. Dallas was not so sure. He had come to know Duane too well to think that one defeat would stop the editor. The proceedings at Lancaster convinced Dallas that a momentous crisis was at hand, a social crisis of leadership in which editors, their cohorts, and dupes (be they the artisans and shopkeepers who followed Duane and Leib in Philadelphia or the rural bumpkins in the legislature who thought nothing of wrecking a time-honored legal system to gratify their ignorant antipathies to wealth and learning) would drag the state and the nation into chaos if the "men of character and talents" did not act, and soon. If those men could not

> be drawn from professional and private pursuits, into the Legislative bodies of our governments . . . Republicanism will moulder into anarchy, and the labor & hope of our lives will terminate in disappointment and wretchedness. Perhaps, the crisis is arrived, when some attempt should be made to rally the genuine Republicans round the standard of reason, order, and law. At present we are the slaves of men, whose passions are the origin, and whose interests are the object of all their actions. I mean, your Duanes, Cheethams, Leibs, &c. They have the press in their power; and . . . it is too plain, that we have not spirit enough to resist the tyranny of the Printers.[83]

Duane, incensed by the judges' acquittal and more convinced than ever of the uselessness of impeachment as an effective check, quickly confirmed Dallas's fears by launching a campaign for a convention to revise the state constitution. The radicals' main goal was to fashion a new frame of government that more nearly embodied the democratic aspirations, if not the precise form, of the state's original constitution of 1776. In the process, they intended to "sweep away what yet remains of the dregs of British laws and lawyers." Among the specific reforms proposed were annual election of senators, reduction of the governor's powers, and election or appointment of judges for limited terms, along with drastic changes and simplifications in court procedures. Some talked of even more radical changes such as mandatory use of arbitrators, limitations on appeals, and state regulation of lawyers' fees.[84]

Radical Republicans also began to array themselves behind a candidate to compete against Governor McKean, who was up for reelection in 1805 and who had sealed his fate with the legislature by publicly referring to the constitutional reformers as "a set of clodpoles and ignoramuses." The radical candidate was Speaker of the House Simon Snyder, an obscure German farmer who had risen to prominence in the legislature for his leadership on the judicial reform issue. The selection filled the moderates with contempt and disbelief. "Don't laugh," one Quid wrote to Dallas when informing him of the likely nomination.[85]

At the same time, Dallas began the moderate counterattack by organizing the Society of Constitutional Republicans, a kind of counter-Tammany Society that pledged to defend McKean and the present state constitution while remaining within the national Republican party. To many, this last goal seemed especially difficult to achieve. Duane was too heavily identified with the great Republican victory of 1800 to be successfully written out of the party. "The extensive circulation of the Aurora . . . may do infinite mischief," worried one of Dallas's allies. "I sincerely lament the depravity of that man [Duane] he has been usefull to his country & thereby acquired the confidence of the people which now . . . renders him the more dangerous."[86]

During the gubernatorial campaign, Duane set out to read Dallas and McKean out of the Republican party. The moderates, and historians after them, criticized the scurrility of this campaign, but while Duane's rhetoric was severe and his facts occasionally exaggerated, his attacks were strictly political rather than personal. The *Aurora* concentrated on making the highly relevant point that it was the Quids, alias the moderates, "alias John Doe & Richard Roe," who had betrayed the Revolution of 1800 and caused the split in the party by tending constantly toward a rapprochement with the Federalists and their philosophy. McKean was damned with his many past political shifts and his intemperate remarks against judicial reform and the majority of the state legislature. Dallas was blamed for most of the developments that had distressed the radical wing of the party and accused of showing his true loyalties by the *"company he kept"* in the legal profession and Federalist-dominated polite society. Meanwhile, Duane argued, the really democratic Republicans had "learned their own strength" and seen "the necessity of totally throwing off the unsound parts of the party."[87]

In June Alexander Dallas produced the central document of the Constitutional Republican side of the campaign, an open memorial to the legislature against the call for a constitutional convention. The memorial went through all the arguments against the proposed constitutional changes and radical judicial reforms, but it expended considerably more passion declaiming against the excesses of newspaper politics. "The citizens of America begin at length to perceive," Dallas wrote, "that advantage has been taken of their just veneration for the liberty of the press to shackle them with the tyranny of printers."[88]

The memorial recounted at some length the methods by which printers had placed Pennsylvania in its present precarious position, at the mercy of the radical "malcontents" and their visionary designs. Disappointed in their hopes for places of honor within the party and frustrated at the failure of party colleagues to go along with their schemes, Duane and his friends had "resolved to coerce whom they could not persuade, and to ruin what they could not enjoy. They quickly, therefore, exchanged the arts of solicitation and deception for the weapons of denunciation and terror" against the reputations of the more substantial leaders of the party. "The whole machinery of confidential letters, essays upon the state of parties, anonymous hints, admonitions, and accusations"—in short, all the typical methods of newspaper politics—"has been set in motion." Those who disagreed politically were charged with *"heresy," "apostasy," "political defection,"* and similar crimes.[89]

Even worse was the way that the tyranny of printers had made men of wealth, education, and breeding unwelcome and uncomfortable in the Republican party. According to Dallas, men who "disdained to carry the prejudices of party into the circles of social life, or to declare all learning, learned men, and good manners hostile to the dignity of republican virtue—the malcontents have arbitrarily enrolled as *a Quid* or *a Federalist,* a *traitor* or a *Tory.*" At a party meeting in Harrisburg, it was claimed, "merchants and lawyers, men of education and men of wealth, were indiscriminately excluded from the honors of the sitting."

These depredations followed naturally from the "impious and visionary" philosophy on which the tyranny of printers was predicated, deriding that which "was prepared for us by our venerable ancestors" and proclaiming "*human perfectibility . . .* to be the only rational guide in the formation of a free government." The remarkably Federalist-sounding memorial concluded with a call for the Republican gentry to throw off the printers' yoke, couched in language that revealed the remarkable depth of the Quids' bigotry toward their onetime party comrades: "For ourselves, we think that it is time to evince to the world that a democratic republic can enjoy energy without tyranny, and liberty without anarchy. It is time to brush from the skirts of the Republican party the moths that stain the purity of its color and feed upon the consistency of its texture."[90]

As it turned out, the "moths" could not be brushed off so easily. At first glance, the moderates seemed to have won the 1805 campaign; McKean was reelected and the drive for constitutional reform was derailed in the legislative contests. But according to Albert Gallatin, it was Duane who, "possessed of an engine which gives him irresistible controul over public opinion," had "gained the victory for his friends." Gallatin called it victory, because at least two-thirds of the Republican voters had followed the *Aurora* editor's lead. "McKean owes his reelection to the federalists," the treasury secretary sighed. Dallas and the moderates had won the campaign but lost the Republican party in the process. His pride and political standing battered by Duane's barrages, A. J. Dallas was forced (at least temporarily) to join Tench Coxe in the political beyond.[91]

THE DECLINE OF DUANE, BUT NOT THE EDITORS

William Duane emerged from the 1805 rebellion as not just the Republican party's leading editor but one of its most influential power brokers as well. In other parts of the nation, he was regarded as leader of the party in Pennsylvania. In Richmond to observe Aaron Burr's treason trial in 1807, Duane found himself courted by all sides of the coming contest for the Republican presidential nomination. Yet he was also one of the party's most controversial figures. To Federalists and disgruntled Republican moderates alike, his name was a byword for everything they hated about the new political order that newspaper politicians had helped create.

In fact, the hatred Duane and his role had inspired over the years was too powerful a force to stop forever. The beginning of his downfall can be traced to this same peak period. The problems began when Duane decided to take the next logical step in his political career and run for office himself. A longtime ally was retiring from Congress, and Duane hoped to take his place. But, finding himself ineligible for Congress (thanks to Federalist lawsuits) because his citizenship was too recently acquired, the editor accepted a nomination for state senate instead.

This led to one of Duane's worst political humiliations. His Federalist and Quid enemies were galvanized into action by the opportunity to humble their least-favorite editor. Open social and ethnic bigotry was once again the order of the day. Two satirical weeklies, the *Tickler* and the *Spirit of the Press,* made Duane the star of their columns, fabricating stories about Duane's past such as that he was the illegitimate offspring of a French and Indian War camp follower and that he had a raped a girl in Ireland and left her to die. Occasionally, the tales were illustrated with woodcuts. Hundreds of Federalists who had not voted in years turned out this time and sent Duane and the local ticket down to a smashing defeat. In the city's more fashionable neighborhoods, he was crushed by margins of three to one or worse.[92] A powerful editor did not necessarily make for a popular candidate. In fact, the relationship seemed to work rather in reverse, an editor being a lightning rod and scapegoat for his party in a way that few individual politicians were.

The run for office, the first and last of Duane's life, was only one of many instances during this period in which the editor miscalculated and pushed his power to set the terms of party membership too far. In one case, Duane and Leib tried to impeach Governor McKean over a minor incident in which the governor had refused to deliver the commission of an *Aurora* stalwart who seemed to have won a disputed sheriff's election. Gen. John Barker, the incumbent sheriff, was deputed by Duane to change McKean's mind on the subject, failed, and then published a letter describing his mission in a Federalist newspaper. For this infraction, Duane attacked the popular Barker in the *Aurora* and tried to politically excommunicate him. The governor probably did treat Duane's friend unfairly, and Barker was an undoubtedly a weak link in the local party, but the editor also seemed to be abusing his special role as definer of the party to settle personal scores rather than to police ideology and maintain unity.[93]

For our purposes, the most important aspect of Duane's eclipse was the success of his enemies' efforts to supplant the *Aurora*. Coxe and Dallas had failed when they tried to use William McCorkle as a front, but a wider circle of enemies did better when they found another strong and independent editor to replace Duane. This process began in 1807, when Duane's friend and fellow Irish radical exile, John Binns, was asked by unnamed Philadelphia Republicans to start a newspaper there. Once a prospective *Aurora* employee, Binns had instead made himself the William Duane of the Susquehanna Valley with the Northumberland *Republican Argus*, a newspaper that had been highly praised and often quoted in the *Aurora*. Binns's prominence also owed to his role as a kind of political mentor to Simon Snyder, the popular German farmer-politician who had run against Governor McKean in 1805.

Duane did not thrill to the idea of another Republican newspaper in the crowded Philadelphia market, but Binns planned an evening paper and the *Aurora* editor sincerely believed he was gaining an ally. Binns allayed remaining suspicions by taking the trouble to swear "upon the altar of my conscience," at a public meeting, that his new paper was intended to help the *Aurora,* not oppose, undercut, or supersede it. Thus reassured, Duane helped Binns become a major figure in Philadelphia Republican circles overnight, inviting him into several clubs and his militia company and arranging for Binns to give the Tammany Society's annual "Long Talk" in May 1807.[94]

The new editor puffed and praised Duane and Leib in his early issues but soon after became a dangerous political competitor. Binns's general strategy was to outflank the *Aurora* in rhetorical populism while quietly maintaining better relations than Duane did with powerful figures in government and the local business community. Stealing an ideological march on Duane, Binns called his paper the *Democratic Press,* becoming one of the first Republican editors to use the *D* word in his title, and gave it the motto, "The Tyrant's Foe . . . the People's Friend." (Duane was an avid democrat himself, but believed the party should stick with the name "Republican" because that was what Jefferson used.) The title and motto were just a taste of the more blustery and less sophisticated political style that, in addition to good timing and connections, would allow Binns to beat Duane at his own game.[95]

Binns first revealed his hand by attacking Michael Leib and failing to defend Duane during the disastrous 1807 election, but the key to the new editor's accession was his relationship with Simon Snyder. Snyder's narrow loss to McKean had made him a folk hero among the farmers of the Pennsylvania interior, especially his fellow Germans, who were eager to elect one of their own after years of subservience to Philadelphia. Duane generally supported Snyder, but the *Aurora* had initially opposed his nomination, and Leib was jealous of any rival for leadership of the state's German population. Duane and Leib joined almost all other Republicans in backing Snyder when he ran again in 1808, but the *Democratic Press* was the campaign's clear statewide voice and swiftly became the more popular Philadelphia paper among the interior Republicans. At the same time, Binns and the Philadelphia Snyderites undercut Duane at home by quietly welcoming Dallas and many of the Quids back into the Republican fold.

When Snyder won, Duane found himself on the outs even though he had chosen the winning side. Binns became the governor's more or less openly acknowledged speechwriter, chief adviser, and distributor of patronage. Duane was boxed in, with Binns both claiming the loyalty of rural populists and cooperating with Quid conservatives. More important, the *Aurora* lost its ability to set the terms of party regularity, an authority that clearly settled on the *Democratic Press* as the organ of a popular Republican governor.[96]

Subsequent issues exacerbated the situation created in 1808, with Binns solidifying his alliances and Duane increasing his alienation from both the rural democrats who followed Snyder and the urban grandees associated with Dallas. Most crucial were the economic issues generated by the impact of Jefferson's embargo.

The cessation of foreign trade freed a huge amount of Philadelphia capital usually tied up in commerce, and it was used to fuel a sudden manufacturing boom. When the embargo was lifted in 1809 and merchants began absorbing much of the capital again, there was a sudden credit crunch, which in turn led to a push for new banks to keep the manufacturing boom going. Philadelphia Republicans had always been more development oriented than their southern counterparts, but the boom got many of them thinking in positively Hamiltonian terms about the need for government action to expand the nation's banking facilities and protect and encourage manufacturing. The Philadelphia party divided into a "New School" that welcomed all new schemes for economic development and an "Old School" that was disturbed by the corrupting influence and inegalitarian social consequences of rapid development. Binns and the old Quids found common ground in the new approach, while William Duane and his ever more visibly plebeian following stuck with the old.[97]

Meanwhile, Duane's feud with New School allies in Washington, led by Albert Gallatin, lost him the support of the national administration. Previously, Duane's closeness and loyalty to Jefferson (despite mistreatment in patronage matters) had been a source of strength at home, but he had no such relationship with James Madison. Binns had much better relations with the Madison administration through an alliance with Richard Rush, a young New Schooler who became comptroller of the treasury in 1811.[98]

The Old and New Schools fought several battles over state banking just after the embargo, but a dangerous turning point for Duane came in 1811, with the proposed recharter of the Bank of the United States. Standing by the critique of the bank that the *Aurora* and other Republican newspapers had been making for twenty years, Duane strongly opposed recharter, at a time when many Philadelphia Republicans had come to regard the bank as a highly beneficial hometown institution. As a supporter of deliberate, broad-based economic development, Duane proposed a new institution that would be fully under government control, as the Bank of the United States was not. The Madison administration was itself divided on the issue, and the *Aurora* was an important factor in the national bank's one-vote defeat in Congress. Duane's antibank stance lost him many old local allies who had become development enthusiasts or simply saw him as a traitor to Philadelphia on the issue. Most important, it lost Duane a principal financial backer in Thomas Leiper, the wealthy tobacconist whose credit had long been the *Aurora*'s fiscal backbone, supporting loans that serviced the huge debt left over from the aborted expansion to Washington. "Leiper says that in writing against the Bank I was writing against my own interest," Duane lamented.[99]

An important point underlined by Leiper's comment is how much more a loss of political influence meant to a partisan editor than to a conventional politician with another income or occupation to fall back on. Every political blow against Duane also inflicted heavy financial losses. The battles with McKean and Snyder lost him state printing contracts and robbed him of needed aid in dealing with his many lawsuits, while Gallatin's enmity squeezed Duane out of federal printing contracts and prevented or delayed payments on others. The fight over banking cut off most of his sources of credit and led to myriad other pressures and reprisals. Duane found that no part of his life was safe. Alexander Dallas even tried to turn Duane's eldest son, William John, into his own protégé, by offering him the chance to read law in Dallas's office, a step that would have required the son to sever relations with his father in addition to violating their joint antilawyer principles. Dallas also used his influence to see that Duane received as little benefit as possible from the Franklin-Bache family fortune, even though he was raising several of Benjamin Franklin's great-grandchildren and had paid off their father's huge debts.[100]

Though Duane had many years and several political comebacks left, most notably a rollicking tour as federal adjutant general for Pennsylvania during the War of 1812, his power broker days were mostly over after 1811. The editor and his newspaper were reduced to the roles of sparring partner and ideological gadfly to the New Schoolers, who gradually established themselves as the "regular" Democratic Republican organization thanks to Duane's growing disaffection with the national administrations and flirtation with the presidential candidacy of De Witt Clinton. Events probably reached their nadir for Duane at the end of the war, when his archnemesis Alexander Dallas became secretary of the treasury and helped create a brand-new Bank of the United States. In the 1810s Duane even occasionally allied himself with reformed Federalists in his desperation to bring down the New School.[101]

Yet if Duane's personal power was broken, the "tyranny of printers" in Philadelphia continued unabated. In 1811 Dallas decried "a newspaper government" as "the most execrable of all things" and begged administration officials to pay less attention to both Duane's denunciations and Binns's blandishments. The two editors kept up a running verbal firefight with each other, but they both worked to maintain the newspaper influence over local politics and even joined forces on some substantive matters. Regarding the foreign policy crisis of 1807–12 and the subsequent war, both editors were substantially more bellicose against the British than many people of "wealth and talents" in their city. Binns and Duane often seemed to be competing to see who could beat the drums more loudly, and together with editors in other cities, they provided the war policy with badly needed support that it was not getting in other parts of the North. In 1813 Richard Rush expended a seventeen-page letter trying to convince his Federalist mother—against her distinct impression—that "this war was not made by John Binns or William Duane" or other "low, vulgar fellows."[102]

It is doubtful that Richard Rush won the argument. While John Binns never managed to match Duane in terms of national influence, within a few years of his takeover as leading Philadelphia editor he had become almost as intolerable as Duane to genteel Philadelphia politicians. Indeed, at times the Binns regime seemed worse. It was complained that the new boss was less talented than the old boss but even more dictatorial and rapacious. This was true partly because Binns simply had more power than Duane. Besides reading individuals in and out of the party with his newspaper, Binns's close relationship with Governor Snyder, who stayed in office nine years, allowed him to keep an iron, long-term grip on the state government's vast patronage. Moreover, Binns was much greedier for offices and wealth than Duane, and more single-minded and successful in pursuing them.

While Duane was fighting banks, for instance, Binns was promoting them and then arranging directorships for himself. "Binns and Duane have very different dispositions," wrote the Federalist turned conservative Republican Edward Fox. "Duane appears not to have any idea of the value of property; I believe Binns is very well convinced that it is 'the one thing needful.'"

Ultimately, Fox argued, the deeper problem was not one editor or the other but the whole system that had granted them their power in the first place. "The misfortune of the republican party always has been making too much of their printers," he commiserated with an ally, "setting them above the party, and putting them as the leaders, instead of the *tools* of the party."[103]

This "misfortune" was not to be alleviated any time soon. As long as partisan newspapers were so central to Pennsylvania (and American) politics, partisan editors would be, too. The tensions between editors and their ostensible party allies highlight the fact that the rise of these political professionals represented a fundamental change not only in the practice of American politics, but in its very character. Men of different backgrounds and different values than the typical gentleman officeholder of the revolutionary era had come to have an important place in political life and, increasingly, a share in political power as well. Their presence was quickly propelling American political culture—in terms of its methods, its personnel, its style of discourse, and sometimes even the basic values it expressed—into unexpected and, for many, unwanted areas.

Binns would eventually be deposed but would no more fade away than Duane had, and their replacements would also be troublesome and powerful, if not so all-encompassing as the two old radicals. A testament to their staying power came when the New School faction was temporarily thrown out of power in the gubernatorial election of 1820 with the help of both the *Aurora* and the *Democratic Press.* The new governor, Joseph Hiester, then named both Binns and Duane Philadelphia city aldermen. This was simultaneously a favor to the editors and an intentional affront to their enemies; a decade past his prime, Duane was still a potent political symbol. He desperately needed the money, and he and Binns actually became friends again while serving together. Another governor would later make Duane Philadelphia county "prothonotary," a type of court clerk, for similar reasons—insulting the old editor's still-ascendant enemies in Philadelphia.[104]

The *Aurora* editor's son and sometime coeditor William J. Duane confirmed his father's fears and became a prominent attorney (though not in Alexander Dallas's firm), but in most other ways stayed true to his father's ideals. He ignored his Federalist law teacher Joseph Hopkinson's advice to abandon Republican politics, thoughtfully crusading for many of his father's causes. The younger Duane also horrified many of his legal colleagues with what they regarded as an unprofessional attitude, voluntarily limiting his income by never trying "to prevail in an unjust cause." The younger Duane's public life culminated in a short stint as secretary of the treasury under Andrew Jackson. He got the job partly because of President Jackson and his advisers' admiration for the *Aurora,* the favorite political newspaper of their youth. It probably did not hurt that the leading Jacksonians were all products or beneficiaries of the newspaper politics that the elder Duane had helped create.[105]

13

Ordinary Editors and Everyday Politics

How the System Worked

◈

Heretofore this study has focused mostly on national trends and editors of national import. This chapter analyzes the workings of newspaper politics on a more mundane and local level. Once again, the approach is primarily biographical. The following vignettes use the experiences of several "ordinary" newspaper politicians to illuminate the everyday workings of newspaper-based parties: Where exactly did newspapers and editors fit into (and shape) the structure of the political system? What roles did editors play in local parties? What were an average editor's limits and possibilities in a polity that the revolutionary gentry had designed and still controlled?

THE WAGES OF MOBILITY: THE RISE AND FALL OF JAMES J. WILSON

In the years after 1800, some partisan printers became important local political figures or officeholders, and at least a few sought elective political careers like those of the politicians their newspapers promoted. The odds against such desires being realized were rather high initially, with voters resistant and other politicians actively hostile to these aspirations, but editors were too well placed in the post-1800 political system to be held back completely or indefinitely. Thus, a handful of printers found their way into Congress in the first two decades of the nineteenth century.[1]

The most precociously successful player of the new system was James Jefferson Wilson of New Jersey, whose career can be seen as both a harbinger of democratization to come and an index of the degree to which democratization had not yet occurred. Using his position as the state's leading Republican editor, Wilson became a dominant force in the state's politics while still in his twenties, with influence sufficient to make him the first printer ever elected to the United States Senate.

Wilson was one of that fairly numerous class of young printers for whom the onset of party politics in the 1790s was a kind of godsend. Born in 1780 to an ordinary farming family in Scotch Plains (possibly as one of the first children in America to be named after Thomas Jefferson), he was an apprentice in the office of the Elizabethtown *New-Jersey Journal,* an old revolutionary paper that later sided with the Republicans. Wilson finished his apprenticeship in 1799 and quickly found a more exciting job than the typical journeyman printer of the past: he moved to Delaware to become foreman printer and apparently chief writer for the Wilmington *Mirror of the Times,* one of the partisan Republican newspapers started in response to the Sedition Act.[2]

In Delaware Wilson earned some notoriety for his writings and for bravely defending himself and his right to political involvement from Federalist snubs and violence. In November 1800 Wilson wrote an item attributing a certain remark (the relevant issue of the paper is missing) to a young Federalist gentleman named Richard Stockton. On the evening the piece was published, Stockton visited the *Mirror* office armed with a whip, intent on chastising Wilson. Under the code of honor that many gentlemen of the period tried to follow, a whipping was the appropriate mode of redressing an insult from an inferior. There had been many threats against the printers of the *Mirror,* so Wilson answered the door with a pistol in his pocket. An argument and scuffle ensued that ended with Wilson's coworkers hauling Stockton outside as he shouted that the printer was a "Damn'd Villain, Damn'd Upstart, Damn'd Coward."

The aspiring Wilson tried to resolve the situation in what he imagined to be a genteel manner, sending Stockton a conciliatory note. When that overture was ignored, he made "recourse to a system which the world term *honorable*" and sent another note challenging Stockton to a duel. Much to the young printer's shock, Stockton sent both notes back, "and declared me *unworthy his notice!*" Duels were conceived as a contest for honor between equals, so there was no dishonor for Stockton in refusing a challenge from someone the community deemed his inferior. This was a judgment that Wilson could not accept. In the *Mirror,* he questioned Stockton's calling him a "damn'd upstart," a political child to be seen and not heard: "If he meant by it, as he apparently did, that I depended on my own industry for support, that I wished no surreptitious merit, and that I would rise, if I rose at all, by personal exertion, in an honest occupation.— I acknowledge the justness of the epithet."[3]

The Stockton incident displayed a characteristic that Wilson shared with many other Republican printers, an inability to read (or unwillingness to recognize) the social realities of many situations he encountered. This trait was marked especially deeply in Wilson by the experience of forming close friendships with several better-educated young gentlemen while he was working in Wilmington, especially William Darlington, a physician trained at the University of Pennsylvania. Wilson's utter disregard for social boundaries and niceties may have allowed him to rise higher in politics than most members of his class—he simply could not perceive that artisans were not supposed to become senators—but it would render him a buffoonish (if feared) figure to gentleman political colleagues who would do all in their power to bring him down.[4]

In some respects, the rest of Wilson's career can be read as a crusade to show the Richard Stocktons of the world just how worthy of their notice an "upstart" could become. This meant not only winning political power himself, but also trying to delegitimize the power and culture of New Jersey's reigning political elite of wealthy, educated gentleman and professionals. Wilson's subsequent newspaper work contained an especially doctrinaire brand of democracy and stark sense of class antagonism. "Who made men Democrats?" began a "Political Catechism" in the *Mirror of the Times*. "Such the Almighty created them," came the answer, "all being born free and equal." In a less evangelistic mood, Wilson wrote matter-of-factly that "Judges, Lawyers, the Clergy, and Merchants" were always the "most active and dangerous enemies of our civil and religious liberties," while "Farmers, Mechanics, and Laborers are generally . . . attached to equal rights and rational liberty." Going beyond mere denunciations to specific reforms, he called for legal reforms like the ones William Duane supported in Pennsylvania and ridiculed the genteel custom that embarrassed him in Wilmington, dueling. Following Richard Stockton's example, aggrieved members of the learned professions would repay Wilson's hostility in kind over the years. Lawyers in his own party would work to undermine him, and in 1803 a gang of Federalist law and medical students would drag the editor out of his newspaper office and beat him for criticizing their Fourth of July gathering.[5]

While splashing cold water on his social identity, Wilson's confrontations with the Wilmington Federalists may have brought him to the attention of the people who soon after provided his great political opportunity. This came in the summer of 1801, when he became a partner in New Jersey's new Republican organ, the Trenton *True American,* joining the original proprietors, Matthias Day and Jacob Mann.

Day and Mann appear to have been trade-oriented printers who, while promising "to conduct a press in support of original republican principles," needed and confidently expected the assistance of local Republican gentlemen ("such friends of freedom . . . whose situations and opportunities have been advantageous") in filling their pages. Apparently their confidence was misplaced, because the *True American* carried virtually no original material for nearly four months after the opening address, until the week James J. Wilson joined the firm. After that, it showed immediate and sweeping political improvements. One of his early efforts was an encomium and survey of the Republican newspaper network that, significantly, put great emphasis on the active political role of "*Republican Printers . . .* the vigilant centinels, who watched at the portals of Liberty . . . the valiant heroes, who combatted for the People, in contempt of threats and bribes—of persecution and prosecution—of dungeons and death." A fan of William Duane, Wilson began his work in New Jersey with an exalted sense of his own mission as editor.[6]

In joining Mann and Day's firm, the twenty-one-year-old Wilson was more or less handed the management of the local Republican party organization. A little more than a week after he had arrived in town, Wilson and Mann were invited to a public Fourth of July dinner held by the area's "more elderly and respectable Republicans." This invitation marked their special status in the party. Many other young Republicans of longer residence were left out and resented an outsider receiving such preferential treatment. Five months later, Republican chieftain Joseph Bloomfield and several allies lent Wilson the money to buy Day out. Under Wilson's direction, the *True American* immediately became the centerpiece of state Republican politics. While the state legislature was in session, Wilson told his Wilmington friend (and future congressional colleague) William Darlington, he did "not lack for Society . . . as our office is a place of general rendezvous for all the Jacobin members." Little more than a year after moving to Trenton, Wilson was considered so indispensable by the Republican members of the legislature that when he announced plans to go on a business trip during the legislative session, they implored him to send his partner instead.[7]

Though Wilson detested Trenton as a place to live, he was eager to help his home state see the error of its political ways. The task had several attractions. Foremost was the chance to promote "the glorious principles of our revolution." Though Wilson had no memories of that event, he had no doubt that two of its major principles were democracy and equality, at least for free white men. (Wilson himself did not make this disclaimer explicitly, and his newspaper would avidly support the gradual abolition of slavery in New Jersey, a measure he helped pass through a Republican-controlled legislature in 1804.)

Having missed the original struggle, Wilson was anxious to join in what he saw as its continuation. The Federalists represented a headlong retreat from the Revolution's promise, and were composed (in his mind) of many actual and tacit opponents of it. Wilson wanted to rescue his state, and the Revolution's legacy, from them. "If we are to be governed by a few *ambitious lawyers* and *Old Tories*, the blood of our best and bravest Patriots has been shed in vain, and our treasures exhausted for a name without meaning." Fortunately for his peace of mind, Wilson believed that the Federalists' dominance up to 1800 (and continued strength) was an aberration that resulted only from the lack of Republican newspapers serving the rural areas of the state. New Jersey's farmers, he opined, "are perhaps as real Republicans, and as great practisers of Equality" as any people in the Union, and they would have "long since . . . execrated" the "profligate and tyrannical" Federalists "had the *truth* been permitted to reach them."[8]

Another attraction of running a partisan newspaper like the *True American* was the political lifestyle itself, which to Wilson epitomized egalitarian republicanism. While Joseph Bloomfield was governor, the editor was flattered to be a regular dinner guest in the chief executive's home. The printer was dazzled by both by the seeming elegance of these affairs—Bloomfield served "excellent wine which he had had in his cellar sixteen years," Wilson burbled—and the substitution of ideological affinities for class distinctions that they represented. "Our conversation, as our company, was wholly and purely Republican," he told Darlington.[9]

Governor Bloomfield gave other tangible signs of his support besides the free meals. Wilson's printing office received as much of the state's printing work as the governor could give him, and the editor saw his circulation shoot up to the very respectable (for this period) figure of 1,700.[10]

Wilson tried to run his newspaper office in an equally republican fashion; he and his partner, both single men in the early days, lived there with

their journeymen and apprentices. This was a typical artisanal arrangement, of course, but instead of acting as the traditional authoritarian father of his shop, Wilson ran it as a democracy. He invited Darlington up
to Trenton so he could "see Republican equality in its highest pitch of perfection, as we all eat and drink the same victuals and liquor, and at the
same table; and decide all disputes by vote, in which the boys, and journeymen, and employers have an equal voice."[11]

Wilson soon applied his egalitarian principles to a major reform of the
local party organization. Despite Wilson's faith in their natural Republicanism, the farmers of rural New Jersey stubbornly continued to vote Federalist during Wilson's first two years in Trenton. During the 1801 and
1802 campaigns, rampant corruption and infighting among the Republicans embarrassed the party. They lost ground in the legislature in 1801,
and incumbent Governor Bloomfield went down to defeat. The "Association for the Preservation of Our Electoral Rights," introduced by Wilson
at a public meeting in late December 1802, aimed to rectify all these problems by systematizing the Republican organization and encouraging
wider participation in the party through a better-defined, more open and
egalitarian structure.

In essence, Wilson's plan created a series of open conventions, stretch-
ing from the township level to the state level, that made nominations and
elected delegates to the higher conventions. The system aimed to make
nominations more formal, authoritative, and clearly backed by popular
support than earlier ones had been. Previously, nominations had been
made by caucuses or simply printed in the newspapers as the decision of
some unknown party meeting. Convention nominations speaking the unmistakable sense of the party were much harder for Federalists to infiltrate
or for party renegades to flout, sabotage, or ignore.[12]

Though more democratic in form, one of the most significant aspects
of these nominating conventions, compared with legislative caucuses or
closed meetings, was the large potential role they afforded to mid-level
party activists such as newspaper editors. Though the Hunterdon County
meetings were attended by large crowds and were democratically conducted, they had the effect of concentrating influence in the hands of the
county's leading political professional, James J. Wilson. The most important official duties were handled by the secretary that each convention
elected, and between 1803 and 1812 Wilson almost always held that
office.[13]

A better systematized party structure also placed a higher premium on party organization and loyalty, matters of great concern and personal interest to Wilson. As party editor, Wilson was the person most responsible for expounding the "party line," and he thus had the greatest stake in maintaining the party's ideological consistency and enforcing party discipline. The more seriously voters and elected officials took such matters, the more powerful the editor was. Wilson tended (often correctly) to interpret party schisms as the results of "the avarice and ambition of unprincipled men who are scrambling for profitable offices or scuffling for posts of honor and influence"; it was the editor's task to expose such men in his newspaper and thus thwart their schemes. In the process, he gained something approaching the power of political life or death over his fellow politicians, as long as the voters heeded his pleas for party loyalty.[14]

With the new, reformed party structure in place, Wilson felt sure that, "though our political body" was still in a "high fever" of Federalism, he could "restore the patient to perfect health." There would be "no blood . . . drawn," but "a great deal of ink will be shed."[15] The patient responded to Wilson's therapy. In the 1803 elections, just after the convention system was instituted, the Republicans took control of the state legislature for the first time. Bloomfield returned to the governor's chair, and would remain there until 1812.

The triumph made Wilson the key man in state politics and allowed him to practice political professionalism on the largest scale of any editor to date. Besides the state's printing patronage, he began to receive numerous offices. When the 1803 General Assembly convened, it elected Wilson its clerk, an honor that it would confer repeatedly thereafter. At around the same time, he was appointed surrogate of Hunterdon County (equivalent to a county clerk or register). In 1811 he became president of a newly chartered state bank, against the wishes of the bank's board, which was simply told that it was useless to oppose the editor because the legislature would appoint him if the board refused. Wilson clearly enjoyed overpowering those he considered moneyed aristocrats when he had the chance. By 1812 a Republican critic seems not to have exaggerated in calling Wilson "the most influential and powerful individual in the state," in public life, if not in the broader society.[16]

While Wilson was not immune to avarice, it is important to note that at least some of these official salaries were absolutely necessary to him. The need for supplementary income was built into the structure of the role he played in the party. Though the *True American*'s circulation increased along with its political standing, Wilson had the usual troubles collecting the money his subscribers and advertisers owed him. "Your compassion for printers is not misplaced," Wilson told his friend Darlington. "I verily believe there is no other profession . . . so badly treated" in the area of collections.

Like other editor-politicians, Wilson's policies in managing the *True American* were driven by politics rather than economics. The party's message had to be gotten out to as many people as possible, in a form (quality of paper and type) that reflected well on the party. Reducing the paper's circulation or attractiveness in order to reduce costs would have defeated its fundamental purpose. Reporting on his personal affairs to Darlington, Wilson lamented that "in property I am not, and can never expect to be, gaining much, as long as I print a paper."

Political offices allowed the *True American* to keep publishing and the editor to make a living. He would not have accepted so many petty offices, Wilson told Darlington, "had not the expence of maintaining the establishment of the paper been so great as to require some other resource for supporting it than it furnished itself." Nevertheless, Wilson's plural office-holding and political professionalism came under attack, especially from more genteel and "moderate" politicians who resented his power and disapproved of the efficiency of the organization he had created.[17]

It was also possible to attack the ascendant Wilson (at least rhetorically) from a more democratic and egalitarian point of view. A pamphlet under the signature "A Democratic Republican" appeared in 1812, expressing the feelings of some in the party who lamented "to see *the Editor* of their Paper transformed into a haughty and overbearing Aristocrat." Arguing that Wilson had betrayed his earlier ideals (including rotation in office), the pamphlet concluded that throwing him out of the legislature immediately was the only step that would lead the editor "to *reflection*," and, some Republicans hoped, "to *reformation*." Moreover, Wilson's case made it clear that a Republican editor should always "confine himself to his printing profession."[18]

True to the pamphlet's analysis, if not its hopes, the 1812 attack on Wilson failed. According to his enemies, the editor had come to exercise almost dictatorial control over Hunterdon County and the Republican majority of the state legislature. As clerk, he was certainly in a position to monitor and manage the legislature's doings, and he did wield much influence over nominations and patronage. However, he was also clearly the leader, in a more conventional and less sinister sense, of the state's rural and "radical" Republicans. Many obscure farmers in the state legislature got their political educations from the *True American* and genuinely admired Wilson, seeing in him a "Clod Hopper" like themselves made good.

After the War of 1812, during which Wilson served as New Jersey's adjutant general, his loyal legislative supporters honored him, over determined resistance, with election to the United States Senate. The election required numerous ballots, because Wilson's Republican enemies refused the normal courtesy of uniting behind the leading Republican candidate after the first vote, preventing him from gaining the necessary majority. His detractors even voted Federalist on a few ballots. The issue was finally resolved when Wilson arranged for the opposing faction's Senate candidate, Mahlon Dickerson, to be nominated for governor.[19]

Though it made him the first printer to reach the Senate, Wilson's elevation was a decidedly mixed blessing, tangling him in the same sort of class barriers he had previously overleaped in rising so far. He might have been better advised to refuse (or not seek) the honor no matter how much it flattered him. Though by no means uncomfortable with political power, the new senator was suddenly self-conscious, wondered whether a tradesman like himself possessed the kinds of skills and training he would be expected to display in a body full of lawyer-orators. Though in "fidelity and zeal, I yield to no one," Wilson wrote to William Darlington, he felt inferior as to "talents and learning." The new senator resolved "to supply these deficiencies by application and industry, and to draw upon the resources of others" more educated than himself.[20] He looked mostly to his lifelong friend Darlington, who was fortuitously elected to Congress from Pennsylvania in the same year that Wilson joined the Senate. The two roomed together in Washington and were constant companions during their joint service. Even with this help, Wilson spoke little on the Senate floor and apparently made little impression on his colleagues.[21]

Besides feeling out of his depth for the first time, Wilson faced a number of personal difficulties arising from his Senate service, the worst being a severe reduction in his income and huge increase in his expenses. He had to give up his New Jersey posts in order to take his Senate seat and also hire an assistant to conduct the *True American* while he was away. In addition, Wilson had to increase the newspaper's subscription price, explaining to readers that without lucrative offices to subsidize the paper, it had to cost more. The *True American* would now be his principal source of income, along with a six-dollar-a-day allowance as a member of Congress.

Though relatively lavish by artisanal standards, congressional pay was not enough to support Wilson's large family in the style to which they had become accustomed as well as defray the travel and lodging expenses involved in congressional service. The new senator had to sell many of his assets to stay afloat and soon found his creditors threatening foreclosure on his home and the *True American* office. All these adversities took their toll on Wilson and brought his Senate term and political career to a tragic end. Printers had a reputation as problem drinkers, and the stress of Wilson's Senate service seems to have worsened what was probably a lifelong habit. By the middle of his Senate term, Wilson often spent the day in bed instead of on the Senate floor, and his lawyer colleagues in the New Jersey delegation, jealous of his power and personally contemptuous in any case, saw to it that the news of his condition reached home. Though Wilson rallied somewhat for the 1820 election, the now moderate-controlled legislature sent the lawyer and Princeton graduate Samuel Southard—the son of one of Wilson's tattling congressional colleagues— to Washington in his place. In the wake of his defeat, Wilson began drinking more heavily than ever. He died a few years later, allegedly in a drunken fall.[22] Pioneering the democratization of the Senate had almost literally been the death of him.

SENATOR ROBERTS AND THE EDITORS: MEDIATING AMERICAN POLITICS THROUGH INFORMATION AND INFLUENCE

Since no complete collection of an early national editor's papers survives, the day-to-day workings of newspaper-based politics can best be observed in the correspondence of a more conventional type of political leader, not a famous statesman who was completely absorbed in setting national policy or leading congressional debates, but a politician who built a successful career of local repute and stayed in close touch with his local community. Jonathan Roberts of Norristown, Pennsylvania, fits this description. He was a farmer and wheelwright who served successively as a Republican state senator, congressman, and U.S. senator between 1807 and 1821.[23]

Besides corresponding with his family and fellow members of Congress, Roberts kept in contact with a remarkable number of newspaper editors, exchanging information and influence in a way that cemented party ties and strengthened both the editors and the senator in their respective spheres. Editors kept Roberts abreast of public opinion at home, defended his actions in Washington, and provided him with a means of communicating with his constituents, while exercising their primary function in the party, the oversight of day-to-day political affairs in their local area. Roberts in turn furnished local editors with the information they needed to defend national Republican policy effectively, helped with patronage requests (usually on behalf of others) that built the editors' reputation for influence in their communities, and aided them in their respective quests for indispensable government aid.

Partisan newspapers "mediated" the gaps in the American political system in their pages, for instance by framing a national issue in locally resonant terms. A review of Roberts's editorial correspondents reveals how editors themselves could mediate in more subtle ways that often did not appear in their newspapers. In the local constituency, editors could become almost the unofficial agents for the state and national party and higher-level political associates, and in turn, conduits for (and controllers of) the political information, influence, and benefits that passed between the local community and higher levels of government.[24]

We can begin with Roberts's hometown editor, James Winnard, an Irish-born printer who began publishing the *Norristown Register* in 1803, replacing the area's first Republican journal, the *True Republican*. Winnard was no William Duane and his paper was no *Aurora*, but a local memorialist wrote that "no man ever lived in Montgomery County who wielded a more decided influence in moulding our people into the doctrines of Jefferson." Historically, the area had been Federalist, but Roberts and Winnard turned it around quickly and permanently.[25]

Winnard wrote relatively little himself, but he dutifully publicized local Republican party activities and reprinted much choice material from more radical Republican journals such as the *Aurora,* New London *Bee,* and Trenton *True American.* He was so dependent on his postally subsidized exchange papers, in fact, that when there was nothing worth printing in them, he led off his editorial column with a business notice and an apology. His selections emphasized defending Jefferson and encouraging ordinary voters to participate in elections, often using James J. Wilson's material. Winnard covered the entire front page of one issue with a selection from an edition of the *Spirit of Despotism* published by Wilson, headed "The indifference of the middle and lower classes of the people to public affairs, highly favorable to the encroachments of the tory principle, and therefore to the spirit of despotism." (Winnard liked this work so much he issued his own edition in 1807 and offered it as a premium to any Republican who sold twelve subscriptions to the *Register*.)[26]

Like other editors, Winnard also took advantage of the party press network's decentralization to adapt the Republican creed to local predilections, in this case to a Quaker-settled area where antislavery sentiment was strong. Though his party was headed by a large-scale slaveholder, Winnard used one of his few original pieces to praise a 22-6 Senate vote to outlaw the international slave trade, contrasting it with the actions of the Republican-controlled South Carolina legislature: "who have passed a law for the *importation* of slaves into that state; the one is deserving of encomiums, while the other deserves the execration of the human race—yet, reader, they bestow on themselves the appellation of *republicans!!!* . . . What inconsistency!"[27]

From his earliest days in politics, Jonathan Roberts helped his local editor fill the paper. First from the state legislature, and later from Congress, Roberts regularly sent Winnard his impressions of the proceedings as well as relevant documents, and the editor gratefully published them all. Roberts also helped Winnard in his business dealings with the state and national governments. Roberts was elected to the state senate in 1807, and it was around the same time that the *Register* seems to have acquired state printing contracts. Both the state and national legislatures paid for members' newspaper subscriptions, allowing them to stay abreast of opinion back home and (because they got many free subscriptions) curry favor with a large number of editors. In several of his letters to Roberts, Winnard enclosed a bill for legislators' subscriptions to his newspaper, to be submitted to the proper authorities by the senator personally (and thus presumably expedited).

Winnard provided many services in return for Roberts's help, most revolving around maintaining his support at home. Roberts's every political act was highlighted (though not brazenly so) in the pages of the *Register*, from his first work on the Republican county committee of correspondence to his participation in congressional debates. The coverage reached a kind of peak in early 1812, when Roberts was a leading advocate of war at a time when that position was not very popular in rural eastern Pennsylvania. The *Register* rarely carried congressional debates, but several of Roberts's speeches were printed in full, including an oration on a naval bill that covered nearly seven columns—almost half the paper's total space—in the February 12 issue. In addition to promoting Roberts's career directly, Winnard also fed him helpful political information, reporting privately on such matters as the divided opinion around Norristown over a certain state turnpike bill and the political background of a bitterly disputed local legislative election.[28]

It should be noted that Winnard was no mere cipher or retainer. He was a founding member of Norristown's borough council and a power in local politics until his death in 1837. His letters to Roberts displayed a sense of personal responsibility for managing the political situation on the ground in Norristown. With regard to a Federalist maneuver that had blind-sided the local Republicans, Winnard apologized that "Not an individual in this place, as far as my information extends, was apprized of any such procedure—for, if it was known that any such movements were going forward, every exertion wd. be exercised to arrest its progress." Winnard and his newspaper were nothing more or less than the local branch office of the Republican party.[29]

Another of Roberts's editorial contacts was Samuel Maffett of the Wilkes-Barre *Susquehanna Democrat,* "a paper that circulates pretty largely among . . . your constituents." A recently graduated apprentice of John Binns's *Democratic Press,* Maffett was barely twenty-one when he founded his paper in 1810. After only five years in Wilkes-Barre, Maffett was appointed to the first of a series of county offices, in which he would serve consecutively, while also editing his paper, until his death in 1825. Engaged in a close battle over the merits of President Madison's policy toward Britain in early 1812, he urgently asked Roberts for detailed information on the thinking behind some of the administration's recent actions: "I am placed in rather a disagreeable situation, attacked on all sides by the loyal subjects of his majesty in this place—and I scarcely know what answer to make to their taunts—By giving me the information desired you will enable me to take grounds . . . to contradict them, oppose their falsehoods, [and] justify government." In return for this crucial aid, Maffett answered a query from Roberts about the qualifications of a local man being considered for a federal appointment. Roberts must undoubtedly have recommended or assented to Maffett's own later appointments.[30]

The editor with whom Jonathan Roberts apparently worked most closely of all was Thomas J. Rogers, a young Irish printer who established Easton, Pennsylvania's, first Republican paper, the *Northampton Farmer,* in 1805. Rogers's parents had emigrated to Philadelphia in 1786, in time for their young son to spend his formative years in an atmosphere charged with newspaper-driven partisanship. Thomas apprenticed with Samuel Harrison Smith in Philadelphia, then moved with his employer to Washington City, where he worked for several years (some as a journeyman) on the *National Intelligencer.* By 1805 Rogers was back in Philadelphia, working for one of the local Republican papers and waiting for a chance to acquire a newspaper of his own. He served as a junior officer in William Duane's highly politicized Militia Legion and took part in city politics. In the fall of that year, Rogers bought the printing office of Samuel Longcope, publisher of the nominally Federalist but mostly apolitical *American Eagle* in Easton, the seat of Northampton County.[31]

Rogers's proposals promised that the "political complexion" of his new paper would be "strict impartiality at all times," but this disclaimer was made merely out of custom, or perhaps it aimed to hoodwink the old paper's Federalist customers. When Rogers's *Northampton Farmer* made its appearance in December, the editor had exchanged the *Eagle's* masthead quotation from George Washington for a new one from Thomas Jefferson, proclaiming "equal and exact justice for all men, of whatever state or persuasion, religious or political." While repeating the pledges of impartiality in his opening address to readers, Rogers added the rather contrapuntal proviso that, in a republican government, it was "not only proper, but . . . absolutely necessary, that the conduct of public men should be investigated with a scrutinizing pen." Scrutinize Rogers did, but as a sentinel of the Republican party rather than a neutral defender of the public, though this was a distinction that Rogers rarely made.[32]

Rogers swiftly joined Duane, Binns, and other Pennsylvania editors in crusading against Governor McKean, while simultaneously performing many more workaday political tasks. While the *Aurora* and *Democratic Press* battled for control of the state party, Rogers tried to define Republican orthodoxy on the local level, where he had to deal with his own set of "Constitutional Republicans," whom he labeled "new federalists." He also faced the more delicate task of convincing voters in a heavily German, relatively apolitical region that they should think and vote like partisans. "Give your votes to none but firm and undeviating republicans," the editor asked his readers, and in issue after issue, he tried to supply them with the necessary information to do this. By his paper's first birthday, Rogers was making the more accurate claim that while the *Farmer* was impartial regarding "private character," it could not fail to "sound the alarm when the public's rights were conceived to be in danger."[33]

Easton's Republican-sympathizing congressman, a local war hero named Robert Brown, was facing a tough reelection battle in 1806, so Rogers set himself the task of saving Brown's seat. Apparently Brown had little to offer in the way of charisma and oratorical skills. He had not cut much of a figure in the House, so Rogers plugged Brown's faithfulness to his constituents, ideological consistency, and regular attendance. Readers might never see Brown's speeches in the newspaper-published congressional proceedings, but if they scanned the "yeas and nays," Rogers argued, they would always find Brown on the right side of an issue, in this case, in favor of Jefferson's anti-British trade measures. "Has not General Brown, citizens of Northampton, always been your friend and the friend of your country? Has he ever acted contrary to your will or opinion?"[34]

One of the other Republican candidates in the northeastern Pennsylvania three-man district was an even more colorless man named Dr. John Hahn. Rogers praised Hahn's "worth, talents, and integrity," which primarily showed up in his "firm and undeviating republicanism." Thus Rogers equated party loyalty with integrity and even manliness, two qualities more traditionally associated with the disinterestedness and nonpartisanship of the classical republican statesman. In contrast, Hahn's Constitutional Republican opponent, Frederick Conrad, was not a "firm and decided politician," but instead *"a political trimmer"* who had once denounced Republicans as "d——d Jacobins." For good measure, Rogers threw in the charge that Conrad, an incumbent, had gone home for several weeks while Congress was in session and still collected his per diem.[35]

When the returns were in, Brown was the top vote getter in a six-way race, and Hahn missed election by eleven votes. The Northampton Republicans had "made a noble stand" at the election and "apostasy" was in decline. With these victories under his belt, the newly arrived Rogers emerged as a power in eastern Pennsylvania, one clear sign of which was his sudden appearance as an officer in the Easton Light Infantry militia company. Rogers would rise from a company lieutenant in 1807 all the way to state brigadier general. Militia officers were elected, of course, and Rogers made sure that company doings always received prominent play in the *Northampton Farmer*. Following the example of Duane in Philadelphia, Rogers used the militia as the base for all his future endeavors, in terms of both supplying votes and providing an organizational imprimatur under which various Rogers-inspired political messages could be sent.[36]

Like James J. Wilson, Rogers discovered that seemingly no amount of influence could make a partisan newspaper profitable, so he used his political leverage to secure offices to make ends meet. In 1808 he was appointed clerk of the Northampton County Orphans Court. Even with the *Northampton Farmer* long established and relatively well-stocked with advertising, Rogers admitted, "If were not for the office I hold, I could not live by publishing my paper."[37]

The quick rise of an interloping printer was bitterly resented by Easton's established families and politicians. Rogers had begun to interfere with the local power structure, antagonizing the leading Germans and lawyers in particular. In the spring of 1807, Rogers excoriated three German assemblymen from the area because they had voted against a bill to improve navigation on the Delaware near Easton. In that fall's election, he got one of the Germans replaced with a non-German newcomer like himself. Unable to take much more, the local Constitutional Republicans (probably coopcrating with Federalists) encouraged Christian J. Hütter, a veteran printer who published the German-language *Northampton Correspondent*, first to politicize his existing paper and then to start one in English, which appeared as the *Pennsylvania Herald and Easton Intelligencer* in August 1808. A report reached Rogers that the new paper had been founded "for the express purpose of *breaking me up.*" Virtually the day Hütter's proposals came off the press, Rogers warned that his enemies were "miserably mistaken" if they thought he could be silenced.[38]

By way of making good on this threat, Rogers became the region's most potent advocate of Simon Snyder's 1808 race against "his majesty" Thomas McKean. The *Northampton Farmer* successfully attached a Federalist label to the Constitutional Republicans and needled Hütter as a "resplendent genius" whose paper was written by Federalist lawyers. In September Rogers made lawyer domination of officeholding a major and personally resonant issue of the campaign, labeling the two candidate slates the "Republican Farmers' Ticket" and the "Federal Lawyers Ticket." The *Herald* writers sneered (not always accurately) about Rogers's background and attacked his placement of commas, but to little avail. Snyder won, and Rogers got his appointment with the Orphans Court, displacing George Wolf, a German and a leading member of the Easton bar. The

Herald expressed the feelings of many old-time Easton politicians in describing Rogers (on the occasion of his appointment) as "an unprincipled . . . printer . . . without family or property, and without any thing to recommend him but want." This was a sentiment shared by many opponents of rising political editors.[39]

Thomas J. Rogers and Jonathan Roberts made their political acquaintance under circumstances that are revealing of an ordinary editor's role in small-town politics. Trying to coordinate with neighboring counties early in the Snyder campaign, Roberts sought to contact the most active Republican in Easton. Supposedly the key man was one Dr. John Cooper, but a Roberts letter requesting that Northampton hold an anti-McKean meeting ended up with Rogers instead, who simply called the meeting himself.

When Roberts wrote Rogers to ask where Easton political correspondence should be addressed in the future, Rogers answered himself, and only himself. "We have no society or even a standing committee of correspondence in this county; indeed, those Democrats in this county who might be useful to the cause are not active, which I am sorry to mention. I have repeatedly urged . . . the necessity of making every exertion, but to no effect." Indeed, the procedure followed in the recent case was habitual. When Dr. Cooper received a political letter, "he generally hands it to me, in order that I may communicate it to the Democrats in the county." In fact, whenever any of the county Democratic leaders came to Easton, they stopped by the *Farmer* office; "consequently I will have the best opportunity of making known" any plans or ideas that other Democrats around the state wanted to disseminate. So why not cut out the middleman? The office was the political hub of the county, and Rogers was trying to make it more so by installing himself as the county's sole liaison with the rest of the Republican political world.[40]

Rogers and Roberts established a political relationship that maximized the potentialities of newspaper politics. The editor and the legislator conducted a series of reciprocal exchanges that strengthened each politically and often personally, while cementing the support of the other. Rogers kept Roberts minutely informed of political developments in northeastern Pennsylvania and made it his business to see that Roberts's political interest and their mutual political views were industriously and vigorously promoted. Most of the extant letters between the two were written between 1808 and 1812, especially toward the end of that span, so the policies they were most often championing were trade sanctions and military action against Great Britain. Rogers warned Roberts that the taxes being proposed to fund the prospective war with Britain would "make a great noise here." When Northampton County's flour millers began mounting an organized protest against the trade embargo with Britain, Rogers sent along regular updates, while personally mobilizing a political response to the "bawling millers."[41]

In return for Rogers's services, Roberts sent back similarly detailed reports on political happenings at the capital, much as he did to the *Norristown Register,* sometimes along with essays for Rogers's paper. The kind of informed insight that only a member of Congress could provide raised the stature of a rural newspaper like the *Farmer,* along with that of its editor. "It is certainly of much importance to one in my situation to have a punctual correspondent at Washington and Lancaster during the Sessions," Rogers explained in thanking Roberts.[42]

There were also exchanges between the two in matters of influence. When people in Northampton County wanted a favor or appointment from the government—often military commissions in this war period—they went to Rogers, and he in turn wrote to Roberts. When Roberts needed the name of a reliable man to fill some office in the Easton area, he consulted Rogers, often effectively placing the office in the editor's gift. The effect of all this was to increase Rogers's influence in his community, while enhancing Roberts's standing with a key local activist and his newspaper.[43]

One area in which Rogers constantly needed Roberts's clout was the editor's numerous schemes to supplement his paper's income. For instance, Rogers asked for the senator's help in wresting the printing of the U.S. laws away from a Lancaster printer, claiming with some justice that Lancaster had easy access to the Philadelphia newspapers, while there were no publishers of the laws anywhere in the relatively isolated hills of northeastern Pennsylvania and northwestern New Jersey. Rogers employed a typical argument of editors asking for much-needed government favors: "The expence will be but a trifle to the United States, while it would be of considerable importance to me."[44]

To a greater extent than many editors, Rogers also tried his hand at other forms of political publishing besides newspapers and the laws. Senator Roberts acted as agent for promoting Rogers's various publications; elected officials interested in gaining newspaper editors' support were of-

ten a captive market for such solicitations. In particular, Roberts helped
with Rogers's most ambitious publishing venture, the *American Biographical Dictionary*. The entries in the *Dictionary* primarily covered heroes of
the Revolution and were actually memoirs solicited by Rogers from a
child or friend of each subject. It was to be sold, like most large works of
the day, by subscription. Roberts dutifully passed Rogers's proposal papers
around Washington and sent them back filled with signatures.[45]

Rogers's *Biographical Dictionary* was a classic case of the urge to do well
by doing good that characterized many early political and literary entrepreneurs. The editor designed the book "to perpetuate the memory, and
. . . extend the benefits of patriotic virtues and achievements," and fervently believed in his work's educational and social benefits. Like his fellow literary entrepreneur Mason Locke Weems, of George Washington
and the cherry tree fame, Rogers wanted to offer the heroes of the Revolution as positive role models for American children. By "contemplating
the characters of those illustrious men, who have been emphatically called
the founders of our republic," Rogers wrote, young Americans could make
themselves "models of every public and private virtue" and secure a bright,
democratic, and republican future for the nation.[46]

At the same time, Rogers tirelessly exploited his political connections
in "making some interest in favour of my book," prevailing upon his political associates either to buy copies themselves or help him sell them to
others. Wherever Rogers went, whether to Congress or a state convention, he rarely failed to promote his *Dictionary*. His most creative idea involved having the work officially adopted as a school textbook (and thus
purchased in bulk with public money), both in the United States and in
the fledgling republics of South America. He got influential political leaders to support the former proposal, and regarding the latter, Rogers wrote
to Simón Bolívar himself!

Rogers sincerely believed that wide knowledge of the lives of American
patriots would help sustain democracy and republicanism around the
globe, but he also dreamed of the vast profits that would ensue if he succeeded in having governments purchase thousands of copies of his book.
While it is unlikely that any South American schoolchild ever learned liberty from Thomas J. Rogers, the textbook project was at least partly successful. The *American Biographical Dictionary* went through three editions,
and in 1827 the Pennsylvania legislature passed a resolution recommending that county commissioners buy the book for public school students.

The vast profits seem not to have materialized, however, because Rogers spent the last years of his life holding down an office in the Philadelphia custom house.[47]

The Rogers-Roberts letters reveal much more than just the relationship of editors to officeholders. They also provide a glimpse into the way editors held together and shaped the development of the entire political system. As James J. Wilson did in New Jersey, Rogers pushed the politics of northeastern Pennsylvania toward the typical nineteenth-century pattern of popular campaigning, seemingly open conventions, and strong parties. Organized political parties had a place for editors in a way that other modes of conducting public affairs did not. Thus editors placed a high premium on party loyalty, the terms of which their newspapers set. The use of nominating conventions, known as "delegate meetings" or "conferences," had become common in Pennsylvania, and Thomas J. Rogers ardently defended the practice, which placed decision making in the hands of local party organizers like himself.

Not everyone in politics liked the new system as well as he did. Rogers was outraged during the 1811 election season when, after a ticket had already been nominated by the county delegate meeting (where Rogers himself had been a delegate), a group of renegade Republicans joined with Federalists to form a second ticket. Rogers fumed to Roberts that any politician who would "suffer himself [to] be made use of after the will of the majority has been fairly . . . expressed, cannot be a democrat, for he would, to obtain office, suffer himself to be made use of by any party." Rogers wished that his erstwhile Republican colleagues had resolved their differences within the bounds of party unity, showing both more commitment to the organization and a greater sense of what can only be called professionalism. "How much better would it have been for those who did not like the Delegate ticket to have said, 'we will support the Delegate ticket this year, to prevent division, and we will endeavour to select a ticket next year we like better.'" Rogers asked Roberts to write a series of articles on delegate meetings, defending their legitimacy so that their nominations would be better respected, restraining individualistic ambitions and making the party a more stable and effective political unit: "If we go on as we have . . . , the Democrats in this state will be like a flock of lost geese, have no fixed plan, while our enemies will take advantage of our want of *system*, and may succeed through . . . our divisions."[48]

Regarding himself as a colleague of Senator Roberts rather than a satellite, Rogers was quite self-aware about his role as the party's chief operative in Easton. As a party editor, Rogers saw it as his job not only to influence public opinion in his party's favor, but also to manage the local party itself, working to keep it unified and electorally strong. "As our county is now divided," Rogers told Roberts at one point, "I must double the exertions of my Printing office." Campaigning was uniquely an editor's role, because even in ultrapoliticized Pennsylvania, candidates were supposed to stand aloof from their own races. "Nothing can be more disgraceful," wrote the surrogate campaigner Rogers of an opposition candidate, "than to see a man riding around the country soliciting votes for *himself.*"

Rogers's managerial work went far beyond what was printed in the newspaper. He was always in attendance at local party gatherings and usually the leading spirit. When the Easton Democratic Republicans held a borough meeting, Rogers drafted the resolutions in advance and had alternative sets of resolutions ready to suit whatever the mood of the crowd turned out to be. To free his time for politics, Rogers hired an assistant to gather news from the exchange papers, and if the assistant was sick or politics got too intense, the news was left out altogether.[49]

An episode that demonstrated Rogers's decisive role in the local party was the ouster of Congressman William Rodman, engineered by the editor in 1812. Dissatisfied with Rodman's apparent opposition to strong measures against Great Britain, Rogers took the opportunity of a trip to Philadelphia to travel through the rest of the congressional district and lay the groundwork for a movement to deny Rodman the next Democratic Republican nomination. As a replacement, Rogers had in mind Samuel D. Ingham, a Bucks County paper manufacturer and former state legislator. As the leading party manager in Northampton County, the other half of the district, Rogers sent word for Ingham to come and visit him in Easton. After the visit, Rogers initiated a stream of anti-Rodman, pro-Ingham newspaper items and meeting resolutions. By August the editor was convinced the voters would "suffer our former friend Rodman to retire and reflect on his treachery and apostasy . . . nothing shall be wanting on my part in this quarter to endeavor to oust him."[50]

Nothing was wanting, apparently, because in October both Ingham and Roberts gave Rogers the credit for Ingham's landslide victory, led by a thousand-vote margin in Rogers's own Northampton County. Writing to Roberts after the election, the editor implicitly revealed the key to his success as a campaigner: Rogers had politics for his profession, his one over-riding concern and main income source, while the millers, his main local opponents in this and other recent battles, "do not care about elections as long as flour is so much in demand." This singular focus had made Rogers the Easton area's major political manager.[51]

MERINO RAMS AND MUTTON SOUP: TO CONGRESS AND BACK WITH THOMAS J. ROGERS

At this point, it is appropriate to switch focus from editors' relation-ships with officeholders to the way in which one editor built upon those relationships and took the next step, seeking election to office in his own right. Jonathan Roberts's most prolific correspondent, Thomas J. Rogers, happens to provide one of the best examples available.

He and Samuel Ingham, the congressman he had more or less created in 1812, worked themselves into the graces of the officeholder-dominated "Family" faction in Philadelphia, named after the three brothers-in-law, including Alexander Dallas's son George Mifflin Dallas and Philadelphia postmaster Richard Bache, who headed it. The Family had inherited the mantle of the wealthy, conservative "Constitutional Republicans" who had defended Thomas McKean, opposed reform of the legal system, and com-peted with William Duane's faction for control of the party.

Rogers himself had been a bitter detractor of the Constitutional Re-publicans. By the 1810s he was gravitating toward Pennsylvania's burgeon-ing manufacturing and transportation interests and saw more opportunity with the wealthy, well-connected Philadelphians than the state party's other wing, the base of which was much poorer, and more rural, German, even western. The Family's other appeal, perhaps reflecting more favor-ably on Rogers, was that they could make the most convincing claim to be the regular Republican organization that had supported the national Re-publican administrations through all the state's various upheavals.[52]

The War of 1812 gave Rogers his opportunity to run for office. More and more heavily involved in the militia, Rogers served in Pennsylvania's 1814 mobilization (the same one that made William Duane adjutant gen-eral) and found an issue for himself in the mistreatment (especially non-payment) of the Pennsylvania troops by the federal authorities. In the summer and fall of 1815, Rogers sold the *Northampton Farmer,* organized protest meetings for militia pay, and got himself nominated for the state senate. The printers who bought Rogers's paper (renaming it the *Spirit of*

Pennsylvania) pledged to favor no particular party and even apologized that "the warm politician will denounce our journal as insipid," yet they managed to find room for prominent notices of Rogers's political activities. His opponent was old rival George Wolf, the German lawyer who once lost a valuable county office to Rogers. The voting patterns in Rogers's victory were revealing of where a party editor's actual popularity may have lain. Wolf won handily in the town of Easton, where Rogers had been known as a working printer and patronage appointee, but the editor's strength increased with the distance from Easton. In neighboring towns and rural areas, Rogers was known more impersonally as the editor of a highly regarded newspaper and a popular militia officer.[53]

In the state senate, Rogers made militia reform his issue and laid the groundwork for higher office. He wrote letters on the legislature's proceedings for John Binns's *Democratic Press* and, at the same time, attached himself to State Treasurer William Findlay, who would be the "regular" (and Family-supported) Republican candidate for governor in 1817 despite grave reservations about his integrity and politics in some circles. This shift was a delicate operation for Rogers, since it involved potentially alienating former allies from the newspaper wars, including Binns.

Other shifts were in the offing as Rogers bid for the brass ring. At home in Easton, he lost his hold over the *Spirit of Pennsylvania* but soon made common cause with his old editorial sparring partner Christian J. Hütter, who founded a pro-Findlay Republican paper called the *Easton Centinel* in July 1817. Rogers and Hütter joined forces to campaign for Findlay, and in the aftermath Rogers worked hard but carefully, through intermediaries, to place his own supporters on the district nominating conference that would choose a congressional candidate in 1818. Mirabile dictu, Rogers emerged as the conference's consensus choice and, with the *Easton Centinel*'s support, won the election over token opposition. Thus in 1818 Rogers became only the seventh printer-editor (after Matthew Lyon, James J. Wilson, William Hendricks of Indiana, Daniel Cruger of New York, Salma Hale of New Hampshire, and Orasmus C. Merrill of Vermont) to be elected to Congress. Wilson and Rogers were the only working printers elected to Congress through 1818. All the others but Lyon had become lawyers and had shed their printerly identities years before their elevation to the national legislature.[54]

Ensconced in Washington, Rogers established the same relationship with Hütter that he had once had with Jonathan Roberts. Hütter reported on political movements and public opinion at home—who planned to run against Rogers at the next election, what local people thought of a proposed tax, the progress of efforts to pass a new militia law. Knowing from experience that editorial support back home was crucial to his political welfare, Rogers inundated Hütter with mail. "I must confess that you are the most faithful correspondent I ever had," Hütter wrote the congressman at one point, struggling to keep up an equally heavy output in return.[55]

Rogers was much more comfortable in Washington than James J. Wilson, and he eventually became an influential man in the House. (Yet perhaps because of their common background in the printing trade, Rogers and Wilson recognized each other as kindred spirits and roomed together during the Sixteenth Congress.) Along with now-colleague Samuel Ingham, Rogers became one of presidential candidate and Secretary of War John C. Calhoun's chief northern lieutenants, planting newspaper pieces boosting the South Carolinian's nationalist credentials around the state. Like most other Pennsylvania politicians, Rogers also became a zealous advocate of tariff protection for American manufactures.[56]

Rogers's career as an elective politician would be unpleasantly eventful. His choice of state political factions turned out to be unfortunate. While Rogers was far away in Washington, William Findlay's administration descended into a morass of financial scandals, opening the governor and all his supporters to attacks on their integrity and strong challenges at reelection time. Almost simultaneously, the Panic of 1819 unleashed great hostility to the cliques of officeholders that were seen as controlling politics all over the nation, a description that unquestionably applied to the Pennsylvania Findlayites. In some eyes, the power now held by men like Rogers showed just how shamefully the republic had declined since the days of the revolutionary heroes. Seen justly as a tireless political entrepreneur, Rogers was never especially popular in Easton. Many in Easton's upper crust had never reconciled themselves to his rise and would take strong action to reverse it.

The intensity of and the resources behind the hostility to Rogers show most clearly in the fact that each of his bids for reelection inspired the founding of special newspapers devoted almost exclusively to his political destruction. The Easton *Mountaineer*, which appeared in January 1820, looked like a conventional newspaper, with advertisements and news and reprinted essays from other papers. Yet from June until the paper went out of business roughly a year later, hardly an issue was published without some anti-Rogers material, usually several columns of it, sometimes interspersed with slaps at the Findlay administration and Hütter of the *Centinel*. In spite of these efforts, Rogers just barely survived an electoral debacle that swept Findlay out of office. The former editor even added to his laurels, winning another election for brigadier general of the state militia a few months later.[57]

In 1822 Rogers's enemies subjected him to an even more ferocious pounding. A former close ally of the congressman's named Hugh Ross was induced—probably hired or heavily subsidized—to turn coat. Ross established a newspaper called *The Expositor*, which dispensed with all pretenses about its purpose: each issue contained four pages of solid type assaulting Rogers and his associates with no advertising and only occasional news items to dilute the venom. Much of Ross's material came from information, letters, and documents obtained while working with Rogers. The questionable ethics and malevolent intentions of the whole enterprise were laid bare in its banner motto, "That which the welfare of the people demands, is justifiable." In his final issue, Ross belatedly announced that he would not exchange his paper with other editors because, frankly, "the matter . . . in it related merely to local politics, and included nothing of general interest." It existed solely to do in Thomas J. Rogers. It was a testament to Rogers's resourcefulness that he survived even this second onslaught, again winning reelection by a few hundred votes.[58]

In their sheer volume and substance, the *Mountaineer* and *Expositor* attacks on Rogers provide a remarkable window into how ordinary editorial politicians were perceived by some in their communities. Both papers bored in on Rogers's political professionalism. He had won many battles over the years by simply working harder and more creatively at campaigning than others, but this now became a serious demerit. It was said that Rogers was too much "[his] own trumpeter." Allegedly, he spent too much of his time in Congress currying favor with constituents by writing letters home and franking copies of the *National Intelligencer*. He had arranged his own renomination by holding meetings in out-of-the-way places and packing them with his own supporters.

Then there were charges of bribing voters. One of his lackeys had supposedly offered a popular local farmer a Merino ram if he would support Rogers for Congress. The *Mountaineer* made a major issue out of this anecdote, at one point listing Rogers and his allies as the "Merino Ram

Ticket," complete with illustration. Perhaps most damning of all, the *Mountaineer* charged that Rogers had toured the district campaigning for himself: "I never knew an instance before in this district," wrote an *Expositor* correspondent, "that the candidate himself would be continually out begging for votes. Such a course . . . is too degrading, too little. If he has not friends that will push him, then he had better not run."[59]

Rogers needed to stoop so low, his enemies argued, because he was an unworthy candidate: an immoral man, an immigrant, a climber who had risen above his station and lacked the respect of his community. Without aggressive self-promotion and partisan overkill, he was nothing. The *Mountaineer* urged voters to choose "an honest German farmer" native to the county over someone who was "not born in the district, state, or even in the United States" and predicted that Rogers could not win twenty votes in his own heavily Republican neighborhood. Chided for insulting the Irish, one editor hastened to add that Rogers came from "the *lowest class* of Irish," which "every well bred man" would admit were "the most profane and vulgar beings in the human family." Especially in the *Expositor*, Rogers was depicted as a drunken lout who swore incessantly and enjoyed fighting in taverns, when not physically threatening enemies or mistreating his own family.[60]

Even when the prophecies of Rogers' sinking voter support turned out to be wrong, it was said to prove nothing about the congressman's personal popularity or community standing. Utterly lacking in the traditional attributes of leadership, Rogers's electoral success was attributed solely to excessive partisanship and campaigning, an analysis that was not without merit: "Party spirit obtained for him those offices . . . he could never have looked or even hoped for. Yes, party spirit placed him on the 'top of the wheel,' passed him from one office to another, and at last ushered him into the National Legislature." Rogers's vulgarity and political overexertion had disgusted more respectable men and discouraged them from running: "They are as much afraid of a competition 'with *Gen. Rogers*, as a well-dressed gentleman would be of encountering a chimney sweep.'" Open letters were addressed to John C. Calhoun to the effect that he was disgracing himself by accepting the aid of "miserable and forlorn tools" like Rogers.[61]

Naturally, a man of such low breeding was venal and proprietary in his approach to office, the *Mountaineer* and *Expositor* argued, an impression that Rogers sometimes could not help but foster, since he actually lived on his official earnings. Supposedly Rogers had prevailed upon the Findlay administration to appoint his elderly father in Philadelphia a justice of peace, with the agreement that the income of the office would go to his son. This may well have been true. Suffering heavy losses from his congressional travel and living expenses, Rogers allegedly declared that this arrangement was a "damn'd fine thing for him in his embarrassed situation, and would help him; and every man was a damn'd fool for not looking out for himself."[62]

Nor did Rogers make up for his coarseness and greed with political consistency, his enemies charged. He had switched state factions, of course, and embraced onetime mortal enemies such as Hütter. What the *Expositor* roasted Rogers for particularly was his course on the Missouri statehood issue. Initially Rogers had joined other northern Republican congressmen in supporting the Tallmadge Amendment and written numerous impassioned letters home to Easton expressing his hatred of slavery. Then after a few weeks of deadlock and some strong pressure from Ingham and the Calhounites, he caved in and voted to admit Missouri without restriction. While the vote was understandable in terms of Rogers's nationalism, commitment to party unity, and genuine admiration for Calhoun, it was easy to depict as a violation of his own conscience in the name of selfish, weak-minded partisanship.[63]

The anti-Rogers newspapers doubtless exaggerated, but their overall theme that his life and identity were wholly and unattractively consumed by politics cut deeply. So did the allusions to his personal habits. Printing offices were not exactly schools for good manners and healthy living, and political life took place in an endless series of taverns, banquet halls, and well-liquored outdoor gatherings. One of the *Expositor's* ugliest stories seems likeliest to be true. The allegation was that Rogers had spent an entire weekend in September 1822 on a binge of drinking and politicking, while his family was home sick. The fun began with a political meeting on Friday night and continued with a quarrelsome bender at the Salt Box Tavern. When challenged about why he had stayed in town all night, Rogers lamely explained that he had been buying meat for his family, in order to make some restorative mutton soup.[64]

Though the voters twice vindicated Rogers in the face of these attacks, the end of his third term found him with little stomach to go on as an elected official. His reputation was in tatters, and, after six years of congressional service, so were his finances. This was the fate of most early congressmen without substantial wealth or a profession that they could practice in Washington. In 1824 a new Family governor, John A. Shulze, appointed Rogers as register and recorder of Northampton County, and he quietly resigned his seat in Congress to be replaced by longtime rival George Wolf. For the next few years, he worked on his textbook project and put himself quietly out to pasture, a political has-been at age forty-three. Or so Rogers may have thought, until he became one of the hundreds of newspaper editors who abetted and benefited from the reconstruction of the party system that coincided with the political rise of Andrew Jackson. It is to this subject that we now turn.[65]

14

Newspaper Editors and the
Reconstruction of Party Politics

༄

T*he years from* Thomas Jefferson's second administration to the end of
the War of 1812, the period in which Thomas J. Rogers and James J.
Wilson rose to power, were some of the most intense, chaotic, and confus-
ing in American political history. The Republican administrations' policies of trade war and then shooting war against Great Britain inspired
both support and opposition that recalled and sometimes exceeded the
bitterness of the 1790s. Riots and disturbances wracked the cities, federal
troops were needed to enforce the trade laws, and state governments actively hindered the war effort. Some Federalist leaders plotted secession
and others made secret contacts with the British, while more moderate
Federalists only proposed major constitutional surgery at the Hartford
Convention of 1814–15.

The impact of the War of 1812 era on the American political system
was both profound and contradictory. The Republican-Federalist conflict
was powerfully reenergized before and during the war, only to be damp-
ened nearly to death in its aftermath. Federalism collapsed as a national
force amid a wave of revulsion against the partisan excesses of the previous decades, of which the Federalists' wartime obstructionism and apparent disloyalty seemed to some only a logical extension.

The impact of these years was especially contradictory in the area of
newspaper politics. On the one hand, the 1807–15 period was an important
stage in the growth and development of the political newspaper networks,
as the system attracted fresh, committed recruits and became ever more
firmly rooted and professionalized. On the other hand, the national events
of the period conspired to destroy the national party conflict that partisan

newspaper editors were so devoted to tending. The aftermath was a volatile situation, during the so-called "Era of Good Feelings," in which national party alignments were nonexistent, but a vast infrastructure of political conflict continued to function in communities across the land.

It was out of this situation that the Jacksonian-era mass party system (and the nineteenth-century political order more generally) developed, and partisan newspaper editors were one of the most important forces behind that change. More than any single group of politicians, Republican editors worked to keep the party alive after the collapse of Federalism, using whatever materials came to hand. Tapping into political energy sources such as public distress over the Panic of 1819 and the popularity of Gen. Andrew Jackson, editors and other pro-party politicians were eventually able to reassemble the pieces of the old party conflict and improve on it, producing a new party system that would surpass the old Republican versus Federalist arrangement in penetration, institutionalization, and apparent popularity.

In the process, editors materially changed their own position in the political system. Before the 1820s, editors were influential but disdained henchmen who (like James J. Wilson or Thomas J. Rogers) occasionally fought their way into positions of honor or authority, but were then usually undermined or betrayed by their own allies. By the 1830s editors had forged the decisive role in American political life that they enjoyed for most of the rest of the century. Having once obtained offices only by sheer political force and almost never by presidential appointment, in the 1830s editors became the most disproportionately represented occupational group in politics besides lawyers, maintaining a large presence in Congress, the postal service, and many other officeholding categories. Once ignored or schemed against by high officials, editors were pushed forward by statesmen and welcomed into national administrations. Out of the gentry-dominated political order of the founders, the editors helped create one in which they themselves were among the principal figures. Quite naturally and fittingly from the editorial viewpoint, this order was one in which party loyalty and political service were the most highly valued qualities, largely determining the distribution of government benefits and offices.

This final chapter provides an overview of editors' roles in the maintenance and revival of party, culminating in the Democratic victories that brought Andrew Jackson, Martin Van Buren, and, to some extent, the editors themselves, to power.

"AN ARMY OF PRINTERS": THE WAR OF 1812 ERA AND
THE ORIGINS OF JACKSONIAN NEWSPAPER POLITICS

The ongoing integration of newspapers and editors with party politics was perhaps finally cemented (and the press networks given another major growth spurt) by the events leading up to the War of 1812. Thomas Jefferson's mostly successful plan to neutralize the Federalist party by moderation and conversion foundered when he imposed an embargo on all foreign trade in 1807. The Republican president's first truly divisive policy initiative (and major policy failure), "peaceable coercion" devastated New England's maritime economy and seemed to vindicate Federalist warnings about the dangers of Virginia domination. The Federalist party was handed its first popular issue since the XYZ Affair and a sufficient injection of voter support to stave off death for a few more years. Federalists rolled back many of the Republican gains in New England and mustered enough national strength to run their own presidential candidate respectably and make a renegade Republican, De Witt Clinton, a serious contender against James Madison.[1]

The seeming resurrection of Federalism, which included renewed organizational efforts and multiple newspaper foundings, called forth furious Republican exertions in response. The two parties together pushed the level of newspaper creation to new highs: eighty journals were founded in 1808 and eighty-two in 1809 (see appendix 1). The new papers spread even farther afield—and stacked on top of one another in many places because of continuing Republican factionalism. (See map 6.)

The Jefferson and Madison administrations' desperate need for political support and willing soldiers even led to a temporary relaxation of the standards that had barred printers from being appointed to office in the past. Thus William Duane was named first a lieutenant colonel in the expanded army and then adjutant general for Pennsylvania (over the objections of Treasury Secretary Albert Gallatin, who left the cabinet in disgust); New Brunswick *Fredonian* printer-editor James Fitz Randolph became a federal revenue collector; and several other editors, including "little lunatic" William Pechin of the Baltimore *American* and Selleck Osborn, then of Boston, received military commissions. "AN ARMY OF PRINTERS!!!," shrieked the Baltimore *Federal Republican* in response. "The cheek burns and the hand trembles while we write it." The arch-Federalist journal correctly recognized these appointments as an impor-

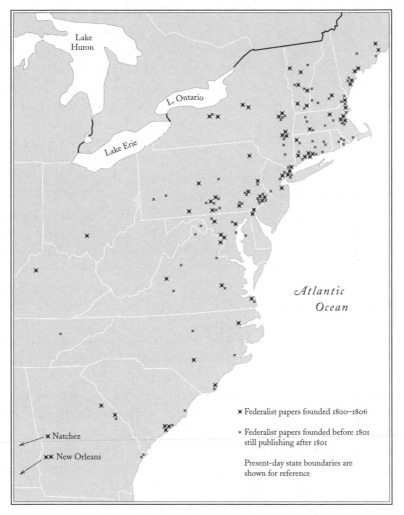

Lake
Huron

L. Ontario

Lake Erie

*Atlantic
Ocean*

✖ Federalist papers founded 1800–1806

✕ Federalist papers founded before 1801
still publishing after 1801

Present-day state boundaries are
shown for reference

✖ Natchez

✖✖ New Orleans

MAP 6. The Political Wars of 1812: Republican and Federalist
Newspapers Founded 1807–1814.

tant act of democratization on Jefferson's part, which editor Alexander
Contee Hanson naturally deplored. The appointments would "give *heart-
felt satisfaction* to every *Printer's Devil*, who aspires after fame and honour
and glory"; Jefferson had "disregarded the solemn responsibility of office
in giving . . . importance and influence to the most hateful and dangerous
members of the republick."[2]

Rapid expansion also brought a large and important new cohort of editors into the business. Many editors who would be dominant figures and tone setters in the Jacksonian-era party press all first picked up the pen around this time, including Thurlow Weed, Amos Kendall, and a host of more obscure figures, such as Jefferson's young printer-correspondent John Norvell, who were very important in their own time and places. Besides zealotry, one characteristic of this cohort was an inveterate devotion to party organization and continuing political warfare, both as ways of life and the proper modes of conducting the republic. A thoroughgoing professionalism and a deep commitment to making their careers in politics allowed many members of this cohort to weather the collapse of the old parties and help foster the creation of new ones.

The rise of New Hampshire's Isaac Hill provides a useful example of what the editors in this cohort were like and how they changed the political system as they rose through it. The editors who emerged during the war years not only democratized the ranks of politicians by their presence, but they also changed the rhetoric, style, and sometimes even the content of politics, for better or worse. Hill was one of the most infamous editors whoever worked in the partisan press. Wearing his common background on his sleeve, he was the kind of man who injected a sharp flavor of class resentment into the politics of the period—sometimes out of any proportion or even close relation to the issue at hand.[3]

In 1809 the twenty-one-year-old Hill was completing his apprenticeship in the Amherst, New Hampshire, office of Joseph Cushing, an oldfashioned, moderately Federalist printer. Though close to his master, Hill's own political principles were violently Republican and democratic. Hill had grown up in Massachusetts, the unhappy son of a poor farmer prone to fits of insanity. Physically disabled by a childhood accident, Isaac was also a strenuously ambitious boy who, like many other young men of his background, took up the printing trade to escape from the "drudgery of a small farm" to a situation that afforded a modicum of intellectual stimulation.

Hill educated himself by reading the wares of Cushing's bookshop, and honed his political skills by writing for his master's paper and joining a local debating society. Without the connections or money required to attend college or study law, Hill jumped at the chance, when it offered, to "commence the life of the editor of a political newspaper." For $300 (possibly borrowed from John Langdon, the just-defeated Republican governor), he bought out one of New Hampshire's two Republican newspapers and launched his own, the Concord *New-Hampshire Patriot*, in 1809.[4]

In the beginning, Hill's prospects were not bright. His printing press was of revolutionary vintage, and his used types were worn down from having been previously used to print a full edition of the Bible. While the local Federalist paper had most of Concord's professional men for a stable of writers, Hill did almost all of his paper's writing and much of the printing himself, having only a younger brother and one journeyman for a staff. All these deficiencies could be seen in the printed product, which was barely legible at times and largely free of the classical pen names and literary allusions that gentleman essayists typically employed.[5]

Despite these disadvantages, Hill was a smashing success. Swearing eternal hostility to the "evil spirit of Federalism" that was "stalking up and down the land seeking whom it may devour," Hill brought a blunt, angry rhetoric and a take-no-prisoners political style that seemed to strike a chord with the state's flinty populace. His lack of education unredeemed by any gift for political theory or elegant prose, Hill channeled his rage, energy, and Yankee moral absolutism into creating a very effective political newspaper. Rhetorically, the *Patriot* tapped into the fervid, often luridly expressed religious emotionalism that had fallen out of favor with New England's educated elites but remained strong in its popular culture.[6]

Hill's very first editorial column struck a typical note by framing his opposition to the Federalists in terms of revenge for childhood tragedies. "Theirs is the cause of Great Britain," Hill wrote, which he had learned to hate while "feeling the loss of personal connexions, the fruit of British barbarism at Menotomy and Bunker-Hill." In a later article, Hill's Federalists were in league with worse powers than the British. It was the Republicans' duty, he wrote, to "counteract [the] evil machinations" of those who had "bowed the knee to this political Baal." In 1812 he was able to strip the complex debate surrounding the Jefferson and Madison embargoes down to a stark opposition of good versus evil and haves versus have-nots. According to Hill, the embargo was "beneficial to *poor people* . . . the *manufacturer*," and "the *farmer*," and "injurious . . . not to the fair and honorable merchant," but only to "such as have been in the habit of sponging the country people and have made themselves rich at other's expense." When not pronounced demonic and overbearing lordlings, Federalist officeholders were flatly dismissed in the *Patriot* as incompetents and nonentities. On the performance of New Hampshire's incumbent congressmen, Hill commented that they had, "with a prudence becoming their several abilities, wisely concluded to hold their tongues in public discussions."[7]

When criticized for his vitriol, Hill pleaded "youth and inexperience," but also made a case for vitriol as a positive good: "Assailed, as our republican institutions are, by corruption and foreign intrigue, by the advocates and palliators of foreign injustice and wickedness," the editor suggested, it would be "criminal not to advocate our rights with ardor and a degree of warmth." Hill clearly did not regard the party conflict as a momentary crisis that would end with the Federalists' defeat or conversion; it was instead an ongoing competition that was inevitable and natural. Since the late 1790s, editors had periodically attacked the hypocrisy of traditional commercial "impartiality" and defended partisanship in terms of their duty to defend the republic. William Duane had memorably denounced Republican moderates who shied away from extreme partisanship as "hermaphrodites" made from "the combination of good and evil, of the *mule kind*, incapable of propagating." Hill introduced a note of relativism into this line of argument, implying that any strong party affiliation was better than none, even if the affiliation was evil:

> In the first place, we view the idea of an impartial paper as preposterous; for there is no man in his senses who does not view one of the great parties . . . as being essentially right, and the other wrong; and the man thus convinced of right and wrong would, in our opinion, be equally guilty for treating both parties alike with him who advocated a bad cause knowing it to be such.[8]

To a greater degree and in a franker manner than earlier cohorts of editors, Hill and his contemporaries embodied an uneasy combination of real zeal for the cause with the practical, results-oriented approach of entrepreneurs in the business of politics. Hill was a relentless political organizer and highly focused campaigner. It had become standard practice for editors to print tickets, exhort party workers to "exertion," and defend their leading candidates, but Hill went much further. Deposed governor and possible *Patriot* benefactor John Langdon was puffed ("We enquire in vain even for an error in judgment in the public life of Gov. Langdon") and virtually renominated the moment he left office. As the state election of 1809 drew near, the *Patriot* issued a long string of short responses—suitable for use in a tavern or post office discussion—to Federalist-circulated rumors against Langdon and the Republicans, many under exclamation-pointed headlines. "Suggestions" were issued that local campaign committees be formed to use "every fair and honorable means" to win the election.[9]

At the same time, Hill was careful to make sure that the political effectiveness of his newspaper translated into prosperity for its proprietor. He sold more advertising than most Republican papers and also seems to have been more effective in his debt collections. Rather than issue petulant dun notices years later, he began the paper with the jaded admonition that "when a person subscribes, he should always count on sometime paying." Many editors complained about enemies interfering with the distribution of their newspapers. Hill cut to the chase and offered a reward for anyone caught destroying or misdirecting his. Like many rural editors in settled areas, he reduced his subscription risk by delivering the *Patriot* through post riders, who bought discounted papers from the printer and then became responsible for collecting subscription payments along their routes.

In this and other areas, Hill tried to ensure that the politics and economics of his business worked together rather than at cross purposes. Concerned about low circulation in a particular town, he sent a new post rider out with a letter to a local Republican leader on the route, suggesting that by helping the rider get "good encouragement," he would be both helping the Republican cause and earning the editor's favor. Close attention to finances is one area where Isaac Hill may not have been such a representative partisan editor. Most tried to use their political connections to earn a living, but Hill actually succeeded, becoming wealthy in real estate and banking over his editorial career.[10]

Appalled and alarmed by Hill, the Federalists retaliated viciously. Their newspapers publicized his painful family background, and the disabled editor was attacked in a Concord street. Yet he proved incredibly resilient. When Langdon won back the governor's chair and the Republicans regained control of the state legislature within a year of Hill's buying the *Patriot,* the editor gained a reputation for great political skill. This and subsequent exploits swiftly made Hill one of the preeminent figures in New Hampshire politics, overshadowing most of the state's elected officeholders. His partisan rage never died—especially toward real, former, or imagined Federalists—but as a practical politician, Hill was able to adjust his specific targets as conditions warranted. A vehement supporter of John Quincy Adams during the war years and a critic of the political ambitions of Andrew Jackson as late as March 1824, Hill switched sides soon after and made himself one of Jackson's most notorious partisans by charging, in a footnote to a campaign biography of Jackson, that the diplomat

Adams had once "procured" a virginal American governess for the "imperial lust" of the tsar of Russia.[11]

Isaac Hill drove his political opponents (and many historians after them) to distraction, but he and his ilk—editors who were professional politicians, hyperactive organizers, and vituperators by trade—were to some extent the natural offspring of the newspaper-based political system that was consolidated after 1800. Having grown up with newspaper politics and embraced it as a vocation, they cheerfully accepted its ethos and exigencies. These could include rhetorical brutality, fanatic zeal, and intense competitiveness, along with a moral code flexible enough to accommodate the occasional ideological inconsistency or bout of opportunism regarding public offices and printing contracts.

So Isaac Hill's contemporary John Norvell could ply his trade with equal aplomb for five different newspapers in three different states, act as an energetic editorial supporter of first Vice President John C. Calhoun and then his archenemy and successor Martin Van Buren, and hold appointive offices under the Democratic presidents Andrew Jackson and James K. Polk, as well as Polk's Whig replacement, Zachary Taylor. Throughout life, Norvell brushed off charges of excessive partisanship with the argument that it was self-defeating, unworthy, and, in essence, unprofessional, to advance a cause with anything less than the highest possible level of energy, efficiency, and fervor. Asked in midcareer for a reply to the criticism that he and his allies had shown "indiscreet zeal" in promoting a candidate, Norvell scoffed: "To be afraid of our own shadows is the most pernicious thing in politics. I must confess that I prefer even that *'indiscreet zeal'* of which . . . we have been accused."[12] While often coarse, always aspiring, and sometimes unappealing, editors with these sorts of attitudes were a potent political force, one which began to coalesce before and during the War of 1812.

NEWSPAPER EDITORS AND THE WAR ON GOOD FEELINGS

Unfortunately for professional partisan zealots like Norvell and Hill, the years immediately following the war (and their emergence on the political scene) were not very favorable ones for party politics in the United States. The aging revolutionary gentry and their successor statesmen had been growing uneasy over the direction of American political culture for many years, feelings in which the rise of newspaper politics played no small part. Partisan excesses during the embargo and the war, especially

Federalist opposition that verged on and sometimes crossed over the line into disloyalty, brought out the latent antipartyism of many older Republican leaders and caused many others to identify themselves as strident nationalists rather than Republican partisans. At the same time, many of the substantive bases for the old party distinctions seemed to be fading, as the national government's financial and military embarrassments caused many Republicans (especially in Congress and the Madison administration) to embrace policies—such as a national bank, the encouragement of manufacturing, and more flexible standards of constitutional interpretation— formerly associated with the Federalists. The end of the war itself shut down one of the last issues that strongly divided Federalist and Republican gentlemen.[13]

Given this atmosphere, it is not surprising that party politics came under a sustained and effective attack, most influentially in the form of *The Olive Branch: or, Faults on Both Sides, Federal and Democratic,* by Mathew Carey. Another Irish radical printer transplanted to Philadelphia, Carey had followed a different path in America than contemporaries such as William Duane and John Binns. Focusing on his publishing business, Carey had become a wealthy man by eschewing political newspapers in favor of more profitable literary commodities such as Bibles. After 1800 he mostly stayed aloof from party politics, while moving into a second career as a tireless promoter of national economic development, especially in the form of the protective tariff. Clashing with Duane and other partisan Republican editors over issues such as the recharter of the Bank of the United States, Carey became a harsh critic of newspaper politics, seeing his former friends' neediness as an unanswerable argument in favor of his own decision to abandon political publishing. He wrote *The Olive Branch* at the time of the Hartford Convention in 1814, addressing the current crisis but also looking forward to a postwar reform of American politics and government. Going through ten editions and doubling in size over four years, Carey's vast compendium of documents, arguments, and historical narrative became one of the bestselling books in American history up to that time.[14]

The *Olive Branch* aimed to replace the party conflict with a patriotic consensus in support of the war and a larger program of increasing the nation's strength and wealth through systematic government action. Carey began by rehearsing the standard classical republican indictment of "party and faction" as "the bane and destruction of the ancient republics," arguing that the American republic was about to go the way of Rome and Sparta, torn apart and exposed to despotism or conquest. He then reviewed the political controversies and national policies of the previous twenty-five years, blaming the errors that led to the war and hobbled its prosecution on the ideological bigotry and extremity of both parties.[15]

While his specific charges were mostly aimed at Federalist obstructors of the war effort, Carey's strictures against partisanship per se also applied to the Republicans, who had introduced party politics to the national scene. Editors and other political writers were particularly blameworthy, having driven the country to the brink of disaster by fomenting "a satanical spirit of hatred, malice, and abhorrence" that they "daily increased by inflammatory publications."[16] This analysis provided the basis for Carey's most startling criticism of past Republican policies. "The factious clamor excited against the sedition and alien laws" in 1798–1800, so potent in removing the Federalists from power, he classed "among the sins of the [Republican] party." Any "reasonable man" could now agree, Carey wrote, that the Sedition Act, "so far from being an outrageous infringement of liberty" as the Republicans had then claimed, was "not merely defensible, but absolutely necessary and indispensable towards the support of [the] government."[17]

Carey made it clear that abandoning party politics would go hand in hand with halting or reversing many concurrent political trends, particularly those involving any form of democratization. The new patriotic consensus would be forged among "a few influential men in the different states," who would transmit their enlarged views to their less well-informed neighbors and expect that their advice would be followed. Carey was explicit about the need for a retreat from the democratic rhetoric and vigorous criticism of government officials that had come with the rise of the partisan press. The *Olive Branch* condemned radical democrats along with hard-core Federalists and argued for the government's absolute power to protect itself from newspaper interference. Carey asked editors to tone down their criticism of even so agreed-upon an evil as monarchy, specifically citing Paine's attack on "crowned ruffians" in *Common Sense.* Besides offending "good taste and decency," such remarks might anger European monarchs and lead to wars. The major beneficiaries of the hostility stirred up by such alleged rhetorical indecency were those upstart politicians "whose influence and consequence depend on fomenting discord, and who would sink into insignificance in times of tranquility."[18]

Here Carey was participating in, and promoting, the culmination of the political gentrification campaign that had begun shortly after 1800. Wealthier and more genteel Republicans had long been concerned about restraining their party's partisanship and maintaining its respectability, and, particularly when facing off in factional battles against strong partisan newspaper editors, they were not immune to the more commonly Federalist feeling that the young nation's political culture was already in a dangerous state of decline. The very word "politician" changed meanings, acquiring a newly pejorative connotation.

In the eighteenth century, "politician" had "denoted simply persons engaged in public affairs," including political theorists as well as candidates and officials. A "wise politician" was someone expert in the enlightened science of politics, understood as a field devoted to regulating society so as to maximize human prosperity, freedom, and happiness. In the early nineteenth century, "politician" was narrowing toward its modern application, denoting someone devoted to advancing themselves in public life, whose only expertise was in the more narrow political science of winning elections and securing official salaries. The word was often applied even more specifically, to those who occupied the lower echelons and strategic points of the political system and manipulated it from behind the scenes. The opposites of the "politicians" were the gentleman "statesmen," the founders of the republic and their successors. The rise of the political parties, and the newspaper politics that came with it, had allowed the politicians to gain the upper hand. Now that Federalism was no longer a threat and national honor had been vindicated, it was time for the statesmen to take command once more.[19]

Though few incumbent or expectant officeholders ventured to join Mathew Carey in defending sedition prosecutions and monarchy, large numbers publicly endorsed the *Olive Branch,* and national Republican leaders pushed forward with many of Carey's other suggestions. This was especially true of the Fourteenth Congress, elected in 1814 at the darkest stage of the war and generally regarded as one of the most distinguished congresses ever, rivaling even the First Congress in terms of the talent, energy, education, wealth, and eloquence of its members. Headlined in the House by the future "great triumvirate" of Henry Clay, John C. Calhoun, and Daniel Webster, the men of the Fourteenth Congress were bent on achieving national greatness in the wake of the war's humiliations. Though overwhelmingly Jeffersonian in their political affiliations, the postwar legislature embarked on an economic development program of Hamiltonian scope and substance, even going beyond Hamilton by including a plan (eventually vetoed) to systematically improve the nation's transportation system.

Along with the new departures in policy went concomitant departures in political style, both changes reflecting newly expansive notions of the federal government's role in American society. Insulated from partisan pressures by the lack of effective party competition, Republicans in national office increasingly conducted themselves as a leadership class to which a certain status and income were due. Whereas, under Jefferson, the ruling gentlemen had shown at least some cosmetic respect for popular sensibilities, the Fourteenth Congress openly disregarded those sensibilities by voting itself a pay raise. Complaining of high living costs and depreciated currency, the House and Senate took only two weeks in March 1816 to pass a bill converting members' $6 per diem to a $1,500 salary.[20]

The expanded size and population of the country had increased the "weight and responsibility" of members, explained one congressional supporter of the Compensation Act. It was impossible to "live in the style of a gentleman" (two horses, a servant, and residence in a genteel boarding-house) on the current allowance, complained another. The possibility of adverse public reaction was brushed aside. Voters would never have the "poorness of spirit" to demand that their representatives "degrade themselves . . . , or . . . sacrifice their private property" in order to serve, Samuel W. Dana of Connecticut assured his colleagues.[21] As the historian Michael Wallace has put it, "the rule of the statesmen had begun again."[22]

Though some Compensation Act advocates argued that higher pay would allow politicians of more modest means to serve, the bill is best seen as an effort to gentrify Congress, not democratize it. John C. Calhoun made this clear in mounting an elaborate defense of the pay raise. The "best materials for politics," Calhoun argued, meaning young men of property who had obtained liberal educations and pursued learned professions, were avoiding Congress in favor of the executive branch, state government, or private life. An increased income would improve the social "tone of parties" in both Congress and the country at large. "Make a seat in Congress what it ought to be, the first post in the community," Calhoun predicted, "and men of the greatest distinction . . . will seek it."[23]

Significantly, one of the few senators to speak up against the original bill was the only Republican printer in Congress at that point, James J. Wilson of New Jersey, who needed the money as much as anyone in Washington. Wilson noted the terrible political timing of the pay raise, "just at the close of a very expensive war, when many of the internal taxes and high impost duties are yet continued." All outstanding claims from the war ought to be paid, and the war taxes repealed, before Congress even considered rewarding itself. The editor-senator asked his colleagues to consider the matter from the viewpoint of politicians and ordinary citizens outside of Washington. In his own state, Wilson explained, no official except the governor made any amount close to the proposed new salary.

The next Republican editor to arrive in the Senate after Wilson, William Hendricks from the new state of Indiana, was more explicit on this point when the pay raise issue was reopened in December 1816. Living in an area that was only tenuously connected to the national market, where the "sources of wealth, means of procuring money, were few and narrow," and families sustained themselves by in-kind exchanges and subsistence farming, the citizens of Indiana held "ideas of expenditure . . . very unlike those of all the Eastern cities. Six dollars per day sounded large enough to them." Indeed, the new $1,500 salary was more money than a frontier family would see over a period of years, and many times the income of a typical urban artisan. Wilson and Hendricks were making elementary points of democratic politics—gauging how the voters would perceive the government's actions—but the statesmen in Congress apparently needed newspaper politicians to explain them.[24]

In retrospect, the sequel to Compensation Act seems unsurprising: a crushing popular backlash that both Republican and Federalist editors helped to generate and direct. Republican editors who had worked to maintain party regularity over the years, and other Republicans unhappy with the new direction of their national leaders, took full advantage of the weapon they had been handed, as did diehard Federalists eager to discredit the Republican Congress. Political editors everywhere denounced the act or avoided defending it if a local political ally happened to have supported the pay raise. Denunciation quickly escalated into concrete action. Protest meetings were held all over the country and heavily publicized in the newspapers. Several state legislatures passed resolutions instructing their representatives to reverse the pay raise.

Having failed to stop the bill in Congress, Sen. James J. Wilson planned to hold several apostate Republicans accountable in the fall election. Dr. Lewis Condict would be dropped from the congressional ticket outright for voting for the bill, Wilson decided, and others would be disciplined: "Some are even for dismissing the entire delegation on the grounds that the receiver [of the pay raise] is as bad as the *thief.*"

The protests against the pay raise achieved stunning results. Even in the remotest frontier settlements, it was reported, "There was scarcely a man . . . who had not heard [of] and reprobated the law." The displeasure translated directly into votes. More than two-thirds of the Congress that passed the Compensation Act was not reelected in 1816, including more than four-fifths of the members who had voted for it. Many of the remaining one-fifth had to work hard to survive, and sometimes abase themselves before the voters. The bill's sponsor, Rep. Richard Mentor Johnson of Kentucky, went out stumping in its defense. To the amusement of Amos Kendall, recently ensconced by Johnson as the local newspaper editor (but nevertheless a measured opponent of the Compensation Act), the congressman found his constituents' opposition so intense that "after a passionate speech in favor of the measure," he would often "conclude by promising to vote for its repeal, because such was the will of the people."[25]

Forced to redeem themselves and reverse the pay raise at the next session, many supporters blamed the professional jealousy and sordid ambition of editors trying to hold onto the undeserved power they had gained. "Party printers, who are fond of exercising all the influence that they possess," complained Wilson's home state rival Henry Southard, "seized the compensation bill as a measure that would produce murmuring and discontent, and attempted to wield it to their advantage." Robert Wright of Maryland growled that "party printers"—the artisanal designation was used purposefully—"from one end of the United States to the other, have been engaged in fanning the unhallowed flame, to destroy the fair fame of patriots."[26]

The voters' outrage at the Compensation Act and Congress's rush to placate them inspired misgivings that went even deeper than the role of newspaper editors in politics. When the bill was first considered and especially during the long, bitter debates over its repeal, many pay raise supporters made no secret of their contempt for a politics that forced leaders to regulate themselves according to the values of ordinary voters. When it was suggested that members consult their constituents before proceeding with the pay raise, Virginia's John Randolph snorted, "Consult them for what?" John C. Calhoun and several other speakers in the repeal debates cited Edmund Burke and attacked the whole notion that Congress should consider itself bound by voter preferences. "Have the people of this country snatched the power of deliberation from this body?" Calhoun cried, frustrated over the repudiation of a Congress he had led through bold new departures in national policy.[27]

It was a sign of the success of Mathew Carey's crusade against party that this mighty upheaval against Congress in 1816 had little impact on other elections or on the neo-Federalist direction of the governing Republican elite. The *Olive Branch,* the Hartford Convention, and the Fourteenth Congress had ushered in an era of nonpartisan national politics in which major elections and policy decisions became nearly disjoined from popular majorities.

This became glaringly obvious in the 1816 presidential race. While congressional incumbents were being swept away by an anti-incumbent tidal wave, Secretary of State and presidential heir apparent James Monroe faced his only serious opposition from another member of Madison's cabinet, Treasury Secretary William Crawford. William Duane and other editors had savaged the practice of nominating the Republican presidential candidate by a congressional caucus when it was employed in 1808, but they could not yet stop it. The oligarchic, backroom character of the caucus was heightened in 1816 when Crawford privately stepped aside, intending to remain in the cabinet as Monroe's understudy. The succession thus arranged, the general election went nearly uncontested, Monroe carrying all but the diehard Federalist states of Massachusetts, Connecticut, and Delaware. For the first time since 1792, Monroe's modern biographer writes, "the Presidency seemed to be offered as a reward for meritorious service or as an honor bestowed on a respected public servant, rather than as a prize to be carried by the strongest party in a bitterly fought contest."[28]

True to the circumstances of his election and his own increasingly nostalgic outlook, Monroe made "a union of parties in support of our republican govt" one of the major goals of his new administration. He picked John Quincy Adams, a supporter of the war who remained a Federalist in most of his personal and political values, as secretary of state, and began his term with a symbolic journey to Boston, the headquarters of the once-disloyal opposition. Most of the nation's political elite responded in kind, with Republicans and Federalists alike feting Monroe as he passed along his route. The arch-Federalist Boston *Columbian Centinel,* a paper that had recently preached secession and a separate peace with Great Britain, observed that the president's visit had brought about an "Era of Good Feelings," in which "many persons have met . . . whom party politics had long severed." Old Federalists began applying for jobs in the new administration.[29]

While largely successful in eliminating organized national party competition, Monroe's efforts produced no "era" of political harmony. Within the cabinet, a bruising backstage battle to succeed the president began almost immediately. Speaker of the House Henry Clay, miffed at his exclusion from the cabinet and thus the succession sweepstakes, used his power to thwart and embarrass the administration whenever possible. Congress was thus convulsed with a rancorous, Clay-fueled controversy over Gen. Andrew Jackson's invasion of Spanish Florida, followed quickly by a crisis over slavery in the proposed state of Missouri. The latter situation was partly generated by the inability of now-weak party loyalties to keep sectional antipathies in check. Politics continued to roil feverishly in most of the states as well, in conflicts that often pitted former Republican allies against each other. The local discontent became immeasurably more intense beginning in 1819, when the mismanagement of the new Second Bank of the United States helped trigger an economic collapse that was particularly devastating in the West and South. For many Americans, this seemed to discredit the neo-Hamiltonian economic policies of the postwar era.[30]

How did Republican newspaper editors respond to all this? Though most editors supported one national leader or another, the blurring of party lines and the flight from political competition and direct accountability to the voters profoundly disturbed many of them. More than any other political actors, newspaper editors were emotionally and financially invested in a continuing party conflict. Editors were usually the most partisan and ideological members of their particular party, group, or faction, or at least they conducted themselves as such. Partly this was driven by their political professionalism. It was their job to define party orthodoxy and generate partisan fervor among activists and voters. Declining partisanship meant less demand for these services and thus declining incomes for editors. Who would subscribe to a partisan journal without a party conflict? Why would high officials steer printing contracts or supply information to allied printers if no partisan opposition threatened them?

There was, moreover, something inherently radicalizing in the process of political editing. Officeholders could make compromises and still have a legislative or diplomatic accomplishment to boast of, but an editor could make his name and expand his influence only by establishing a bright, consistent party line and defending it eloquently or scabrously enough to deter other politicians from crossing.[31]

Of course, most editors hardly needed financial or professional incentives to become party ideologues. Few nonideologues could long stomach a party editor's work: the constant, unrelenting production of strident and repetitious partisan rhetoric. After staking themselves to such rhetoric, editors had far more prestige to lose than other politicians did when old positions were reversed or old enemies embraced. Their contradictions were available in print to anyone who had kept back files of their paper, as many politicians, printers, and citizens did in this period.

A detailed definition of exactly what beliefs Republican editors defended lies outside the scope of this work. The ideology varied by locality and faction in any case, but for the typical Republican editor the foundation of it was democracy. This was not necessarily the spontaneous, all-inclusive "participatory" democracy favored by twentieth-century radicals and scholars, but a less utopian nineteenth-century variety—radical enough for its time—demanding that citizenship, political participation, and offices be open to all white men and that government abide by the wishes and values of this mass electorate as expressed through the political process.

In the face of the postwar campaign against party, many editors came to realize how integral party politics was to their vision of democracy, because it provided a mechanism that allowed democracy to work, bringing popular majorities and "public opinion" to bear on the selection of government officials and the evaluation of their performance in office. As we have seen, this mechanism also created a large role for editors themselves, especially in generating that public opinion or in creating impressions among other politicians about what their publics were thinking. This self-serving feature of party politics only added to editors' sense of the democratic benefits of party, because while they formed one elite of party activists, they were by and large far from the only elite in social origins, manners, or educational credentials.

The upshot of all this was that many Republican newspaper editors resisted the upper-echelon drive to end party politics. Monroe's tour was widely and favorably reported, but the Federalists' obsequious reaction to it raised hackles and criticism. Many Republican papers marveled at the "grossest flattery" being directed at Monroe from men who had previously derided him as a traitor and coward. A *Richmond Enquirer* writer detected the Federalists' old monarchical tendencies in the adulation they showed to Monroe—they insisted on treating the president like a king even when pretending to embrace republicanism—and expressed some disgust with the president himself for allowing such unrepublican tributes: "It is much to be regretted that a trip of this kind ever entered his head." More often it was argued that the only sincere motive behind the Federalists' sudden sycophancy was a desire to regain high office by stealth. When the president's annual message brought another show of "good feelings" in December 1817, the Hartford *Times* announced that "the policy of the Federalists is now no secret. Despairing of success . . . they have resolved to sell themselves for what they can get."[32]

Beyond new attacks on Federalism, Monroe's antiparty campaign inspired editors to reflect more deeply on the political changes that were occurring. Many concluded parties would always be with the United States, whether the president wanted them or not. "Republics will be divided into opposite parties," wrote Thomas Ritchie of the *Richmond Enquirer.* "When men can think with freedom and act with decision, they will split according to their views of national interests." Of course, it had long been common to write of the inevitability of parties, as Madison had in the tenth *Federalist* essay, but they had usually been portrayed as one of the ineffable forces that undermined fragile republics and needed to be guarded against. Responding to the "Era of Good Feelings," editors began to treat party competition as a natural and appropriate outgrowth of a free government and a relatively open, fluid, and diverse society. More than one Republican editor compared the end of party competition to the Christian millennium, a visionary hope that all revered in principle but the actual occurrence of which few expected or really wanted any time soon.

Using this metaphor, editors in both Delaware and Connecticut took the Jeffersonian justification for party organization—a distasteful expedient to be used only in emergencies—to its vanishing point: "The extinction of party spirit is *desirable;* and so is the Millennium; but we cannot expect one more than the other until a regeneration of the human mind has been wrought. From the very nature of our government, and the ambitious and enterprising character of our people, party must exist."[33]

In New England, the Republican newspapers welcomed Monroe's visit

to their dishonored region as cordially as the Federalists, but some carefully demurred as to the visit's political meaning. The Federalists styled the
new political developments, "'You come over . . . to our measures—we go
over to your men,'" but the Boston *Chronicle & Patriot* (successor to the
old *Independent Chronicle*) disputed this analysis. While the paper applauded the restoration of social contact between Federalists and Republicans, it denied that a "Union of Parties" was taking place, and also questioned the goal. Republicans should "never consent to purchase their
adhesion by even the appearance of apostasy from republican principles."
The paper defined these principles simply but convincingly, though in
terms that applied better to Republican editors than to their members of
Congress: "The difference between the parties was originally and always
has been . . . that the republicans were for a purely popular government,"
while the Federalists "in their hearts still consider the British the best
model existing, and ours as at best a dangerous experiment." They would
never give up "their doubts about the practicality of our purely democratic
system."[34]

Exiled New England editor Selleck Osborn took a similar approach.
Taking over the primary Republican paper in Delaware, the Wilmington
American Watchman, he maintained a steady fire on the idea that the two
parties could ever establish a meaningful relationship without betraying
themselves. One of his cleverer pieces was a mock marriage notice:

THE BANNS FORBIDDEN.

"Marriage is intended between **American Democracy** and **New England
Federalism.**—Whoever may know of any impediment . . . why these parties
should not be joined in wedlock, let them now speak or forever hold their
peace!"

—WE FORBID THE BANNS—

"You do? Then please to shew cause."
Then, and please your reverence, the cause is . . . no less than absolute and ir-
removable **incompatibility** . . . . If you would have the parties peaceable, do
not bring them *too near* together. Your reverence undoubtedly knows some of
some, who get along very well as friends and neighbors; but marry them, and
they would soon quarrel.[35]

Osborn's notice implied a direction that many editors were taking, toward
a sense of the utility and even positive benefits of a stable system of party
competition. Osborn and others were doing this independently and a few

years in advance of the more famous pro-party arguments made by Martin Van Buren's New York "Bucktail" faction.[36] Other essays in the *American Watchman* made the argument explicitly. "So far from finding this party conflict a curse to our country," Osborn wrote, "we have seen that much light and much benefit has been elicited by its operation." While modern readers may smile at the idea of gaining enlightenment from political campaigns, editors like Osborn, who truly believed that the Republican party and its newspapers had rescued liberty from British and Federalist tyrants, could also believe that party competition, as conducted in their pages, provided a crucial form of political education to the reading and voting public. "A spirit of honorable contention calls forth the talents of the community," wrote a *Watchman* contributor, "and expands the mass of national intellect by a general diffusion of knowledge." The dangers of party, on the other hand, had been vastly overrated. The ancient republics that party strife destroyed were corrupt or poorly constructed: "None but a rotten constitution need shrink from the light."

Far from threatening the American republic, party competition strengthened it almost like physical exertion strengthened the body. Quoting an Irish orator's famous remark that "the condition on which God has given Liberty to man, is that of eternal vigilance," Osborn suggested that parties helped protect liberty by fixing attention on the government's actions and sparking constant political discussions. A lack of party competition allowed politicians and voters alike to grow flabby, in terms of both their political values and their level of political engagement. This was bad for the republic, but the more immediate danger was that "political supineness" on the part of the Republicans would allow the Federalists to carry out their schemes undetected.[37]

In Osborn's estimation, the "Era of Good Feelings" had accomplished one valuable task: it smoothed the rough edges of party conflict by restoring some personal contact and civility between longtime opponents. "The *personal* spirit of party—all pistolling, cudgelling, nose-pulling, abusive, slanderous party spirit, (such as that of '98) is already pretty much at an end," and good riddance to such extremities of party spirit, which militated "against good neighborhood." These forms of party competition had always fallen hardest on editors anyway. Monroe's temporary cease-fire would strengthen parties in the long run, Osborn argued, by making them more stable and less disruptive to society and the nation. The decline of personal violence and disputation would allow party battles to focus on the substantive differences of policy and philosophy that were the only legitimate basis for party distinctions. Controversies could now be "conducted in an open manner and upon general principles." On that basis, parties might become bulwarks rather than threats to the national feeling that had been so lacking in the late war.

The president's tour had shown "political antagonists the practicability of acting and feeling together" when patriotism required it, Osborn argued. This experience might prevent future opposition parties from venturing as close to treason as the wartime Federalists had. Monroe had inadvertently laid the groundwork for the emergence of a truly loyal opposition party, one that opposed the current national leaders but supported the legitimacy of the government and agreed on the fundamental rules of the political game. If parties thus learned to behave themselves, the substantive basis of the antiparty argument would be destroyed.[38]

However, the most widespread and effective form of editorial resistance to "good feelings" was not the intellectual defense of party, but the more practical method of simply continuing to engage in party battles when others tried to sidestep them. Editors picked partisan fights, maintained old party labels or invented new ones, and fought for reforms that helped build a stronger institutional basis for democratic politics.

One of the better and earlier examples of editors' directly confronting the new nonpartisanship occurred in Kentucky, where the principals were the young printer and Kentucky native John Norvell, just returned from a tour with Baltimore's ultrapartisan Republican press, and Amos Kendall, who would eventually become the most infamous member of Andrew Jackson's "Kitchen Cabinet." Kendall can also serve as an exemplar of a type of newspaper politician that became increasingly common after 1815. Neither a printer nor a blue-blooded attorney or man of letters, this new-model editor was a low-grade (or self-styled) lawyer of relatively undistinguished social origins, the type of person who might easily have taken up printing in earlier times. The son of a poor but respected Massachusetts farmer, Kendall had managed to get a college education by schoolteaching his way through Dartmouth College, then a second-rate institution whose constituency was country boys socially and financially unqualified for Harvard. He obtained his legal training by reading for a year in the office of a hometown Republican politician.

With no prospects in the Massachusetts bar, Kendall went west, armed with what he thought was an offer to tutor a Kentucky senator's children.

Unfortunately, he arrived in Lexington to discover that the senator's offer had not been serious and found himself stuck in a highly uncongenial location. Henry Clay's wife hired the young New Englander as a tutor, but other doors failed to open. The legal profession and female society alike seemed wired shut against a shy, homely, impoverished, unconnected Yankee. Kendall imagined himself orating on the floor of Congress, but in a region where military laurels and physical prowess were deeply revered, his diminutive stature and tendency to get faint and sweaty at the thought of bloodshed left little hope that he would ever be popular. "Drink whiskey and talk loud . . . and you will hardly fail of being called a clever fellow," Kendall wrote contemptuously of his new home, knowing that he would never be convincing in the role of swaggering southern blade.[39]

About the only aspect of Kendall that did impress the Kentuckians was his writing ability. Beginning with poetry written to impress the ladies and prove his own gentility at evening parties, Kendall soon found himself writing speeches for local politicians and, taking the only employment opportunity (besides teaching) that anyone would offer, the editing of a newspaper. Editing also turned out to be his only realistic avenue into politics. In 1815 he bought the local paper in Georgetown, Kentucky, and the postmastership that went with it. The patron of Kendall's first venture was the local war hero and congressman Richard M. Johnson, who also happened to be the principal sponsor of the Compensation Act. Contrary to the editor's expectations, Johnson considered the paper his personal organ, existing to defend him and rhetorically slaughter his enemies no matter what. Kendall managed to save Johnson's seat in the 1816 elections without too much cost to his own integrity, but he was glad later that year when Bank of Kentucky president William Gerard offered to sell him, with financing, the Frankfort *Argus of Western America,* an established journal with a statewide circulation.[40]

Taking over in Frankfort, Kendall immediately declared war on good, antipartisan feelings. Finding "little party spirit in the State," he launched an attack on a rival paper "as well for amusement as in support of the Republican party." The most effective and professional editors had to enjoy their work, and Kendall's frustrations with his place in Kentucky society made him eager to shake it up. John Norvell, who took over the Lexington *Kentucky Gazette* shortly after Kendall's move to Frankfort, probably felt similar frustrations, being an opponent of slavery who had already fled Kentucky for lack of opportunity once before.[41]

Their chance came in the "New Election" controversy arising from the death of recently elected Gov. George Madison. Like many state-level furors of this period, the battle lines over this issue largely replaced older divisions derived from national politics. Lt. Gov. Gabriel Slaughter had filled Madison's place and then shocked many Kentucky Republicans by appointing John Pope, formerly a leading Federalist but now a professed "no party" man, as secretary of state. Slaughter's appointment of Pope gave "good feelings" a palpable form that even President Monroe (who mostly avoided appointing Federalists despite his nonpartisan rhetoric) had not yet attempted. This was highly threatening to people who depended on partisanship for their livelihood and importance, and the threat became clearer when the Slaughter-Pope forces began to justify their actions in Monrovian terms.

Kendall, Norvell, and their papers quickly joined a group of ambitious young politicians in campaigning for a new gubernatorial election. The editors led the "New Election" forces to a substantial victory in the election of 1818, and they would probably have unseated Slaughter and Pope if the Panic of 1819 had not devastated the state and created new political issues a few months later. According to one historian, it was during this controversy that political newspapers first emerged as a decisive force in Kentucky politics.[42]

The victory was accomplished by turning the election into a kind of referendum on party politics. Norvell and Kendall were generally supportive of Monroe and eager participants in the new Republican enthusiasm for banking, manufacturing, and other forms of economic development. Yet they could never accept political fellowship with those who had once undermined the late war effort or had cast aspersions on democracy. The *Kentucky Gazette* denounced the "'No Party Governor'" and condemned "the infatuation of many republicans" with "party amalgamation" on both ideological and practical grounds. "The truth is, that never did a more gross delusion seize the minds of rational men," then the currently fashionable notion "that a cordial union could be effected between two parties so hostile in their feelings, so opposite in their principles."

The delusion had tactical disadvantages in addition to its ideological impossibility. "The experiment has tended to depress the republicans and give advantage to the federalists," Norvell wrote. Worse yet, dispensing so quickly and lightly with party distinctions impugned the seriousness of the old conflict: "It has induced weak republicans to . . . propagate the fallacious notion, that the federalists as a party were a patriotic set of men; that between the two parties only a slight shade of difference existed." The editor hoped that the Republicans would desist from such efforts at "an unholy alliance" in the future and not be fooled when abhorrent principles and politicians came "disguised under the cloak of canting hypocrisy and smiling moderation."[43]

At the same time, the *Kentucky Gazette* went further than condemning amalgamation, and worked to convince voters that party could be a positive political good, based on what political scientists would later come to call the theory of "responsible" party government. Party politicians pledged themselves to a particular set of principles, which they could then be held accountable to once they took office. George Madison and his predecessor governors had been elected as Republicans and "were as much bound by their plighted faith to the republican party, by every principle of probity and honor, to consider themselves, and to act, as *party* men, after they were elected to that chair, as while they were candidates for that chair." Those who abjured party sought office merely for themselves, or to insulate themselves from the popular will, by making no commitments about their future course of action. Norvell argued strongly for a party-based political system in which editors like himself would be powerful figures. Elected representatives should subordinate themselves to party dictates, which were derived from public opinion and would inevitably be expressed "through the chastening and correcting animadversion of a free press."[44]

Few issues of Amos Kendall's *Argus of Western America* remain extant for 1817 and 1818, limiting how much we can know about the specific terms of its case against "acting" Governor Slaughter and party amalgamation. Kendall definitely did show himself to be a strong party man, who would not be turned aside by the personal politics that many Kentucky gentlemen employed. Suddenly befriended by John Pope and other Federalists at the beginning of the controversy, Kendall found it amusing "to see men who ought to know better, expect that we would yield our political principles" so easily to personal blandishments. "Those men found their civilities useless, and entirely discontinued them."

Instead of laying down with Federalists, Kendall mounted a systematic campaign for the new election and then following his articles up with a pamphlet called "Free Suffrage," 5,000 copies of which were printed and distributed throughout the state. At some point, however, the *Argus* softened its position enough to be criticized by the *Kentucky Gazette* and other journals, and later Kendall expressed the opinion "that the lines of demarkation between the two great political parties which formerly divided this country are obliterated and gone." Yet he fully expected a new and similar party conflict to arise again, and soon. The evil, antidemocratic principles underpinning Federalism lurked "in the bosom of society," in the form of inequalities of wealth, status, and power, and would creep back out in some other form. Indeed, he could already "perceive too much of them in the councils of the nation."[45]

If Kendall was less doctrinaire about the Republican party than were the *Kentucky Gazette*'s editors, he fully concurred with them in valuing partisan politics. To him, party competition served as a healthy alternative to the violence and coercion he saw dominating the politics of other nations. Despite the bitterness of the "New Election" controversy, the manner in which the battle was conducted demonstrated to Kendall "more forcibly than language can do the excellence of our system of government." In other countries, basic questions such as "who is entitled to the chief magistracy" had to be "referred to the God of battles": whoever could command the greater financial resources "or direct the greatest number of bayonets" would take the prize, and might would make right. In America, by contrast, the "pen and tongue" were the "only weapons" with which such battles were fought, and they were both far less destructive and far more democratic than other political weapons, being intended to persuade an electorate that would make the final decision.[46]

The basic divisions created in the "New Election" fracas carried over into what became one of the Jacksonian era's defining political conflicts, over banking and debtor relief before, during, and after the Panic of 1819. A long, credit-financed land boom collapsed and a wide cross-section of Kentucky's population found themselves with massive debts they had no prospects of paying. Amos Kendall and other former New Electionists became the leaders of the pro-relief forces, representing the state's farmers, recent migrants, and middle-class urbanites against the entrenched planter wealth of the Bluegrass region around Lexington. Kendall's chief henchman was another nonpracticing lawyer named Francis Preston Blair, who often wrote for Kendall's *Argus* in the spare time left over from his job as clerk of courts for Franklin County, where the state capital was located. Their efforts culminated in the creation of the Bank of the Commonwealth of Kentucky, an institution without specie reserves whose sole purpose was to issue paper money loans that would allow small debtors to meet their obligations and keep their property. Creditors who refused to accept these notes at face value lost the right to use the courts to collect their debts.

The controversy entered its bitterest and most political phase when the state and federal courts invalidated much of the debtor relief program. Kendall, Blair, and the *Argus* created a new state party organization and elected a pro-relief governor and legislature in 1824 with 63 percent of the vote. Lacking the two-thirds majority necessary to remove the offending state court judges, the new legislature simply repealed all the statutes that had established the state court of appeals and then created a new court. The old court of appeals refused to disband and promptly declared the new one unconstitutional. The "New Court" and "Old Court" parties battled it out through the middle of the 1820s, spurring ever more furious campaigning and the first evenly matched, organized party conflict in Kentucky history.[47]

Good feelings broke down most colorfully in Kentucky, but similar situations appeared in numerous other localities, with editors usually leading the charge back toward partisanship and often using the economic depression as fuel. In Philadelphia, William Duane's Old School Democrats, allied with a small network of editors in the Pennsylvania interior, rebelled over state promotion of banks, the oligarchic caucus system of nominations, and the rampant cronyism of "Family" party rule. They even succeeded in deposing the "Family" for a time in 1820.[48]

Turmoil over similar issues in Ohio led to the rise of several major newspaper politicians, including Moses Dawson, a kind of frontier version of William Duane and John Binns. A draper and active United Irishman from Belfast, Dawson had been jailed (and nearly hung) by the British; his life was probably saved by the fact that he was already in custody when the Irish rebellion of 1798 broke out. Returning to his trade for a time, then reinventing himself as a promoter of Lancastrian schools, Dawson turned back to politics in the 1810s, pamphleteering and speaking for parliamentary reform in Scotland. Arrest warrants were issued in 1817, and Dawson was finally forced to join the ranks of radical exiles to America, two decades late. After a brief stay in Philadelphia, he was hired to run a Lancastrian school in the boom city of Cincinnati, where he soon after started a new school of his own. Unfortunately, the Panic of 1819 wiped out Dawson's school along with the rest of the Cincinnati economy, and in 1821 he found work doing what radical exiles seemed to do best, writing for a political newspaper, the *Inquisitor and Cincinnati Advertiser.*

An experienced political writer in a region where such were in short supply, Dawson set out to upset political calculations in Washington by promoting presidential candidates who seemed to him more popular with the people and less associated with the new political directions in Washington. While his first choice, native son William Henry Harrison, did not pan out, Dawson's luck was better when he became one of the first editors in the Old Northwest to champion the dark-horse candidacy of a general named Jackson.[49]

In Missouri, a young lawyer named Thomas Hart Benton used the *St. Louis Enquirer* to transform himself into the territory's political colossus in the space of two years. Of North Carolina planter stock, the once-promising Benton had become severely damaged goods at home after cheating in college at Chapel Hill. Redeemed after a move to Tennessee, Benton's budding career was again cut short (nearly along with his life) by a falling out with that state's most powerful and dangerous man, Andrew Jackson. Landing on his second frontier at St. Louis, Benton gained entree into the local elite there, too, but could not even get elected to the town council until after he took up the editorial pen. In 1818 he and a partner bought a local newspaper called the *Western Emigrant,* changed its name, and immediately began to crusade on a number of issues: for expansion into the Spanish Southwest and Pacific Northwest, for better transportation to the West, against unsound western banking practices and paper money, for Missouri statehood, and against northeastern efforts to exclude slavery from the new state. Benton and his newspaper's leadership in the drive for statehood without restrictions on slavery earned him not only the town council seat he had once been denied, but also one of the new state's first two Senate seats. Benton would define party politics in Missouri for the next three decades and become one of the new Democratic party's preeminent national leaders.[50]

The most famous local conflict of all occurred in New York, between Martin Van Buren's Bucktails and the followers of De Witt Clinton, spanning issues such as the Erie Canal, Clinton's flirtations with Federalist support, and the rewriting of the state constitution. Van Buren and his allies also made the most extended and best-remembered case for the positive benefits of party politics. Under their other sobriquet, the "Albany Regency," they became renowned as the most highly effective, professional, and unapologetic party organization in the country. While not as clear-ly editor-led as other state parties, the Bucktails were assiduous practi-tioners of newspaper politics and included several newspaper editors among their brain trust, notably the printers Azariah C. Flagg, of the *Plattsburgh Republican,* and Edwin Croswell, nephew of Harry and editor of Van Buren's state capital organ, the *Albany Argus.*[51]

JOHN MILTON NILES AND THE

DEMOCRATIZATION OF CONNECTICUT

Possibly the most transformative example of editorial party building occurred in Connecticut, the state most resistant to both newspaper poli-tics and Jeffersonian Republicanism. The political situation in the "Land of Steady Habits" had changed little since the days of Charles Holt. Even the Hartford Convention had failed to dislodge the "Standing Order," the state's oligarchy of Federalist officeholders and tax-supported Congrega-tional clergymen. Many of the old Republican activists had given up, left the state, or died, having never come close to winning a statewide election or even a congressional seat. One-time party firebrand Abraham Bishop and several others whom Jefferson had appointed to federal offices were growing rich and, after 1806 or so, somewhat less inclined to their old lev-els of exertion and radicalism. Since the appointees were all Yale men and lawyers like their Federalist opponents, their disbarment from the Stand-ing Order was relatively easy to reverse.[52]

In the newspaper realm, matters in Connecticut were even worse by the early 1810s. After Selleck Osborn's *Witness* and several other papers from the later Jefferson administration were stamped out, there were seemingly no printers brave enough to try again. Out-of-state Republi-cans wondered why nothing was being done. By the outbreak of the war, the state's first Republican paper, the Hartford *American Mercury,* was the only one left publishing, and it was increasingly inadequate. The *Mercury's* aging printer, Elisha Babcock, and his son had become more reluctant to publish "high-seasoned" political fare and were beginning to earn some critical comment even from longtime contributors. After 1811 the Federal-ist *Connecticut Courant* rarely even bothered to attack its rival anymore.[53] The "long-felt want" for more Republican journalism was partly met in 1812, when the printer Joseph Barber founded the *Columbian Register* in New Haven.[54]

The postwar ideological détente had a strange and ironic impact on

Connecticut. Bishop and many of the other Republicans changed their minds on some issues, most notably the Bank of the United States. They also learned to behave, write, and speak somewhat more respectably and conventionally, especially in the area of religion. Once they had been prone to using words like conspiracy, delusion, and popery to describe the Standing Order and its methods, but by the late 1810s, even Bishop had learned to rein in his "profane raillery" and "wicked eloquence." At the same time, a key group of Federalists, the Episcopalians, began to disengage from the Standing Order. Though wealthy, well connected, and more favorably treated than other dissenters, after 1800 the Episcopalians began to chafe under the realization that the ruling Congregationalists would never allow them a significant share of power under the Standing Order. The legislature repeatedly refused to charter an Episcopal college and then swindled the Bishop's Fund out of $20,000 it was supposed to receive from a bonus paid the state for chartering an Episcopalian-controlled bank.[55]

By early 1816 the Episcopalians were ready for an open break. New Haven had a particularly large and powerful contingent (with the former Federalist editor Harry Croswell as their rector!), and Abraham Bishop extracted a promise that they would "walk no more with their Congregational brethren." In February, a joint meeting of Republicans and Federalist Episcopalians engaged in the ultimate act of "good feelings," nominating Oliver Wolcott Jr. for governor with an Episcopalian Federalist running mate.

The son and grandson of former Connecticut governors, Wolcott had been Alexander Hamilton's assistant and successor at the Treasury Department, but he had conveniently lived out of state during the war years and become somewhat estranged from the Standing Order. The Wolcott-headed slate was labeled the "American Toleration and Reform Ticket," and the coalition behind it was generally known as the Toleration Party. Most of its campaigners were Republicans, but they now submerged their identity and fought to put renegade Federalists in office. "We take *toleration* ground only, carefully avoiding the old ground," announced Bishop, temporarily reenergized and writing much of the *Columbian Register's* material. Large numbers of Republicans, both old and young, were similarly galvanized by the sudden possibility that they might actually win an election. Thus the abandonment of party in Connecticut led to the most vigorously contested campaign in years.[56]

Reform of the state's religious establishment was the main theme of the campaign, with heavy emphasis on its discrimination against Episcopalians and smaller doses of the anticlericalism that the Republicans had hurled forth in earlier years. At the same time, the Republican Tolerationists renewed their drive, begun in 1804, for a written constitution to replace the state's 1662 colonial charter. Besides separation of church and state, they wanted a constitution that would implement reforms in the suffrage, the basis of representation, and the state's highly regressive revenue system, which taxed farmland, livestock, and people at many times the rate of bank stock, capital, and silver plate. The Tolerationists lost the election by a little over 1,000 votes, but they won more legislative seats than the Republicans ever had. In the fall 1816 legislative elections (Connecticut had them twice a year), they did a bit better but still fell short of a majority.[57]

Clearly, the Toleration movement had the Standing Order on the run, but apparently there was still an element missing. It was supplied on the first day of 1817, when the printer F. D. Bolles and the young Republican lawyer John Milton Niles launched the Hartford *Times,* a new newspaper expressly dedicated to "the diffusion of correct political information . . . the support of Republican principles . . . and . . . the encouragement of TOLERATION." Thus, the new party was embodied in the state capital for the first time.[58]

Newspaper politics in Connecticut achieved a new level of intensity and maturity with the rise of Niles and the *Times.* The editor began the spring 1817 campaign earlier than usual, in early February for an April election, and frankly devoted his whole paper to the effort. The "TOLERATION TICKET" of Oliver Wolcott and Jonathan Ingersoll was announced in a large box, spanning two columns at the top of one of the main editorial pages and often on the front. Over the next two months, the *Times* ran two long and unusually effective series, a broad and philosophical one entitled "The Age of Improvements" and a lighter, pseudo-travelogue purporting to be the reflections of a "Virginian in Connecticut." Closer to election time, pointed stand-alone essays and editorials were added to the mix.[59]

The major essays developed a campaign theme that Niles had already introduced in previous issues. The essential message was that the Standing Order's Connecticut, despite the sterling qualities of its people and the claims of its leaders to be "an extraordinary race of men" whose government "had produced the greatest portion of civil and social happiness that ever fell to the lot of people on earth," was an embarrassment to the republic. "Connecticut has always been an aristocracy," wrote "Laurens," and now it was time to catch up with the rest of the nation and begin to implement the enlightened principles of the Revolution. "Is not the general sense of mankind entitled to some respect? Is not the example of every other state worthy of imitation?" Niles even blamed the flood of emigrants then leaving Connecticut on the state's political backwardness.[60]

Niles and the *Times* presented a version of Tolerationism that was much more explicitly Republican and democratic than the coalition of elites that first nominated Oliver Wolcott. Abraham Bishop had advised abandoning the "old ground," but Niles took a different approach, linking "Republicanism and Toleration" in an effort to keep the old Republican party alive inside the Toleration shell. While the *American Mercury* and *Columbian Register* harped on narrower issues such as the Bishop's Fund, Niles laid out a broad agenda for democratizing the state.[61]

Niles's agenda of "radical reform" can be summarized as follows. It only began with an immediate end to the Congregational religious establishment, which Niles, as a practicing Universalist, had more than political reasons for opposing. The state also needed a written constitution and an end to the management of its affairs according to mere customs. The most obvious example was the tradition by which many officeholders stood for reelection twice a year but were in reality granted life tenure and immunity from opposition. The property requirement for voting, along with all other impediments to universal white male suffrage, had to be eliminated and all significant offices opened up to popular election, including presidential electors. What was more, steps needed to be taken to guarantee that voters could exercise their suffrage freely and equally. This meant not only the repeal of the hated "Stand-Up Law" but also the liberalization of the debt laws, to prevent Federalist creditors from attaching the property and causing the imprisonment of poor Republican debtors, alleged to be a common form of political intimidation in the state. The taxation system needed to be modernized and its favoritism for the rich ended.

For purposes of representation, the *Times* demanded that the state be districted for legislative and congressional elections in place of the existing system of town representation, which slighted the growing cities and had created something akin to rotten boroughs in some declining rural areas.

In addition to these legal reforms, the *Times* called for changes in the state's underlying political culture that would bring about some much-needed "rotation in office." Opposing an incumbent officer should be accepted as a legitimate practice, Niles argued, and voters should learn to occasionally heed opposition campaigners and elect a challenger. In their appointments, governors should sometimes reach outside the narrow stratum of Yale-educated Congregationalist lawyers who dominated the Standing Order.[62]

The reform agenda revealed the Republican base beneath the *Times*'s Toleration superstructure, and the paper carried plenty of other material displaying decidedly "bad," partisan feelings toward Federalists, with the single exception of Toleration gubernatorial candidate Oliver Wolcott. Niles frequently reminded voters of the Hartford Convention, and the "opprobrium which is already too deeply, and, we fear, incurably attached to this ill-fated city." Of course, Wolcott and the other Federalist renegades now disapproved of the convention, too, but not in the bitter terms used by Niles. The *Times* dilated on the indelible nature of the reputation for "treason," "disunion," and "criminality" that Federalist behavior during the war had fixed on the region. "Like an *acid*," their deeds had "*neutralized* those glorious traits in our character . . . acquired in the revolutionary war." While professing to regret the need to bring up the Hartford Convention, Niles added new details, such as depositions concerning a case in which Hartford officials had charged a federal military recruiter with creating a public nuisance (in the course of his duty) and then pressured a wavering jury into convicting him.[63]

On this and countless other issues, the *Times* showed little regard for the sensibilities of the Toleration party's ex-Federalist wing in expressing its radically democratic views. For instance, Niles dismissed the Standing Order's boasts of its support for education, especially in the form of Yale College, by attacking Yale's lavish state support as a prime example of the Connecticut elite's self-serving approach to government. Working through a long list of "What have our Rulers done for the State," a *Times* essay commented that the topic of Yale should be discussed under the heading "what our rulers have done for themselves," even though the paper was supporting a Yale man for governor.[64]

Niles also maintained the Republican journalistic tradition of following the travails of brother editors in his pages, presenting both himself and them as part of a national Republican community. For example, he noted

Selleck Osborn's move to the *American Watchman* and recalled his perse-cution in Connecticut. Perhaps his closest out-of-state ally was Isaac Hill of the *New Hampshire Patriot,* an editor doubtless little admired by gen-teel Federal or Episcopalian Tolerationists. The "able and indefatigable" Hill, who was the editorial leader of a similar toleration campaign in his own state, first showed up in the *Times* as the victim of a legislative con-tempt proceeding brought for allegedly misquoting a Federalist legislator's speech. He and Niles would report on, work with, and visit each other for years to come.[65]

Niles and the *Times* finessed the question of party in this first cam-paign. "No man more fully recognized the utility and necessity of party organization to accomplish and carry into effect important measures based on fundamental principles," one of Niles's close allies observed, but this position was somewhat problematic in 1817.[66] In keeping with the bi-partisan origins of the Toleration movement, the editor and his writers decried Federalist intolerance and "party spirit" and welcomed the cooper-ation of Wolcott and the Episcopalians. However, they carefully avoided attacks on party politics per se and evinced a firm commitment to party as they believed the Republicans practiced it. The first installment of the "Age of Improvements" condemned parties rooted in "causes . . . of a fixed and permanent nature, such˙ as WEALTH, or *sectarian religious systems.*" The Federalists were a party like this, secretive, exclusive, and class-based, and like all such parties, when they attained power, they became "a kind of *practical* ARISTOCRACY." Parties that cohered around a "particular policy of the government" and conducted themselves more openly and demo-cratically, as Niles believed the Republicans did, were entirely another matter.

When the desperate Federalists openly announced their gubernatorial nomination for the first time in March 1817, Niles sarcastically celebrated their sudden embrace of Republican methods. "Yes, fellow citizens, a *fed-eral* nomination has appeared for the first time in Connecticut!" the *Times* announced, noting that this was mentioned not "because *we* consider that it is improper, but only because *they* have always considered it so."[67]

By the issue before the April 7 election, the *Times* had dropped any pretense of reticence about practicing popular party politics. An illustrated "Toleration Ticket" took up a large chunk of the front page, and essays within addressed themselves to particular groups of voters, such as former Republicans, the militia, and young men. The youths of Connecticut were urged to set aside their elder's doubts about partisanship. They might not completely support every position or candidate of either party, but it showed an immature "levity of mind" to hesitate or waver in making one's choice.[68]

The barrages from the *Times* appear to have been effective. More votes were cast in April 1817 than in any previous Connecticut election, and the Tolerationists finally elected Oliver Wolcott and majority of the legislature. The nation's most entrenched political dynasty had toppled in the first election of the *Times*'s existence. Niles exulted that it was because of the Toleration campaign's "unusual strength and activity, that the election . . . resulted so differently from any former one that has ever taken place" in Connecticut. In later years, observers from both camps agreed, and named John Niles "more than any other single person, the instrument of overturning the Federal Party in the State."[69]

Niles's career involved as well as promoted democratization. He was not a printer, but he came from background equally common.[70] He was born in 1787 to a family that had been farming smaller and smaller plots of land around Windsor, Connecticut, for generations. Losing his father at a young age, Niles spent his childhood working with an older brother on the family's small farm, trying to wrest a living from the recalcitrant Connecticut soil that was driving thousands of their peers to decamp the state. Niles's only formal education was a winters-only common school, but like so many northern political professionals, he had Benjamin Franklin's bookish inclination and took his opportunities where he found them. Before he was very old, Niles had so far mastered the common school curriculum that he was teaching rather than merely attending it.[71]

Niles continued as a farmer-schoolteacher until he was twenty-one, when younger siblings were ready to take over supporting his mother. Ambitious, restless, and intellectually undernourished, but feeling himself too old and too poor for college, he embarked upon a "systematic and laborious" course of self-education. Niles threw himself into his studies with the earnest ferocity that marked all of his later activities, turning his mind into a "great storehouse of facts." According to Gideon Welles, a disciple of Niles who would succeed him as editor of the *Times*, this autodidacticism made Niles "always formidable," even to his better-educated opponents.

While building his mind into a mightier engine than any college of the day could have produced, Niles was also missing out on the training in public speaking, polite letters, and genteel manners that college men did acquire. These deficiencies would hamper and embarrass him in his later career. Cursed with a stumpy, awkward physique, Niles rarely made a good impression and was often "treated and regarded with some degree of contempt" by legal and political colleagues. He would always have to prove himself, by engineering electoral victories for allies, administering defeats to foes, and winning debates with knowledge and logic rather than personal presence or classical eloquence.[72]

The capstone of Niles's self-improvement campaign was acquiring a learned profession, and with his literary and political interests, the law was a natural choice. So Niles apprenticed himself to a charitable country lawyer who was also a minor Republican politician. Either the young man or his mentor must have believed in a more extensive and rigorous legal education than was typical of law office apprenticeships, because it was only after five long years of study and clerical work that Niles hung out his own shingle.[73]

In becoming a lawyer, Niles was taking part in a trend that would have a strong impact on the partisan press. Colonial lawyers had worked assiduously to increase the power, prestige, and exclusiveness of the legal profession, but after 1800 things began to move in the opposite direction. Apprenticeship requirements for admission to the bar were cut back, and bar associations aimed at raising standards and controlling access to the profession fell into decline. The end result was not so much the democratization of the profession as its stratification, a situation in which almost any young man could become a lawyer but only those with elite contacts or formal education could find clients enough to prosper. The number of lawyers exploded while their levels of wealth and attainment dropped, and the prestige of the profession as a whole suffered. The most lucrative business was engrossed by the elite bars of the major cities, which became even more exclusive and distinguished. The vast majority of lawyers, especially newly minted and upwardly mobile practitioners, found themselves underemployed and available for other pursuits, such as editing political newspapers.[74]

Thus struggling lawyers came to make up an increasingly large contingent of the editorial corps. Indeed, anecdotal evidence suggests that printer-editors were no longer the norm by the middle of the nineteenth century. But this was not necessarily a process of gentrifying the press or crowding the common man out of journalism. At least among the Democratic Republicans, the new editors tended to come from backgrounds very similar to the old partisan printers. By and large, they were still bright boys of modest means whose main goal was exchanging their parents' lives of manual labor (typically on a small farm) for more intellectual kinds of work.[75]

This was the path that John Niles took into journalism. Bogged down by his lack of education and connections, Niles's law practice languished. The Federalist *Connecticut Mirror* later charged, with great accuracy, that Niles had "long been dragging at the tail of the [legal] profession like a canister on the tail of a dog," failing to attain even "the celebrity of a common pettifogger."[76] With spare time in abundance, Niles filled his days by continuing his studies and, more significantly, turning his hand to political publishing. He began by submitting pro-Republican essays to the Hartford *American Mercury* during the War of 1812.[77]

"With a mind deeply imbued with democratic ideas and an ardent temperament," he soon threw himself wholly into opposing the local Federalists, whose disloyalty to the war government and the legacy of the Revolution filled him with chagrin for his state and region. As for many other Republican editors who came of age in this period, "Hartford Convention Federalist" would long be his ultimate term of opprobrium. With the war and his now-vocal Republicanism cutting off "all hope of present success" as a lawyer in Connecticut, Niles's poverty seemed to demand "that he attend to something else than political controversies for a livelihood." He considered fleeing the state, as many other Connecticut Republicans already had. Touring Vermont, New York, and Pennsylvania, Niles searched for a place where his prospects might be better. At Harrisburg, he met several young politicians serving their first terms in the state legislature. One of them may have had a particular influence on Niles's eventual career choice: William J. Duane, son and assistant of the *Aurora* editor.[78]

Upon his return from Pennsylvania, Niles decided to remain in Connecticut and take up political publishing on a full-time basis. In 1816, in conjunction with the first Toleration campaigns, he edited and saw to press the first American edition of John Trenchard and Thomas Gordon's *The Independent Whig,* a classic eighteenth-century British republican tract that took aim at England's established church. This was a subject of obvious contemporary relevance in Connecticut, and the edition was produced for political use, with an eye to "cheapness and convenience." In a long, impassioned preface to the work, Niles expressed a budding political professional's hope that the work would make money as well as promote the cause he supported: "It is hoped that it will meet with encouragement and *expected* that it will do good."[79] Soon after the *Independent Whig* was published, Niles started the *Times,* and three months later, he helped consign the Standing Order to the dustbin of Connecticut history.

Or so Niles hoped. "It is only the dawn of reformation," the editor had written when the first positive election results came in, but it soon became apparent that the new day would bring less than he had expected. Governor Wolcott showed little inclination to "rotate" many of the old Federalist officials, and the substantive reforms were slow in coming. The Stand-Up Law was repealed at the fall session of the legislature, and later some minor reforms in the tax code and debt laws were implemented, but that was all. It took a year after the first victory, and strong pressure from Niles and the younger Republican Tolerationists, to get a constitutional convention called, and the document that finally was written in August and September 1818 profoundly disappointed Niles. While ending the religious establishment and providing nearly universal white male suffrage, it retained representation by towns and made no provision for districting.

Worse than these failures for Niles was the step backward the convention took regarding the judiciary. Formerly, Connecticut judges had served one-year terms but had been perpetually reappointed by custom. The new constitution codified rather than eliminated this system by introducing an "independent judiciary" (that is, judges appointed for life) as it existed in other states. Niles himself was not elected to the convention, but his closest ideological soul mates who did participate voted against the final document, considering it "defective . . . unjust . . . as founded on no basis of republican equality, as avoiding . . . accountability and responsibility." Editorially, Niles gritted his teeth and used the *Times* to support ratification, any constitution being preferable to a royal charter, but he did so with little of his usual enthusiasm.[80]

Niles found the business side of newspaper politics just as unsatisfying as the results of his reform movement. In some financial respects, the *Times* was luckier than most Republican newspapers. The inclusion of Federalists and Episcopalians in the Toleration coalition and association with the ruling party gave Niles's paper a patina of respectability that enabled him to attract more advertisers than usual. The *Times* became a seemingly viable enterprise as Toleration victories mounted, with the number of ads jumping sharply after each election.[81]

However, Niles's collection problems early reached the typical, chronic level, and many of his supposed allies seemed little disposed to help. Given what the *Times* had meant to the party in power, it seemed to Niles that the paper was entitled to at least a share in the local, national, and state government printing contracts. This was especially true because the *Times* contained more political matter than many papers, an "additional expence . . . necessary only for the objects of the party." Yet nothing was done, and Niles lost money on the paper that he was not making in his law practice. There seemed to be little appreciation, or even understanding, among his Tolerationist colleagues of a party editor's needs and interests.[82]

Niles came to realize, with some bitterness, that while publishing might be the only way he could make a living out of politics, it was not going to be an easy or lucrative way; nor did it seem likely to bring the social respect he craved. Reporting on the suicide of an Ohio editor only eight months into his first year with the *Times,* Niles expressed "surprise that *all* editors . . . of newspapers do not *kill themselves.*" Though he ably performed the duties of a "Public Sensor"; that is, "to guard and correct the morals and manners of the people; and . . . the spirit of the civil and religious institutions of the republic," an editor's reward was often "injustice, ingratitude, embarrassment, poverty, distress and suicide."[83]

Niles did not meet such a fate, but only by refusing to settle into the role of contented auxiliary to the new regime. While remaining a nominal supporter of Governor Wolcott, Niles and his newspaper kept up the pressure for his program of democratic reforms and continued to express a much more frank and unapologetic Democratic Republicanism than the ruling party's officeholders. Niles emerged as the leader, and the *Times* as the organ, of what was variously thought of as a young or radical Republican faction, for the moment merely in tension with ex-Federal Tolerationists and older Republicans over the very moderate level of change embodied in the Constitution of 1818 and the policies of Wolcott.

The *Times* group held out for the districting and reapportionment plan that other Republicans had dropped and joined similar factions in other states (such as William Duane's Old School) in attacking caucus nominations and secretive party organizations. Niles also argued for what seemed to be the most neglected aspect of his reform program, "rotation in office." Connecticut's corps of officeholders had changed little, and in character not at all. It was still composed almost exclusively of Yale-educated lawyers.[84] While trying to avoid criticizing Wolcott, the *Times*'s demands for removals had escalated by 1819 to the point of suggesting, after another victory, that all offices be declared vacant and the whole state bureaucracy and judiciary filled anew.[85]

One source of Niles's ardor for rotation was undoubtedly the desire to hold a rotated office himself, but his demands should not be dismissed as mere jealousy. Governor Wolcott tried to buy the editor off in 1821 with a Hartford County judgeship, but he merely used the position to support his partisan politicking, combining his duties with writing for the *Times*.[86]

At stake in the rotation issue was one of the Standing Order's most offensive premises: that its oligarchic, autocratic rule was justified by the fact that only a certain narrow category of men had the necessary abilities and knowledge to make, execute, and interpret the laws. This conflicted not only with Niles's personal interests and feelings, but also with the thoroughgoing egalitarianism he seems to have carried from his hard-scrabble youth. This philosophy was also based partly on religious faith, in the doctrine of spiritual equality espoused by many evangelical Protestant sects. Niles's own denomination, the Universalists, proclaimed that all alike would eventually be saved. Universalism was rooted in, and fero-ciously defended, the unaided spiritual insights of common, uneducated Christians. It took special aim at Calvinist doctrines that inculcated feel-ings of unworthiness and futility in the individual believer, feelings that were exacerbated by the personal arrogance, ostentatious erudition, and complex theologies of learned clergy.[87]

Niles's Universalist social thought, and something of its political impli-cations, came out in a New Year's essay published during a period when the paper was filled with demands for removals of Federalist officeholders:

> The fact is, though pride, prejudice, and superstition may teach a different doctrine, *mankind are essentially alike*—none perfectly good—none perfectly bad—none wholly active—none wholly indolent . . . Hence we establish the first law of our nature—that all mankind are essentially EQUAL. . . . This shews the wisdom and goodness of the great creator, and the vanity and emptiness of wealth, power, and every circumstance of human greatness.[88]

A fall 1817 campaign essay applied these ideas more directly to politics and officeholding, sketching the salutary effects of such political Universalism and advising Connecticut voters to throw off the soul-crushing Calvinism of their political culture. "Let the people learn to respect *themselves*," a *Times* writer predicted, "and they will soon lose all false respect" for incumbent officeholders and politicians who flaunted their expensive educations. "They will cease to think that men in place possess any extraordinary *qualifications;* or, indeed, that any are required. . . . They will cease to believe that any one class of citizens have *superior claims* to public consideration." Of course, everyone knew what class seemed to make this claim: "They will cease to believe that the lawyers have any better qualifications, or higher claims for preferment than others, and begin to enquire into their monopoly of public office."[89]

Niles tried to promote his belief in common officeholders (and, typically, to make some money at the same time) by writing a manual for local officials. Believing that government by custom was retrograde and aristocratic, Niles produced a detailed, fully indexed guide to all the legal duties of justices of the peace, constables, and similar officials. The idea was to supply everything needed, even forms for common legal processes with directions for use, so that any literate person could hold a government office with credit. It was some time before the intended audience was in a position to use the book, but it would become a standard reference.[90]

Niles perceived that one of the major factors blocking the democratization of officeholding through massive removals was the atmosphere of "good feelings" that both President Monroe and Governor Wolcott had fostered. He became convinced that the blurring of party lines and delegitimation of strong partisanship had given Federalists the cover they needed to subvert the Toleration victory. After their defeat, the cannier Federalist officeholders in the state had toned down their anti-Republican and antidemocratic rhetoric and celebrated the death of party spirit, turning the new spirit of tolerance into a powerful argument for lenience in removals. Many of the old Federal Tolerationists were inclined to agree. Niles saw in Connecticut's "era of good feelings" a largely successful effort to maintain the old oligarchy under new names.[91]

Hence Niles warred furiously against all efforts to end the party conflict. His formerly subtle defenses of party politics became open arguments for the benefits of a party based on "fixed principles," as opposed to the personal, vindictive "party spirit" formerly practiced by the Federalists. The *Times* denounced Federalist conciliation and suggestions for a "union of parties" as a "political gull-trap." A front page address in September 1817 warned voters and politicians what type of union the Federalists wanted: "Give us all the honors, all the power, and be content to be hewers of wood and drawers of water, to plough, hoe, and go to meeting and then we will unite. We will suffer you to vote for us, honor us, and to support us. This is the union the federalists seek for . . . and the only one they will accept, until forced to do so by your votes."[92] By 1819 the *Times's* partisan flame fanning had become so intense and incessant enough that Niles felt the need to deny that a "state of strife" was his element. He claimed to find no "gratification in keeping alive party spirit," though the truth was probably otherwise.[93]

By 1822, amid a continuing lack of change in Connecticut and many signs of the further decline of partisan ties at the national level, Niles had become convinced that a thorough reconstruction of the political system was in order. The Republican party had to be reassembled and reorganized on a stronger and more permanent basis. Upon hearing of a Federalist manor lord being appointed to a federal office in New York, Niles exploded to a correspondent that it amounted to "open and barefaced disrespect and even contempt for popular opinion, and the rights and feelings of the people." He vowed that "if the 'powers that be' at Washington do not adopt a different policy it does not require the gift of prophecy to foresee that a vigorous and I trust a successful effort will be made to reorganize the scattered elements of the Republican party, the destruction of which seems to have been a leading object of Mr. M[onroe]'s administration."[94] Unfortunately for Niles, party building on its own rarely generated much enthusiasm with voters. What he needed was a vehicle for his project, a cause or figure popular enough to power the creation of a new national party.

ANDREW JACKSON AND THE COMING OF THE EDITORIAL "MILLENNIUM"

The vehicle Niles would need was taking shape around the time of his vow, in the form of Andrew Jackson's rise as a presidential candidate. While Jackson was already a major public figure, the origins of his presidential candidacy can be traced to the old Republican editors, including William Duane himself. The *Aurora* first raised the Jacksonian presidential flag in January 1822, somewhat speculatively associating Jackson with such Old School views as restraints on banking and opposition to the control of political parties by legislative caucuses. The venerable newspaper expired soon thereafter, but it was replaced by the *Columbian Observer,* edited by a former assistant of Duane's named Stephen Simpson. Simpson was joined by a small network of like-minded newspapers around the state.

When the Tennessee legislature nominated Jackson for president as part of a complex political ruse a few months later, the remnants of the Old School were ready. Pennsylvania exploded in mass meetings supporting Jackson, allowing the Old School and their western Pennsylvania allies to hijack the Republican party out from under Duane's old enemies, the New School or "Family" party, who hoped to throw the state's support behind John C. Calhoun. A state convention in early 1823, planned as the launch of Calhoun's candidacy, nominated Jackson instead, and the prospect of his winning Pennsylvania's electoral votes instantly turned Jackson into a national contender. The *Columbian Observer*-led Old School won Philadelphia in 1824, sparking a campaign that carried the state for Jackson in the presidential election. Combined with southern and western support, Pennsylvania's electoral votes gave Jackson a national plurality and set the stage for the "Corrupt Bargain" that made John Quincy Adams president and launched the Jackson campaign in earnest.[95]

Before the 1824 election, party rebuilders and "radical" or "old" Republican state factions had been much more likely to support Georgia's William Crawford or some local favorite. The most prominent Crawfordites were Martin Van Buren and Thomas Ritchie, whose *Richmond Enquirer* was viewed in some quarters as speaking for all the old Jeffersonians of the South. Crawford suffered a serious stroke before he could be nominated, but Van Buren and Ritchie carried their notions of party regularity so far as to have their man put forward anyway, by a congressional caucus that most of the members failed to attend.

With the caucus thus discredited for all time and their plans for Crawford immolated, the two shifted their allegiance, and their hope for a revived Republican party, over to Jackson. This was no small trick. Ritchie in particular had once strongly opposed Jackson as too unstable and dictatorial a personality to be trusted with executive power. By early 1827, however, the two had come to see that Jackson's popularity with the voters would get him elected in any case and that their best chance for a "substantial reorganization of the old Republican party" after years of chaos and good feelings was to harness Jackson to it. Van Buren even wanted Ritchie to start an "old Republican" Jacksonian newspaper in Washington and lead the campaign himself, but Vice President John C. Calhoun, another party to the alliance, convinced him to confer that role on the *United States Telegraph*, edited by a Calhoun loyalist and former St. Louis editor named Duff Green.[96]

Over the same period (roughly 1825–27), almost all the other party builders, dissident factions, and editorial rebels against good feelings made a similar decision to cast their lot with Jackson. These included the New Court forces in Kentucky, Thomas Hart Benton and his supporters in Missouri, Moses Dawson and another Cincinnati editor named Elijah Hayward in Ohio, and factions centered around several different newspapers in New England: the Boston *Statesman,* Isaac Hill's *New Hampshire Patriot,* and John Niles's Hartford *Times.* While some of these groups and editors had longstanding affinities for Jackson, others were clearly hopping aboard a lumbering political bandwagon.[97]

The 1828 campaign saw newspaper politics deployed on a scale that dwarfed the Revolution of 1800. Even as the most partisan of the old Republican journals gravitated to Jackson, a huge number of new Jacksonian papers appeared. The Jacksonians had a national flagship in the *United States Telegraph,* but their newspaper network was as decentralized as the old Republican one had been, with large numbers of papers in far-flung locations being widely reprinted.[98] The new wave of newspaper foundings created a new generation of young political professionals. It also reenergized a number of the old printers, though in some cases for opportunistic reasons. Thomas J. Rogers, for instance, suddenly came out of his early retirement in 1827 to found the *Delaware Democrat* as the Jacksonian organ in Easton.[99]

Meanwhile, yet other Republican editors were organizing parties, founding newspapers, and mounting state campaigns against Jackson, whose larger-than-life image lent itself nearly as well to demonization as adulation. Love him or loathe him, the old general inspired intense emotions that political entrepreneurs across the spectrum could exploit. For instance, former refugee radical and onetime Pennsylvania printer-"tyrant" John Binns suddenly resurfaced, now as one of Jackson's most effective detractors. Binns flooded the country with copies of his innovative "Coffin Handbills," graphically detailing Jackson's penchant for personal violence and ruthless, autocratic decisions.

Of greater long-term significance to the anti-Jacksonian forces was the emergence of Thurlow Weed, a young Republican printer in central New York who was leading the politicization of antimasonry just as Jackson was being elected. Under Weed's influence, the Antimasons broadened from a one-issue crusade into a major anti-Jackson party, becoming the first party to hold a national nominating convention and supplying the opposition to Jackson with a badly needed dose of populistic fervor. In subsequent years, Weed would remain the most powerful voice within the anti-Democratic forces arguing for the need to match the Jacksonians in organization and mass appeal.

Fittingly, the most vicious, personal, elaborate, and inaccurate attacks on Jackson in 1828 came from a former Federalist editor, carrying on the grand Federalist press tradition of high-mindedly "wading knee-deep in smut" in order to save the republic from an immoral leader. This was Charles Hammond, whose pro-Adams *Cincinnati Gazette* and separate campaign publications (including one brazenly entitled *Truth's Advocate*) broadcast the heavily embellished fruits of some opposition research the editor had done in Kentucky and Tennessee. Hammond's most famous revelations concerned Jackson's accidentally bigamous marriage and the questionable circumstances surrounding it, supposedly revealing the Jacksons as "a convicted adulteress" and her home-wrecking "paramour" whose examples would surely corrupt America's youth. Nor did Hammond stop with these fact-based tales. Pious readers also learned that Jackson's mother was a "COMMON PROSTITUTE" and his father a "MULATTO MAN."[100]

Andrew Jackson's presidency marked a major turning point in the history of newspaper politics. Understanding exactly the role that newspaper editors played in his campaigns, Jackson amply expressed his gratitude to the network of editors that supported him, not only by doling out printing contracts but also by appointing at least seventy editors to federal offices and allowing several key editors to play crucial roles in his administration. Isaac Hill and Amos Kendall were named to high positions in the Treasury Department, and Kendall became perhaps the central figure in Jackson's "Kitchen Cabinet" of advisers, the beginnings of the White House staff. This group also included Kendall's Kentucky coworker Francis P. Blair, recruited to edit the new Jackson administration organ, the *Washington Globe*. Blair was given vast federal patronage, when it could be wrested from Duff Green, and became one of the national Democratic party's primary managers and spokesmen. Kendall would later be elevated to the cabinet, as postmaster general.

At the same time, lower-level jobs all over the nation went to other Jacksonian editors. If they wanted rewards of this type (as Thomas Ritchie did not), most of the major state party editors got them. Various editors and writers of the Boston *Statesman* were appointed to key posi-

tions in the city's custom house. Moses Dawson of the *Cincinnati Advertiser* was put in charge of the local land office, while his cohort Elijah
Hayward of the incongruously named Cincinnati *National Republican*
went to Washington to become chief of the General Land Office. At least
twenty-five editors were given local postmasterships, usually in the towns
where they published.

While many of the posts went to ambitious newcomers who entered
the newspaper business just in time to join the Jackson campaign, a number of the jobs went to veteran Republican printers. By dint of furious
lobbying, Thomas J. Rogers converted his work on the *Delaware Democrat*
into an appointment as naval officer in the Philadelphia custom house.
Through a complex sequence of events, Amos Kendall's former Kentucky
ally John Norvell, who had most recently spent a decade editing Philadelphia Democratic Republican newspapers (including the original Philadelphia *Inquirer*), was made postmaster of Detroit in Michigan Territory.
Other awardees included at least three participants in the 1800 campaign,
William Dickson of the Lancaster *Intelligencer* (via his widow or daughter
Mary), William J. Duane, and Charles Holt.[101]

The editorial appointments horrified Jackson's opponents and even
some of his supporters. The Washington *Daily National Journal,* an
Adams paper, compared the appointments to Sir Robert Walpole's bribery
of the British press and amassed a running roster of the lucky editors to
document the extent of the "corruption." The *Journal* and many other papers lashed Jackson for turning a group of obscure, dishonest printers into
a privileged class.[102] Reports came to Jackson from Virginia that he was
losing his "most respectable and staunch supporters" because of his close
association with newspaper editors. Under the lead of "truehearted Virginians," the Senate refused to "swallow the printers" and denied confirmation to Hill and several others. The rejections were based on about
equal parts social snobbery, classical republican scruples, and lawyerly occupational jealousy.[103]

In contrast, Jackson saw no reason to uniquely disqualify editors from
office. Though unsympathetic historians have always exaggerated his role
in the advent of the so-called "spoils system," his editorial appointments
did set the important precedent of a president's openly acknowledging, rewarding, and even verbally honoring his campaigners. "Those who stept
forward and advocated the question termed the side of the people" did so
out of a "generous and patriotic impulse" and ought not to be punished,

Jackson told critics. To appoint newspaper editors to office was merely to make "the road to office and preferment . . . accessible alike to the rich and the poor, the farmer and the printer." Here was the full acceptance and facilitation of their role in politics that newspaper editors had craved since the 1790s. Newspaper politics and its attendant political professionalism had come of age.[104]

However, the impact of the 1828 election and its patronage sequel went beyond merely forcing the presidents and statesmen to acknowledge the newspaper politicians. Editors had already been strong agents in reviving party spirit, but Jackson's victory allowed them to emerge as key architects of the new, better-organized, more broadly based mass party system that developed during the 1830s.[105] The appointments aided (and often funded) this process, but what was more, they gave large numbers of editors the necessary platform and legitimacy to move beyond the role of henchmen, spokesmen, and party managers to become major elected officials and statesmen themselves. The vanguard of this trend was none other than Isaac Hill. After the Senate found him too distasteful to confirm as second comptroller of the treasury, Hill went back to New Hampshire, flexed the power of the *Patriot* and the Jacksonian organization, and promptly got himself sent back to Washington as a senator.[106]

Hill's friend John Milton Niles took part in all these developments and was one of their chief promoters and beneficiaries in Connecticut. Jackson's defense of his editorial appointments contained exactly the sort of equation between democratization and offices for partisan campaigners that Niles had long been making. While self-serving, Niles's views should be taken seriously, for the change they demanded was significant, especially in Connecticut.

Niles was considerably less opportunistic in his Jacksonianism than many of his editorial colleagues. The Hartford *Times* had been one of the few newspapers in New England to defend Jackson when he was being roasted in Congress over his invasion of Spanish Florida in 1818.[107] Later, it became the first newspaper in the region to support the Old Hero's presidential candidacy, as members of Niles's Republican faction transformed themselves into the state's Jacksonian Democrats. However, Old Hickory was anything but an easy sell in the "Land of Steady Habits," where his violent, willful frontier hero image held little allure. The *Times* slowly built Jackson up as both a repository of the old Jeffersonian faith and a harbinger of a more open and democratic society in New England, but it was an uphill fight, requiring extraordinary efforts.

Niles built a strong electoral base for Jackson in the cities, running a tightly disciplined, New York-style organization out of the *Times* office with the party central committee composed largely of staff members. In 1826 he represented Hartford in the state assembly and the following year narrowly missed election to the state senate. By the time of the 1828 presidential election, Niles and his allies had managed to realize several long-term goals: forcing the retirement of old Governor Wolcott, passing a districting bill through the legislature, and, as many editors had done elsewhere, pushing the state's political parties away from legislative caucuses and toward delegate conventions as the chief method of making nominations and other party decisions. Yet in many other ways, victory seemed far off. The state's Republicans divided bitterly over the Jackson candidacy, with the majority supporting John Quincy Adams. Jackson did not come close to carrying Connecticut in 1828, and the Jacksonian faction of the state legislature was as yet painfully small.[108]

In the aftermath of his candidate's victory, Niles ironically found himself in serious personal and political trouble. His rivals for control of the Republican party (most of whom would eventually become Whigs) were ascendant and rhetorically pummeling him and his increasingly isolated newspaper. Others were plotting to supplant Niles as Connecticut's leading Jacksonian. To add injury to these insults, Niles (like many other Jacksonian editors) had gotten into financial difficulties during the campaign, sinking far too much of his relatively meager earnings into the *Times* and the Jackson cause. Needing tangible help and a sign of favor from the new administration, his eye fell on the $3,000-a-year Hartford postmastership, a post that would finance future campaigns and prove to both his blue-blooded opponents and society at large that he was a man of great influence, to be feared or respected.

Too shy and too proud to go begging offices himself, Niles sent his young lieutenant Gideon Welles (since 1826 the primary editor of the *Times*) to Washington with a mission: bring back the postmastership for Niles and influence the administration's decisions on other Connecticut offices. So many expectant journalists were swarming the capital that Welles and twelve others, "all Jackson editors," had to visit the president en masse, like troops passing for review. Also in the delegation were Duff Green, Amos Kendall, Isaac Hill, Thomas Ritchie, Mordecai M. Noah of the New York *National Advocate,* and Nathaniel Greene of the Boston *Statesman.* Understandably, young Welles got to do very little of the talking.

Welles spent the rest of the time he was in Washington loitering around the offices of Green's *U.S. Telegraph* and hobnobbing at the home of the Rev. Obadiah Brown, a Baptist minister, whose parlor became a rendezvous for visiting journalists. Less enjoyable were Welles's other lobbying tasks: sheepishly buttonholing congressmen and working to head off competitors from home who had showed up at their own behest. Welles and his new editor friends naturally joined the infamously rowdy crowd of revelers at Jackson's inauguration. The White House furnishings were trampled, dishes broken, and the president-elect himself nearly crushed against one wall of the East Room, in a scene that signaled the dawn of mob rule to several fearful observers. Gideon Welles had to sleep late the next day to recover from his share of the revelry, forgoing his usual lengthy report home to Niles.[109]

Apparently Welles's mission succeeded. Niles was appointed postmaster of Hartford, and at the same time, Jackson removed a number of longtime Republican officials who, in the Hartford *Times* view of things, had fallen away from the true faith. The postmastership would sustain Niles and his allies through many lean years of factional infighting and continued electoral futility. Previously, disastrous pro-Jackson coalitions had been attempted with former Adams supporters and even converted Federalists. The appointment gave Niles the wherewithal to hold out and follow his own inclinations, which were for the hard-core Jacksonian Democrats around the *Times* "to stand upon our own principles and fight it out" for control of the party and state. This was, he told a fellow New England editor, "not only the most consistent, but the most expedient course," a combination few editor-politicians could resist. Niles would be further fortified, and even grow rather wealthy, through the same political channels that brought his postmastership. He started a papermaking business and found a highly lucrative customer in none other than Francis P. Blair's *Washington Globe*.[110]

Connecticut voters spurned Jackson even amidst the relative landslide of 1832, but in the wake of the Bank War, Niles's tenacity and ideological rigor began to pay off at last. The *Times* had long been a critic of banking, paper money, and the inegalitarian effects of the market revolution. This put Niles and company on the administration's side of the split in Jacksonian ranks that appeared over Jackson's measures to not just refuse to recharter the national bank, but actually to kill it and replace bank paper with hard currency. Though they had to fight off a competing Democratic newspaper funded by a local bank, the *Times* faction's fortunes changed rapidly for the better, aided by the beginning of significant foreign immigration into Connecticut's cities. In 1833 they finally managed to elect a relatively congenial governor. Jackson visited Hartford that same year and showed marked respect to Niles and other members of the *Times* coterie. When incumbent senator Nathan Smith died in 1835, Niles's high standing in Washington got him appointed to the vacancy, and Welles was named to fill his old place as postmaster.[111]

After Martin Van Buren's 1836 presidential candidacy finally brought Connecticut into the Jacksonian fold, Niles won a full Senate term and went on to be one of the truly outstanding and independent northern Democrats in Washington during the 1830s and 1840s. He took a brief hiatus from the Senate at the end of Van Buren's presidency to accept his highest office, replacing Amos Kendall as postmaster general. Always uncompromising, he fought the proslavery takeover of the Democratic party during the Polk administration, and later (like Van Buren, but for more idealistic reasons) became a Free Soiler.[112]

CODA: COMMON MEN IN HIGH OFFICE

At the time of Niles's Senate exploits, editors would no longer be a novelty at the highest levels of national politics. By the late 1830s, newspaper politicians enjoyed a kind of ascendancy—Theodore Roosevelt's "millennium" of ignorant, small-fry politicians—that the newspaper role in building the mass party system had helped bring about. In his first Congress, Niles was one of seven former editors in the Senate, including Isaac Hill and John Norvell, who had parlayed his Detroit postmastership into one of Michigan's first two Senate seats. In all, at least thirty-five printers, editors, and publishers sat in Niles's first two Congresses, the twenty-fourth and twenty-fifth. During his second Senate tour, from 1843 to 1849, Niles served with at least forty other printers, editors, and publishers. Other than lawyers, partisan journalists were probably the most disproportionately well-represented occupational group in Congress.[113]

This was a situation rife with ambiguities. On the one hand, this editorial invasion of Congress constituted a significant democratization of high American political leadership. Roughly one quarter of the editor-congressmen were printers by training, and hence former tradesmen and manual laborers. Most of the rest, at least the northerners among them, were far from polished aristocrats. As a group, they lacked the poise, presence, and trained oratorical abilities of congressional statesman such as Henry Clay and Daniel Webster. Old printers like Hill and raw farm boys like Niles found that their rough manners, plain dress, and misshapen bodies set them apart, unpleasantly. Having been laughed at when he had tried to speak extemporaneously in the New Hampshire legislature, Hill woodenly read his maiden Senate speech from a prepared text, a stylistic faux pas that earned him the derision of his new colleagues. Both Hill and Niles actually became frequent speakers, but they would be noted for the cogency of their arguments and the extent of their preparation rather than the eloquence or emotional power of their oratory. Niles's speeches were frequently reprinted as political pamphlets but rarely memorized by schoolchildren.[114]

Social life at the capital was a particular trial for editors in Congress. Decades of newspaper writing and political power never took Niles or Hill far from the social identity and manners of their youths. A better-bred contemporary remembered Niles and Hill leaving a Washington dinner party together. Facing with the challenge of paying their respects to the ladies, the two were obviously discomfited. The brusque Hill simply bolted, and though inclined by his shyness to follow suit, Niles was stopped short by the sight of his friend, ally, and fellow former editor, Thomas Hart Benton, bowing to the women individually:

> as Benton was actually performing his courtesies, [Niles] felt it impossible wholly to disregard such a pattern. Setting out first for the door, he soon diverged toward the fireside; when near the ladies, he was suddenly seized with panic, and pulling out a red . . . handkerchief from his pocket, gave a loud blast upon his nose, shot out the door, and thus safely effected his retreat.[115]

On other hand, the accession of editors to high national office inaugurated an era decried by many contemporaries and historians as rife with graft, corruption, and self-aggrandizing politicians whose democracy was far more rhetorical than real.[116] Both views have much to recommend them. Political professionalism did become an end in itself for many editorial politicians, especially after their battles for white male democracy were won.

Moreover, while clearly an effective system for building parties and mediating a federalized political system, newspaper politics was surely a problematic thing to build into the heart of the government. The chronic, inherent financial debilities of political newspapers turned newspaper editors into a major and powerful market for what clearly was a form of graft, but a highly resilient and difficult-to-reform type precisely because it was essentially honest and well intended. In the hands of editors like John Niles, printing contracts, postmasterships, and the like amounted to a primitive, necessary form of public campaign financing. Once such funding became easily available, as it was from the Jackson administration on, less honest and more selfish politicians would have ample opportunities to abuse the indirection and lack of oversight inherent in such informal arrangements. To a certain extent, real corruption may have been the price of real democratization. A fuller exploration of this problem will have to await a future volume.

APPENDIX I

Charts on the Growth of the American Press

NOTE ON SOURCES

The maps, charts, and statistics on newspaper partisanship in this work are based on my own database of partisan newspapers, 1795–1815. The original list was constructed using Brigham, *History and Bibliography of American Newspapers,* and Lathem, *Chronological Tables of American Newspapers.* Newspapers were then assigned partisan identities, using a number of sources: actual inspection of the papers themselves in the course of my primary research, comments in other newspapers, local histories, state and local histories of printing and journalism, and three previous national surveys of early newspaper partisanship: Thomas, *History of Printing in America,* 517–25; Donald H. Stewart, "Appendix: Annotated List of Newspapers," in his *Opposition Press of the Federalist Period,* 867–93; and David Hackett Fischer, "Political Affiliation of American Newspapers, October 1, 1800," and "Federalist Electioneering Newspapers, 1800–1820," in *Revolution of American Conservatism,* 413–29. Newspapers were assigned partisan identities only where some reasonably convincing evidence was available, and some mistakes and exaggerations of the Thomas, Stewart, and Fischer lists were corrected. For newspapers that I did not personally read or have independent information on, I only assigned a partisan identity where the various lists were in substantial agreement on the political complexion of a given journal. Given the unavailability or inaccessibility of many early newspapers, the maps, charts and statistics probably underestimate the actual extent of the newspaper partisanship. In any case, the statistics are intended to convey a broad sense of proportion and pattern, not scientifically precise measurements.

It should also be noted that charts 1 through 4 analyze the growth of the entire press, rather than just its partisan sector. These charts are derived from the works by Brigham and Lathem just cited, along with Weiss, *Graphic Summary of the Growth of Newspapers.*

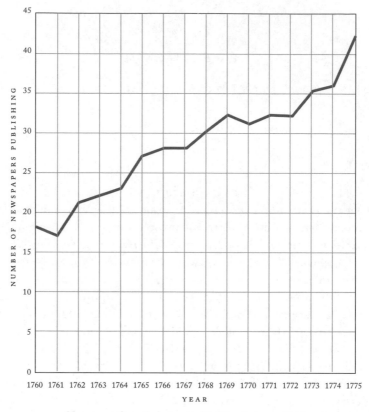

CHART I. Newspaper Growth during the Pre-Revolutionary Crisis, 1760–1775.

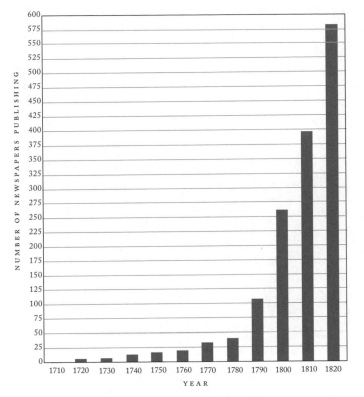

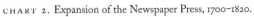

CHART 2. Expansion of the Newspaper Press, 1700–1820.

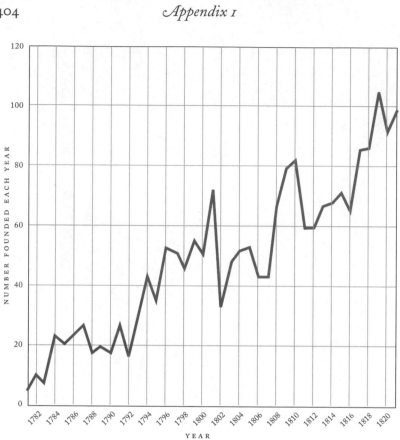

CHART 3. The Pace of Newspaper Creation, 1780–1820.

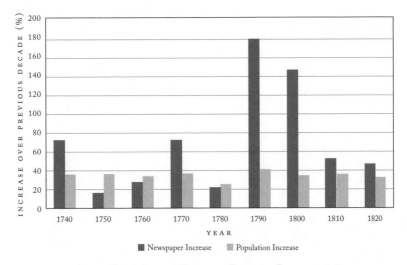

CHART 4. Population and Newspaper Expansion Rates, 1730s–1810s.

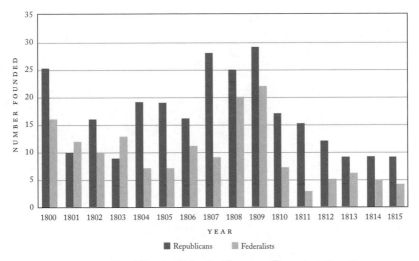

CHART 5. Republican vs. Federalist Newspaper Expansion, 1800–1815.

APPENDIX 2

The Sedition Act and the Expansion of the Republican Press

Listed below are all partisan Republican or Republican-leaning newspapers that were active during the election year of 1800, arranged by time of founding. Slashes indicate changed titles, brackets a simultaneous "country" edition. The right column gives each paper's known lifespan. For sources, see the source note to appendix 1.

BEFORE 1789

Boston	Mass.	*Independent Chronicle*	1784–1817
New York	N.Y.	*New-York Journal/*	
		Greenleaf's New-York Journal	1784–1800
Hartford	Conn.	*American Mercury*	1784–1833
Carlisle	Pa.	*Carlisle Gazette*	1785–1817
Augusta	Ga.	*Augusta Chronicle*	1785–1820+
Elizabeth Town	N.J.	*New-Jersey Journal*	1786–1820+
Petersburg	Va.	*Virginia Gazette/*	
		Petersburg Intelligencer	1786–1820+
Charleston	S.C.	*City Gazette*	1786–1840
Lexington	Ky.	*Kentucky Gazette*	1787–1820+
Albany	N.Y.	*Albany Register*	1788–1820+

1790–94

Philadelphia	Pa.	*Aurora and General Advertiser*	1790–1822
Philadelphia	Pa.	*Neue Philadelphische Correspondenz*	1790–1812
Martinsburg	W.Va.	*Potowmac Guardian*	1790–1800
Frederick	Md.	*Bartgis's Federal Gazette*	1792–1800
Richmond	Va.	*Virginia Argus*	1793–1816
Frederick	Md.	*Rights of Man*	1794–1800

1795–96

Columbia	S.C.	*State Gazette*	1795–1820+
Lexington	Ky.	*Stewart's Kentucky Herald*	1795–1805

Baltimore	Md.	*Baltimore Telegraphe/City Gazette*	1795–1807
New York	N.Y.	*Argus*	1795–1800
York	Pa.	*Unpartheyische York Gazette*	1796–1803
Dedham	Mass.	*Minerva/Columbian Minerva*	1796–1804
Newark	N.J.	*Centinel of Freedom*	1796–1820+
Reading	Pa.	*Readinger Adler*	1796–1820+

JAN. 1797–MAY 1798

Hagerstown	Md.	*Maryland Herald*	1797–1820+
Alexandria	Va.	*Alexandria Times/ Columbian Advertiser*	1797–1802
Mount Pleasant	N.Y.	*Mount Pleasant Register*	1797–1800
New London	Conn.	*Bee*	1797–1802
Bennington	Vt.	*Vermont Gazette/World/ Green Mountain Farmer*	1797–1820+
Fredericksburg	Va.	*Genius of Liberty/Courier*	1797–1801
Philadelphia	Pa.	*Universal Gazette*	1797–1800
Wilkes-Barre	Pa.	*Wilkesbarre Gazette*	1797–1801
Charleston	S.C.	*Carolina Gazette*	Jan. 1798–1820+
Washington	Pa.	*Herald of Liberty*	Feb. 1798–1802
Norfolk	Va.	*Epitome of the Times*	Mar. 1798–1802
Frankfort	Ky.	*Guardian of Freedom*	May 1798–1805
Morristown	N.J.	*Genius of Liberty*	May 1798–1801

PASSAGE OF THE SEDITION ACT, JUNE–JULY 1798

JUNE 1798–DEC. 1799

Frankfort	Ky.	*Palladium*	Aug. 1798–1816
Stonington	Conn.	*Journal of the Times/ Impartial Journal*	Oct. 1798–1804
Louisville	Ga.	*Gazette/State Gazette/ Republican Trumpet*	Nov. 1798–1811
Leesburg	Va.	*True American*	Nov. 1798–1800
Richmond	Va.	*Examiner*	Dec. 1798–1804
Baltimore	Md.	*American*	May 1799–1820+
Greensburg	Pa.	*Farmers' Register*	May 1799–1818
Lancaster	Pa.	*Lancaster Correspondent (German)*	May 1799–1803
Lancaster	Pa.	*Intelligencer*	July 1799–1820+
Winchester	Va.	*Winchester Triumph of Liberty*	July 1799–1803
Easton	Md.	*Republican Star*	Aug. 1799–1832
Portsmouth	N.H.	*Republican Ledger*	Aug. 1799–1803
Boston	Mass.	*Constitutional Telegraphe/ Republican Gazetteer*	Oct. 1799–1803

Raleigh	N.C.	*Raleigh Register*	Oct. 1799–1856
Wilmington	Del.	*Mirror of the Times*	Nov.1799–1806
Newburgh	N.Y.	*Rights of Man*	Nov. 1799–1806
Huntingdon	Pa.	*Guardian of Liberty*	Nov. 1799–1800
Philadelphia	Pa.	*Constitutional Diary*	Dec. 1799–1800
Petersburg	Va.	*Republican/Old Dominion*	Dec. 1799–1830

1800

Goshen	N.Y.	*Orange Patrol*	Jan. 1800–1802
Nashville	Tenn.	*Tennessee Gazette*	Jan. 1800–1806
Richmond	Va.	*Press*	Jan.–Feb.1800
Staunton	Va.	*Political Mirror*	Jan. 1800–1802
Geneva	N.Y.	*Impartial American*	Feb. 1800–1801
New York	N.Y.	*American Citizen* [*Republican Watch-Tower*]	Mar. 1800–1810
New York	N.Y.	*Forlorn Hope*	Mar.–Sept. 1800
Martinsburg	W.Va.	*Republican Atlas*	Apr. 1800–1801
Salem	Mass.	*Impartial Register/Salem Register/Essex Register*	May 1800–1854
Catskill	N.Y.	*Western Constellation*	May 1800–1804
Richmond	Va.	*Friend of the People*	May–July 1800
Danbury/Norwalk/ New Haven	Conn.	*Sun of Liberty*	June 1800–1801
Georgetown	D.C.	*Cabinet*	Aug. 1800–1801
Georgetown	D.C.	*Friend of the People*	Aug.–Nov. 1800
Pittsburgh	Pa.	*Tree of Liberty*	Aug. 1800–1810
Providence	R.I.	*Impartial Observer/ Liberty's Sentinel*	Aug. 1800–1802
Washington	D.C.	*Universal Gazette*	Sept. 1800–1814
Pittsfield	Mass.	*Sun*	Sept. 1800–1820+
Washington	D.C.	*National Intelligencer*	Oct. 1800–1869
Chillicothe	Ohio	*Scioto Gazette*	Oct. 1800–1926
Newport	R.I.	*Guardian of Liberty/ Rhode Island Republican*	Oct. 1800–1806
New York	N.Y.	*Temple of Reason*	Nov. 1800–1801
Greensburg	Pa.	*Deutsche Bauer's Register*	Nov. 1800–1803
Lewistown	Pa.	*Western Star*	Nov. 1800–1812
Norristown	Pa.	*True Republican*	Nov. 1800–1803

NOTES

ABBREVIATIONS

AAS   American Antiquarian Society, Worcester, Mass.

APS   American Philosophical Society Library, Philadelphia, Pa.

Annals of Congress Joseph Gales Sr., et al., eds. *The Debates and Proceedings of the Congress of the United States.* Washington, D.C., 1834–56.

Aurora   Philadelphia *Aurora and General Advertiser.*

BDUSC   Kathryn Allamong Jacob and Bruce A. Ragsdale, eds. *Biographical Directory of the United States Congress, 1774–1989: Bicentennial Edition.* Washington, D.C., 1989.

BIIC-DPL   Burton Historical Collection, Detroit Public Library, Detroit, Mich.

BP-CC   Bache Papers, Castle Collection.

CHS   Connecticut Historical Society, Hartford, Conn.

CWM   College of William and Mary, Earl Gregg Swem Library, Manuscripts and Rare Books Department, Williamsburg, Va.

DAB   Allen Johnson and Dumas Malone, eds. *Dictionary of American Biography.* New York, 1928–36.

DHRC   Merrill Jensen, John P. Kaminski and Gaspare J. Saladino, eds. *The Documentary History of the Ratification of the Constitution.* Madison, Wisc. 1976–.

DU   Duke University, William R. Perkins Library, Special Collections Department, Durham, N.C.

GA   Philadelphia *General Advertiser, 1790–94.*

GUS   New York *Gazette of the United States,* 1789–90; Philadelphia *Gazette of the United States,* 1790–1804.

HBAN   Clarence S. Brigham. *History and Bibliography of American Newspapers, 1690–1820, including Additions and Corrections (1961).* Hamden, Conn., 1962.

HSP   Historical Society of Pennsylvania, Philadelphia, Pa.

LCP   Library Company of Philadelphia, Pa.

LC   Library of Congress, Washington, D.C.

NA   National Archives, Washington, D.C.

NG   Philadelphia *National Gazette,* 1791–93.

N-YHS   New York Historical Society, New York City, N.Y.

NYPL   New York Public Library, New York City, N.Y.

PAH   Harold C. Syrett and Jacob E. Cooke, eds. *The Papers of Alexander Hamilton.* New York, 1961–87.

PJM   William T. Hutchinson, et al., eds. *The Papers of James Madison.* Vols. 1–10, Chicago, 1962–77; vols. 11–17, Charlottesville, Va. 1977–91.

PTJ   Julian P. Boyd, et al., eds. *The Papers of Thomas Jefferson.* Princeton, N.J. 1950–.

RG59-NA   Record Group 59, General Records of the Department of State, National Archives, Washington, D.C.

UVA   University of Virginia, Alderman Library, Charlottesville, Va.

VHS   Virginia Historical Society, Richmond, Va.

WTJ   Paul Leicester Ford, ed. *The Writings of Thomas Jefferson.* New York and London, 1892–99.

1. THE NEWSPAPER-BASED POLITICAL SYSTEM OF THE ANTEBELLUM UNITED STATES

1. Iyengar and Reeves, *Do the Media Govern?*

2. Cox, *Journey through My Years,* 235–37; Sinclair, *Available Man,* 22.

3. H. L. Mencken, "Bayard vs. Lionheart," in *Carnival of Buncombe,* 15.

4. Marvin, "Space, Time, and Captive Communications History," 20–38. Many modern-day journalists and citizens also believe that the media should function as a "watchdog" against abuses by government. However, the only acceptable mode of performing this function, in current journalistic ideology, is to expose wrongdoing in news reports, thereby fulfilling the public's "right to know." Nothing in current mainstream journalistic culture, including the "public journalism" movement, authorizes journalists acting as engaged, critical partisans, except (occasionally) within the limited confines of the op-ed pages. See Gleason, *Watchdog Concept;* Weaver and Wilhoit, *American Journalist,* 104–45; Klaidman and Beauchamp, *Virtuous Journalist,* 126–43, 154–55. In many other parts of the world, the modern journalistic traditions are quite different, with most newspapers maintaining frank political identities and journalists acting as engaged partisans up to very recent times. A number of European nations (including France, Italy, Norway, and Sweden) have considered a politically engaged press important enough to provide government subsidies aimed at maintaining newspapers affiliated with each major political party in each major locality, in defiance of worldwide economic trends toward apolitical, profit-oriented newspaper monopolies. See Smith, *The Newspaper, An International History* especially 164–68; Smith, *Newspapers and Democracy;* Koss, *Rise and Fall of the Political Press in Britain.* Koss dates the demise of the British party press approximately to the 1960s, but the British press still strikes most American readers as much more politicized than their own.

5. For the late development of the "news function" in newspapers other than the large urban dailies, see Russo, "Origins of Local News"; Baldasty, *Commercialization of News;* Clark, *Southern Country Editor.* Even that most whiggish of journalism historians, Frank Luther Mott had to admit that the "partisan press dominated American journalism" up through the Civil War (*American Journalism*, 253).

6. Tocqueville, *Democracy in America*, 185–86.

7. Schudson, "Troubleshooting Manual for Journalism History," 463–66. For works dispelling commonly accepted myths about the impact of the watchdog press in the Vietnam War and the Watergate scandal, see Hallin, *"Uncensored War";* and Lang and Lang, *Battle for Public Opinion.*

8. Political historians have been the heaviest consumers of newspaper sources, but they have rarely given extensive or explicit treatment to the political role of newspapers and newspaper editors, even in otherwise exhaustive works. According to J. Mills Thornton III (*Politics and Power in a Slave Society*, 128), the press was "third great element in party governance," along with party conventions and legislative caucuses, but it has also been "perhaps the most infrequently noticed" by historians. A survey of the literature more than bears out Thornton's assumption. Two major synthetic works on the evolution of the party system completely ignore the role of the press: Chambers and Burnham, *American Party Systems;* and Kleppner et al., *Evolution of American Electoral Systems.* Though newspapers were, after Bibles and almanacs, the most widely circulated type of printed matter in the early American republic (Gilmore, *Reading Becomes a Necessity of Life*, 193), even historians of print culture and popular reading have devoted relatively little attention to them. Two essay collections intended to present representative samples of work in the "print culture" field either omit the partisan press entirely or restrict the subject to part of one chapter: Davidson, *Reading in America;* and Joyce et al., *Printing and Society in Early America.*

9. For influential examples of these interpretations, see "The Dark Ages of Partisan Journalism," in Mott, *American Journalism*, 167–80; and Park, "Natural History of the Newspaper."

10. Sloan, "Journalism Historians Lost in the Past, Need Direction," 4–7, 48. Other surveys and critiques of the historiography of journalism can be found in Startt and Sloan, *Significance of the Media*, 1–15, 78–105; Nord, "A Plea for *Journalism* History"; Nerone, "Mythology of the Penny Press"; Marvin, "Space, Time, and Captive Communications History"; Carey, "Problem of Journalism History." The textbooks mentioned are Mott, *American Journalism;* and Emery and Emery, *Press and America.* Michael Schudson, in his 1997 article "Troubleshooting Manual for Journalism History," argued that journalism historiography was still just beginning to move beyond the whiggish concerns and questions of these textbooks, and Schudson, Andie Tucher, and James Carey all essentially endorsed that view again in a panel at the 2000 meeting of the Organization of American Historians.

11. The political scientist Thomas E. Patterson argues that the media have taken over many former functions of the political parties, including the screening of presidential candidates. See Patterson, *Out of Order*, 29, 35.

12. Overviews of the present state of the field can be found in: Hench, *Three Hundred Years of the American Newspaper;* Solomon and McChesney, *Ruthless Criticism;* Sloan and Startt, *Significance of the Media.* A recent synthesis of the new journalism history for the early national period is Humphrey, *Press of the Young Republic.* There re-

mains a tendency among even the most sophisticated historians of journalism to treat aggressive news reporting as the press's preeminent, essential, teleological function. They tend to write with automatic approval whenever they find newspapers becoming independent of party politics, and tend to construct their studies as searches for origin points, or early examples, of modern characteristics such as the ideology of objectivity, "coverage" of major events, and typical stylistic devices such as the "inverted pyramid" story structure. Though written in a non-whiggish tone and often aimed at subverting modern myths about the journalism profession, these studies are nevertheless engaged in an inherently limiting enterprise. They are virtually forced to focus on the relative handful of big-city newspapers that can be considered potential precursors to modern journalism, and deal with the vast majority of the nineteenth-century press only as foils or points of contrast, if at all. For cases in point, see Rutenbeck, "Editorial Perception of Newspaper Independence"; Rutenbeck, "Newspaper Trends in the 1870s"; Schudson, *Discovering the News;* Schiller, *Objectivity and the News;* Mindich, *Just the Facts.*

13. Fallows, *Breaking the News,* 182; Patterson, *Out of Order,* 39–42, 52, 141, 154, 156; Crouse, *Boys on the Bus,* 57, 344–53; Entman, *Democracy without Citizens,* 8–9. Entman cogently describes the modern media as exercising "power without control," in a list of characteristics revolving around the sterility of the media's present-day political role: "abundance [of information] without growth" in citizen participation or understanding; "aggressiveness without accountability," and "pressure without reform."

14. Silbey, *American Political Nation,* 54. Despite this statement, Silbey's text makes only scattered references to the role of the press. Though some works of political history have considered the role of the press in politics more thoroughly, even they have portrayed partisan newspapers merely as useful adjuncts to the political parties—"a kind of public address system to supporters," according to Ronald Formisano (*Transformation of Political Culture,* 16). Standard works that deal rather extensively with the role of political newspapers and newspaper editors while still treating them as appendages to the political system are: Cunningham, *Jeffersonian Republicans;* Cunningham, *Republicans in Power;* Fischer, *Revolution of American Conservatism;* McCormick, *Second American Party System;* and Remini, *Election of Andrew Jackson.*

15. On newspapers and party politics in the late nineteenth century, see Summers, *Press Gang;* and McGerr, *Decline of Popular Politics.*

16. Except where noted, the following general discussion of the press's role in nineteenth-century politics is grounded in my own research and in the general literature on journalism history and party history. Besides those already cited, works that have strongly influenced my ideas include: Bailyn and Hench, *Press and the American Revolution;* Hench, "Newspaper in a Republic"; Baldasty, *Commercialization of News,* 11–46; Sloan, "Early Party Press"; Sloan, "Purse and Pen"; Smith, *Press, Politics, and Patronage;* Stewart, *Opposition Press of the Federalist Period,* 3–32; Hamilton, *Country Printer;* Lyon, *Pioneer Editor in Missouri;* Cole, *Jacksonian Democracy in New Hampshire;* Kehl, *Ill Feeling in the Era of Good Feeling;* Gienapp, *Origins of the Republican Party;* Van Deusen, *Thurlow Weed;* Niven, *Gideon Welles;* Robertson, *Language of Democracy;* John, *Spreading the News;* McGerr, *Decline of Popular Politics,* 14–22.

17. Tocqueville, *Democracy in America,* 517.

18. Ketcham, *Presidents above Party;* Troy, *See How They Ran.*

19. In addition to my own research and the works on party history already cited, the

description of early campaigning in the next few paragraphs rests primarily on the following works: Isaac, *Transformation of Virginia;* Sydnor, *Gentlemen Freeholders;* Maier, *From Resistance to Revolution;* Dinkin, *Voting in Provincial America;* Dinkin, *Voting in Revolutionary America;* Dinkin, *Campaigning in America;* Taylor, "'Art of Hook and Snivey'"; Dupre, "Barbecues and Pledges"; Jordan, *Political Leadership in Jefferson's Virginia;* Heale, *Making of American Politics;* Heale, *Presidential Quest.* On celebrations and toasting, see Koschnik, "Political Conflict and Public Contest"; Newman, "Principles or Men?"; Newman, *Parades and the Politics of the Street;* Travers, *Celebrating the Fourth,* 69–106; Waldstreicher, "Rites of Rebellion"; Waldstreicher, *Perpetual Fetes.*

20. Dupre, "Barbecues and Pledges," 483; Baltimore *Whig,* 8, 23, 24, 28, 29 Sept., 1, 2, 5, 6, 7 Oct. 1813.

21. Tocqueville, *Democracy in America,* 518.

22. Similar points are made in Koschnik, "Political Conflict and Public Contest," 228–29; and Grasso, *Speaking Aristocracy,* 473–74. The critical role of print in turning local celebrations and meetings into a powerful force for nationalism is a major theme of Waldstreicher, "Rites of Rebellion" and *Perpetual Fetes.*

23. Trenton *True American,* 29 July 1816. Editors could also manipulate the readings of public opinion that were taken from the pages by printing toasts selectively, as the True Americans editor did by including a large number of toasts condemning a congressional pay raise that he and the paper were campaigning against.

24. John Binns to Thomas J. Rogers, 5 Feb. 1816, Binns file, Dreer Collection, HSP.

25. Tocqueville, *Democracy in America,* 517.

26. Leonard, *News for All,* 3–61; Brown, *Knowledge Is Power,* especially 132–59, 218–96; Conroy, *In Public Houses,* 234–36, 279–80, 304–305, 313; Smith, *The Newspaper: An International History,* 95. Space and time considerations have made it impossible to address the important question of readership very extensively in this book. The only way to generate hard information on newspaper readership for this period is to undertake painstaking social history research, examining, through estate inventories and similar records, exactly what reading material individual families had on hand. The most thorough study of this infrequently seen type (Gilmore, *Reading Becomes a Necessity of Life*) confirms the anecdotal evidence presented here about the penetration of early newspapers. Wowed by the claimed circulation figures of the sold-on-the-street commercial dailies that first began to appear in the 1830s (the "penny press"), scholars have tended to overestimate the change in newspaper readership levels that the new cheap newspapers represented, depicting them as America's first "mass medium." For examples, see Tucher, *Froth and Scum;* Schudson, *Discovering the News,* 12–60; Schiller, *Objectivity and the News;* and Mott, *American Journalism,* 215–53. While penny newspapers such as the *New York Herald* may have been the first to achieve huge individual circulations, the evidence for their supposedly revolutionary impact on newspaper readership as a whole has been more assumed than demonstrated. (A common source for claims about the revolution in readership are some highly speculative circulation statistics, mostly mere estimates before 1830, presented in Lee, *Daily Newspaper,* 711–45.) The penny press may have heralded the centralization of newspaper production as much as the expansion or democratization of newspaper reading. It was also a phenomenon that was for decades largely limited to a few major eastern cities. For a strong critique of the historiography on the penny press, see Nerone, "Mythology of the Penny Press." A recent account, Henkin, *City Reading,* 101–135, basically endorses

the "mythology" but makes an advance by emphasizing that the penny press was a "decidedly urban," or even decidedly New York, phenomenon.

27. Mesick, *English Traveller in America,* 225–29; Farkas, *Journey in North America,* 60–61, 151–52.

28. For "mediation" as one of the primary tasks of newspaper editors and other early party activists, see Waldstreicher and Grossbart, "Abraham Bishop's Vocation."

29. The best source on these matters is John, *Spreading the News,* which shows that the early postal service was a powerful instrument of public policy.

30. "Credit to Whom Credit is Due," Trenton *True American,* 5 Jan. 1802.

31. Smith, *Press, Politics and Patronage,* 114–26.

32. Wilson, *Presidency of Van Buren,* 64.

33. Van Deusen, *Thurlow Weed,* 38–69; Baldasty, "New York State Press and Antimasonry."

34. Filler, *Crusade against Slavery,* 55–62; Stewart, *Holy Warriors,* 133.

35. McCormick, *Second American Party System;* Kleppner, et al., *Evolution of American Electoral Systems,* 77–111; Silbey, *American Political Nation,* 5–32.

36. McWilliams, "Parties as Civic Associations."

37. The most thorough work on Tammany Hall is Mushkat, *Tammany.*

38. Quotation from Silbey, *American Political Nation,* 52. On the national party committees, which remained weak and seminomadic as late as the 1960s, see Cotter and Hennessey, *Politics without Power,* 1–38. The party chairman became a somewhat more authoritative figure after the Civil War, as an intermittent tradition developed of giving the chairman a patronage-heavy cabinet post such as postmaster general. (ibid., 92–94; and also see, Fowler, *Cabinet Politician.* Parties in the U.S. Congress shared a similarly uneven pattern of development, with strong partisanship long preceding institutionalization. See Polsby, "Institutionalization of the House." The weakness and general invisibility of the old national party committees stood in marked contrast to the thorough institutionalization of formal party organizations that took place in other democratic nations such as Great Britain.

39. Tocqueville, *Democracy in America,* 518. The patterns of newspaper expansion in the early republic bear out Tocqueville's assertion. Political crises and transformations coincided frequently with the establishment of large numbers of new newspapers. See chapters 6 and 14 and the charts in appendix 1 below.

40. Anderson, *Imagined Communities,* 62. See also, Clark, *Public Prints,* 252–53.

41. Baltimore *Whig,* 8 Sept., 2, 5 Oct. 1813. For a similar case of candidate authentication, see Baltimore *Patriot,* 22 May 1815, 13, 22, 25, 31 Jan., 9 Sept. 1816.

42. Thornton, *Politics and Power,* 129; Niven, *Gideon Welles,* 60–61; Miller, *Historical Sketches of Hudson,* 64–67; Detroit *Democratic Free Press,* 5 November 1832, 3 April 1833.

43. Three important exceptions are Baldasty, "Press and Politics in the Age of Jackson"; Hamilton, *Country Printer;* and Smith, *Press, Politics, and Patronage.* A broad, international survey of newspaper history published in Great Britain but little known in the United States, declares that "the editor had become the linchpin of all party political activity" all over Europe by the 1880s, many decades after the same situation had developed in America: Smith, *The Newspaper: An International History,* 105.

44. Heale, *Making of American Politics,* 157–58.

45. McCormick, *Second American Party System,* 352.

46. Baldasty, "Press and Politics in the Age of Jackson," 7–13.

47. Quotation from *To the Republicans of Hunterdon,* 15. For the idea of editors as party whips, I am indebted to Thornton, *Politics and Power,* 129.

48. *To the Republicans of Hunterdon,* 7.

49. New York *World,* 23 November 1882, quoted in Gienapp, *Origins of the Republican Party,* 151–52.

50. Remini, *Van Buren and the Making of the Democratic Party,* 125–33.

51. Weber, "Politics as a Vocation," 83–87.

52. Philadelphia *Franklin Gazette,* 21 May, 18, 19, 21 June 1819; Pasley, "'Indiscreet Zeal' of John Norvell."

53. "Editorial Courtesy," *Hartford Times,* 4 March 1833.

54. Quotation from enclosure with Duff Green to Cabell and Co., 4 June 1831, Duff Green Papers, LC. On the Washington Institute affair, see Pretzer, "The British, Duff Green, the Rats and the Devil."

55. Weber, "Politics as a Vocation," 101.

56. The decline of newspaper-based politics at the national level can be traced to the creation of the Government Printing Office in 1860 and the attendant end of heavy government patronage of Washington newspapers. See Smith, *Press, Politics, and Patronage,* 219–48. The best sources on the continuation of newspaper-based politics into the twentieth century are the autobiographies of party editors in small cities and towns, such as Josephus Daniels of Raleigh, North Carolina (*Tar Heel Editor* and *Editor in Politics*), navy secretary under Woodrow Wilson and a mentor of Franklin D. Roosevelt; and William Allen White of Emporia, Kansas (*Autobiography of William Allen White*).

57. One of the very few recent monographs to directly tackle democratization is Shade, *Democratizing the Old Dominion,* dealing with one state and taking democracy largely as a given for the rest of the country. The democratization of political language is analyzed in Robertson, *Language of Democracy.*

58. For two statements of this view, among many that could be cited, see Roediger, *Wages of Whiteness,* 55–60; and Baker, "Domestication of Politics," 622–632.

59. Attacks on the idea that meaningful democratization occurred before the Civil War include Pessen, *Riches, Class and Power,* and Altschuler and Blumin, *Rude Republic.* My own views on this question are given more fully in Pasley, "Party Politics, Citizenship, and Collective Action."

60. Wilentz, "On Class and Politics," 45. This same essay provides a thorough review of the relevant literature, which is far too voluminous to cite here.

61. Ibid., 56.

62. Formisano, "Deferential-Participant Politics," 478–79. For an elaboration of this argument, and a review of the historiography on the rise of "professional politicians" (including a fuller effort to define the term), see Pasley, "Artful and Designing Men."

63. Ridgway, *Community Leadership in Maryland.*

64. Blumin, *Emergence of the Middle Class,* xi, 1–65.

65. Appleby, *Capitalism and a New Social Order,* 51–78.

66. On this antiparty political morality and its canons of "patriot" leadership, see Ketcham, *Presidents Above Party,* and Hofstadter, *Idea of Party System,* chaps. 1 and 2. For a strong case that "classical republican" is a good general term for this political culture (among many that could be used), see Richard, *Founders and Classics.*

67. While I do not make the argument in quite the same terms, my findings are

consonant with those of Rosenberg, *Protecting the Best Men.* Both the "new libertarian-ism" and the later betrayals of it are described in Leonard Levy's books, *Emergence of a Free Press* and *Jefferson and Civil Liberties.*

68. On the relatively high voter turnouts in the Federalist-Republican contests, see McCormick, "New Perspectives on Jacksonian Politics."

69. See the highly influential works, Wallace, "Changing Concepts of Party," and Hofstadter, *Idea of Party System.*

70. Roosevelt, *Benton,* 78.

2. THE PRINTING TRADE IN EARLY AMERICAN POLITICS

1. Except where noted, the account of the printing trade in the following pages draws especially on: Botein, "Printers and the Revolution"; Botein, "Meer Mechanics"; Hamilton, *Country Printer;* Wroth, *Colonial Printer;* Clark, *Public Prints;* Remer, *Printers and Men of Capital;* Silver, *American Printer;* Silver, "Aprons instead of Uni-forms"; Pretzer, "Tramp Printers"; Rorabaugh, *Craft Apprentice;* Leonard, *Power of the Press,* 13–53; Brigham, *Journals and Journeymen;* Smith, *One Hundred Years of Hartford's "Courant";* Morse, *Connecticut Newspapers.*

2. Franklin, *Franklin's Autobiography,* 9–10; Prentiss Autobiography, AAS, 65; Clark, *Public Prints,* 194–95; Botein, "Printers and the Revolution," 12–13, 16–17; Botein, "Meer Mechanics," 140–50.

3. Wroth, *Colonial Printer,* 79–86, 115–21; Rorabaugh, *Craft Apprentice,* 11–14; Moran, *Printing Presses,* 17–47, 59–62; Silver, *American Printer,* 28–49; Hamilton, *Country Printer,* 5–12, 15–16; Prentiss Autobiography, AAS, 41–42.

4. Wood, *Radicalism,* 11–56. Even into the nineteenth century, according to one re-cent study, "physical labor's traditional association with poverty, brutishness, and lack of mental content" remained in force. See Glickstein, *Concepts of Free Labor,* 10.

5. Botein, "Meer Mechanics," 157–58.

6. Weed, *Autobiography of Thurlow Weed,* 58; Franklin, *Franklin's Autobiography,* 26, 36, 42, 44, 50, 52; Pretzer, "Tramp Printers," 3–5; Silver, *American Printer,* 8–10; Hamil-ton, *Country Printer,* 22–25; Greeley, *Recollections,* 83–105. On the large role of appear-ance, including an upright posture, symmetrical body, and graceful movements, in es-tablishing one's gentility, see Bushman, *Refinement of America,* especially 30–78. On the general early American drinking problem, see Rorabaugh, *Alcoholic Republic.*

7. James Parker, "A Letter to a Gentleman in the City of New-York," Broadsheet, 2 Nov. 1759, in MacAnear, "James Parker versus New York Province," 323, 329; Botein, "Meer Mechanics," 156–160; Thomas, *History of Printing,* ed. McCorison, 464–71; Wood, *Radicalism,* 35, 85–86.

8. Botein, "Meer Mechanics," 180; Botein, "Printers and the Revolution," 20.

9. Botein, "Printers and the Revolution," 20–21; Botein, "Meer Mechanics," 182–83; Benjamin Franklin, "An Apology for Printers," Franklin, *Writings of Franklin,* ed. Smyth 2:174.

10. Brown, *Knowledge Is Power,* 16–41; Clark, *Public Prints,* 70–71; Mott, *American Journalism,* 8–9.

11. Mott, *American Journalism,* 9–10; Duniway, *Freedom of the Press in Massachusetts,* 68–69; Clark, *Public Prints,* 71–73.

12. Clark, *Public Prints,* 77–102; Mott, *American Journalism,* 11–14; Steele, *English Atlantic,* 132–67.

13. James Parker, "Letter to Gentleman," in MacAnear, "Parker versus New York," 324; Alexander, *Narrative*, 1–35; Botein, *Zenger's Malice;* Mott, *American Journalism*, 31–38. The famous case of James Franklin's *New England Courant,* a paper bitterly critical of Boston's Puritan oligarchy but written by a "club" of local gentlemen, can be interpreted in a similar fashion. See Leonard, *Power of the Press*, 18–24; Duniway, *Freedom of the Press in Massachusetts*, 94–103, 163–66; Botein, "Meer Mechanics," 204; Thomas, *History of Printing*, ed. McCorison, 104–10; Mott, *American Journalism*, 15–21.

14. Botein, "Meer Mechanics," 204–209. Nash, *Urban Crucible*, 199–202, argues that newspapers had became an "indispensable" part of colonial politics by the 1740.

15. The term "correspondent" was used literally, meaning a gentlemen who wrote letters describing or commenting on news events, not a paid news gatherer.

16. Abraham Bishop to Jonathan Law, 1 May 1811, Bishop Letterbook, Yale.

17. Levy, *Emergence of a Free Press*, 16–61; Buel, "Freedom of the Press," 72–76. The newspaper's role in the growth of appeals to popular rights and public opinion, and the attendant increase in colonial paeans to and defenses of the press, can be seen, from wildly different perspectives, in Morgan, *Inventing the People*, 122–48; Smith, *Printers and Press Freedom;* and Warner, *Letters of the Republic.*

18. Warner, *Letters of the Republic*, 1–4, 34–72, 179n5; Schlesinger, *Prelude to Independence*, xiii–xiv, 281–301; Kobre, *Development of the Colonial Newspaper*, 95–173; Davidson, *Propaganda and the American Revolution*, 225–45; Leonard, *Power of the Press*, 33–53; Bailyn and Hench, *Press and the American Revolution;* Humphrey, *This Popular Engine.*

19. Martin, *Men in Rebellion;* Buel, "Freedom of the Press," 72. Actually, Buel writes that "colonial Americans" held this belief, but it is more accurately located in the minds of the educated white male gentry who made up the active political leadership of the colonies.

20. "Address to the Inhabitants of Quebec, 1774," in Schwartz, *Bill of Rights*, vol. 1, 223.

21. Levy, *Emergence of Free Press*, 62–88; Buel, "Freedom of the Press," 75–81; Nerone, *Violence against the Press*, 18–52.

22. Warner, *Letters of the Republic*, 67–68; Davidson, *Propaganda and the American Revolution*, 15, 242; Morgan, *Inventing the People.* This interpretation departs somewhat from the German philosopher Jürgen Habermas's original formulation of the "public sphere" (in *Structural Transformation*) as being truly rather than just apparently open to all and personless. It is also important to acknowledge that the "public sphere" (and the concept of public opinion it helped foster) had an even more important political purpose than the concealment described here. It served to partially neutralize the enormous personal authority and prestige of monarchs and nobles, as well as to provide (to use the modern political vernacular) a more level rhetorical playing field for critics of monarchical government such as the American Revolutionaries. On the debate over Habermas's ideas, see Brooke, "Ancient Lodges and Self-Created Societies"; Calhoun, *Habermas and the Public Sphere.*

23. Rush, *Autobiography*, 113–14.

24. Botein "Meer Mechanics," 210–25; Botein, "Printers and the Revolution," 23–49; Thomas, *History of Printing*, ed. McCorison, 163–64.

25. Thomas Jefferson to Isaiah Thomas, 1809, quoted in Thomas, *History of Printing*, ed. McCorison, 556n; Schlesinger, *Prelude to Independence*, 79. This was only the

first of Jefferson's many forays into the founding of newspapers, and may mark the beginnings of his deep belief in their efficacy. On similar dealings in another region, see Yodelis, "Who Paid the Piper?," 1–49.

26. Davidson, *Propaganda and the American Revolution*, 225. See also, Schlesinger, *Prelude to Independence*, 297.

27. Botein, "Meer Mechanics," 210–11; Silver, "Edes," 248–53, quotation on 252. Silver's article reprints much source material verbatim.

28. Silver, "Edes," 250–61; Buckingham, *Specimens*, 1:165–96; Schlesinger, *Prelude to Independence*, 71–72, 91–93, 178–79; Thomas, *History of Printing*, ed. McCorison, 134–37; Kobre, *Development of the Colonial Newspaper*, 118–27. For Hancock's and Church's advertisements, see almost any issue of the *Boston Gazette* during the 1760s.

29. Thomas, *History of Printing*, ed. McCorison, 137; *Boston Gazette*, 1 January 1797, reprinted in Buckingham, *Specimens*, 1:201–202.

30. Thomas, *History of Printing*, ed. McCorison, 136–37; Buckingham, *Specimens*, 1:196–205; Silver, "Edes," 262–68.

31. Silver, "Edes"; *Boston Gazette*, 1 Jan. 1797; Buckingham, *Specimens*, 1:201–202, 199, 202, 204–205.

32. Cutler, *Connecticut's Revolutionary Press*, 60; Morse, *Connecticut Newspapers*, 15–16; Buckingham, *Specimens*, 1:240–45; Shipton, *Isaiah Thomas*, 32–67.

33. On Russell, see Hench, "Newspaper in a Republic"; and Buckingham, *Specimens*, 2:1–117. On Goodwin, see Smith, *One Hundred Years of Hartford's "Courant"*. A good account of the backlash among the Revolutionary gentry against some aspects of the Revolution, especially the volatile, populistic politics that had come to characterize the state governments, can be found in Wood, "Interests and Disinterestedness."

34. Ebenezer Hazard to Jeremy Belknap, 18 Dec. 1782, "Belknap Papers," 2:168.

35. Brunhouse, *Counter-Revolution in Pennsylvania*, 5–6, 121–26. Oswald was the most controversial editor of the 1780s by far. See Teeter, "Printer and Chief Justice," 235–42; Teeter, "Press Freedom and Public Printing," 445–51; Ashley, *American Newspaper Journalists*, 334–38.

36. Thomas Jefferson to Edward Carrington, 16 Jan. 1787, *PTJ*, 11:49.

37. Cranfield, *Press and Society*, 11–30.

38. Ibid., 41–48; Black, *English Press in the Eighteenth Century*, 135–51; Aspinall, *Politics and the Press*, especially 67–68; Harris, *London Newspapers in the Age of Walpole*, especially 119–21, 117; Boyce et al., *Newspaper History*, 82–97.

39. Alexander, *Selling of the Constitutional Convention*.

40. Heideking, "Die amerikanische Presse und die Verfassungsdebatte"; Charles E. Clark, *Printers, the People and Politics*; Rutland, "First Great Newspaper Debate," 43–58. I am grateful to John P. Kaminski for calling my attention to Heideking's study. Obviously the Constitution's opponents produced a large body of writings as well, as found in modern collections like the *DHRC*, but the evidence is clear that the antifederalist writings were much less widely disseminated. Supporters of the proposed federal constitution in 1787–88 are referred to in the text as "federalists" (lower-case), in order to distinguish them from supporters of the later Federalist party. While overlapping, the two groups were not the same.

41. Clark, *Printers, People and Politics*, 12–18, 35–37; *DHRC: Rat. by States*, 3:329–30; Morse, *Connecticut Newspapers*, 15; Hartford *Connecticut Courant*, 10, 24 Dec. 1787, in *DHRC: Rat. by States*, 3:492–93; "The Landloser," Hartford *American Mercury*, 7 Jan. 1788, in *DHRC: Rat. by States*, Microfiche Supplement, Connecticut document no. 64.

42. Hofstadter, *Idea of a Party System;* Ketcham, *Presidents above Party;* Wallace, "Ideologies of Party."

43. "A Pennsylvania Mechanic," Philadelphia *Independent Gazetteer,* 29 Oct. 1787, in *DHRC: Rat. by States,* Microfiche Supplement, Pa. Doc. no. 170. The practice of polite writers using literary personae that were well known in their set is described in Shields, *Civil Tongues and Polite Letters.* The problem may have been that the antifederal writer really was unknown to elite readers, because an outsider to their social circles. The federalist irritation with such a contribution to the printed public sphere reveals the truly fictional nature of its outward personlessness and inclusiveness.

44. "Galba," Philadelphia *Independent Gazetteer,* 31 Oct. 1787, in *DHRC: Rat. by States,* Microfiche Supplement, Pa. doc. no. 174; also see Pa. doc. no. 185; "PROPOSALS for a Literary Register," *Gazette of the State of Georgia,* 29 Nov. 1787, in *DHRC: Rat. by States,* 3:248–51; "Philadelphiensis I," Philadelphia *Freeman's Journal,* 7 Nov. 1787, in *DHRC: Rat. by States.,* 2:280–85.

45. Nerone, *Violence against the Press,* 60–63; Walters, *Dallas,* 18–20. For an overview of federalist reprisals nationwide, see Rutland, "Great Newspaper Debate," 50–51.

46. At this point, I depart somewhat from Stephen Botein's interpretation, especially the part of it summed up in the following statement: "During the Revolutionary years, the trade adapted to a new politics of controversy. By so doing, printers seemed assured of recognition as major figures in the political life of the republic. . . . they would be expected not only to register events but to make and modify them." ("Printers and the Revolution," 49) Clearly, the Revolutionary gentry expected to "make and modify" events using the press, but there is really no evidence of printers taking the lead in politics before the late 1790s. Even then, and for long after, printers became political actors in their own right only over the resistance of more traditional political leaders.

47. Botein, "Printers and the Revolution," 6, 11, 51, 49–57; Silver, *American Printer,* 22–25, 14; Stewart, *Documentary History,* 6, 59 (quoted).

48. Bailyn and Hench, *Press and the Revolution,* 1, 9–10, 53; Thomas, *History of Printing in America;* Buckingham, *Specimens;* Stewart, *Documentary History,* 59.

49. Rosalind Remer describes specialization of printing during the 1790s in *Printers and Men of Capital,* with pages 24–38 focusing on the emergence of a political specialty.

50. On "competency" as the typical life goal of early American artisans and farmers, see Vickers, "Competency and Competition."

3. THE TWO NATIONAL *GAZETTES* AND THE BEGINNINGS OF NEWSPAPER POLITICS

1. Smith, *Press, Politics, and Patronage,* 1–11; John, *Spreading the News,* 30–42. Postal policy had its greatest impact in helping newspapers circulate nationally and within areas of dispersed settlement such as the South and West. Private carriers usually distributed newspapers to local subscribers. Newsboys, often the printer's own apprentices, did the job in urban areas, while in thickly settled rural districts, local newspapers were delivered by post riders who also performed various other jobs for people along the route, such as bringing mail from the local post office and running errands. See Mott, *American Journalism,* 105–106; Prentiss Autobiography, AAS, 41; Hamilton, *Country Printer,* 216–22.

2. The highest circulation figure I have seen cited (for the late eighteenth century) is 4,000 for the Boston *Columbian Centinel*, and this is probably exaggerated. A figure approaching 2,000 was probably more common for the most successful urban newspapers, and even that many copies required many workers, multiple presses, or more expensive iron presses that were rare in America before the 1820s. Cylinder and steam-powered presses were first developed in the 1790s and 1820s, respectively, but had little impact on the newspaper industry until much later. See Mott, *American Journalism*, 158–59; Brigham, *Journals and Journeymen*, 19–22; Wroth, *Colonial Printer*, 79–86; Moran, *Printing Presses*, 47–141; Silver, *American Printer*, 37–59.

3. For a study of the fully developed party press of the 1830s that bears these observations out, see Kielbowicz, "Party Press Cohesiveness."

4. The most judicious secondary treatment of Fenno is John B. Hench's introduction to "Letters of Fenno," 89: 299–306, while chapter 1 of Marcus Daniel's recently completed dissertation, "Ribaldry and Billingsgate," is probably the most thorough. On Fenno's father and his work for Russell, see Jeremy Belknap to Ebenezer Hazard, 2, 8 May 1789, "Belknap Papers," 3:123–25; and John Fenno to Joseph Ward, 20 Dec. 1789, Hench, "Letters of Fenno," 89:352.

5. Christopher Gore to Rufus King, 18 Jan. 1789, *Life and Correspondence of King*, 1:357; John Fenno, "An Address," 1 Jan. 1789, Agreement of John Fenno with John Lucas, Joseph Ward, Christopher Gore, Thomas Russell, James Bowdoin, Saml. Eliot, Jonathan Mason, and Caleb Davis, 1 Jan. 1789, in Hench, "Letters of Fenno," 89:312–14, 311; John Fenno to Mary Curtiss Fenno, 4 Feb. 1789, Fenno-Hoffman Papers, Clements Library.

6. Belknap to Hazard, 2 May [1789], "Belknap Papers," 3:123; John Fenno to Joseph Ward, 5 April 1789, Hench, "Letters of Fenno," 89:325.

7. Botein, "Printers and the Revolution," 11–57; Humphrey, *This Popular Engine*, 23–43; Wroth, *Colonial Printer*, 169–90, 230–36; Hamilton, *Country Printer*, 47–92; Yodelis, "Who Paid the Piper?"; Clark, *Public Prints*, 193–214. Statistics taken from Weiss, *Graphic Summary*, 7–9.

8. Franklin, *Benjamin Franklin's Autobiography*, 85, 91; Van Doren, *Franklin*, 106–23, 127–29; Wright, *Franklin of Philadelphia*, 53–55; Clark, *Public Prints*, 205–207.

9. Botein, "Printers and the Revolution," 17.

10. *GUS*, 15 April 1789; Anderson, *Imagined Communities*, 62.

11. *GUS*, 15 April 1789. Fenno's avoidance of local ties and references resembles the intentionally vague, "generic" quality that David Waldstreicher (*Perpetual Fetes*, 30–39) has noted in nationalist celebrations during the American Revolution.

12. John Fenno to Joseph Ward, 5 April 1789, Hench, "Letters of Fenno," 89:324; John Fenno to Mary Curtiss Fenno, 22 March 1789, Fenno-Hoffman Papers, Clements Library.

13. John Fenno to Joseph Ward, 28 Jan., 17, 23 Feb. 1789, Hench, "Letters of Fenno," 89:315, 320–21; John Fenno to Mary Curtiss Fenno, 4 , 7 Feb., 8 March 1789, Fenno-Hoffman Papers, Clements Library.

14. Fenno to Ward, 5 Aug. ("auxiliary"), 5 April ("Men of Sense") 1789, Hench, "Letters of Fenno," 89:334, 324; Miller, *Federalist Era*, 6–8. On the use of monarchs' images to build national loyalty, see Colley, *Britons*, 195–236.

15. *GUS*, 22, 28, 25 April, 6 May, 14 Nov. 1789.

16. Ibid., 15 April 1789; John Fenno to Joseph Ward, 9 Oct. 1789, Hench, "Letters of Fenno," 89:342.

17. John Fenno to Joseph Ward, 5 July, 5 April 1789, Hench, "Letters of Fenno," 89:329, 324.

18. *GUS*, 12 Dec. 1789 (quoting Stockbridge *Western Star*), 18 Sept., 21 April 1790; Fenno to Ward, 28 Nov. 1789, Hench, "Letters of Fenno," 89:348.

19. John Fenno to Joseph Ward, 26 July, 5 Aug. 1789, Hench, "Letters of Fenno," 89:332, 334.

20. John Fenno to Joseph Ward, 8 Oct., 5 Aug. 1789, ibid., 89:339, 334.

21. Handover, *History of London Gazette*, 19–66.

22. *GUS*, 27 April 1791; Fenno to Hamilton, 9 Nov. 1793, *PAH*, 15:393–94; John Fenno to Mary Curtiss Fenno, 31 May, 20 and 27 July 1798, Fenno-Hoffman Papers, Clements Library. While women had been mobilized to a degree during the Revolution, male disapproval of females discussing or involving themselves in politics outside of certain ritualized occasions such as parades reasserted itself and grew stronger as parties developed and political campaigns became more rough and intense. See Baker, "Domestication of American Politics."

23. John Fenno to Joseph Ward, 28 Nov., 9 Oct., 28 Nov. 1789, Hench, "Letters of Fenno," 89:348,340–42, 348; *GUS*, 28 Nov. 1789. Johnson quoted in Handover, *History of London Gazette*, 53.

24. John Fenno to Joseph Ward, 11 April 1790, Hench, "Letters of Fenno," 89:360; Treasury Department accounts, *PAH*, 13:106, 142; Hamilton's "Cash Book," *PAH*, 3:58.

25. John Fenno to Joseph Ward, 14 Nov. 1793, Hench, "Letters of Fenno," 90:187.

26. Ibid.; John Fenno to Alexander Hamilton, 9 Nov. 1793, Alexander Hamilton to Rufus King, [11 Nov. 1793], Hamilton to John Kean, 29 Nov. 1793, *PAH*, 15:393–94, 395–96, 418.

27. Fenno to Ward, 14 Nov. 1793, Hench, "Letters of Fenno," 90:187.

28. John Fenno to Joseph Ward, 8 Oct. 1789, ibid., 89:339.

29. Fenno to Ward, 11 April 1790, ibid., 89:360.

30. Thomas Jefferson to James Madison, 9 May 1791, *PTJ*, 20:293. A balanced assessment of Adams's views can be found in Shaw, *Character of John Adams*, 230–36

31. Thomas Jefferson, "Notes of a Conversation with George Washington," 1 Oct. 1792, *PTJ*, 24:435; McCoy, *Elusive Republic*, 136–65; Banning, *Jeffersonian Persuasion*, 126–60.

32. Thomas Jefferson to Thomas Mann Randolph, 15 May 1791, *PTJ*, 20:416; Popkin, *News and Politics in the Age of Revolution*, 8–9, 122–23; Thomas Jefferson to George Washington, 9 Sept. 1792, *PTJ*, 24:356–57; *GUS*, 6 November 1790 ff., 11 Dec. 1790 ff., 27 April 1791 ff.

33. Jefferson to Carrington, 16 Jan. 1787, *PTJ*, 11:49.

34. Ibid.

35. Thomas Jefferson to [Benjamin Franklin Bache], 28 April 1791, Bache Papers, Castle Collection, APS.

36. Jefferson to Randolph, 15 May 1791, *PTJ*, 20:416. There are many secondary accounts of Jefferson's newspaper project, the best of which are Cunningham, *Jeffersonian Republicans*, 13–19; Smith, *Press, Politics and Patronage*, 12–23; and Editorial Note, "Jefferson, Freneau and the Founding of the *National Gazette*," in *PTJ*, 20:718–53. See also Daniel, "Ribaldry and Billingsgate," chap. 2.

37. James Madison to Edmund Randolph, 13 Sept. 1792, *PJM*, 14:365.

38. Ibid.; James Madison to Thomas Jefferson, 1 May 1791, *PJM*, 14:15; Jefferson to Madison, 21 July 1791, *PTJ*, 20:657.

39. Among the many works describing the founding generation's political morality are Ketcham, *Presidents above Party;* and Hofstadter, *Idea of a Party System,* 1–73. For Madison's acknowledgment that the incipient opposition was a party, see his essays "Parties" and "A Candid State of Parties," Philadelphia *National Gazette,* 23 Jan., 26 Sept. 1792, and *PJM,* 14:197–98, 370–72. The former essay roundly condemns parties even as it suggests that some might be inevitable and even necessary. Madison made a distinction between "natural" and "artificial" parties, of which the emerging Republicans were the former and Hamilton's Federalists the latter. For a perceptive account of the evolution of Madison's thought on parties, see Elkins and McKitrick, *Age of Federalism,* 263–70.

40. Jefferson to Washington, 9 Sept. 1792, *PTJ,* 24:356–57.

41. "An American, No. II," *GUS,* 11 August 1792, in *PAH,* 12:192.

42. Thomas Jefferson, "Anas," 11 March 1800, in Bergh, *Writings of Jefferson,* 1:435; Matthew Livingston Davis Memorandum Book, Rufus King Papers, Vol. 57, N-YHS, 25–26; Pasley, "Journeyman, Either in Law or Politics," 550–52, 560. A convenient summary of Jefferson's many entanglements with the press can be found in Mott, *Jefferson and the Press.*

43. Leary, *That Rascal,* 166–86; Thomas Jefferson to Philip Freneau, 28 Feb. 1791, Jefferson to Madison, 21 July 1791, *PTJ,* 19:351, 20:657.

44. Philip Freneau to Thomas Jefferson, 5 March 1791, *PTJ,* 19:416–17; Freneau, "The Country Printer," in *Poems of Freneau,* ed. Pattee, 3:63–64; James Madison to Thomas Jefferson, 24 July 1791, *PTJ,* 20:667; Philip Freneau to James Madison, 25 July 1791, *PJM,* 14:57; Cunningham, *Jeffersonian Republicans,* 17.

45. James Madison to Charles Simms, [post 23] Aug. 1791, Madison to Joseph Jones, Madison to Mann Page Jr., 23 Aug. 1791, Madison to James Madison Sr., 13 Nov. 1791, Daniel Carroll to Madison Jr., 22 Nov. 1791; William Madison to Madison Jr., 3 Dec. 1791, Carroll to Madison Jr., 12 December 1791, Madison Jr. to Henry Lee, 18 Dec. 1791, *PJM,* 14:73, 71–72, 107, 122–23, 137, 147, 154; Cunningham, *Jeffersonian Republicans,* 17–18; Thomas Jefferson to Philip Freneau, 13 March 1792, Jefferson to Thomas Bell, 16 March 1792, Jefferson to Washington, 9 Sept. 1792, Editorial Note, "*National Gazette,*" *PTJ,* 20:758–59, 24:357, 20:730–31; Daniel Carroll to James Madison, 21 Dec. 1791, 8 Jan. 1792, Henry Lee to Madison, 8 Jan. 1792, Madison to Lee, 21 Jan. 1792, Lee to Madison, *PJM,* 14:175, 182–83, 183, 193, 219.

46. Philadelphia *National Gazette,* 31 Oct., 1, 8 Dec., 1791, 22 Dec., 9, 16 Apr., 3, 7 May 1792. The *National Gazette's* advertising peaked at slightly more than two columns in the issue of 16 April and dropped off from there as the editorial content became more partisan.

47. Ibid., 31 Oct. 1791–15 March 1792; Leary, *That Rascal,* 197–99. The first clearly partisan essay series, an attack "On the Funding System," by "Brutus," began 15 March 1792.

48. For Madison's eighteen essays for the *National Gazette,* see *PJM,* beginning with the editorial note at 14:110–12.

49. Philadelphia *National Gazette,* 2 April 1792.

50. Ibid., 26 April 1792. Much of the *National Gazette's* best material has been reprinted in Freneau, *Prose of Freneau,* ed. Marsh.

51. I am not claiming that they wanted a permanent party system at this point, which they did not, only that "republican" was being used to identify a particular group

of politicians, rather than merely a philosophical preference. James Roger Sharp makes a similar argument and calls the Federalists and Republicans "proto-parties" in *American Politics in the Early Republic.*

52. Philadelphia *National Gazette,* 30 April 1792.

53. Ibid., 7 May, 4 July , "A Farmer," 25 July, "Brutus," 1 Aug., 11 June 1792.

54. Ibid., 26 Sept. 1792.

55. Ibid., 22 Dec. 1792.

56. Ibid., 5 Sept. 1792.

57. Ibid., 22 Aug. 1792, 12, 15, 19, 29 Sept., 6 Oct. 1792. A good brief account of the 1792 election in Pennsylvania can be found in Walters, *Dallas,* 32–42.

58. Philadelphia *National Gazette.,* 12, 19 Sept., 10, 24 Oct., 17, 24 Nov., 1, 5, 8. 12, 22, 29 Dec. 1792.

59. Ibid., 4, 7, 25 July 1792, 24 April, 5 Jan. 1793; Freneau, *Prose,* 281–82, 288–89, 294–95.

60. *GUS,* 26 Jan. ("cacklers"), 2 ("wits"), 5 ("villains"), 26 May ("worst"), 6 ("effrontery"), 23 ("propagators"), 27 June ("brawler"), 1 Aug. ("enemies"), 4 Aug. 1792.

61. Ibid., 2 May 1792. This narrow, traditional "public sphere" is described in Habermas, *Structural Transformation,* 1–26.

62. *GUS,* 8 Aug., 26 May, 9 June 1792; Leary, *That Rascal,* 203– 204.

63. *GUS,* 26 Jan., 2, 19 May 1792, 13 Feb. 1793.

64. Sawvel, *Complete Anas of Jefferson,* 124.

65. Alexander Hamilton to Edward Carrington, 26 May 1792, *PAH,* 11:429 ("faction"), 431–32, ("malignant"), 435–36.

66. Hamilton to Carrington, 26 May 1792, *PAH,* 11:444, 442.

67. "T. L. No. 1," *GUS,* 25 July 1792, in *PAH,* 12:107; Leary, *That Rascal,* 209.

68. Philadelphia *National Gazette,* 28 July 1792, and *GUS,* 1 Aug. 1792, both in *PAH,* 12:123–25.

69. "An American, No. 1," *GUS,* 4 Aug. 1792, in *PAH,* 12:159.

70. Madison to E. Randolph, 13 Sept. 1792, *PJM,* 14:364–65.

71. Freneau's affidavit was published in the *GUS,* 8 Aug. 1792, and has been reprinted in *PAH,* 14:188n3–189n3.

72. Editorial Note, "National Gazette" in *PTJ,* 20:748–51; Granato, "Freneau, Jefferson and Genet"; Leary, *That Rascal,* 238–45.

73. *GUS,* 4 Aug. 1792.

74. On the fear of conspiracy as a political and intellectual force in early America, see Bailyn, *Ideological Origins,* 22–159; Wood, "Conspiracy and the Paranoid Style"; Hutson, "Origins of 'Paranoid Style.'"

75. "An American, No. 1," in *PAH,* 12:158–59. For other examples, among many, see *GUS,* 2 May, 8 Aug. 1792.

76. Philadelphia *National Gazette,* 24 April 1793, reprinted in Freneau, *Prose of Freneau,* 297–98. See also, Jefferson to Washington, 9 Sept. 1792, *PTJ,* 24:355.

77. Jefferson to Washington, 9 Sept. 1792, *PTJ,* 24:357.

78. Elkins and McKitrick, *Age of Federalism,* 282; Editorial Note, "National Gazette," *PTJ,* 20:752–53.

79. Carroll to Madison, 21 Dec. 1791, Henry Lee to Madison, 8 Jan. 1792, Madison to Henry Lee, 21 Jan. 1792, Lee to Madison, 6 Feb. 1792, *PJM,* 14:175–76, 183–84, 193, 219.

80. For example, a scan of one widely circulated journal, the weekly Boston *Inde-*

pendent Chronicle, turns up at least seven substantial *National Gazette* pieces appearing between 15 Dec. 1791 and March 1792, and four between 19 April and 4 July 1793, to take only two randomly selected periods. And this was a newspaper that had its own writers and took relatively little from the exchange papers.

81. Philadelphia *National Gazette,* 9, 27 Oct. 1793; Leary, *That Rascal,* 245–46.

4. BENJAMIN FRANKLIN BACHE AND
THE PRICE OF PARTISANSHIP

1. Gordon Wood has aptly described the revolutionary elite's political and social values as a "republicanism" that was opposed to both monarchy and democracy. Rather than out-and-out proponents of hierarchy, they tended to be "enlightened paternalists," willing to grant varying degrees of influence to popular opinion but preferring a polity in which patriotic statesmen of weight could lead as their consciences dictated, without the need of constant competition or incessant popular supervision. On this score, the leading Republicans had more in common with Federalist leaders than they did with activists such as Bache and John Beckley. See Wood, *Radicalism,* 95–225; Ketcham, *Presidents above Party;* Pasley, "A Journeyman, Either in Law or Politics."

2. In the past decade or so, Benjamin Franklin Bache has suddenly become a popular historical subject. Jeffery A. Smith has produced two works in which Bache is a major focus, *Franklin and Bache* and *Printers and Press Freedom,* while James Tagg has published a thorough biography. The most recent book involving Bache is Rosenfeld, *American Aurora,* a hybrid of history, anthology, and novel in which the author assumes the persona of Bache's partner and successor William Duane. See also Daniel, "Ribaldry and Billingsgate," chap. 3.

3. Benjamin Franklin to Richard Bache [Sr.], 11 Nov. 1784, Franklin, *Writings of Franklin,* 9:279; Smith, *Franklin and Bache,* 81–82; Tagg, *Bache,* 44–45.

4. Benjamin Franklin Bache Diary, 5 April 1785, Benjamin Franklin Bache Papers, APS; B. F. Bache to Richard and Sarah Bache, 11 May 1785, Society Collection, HSP (quoted); Tagg, *Bache,* 45–46; Smith, *Franklin and Bache,* 88–89.

5. Benjamin Franklin Bache to Benjamin Franklin, 1 Aug. 1787, BP-CC, APS; Smith, *Franklin and Bache,* 100–101; Tagg, *Bache,* 59–65.

6. Benjamin Franklin Bache to Richard Bache, 10 Jan. 1793, BP-CC, APS.

7. Benjamin Franklin Bache to Benjamin Franklin, 21 Dec. 1779, B. F. Bache Papers, APS; B. F. Bache Diary, 30 Sept., 2 Feb., June–July 1784, B.F. Bache Papers, APS; Tagg, *Bache,* 39, 27, 127; Smith, *Franklin and Bache,* 60.

8. Van Doren, *Franklin,* 655–58, 709–10; Tagg, *Bache,* 127–28. On these men as journalist-politicians, see Popkin, *Revolutionary News,* especially 35–95.

9. Darnton, *Literary Underground,* 14–70; Darnton and Roche, *Revolution in Print,* 3–66. On Bache forgetting his English, see Benjamin Franklin Bache to [Richard Bache], 15 Sept. 1782, B.F. Bache to [Sarah Bache], 27 July 1783, 9 Feb. 1785, B. F. Bache Papers, APS; Tagg, *Bache,* 29.

10. Benjamin Franklin Bache to Margaret Hartman Markoe, 6 Dec. 1789 (quoted), 20–22, 22–24 March 1790, BP-CC, APS; Tagg, *Bache,* 72–77.

11. Benjamin Franklin Bache to Margaret Hartman Markoe, 2, 10 May 1790, B. F. Bache Papers, APS; Bache to Fermin Didot, 7 May 1790, Typographic Library Manuscripts, Columbia Univ.; Robert Morris to Benjamin Franklin Bache, 28 July 1790, BP-CC, APS.

12. *GA,* 2 Oct. 1790; Benjamin Vaughn to Benjamin Franklin Bache, 1 Sept. 1790, 1, 3 Sept. 1790, BP-CC, APS; B. F. Bache to F. Didot, 7 May 1790, Typographic Library Manuscripts, Columbia University; Tagg, *Bache,* 100–101.

13. *GA,* 23 Oct. 1790; Tagg, *Bache,* 99; Benjamin Franklin Bache to Margaret Hartman Markoe, 21 June 1791, BP-CC, APS.

14. Jefferson to T. M. Randolph, 15 May 1791, *PTJ,* 20:416; *GA,* 1 ("Hydra"), 4, 5, 6 Dec. 1792.

15. *GA,* 7 Dec. 1792. The political upheavals in revolutionary Philadelphia are covered in Rosswurm, *Arms, Country, and Class;* and Foner, *Tom Paine and Revolutionary America,* 107–44.

16. *GA,* 23 Jan. 1793.

17. Benjamin Franklin Bache to Richard Bache, 3 Feb. 1793, BP-CC, APS.

18. Tagg, *Bache,* 165–66.

19. Benjamin Franklin Bache to Richard Bache, 3 Feb. 1793, BP-CC, APS.

20. Tagg, "Bache's Attack on Washington." Simon Newman, in "Principles or Men?" has recently shown that the "forms and manners" with which the Federalists surrounded Washington, such as birthday celebrations and triumphal "progresses," were continuations of the rituals that had formerly been used to honor the king. Thus it was far from unreasonable for radical Republicans like Bache to see these as signs of creeping monarchy.

21. *GA,* 31 Jan. 1793.

22. Ibid., 1 Jan. 1794.

23. [Bache], *Remarks Occasioned by the Late Conduct of Mr. Washington,* 65.

24. The eighteenth-century "public sphere" is conceptualized in Habermas, *Structural Transformation,* 27–117, and further conceptualized, more concretely described, and then critiqued in Michael Warner's works, *Letters of the Republic* and "Mass Public and Mass Subject." The most informative treatment of the founders' use of classical pseudonyms is Richard, *Founders and Classics.*

25. *Aurora,* 23 Nov. 1795.

26. [Bache], *Remarks Occasioned,* iv (quoted), passim. This pamphlet is attributed to Bache by James Tagg in *Bache,* 286–87.

27. *Aurora,* 5 March 1797.

28. Carey, *Autobiography,* 39; Remer, *Printers and Men of Capital,* 37–38; Carter, "Political Activities of Carey."

29. *Aurora,* 5 June 1798 (quoted), 11 Aug. 1802.

30. Samuel C. Johonnot to Benjamin Franklin Bache, 18 Aug. 1790, BP-CC, APS.

31. Wood, *Radicalism,* 298.

32. B. F. Bache to R. Bache [Sr.], 3 Feb. 1793, BP-CC, APS.

33. Elizabeth Hewson to Thomas T. Hewson, 24 Oct. 1796, Hewson Family Papers, APS, quoted in Smith, *Franklin and Bache,* 147; Elizabeth Hewson to Thomas T. Hewson, 5 June 1797, Hewson Papers, APS, quoted in Tagg, *Bache,* 287.

34. Minutes of the Democratic Society of Pennsylvania, HSP, 2 Jan 1794; Tagg, *Bache,* 207–208. Donald Stewart calculated that at least thirty-two printers were members of various Democratic societies, and many of these were or became prominent Republican party editors. See Stewart, *Opposition Press,* 648–649n42.

35. Democratic Society Minutes, HSP, 5 June 1794; Foner, *Democratic-Republican Societies,* 84.

36. Democratic Society Minutes, HSP, 11 Sept. 1794, also reprinted in Foner, *Democratic-Republican Societies,* 91–93; Tinkcom, *Republicans and Federalists,* 108–109; Phillips, *William Duane,* 104–107; Michael Leib to Lydia Leib, 5, 11, 20 Oct. 1794, Leib-Harrison Papers, Society Collection, HSP.

37. *Aurora,* 8 Nov. 1794.

38. Tagg, *Bache,* 246–49. On the southern mission, see Margaret H. Bache to Benjamin Franklin Bache, 10 July 1795, BP-CC, APS.

39. Benjamin Franklin Bache to Margaret H. Bache, 8, 10 ("tool") July 1795, 15 July 1795 ("patriot"), New York, 18, 21 July 1795, BP-CC, APS.

40. Margaret H. Bache to Benjamin F. Bache, 2, 4 July 1795, BP-CC, APS.

41. The best account of the Philadelphia Republican "Grub Street" is Durey, *With the Hammer,* 74–79, quotation on 75. On Reynolds, see Twomey, *Jacobins and Jeffersonians,* 214–40; and Tagg, *Bache,* 285, 402–403. On the immigrant radicals generally see Phillips, *William Duane;* Durey, "Thomas Paine's Apostles"; Durey, *Transatlantic Radicals;* Jacob and Jacob, *Origins of Anglo-American Radicalism,* 313–28.

42. Matilda Tone to Margaret H. Bache, [circa fall 1796], BP-CC, APS.

43. Benjamin Franklin Bache to Margaret H. Bache, New York, 3 ("sold") July 1795, 3 July 1795, 5 July 1795, 8 ("not so well"), 10, 15 ("toad eaters") July 1795, BP-CC, APS.

44. Benjamin Franklin Bache to Charles Debrett, 3 Dec. 1796, BP-CC, APS.

45. These examples are taken from an advertisement headed "Political Novelties" that began running in the *Aurora* of 21 May 1796.

46. Remer, *Printers and Men of Capital,* 26–31.

47. When I call the *Aurora* a "party paper" here, I do not mean to portray it as a mere tool of a party organization. Instead, the term is meant to convey the fact that Bache's paper both promoted a set of beliefs and worked hard in election campaigns to elevate a particular set of men to office.

Bache biographer James Tagg argues that the editor was a "transitional figure," an "ideologue" fundamentally different or even superior to "the many who embraced mere party politics after 1800." (*Bache,* 401) To me, this obfuscates the nature of Bache's activities. The editor was indeed an "ideologue," but that by itself does not make him distinct from a party politician. Ideology was what drove Bache to be a party politician. After 1795, Bache and his *Aurora* successors were material and integral participants in every election that would be held in Philadelphia for thirty years. They were consummate party men. At the same time, they also held and fought for democratic beliefs as radical as any in the Anglo-American world of their day. Tagg tries to distinguish between "radicalism" and "partisanship" (ibid., 402–403), but in reality the two usually went hand in hand. Tagg demonstrates the problematic nature of the distinction when he lists Bache's successor William Duane among the party men or politicos and Dr. Michael Leib among the radicals. In fact, Duane and Leib were close political partners and together they would be one of the strongest forces in Pennsylvania politics in the early nineteenth century. On the Duane-Leib relationship, see Phillips, "Duane and the Origins of Modern Politics," and Phillips, *William Duane.*

48. For Bache's earlier regrets about the use of tickets, see *GA,* 11 Oct. 1794. For the 1795 campaign, see *Aurora,* 5 Oct.–24 Oct. 1795. For secondary accounts, see Miller, *Philadelphia,* 75–78; Tagg, *Bache,* 257.

49. *Aurora,* 9, 12, 13 Oct. 1795.

50. This sentence paraphrases Anderson, *Imagined Communities,* 62.

51. *Aurora*, 13 Oct. 1795.

52. Ibid., 13 Sept. 1796.

53. Ibid., 13 Sept.–28 Dec. 1796; Tagg, *Bache*, 290–96.

54. *Aurora*, 8, 15 Oct. 1796; Tagg, *Bache*, 294; Miller, *Philadelphia*, 86.

55. Tagg, *Bache*, 311–52.

56. Benjamin Franklin Bache to an unnamed *Aurora* subscriber, 8 June 1798, copy, BP-CC, APS (quoted); [Bache], *Truth Will Out!*, iii–iv; *Aurora*, 9 May, 9 Aug. 1798; Tagg, *Bache*, 328, 346–47, 370.

57. On Bache as the Sedition Law's "chief target," see Thomas Jefferson to James Madison, 26 April, 3 May 1798, *PJM*, 17:120–21, 124; Smith, *Freedom's Fetters*, 95, 107, 188.

58. *Aurora*, 9 May, 28 June 1798; Smith, *Freedom's Fetters*, 107.

59. *Aurora*, 27 (quoted), 30 June 1798; Smith, *Freedom's Fetters*, 200–202.

60. Tagg, *Bache*, 115n.73; [Bache], *Truth Will Out!*, iii; *Aurora*, 13 July 1798.

61. Francis Markoe to Margaret H. Bache, 4 Aug. 1798, BP-CC, APS.

62. James Monroe to Benjamin Franklin Bache, 8, 9, 30 Oct. 1797, 26 March 1798, BP-CC, APS.

63. Jefferson to Madison, 26 April 1798, *PJM*, 17:120–21.

64. Thomas Jefferson to Samuel Smith, 23 Aug. 1798, *WTJ*, 7:275–80.

65. Of the many secondary sources on Cobbett, the most relevant here is List, "Role of Cobbett in Philadelphia's Party Press." Possibly the most sophisticated discussion of Cobbett's American career (which ended in 1800) appears in Daniel, "Ribaldry and Billingsgate," chapter 5. Though one of the most well-known and frequently quoted editors of the 1790s, William Cobbett is not a major figure in this study because in my view he was (in his American phase, anyway) more of a satirist than a politician. Though the Republicans greatly feared the apparent popularity of Cobbett's publications, he largely stayed out of electoral politics, never writing, for instance, about the presidential election during the election year of 1800 (Daniel, "Ribaldry and Billingsgate," 539). Moreover, he had a distant, sometimes hostile relationship with many more mainstream Federalist leaders and editors. There is no doubt that, as Daniel argues, "the transgressive, iconoclastic" nature of Cobbett's journalism was "profoundly political" (Daniel, "Ribaldry and Billingsgate," 486) in a larger cultural sense. Yet his example was followed relatively rarely in America before the 1830s. Other editors used satire and engaged in personal attacks, in some cases exposing aspects of their victims' private lives. Yet there is no example I know of an American partisan journalist whose jibes and innuendos were anywhere close to as personal, frequent, and extreme as those of Cobbett, who blasted through even such strong taboos as those against attacking women and intimating the homosexuality of a public figure.

66. Cobbett, *Porcupine's Works*, 1:374, 6:52–53, 7:294–95; Philadelphia *Porcupine's Gazette*, 17 March 1798; Smith, *Freedom's Fetters*, 191–92.

67. *Aurora*, 3 July 1798.

68. Ibid., 27 Aug. 1798; William Duane to Tench Coxe, 14 Sept. 1798, Coxe Papers, HSP.

69. William Duane to St. George Tucker, 9 Sept. 1798, Tucker-Coleman Papers, William and Mary; John Fenno to Joseph Ward, 30 Aug. 1798, Hench, "Letters of Fenno," 90:228.

70. Notice dated 11 Sept. 1798, typescript copy, BP-CC, APS.

71. William Duane to Tench Coxe, 12, 14 Sept. 1798, 30 Oct. 1798 (quoted), Coxe to Margaret Bache, n.p., 13 Sept., 22 Nov. 1798, Coxe Papers, HSP.

72. Philadelphia *Porcupine's Gazette*, 3, 6, 30 Nov., 18 Dec. 1798, 27 Feb. 1799, 1, 3 May 1799.

73. Thomas Boylston Adams to William S. Shaw, 29 July 1800, Washburn, "Letters of Thomas Adams," 27:119.

74. These two paragraphs are particularly influenced by Warner, "Mass Public and Mass Subject."

5. THE BACKGROUND AND FAILURE OF THE SEDITION ACT

1. Stewart, *Opposition Press*, 3; Thomas Jefferson to James Monroe, 19 Oct. 1823, *WTJ*, 10:275; "On the Utility of Education," Wilmington *Mirror of the Times*, 4 March 1801; Fisher Ames to Theodore Dwight, 19 March 1801, Allen, *Works of Ames*, 2:1410–11.

2. Thomas Jefferson, "Notes on Professor Ebeling's Letter of July 30, 1795," *WTJ*, 7:48.

3. Stewart, *Opposition Press*, 624; Mott, *American Journalism*, 121–22; Fischer, *Revolution of American Conservatism*, 132. See appendix 1 for an explanation of how my newspaper statistics were constructed.

4. For the number of newspapers founded, see Hench, "Newspaper in a Republic," 280; Lathem, *Chronological Tables of American Newspapers*, 22–43.

5. On older journals in decline by the 1790s, see: Buckingham, *Specimens*, 1:198–205; Anderson, *Shepard Kollock*, 125–26, 142–43; Ashley, *American Newspaper Journalists*, 334–38.

6. See Buckingham, *Specimens*, 1:255, 267–91, quotations on 267 and 272–73; Hench, "Newspaper in a Republic," 48–52; Benjamin Franklin Bache to Margaret H. Bache, 8 July 1795, BP-CC, APS.

7. Hartford *American Mercury*, 8 Sept., 6 Oct. 1794, 20 July, 16 Aug. 1795, 25 April, 23 May 1796, 13 Feb. 1797; Elisha Babcock to Ephraim Kirby, 18 Oct. 1794, 4 Aug. 1795, 13 Nov. 1797, 17, 22 Sept., 20 Oct. 1801; Samuel A. Law to Kirby, 22 July 1795, Kirby Papers, DU; Briceland, "Ephraim Kirby," 139–54, 176–78, 198–99.

8. Another exceptional figure was Thomas Greenleaf of the *New-York Journal*, a committed antifederalist and leader of the Tammany Society. See Hudson, *Journalism in the U.S.*, 144–45; Young, *Democratic Republicans of N.Y.*, 120, 129, 203, 209, 252, 400; Buckingham, *Specimens*, 1:281.

9. Austin, *Matthew Lyon*, 1–89.

10. Matthew Lyon to Albert Gallatin, 4 Dec. 1803, Gallatin Papers, N-YHS (quoted); Austin, *Matthew Lyon*, 64–89; Rutland *Farmers' Library*, 1 April 1793 ff; *HBAN*, 1091, 1083.

11. Lyon's tumultuous early years in Congress are thoroughly covered in Austin, *Matthew Lyon*, 90–102.

12. *Annals of Congress*, 5th Congress, 2d sess., House, 1009–1017

13. Durey, *With the Hammer*, 76–77.

14. Washington *Herald of Liberty*, 12 ("Portrait"), 26 Feb., 16 April ("To Arm") 1798.

15. See John Israel to Israel Israel, 12 Oct. 1804, Coxe Papers, HSP. On Israel's membership in the Democratic Society and his occupational background, see Foner,

Democratic-Republican Societies, 440. A brief secondary work on John Israel is Prince, "John Israel." Quotation from John Israel to Albert Gallatin, 23 Sept. 1798, Gallatin Papers, N-YHS.

16. Israel to Gallatin, 23 Sept. 1798, Gallatin Papers, N-YHS; Washington *Herald of Liberty*, 12 Feb., 16 April, 19 Feb., 3 Sept. 1798.

17. Washington *Herald of Liberty*, 8 Oct. 1798

18. Ibid., 3 Sept.–22 Oct. 1798, quotations from 8, 22 Oct.

19. John Israel to Albert Gallatin, 15 April 1799, Gallatin Papers, N-YHS.

20. Washington *Herald of Liberty*, 11 Feb. 1799.

21. Tinkcom, *Republicans and Federalists*, 232, 235; Ferguson, *Early Western Pennsylvania Politics*, 151.

22. Washington *Herald of Liberty.*, 9 Sept. 1799–22 Oct. 1799, quotations from 9 Sept., 7 Oct., 30 Sept., 21 Oct. 1799; John Israel to Albert Gallatin, 6, 20 Oct. 1799, Gallatin Papers, N-YHS.

23. *Pennsylvania Archives*, 9th ser., 3:1585; John Hamilton to William Hoge, 15 Jan. 1800 (quoted), enclosure in William Hoge to Albert Gallatin, 28 March 1800, Gallatin Papers, N-YHS.

24. Hoge to Gallatin, 28 March 1800, Hamilton to Hoge, 15 Jan. 1800, Gallatin Papers, N-YHS.

25. Snowden and McCorkle to James Madison, 9 Aug. 1797, 25 June 1798, *PJM*, 17:41, 157; Evans, *American Bibliography*, entries 31906, 33485.

26. Chambersburg *Farmers' Register*, 18, 25 April, 2, 9, 16, 23 May, 6 June 1798. The proceedings of an apparently Federalist meeting appeared in the issue of 23 March 1798. The *Register*'s first Republican political essay appeared in the issue of 13 June ("Sidney"), but a Federalist rebuttal appeared in the next issue, that of 20 June ("A Citizen").

27. Alexandria *Times*, 10, 12 April 1797, 11, 31 July, 2, 15 Aug. 1797; Norfolk *Epitome of the Times*, 9, 16 April, 3, 14 May 1798.

28. Smith, *Freedom's Fetters*, 3–93, quotations on 24; Durey, *With the Hammer*, 107–109; Durey, "Thomas Paine's Apostles"; Durey, *Transatlantic Radicals*; Twomey, *Jacobins and Jeffersonians*.

29. Thomas Jefferson to James Madison, 26 Apr. 1798, *PJM*, 17:120; Smith, *Freedom's Fetters*, 95.

30. Addison, *Liberty of Speech and Press*, 18–19.

31. Rosenberg, "Addison and Origins of Federalist Thought"; Rosenberg, *Protecting the Best Men*, 64–87. Rosenberg's work called my attention to the importance of Addison's grand jury charges as sources for understanding Federalist thought on the Sedition Act.

32. Jefferson to Carrington, 16 Jan. 1787, *PTJ*, 11:49; Addison, *Liberty of Speech and Press*, 18, 19.

33. *Annals of Congress*, 5th Cong., 2d sess., House, 2098; Addison, *Reports of Cases*, 205. Allen's was one of the few speeches in the debate that focused on the broad rationale for the act rather than on its constitutionality. The new cultural histories of the French Revolution have rather agreed with the Federalists on the press's role in subverting the ancien régime. For examples, see Chartier, *Cultural Origins of the French Revolution;* Popkin, *Revolutionary News;* Darnton and Roche, *Revolution in Print;* Darnton, *Literary Underground.*

34. Addison, *Liberty of Speech and Press,* 20; *Annals of Congress,* 5th Cong., 2d sess., House, 2098. The text of the act "for the punishment of certain crimes against the United States," is conveniently reprinted in Smith, *Freedom's Fetters,* 441–42. The "cutting edge" nature of the Sedition Act is described in Levy, *Emergence of a Free Press,* 297–98; and Berns, "Freedom of the Press."

35. Stanley Griswold, "To my Children & friends," ms. memoir dated 4 Jan. 1801, Michigan Collection, Clements Library, University of Michigan.

36. Addison, *Reports of Cases,* 211–12.

37. Ibid., 210. Douglass Adair has argued for a similar concept of "fame" as the prime motivation of many of the American Founders. See *Fame and the Founding Fathers,* 3–26.

38. Addison, *Reports of Cases,* 210–11.

39. Addison, *Liberty of Speech and Press,* 20.

40. Addison, *Reports of Cases,* 203; Rosenberg, *Protecting the Best Men,* 82–89.

41. Addison, *Reports of Cases,* 159.

42. Wood, *Radicalism,* 23, 36–38, 63–64, 184–86. On the Federalist commitment to republicanism, see Kerber, *Federalists in Dissent.*

43. Jefferson, *Writings,* 290–91.

44. Quoted in Williamson, *American Suffrage,* 10–11.

45. Addison, *Reports of Cases,* 202–203.

46. Ibid., 213; *Annals of Congress,* 5th Cong., 2d sess., House, 2100.

47. *Annals of Congress,* 5th Cong., 2nd sess., House, 10 July 1798, 2140–2141.

48. Smith, *Freedom's Fetters,* 159–274; Shulim, "John Daly Burk," 19–36.

49. Shulim, "John Daly Burk," 31, 35–36; Smith, *Freedom's Fetters,* 204–220, 398–417; Hench, "Newspaper in a Republic," 174–79.

50. For example, see Levy, *Emergence of a Free Press,* 282–349; Berns, "Freedom of the Press"; Chambers, *Political Parties in a New Nation,* 140–41; Miller, *Federalist Era,* 228–42; Sharp, *American Politics in the Early Republic,* 187–225; Elkins and McKitrick, *Age of Federalism,* 719–26; Koch and Ammon, "Virginia and Kentucky Resolutions."

51. The "new libertarianism" is described in Levy, *Emergence of a Free Press,* 309–37, the latest version of a work first published in 1960. The existence of the new libertarianism is perhaps mostly strongly attacked in Berns, "Freedom of the Press," 135–42, while a milder, less sweeping demurral can be found in Rosenberg, *Protecting the Best Men,* 89–99.

52. Koch and Ammon, "Virginia and Kentucky Resolutions"; Beeman, *Old Dominion and New Nation,* 188–201, 204–206, 209–12, 215–16; Kurtz, *Presidency of John Adams,* 380–82; Gilpatrick, *Jeffersonian Democracy in North Carolina,* 82–123; Miller, *Federalist Era,* 242. On the "new libertarianism" not being implemented, see Rosenberg, *Protecting the Best Men,* 89–234; Dickerson, *Course of Tolerance;* Nelson, *Freedom of the Press From Hamilton to the Warren Court;* and even Levy, *Emergence of a Free Press,* 308–49.

53. Meriwether Jones to St. George Tucker, 2 Jan. 1800, Tucker-Coleman Papers, CWM.

54. Newport *Companion and Commercial Advertiser,* 2 May 1798; Newport *Guardian of Liberty,* 3 Oct. 1800; *HBAN,* 1:258–60, 2:1374; Matthias Bartgis to James Madison, Matthias Bartgis file, 24 Dec. 1802, Letters of Application 1801–1809, RG59-NA.

55. Collection problems are a constant theme in histories of early American printing and publishing. For example, see Hamilton, *Country Printer,* 59–60, 65–67; Brigham, *Journals and Journeymen,* 23–26; Stewart, *Opposition Press,* 17–19.

56. William Duane to Tench Coxe, 15 Oct. 1798, Coxe Papers, HSP; James Lyon to Thomas Jefferson, 14 Dec. 1800, James Lyon file, Letters of Application 1801–1809, RG59-NA.

57. Hench, "Newspaper in a Republic," 111–22.

58. David Chambers to Joseph G. Chambers, 23 Apr. 1796, Benjamin Franklin Bache to Joseph G. Chambers, 14 Sept. 1796, Chambers Papers, AAS; David Chambers Autobiography and Genealogy, Vertical File Manuscripts #3302, Ohio Historical Society.

59. New York *Time Piece*, 25 Sept. 1797.

6. CHARLES HOLT'S GENERATION: FROM COMMERCIAL PRINTERS TO POLITICAL PROFESSIONALS

1. Hofstadter, *Idea of a Party System;* Ketcham, *Presidents above Party;* Bailyn, *Ideological Origins;* Banning, *Jeffersonian Persuasion.* For a convincing application of republicanism to artisans, see Wilentz, *Chants Democratic,* 61–103. As we will see later, classical republican antipartyism was much stronger and more resilient among the political and social elite than in other strata of American society, because republicanism's idealization of social and political consensus and leadership by "disinterested" statesmen made little provision for the aspirations or interests of the middling and lower orders. See Appleby, *Capitalism and New Social Order.* Nevertheless, classical republican rhetoric and antiparty ideas were present in some form at all levels, especially in the 1790s.

2. Except where noted, the descriptions of Connecticut's political culture in the following paragraphs are based on: Collier, *Roger Sherman's Connecticut;* Gilsdorf and Gilsdorf, "Elites and Electorates"; Purcell, *Connecticut in Transition;* Daniels, *Connecticut Town;* Thomas, "Politics in the Land of Steady Habits"; Grasso, *Speaking Aristocracy.*

3. Swift, *System of the Laws of Connecticut,* 67–68, 58.

4. Foster, *Jeffersonian America,* 306.

5. Morse, *Connecticut Newspapers.*

6. Printers File, AAS; Hamilton, *Country Printer,* 278; *HBAN,* 52–53, 1432; New London *Bee,* 14, 21 June 1797.

7. New London *Bee,* 14 June 1797–24 Jan. 1798.

8. Ibid., 6 June 1798.

9. Prince, *Federalists and Civil Service,* 66–72.

10. New London *Bee,* 23 June 1802.

11. Charles Holt to Ephraim Kirby, 21 Dec. 1797, Kirby Papers, DU; Wood, *Radicalism,* 194–96.

12. Charles Holt to Ephraim Kirby, 25 Nov. 1798, 9 May 1799, Kirby Papers, DU; Briceland, "Ephraim Kirby," 199–202; New London *Bee,* 6, 20 June 1798.

13. Hartford *Connecticut Courant,* 30 Sept. 1799.

14. New London *Bee,* 14 Nov. 1798; Charles Holt to Ephraim Kirby, 25 Nov. 1798, Kirby Papers, DU.

15. Hartford *Connecticut Courant,* 30 Sept. 1799.

16. New London *Bee,* 23 June 1802, 14, 28 Nov. 1798; Charles Holt to Albert Gallatin, 29 Nov. 1801, Gallatin Papers, N-YHS.

17. Wright, *Anti-Shepherd-Crat,* 13.

18. Alexandria *Times,* June 1798–Mar. 1801.

19. James D. Westcott to Thomas Jefferson, 18 Mar. 1801; Westcott to Levi Lincoln, 18 Mar. 1801, Westcott file, Letters of Application 1801–1809, RG59-NA.

20. New London *Bee,* 12 June 1799.

21. Smith, *Freedom's Fetters,* 375–84; Grasso, *Speaking Aristocracy,* 454–55. On the accuracy of the charge, see Kohn, *Eagle and Sword,* 219–38.

22. New London, *Bee,* 21 May, 27 Aug., 24 Sept. 1800.

23. Morse, *Connecticut Newspapers,* 25–27; Stewart, *Opposition Press,* 617; Thomas Jefferson to Charles Holt, 23 Nov. 1810, Jefferson Papers, LC (quoted).

24. Buckingham, *Specimens,* 2:310–14; Duniway, *Development of Freedom of the Press,* 146.

25. Smith, *Freedom's Fetters,* 379–80.

26. Cunningham, *Republicans in Power,* 12–29; Briceland, "Ephraim Kirby," 300–342.

27. Holt to Gallatin, 29 Nov. 1801, Gallatin Papers, N-YHS; Vickers, "Competency and Competition."

28. Aronson, *Status and Kinship in the Higher Civil Service,* 10–14; Smith, *Press, Politics and Patronage,* 46–47; White, *Jeffersonians,* 347–54.

29. Prince, *Federalists and Civil Service,* 72.

30. New London *Bee,* 23 June, 28 Apr. 1802; Charles Johnson to Thomas Jefferson, 26 Apr. 1802, James Shannonhouse file, Letters of Application 1801–1809, RG59-NA.

31. Charles Holt to Ephraim Kirby, 21 June 1802, Kirby Papers, DU; Hudson *Wasp,* 12 Aug. 1802.

32. New London *Bee,* 23 June 1802.

33. *HBAN,* 1:583–85, 588–89; Miller, *Historical Sketches of Hudson,* 64–67; Matthew Livingston Davis to William P. Van Ness, 4 Feb. 1807, Davis Papers, N-YHS.

34. Hamilton, *Country Printer,* 175–76, 187–188; *HBAN,* 588; Hudson *Wasp,* 7 July, 12 Aug. 1802.

35. Hudson *Bee,* 17, 24, 31 Aug., 7, 14, 21, 28 Sept. 1802.

36. Hudson *Wasp,* 7, 17 July, 12, 30 Aug. 1802.

37. *HBAN,* 528, 583, 614; Hudson *Balance,* 18 Jan. 1803 ff.; Hudson, *Journalism in the United States,* 225; Mushkat, *Tammany,* 39–40.

38. Charles Holt to B. F. Thompson, 23 Feb. 1816, Book Trades Collection, AAS.

39. Charles Holt to Jabez D. Hammond, 7 Apr. 1818, Misc. Uncatalogued Manuscripts, NYPL; Hamilton, *Country Printer,* 124, 278; Munsell, *Typographical Miscellany,* 148–49.

40. New London *Bee,* 23 Sept. 1801.

41. Based on a biographical database created primarily from information in the Printers File, AAS, and *BDUSC.*

42. Pittsfield *Sun,* 16 Sept. 1800.

43. Detweiler, "Changing Reputation of the Declaration"; Travers, *Celebrating the Fourth,* 69–106, 161–63, 169–80; Maier, *American Scripture,* 170–72. Maier's focus on debunking the Declaration's importance as a legal document causes her to underestimate its powerful, posthumous role in tying the memory of the Revolution to popular aspirations for political democracy and equal rights. Ordinary Americans perceived, remembered, and interpreted the Revolution very differently than the statesmen who penned most of the founding documents. The most eloquent statement on this theme remains Young, "George Robert Twelves Hewes."

44. Levy, *Emergence of Free Press,* 297–98; Smith, *Printers and Press Freedom,* 156–67. I would distinguish this popular constitutionalism from both the theoretical "new libertarianism" discerned by Levy and the libertarian "trade ideology" of the colonial printers depicted by Jeffery Smith.

45. Chambersburg *Farmers' Register,* 18 April, 2, 9, 16, 23 May, 6, 13 (quoted), 20 June, 4 (quoted) July 1798, 20 Feb. 1799; *HBAN,* 836–38, 1426; Stewart, *Opposition Press,* 884.

46. Chambersburg *Farmers' Register,* 13, 20, 27 June, 4, 18 July, 22 Aug., 19 Sept., 17 (quoted), 24, 31 Oct. 1798, 27 Feb., 6, 20 March, 3 April 1799.

47. *HBAN,* 1448, 1485; Pittsburgh *Mercury,* 1812–1817; Printers File, AAS.

48. Norfolk *Epitome of the Times,* 17, 21 May 1798.

49. Wood, *Creation,* 393–564.

50. Norfolk *Epitome of the Times,* 21 May 1798.

51. Appleby, *Capitalism and New Social Order,* 51–78.

52. *Aurora,* 24, 25, 27, 30 April 1799. A good account of Fries Rebellion and the troops' behavior can be found in Elkins and McKitrick, *Age of Federalism,* 696–700.

7. THE EXPANSION OF THE REPUBLICAN NEWSPAPER NETWORK, 1798–1800

1. Cunningham, *Jeffersonian Republicans,* 168–74.

2. Uriah Tracy to Oliver Wolcott, 7 Aug. 1800, Gibbs, *Memoirs of the Administrations of Washington and Adams,* 2:399–400.

3. Cunningham, *Jeffersonian Republicans,* 166–74.

4. Thomas Jefferson to James Madison, 5 Feb. 1799, *PJM,* 17:225–26.

5. Cunningham, *Jeffersonian Republicans,* 169–172; Durey, *With the Hammer,* 104–106, 110–13, 119–20.

6. Thomas Jefferson to James Madison, 19 Feb. 1799, *PJM,* 17:234; Jefferson to James Monroe, 19 Feb. 1799, Jefferson to Tench Coxe, 21 May 1799, *WTJ,* 7:365, 378–80; Hugh Henry Brackenridge to Coxe, 3 Feb. 1800, Coxe Papers, HSP; Cooke, *Tench Coxe,* 352–53; Cunningham, *Jeffersonian Republicans,* 131–33; Ames, *History of Intelligencer,* 3–36; Washington *National Intelligencer,* 31 Oct. 1800.

7. Gilpatrick, *Jeffersonian Democracy in North Carolina,* 104–106, 108–109, 119–23, 129, 136; Elliott, *Raleigh Register,* 18–22; Ames, *History of Intelligencer,* 68–80; Twomey, *Jacobins and Jeffersonians,* 30–32, 52–53; Cunningham, *Jeffersonian Republicans,* 173; Stewart, *Opposition Press,* 11; *Raleigh Register,* 4 Feb.–11 Nov. 1800.

8. Andrews, *Pittsburgh's Post-Gazette,* 1–6; Newlin, *Brackenridge,* 209–10.

9. Brackenridge to Coxe, 3 Feb. 1800, Ezekiel Forman to Coxe, 14 Jan., 13 March 1800 Coxe Papers, HSP.

10. H. H. Brackenridge to John Israel, 10 April 1800, in Pittsburgh *Tree of Liberty,* 23 Aug. 1800; Field, "Press in Western Pennsylvania," 231–32; Alexander Fowler to Albert Gallatin, 25 Sept. 1801, Gallatin Papers, N-YHS; Cunningham, *Jeffersonian Republicans,* 173; Stewart, *Opposition Press,* 11; Brackenridge, *Recollections,* 70; Pittsburgh *Gazette,* 16, 23 Aug. 1800; Tarleton Bates to Tench Coxe, 15 May 1804, Coxe Papers, HSP; Pittsburgh *Tree of Liberty,* 23 Aug. 1800.

11. Cunningham, *Jeffersonian Republicans,* 173; *HBAN,* 2:1141.

12. Solomon Myer to Albert Gallatin, 25 May 1799, Gallatin Papers, N-YHS; *HBAN,* 2:992, 854; Field, "Press in Western Pennsylvania," 240.

13. Of 107 editors of strongly Republican newspapers who were identified, occupational information could be found for 93. Among that group, the three leading occupations were: printers, 80; lawyers,6; schoolteachers, 4. On average, each editor spent 13.2 years publishing newspapers, a figure that is somewhat low, because (except in a few cases where the information is unusually complete), it counts only newspaper work for which the editor was listed on a masthead, thus omitting time spent as an uncredited apprentice or editorial assistant. These statistics are based on a biographical database of partisan editors that was created using the Printers File, AAS; *BDUSC,* and myriad biographical works and local histories, most of them listed in the bibliography. For more information, see this book's companion web site at <http://pasley-brothers.com/newspols>.

14. For runaway slave advertisements in the *Raleigh Register* and other North Carolina journals, see Parker, *Stealing a Little Freedom.* The literature on this topic understandably focuses on the content of the ads and on what can be learned about slavery from them rather than on their role in the economics of the press. For an argument that slave advertisements played a strong role in buttressing the colonial press, and vice versa, see Waldstreicher, "Reading the Runaways."

15. Garnett, "James Mercer"; Egerton, *Charles Fenton Mercer,* 1–8.

16. Advertisement in Alexandria *Times,* 17 Aug. 1798; *HBAN,* 2:1114–15; Fredericksburg *Genius of Liberty,* 7 Dec. 1798; Robert Mercer to John Francis Mercer, 7 Jan. 1799, Landon Carter to John Francis Mercer, 7 Feb. 1800, Mercer Family Papers, VHS.

17. Durey, *"With the Hammer",* 114–15, 152–56. For an account of one of Jones's duels, against a rival editor, see William Radford to Gen. John Preston, 15 April 1800, Preston Family Papers, VHS.

18. Meriwether Jones to Creed Taylor, 9 April 1799, Taylor Correspondence, UVA; Palmer, *Calendar of Virginia State Papers,* 8:531; *HBAN,* 1403; Printers File, AAS.

19. *HBAN,* 2:1139, 1141; Durey, *"With the Hammer,"* 114–27.

20. Meriwether Jones to St. George Tucker, 2 Jan., 12 May 1800, Tucker-Coleman Papers, CWM; Jones to Albert Gallatin, 26 June 1801, Gallatin Papers, N-YHS; Jones to Taylor 9 Apr. 1799, Taylor Correspondence, UVA.

21. On the General Committee, see Cunningham, *Jeffersonian Republicans,* 149, 154; Cunningham, *Republicans in Power,* 180–87, 238; Ammon, "Richmond Junto." An original document showing the committee's membership and operations is Philip Norborne Nicholas, George Hay, Meriwether Jones, et al., to John Ambler, 1 Feb. 1804, printed but hand-addressed circular, Ambler Papers, VHS. For the membership of the committee and each of its county-level subcommittees during 1800, see Palmer, *Calendar of Virginia State Papers,* 9:77–87. On Jones's death, see Printers File, AAS.

22. Robert Mercer to J. F. Mercer, 7 Jan. 1799, Landon Carter to J. F. Mercer, 7 Feb. 1800, Mercer Family Papers, VHS; Meriwether Jones to James Madison, 13 March 1801, Meriwether Jones file, Letters of Application 1801–1809, RG59-NA (quoted); Jones to Taylor, 9 April 1799, Taylor Correspondence, UVA.

23. Baltimore *American,* 16–18 May 1799, 16, 18 May 1800. Also quoted in Cunningham, *Jeffersonian Republicans,* 168.

24. Pittsburgh *Tree of Liberty,* 16 Aug. 1800.

25. New York *American Citizen,* 10 March 1800; Cunningham, *Jeffersonian Republicans,* 168.

26. Samuel Morse to Ephraim Kirby, 2 July 1800, Kirby Papers, DU; Morse to Thomas Jefferson, 4 Feb. 1802, Jefferson Papers, LC.

27. Samuel Morse to Thomas Jefferson, 26 June 1800, Jefferson Papers, LC.

28. Danbury *Sun of Liberty,* 24 June 1800, reprinted in *Aurora,* 2 July 1800; Morse to Kirby, 2 July 1800, Kirby Papers, DU.

29. Lancaster *Intelligencer,* 31 July 1799.

30. Pittsfield *Sun,* 16 Sept. 1800.

31. Danbury *Sun of Liberty,* 24 June 1800, reprinted in *Aurora,* 2 July 1800.

32. Bailyn, *Ideological Origins,* 55–93, quotation on 56; Hench, "Newspaper in a Republic," 5–7, 181–233, quotations on 186–87.

33. Danbury *Sun of Liberty,* 24 June 1800, reprinted in *Aurora,* 2 July 1800.

34. Goshen *Orange Patrol,* 13, 27 May, 10 June 1800; *HBAN,* 1:577. Hurtin had previously published a nonpartisan paper called the *Goshen Repository.*

35. Portsmouth *Republican Ledger,* 29 July 1800.

36. Lancaster *Intelligencer,* 31 July, 7, 14, 21, 28 Aug., 4, 11 (chart) Sept. 1799; Higginbotham, *Keystone in Democratic Arch,* 110, 231, 353; Riddle, *Story of Lancaster,* 115–16.

37. New York *American Citizen,* 10 March 1800; Boston *Constitutional Telegraph,* 2 Oct. 1799.

38. An updated roster of 1790s editors who held office can be found at <http://pasleybrothers.com/newspols>.

39. For the application of the term "cadres" to Federalist editors, see Prince, *Federalists and Civil Service.* For a similar view of the basically deferential and traditional role played by Federalist editors of the 1790s, see Fischer, *Revolution of American Conservatism,* 129–34.

40. Washington, Pa., *Herald of Liberty,* 12 Feb. 1798; Wolf and Whiteman, *Jews of Philadelphia,* 31–32.

41. *Pittsburgh Gazette,* 23, 29 Aug. 1800; Newlin, *Brackenridge,* 214. See also, Prince, "John Israel," 50–51. Like many a Federalist printer, Scull was basically commercial in orientation. His bile against Israel and Brackenridge originated mostly in his irritation that his fourteen-year monopoly of the Pittsburgh printing business was at an end. See Andrews, *Pittsburgh's Post-Gazette,* 38–52.

42. Pittsburgh *Tree of Liberty,* 23 Aug. 1800; Washington *Herald of Liberty,* 12 Feb. 1798; Goshen *Orange Patrol,* 13 May 1800; John Israel to Albert Gallatin, 6 Oct. 1799, 2 July (with enclosure, ms. copy of indictment in case of *James Ross v. John Israel,* Allegheny County Court, Dec. term, 1800), 12 Aug. 1801, Gallatin Papers, N-YHS; Andrews, *Pittsburgh's Post-Gazette,* 49.

43. John Israel, "Address to the Citizens of Allegheny and Crawford Counties," Pittsburgh *Tree of Liberty,* 16, 23 Aug. 1800.

44. Pittsburgh *Tree of Liberty,* 23 Aug. 1800.

45. Wilmington *Mirror of the Times,* 29 March, 6 Aug. 1800.

46. This attempted newspaper organization preceded the development of a formal national party. The famous Republican "congressional caucus," often regarded as a precursor to the national party conventions, was in fact a completely informal gathering, with no official authority whatever. There were exactly two "caucuses" in the 1790s. A group of congressmen met in early 1796 to plot strategy on the Jay Treaty but did nothing about the presidential or any other election race. In early 1800, a random group of Republican congressmen got together at James Madison's boarding house to clear up confusion over the vice presidential race. That was the national Republican "organization" in a nutshell. See Chase, *Emergence of Nominating Convention,* 9–12.

47. *HBAN,* 2:1447; James Lyon, "Proposals for Publishing . . . the National Magazine," in New London *Bee,* 31 July 1799; Richmond *Friend of the People,* 5 July 1800. For Lyon's ads, see almost any issue of the *Aurora* from 1799 to 1801.

48. Benjamin Russell to Charles Prentiss, 20 Dec. 1806, Charles Prentiss Correspondence, AAS

49. Hartford *American Mercury,* 19 March 1801. For a lengthy contemporary essay on the Republican newspaper network, complete with reviews of how the most prominent journals performed in the 1800 campaign, see "Republican News-Papers," Trenton *True American,* 21 July 1801.

50. Donald Stewart reached a similar conclusion: "Quotations from [the *Aurora*] far outnumbered those from any other [publication] in the Republican press." See his *Opposition Press,* 612.

51. Trenton *True American,* 21 July 1801.

52. *Aurora,* 27 Jan., 19 Feb. 1800.

8. A PRESENCE IN THE PUBLIC SPHERE: WILLIAM DUANE AND THE TRIUMPH OF NEWSPAPER POLITICS

1. Duane has long been well-known to specialists in this period, of course, and his profile with general readers has recently been raised by his appearance as the "narrator" of Rosenfeld, *American Aurora.* The best secondary treatments of Duane, providing rich insights into the importance of his transatlantic perspective on American politics, can be found in Phillips, *William Duane,* and Durey, *Transatlantic Radicals.* The former work is a verbatim reprint of Phillips's 1968 University of California-Berkeley dissertation, in which form I originally read it. The book version has a new title, but the text remains unchanged down to the pagination. Besides being the best study of William Duane, Phillip's book is indispensable for understanding the political, social, and economic history of Philadelphia and the nation from the 1790s to the 1830s, and covers far more than William Duane's career.

2. William Duane to Tench Coxe, 13 June 1801, Coxe Papers, HSP.

3. Duane, *Biographical Memoir,* 1–2; Phillips, *William Duane,* 35, 5–6; *Memoirs of John Quincy Adams,* 4:508.

4. Duane, *Biographical Memoir,* 2–3; Phillips, *William Duane,* 5–10.

5. Phillips, *William Duane,* 11–21.

6. Ibid., 21–30; William Duane, Bill of Sale to Edward Shaw, [1794], Duane Family Papers, APS; John Kelly to Mathew Carey, 23 Jan. 1795, Lea and Febiger Collection, HSP (quoted), reference courtesy of James N. Green.

7. Phillips, *William Duane,* 30–32; W[illiam Duane], Memorial to Court, 26 Aug. 1795, draft, Duane Family Papers, APS; Hudson, *Journalism in the U.S.,* 211–12.

8. [William Duane] to I. E. Hay, [Dec. 1794], draft, W[illiam] D[uane] to Governor of St. Helena, 1795, draft, Duane Family Papers, APS; Phillips, *William Duane,* 32–33; Kelly to Carey, 23 Jan. 1795, Lea and Febiger Coll., HSP.

9. Phillips, *William Duane,* 37.

10. [William Duane] to Commander of St. Helena, n.d., Duane Family Papers, APS.

11. Phillips, *William Duane,* 34, 36–46; Duane, Memorial to Court, 26 Aug. 1795, Duane Family Papers, APS; Thale, *Selections from LCS Papers,* 312–13, 322–25, 328–31, 371n.

12. Thackara Diary, HSP (quoted); William Duane to James Thackara, 5 June 179[8], in Thackara Diary, HSP; Phillips, *William Duane,* 49.

13. Dwight, *Letter to George Washington,* 17–18, 47–48.

14. Duane to James Thackara, 5, 7 June 1798, in Thackara Diary, HSP; William Duane to Richard Bache, 11 Sept. 1798, copy, William Duane to Tench Coxe, 12, 14, 28 Sept., Oct. 1798 Coxe Papers, HSP; Phillips, *William Duane,* 54–61; Duane, *Biographical Memoir,* 6; *HBAN,* 2:891–92.

15. Duane to Coxe, 12, 14 Sept. 1798, 30 Oct. 1798, Coxe to Margaret Bache, 13 Sept., 22 Nov. 1798, John Beckley to Coxe, 12 Nov. 1798, Coxe Papers, HSP; Cooke, *Tench Coxe,* 346–47; *HBAN,* 2:891.

16. Stewart, *Opposition Press,* 235, 242–47, 333, 480, 500; William Duane to Ephraim Kirby, 3 July 1800, Kirby Papers, DU; *Aurora,* 12, 22, 24 Aug., 3 Sept., 5 Oct. 1799, 12 Feb. 1800.

17. William Duane to Tench Coxe, 7 July 1800, Coxe Papers, HSP.

18. Berkeley and Berkeley, *John Beckley,* 196–99; Duane to Kirby, 3 July 1800, Kirby Papers, DU; *Aurora,* 17 June 1800ff.

19. On Washington and Adams administration personnel policies, see White, *Federalists,* 253–322.

20. *Aurora,* 17, 18, 19, 20, 21, 23, 24, 25 June, 2 July, 5, 8, 23, 26 Aug., 2 Sept. 1800; Duane to Kirby, 3 July 1800, Kirby Papers, DU.

21. Baltimore *American,* reprinted in *Aurora,* 2 July 1800.

22. Pretzer, "Tramp Printers," 4; Silver, *American Printer,* 16, 25.

23. *Aurora,* 3 Aug. 1800.

24. A[rthur] Campbell to David Campbell, 21 (quoted), 26 Feb. 1800, Campbell Family Papers, DU.

25. Phillips, *William Duane,* 56–100.

26. *Aurora,* 4 Aug. 1800; William Duane to Tench Coxe, 3 Nov. 1800, Coxe Papers, HSP.

27. James McHenry to Philemon Dickerson, 3 Sept. 1800, *PAH,* 25:116; Hartford *Connecticut Courant,* 18 Aug. 1800.

28. "Circular," Nov. 1834, in Duane, "Letters of Duane," 391–94.

29. Phillips, *William Duane,* 71–74; *Aurora,* 16, 21 May 1799.

30. *Aurora,* 24, 25, 27, 28 March, 12, 14, 15, 16, 17, 19 May 1800; Phillips, *William Duane,* 84–92.

31. New London *Bee,* 26 March 1800; Trenton *True American,* 21 July 1800.

32. William Duane to James Madison, 10 May 1801, *PJM: Sec. of State Ser.,* 1:153.

33. William Duane to Thomas Jefferson, 10 June 1801, Duane, "Letters of Duane," 267–68; Duane to Albert Gallatin, 13 Dec. 1801, Gallatin Papers, N-YHS.

34. William Duane to Thomas Jefferson, 10 May 1801, Duane, "Letters of Duane," 262; Duane to Madison, 10 May 1801, *PJM: Sec. of State Ser.,* 1:153.

35. Duane to Jefferson, 10 May 1801, Duane, "Letters of Duane," 262.

36. Holt to Gallatin, 29 Nov. 1801, Duane to Gallatin, 13 Dec. 1801, Gallatin Papers, N-YHS; William Duane to Joseph Nancrede, 30 Sept. 1801, Duane, "Letters of Duane," 268–69.

37. *Memoirs of John Quincy Adams,* 5:117.

38. *Aurora,* 1 Sept. 1802; Salem *Register,* 10 Sept. 1802.

39. Trenton *True American,* 21 July 1801; *Memoirs of John Quincy Adams,* 4:508, 117, 5:112.

9. THE NEW CONVENTIONAL WISDOM: CONSOLIDATING AND
EXPANDING A NEWSPAPER-BASED POLITICAL SYSTEM

1. Miller, *Brief Retrospect*, 2:247–51, quotation on 251.

2. Ibid., 2:249.

3. Ibid., 2:253. As one example of this point, Miller might have cited William Duane's *Aurora*, the circulation of which, even according to a hostile observer, was "universal throughout the United States—and in every hovel of Pennsylvania it is to be found and read." (Quoted in Cunningham, *Republicans in Power*, 273.)

4. Miller, *Brief Retrospect*, 2:252–53.

5. Ibid., 2:254–55.

6. Thomas, *History of Printing*, ed. McCorison, 18–21, Thomas remarks at 20n.

7. There is a vast literature in political science defining and refining the idea of "critical elections" and realignments, the technical aspects of which I do not mean to engage. Works that I found particularly helpful include: Key, "Theory of Critical Elections"; Burnham, *Critical Elections*; Clubb, Flanigan, and Zingale, *Partisan Realignment*; Shefter, *Political Parties and the State*. "Critical elections" and their attendant realignments form the theoretical basis for the successive "party systems" that historians have described in Chambers and Burnham, *American Party Systems*; and Kleppner, et al., *Evolution of American Electoral Systems*.

8. Taylor, "From Fathers to Friends of the People." David Hackett Fischer makes a similar argument in *Revolution of American Conservatism*.

9. Historians might well dispute the lesson and credit Jefferson's win to Aaron Burr's work in New York or some other cause, but the widespread perception about newspapers is undeniable, as the evidence presented in this chapter shows. For overviews of the strong interest that both sets of party leaders took in partisan newspapers after 1800, see Cunningham, *Republicans in Power*, 236–74; and Fischer, *Revolution of American Conservatism*, 129–49, 424–29.

10. Dill, *Growth of Newspapers*, 22; Weiss, *Graphic Summary*, 4–5; Melish, *Travels*, 577; Thomas, *History of Printing*, 2:517–25. Thomas's figure of 359 newspapers in 1810 falls somewhat short of the 396 found by Weiss, using *HBAN*. I have used Weiss's figures to calculate the rate of increase. Two dissenting opinions against the thesis that the press was largely political in this period can be found in Nerone, *Culture of the Press*, and Fearon, *Sketches of America*, 228–30. Both books based their conclusions on the early newspapers of Cincinnati, a place where party politics was not yet well developed, and, problematically, take them as representative of the whole American press.

11. Lambert, *Travels*, 2:217–18, 3:124, 186, 247–51; Melish, *Travels*, 59–60; Tudor, *Letters on the Eastern States*, 124–25; Bristed, *America and Her Resources*, 316, 311; Holmes, *Account of U.S.A.*, 381–82.

12. Smith, *Press, Politics, and Patronage*, 41–55.

13. See the many references to Lincoln and Granger in Cunningham, *Republicans in Power*, as well as their many letters to Jefferson in the Jefferson Papers, LC, especially in the early years of his presidency. One of Granger's more extended descriptions of New England politics, immediately preceding his appointment as postmaster general, can be found in Granger to Jefferson, 15 April 1801, Elizur Goodrich file, Letters of Application 1801–1809, RG59-NA. Home in Worcester, Lincoln sent particularly detailed reports in his letters to Jefferson of 28 July 1801, 25 July 1802, 16 Oct. 1802, Jef-

ferson Papers, LC, and 24 Oct. 1801, John M. Forbes file, Letters of Application 1801–1809, RG59-NA.

14. Elisha Babcock to Ephraim Kirby, 29 March 1803, Kirby Papers, DU; Granger to Jefferson, 4 June 1800, 5 Sept. 1802, Granger to Jefferson, 18 Oct. 1800, Lincoln to Jefferson, 28 July 1801, 25 July 1802, Jefferson Papers, LC.

15. Lincoln to Jefferson, 28 July 1801, Jefferson Papers, LC.

16. Ketcham, *Presidents above Party*, 100–13; Hofstadter, *Idea of a Party System;* Jefferson to Francis Hopkinson, 13 March 1789, Jefferson to John Dickinson, 6 March 1801, in Jefferson, *Writings*, 940–42, 1084; Lincoln to Jefferson, 15 June 1801, Jefferson Papers, LC.

17. Lincoln to Jefferson, 25 July 1802, 15 June 1801, Jefferson Papers, LC.

18. Granger to Kirby, 8 March 1802, Kirby Papers, DU.

19. Lincoln to Jefferson, 28 July, 16 Sept. 1801, 1 Apr. 1808, Jefferson Papers, LC; William Lincoln, Manuscript History of Worcester Newspapers, Lincoln Family Papers, folio vol. 45, Lincoln AAS; William Lincoln, *History of Worcester*, 332–34; *HBAN*, 1:418–19; Collection Notes, *National Aegis* Business Records, AAS.

20. William Lincoln, *History of Worcester*, 235–36, 333–34; [Francis Blake], "The National Aegis; By Hector Ironside, Esq.," broadside circular included at beginning of the microfilm edition of the Worcester *National Aegis;* Worcester *National Aegis*, 2, 9, 16, 23, 30 Dec. 1801.

21. *National Aegis*, 13, 20, 27 Oct. 1802.

22. Ibid., 6, 13, 27 Oct., 3, 17, 24 Nov. 1802.

23. Ibid., 13 Oct., 17, 24 Nov., 15 Dec. 1802. Lincoln and Granger both approved and sometimes even urged the regional equivocation regarding Paine. See Lincoln to Jefferson, 6 Dec 1802, Jefferson Papers, LC; Granger to Ephraim Kirby, 19 Nov. 1802, Kirby Papers, DU.

24. Portsmouth *New Hampshire Gazette*, 9 Feb., 19 Jan. ff., 14, 21 Dec. 1802, 11 Jan. ff., 1 Feb. 1803.

25. Salem *Impartial Register*, 12 May 1800 ff.; Bentley, *Diary*, 2:112, 335–36; 4:53; Whitney, "Crowninshields of Salem," 8–13; Tapley, *Salem Imprints*, 79–83, 112. The Crowninshields are treated (perhaps somewhat inaccurately) as representative Jeffersonians in Goodman, *Democratic-Republicans of Massachusetts*, 113–18.

26. Salem *Register*, 4 Jan. 1802 ff.; Whitney, "Crowninshields of Salem," 18–29; Buckingham, *Specimens*, 2:333–34; Tapley, *Salem Imprints*, 113–27; Bentley, *Diary*, 2:452–56; Levi Lincoln to Thomas Jefferson, 13 Dec. 1802, Samuel Bedford file, Letters of Application 1801–1809, RG59-NA.

27. Bentley, *Diary*, 3:54–55.

28. On the *Political Observatory*, see Stanley Griswold to David McClure, 19 March 1804, Gratz Collection, HSP; Griswold to Stephen R. Bradley, 13, 24 Dec. 1804, 10 Dec. 1805, Griswold Papers, BHC-DPL. On the *Eastern Argus*, see Nathaniel Willis, "Autobiography of a Journalist" (1858), reprinted in Hudson, *Journalism in U.S.*, 290; and Fassett, *Newspapers in the District of Maine*, 107–108.

29. Wilmington *Mirror of the Times*, 8 Nov. 1800; Prince, *New Jersey's Jeffersonian Republicans*, 89–90; James J. Wilson to William Darlington, 22 July, 20 Aug., 26 Nov. 1801, Darlington Papers, LC; Cunningham, *Republicans in Power*, 240.

30. See the perhaps overly rosy discussion of Republican leaders' aid to newspapers in Cunningham, *Republicans in Power*, 243–46. If as heavily subsidized as Cunningham suggests, Republican newspapers should have been much more stable and profitable

than they were. For an example of a politician subscribing to distant newspapers, see the personal ledgers of western territorial official and former editor Stanley Griswold, which record subscriptions to newspapers in Cincinnati and Chillicothe, Ohio; New Brunswick, New Jersey; Pittsburgh and Philadelphia, Pennsylvania; Washington, D.C.; and Hartford and Litchfield, Connecticut. See Ledger, 11 July 1805–14 Dec. 1810, Griswold Family Papers, Baker Library, Harvard Business School.

31. Stanley Griswold to David McClure, 19 March 1804, Gratz Collection, HSP; Worcester *National Aegis,* 6 June 1804.

32. Robinson, *Jeffersonian Democracy in New England,* 68–70; Lodge, *Life and Letters of Cabot,* 349; Adams, *New England in the Republic,* 235–39; Paullin, *Atlas of Historical Geography,* 90.

33. *National Aegis,* 6 Sept. 1804 ff., 31 Oct. 1804 (quoted). This theme was general in the New England Republican press during 1804. The Portland *Eastern Argus* (23 Aug. 1804 ff.) was less single-minded but much more prolific than the Worcester paper, printing not only essay after essay of its own, but also reprinting extensively from the *Independent Chronicle,* Walpole *Political Observatory,* Norwich *True Republican,* and other journals. See also, Adams, *New England in the Republic,* 238–39.

34. Robinson, *Jeffersonian Democracy in New England,* 36–51; Purcell, *Connecticut in Transition,* 125, 139–68; Adams, *New England in the Republic,* 230–39.

35. Portland *Eastern Argus,* 6 Jan., 30 Aug., 16 Nov. 1804, 4 Jan., 24 May, 30 Aug. 1805. See also Fassett, *Newspapers in the District of Maine,* 118–19, 195–201.

36. Matthew Livingston Davis Memorandum Book, King Papers, vol. 57, N-YHS, 34–35; Matthew Livingston Davis to William P. Van Ness, 15 Aug. (quoted), 28 Aug. 1805, 1 Aug. 1809, Davis Papers, N-YHS. On the publishing history of the *Morning Chronicle,* see Kline, *Correspondence of Burr,* 724–27, 738; *HBAN,* 667–68.

37. Besides the *National Aegis,* examples of newspapers as politicians' fronts may be found in Cooke, *Coxe and the Early Republic,* 439; and Partridge, "Press of Mississippi."

38. Wright, *Anti-Shepherd-Crat,* quotation on 5; [Shepherd], *Report on the Trial of Andrew Wright; HBAN,* 389.

39. Tapley, *Salem Imprints,* 118–19, 134–40; Bentley, *Diary,* 2:453, 3:175, 178–79, 185, 188, 204, 244, 305; Buckingham, *Specimens,* 2:336–38.

40. Partridge, "Press of Mississippi," 502; Claiborne, *Mississippi,* 396–97.

41. *National Aegis,* 3 Feb., 24 Nov. 1802; Lincoln, *History of Worcester,* 233–37, 244–49, 333–34; Worcester *Massachusetts Spy,* 19 Dec. 1804, 16 Jan. 1805.

42. Orcutt, *History of New Milford and Bridgewater,* 170, 185, 256–57, 265–72, 597–99; Dexter, *Graduates of Yale College,* 4:476–77; Stanley Griswold, "To My Children & Friends," Ms. memoir, 4 Jan. 1801, Michigan Collection, Clements Library; Bishop, *Church and State;* Griswold to Ephraim Kirby, 14 Nov. 1801, 1, 6 Feb., 24 May, 28 June 1802, 15 June 1803 (quoted), Griswold to Kirby, 18 Jan. 1802, Griswold to Kirby, 10 Dec. 1802, Kirby Papers, DU; Griswold to Thomas Jefferson, 12 Nov. 1804, Griswold file, Letters of Application 1801–1809, RG59-NA; *HBAN,* 489–90.

43. Stanley Griswold to Thomas Jefferson, 12 Nov. 1804, Griswold to Henry Dearborn, 26 Nov. 1804, John Langdon to James Madison, 20 Dec. 1804, Stephen R. Bradley to Madison, 25 Jan. 1805, Griswold to Madison, 4 Apr. 1805, Griswold file, Letters of Application 1801–1809, RG59-NA; Griswold to Bradley, 13, 24 Dec. 1804, Griswold Papers, BHC-DPL. On the *Political Observatory*'s reputation, see most issues of the Hartford *American Mercury, Salem Register,* and Portsmouth *New Hampshire Gazette* during Griswold's tenure, especially in the last eight months of 1804.

44. Worcester *National Aegis* (Cotting), 16 July 1806 (and most issues from 9 July to 3 Dec. 1806); Worcester *National Aegis* (Trustees), 9 July; 10 Sept., 17 Dec. 1806; William Lincoln, Manuscript History of Worcester Newspapers, Lincoln Family Papers, AAS; *HBAN*, 418–19.

45. Stanley Griswold to Henry Dearborn, 26 Dec. 1804, Griswold file, Letters of Application 1801–1809, RG59-NA; Bentley, *Diary*, 3:341–42; Tapley, *Salem Imprints*, 138–47; Buckingham, *Specimens*, 2:336–40.

46. Binns, *Recollections*, 36–178, quotation on 160; *DAB*, s.v.; Higginbotham, *Keystone*. On the radical exiles generally, see Durey, *Transatlantic Radicals*.

47. Prentiss Autobiography, AAS, 36, 40, 51 (quoted); Higginbotham, *Keystone*, 99, 117, 235; Printers File, AAS; Field, "Press in Western Pennsylvania," 234–35; Pittsburgh *Commonwealth*, 31 July, 7 Aug. 1805; Hudson, *Journalism in U.S.*, 290.

48. Doggett, *Long Island Printing*, 10; Hamilton, *Country Printer*, 55–57, 289; *HBAN*, 1462, supplement:5.

49. Frasca, "Franklin's Printing Network"; Frasca, "Apprentice to Journeyman to Partner"; Pretzer, "Tramp Printers," 3–16.

50. Rorabaugh, *Craft Apprentice*, 76–96; Wilentz, *Chants Democratic*, 129–32; Pretzer, "Tramp Printers"; Botein, "Printers and the Revolution," 49–52.

51. John Norvell to Thomas Jefferson, 9 May 1807, Jefferson Papers, Missouri Historical Society. On Norvell himself, see Pasley, "Indiscreet Zeal of John Norvell"; *BDUSC*; *HBAN*, 1461.

52. Weed, *Autobiography*, 33.

53. Silver, *American Printer*, 58–61; Rorabaugh, *Craft Apprentice*, 76.

54. H. Chapin to Thurlow Weed, 13 Dec. 1816; James R. Reynolds to Weed, 15 Aug. 1817, 31 Jan., 30 July 1818; Samuel H. Moore to Weed, 16 Aug. 1817, 6, 13 Oct. 1817; Graham Klinck to Weed, 30 Sept. 1817; Augustin P. Searing to Weed, 11 Dec. 1817; J. Howe to Weed, 5 May 1818, Weed Papers, University of Rochester.

55. Weed, *Autobiography*, 69–70; Stevens, *New York Typographical Union No. 6*, 75–81, 98–100.

56. Weed, *Autobiography*, 70, 76–84; Reynolds to Weed, 30 July 1818, Weed Papers, University of Rochester.

57. This general conclusion is based on the Weed Papers at the University of Rochester, where a stark shift in the pattern of correspondence, away from journeyman printers and labor troubles, occurs in early 1819. On specific points mentioned in this paragraph, see Israel W. Clark to Thurlow Weed, 17 Jan. 1819; Solomon Southwick to Weed, 30 Jan., 18 Feb., 4, 11 April, 18 June 1819, 8 Mar. 1822; Obadiah German to Weed, 24 April 1819; Charles G. Haines to Weed, 7 Feb. 1820; Alden Spooner to Weed, 27 Jan. 1821; Benjamin Smead to Weed, 20 Aug. 1821; Charles Galpin to Weed, 18 Sept. 1821, Weed Papers, University of Rochester; Weed, *Autobiography*, 76–78.

58. Van Deusen, *Weed*, 22–37.

59. Thomas listed 172 Republican editors, for 126 of whom some biographical information could be found in the Printers File, AAS, or in standard reference works. There were 96 printers in this group (76 percent) and 54 officeholders (43 percent). Of the 54 editor-officeholders, 44 (81 percent) had been initially trained as printers. Given the frequent sketchiness of the Printers File on matters other than an individual's printing career and on areas other than New England and the Middle Atlantic states, the officeholding figures should be considered minimums. The detailed data on which

these figures are based can be found on this book's companion web site, <http://pasleybrothers.com/newspols>.

60. Wilentz, "On Class and Politics," 56. For two accounts of social mobility in the partisan newspaper business that emphasize its ambiguity and impermanence, see Gary R. Kornblith, "Becoming Joseph T. Buckingham: The Struggle for Artisanal Independence in Early Nineteenth-Century Boston" and William S. Pretzer, "From Artisan to Alderman: The Career of William W. Moore, 1803–1886," in Rock, et al., *American Artisans*, 123–52.

10. THE FEDERALISTS STRIKE BACK

1. *Washington Federalist*, 30 Sept. 1800.

2. Fisher Ames, "The Dangers of American Liberty," Ames to Jeremiah Smith, 14 Dec. 1802, Allen, *Works of Ames*, 1:135, 2:1450.

3. John Nicholas to Alexander Hamilton, 4 Aug. 1803, *PAH*, 26:139–40; Fischer, *Revolution of American Conservatism*, 129–34; Nevins, *Evening Post*, 12–13.

4. Keene *New Hampshire Sentinel*, 23 March, 20 April, 15 June, 25 May , 9, 16 Nov. 1799, 1 March, 20 Sept., 22, 29 Nov. 1800.

5. Ibid., 23 March 1799.

6. This paragraph reflects the overall theme of Fischer, *Revolution of American Conservatism;* and Banner, *To the Hartford Convention*, 216–67. See also Adams, *New England in the Republic*, 230–80. It will be seen below that I do not completely accept Fischer's argument that "young Federalists," a category not as clear-cut as Fischer portrays it, were able to make the Federalists into a "modern," viable party. In my view, the irreducible elitism and social organicism of Federalist ideology made this impossible.

7. Prentiss Autobiography, AAS, 53; Buckingham, *Specimens*, 24–112, especially 57, 110–111; Fischer, *Revolution of American Conservatism*, 261–62.

8. For the derivation of these statistics, see appendix 1.

9. *Washington Federalist*, 25 Sept. 1800. A similar statement from the Portland *Gazette*, founded 1798, can be found in Fassett, *Newspapers in the District of Maine*, 61–62.

10. Printers File, AAS; Hamilton, *Country Printer*, 261; Munsell, *Typographical Miscellany*, 146–47; Richardson and Richardson, *Charles Miner*, 20–23, 27–28, 52–58.

11. For somewhat overstated arguments about the change in the rhetoric of Federalist newspapers around this time, see Banner, *To the Hartford Convention*, 257–60; and Fischer, *Revolution of American Conservatism*, 129–49.

12. Morison, *Life and Letters of Otis*, 1:286–320; Fischer, *Revolution of American Conservatism*, 110–28, 150–81, 424–29.

13. Morison, *Life and Letters of Otis*, 1:299–300; Fischer, *Revolution of American Conservatism*, 140–49; Taylor, *William Cooper's Town*, 353–54.

14. Benjamin Russell to Charles Prentiss, 20 Dec. 1806, Charles Prentiss Corr., AAS.

15. Ibid.

16. Nevins, *Evening Post*, 19–20; Fischer, *Revolution of American Conservatism*, 137–38; Edward D. Bangs to Nathaniel Howe, 28 Feb. 1814, Bangs Family Papers, AAS.

17. Hudson *Wasp*, 7 July 1802 ff.

18. Nicholas to Hamilton, 4 Aug. 1803, *PAH*, 26:139–40; Ames to Smith, 14 Dec. 1802, Ames to Christopher Gore, 13 Dec. 1802, Ames to Theodore Dwight, 19 Mar. 1801, Allen, *Works of Fisher Ames*, 2:1451, 1446, 1411; Fischer, *Revolution of American Conservatism*, 133–38.

19. Buckingham, *Specimens*, 2:156–169; *HBAN*, 317–18; Bernhard, *Fisher Ames*, 332–34; Fischer, *Revolution of American Conservatism*, 136.

20. Mason, "Autobiography," 32–33; Buckingham, *Specimens*, 2:319; Nevins, *Evening Post*, 14–17; Hudson, *Journalism in U.S.*, 217–21; Mott, *American Journalism*, 184–85; *DAB*, s.v.

21. Fischer, *Revolution of American Conservatism*, 140, 364–65, 138, 346, 340; John Prentiss Autobiography, AAS, 42, 61–64; Charles Prentiss Corr., AAS; Konkle, "Enos Bronson"; Scharf and Westcott, *History of Philadelphia*, 3:1982.

22. Schauinger, "Hanson, Federalist Partisan"; Fischer, *Revolution of American Conservatism*, 366–67; Renzulli, *Maryland: Federalist Years*, passim.

23. Baltimore *Federal Republican*, 14 Sept., 29 July, 26 Aug. 1808.

24. Ibid., 4 July 1811; Schauinger, "Hanson, Federalist Partisan," 355.

25. Calderhead, "Strange Career in the Young Navy," 380–81.

26. Fisher, "Francis James Jackson and Newspaper Propaganda," 98–109; [Hanson], *Reflections upon the Late Correspondence; Trial of Alexander Contee Hanson;* Baltimore *Federal Republican*, 30 Nov. 1808.

27. Baltimore *Federal Republican*, 25 July 1808.

28. Ibid., 12, 16, 26 Sept., 2 Dec. 1808.

29. Ibid., 13 July, 30 Sept. 1808.

30. Fischer, *Revolution of American Conservatism*, 366–67.

31. Hanson, *Accurate Report of Argument against Baptis Irvine*, 39–40; Baltimore *Federal Republican*, 13 July 1808.

32. Baltimore *Federal Republican*, 13 July, 26, 31 Aug., 5, 7, 9, 14, 16, 21, 30 Sept. 1808.

33. These statements are based on my readings of Maryland newspapers for the 1808–15 period, when numerous reports of such debates appeared, and the long-forgotten work of David A. Bohmer: "Maryland Electorate and the Concept of a Party System" and "Voting Behavior during the First Party System." On the rarity of campaign speeches and debates in the Federalist-Jeffersonian period, see Dinkin, *Campaigning in America*, 12–13, 36.

34. In *Revolution of American Conservatism*, David Hackett Fischer has written eloquently of Federalist attempts to adapt their philosophy and methods to democracy, but in my view he overestimates their success.

35. Baltimore *Federal Republican*, 22 Aug. 1808.

36. Schauinger, "Hanson, Federalist Partisan"; Steffen, *Mechanics of Baltimore*, 155–66, 239–43, 279–81.

37. Baltimore *Federal Republican*, 20 June 1812. The article is reprinted in Scharf, *History of Maryland*, 3:4.

38. Steffen, *Mechanics of Baltimore*, 228–50; Swisher, *Taney*, 57–59; Renzulli, *Maryland: Federalist Years*, 247–321; Nerone, *Violence against the Press*, 67–70; Hickey, *War of 1812*, 56–67.

39. *HBAN*, 235–36; Georgetown *Federal Republican*, 18 Nov. 1808, 28 April 1815.

40. Georgetown *Federal Republican*, 10 March 1815. Hanson's election to Congress has sometimes been misinterpreted as indicating popular approval of his views and the

Federal Republican. The continuing Republican hold over Baltimore, and the safe Federalist nature of Hanson's congressional seat, can be seen in Martis, *Historical Atlas of Political Parties in Congress*, 73–84; and Martis, *Historical Atlas of Congressional Districts*, 234.

41. Schauinger, "Hanson, Federalist Partisan," 355–58, 361–64; Daniel Webster to Charles March, 7 June 1813, *Papers of Webster*, 1:147; Renzulli, *Maryland: Federalist Years*, 303–18.

42. Ferguson, *Law and Letters in American Culture*.

43. Ellis, *Joseph Dennie and His Circle*, 108–13; *HBAN*, 1402; Philadelphia *Port Folio*, 10 Jan. 1801 ff.

44. Goodrich, *Recollections*, 1:435, 2:118–22; Good, "Theodore Dwight," 87–96; Parrington, *Connecticut Wits*, xxxiii–xxxv; Fischer, *Revolution of American Conservatism*, 296–97.

45. "Mr. Hill's Letter to the Typographical Festival," 18 Nov. 1833, in [Bradley], *Biography of Isaac Hill*, 207; Buckingham, *Specimens*, 2:318; William Coleman to Charles Prentiss, 20 Jan. 1817, Charles Prentiss Corr., AAS.

46. Of 166 Federalist editors on Thomas's 1810 list, there were 138 for whom some information could be found. At least 109 of them (79 percent) were printers by training, comparable to the proportion of printers among the Republican editors (76 percent). (It will be remembered that a sizable, but unverifiable, number of these Federalist printer-editors were like Thomas Dickman and Jesse C. Tuttle, editors in name only.) However, only thirty-six Federalist editors ever held public office (26 percent), a much lower proportion than the Republicans (43 percent). Moreover, only 66 percent of the Federalist editor-officeholders were printers, as opposed to 81 percent of the Republicans. The differences are magnified if one removes from the Federalist numbers seven printer-editors who held postmasterships under the Washington and Adams administrations, on a mostly nonpolitical basis.

47. Figures based on *BDUSC*. See this book's companion web site <http://pasleybrothers.com/newspols> for a complete roster of newspaper editors who served in Congress through 1860.

48. To see the much greater volume of Federalist leaders' contributions, contrast *PAH* and Allen, *Works of Ames*, with *PJM* and *PTJ*.

49. Mason, "Autobiography," 32–33; Nevins, *Evening Post*, 25–34.

50. Baltimore *Federal Republican*, 9, 12, 14 Sept. 1808.

51. There were some notable exceptions to these generalizations, especially in New England and especially among the handful of politically active Federalist printers. For the close attention to politics paid by George Goodwin of the Hartford *Connecticut Courant*, see Goodwin to David Daggett, 28 Oct., 20 Dec. 1802, 28 March, 1, 9 April, 22 Aug., 15 Oct. 1803, 10 April 1805, 10 April, 23 Sept. 1806, 10 April 1809, 9 April 1810, 12 April 1811, 16 Oct. 1815, 27 Feb., 5 March, 9, 10, 11 April 1816, 9 April 1817, 22, 24, 25, 5 Oct. 1818, Daggett Papers, Yale; Smith, *One Hundred Years of Hartford's "Courant"*, 80–100.

52. *Washington Federalist*, Oct.–Dec. 1804; Hudson *Balance*, 16 Feb., 23 March, 6, 13 April, 1 June 1802.

53. Goodrich, *Recollections*, 2:143–160; *DAB*, s.v.

54. Philadelphia *Port Folio*, 10 Jan. 1801.

55. Ibid., 1 Jan. 1803.

56. Ibid., 4, 11 April, 2 May 1801, 18 Dec. 1802, 15 Jan., 23, 30 April 1803; "Equality III," *Works of Ames,* 1:245.

57. Philadelphia *Port Folio,* prospectus, included at beginning of the microfilmed edition.

58. Kerber, *Federalists in Dissent,* 1–22, 173–215. For a footnoted Federalist satire, see "The Triumph of Democracy," *Washington Federalist,* 8 January 1801. On the "insider" character of polite literature, see Shields, *Civil Tongues and Polite Letters.*

59. Fischer, *Revolution of American Conservatism,* 141ff., 424–29.

60. Hudson *Balance,* 22 June 1802; Hudson *Wasp,* 7 July 1802.

61. Worcester *Scorpion,* 26 July, 2, 9 Aug. 1809. On the Federalist self-image, see Taylor, "From Fathers to Friends of the People."

62. Hudson *Wasp,* 7, 17, 31 July, 12, 23, 30 Aug., 9, 23 Sept., 14 Oct., 2, 25 Nov. 1802, 26 Jan. 1803; *DAB,* s.v.

63. Boston *New England Palladium,* 7 August 1801.

64. Fisher Ames to Christopher Gore, 24 Feb. 1803, Allen, *Works of Ames,* 2:1457; Bernhard, *Fisher Ames,* 339; Banner, *To the Hartford Convention,* 259.

65. Nevins, *Evening Post,* 52–56; Adams, *New England in the Republic,* 271–75; Kerber, *Federalists in Dissent,* 23–66.

66. Hudson *Wasp,* 7 July 1802.

67. Fischer, *Revolution of American Conservatism,* 140–49; Kerber, *Federalists in Dissent,* 50–51; Malone, *Jefferson the President: First Term,* 230–31. Quotations from Hudson *Wasp,* 23 Aug. 1802; Philadelphia *Port Folio,* 22 Jan. 1803; Worcester *Scorpion,* 2 Aug. 1809. For other Federalist uses of sexual innuendo to attack Republicans, see chap. 4 and Phillips, *William Duane,* 243.

68. Printers File, AAS; *BDUSC;* Hamilton, *Country Printer,* 54, 83, 100, 150, 242, 292, 309; Richardson and Richardson, *Charles Miner;* Taylor, *William Cooper's Town,* 351–54, 358–59, 383, 384, 424.

II. IMPROVING ON THE SEDITION ACT: PRESS FREEDOM AND POLITICAL CULTURE AFTER 1800

1. Thomas Jefferson to John Norvell, 14 June 1807, *WTJ,* 9:73.

2. George W. Campbell, Circular to Constituents, 14 Apr. 1808, in Cunningham, *Circular Letters,* 2:572.

3. Durey, *Transatlantic Radicals,* 264–65.

4. Ames, *History of Intelligencer,* 1–67, quotations on 38.

5. Durey, *With the Hammer,* 143–71; White, *Jeffersonians,* 550.

6. Ambler, *Thomas Ritchie,* 18–20; Hudson, *Journalism in U.S.,* 268.

7. Margaret Ritchie Stone, "Sketch of My Dear Father," Ritchie-Harrison Papers, CWM (quoted); Ambler, *Thomas Ritchie,* 1–20; Malone, *Jefferson the President: First Term,* 225–26; Mott, *Jefferson and the Press,* 50–51.

8. Richmond *Enquirer,* 24 July 1854 (quoted), reprinted in Hudson, *Journalism in the U.S.,* 270; Ambler, *Thomas Ritchie,* 294–95; Dabney, *Richmond,* 129–30.

9. Richmond *Enquirer,* 23 May 1804.

10. Cunningham, *Republicans in Power,* 185, 238; Ambler, *Thomas Ritchie,* passim.

11. Palmer, *Calendar of Virginia State Papers,* 9:390–91. By contrast, the other Richmond newspaper proprietors, most of them conventional printers, simply asked for the office and sometimes even cited the low prices they would charge.

12. Richmond *Enquirer,* 9 May 1804; Malone, *Jefferson the President: First Term,* 225–26.

13. Thomas Jefferson to Charles Holt, 23 Nov. 1810, Jefferson to Thomas Ritchie, 7 Dec. 1818, Jefferson Papers, LC; Jefferson to Nathaniel Macon, 12 Jan. 1819, *WTJ,* 10:120; Mott, *Jefferson and the Press,* 60–61; Thomas Jefferson to John Adams, 9 July 1819, in Cappon, *Adams-Jefferson Letters,* 543.

14. On Grantland's printing background, see Printers File, AAS. The statistics on editors, printers, and publishers who served in Congress are a based on a study of *BDUSC,* the full results and details of which are presented on the companion web site to this book, <http://pasleybrothers.com/newspols>.

15. Cook, *Life and Legacy of David Williams,* 49–50, 52–57, 138–56; King, *Newspaper Press of Charleston,* 55–67, 73–75, 147–55; *BDUSC.*

16. For more examples of southern gentlemen as powerful editors, see Osthaus, *Partisans of the Southern Press;* and Dabney, *Pistols and Pointed Pens.* On Gales, see Ames, *History of Intelligencer,* 68–84; Durey, *Transatlantic Radicals;* Elliott, *Raleigh Register.*

17. See Durey, *Transatlantic Radicals,* 113, 187, 195–97, 285; Griffith and Talmadge, *Georgia Journalism,* 23–25; Bell and Crabbe, *Augusta Chronicle,* 20–27; Samuel Morse to Tench Coxe, 20 July 1804, Coxe Papers, HSP; and the files of the Savannah *Georgia Republican,* 1802–1805.

18. On the suppression of dissent in the antebellum South, see Nerone, *Violence against the Press,* 84–110; John, *Spreading the News,* 257–83; Eaton, *Freedom-of-Thought Struggle in the Old South.*

19. Levy, *Emergence of a Free Press,* 311–37.

20. Thomas Jefferson to Thomas McKean, 19 Feb. 1803, *WTJ,* 8:218.

21. Dickerson, *Course of Tolerance,* 26–27; Rowe, *Thomas McKean,* 337–38, 332–33; Levy, *Emergence of a Free Press,* 341; Thomas McKean, "Opening Address to the Assembly," 11 Dec. 1802, *Pennsylvania Archives,* 4th ser., 4:502.

22. Dickerson, *Course of Tolerance,* 22–25, 29–31; Levy, *Jefferson and Civil Liberties,* 58–69.

23. Hochman, "Liberty of the Press in Virginia."

24. [James Sullivan], *A Dissertation upon the Constitutional Freedom of the Press in the United States of America* (Boston, 1801), quoted in Dickerson, *Course of Tolerance,* 14, 15.

25. *Speeches in People against Croswell,* 47; Hudson *Wasp,* 12, 23, 30 Aug. 1802.

26. *Aurora,* 16 Dec. 1802; Danbury *Republican Farmer,* 30 May 1804.

27. *Aurora,* 5 Jan. 1803; Durey, *"With the Hammer,"* 167.

28. Hudson *Bee,* 17, 24, 31 Aug., 7, 14, 21, 28 Sept. 1802.

29. Ibid., 21 June, 19 July 1803.

30. Ibid., 2 Aug. 1802; Hamilton, *Country Printer,* 199, 274; Smith, *Freedom's Fetters,* 403–14.

31. Hudson *Bee,* 2 Aug. 1803.

32. Ibid., 16 Aug. 1803.

33. Savannah *Georgia Republican,* 6 Sept. 1803. The Republican Litchfield *Witness,* 7 May 1806, expressed similar views in response to the Connecticut prosecutions of Federalists.

34. Hudson, *Journalism in U.S.,* 289–93.

35. Wright, *Anti-Shepherd-Crat,* quotations on 19 and 17.

36. Rosenberg, *Protecting the Best Men.*

37. McKean, "Opening Address," 11 Dec. 1802, *Pa. Archives,* 4th ser., 4:502; Rowe, *Thomas McKean,* 333; *Speeches in People against Croswell,* 64.

38. Tocqueville, *Journey to America,* 64–65; Cohen, "Lawyers and Political Careers"; Eulau and Sprague, *Lawyers in Politics,* 11–12 and passim; Gawalt, *Promise of Power,* 4–5, 38–41, 62–63, 82; Gawalt, "Sources of Anti-Lawyer Sentiment"; Bloomfield, *American Lawyers,* 54–55; Hall, *Magic Mirror,* 49–66; Martin, *Men in Rebellion,* 80–82; Bogue, et al., "Members of the House," 284–85.

39. Gawalt, "Sources of Anti-Lawyer Sentiment"; Gawalt, *Promise of Power,* chaps. 2 and 3; Ellis, *Jeffersonian Crisis,* 111–13.

40. Ellis, *Jeffersonian Crisis,* 113–16; Gawalt, *Promise of Power,* 60–70, 81–82; Bloomfield, *American Lawyers,* 43–48; Hall, *Magic Mirror,* 67–77.

41. This is the overall thesis of Ellis, *Jeffersonian Crisis.* The following paragraphs also draw heavily on this work.

42. Trenton *True American,* 14 July 1801; James J. Wilson to William Darlington, 9 Sept. 1802, Darlington Papers, LC; Boston *Constitutional Telegraphe,* 31 March 1802; Buckingham, *Specimens,* 2:313.

43. Easton *Northampton Farmer,* 17, 24 Sept. 1808; *Easton Centinel,* 24, 27 Sept., 4 Oct. 1822.

44. Not all editors were radical Republicans, and not all lawyers were moderates, to use Richard Ellis's terms for similar points of view. Yet "radical" lawyers tended to be marginal practitioners like Republican activist John Beckley, while moderate editors tended to be more like the Federalist printers, political ciphers whose papers were controlled and written by gentlemen.

45. Litchfield *Witness,* 6, 21 Aug. 1805.

46. This has not been the view of many historians, who have followed Henry Adams (whose histories of the Jefferson and Madison administrations avenged his ancestors' defeats) in arguing there was increasingly little difference between the values and political culture of the Republicans and Federalists after 1800. Supposedly Republicans adopted Federalist policies, while Federalists adopted Republican political methods. The most tendentious examples are Levy, *Jefferson and Civil Liberties,* McDonald, *Presidency of Jefferson,* and Fischer, *Revolution of American Conservatism,* but the general theme has continued through many decades of scholarship and textbook-writing on the early republic. One of the primary pieces of evidence for this view is the way the Republicans and Federalists allegedly exchanged positions on press freedom, a contention that the rest of this chapter attempts to undermine.

47. For an analysis of *People v. Croswell* and an overstated argument for Hamilton's place in the history of libertarianism, see Berns, "Freedom of the Press and Alien and Sedition Laws," 150–59.

48. *Speeches in People against Croswell,* 62–78, quotation at 63.

49. Ibid., 63–64.

50. Ibid., 70–71; Kyo Ho Youm, "Impact of *People v. Croswell*"; Rosenberg, *Protecting the Best Men,* 108–17, quotation on 114; Levy, *Emergence of Free Press,* 338–40.

51. *Commonwealth v. Clap* (1808), 4 Mass. 163.

52. Buckingham, *Specimens,* 2:310–315; Duniway, *Freedom of Press in Massachusetts,* 146.

53. Levi Lincoln to Jefferson, 13 Dec. 1802, Samuel Bedford file, William Carlton to Samuel H. Smith, 6 May 1803, Carlton file, Letters of Application 1801–1809, RG59-NA; Tapley, *Salem Imprints,* 126–31, 134–38; Bentley, *Diary,* 3:175, 178, 186, 4:31; Duniway, *Freedom of the Press in Massachusetts,* 146.

54. Duniway, *Freedom of the Press in Massachusetts,* 147; Dickerson, *Course of Tolerance,* 31–32; Nelson, *Freedom of the Press from Hamilton to Warren,* 117–20.

55. Munsell, *Typographical Miscellanies,* 103; [Shepherd], *Report on Trial of Andrew Wright;* Wright, *Anti-Shepherd-Crat.*

56. *HBAN,* 380–81; Salem *Essex Register,* 9 Feb., 25 June 1811; Bentley, *Diary,* 4:6.

57. New York *Evening Post,* 31 May 1803, reprinted in Hudson *Bee,* 21 June 1803.

58. Rosenberg, *Protecting the Best Men,* 120–128; William Duane to Thomas Jefferson, 4 Feb. 1809, Ford, "Letters of Duane," 317–19; Phillips, *William Duane,* 242; Clark, *William Duane,* 20; Munsell, *Typographical Miscellany,* 102–104, 107, 108, 113.

59. Duane to Jefferson, 4 Feb. 1809, Ford, "Letters of Duane," 318–19; Phillips, *William Duane,* 242.

60. Hudson, *Journalism in the U.S.,* 290–91; Fassett, *Newspapers in the District of Maine,* 123–39.

61. Nevins, *Evening Post,* 51; Munsell, *Typographical Miscellany,* 113.

62. Hamilton, *Country Printer,* 289; White, *History of Litchfield,* 164–65; *DAB,* s.v.; Printers File, AAS.

63. Litchfield *Witness,* 21 Aug., 18 Sept. 1805.

64. Ibid., 4, 25 Sept., 9, 16, 23, 30 Oct. 1805; White, *History of Litchfield,* 164; Wilmington *American Watchman,* 27 Sept. 1817.

65. Litchfield *Witness,* 5, 19 March, 16 April (quoted), 9 July, 30 July, 6, 13 Aug. 1806, April 1806–June 1807, passim; Hartford *Times,* 7 Oct. 1817; Wilmington *American Watchman,* 27 Sept. 1817.

66. Litchfield *Witness,* 30 July, 6, 13 (quoted) Aug. 1806; Meriwether, et al., *Papers of Calhoun,* 1:25, 25n, 8:277–78.

67. Litchfield *Witness,* 3 June 1807; *HBAN,* 34, 1462; Hamilton, *Country Printer,* 289; Printers File, AAS; *DAB,* s.v.

68. Rosenberg, *Protecting the Best Men,* 114–15; Rowe, *Thomas McKean,* 332–89.

69. [Gerry], *Message from His Excellency the Governor;* Billias, *Elbridge Gerry,* 321–23; Duniway, *Freedom of the Press in Massachusetts,* 153–56.

70. Ibid.; *Trial of Alexander Contee Hanson,* 1–12, 47–55; Baltimore *Federal Republican,* 30 Nov. 1808.

71. Levy, *Emergence of Free Press,* 341–42.

72. Smith, *War and Press Freedom,* 91–93; Dickerson, *Course of Tolerance,* 39–46; Billias, *Elbridge Gerry,* 322–24.

73. Hanson, *Accurate Report of Argument Against Baptis Irvine;* Baltimore *Federal Republican,* 29 July 1808.

74. Rosenberg, *Protecting the Best Men,* 130–52.

12. THE "TYRANNY OF PRINTERS"
IN JEFFERSONIAN PHILADELPHIA

1. James J. Wilson to William Darlington, 27 May 1802, Darlington Papers, LC; William Penrose to Alexander J. Dallas, (Nov. 1800), John Dawson to Dallas, 15 Jan.

1801, A. J. Dallas Papers, HSP; William Duane to John Vaughan, 29 July 1801, Vaughan folder, Historical Society of Delaware.

2. [Duane], *Experience the Test of Government,* 7–8.

3. William Duane to Tench Coxe, 13 June 1801, Coxe Papers, HSP.

4. Leven Powell to Burr Powell, 26 March 1800, Leven Powell Papers, CWM.

5. Phillips, *William Duane,* 119–24.

6. Ibid., 124–30, quotations on 129–30.

7. William Duane to William P. Gardner, 11 June 1801, Gardner file, Letters of Application 1801–1809, RG59-NA.

8. Phillips, "Duane, Philadelphia's Republicans, and Origins of Modern Politics"; Phillips, *William Duane,* chap. 4.

9. William Duane to Thomas Jefferson, 10 June 1801, Ford, "Letters of William Duane," 267.

10. The following two paragraphs rely heavily on the brilliant analysis of Pennsylvania political history between 1776 and 1800 in Phillips, *William Duane,* 101–13.

11. Walters, *Alexander Dallas,* 88–89.

12. Phillips, *William Duane,* 103–104.

13. *Aurora,* 6, 9 March 1801.

14. Ibid., 6 March 1801.

15. Ibid., 9 March 1801.

16. Ibid., 6 March 1801.

17. Ibid., 9 March 1801.

18. Phillips, *William Duane,* 139.

19. Quotation from "Theory of Federalism," *Aurora,* 18 April 1801.

20. William Duane to Albert Gallatin, [1801], Gallatin Papers, N-YHS; Phillips, *William Duane,* 141–42.

21. Duane to Gardner, 11 June 1801 (copy), Gardner file, Letters of Application 1801–1809, RG59-NA; *Aurora,* 18 Apr. 1801; Duane to Jefferson, 10 June 1801, Duane, "Letters of William Duane," 265–67.

22. Alexander J. Dallas to Albert Gallatin, 14 June 1801, Gallatin Papers, N-YHS.

23. Though he was not an active radical on the issues of equality for women and racial minorities, Duane was considerably more sympathetic to the rights of those groups than most politicians of his era. For instance, his solution to the government's Indian troubles, earnestly proposed to Jefferson in 1802, was to give them representation in Congress. See Duane to Jefferson, 7 Jan. 1802, Duane, "Letters of William Duane," 273.

24. Dallas to Gallatin, 14 June 1801, Gallatin Papers, N-YHS.

25. Ibid., William Duane to James Madison, 10 May 1801, Brugger et al., *PJM: Sec. State Series,* 1:152; Duane to Jefferson, 10 June 1801, Duane, "Letters of William Duane," 265, 267; Duane to Coxe, 13 June 1801, Coxe Papers, HSP.

26. Alexander J. Dallas to Albert Gallatin, 16 Dec. 1801, Gallatin Papers, N-YHS; Higginbotham, *Keystone,* 41; Dallas to George Latimer, 1 July 1802, A. J. Dallas Papers, G. M. Dallas Coll., HSP.

27. Walters, *Dallas,* 114, 123, 133; Thomas Leiper to Thomas Jefferson, 26 Aug. 1802, Jefferson Papers, LC; Alexander J. Dallas to Jonathan Dayton, 22 Feb. 1802, Gratz Collection, Seventh Administration, HSP. Moreover, he seems to have had personal business dealings with some of the Federalists whose interests he defended to the ad-

ministration, including George Latimer. See Dallas to Latimer, 5 May 1807, A. J. Dallas Papers, G. M. Dallas Coll., HSP.

28. Walters, *Dallas*, 25–31, 100–110, 122–23.

29. Alexander J. Dallas to Albert Gallatin, 30 Sept., 15 March 1801, Gallatin Papers, N-YHS; Thomas Cooper to Dallas, 13 Oct. 1814, Rosenbach Museum and Library; Edward Fox to Jonathan Roberts, 4 Jan. 1813, Roberts Papers, HSP.

30. Albert Gallatin to Thomas Jefferson, 11 Aug. 1803, *Writings of Gallatin*, 1:134.

31. Aronson, *Status and Kinship in Higher Civil Service*, 7–14, 207–210; White, *Jeffersonians*, 345–68; Cunningham, *Process of Government under Jefferson*, 3–26, 165–87; Thomas Jefferson to James Monroe, 10 March 1808, Bergh, *Writings of Jefferson*, 12:5.

32. Stanley Griswold to Thomas Jefferson, 12 Nov. 1804 (quoted), Griswold to James Madison, 4 April 1805, Griswold file, Letters of Application 1801–1809, RG59-NA. Similar tactics won Griswold raises and promotions throughout his western career. See Griswold to Jefferson, 3 Dec. 1805, 5 May 1808, Jefferson Papers, LC; Griswold to Stephen R. Bradley, 10 Dec. 1805, Griswold to Elijah Boardman, 10 Oct. 1806, Griswold Papers, BHC-DPL; Griswold to Abraham Baldwin, 15 Dec. 1806, draft, Griswold Papers, Baker Library, Harvard Business School; Griswold to Jefferson, 14 Nov. 1808, Griswold file, Letters of Application 1801–1809, RG59-NA; Griswold to Samuel Huntington, 2 April 1810, Rice Collection, Ohio Historical Society; and Griswold's entire file in Letters of Application 1809–17, RG59-NA.

33. William Carlton to Samuel H. Smith, 6 May 1803, Carlton file, Levi Lincoln to Jefferson, 13 Dec. 1802, Samuel Bedford file, Letters of Application 1801–1809, RG59-NA; Newmyer, *Justice Joseph Story*, 49.

34. For the quotation from Granger and the statistics on Federalist postmasters, see Prince, "Federalist Party and Creation of Court Press," 238–40.

35. See chart in Smith, *Press, Politics and Patronage*, 46–47.

36. *Memoirs of John Quincy Adams*, 5:112.

37. Phillips, *William Duane*, 131; Cunningham, *Republicans in Power*, 258–67.

38. Duane to Gallatin, 13 Dec. 1801, Gallatin Papers, N-YHS.

39. Smith, *Press, Politics and Patronage*, 43–44; Phillips, *William Duane*, 131ff.; *Memoirs of John Quincy Adams*, 5:112; Duane to Jefferson, 16 Oct. 1807, 4 Feb. 1809, Duane to R. C. Weightman, 20 Dec. 1808, Duane, "Letters of William Duane," 302, 318, 312.

40. Albert Gallatin to William Duane, 5 July 1801, Gallatin Papers, N-YHS; Phillips, *William Duane*, 156–65; Duane to Daniel Parker, 22 Dec. 1814, Parker Papers, HSP.

41. William Duane to Thomas Jefferson, (received 5 Dec. 1807), Duane to James Madison, 8 Feb. 1808, Duane to Weightman, 20 Dec. 1808, Duane to Henry Dearborn, 21 Jan. 1810, Duane to Madison, 16 April 1810, Duane to Jefferson, 17 July 1812, Duane to Jefferson, 8 Nov. 1824, Duane, "Letters of Duane," 304–305, 308–309, 312, 332–33, 349–51, 383–84; Phillips, *William Duane*, 345–47.

42. Duane to Madison, 8 Feb. 1808, Duane, "Letters of Duane," 309.

43. Edward Fox to Jonathan Roberts, 2 June 1812 (first letter), Roberts Papers, HSP; Phillips, *William Duane*, 346, 348.

44. Duane to Jefferson, 8 Nov. 1824, 17 July 1812, 5 Dec. 1807, Duane, "Letters of Duane," 384, 350–51, 305; Duane, *American Military Library*; Crackel, *Mr. Jefferson's Army*, 82–85.

45. William Duane to [William Daggett], 12 Sept. 1811, Boston Public Library;

Duane to Jefferson, 17 July 1812, Duane, "Letters of Duane," 350–51; Duane to Parker, 22 Dec. 1814, Parker Papers, HSP; Phillips, *William Duane*, 378–79.

46. Duane to Parker, 22 Dec. 1814, Parker Papers, HSP; Duane to Jefferson, 8 Nov. 1824, Duane, "Letters of Duane," 384; Phillips, *William Duane*, 404–406.

47. William Duane to Abraham Bishop, 28 Aug. 1802, Duane, "Letters of Duane," 276.

48. Ellis, *Jeffersonian Crisis*, 15–16, 36–52.

49. Higginbotham, *Keystone*, 42–43; Phillips, *William Duane*, 145–148; *Aurora*, 6 Feb. 1802.

50. *Aurora*, 9, 10 Feb. 1802.

51. Ibid., 12 Feb. 1802.

52. Ibid.

53. Ellis, *Jeffersonian Crisis*, 160–63; Higginbotham, *Keystone*, 51–53; Henderson, "Attack on the Judiciary," 115–16, 120–22.

54. *Pa. Archives*, 4th ser., 4:520.

55. Higginbotham, *Keystone*, 56–58; Ellis, *Jeffersonian Crisis*, 165–167; Henderson, "Attack on Judiciary," 119–120.

56. *Aurora*, 31 March 1803; Higginbotham, *Keystone*, 57; Ellis, *Jeffersonian Crisis*, 166–67.

57. Tolles, *Logan of Philadelphia*, 233–34; Higginbotham, *Keystone*, 43–45; Phillips, *William Duane*, 149ff.

58. *Aurora*, 17, 22, 23, 24 Sept. 1802; Cooke, *Tench Coxe*, 436–37; Michael Leib to Mathew Carey, 12 Dec. 1802, Lea and Febiger Papers, HSP; Phillips, *William Duane*, 153.

59. Andrew Gregg, Robert Brown, John A. Hanna, John Smilie, and William Jones to Thomas Jefferson, 12 Feb. 1803, draft, Jones Papers, Smith Collection, HSP; Phillips, *William Duane*, 153–54; Duane to Tench Coxe, 14 Feb. 1803, Coxe Papers, HSP.

60. Andrew Gregg to William Jones, 1 March 1803, Jones Papers, Smith Coll., HSP; Alexander J. Dallas to Albert Gallatin, 30 March 1803, Gallatin Papers, N-YHS; Phillips, *William Duane*, 154–58; Gallatin to Thomas Jefferson, 21 March 1803, Jefferson to Gallatin, 25 July 1803, Jefferson to William Duane, 24 July 1803, draft, Gallatin to Jefferson, 11 Aug. 1803, *Writings of Gallatin*, 1:118, 154, 129–36.

61. Philadelphia *Aurora*, 22 June 1803; Higginbotham, *Keystone*, 63; Cooke, *Tench Coxe*, 438.

62. Cunningham, *Republicans in Power*, 218.

63. *Philadelphia Evening Post*, 26 May 1804; [A. J. Dallas], "Address to the Republicans of Pennsylvania," 10 June 1805, Dallas, *Life and Writings of Alexander Dallas*, 216.

64. Ellis, *Jeffersonian Crisis*, 167–169; Higginbotham, *Keystone*, 64–67; Walters, *Dallas*, 129.

65. William Duane to Henry Dearborn, 8 July 1810, Duane, "Letters of Duane," 335 ("overture"); Philadelphia *Freeman's Journal*, 11 Sept. 1804 ("threatened"); Phillips, *William Duane*, 158–59.

66. "Quiddism, alias Moderation," *Aurora*, 5 Aug. 1805.

67. William Duane to Henry Dearborn, 3 July 1810, Duane, "Letters of Duane," 335.

68. *Philadelphia Evening Post*, 20 Feb. 1804; *HBAN*, 2:904; Higginbotham, *Keystone*, 68; Printers File, AAS.

69. Cooke, *Tench Coxe,* 439.

70. William Duane to Tench Coxe, 6 May 1802, 22 April 1803, 26 Dec. 1802, Coxe Papers, HSP.

71. *Philadelphia Evening Post,* 20 Feb. 1804 ff.

72. Ibid., March (passim), 5, 6, 14, 18 (quoted) April 1804.

73. Ibid., 20 Feb. 1804.

74. Ibid., 26 May 1804.

75. Ibid., 19, 26 May, 1804.

76. Ibid., 22 May 1804.

77. *Aurora,* 12, 13 ("pitied"), 19, 20 June, 17, 18 ("espoused"), 20, 21, 22, 23, 24, 25, 27, 28, 29, 30, 31 Aug., 1, 3, 4 Sept. 1804; Cooke, *Tench Coxe,* 438–46; Higginbotham, *Keystone,* 68–74.

78. Walters, *Dallas,* 134.

79. [A. J.] Dallas to [William] Duane, draft or copy, 20 Aug. 1804, A. J. Dallas Papers, G. M. Dallas Coll., HSP; *Aurora,* 18 Aug. 1804; A. J. Dallas to Albert Gallatin, 16 Oct. 1804, Gallatin Papers, HSP; Phillips, *William Duane,* 169–70.

80. Andrew Ellicott to Tench Coxe, 16 June 1804, Coxe Papers, HSP.

81. Higginbotham, *Keystone,* 77–80; Ellis, *Jeffersonian Crisis,* 169–70.

82. William Barton to [Charles Jared?] Ingersoll, 28 Jan. 1805, A. J. Dallas Papers, G. M. Dallas Coll., HSP.

83. A. J. Dallas to Albert Gallatin, 26 Jan. 1805, Gallatin Papers, N-YHS.

84. Ellis, *Jeffersonian Crisis,* 171–178; Phillips, *William Duane,* 178–79; Higginbotham, *Keystone,* 80–81; Walters, *Dallas,* 136 (quoted).

85. Higginbotham, *Keystone,* 87; Higginbotham, *Keystone,* 85, 50–51, 92–94, 87; Ellis, *Jeffersonian Crisis,* 161–62, 166, 168, 172, 174; John Kean to A. J. Dallas, 20 March 1805, A. J. Dallas Papers, G. M. Dallas Coll., HSP; Phillips, *William Duane,* 182.

86. Kean to Dallas, 20 March 1805, A. J. Dallas Papers, G. M. Dallas Coll., HSP.

87. Representative samples of the attacks can be found in *Aurora,* 3 ("John Doe"), 5 ("company" and "learned"), 6, 7, 8 Aug. 1805. See also, Higginbotham, *Keystone,* 91–92.

88. [A. J. Dallas], "Address to Republicans," in Dallas, *Life and Writings of Alexander Dallas,* 215.

89. Ibid., 214, 216.

90. Ibid., 214, 219, 217, 233.

91. Albert Gallatin to John Badollet, 25 Oct. 1805, Gallatin Papers, N-YHS; Phillips, *William Duane,* 189; Ellis, *Jeffersonian Crisis,* 180–181ff; Higginbotham, *Keystone,* 99–101; Walters, *Dallas,* 142.

92. Phillips, *William Duane,* 245–50, 229–33, 243.

93. Ibid., 222–27.

94. Ibid., 228–29; Binns, *Recollections,* 196–97; Higginbotham, *Keystone,* 137–38; Philadelphia *Democratic Press,* 15 May 1807.

95. *Ibid.,*6, 8 April, 1, 11 May 1807 ff.; Binns, *Recollections,* 197.

96. Binns, *Recollections,* 191–92, 202–11; Phillips, *William Duane,* 216–22, 229–30, 264–66 ff.; Higginbotham, *Keystone,* 130, 133, 136, 137–43, 147–66.

97. Phillips, "Democrats of the Old School."

98. Phillips, *William Duane,* 288–314, 347–51; Richard Rush to John Binns, 4 Feb., 9 July, 10 Sept., 4 Oct., 1, 17 Nov. 1812, 27 Jan., 3 Feb., 19, 22 March, 16 April, 30 July, 1813, 4 Aug. 1814, Gratz Collection, HSP. See also, generally, Richard Rush Letters, C. J. Ingersoll Coll., HSP.

99. Phillips, *William Duane*, 315–44.

100. Ibid., 267–68; William Duane to Caesar A. Rodney, 1 July 1808, Rodney Coll., Box 1, Folder 6, Historical Society of Delaware.

101. Phillips, *William Duane*, 373 ff.

102. Adams, *Life of Gallatin*, 442; Richard Rush to Julia Stockton Rush, 13 March 1813, Rush Papers, Library Company of Philadelphia; Binns. *Recollections*, 211–21, 230–32.

103. Binns. *Recollections*, 202–11, 232–34; Higginbotham, *Keystone*, 136–37, 273; Phillips, *William Duane*, 300, 347–48, 447; Fox to Roberts, 2 June 1812 (first letter), Roberts Papers, HSP.

104. Binns, *Recollections*, 297–301; Phillips, *William Duane*, 528–32, 598–99.

105. [Duane], *Biographical Memoir*, quotation on 13. The younger Duane also lost his cabinet post by sticking to his father's principles, refusing Jackson's order to remove the federal deposits from the Bank of the United States because there was as yet no suitable publicly controlled institution to which they could be transferred. A believer in totally divorcing the government from banking, Duane argued (correctly) that shifting federal money into state banks would only exacerbate the problems that Jacksonian critics had blamed on the national bank. See Phillips, *William Duane*, 619–37.

13. ORDINARY EDITORS AND EVERYDAY POLITICS:
HOW THE SYSTEM WORKED

1. Based on a study of *BDUSC*. See this book's companion web site <http://pasleybrothers.com/newspols> for a complete list of printers, editors, and publishers who served in Congress up to 1860.

2. Prince, "James J. Wilson"; Prince, *N. J.'s Jeffersonian Republicans*, 89–90; Printers File, AAS.

3. Wilmington *Mirror of the Times*, 8 Nov. 1800.

4. See Wilson's early letters to Darlington, in Darlington Papers, LC, a collection almost entirely made up of correspondence from Wilson.

5. Trenton *True American*, 14 July, 29 Sept., 13 Oct. 1801, 23 Feb., 20 Sept. ("Political Definitions") 1802, 28 Feb. 1803. Criticism of dueling can be found in ibid., 30 June 1801, 9 Jan., 16, 23 July, 6 Aug., 10 Sept. 1804. *Norristown Register*, 15 Nov. 1803; Waldstreicher, *Perpetual Fetes*, 229.

6. Trenton *True American*, 10 March (quoted) to 23 June 1801; "REPUBLICAN NEWS-PAPERS," ibid., 21 July 1801.

7. Prince, "James J. Wilson," 25–26; Prince, *N. J.'s Jeffersonian Republicans*, 88–90; Wilson to Darlington, 22 July, 20 Aug., 26 Nov. 1801, 23 Nov. 1802, Darlington Papers, LC.

8. Trenton *True American*, 13 Oct. 1801; Wilson to Darlington, 26 Nov., 22 July 1801, Darlington Papers, LC.

9. Wilson to Darlington, 20 Aug. 1802, Darlington Papers, LC; Prince, "James J. Wilson," 27. For Wilson and the *True American*'s efforts to abolish slavery in New Jersey (partly an effort to prevent the Federalists from painting the Republicans as a southern-dominated, proslavery party), see the issues of 15, 22, 29 Dec. 1801, 2 March, 1 Nov. 1802, 23 Jan., 13 Feb., 9 April, 9 July 1804.

10. James J. Wilson to Gen. Peter Hunt, 22 Dec. 1806, Coxe Papers, HSP; James J. Wilson to William Darlington, 10 Jan. 1803, Darlington Papers, LC.

11. Wilson to Darlington, 20 Aug. 1802 (quoted), 17 Aug. 1805, Darlington Papers, LC.

12. Trenton *True American*, 3, 17 Jan. 1803; Prince, *N. J.'s Jeffersonian Republicans*, 83–88.

13. Ibid.

14. James J. Wilson to William Darlington, 26 June 1810, Darlington Papers, LC.

15. Wilson to Darlington, 21 May, 21 Sept. 1803, Darlington Papers, LC.

16. Prince, "James J. Wilson," 32; *To the Republicans of Hunterdon*, 10, 7.

17. Wilson to Darlington, 27 Feb. 1808, 6 Nov. 1804, Darlington Papers, LC; Prince, "James J. Wilson," 29–32.

18. *To the Republicans of Hunterdon*, quotations on 7, 15.

19. Prince, "James J. Wilson," 32–35.

20. Wilson to Darlington, 4 March 1815, Darlington Papers, LC.

21. Wilson to Darlington, 4 March 1815, 23 Nov., 22 Dec. 1816, 22 Nov. 1819, Darlington Papers, LC. The conclusion as to Wilson's low profile in Congress is based on a study of the *Annals of Congress* as well as the published papers of prominent congressional Republicans, such as Meriwether, *Papers of Calhoun;* and Hopkins, *Papers of Clay.*

22. Prince, "James J. Wilson," 35–37; Elmer, *Constitution and Government of N.J.*, 211–12.

23. On Roberts, see *BDUSC*, 1725; Klein, "Memoirs of a Senator."

24. On political professionals as "mediators," see Waldstreicher and Grossbart, "Abraham Bishop's Vocation."

25. Auge, *Lives of the Eminent Dead*, 412–13; Printers File, AAS.

26. *Norristown Register*, 8 Dec., 20 Oct. 1803, 7 Oct. 1807; Knox, *The Spirit of Despotism.*

27. *Norristown Register*, 14 Feb. 1804.

28. Ibid., 24, 31 Oct. 1805, 30 Sept. 1807ff., 15 Oct., 9, 23, 30 Dec. 1807, 6, 27 Jan., 3 Feb., 9, 16 March 1808, 24, 31 Jan., 14, 21, 28 Feb., 14, 21 March, 26 Sept., 19, 26 Dec. 1810, 24 Dec. 1811, 8, 29 Jan., 12 Feb., 18 April, 17 June, 8 July 1812; James Winnard to Jonathan Roberts, 14 March 1808, 3 March 1810, 29 Dec. 1811, Roberts Papers, HSP.

29. Auge, *Lives of the Eminent Dead*, 412–13; *Norristown Register*, 6 May 1812; Winnard to Roberts, 3 March 1810, Roberts Papers, HSP.

30. Samuel Maffett to Jonathan Roberts, 28 March 1812, Roberts Papers, HSP; Printers File, AAS.

31. Heller, *History of Northampton County*, 1:290–291; Easton *Northampton Farmer*, 3 Sept. 1808; Thomas J. Rogers to Jonathan Roberts, 1 June 1812, Roberts Papers, HSP; Printers File, AAS; *Thomas J. Rogers having purchased the English Printing Office*, Broadside, LCP.

32. Ibid.; *HBAN*, 2:845; Easton *Northampton Farmer*, 21 Dec. 1805.

33. Ibid., 11 Oct. 1806, 3 Jan. 1807.

34. Ibid., 12 April, 3 May, 20, 27 Sept. 1806.

35. Ibid., 4, 11 Oct. 1806.

36. Ibid., 18, 25 Oct., 22 Nov. 1806, 1, 8 Aug. 1807.

37. *Pa. Archives*, 9th ser., 4:2594, 3115; Rogers to Roberts, 26 Jan. 1812, Roberts Papers, HSP.

38. Easton *Northampton Farmer*, 16 May , 19, 26 Sept., 10 Oct. 1807, 4 June, 14 Aug.

1808; Rogers to Roberts, 3 Jan. 1808, Roberts Papers, HSP; *HBAN,* 845–46, 1436; Reeder, *Family of Christian Jacob Hütter,* 3–5.

39. Easton *Northampton Farmer,* 2, 23 July, 14, 20, 27 Aug., 3, 17, 24 Sept., 1, 8, 15 Oct. 1808; Easton *Pa. Herald,* 10 Aug. 1808 ff., 4, 18 Jan. 1809.

40. Rogers to Roberts, 6 Dec. 1807, 3 Jan. 1808 (quoted), Roberts Papers, HSP; Easton *Northampton Farmer,* 22 Nov. 1806.

41. Rogers to Roberts, 26 Jan. (quoted), 20 (quoted), 26 April, 10, 16 May, 7, 14, 21 June 1812, Roberts Papers, HSP. Unfortunately, very few issues of the *Northampton Farmer* are extant after 1810, so the details of Rogers's efforts against the millers are unavailable.

42. Rogers to Roberts, 17 Nov. 1811, Roberts Papers, HSP. For examples of Roberts's reports back to Rogers, see Roberts to Rogers, 30 March 1811, 16 Nov., 17 Dec. 1812, Roberts file, Dreer Collection, HSP.

43. For examples, see Rogers to Roberts, 8, 22 March, 5 April 1812, Roberts Papers, HSP.

44. Rogers to Roberts, 26 Jan. 1812, Roberts Papers, HSP.

45. Rogers to Roberts, 22 March, 5 April, 16 May 1812, Roberts Papers, HSP; Rogers, *Biographical Dictionary.*

46. Rogers to Simon Bolivar, "Liberator of Columbia Peru &c. &c.," 6 Apr. 1826, draft [?], Rogers file, Dreer Collection, HSP; Rogers, *Biographical Dictionary,* 3d ed., v–vi.

47. Rogers to Mathew Carey, 4 Jan. 1819, E. C. Gardiner Papers, Mathew Carey section, HSP; Rogers to Carey, 6, 28 (quoted) Jan. 1819, Lea and Febiger Collection, HSP; Rogers to Lewis Coryell, 31 Jan. 1823, Coryell Papers, HSP; Rogers to Condy Raguet, 23 April 1826, Rogers to Bolívar, 6 April 1826, and "Resolution recommending to county commissioners to furnish children educated at the public expense with Rogers's Biographical Dictionary," copy, 13 April 1827, all in Rogers file, Dreer Collection, HSP.

48. Rogers to Roberts, 4 Nov. 1811, Roberts Papers, HSP.

49. Rogers to Roberts, 1 Dec. 1811, 22 March, 7 June 1812, Roberts Papers, HSP; Easton *Northampton Farmer,* 10 Oct. 1807, 2, 23 Jan. 1808.

50. Rogers to Roberts, 10 May , 1 June, 16 Aug. 1812, Roberts Papers, HSP.

51. Rogers to Roberts, 1 Nov. 1812, Roberts Papers, HSP.

52. Samuel D. Ingham to Rogers, 27 Dec. 1816, 17 Jan., 21 Dec. 1817, Rogers file, Dreer Collection, HSP. For political background see, Higginbotham, *Keystone;* Klein, *Game without Rules.*

53. Easton *Spirit of Pennsylvania,* 16 June, 29 Sept., 6, 13 Oct. 1815.

54. *Easton Centinel,* 11, 18, 25 July, 1, 15, 22 Aug. ff., 17 Oct. 1817, 19 Sept. 1818 ff; John Binns to Rogers, 5 Feb., 7, 23 Dec. 1816, Binns file, Dreer Collection, HSP; Rogers to D. D. Wagener, 19 Jan., 5 March 1818, Nathaniel Michler to Rogers, Easton, 18 Jan. 1818, Rogers file, Dreer Collection, HSP.

55. Christian J. Hütter to Rogers, 16 Feb. 1817, 25 Jan. 1818, 13 Feb. 1819 (quoted), Hütter file, Dreer Collection, HSP. Internal evidence makes it clear that many more letters between the two are missing from the file.

56. Meriwether, *Papers of Calhoun,* 5:672–73, 7:155, 516, 8:xliv–xlvi, 271; *Carlisle Herald,* reprinted in Easton *Expositor,* 19 Aug. 1822; Rogers to Mathew Carey, 20 Jan., 27 Feb. 1819, 10, 14 April 1820, Lea and Febiger Papers, HSP; Rogers to Carey, 4 Jan. 1819,

21 April 1820, Edward Carey Gardiner Collection, HSP; James J. Wilson to William Darlington, 22 Nov. 1819, Darlington Papers, LC.

57. Easton *Mountaineer,* 7 Jan. 1820–22 June 1821.

58. Easton *Expositor,* 19 Aug–2 Nov. 1822.

59. Easton *Mountaineer,* 16 June, 7, 22 July, 18 ("trumpeter") Aug., 22 Sept. 1820, 22 June 1821; Easton *Expositor,* 19, 27 Aug., 4 Oct. ("begging for votes") 1822.

60. Ibid., 27 Aug., 3 Sept., 1, 4 Oct. 1822

61. Easton *Mountaineer,* 16 June, 5 Oct. 1820, 22 June ("party spirit") 1821; Easton *Expositor,* 27 Aug. ("chimney sweep") 3, 10 Sept. ("lowest class") 1822.

62. "A Free Elector," ibid., 1 Oct. 1822.

63. Ibid., 10, 24 Sept., 1, 4, 7, 22 Oct. 1822.

64. Ibid., 3, 10, 17 Sept. 1822.

65. *Easton Centinel,* 24 Sept., 22 Oct., 5 Nov. 1824; Rogers to Coryell, 31 Jan. 1823, Coryell Papers, HSP; Rogers to Condy Raguet, 23 April 1826, Rogers file, Dreer Collection, HSP; *BDUSC.*

14. NEWSPAPER EDITORS AND THE RECONSTRUCTION OF PARTY POLITICS

1. Robinson, *Jeffersonian Democracy in New England,* 69, 76–94; Adams, *New England in the Republic,* 239–80; Fischer, *Revolution of American Conservatism;* Smelser, *Democratic Republic,* 174–89.

2. Baltimore *Federal Republican,* 25, 13, 27 July, 3 Aug. 1808. On Duane, see Phillips, *William Duane,* 375–77. On Fitz Randolph, see Prince, *N. J.'s Jeffersonian Republicans,* 244; *BDUSC.*

3. For an interesting account of how partisan newspapers democratized political rhetoric in this period, including an example or two from Isaac Hill's newspaper, see Robertson, *Language of Democracy,* 36–67.

4. [Bradley], *Biography of Isaac Hill,* 13–19. This is a campaign biography issued with Hill's own cooperation. A substantial appendix reprints much original source material in full. The best modern secondary source on Hill is Cole, *Jacksonian Democracy in N.H.*

5. "Mr. Hill's Letter to the Typographical Festival," 18 Nov. 1833, in [Bradley], *Biography of Isaac Hill,* 206–207; Concord *N.H. Patriot,* 18 April 1809–10 April 1810.

6. Concord *N.H. Patriot,* 18 April 1809. The colonial beginnings of New England's popular religious culture are described in Hall, *Worlds of Wonder,* and its nineteenth-century resurgence and politicization in Hatch, *Democratization of American Christianity.*

7. Concord *N.H. Patriot,* 18 April, 9 May 1809, 27 Feb. 1810, 12 May 1812, 9 Jan. 1810; [Bradley], *Biography of Isaac Hill,* 174.

8. [Bradley], *Biography of Isaac Hill,* 27; *Aurora,* 22 June 1803; Concord *N.H. Patriot,* 10 April 1810.

9. Concord *N.H. Patriot,* 13 June 1809, 27 Feb., 6, 13, 20 March 1810.

10. Ibid., 18 April 1809 ff., 27 Feb. 1810; Isaac Hill to R. Bartlett, 25 Sept. 1816, Misc. Papers, NYPL.

11. [Bradley], *Biography of Isaac Hill,* 25–26, 28–29; Cole, *Jacksonian Democracy in N.H.,* 4–5, 22–23; Hill *Wise Sayings of Isaac Hill,* 1–2, 5–6; [Hill], *Sketch of Andrew Jackson,* 49–50.

12. John Norvell to T. J. Rogers, 29 Jan. 1822, Dreer Collection, HSP; Pasley, "Indiscreet Zeal of John Norvell."

13. Dangerfield, *Awakening of American Nationalism*, 1–16; Sellers, *Market Revolution*, 59–79.

14. Carter, "Mathew Carey and the Olive Branch"; Carter, "Political Activities of Mathew Carey; Green, *Mathew Carey*.

15. Carey, *Olive Branch*, 10th ed., 43 (quoted), 12. On substantive issues, Carey's nonpartisanship was more rhetorical than real. Most of his examples and vitriol were aimed at the Federalist opponents of the war, and the book became a powerful weapon in the hands of Republican partisans eager to obliterate the Federalists with charges of disloyalty.

16. Ibid., 12, 13, 45, 15.

17. Ibid., 45, 50–51.

18. Ibid., 12, 43, 430–32, 45.

19. Ostrogorski, *Democracy and the Organization of Political Parties*, 2:44; Fischer, *Revolution of American Conservatism*, 30–32; *Niles' Register* 23 (15 Feb. 1823): 370–71; Wallace, "Ideologies of Party."

20. Dangerfield, *Awakening of American Nationalism*, 8–16; Skeen, "Compensation Act"; Sellers, *Market Revolution*, 104–107; Heale, *Making of American Politics*, 123.

21. *Annals of Congress*, 14th Cong., 1st sess., House, 1182, 1185, Senate, 201.

22. Wallace, "Ideologies of Party," 108.

23. *Annals of Congress*, 14th Cong., 2d sess., House, 579–81.

24. Ibid., 14th Cong., 1st sess., Senate, 191–192, 2d sess., House, 507–508. For the accuracy of Hendricks's depiction of prairie settler life in this period, see Faragher, *Sugar Creek*. For an argument that this largely cashless, relatively nonmarket-oriented lifestyle was widespread among common American families, and a discussion of the Compensation Act controversy in this context, see Sellers, *Market Revolution*, 3–33, 106–107.

25. Skeen, "Compensation Act"; James J. Wilson to William Darlington, 15 Sept. 1816, Darlington Papers, LC; *Annals of Congress*, 14th Cong., 2d sess., House, 507–508; Kendall, *Autobiography*, 178.

26. *Annals of Congress*, 14th Cong., 2d sess., House, 586, 524, 536, 553.

27. *Annals of Congress*, 14th Cong., 1st sess., House, 1183; 2d sess., House, 548–554, 574–584, 616–637, Calhoun quotation on 576.

28. Chase, *Emergence of Presidential Nominating Convention*, 18–28; Ammon, *James Monroe*, 352–57.

29. Ammon, *James Monroe*, 366–79; Dangerfield, *Era of Good Feelings*, 95–104; Wallace, "Ideologies of Party," 106–109.

30. Sellers, *Market Revolution*, 103–71; Ammon, *James Monroe*, 380–395; Dangerfield, *Awakening of American Nationalism*, 72–140.

31. For a similar point, see Thornton, *Politics and Power*, 129.

32. *Richmond Enquirer*, 5, 12 ("Franklin,") Aug. 1817; Wilmington *American Watchman*, 26 July 1817; Providence *Columbian Phenix*, quoted in Wilmington *American Watchman*, 13 Aug. 1817; Hartford *Times*, 16 Dec. 1817.

33. *Richmond Enquirer*, 5 Aug. 1817; Wilmington *American Watchman*, 26 July 1817; Hartford *Times*, 9 Sept. 1817.

34. Boston *Independent Chronicle & Patriot*, 8, 11 July 1817.

35. Wilmington *American Watchman,* 19 July, 9, 13, 20 Aug., 13, 27, 30 Sept. 1817.

36. Here I refer to several influential works on the origins of party politics: the frequently cited article by Michael Wallace, "Changing Concepts of Party"; his mentor Richard Hofstadter's book, *The Idea of a Party System,* which derives heavily from Wallace's research; and Wallace's later dissertation, "Ideologies of Party." For decades accepted as the definitive statements on this subject, these works give almost entire credit for the new, positive vision of permanently competing parties to Martin Van Buren and his Bucktail faction in New York, dubbed by their enemies the "Albany Regency." While the New York Van Burenites did indeed produce an elaborate defense of party during the early 1820s, their arguments were predated by those of the editors in this chapter by several years. There is little indication that Osborn and the rest were inspired by the Bucktails, and given the timing, the influence might well have flowed in the other direction.

Wallace and Hofstadter did not perceive the unique role of editors in the defense and reconstruction of party competition, and they come dangerously close to depicting the new party system as the personal creation of Martin Van Buren. In fact, it was produced by the activities of a broad spectrum of Republican activists all over the country. Wallace and Hofstadter also forced the pro-party argument into a consensus history framework that does not entirely fit. For instance, they contrasted the new party politicians with ideologues, even though many of the arguments for maintaining party politics hinged on the necessity to maintain ideological purity and to avoid betraying older ideals. In my view, Republican editors expressed not so much a new concept of party as the accepted political values of their particular quadrant of the political system. As ground-level political campaigners by trade, they saw the party system as long established and reasonably well functioning, though in need of some improvements. Editors felt that parties could be more efficiently organized and stable, with plenty of rewards available for campaigners, but they showed little interest in the valueless, mechanical, "modern" party bureaucracy painted by Wallace and Hofstadter. For a strong case against the modernity of the Jacksonian era justification for parties, see Wilson, "Republicanism and the Idea of Party in the Jacksonian Period." John Ashworth, in *Agrarians and Aristocrats,* 205–18, shows that the defense of parties was a key component of radical Democratic thought in the late 1830s and early 1840s. An evocative portrait of the deep values transmitted by parties can be found in Baker, *Affairs of Party.*

37. Wilmington *American Watchman,* 26 July, 20 Aug., 13 Sept. 1817.

38. Ibid., 9, 20 Aug., 26 July 1817.

39. Marshall, "Early Career of Kendall," 1–47, 65–99; Kendall, *Autobiography,* chapters 1–5.

40. Marshall, "Early Career of Kendall," 100–160; *HBAN,* 151, 156–57.

41. Kendall, *Autobiography,* 182–83.

42. Lexington *Kentucky Gazette,* 2, 16 June 1817; Marshall, "Early Career of Kendall," 161–87; Kendall, *Autobiography,* 182–98.

43. Lexington *Kentucky Gazette,* 16 Oct. 1817, 16 Oct. 1818.

44. Ibid., 2, 16, 21, 28 June, 3 July, 2, 9, 16, 30 Aug., 13 Sept. 1817.

45. Kendall, *Autobiography,* 182–90; Frankfort *Argus of Western America,* 30 April, 22 Jan., 29 Oct. 1819.

46. Ibid., 1 Jan. 1819.

47. Marshall, "Early Career of Kendall," 188–399; Smith, *Francis Preston Blair,* 4–25; McCormick, *Second Party System,* 212–16; Sellers, *Market Revolution,* 169–70.

48. Phillips, "Democrats of the Old School"; Phillips, "Pennsylvania Origins of Jackson Movement"; Kehl, *Ill Feeling in Era of Good Feeling*, 119–39, 193–204; Klein, *Game without Rules*, 79–83.

49. Stevens, *Early Jackson Party in Ohio*, 3–5, 7, 15–16, 19–20, 28, 33–34, 39–40, 46–47; Hall, "Moses Dawson," 175–89.

50. Chambers, *Old Bullion Benton*, 3–100, especially 81–96; McCormick, *Second Party System*, 304–306.

51. There is an immense literature on Van Buren's Albany Regency. I have relied especially on Cole, *Van Buren and the Political System*, 66–98; Niven, *Martin Van Buren*, 60–37; Wallace, "Changing Concepts of Party"; and McCormick, *Second Party System*, 114–15. On Flagg, see Hamilton, *Country Printer*, 104–105, 272. On Croswell, see Manning, "Herald of the Albany Regency."

52. Abraham Bishop to Jonathan Law, 2 Feb., 23 April 1809, 26 May, 11, 16 July, 11 Aug. 1810, 1, 3 May 1811, 16 April 1815, Bishop Letterbook, Yale University; Waldstreicher and Grossbart, "Abraham Bishop's Vocation"; Dexter, "Bishop and His Writings"; William H. Crawford to Abraham Bishop, 28 March 1817, New Haven Custom House Papers, New Haven Colony Historical Society. The decline of Connecticut Republican fortunes and activity after 1806 is covered in Purcell, *Connecticut in Transition*, 174–88. Bishop's later conservatism and lower level of political activity are described in Dexter, *Biographical Sketches*, 4:19–20.

53. Abraham Bishop to Jonathan Law, 3 May 1811, 26 March 1815 (quoted), Bishop Letterbook, Yale University; Joel Barlow to Abraham Bishop, 25 Sept. 1807, New Haven Custom House Papers, New Haven Colony Historical Society. According to the Connecticut Historical Society's card file index to the *Courant*, Babcock and the *Mercury* were mentioned exactly once after 1811.

54. Clark and Hill, "Newspapers of Connecticut," 92–93; Abraham Bishop to Jonathan Law, 15 Jan., 13 March, 1 April, 18 Apr., 17 May, 18 July, 24 Aug., 5 Sept. (two letters), 7, 10 Sept. 1816, Bishop Letterbook, Yale University.

55. Purcell, *Connecticut in Transition*, 32–44; Increase Cooke to John Babcock, 12 Feb. 1803, Babcock Papers, CHS.

56. Abraham Bishop to Jonathan Law, 15 Feb., 13 March 1816, Bishop Letterbook, Yale University; Purcell, *Connecticut in Transition*, 211–13.

57. Ibid., 214–18, 230.

58. Niles Autobiography, CHS, 2–3; Hartford *Connecticut Courant*, 1 Oct. 1816; Hartford *Times*, 1 Jan. 1817.

59. Hartford *Times*, 4 Feb.–1 April 1817. The "American Toleration and Reform Ticket" first appeared in the issue of 25 Feb. The 1 April issue featured more than three pages of closely spaced electioneering material.

60. "The Age of Improvements . . . No. IV," ibid., 11 March 1817; "To the Honorable James Hillhouse," ibid., 18 March 1817; "The Age of Improvements . . . No. VII," ibid., 25 March 1817; "Emigration and Toleration," 8 April 1817.

61. Ibid., 23 Feb. 1817. For an overview of what the other Republican newspapers were discussing, see Brownsword, "Connecticut Political Patterns," 35–38.

62. "The Age of Improvements . . . No. VII" and "To the Honourable James Hillhouse," Hartford *Times*, 25 March 1817. The agenda was recapitulated, in numbered list format, in the issue before the election (1 April 1817). On Niles's Universalism, see his receipt for a slip at the First Independent Universalist Church of Hartford, dated 18 Nov. 1824, Niles Papers, CHS.

63. "Capt. Boardman's Trial," Hartford *Times,* 21 Jan. 1817; "Boston and Hartford," 4 Feb. 1817. See also, ibid., 25 Feb. 1817.

64. "The Age of Improvements . . . No. IV," ibid., 11 March 1817.

65. Ibid., 29 July, 21, 28 Jan., 4 March 1817; Isaac Hill to John M. Niles, 9 May, 24 Aug. 1829, Niles Papers, CHS; Hill to Niles, 28 Oct. 1833, John Milton Niles Papers, NYPL. Hill's prosecution came just after the overthrow of Federalism in New Hampshire, and he in fact turned it to great advantage. Holding a slight majority in the state legislature, the Republicans intentionally let the prosecution proceed and gave Hill access to the floor so he could mount a lengthy, grandstanding defense. After subjecting the Federalists to two days of intense embarrassment, Hill's legislative allies triumphantly exonerated him. See Bradley, *Biography of Isaac Hill,* 46–51. On New Hampshire politics in this period, though not the trial, see Cole, *Jacksonian Democracy in N.H.,* 16–46.

66. Gideon Welles, biographical sketch of Niles in Stiles, *History of Ancient Windsor,* 2:535.

67. "Age of Improvements . . . No. I," Hartford *Times,* 18 Feb. 1817; "Party Desperation," ibid., 11 March 1817.

68. Ibid., 1 April 1817.

69. Ibid., 22 April 1817; Goodrich, *Recollections,* 2:429n; Morse, *Neglected Period of Connecticut's History,* 62–63; Stiles, *History of Ancient Windsor,* 2:534–36. For a general account of the spring 1817 election, see Purcell, *Connecticut in Transition,* 220–21.

70. The two basic sources on Niles's early life are an undated, unfinished manuscript autobiography and a manuscript biographical sketch of Niles by his disciple Gideon Welles, both in CHS. The Welles sketch is printed in Stiles, *History of Ancient Windsor,* 2:534–36.

71. Ibid., 2:534; Niles Autobiography, CHS, 1.

72. Stiles, *History of Ancient Windsor,* 2:534; Goodrich, *Recollections,* 2:429n.

73. Niles Autobiography, CHS, 1–2.

74. Abel, *American Lawyers,* 40–41; Chroust, *Rise of the Legal Profession in America,* vol. 2; Miller, *Life of the Mind in America,* 109–16; Friedman, *History of American Law,* 305–306; Nash, "Philadelphia Bench and Bar."

75. For instance, compare the story of Niles's early life with that of the printer Horace Greeley. See Greeley, *Recollections of a Busy Life,* 34–67, 75–82; Van Deusen, *Greeley,* 5–14. There is no denying that printing, editing, and publishing became more and more separate functions during the nineteenth century, especially on larger and more financially successful newspapers, but the social implications of this are more ambiguous than some writers (Hamilton, *Country Printer,* 150–51; Botein, "Printers and the Revolution," 49–57) have claimed. In the Jacksonian period, both lawyering and editing were open to people who would once have been limited to the trades.

76. Hartford *Connecticut Mirror,* 22 March 1819, quoted in Brownsword, "Connecticut Political Patterns," 52.

77. Stiles, *History of Ancient Windsor,* 2:535.

78. Niles Autobiography, CHS, 2; Stiles, *History of Ancient Windsor,* 2:534–35.

79. [Niles], "Preface," in *Independent Whig,* 1st American ed. from 6th London ed., xxii–xxiii.

80. "Glorious Triumph!!!," Hartford *Times,* 1 April 1817 (quoted); Brownsword, "Constitution of 1818"; Trumbull, *Historical Notes,* 56–60; Purcell, *Connecticut in Tran-*

sition, 223–59; John M. Niles, biographical sketch of Alexander Wolcott, in Stiles, *History of Ancient Windsor*, 834–35n (quoted).

81. Elections were held in April and September, and the number of advertising columns in the *Times* increased as follows: March 1817, 4–5; May–June 1817, 8–9; Sept.–Oct. 1817, 9–11; May–June 1818, 13–15.

82. Hartford *Times*, 28 Sept. 1819.

83. Ibid., 26 Aug. 1817.

84. Brownsword, "Connecticut Political Patterns," 73–149; Brownsword, "Constitution of 1818," 7–9; Niven, *Gideon Welles*, 25–27.

85. Hartford *Times*, 26 May 1818, 2 Feb., 21 April, 4, 11 May, 1 June 1819.

86. Stiles, *History of Ancient Windsor*, 2:535.

87. On Universalism, see Hatch, *Democratization of American Christianity*, 40–42, 126–27, 170–72, 177; Robinson, *Unitarians and Universalists*, 47–74.

88. "The New Year," Hartford *Times*, 6 Jan. 1818.

89. "The Prospect before Us, No. IV," ibid., 28 Oct. 1817.

90. On the work's purposes, see Niles, *Connecticut Civil Officer*, iii–iv, viii.

91. Ibid., 3 March 1818, 6 April 1819; Niven, *Gideon Welles*, 27.

92. Hartford *Times*, 7 April 1818, 9 Sept. 1817. See also, ibid., 4, 11 Nov., 16 Dec. 1817, 6 Jan., 3, 31 March, 12 May 1818, 2 March 1819.

93. Ibid., 6 April 1819.

94. John M. Niles to John Russ, 5 Feb. 1822, Niles Papers, CHS.

95. Phillips, "Pennsylvania Origins of Jackson Movement," 494–99; Sellers, *Market Revolution*, 172–74, 187–89, 191–92; Kehl, *Ill Feeling in Era of Good Feeling*, 217, 223–34; McCormick, *Second Party System*, 139–40.

96. McCormick, *Second Party System*, 187–90; Remini, *Election of Andrew Jackson*, 53–58; Cole, *Van Buren and the Political System*, 142–81; Ambler, *Thomas Ritchie*, 85–117; Van Buren, *Autobiography of Martin Van Buren*, 514. The key letter, outlining a coalition of "the planters of the South and the plain Republicans of the North," is Martin Van Buren to Thomas Ritchie, 13 Jan. 1827, Van Buren Papers, LC. On Duff Green, see Green, "Duff Green: Militant Journalist of the Old School"; and Ashley, *American Newspaper Journalists*, 273–77.

97. McCormick, *Second American Party System*, 41–49, 54–69, 214–21, 262–65. 304–307; Sellers, *Market Revolution*, 189; Klein, *Game without Rules*, 150–66, 188–261.

98. Smith, *Press, Politics, and Patronage*, 59–72; Remini, *Election of Andrew Jackson*, 76–80. The absence of detailed reference works like *HBAN* for the period after 1820 makes a definite count of these new Jacksonian papers virtually impossible at this juncture. Remini gives what are probably representative, if not low, figures for a few states. Between 1824 and 1828, he counts eighteen new journals in Ohio and nine in North Carolina.

99. *Delaware Democrat and Easton Gazette*, began 10 May 1827 and folded 20 Nov. 1828, with the very issue that reported the election results.

100. Binns, *Recollections*, 242–57; Remini, *Jackson and the Course of Freedom*, 118–23; Remini, *Election of Andrew Jackson*, 151–56; Weed, *Autobiography*, chaps. 20–26, 29–30, 32, 37; Chase, *Emergence of Nominating Convention*, 121–81; Van Deusen, *Thurlow Weed*, 38–69; Holt, *Rise and Fall of American Whig Party*, 12–32; Hudson *Wasp*, 7 July 1802; Weisenburger, "Life of Charles Hammond," 383–87.

101. Smith, *Press, Politics, and Patronage*, 84–99; Pasley, "Indiscreet Zeal of John

Norvell." Rosters of the editorial appointees were compiled by anti-Jacksonian newspapers. See Washington *Daily National Journal,* 9 Jan. 1829; and Washington *National Intelligencer,* 27 Sept. 1832. My research has uncovered a few errors and several omissions in these rosters, raising the overall number over the fifty-seven listed by the *Intelligencer.* On Rogers's campaign for an appointment, see Samuel D. Ingham to Thomas J. Rogers, 16 Mar. 1828, D. H. Miller to Rogers, 5, 10 April 1830, Rogers to D. H. Miller, 10 April 1830, Dreer Collection, HSP; Rogers to Lewis Coryell, 8 June 1828, 5 May, 20 June 1830, Coryell Papers, HSP; Rogers to Isaac D. Barnard, 14 Dec. 1828, Barnard Papers, Townsend-LeMaistre Collection, HSP.

102. Washington *Daily National Journal,* 5, 9 Jan., 3, 9, 14, 18, 21, 28, 29 April, 1, 14 May, 28, 29 Nov., 3, 4, 5, 23 Dec. 1829, 10, 12, 16, 19, 27 April, 4, 11, 12 May, 28 Aug. 1830; *Niles' Register,* 13 June 1829.

103. John Randolph to Andrew Jackson, 8 Nov. 1831, Bassett, *Correspondence of Jackson,* 4:370; John Campbell to James Campbell, 23 April, 1830, Campbell Family Papers, Duke; Smith, *Press, Politics, and Patronage,* 96–99, 297n45.

104. Andrew Jackson to T. L. Miller, 13 May 1829, Bassett, *Correspondence of Jackson,* 4:32.

105. The standard work on the development of the new mass party system, McCormick, *Second Party System,* does not quite make the point about the editors' role, but it can be seen in the number of newspaper editors that McCormick identifies as key state party figures. "Parties did not 'emerge,'" McCormick writes, "neither did they 'form,' rather, they were formed by astute and energetic politicians. When the process of party formation is examined state by state, it can be seen that at some appropriate opportunity rival leaders, or groups of leaders, took the initiative in creating parties" (351–52). Among a list of nine examples of such leaders, McCormick includes five newspaper editors: Niles of Connecticut, Hill of New Hampshire, Dawson of Ohio, Kendall of Kentucky, and Weed of New York. Elsewhere in the book, McCormick gives prominent party-building roles to more editors, including David Henshaw of Massachusetts, Elijah Hayward of Ohio, Peter K. Wagner of Louisiana, and Thomas Ritchie of Virginia.

106. On Hill's revenge, see Cole, *Jacksonian Democracy in N.H.,* 89–98.

107. Hartford *Times,* 29 Dec. 1818, 5, 12, 19, 26 Jan., 2, 9, 16 Feb. 1819.

108. Morse, *Neglected Period of Connecticut's History,* 62–63, 79–99; Niven, *Gideon Welles,* 26–54; Brownsword, "Connecticut Political Patterns," 183–337; McCormick, *Second Party System,* 65–67. The *Times* party's activities and strategies are amply recorded in their newspaper and (after 1826 or so) in the voluminous Gideon Welles Papers, LC.

109. John M. Niles to Thomas Hart Benton, 28 Jan. 1829, Niles to Gideon Welles, 6, 12, 20, 25 Feb., 5 March 1829, Welles to Niles, 10, 12 (quoted), 19, 22 Feb., 5 March 1829, Noah Phelps to Welles, 12, 13, 22 Feb. 1829, Welles to Phelps, 9 March 1829, Welles Papers, LC; Niven, *Gideon Welles,* 50–70; Robert V. Remini, *Jackson and Course of Freedom,* 166–67, 169–80.

110. Niven, *Gideon Welles,* 71–87; John M. Niles to David Henshaw, 22 Feb. 1830, Misc. Manuscripts, Boston Public Library; F. P. Blair to John Niles, 14 Oct. 1831, 27 June 1832, Niles Papers, CHS; John C. Rives to John M. Niles, 4, 20 Aug., 20 Sept., 15, 25 Oct., 26 Nov. 1832, Niles Papers, NYPL; Rives to Niles, 4 June, 2 Aug. 1833, 17 Feb., 27 Oct. 1834, Misc. Personal Papers, NYPL.

111. Morse, *Neglected Period of Connecticut's History,* 84–118, 288–99; Niven, *Gideon Welles,* 104–49; McCormick, *Second Party System,* 68–69.

112. The best secondary source on Niles's later political career is Niven, *Gideon Welles,* 167–252. See also Niles Autobiography, CHS; Stiles, *History of Ancient Windsor,* 2:534–36; *DAB.*

113. See this book's companion web site <http://pasleybrothers.com/newspols> for a complete roster of printers, editors, and publishers who served in Congress up through 1860.

114. Cole, *Jacksonian Democracy in N.H.,* 97–98; Stiles, *History of Ancient Windsor,* 2:534–36. See the bibliography for examples of Niles speeches reprinted as pamphlets.

115. Goodrich, *Recollections of a Lifetime,* 2:429n–430n.

116. The most thoroughgoing and vitriolic statement of this view can be found in Edward Pessen's works, *Jacksonian America* and *Riches, Class, and Power.*

SELECTED BIBLIOGRAPHY

PRIMARY SOURCES

Manuscript Collections

American Antiquarian Society, Worcester, Mass
John and Sidney Babcock Papers
John Bailhache Autobiography
Bangs Family Papers
Book Trades Collection
David Chambers Papers
Lincoln Family Papers
Charles Prentiss Correspondence
John Prentiss Papers, including a bound manuscript autobiography, "Autobiographical
    and Historical: Recollections of Eighty-eight Years" (1866), cited as Prentiss Auto-
    biography
Printers File

American Philosophical Society Library, Philadelphia, Pa.
Bache Papers—Castle Collection (microfilm)
Benjamin Franklin Bache Papers
Bache Family Papers
Duane Family Papers
William J. Duane Papers

Boston Public Library, Boston, Mass.
Miscellaneous letters of: John Beckley, William Duane, John M. Niles

*College of William and Mary, Earl Gregg Swem Library, Manuscripts
and Rare Books Dept., Williamsburg, Va.*
Leven Powell Papers
Ritchie-Harrison Papers
Tucker-Coleman Papers

Columbia University, Rare Book and Manuscript Library, Columbia, Mo.
De Witt Clinton Papers (microfilm)
Edwin Patrick Kilroe Collection

Charlemagne Tower Papers
Typographic Library Manuscripts

Connecticut Historical Society, Hartford, Conn.
Babcock Papers
Index to the Hartford *Connecticut Courant*
John Niles Autobiography
John Niles Papers

Detroit Public Library, Burton Historical Collection, Detroit, Mich.
Alpheus Felch Papers
Stanley Griswold Papers
Mason Family Papers
John Norvell Papers
Reading Room File
Ross Wilkins Papers
William Woodbridge Papers
Augustus B. Woodward Papers

Duke University, William R. Perkins Library, Special Collections, Durham, N.C.
Campbell Family Papers
Ephraim Kirby Papers
John M. McCalla Papers
John Page Papers

Easton Area Public Library, Marx Room of Local History, Easton, Pa.
Easton, Pa, Newspaper extracts, 1823–35 (typewritten manuscript)
Matthew S. Henry, Manuscript History of Northampton County, 1851 (typewritten copy)

Harvard Business School, Baker Library, Special Collections, Allston, Mass.
Stanley Griswold Papers

Harvard University, Houghton Library, Boston, Mass.
Jacob Bailey Moore Papers
Stanley Griswold Sermon Collection

Historical Society of Delaware, Wilmington, Del.
Miscellaneous Manuscripts
Rodney Collection

Historical Society of Pennsylvania, Philadelphia, Pa.
George Bryan Papers
Lewis Coryell Papers

Tench Coxe Papers (microfilm)
George Mifflin Dallas Collection
Democratic Society of Pennsylvania, Minutes
Ferdinand J. Dreer Autograph Collection
Edward Carey Gardiner Collection, Mathew Carey Papers
Simon Gratz Autograph Collection
Charles Jared Ingersoll Correspondence
William Irvine Papers
Lea and Febiger Papers
Daniel Parker Papers
Jonathan Roberts Papers
John Sergeant Papers
John Smith Papers
Uselma Clarke Smith Collection, William Jones Papers
Society Autograph Collection
Society Miscellaneous Collection
Society Small Collection
Samuel C. Stambaugh Papers
David McNeely Stauffer Collection
William Wood Thackara Diary
Townsend-LeMaistre Collection, I. D. Barnard Papers
Roberts Vaux Papers
Anthony Wayne Papers
George Wolf Papers

Library Company of Philadelphia, Philadelphia, Pa.
Miscellaneous Manuscript Collection
Rush Papers

Library of Congress, Manuscript Division, Washington, D.C.
Blair Family Papers (microfilm)
William Darlington Papers
Peter Force Papers. Series I: General Correspondence
Gales and Seaton Papers
Francis and Gideon Granger Papers (microfilm)
Duff Green Papers (microfilm)
Thomas Jefferson Papers (microfilm)
James Madison Papers (microfilm)
James Monroe Papers (microfilm)
Thomas Ritchie Papers
Martin Van Buren Papers (microfilm)
Gideon Welles Papers (microfilm)

Missouri Historical Society, Library and Collections Center, St. Louis, Mo.
Dougherty Papers
Hamilton R. Gamble Papers

Genealogy collection
Thomas Jefferson Papers (Bixby Collection)
Journals and Diaries collection: William Gilpin letters
Lucas Collection
Ludlow-Maury-Field Collection
Sibley Papers

National Archives, Washington, D.C. (Record Group 59, General Records of the Department of State.)
Letters of Application and Recommendation During the Administration of Thomas Jefferson, 1801–09. Microcopy 418.
Letters of Application and Recommendation During the Administration of James Madison, 1809–17. Microcopy 438.
Letters of Application and Recommendation During the Administration of Andrew Jackson, 1829–37. Microcopy 639.
Letters of Application and Recommendation During the Administrations of Martin Van Buren, William Henry Harrison, and John Tyler, 1837–45. Microcopy 687.

New Haven Colony Historical Society, New Haven, Conn.
New Haven Custom House Papers

New York Historical Society, New York, N.Y.
Matthew Livingston Davis Papers
Albert Gallatin Papers (microfilm)
Rufus King Papers
Allen McLane Papers
Miscellaneous manuscripts, filed under: Abraham Bishop, Gideon Granger, John M. Niles, Gideon Welles

New York Public Library, Rare Book and Manuscript Division, New York, N.Y.
Joseph Clay Papers
Dwight Family Papers
Azariah C. Flagg Papers
James Madison Papers
James Monroe Papers
Miscellaneous Papers (uncataloged), filed under: Benjamin Franklin Bache, Richard Bache Jr., John Beckley, Abraham Bishop, Matthew L. Davis, William Duane, Isaac Hill, Charles Holt, B. Irvine, Thomas Ritchie, Solomon Southwick Jr., John C. Wright
John Milton Niles Papers

Ohio Historical Society, Ohio Historical Center, Columbus, Ohio
Larwill Family Papers
Joseph H. Larwill Papers
Charles Elmer Rice Collection

John Sloane Papers
Vertical File Manuscripts

Rosenbach Library and Museum, Philadelphia, Pa.
Thomas Cooper Letters

University of Michigan, Bentley Historical Library, Ann Arbor, Mich.
Stevens Thomson Mason Papers
Mark Norris Papers
Francis Willett Shearman Papers

University of Michigan, William L. Clements Library, Ann Arbor, Mich.
Lewis Cass Papers
Fenno-Hoffman Papers
Lucius Lyon Papers
Michigan Collection
John Michael O'Connor Papers
War of 1812 Papers
William Wilson Papers

*University of Rochester, Rush Rhees Library, Dept. of Rare Books
and Special Collections*
Thurlow Weed Papers

University of Virginia, Alderman Library, Charlottesville, Va.
Ambler Family Papers
Carr Family Papers
R.H. Coleman Letters
Richard K. Crallé Papers
Gooch Family Papers
Thomas Jefferson Papers
McGregor Collection
Carr-Cary Papers
Miscellaneous Manuscripts
Stone Family Letters
Creed Taylor Correspondence
Micajah T. Woods Papers

Virginia Historical Society, Richmond, Va.
Ambler Family Papers
Gooch Family Papers
Mercer Family Papers
Miscellaneous Manuscripts
Preston Family Papers

Yale University, Sterling Library, Manuscripts and Archives, New Haven, Conn.
Abraham Bishop Letterbook
Col. John Brown and Maj. General Preston Brown Papers
David Daggett Papers
Misc. Manuscript Collection

Newspapers
(consulted on microfilm except where physical location is noted)

Connecticut
Danbury *Republican Farmer,* 1803–1805
Danbury/Norwalk/New Haven *Sun of Liberty,* 1800–1801 (Houghton Library, Harvard University)
Hartford *American Mercury,* 1794–1808
Hartford *Connecticut Courant,* 1800–20
Hartford *Connecticut Mirror,* 1812, 1816–17, 1829
Hartford *Times,* 1817–38 (CHS)
Litchfield *Witness,* 1805–1807
New London *Bee,* 1797–1802
New London *Connecticut Gazette,* 1798–1802
Stonington *Journal of the Times,* 1798–99
Stonington-Port *Patriot, or Scourge of Aristocracy,* 1801–1803

Delaware
Wilmington *American Watchman,* 1809
Wilmington *Mirror of the Times & General Advertiser,* 1799–1801 (Houghton Library)

District of Columbia
Georgetown *Federal Republican,* 1812–15
Washington *National Intelligencer,* 1800–1801, 1832
Washington *Daily National Journal,* 1824, 1829–30 (Center for Research Libraries, Chicago)
Washington Federalist, 1800–1802, 1804.

Georgia
Savannah *Columbian Museum and Savannah Advertiser,* 1802–1805
Savannah *Georgia Republican & State Intelligencer,* 1802–1805

Kentucky
Frankfort *Argus of Western America,* 1816–30
Lancaster *Political Theatre,* 1808–1809
Lexington *Kentucky Gazette,* 1800–1801, 1817–19

Maine
Portland *Eastern Argus,* 1803–1805

Maryland

Baltimore *American,* 1799–1800
Baltimore *Federal Republican and Commercial Gazette,* 1808–1812
Baltimore *Republican,* 1827–30 (AAS)
Baltimore *Patriot,* 1812–17 (AAS)
Baltimore *Whig,* 1813–14 (AAS, LC)
Niles Register

Massachusetts

Boston *Constitutional Telegraph,* 1799–1800 (Houghton)
Boston *New England Palladium,* 1801, 1803–1805
Boston *Independent Chronicle,* 1791–93
Boston *Independent Chronicle & Patriot,* 1817
Pittsfield *Sun,* 1800–1802
Salem *Gazette,* 1800–1802 (Houghton)
Salem *Impartial Register/Register,* 1800–1802
Springfield *Republican Spy,* 1803–1804
Worcester *Massachusetts Spy,* 1801, 1803–1805, 1809
Worcester *National Aegis,* 1801–1806
Worcester *Scorpion,* 1809

Michigan

Detroit *Democratic Free Press,* 1831–36

Mississippi

Natchez *Mississippi Herald and Natchez Gazette,* 1804, 1806–1808

New Hampshire

Concord *American Patriot,* 1808–1809
Concord *New Hampshire Patriot,* 1809–1810, 1817
Keene *New Hampshire Sentinel,* 1799–1805
Portsmouth *New Hampshire Gazette,* 1801–1803
Portsmouth *Republican Ledger,* 1800 (Houghton)
Walpole *Political Observatory,* 1803–1805

New Jersey

Newark *Centinel of Freedom,* 1817
Trenton Federalist, 1802–1803
Trenton *True American,* 1801–1806, 1812–24

New York

Goshen *Orange Patrol,* 1800 (AAS)
Hudson *Balance,* 1802–1803
Hudson *Bee,* 1802–1803
Hudson *Wasp,* 1802 (full run)
New York *American Citizen,* 1800–1801

New York *Evening Post*, 1804
New York *Gazette of the United States*, 1789–90
New York *Time Piece*, 1797–98

North Carolina
Raleigh Register, 1800–1801

Pennsylvania
Chambersburg *Farmers' Register*, 1798–99
Easton *American Eagle*, 1799–1805
Easton *Centinel*, 1817–33
Easton *Delaware Democrat and Easton Gazette*, 1827–28
Easton Expositor, 1822
Easton *Mountaineer*, 1820
Easton *Northampton Farmer*, 1805–11
Easton *Pennsylvania Herald and Easton Intelligencer*, 1808–1809
Easton *Spirit of Pennsylvania*, 1815–20
Lancaster *Intelligencer*, 1799–1801
Norristown *Register*, 1803–1808 (Historical Society of Montgomery County)
Philadelphia *American Sentinel*, 1829 (LCP)
Philadelphia *Aurora and General Advertiser*, 1790–1812
Philadelphia *Democratic Press*, scattered issues
Philadelphia *Franklin Gazette*, 1818–20 (AAS)
Philadelphia *Freeman's Journal*, 1804 (Houghton)
Philadelphia *Gazette of the United States*, 1790–98
Philadelphia *General Advertiser*, 1790–94
Philadelphia *National Gazette*, 1791–93
Philadelphia *Pennsylvania Inquirer*, 1829 (LCP)
Philadelphia Evening Post, 1804
Philadelphia *Porcupine's Gazette*, 1798–99
Philadelphia *Port Folio*, 1801, 1803
Pittsburgh *Commonwealth*, 1805
Pittsburgh *Gazette*, 1800–1801
Pittsburgh *Mercury*, 1812, 1816–17
Pittsburgh *Tree of Liberty*, 1800–1801
Washington *Herald of Liberty*, 1798–1800
West Chester *Village Record*, 1818

Rhode Island
Newport *Companion*, 1798–99
Newport *Guardian of Liberty*, 1800–1801
Newport *Rhode Island Republican*, 1801
Providence *Microcosm*, 1825–27 (AAS)

South Carolina
Charleston *City Gazette and Daily Advertiser*, 1800–1801

Vermont

Rutland *Farmers' Library*, 1793–94
Rutland *Vermont Mercury*, 1802

Virginia

Alexandria *Columbian Advertiser*, 1802
Alexandria *Expositor*, 1802
The Times and Alexandria Advertiser, 1798–1802
Fredericksburg *Genius of Liberty*, 1798–99 (AAS)
Norfolk *Epitome of the Times*, 1798–1801 (AAS)
Richmond *Enquirer*, 1804–1808, 1817
Richmond *Examiner*, 1798–1802
Richmond *Friend of the People*, 1800 (AAS)
Staunton *Political Mirror and Scourge of Aristocracy*, 1800–1801
Williamsburg/Richmond *Virginia Gazette*, 1775–80

Other Published Primary Sources

Adams, John Quincy. *Memoirs of John Quincy Adams, Comprising Portions of His Diary from 1795 to 1848*. Ed. Charles Francis Adams. 12 vols. Philadelphia, 1874.
Addison, Alexander. *Liberty of Speech, and of the Press*. Washington, Pa., 1798.
———. *An Oration on the Rise and Progress of the United States of America, to the Present Crisis; and on the Duties of the Citizens*. Philadelphia, 1798.
———. *Reports of Cases in the County Courts of the Fifth Circuit, and in the High Court of Errors and Appeals, of the State of Pennsylvania, and Charges to the Grand Juries of Those County Courts*. Washington, Pa., 1800.
Alexander, James. *A Brief Narrative of the Case and Trial of John Peter Zenger, Printer of the "New York Weekly Journal"*. Ed. Stanley Nider Katz. Cambridge, Mass., 1963.
Allen, W. B., ed. *Works of Fisher Ames, As Published by Seth Ames*. 2 vols. Indianapolis, 1983.
Auge, M[oses]. *Lives of the Eminent Dead and Biographical Notices of Prominent Living Citizens of Montgomery County, Pa.* Norristown, Pa., 1879.
[Bache, Benjamin Franklin]. *Remarks Occasioned by the Late Conduct of Mr. Washington, as President of the United States*. Philadelphia, 1797.
———. *Truth Will Out! The Foul Charges of the Tories against the Editor of the Aurora Repelled by Positive Proof and Plain Truth, and His Base Calumniators Put to Shame*. Philadelphia, 1798.
Bassett, John Spencer, ed. *Correspondence of Andrew Jackson*. 7 vols. Washington, D.C., 1926–35.
"Belknap Papers." *Collections of the Massachusetts Historical Society*, 5th ser., 2 (1877): 1–500, 3 (1877): 1–373, 445–461.
Bentley, William. *The Diary of William Bentley, D. D.* 4 vols. 1905. Reprint, Gloucester, Mass., 1962.
Bergh, Albert Ellery, ed. *The Writings of Thomas Jefferson*. 20 vols. Washington, D.C.: Thomas Jefferson Memorial Association of the United States, 1905.
Binns, John. *Recollections of the Life of John Binns*. Philadelphia, 1854.
Bishop, Abraham, ed. *Church and State. A Political Union, Formed by the Enemies of Both, Illustrated in the Correspondencies Between the Rev. Stanley Griswold and the*

Rev. Dan Huntington, and Between Col. Ephraim Kirby and the Rev. Joseph Lyman. n.p., 1802.

Botein, Stephen, ed. *'Mr. Zenger's Malice and Falsehood': Six Issues of the New-York Weekly Journal, 1733–34.* Worcester, Mass., 1985.

Boyd, Julian P., et al., eds. *The Papers of Thomas Jefferson.* 28 vols. to date. Princeton, N.J. 1950–.

Brackenridge, H[enry] M[arie]. *Recollections of Person and Places in the West.* 2d ed. Philadelphia, 1868.

[Bradley, Cyrus Parker]. *Biography of Isaac Hill, of New-Hampshire. With an Appendix, Comprising Selections from his Speeches and Miscellaneous Writings.* Concord, N.H., 1835.

Bristed, John. *America and Her Resources.* London, 1818.

Brugger, Robert J., Robert A. Rutland, et al., eds. *The Papers of James Madison: Secretary of State Series.* 4 vols. to date. Charlottesville, Va., 1986–.

Buckingham, Joseph T. *Personal Memoirs and Reflections of Editorial Life.* 2 vols. Boston, 1852.

———, ed. *Specimens of Newspaper Literature.* 2 vols. Boston, 1850.

[Callender, James Thomson]. *The History of the United States for 1796.* Philadelphia, 1797.

Cappon, Lester J. *The Adams-Jefferson Letters: The Complete Correspondence between Thomas Jefferson and Abigail and John Adams.* 1959. Reprint, Chapel Hill, N.C. 1988.

Carey, Mathew. *Autobiography.* 1833–34. Reprint, Brooklyn, 1942.

———. *The Olive Branch: or Faults on Both Sides, Federal and Democratic; a Serious Appeal on the Necessity of Mutual Forgiveness and Harmony.* 10th ed. Philadelphia, 1818.

Cheetham, James. "Letters of James Cheetham." Ed. Worthington C. Ford. *Proceedings of the Massachusetts Historical Society,* 3d ser., 1 (1907): 41–64.

Claiborne, J. F. H. *Mississippi, as a Province, Territory and State, with Biographical Notices of Eminent Citizens.* 1880. Reprint, Baton Rouge, 1964.

Cobbett, William. *Porcupine's Works.* 12 vols. London, 1801.

[———.] *A Prospect from the Congress-Gallery, during the Session Begun December 7, 1795.* Philadelphia, 1796.

Cox, James M. *Journey through My Years.* New York, 1946.

Cunningham, Noble E., Jr., ed. *Circular Letters of Congressman to Their Constituents, 1789–1829.* 3 vols. Chapel Hill, N.C. 1978.

Dallas, George Mifflin. *Life and Writings of Alexander James Dallas.* Philadelphia, 1871.

Daniels, Josephus. *Editor in Politics.* Chapel Hill, N.C., 1941.

———. *Tar Heel Editor.* Chapel Hill, N.C., 1939.

Davis, Matthew L. *A Brief Account of the Epidemical Fever Which Lately Prevailed in the City of New York.* New York, 1795.

———. *Memoirs of Aaron Burr, with Miscellaneous Selections from His Correspondence.* 2 vols. New York, 1836–37.

———. *Oration, Delivered in St. Paul's Church, on the Fourth of July, 1800.* New York, 1800.

Dennie, Joseph. *The Letters of Joseph Dennie, 1768–1812.* Ed. Laura Green Pedder. Orono, Maine, 1936.

Duane, William. *The American Military Library.* 2 vols. Philadelphia, 1807-1809.

———. *Experience the Test of Government: In Eighteen Essays.* Philadelphia, 1807.

————. "Letters of William Duane." Ed. Worthington C. Ford. *Proceedings of the Massachusetts Historical Society*, 2d ser., 20 (1906–1907): 258–394.

————. *Politics for American Farmers; Being a Series of Tracts, Exhibiting the Blessings of Free Government, as It Is Administered in the United States, Compared with the Boasted Stupendous Fabric.* Washington City, 1807.

[Duane, William, II]. *Biographical Memoir of William J. Duane.* Philadelphia, 1868.

Dwight, Jasper [William Duane]. *A Letter to George Washington, President of the United States: Containing Strictures on his Address . . . Notifying his Relinquishment of the Presidential Office.* Philadelphia. 1796.

Elmer, Lucius Q. C. *The Constitution and Government of the Province and State of New Jersey, with Biographical Sketches of the Governors from 1776 to 1845 and Reminiscences of the Bench and Bar during More than Half a Century.* Newark, N.J., 1872.

Farkas, Alexander Bölöni. *Journey in North America.* Trans. and ed. Theodore and Benedek Schoenman. Philadelphia, 1977.

Fearon, Henry Bradshaw. *Sketches of America.* 2d ed. London, 1818.

Foner, Philip S., ed. *The Democratic-Republican Societies, 1790- 1800: A Documentary Sourcebook of Constitutions, Declarations, Addresses, Resolutions, and Toasts.* Westport, Conn., 1976.

Foster, Augustus John. *Jeffersonian America: Notes on the United States of America Collected in the Years 1805–6–7 and 11–12 by Sir Augustus John Foster, Bart.* Ed. Richard Beale Davis. San Marino, Calif., 1954.

Franklin, Benjamin. *Benjamin Franklin's Autobiography.* Norton Critical Edition. Ed. J. A. Leo Lemay and P. M. Zall. New York, 1986.

————. *The Writings of Benjamin Franklin.* Ed. Albert Henry Smyth. 10 vols. New York, 1905-1907.

Freneau, Philip. *The Poems of Philip Freneau.* 3 vols. Ed. Fred Lewis Pattee. Princeton, N.J., 1907.

————. *The Prose of Philip Freneau.* Ed. Philip M. Marsh. New Brunswick, N.J., 1955.

Gales, Joseph, Sr., et al., eds. *The Debates and Proceedings of the Congress of the United States.* Washington, D.C., 1834–56.

Gallatin, Albert. *The Writings of Albert Gallatin.* Ed. Henry Adams. 3 vols. 1879. Reprint, New York, 1960.

[Gerry, Elbridge] *Message from His Excellency the Governor. February 27, 1812.* Boston, 1812.

Gibbs, George, ed. *Memoirs of the Administrations of Washington and John Adams, Edited from the Papers of Oliver Wolcott, Secretary of the Treasury.* 2 vols. New York, 1846.

Goodrich, S[amuel] G[riswold]. *Recollections of a Lifetime, or Men and Things I Have Seen.* 2 vols. New York and Auburn, N.Y., 1856.

Greeley, Horace. *Recollections of a Busy Life.* 1852. Reprint, New York, 1983.

Green, Duff. *Facts and Suggestions, Biographical, Historical, Financial and Political, Addressed to the People of the United States.* New York, 1866.

Griswold, Stanley. *A Statement of the Singular Manner of Proceedings of the Rev. Association of the South Part of Litchfield County, in an Ecclesiastical Prosecution, by Them Instituted against the Rev. Stanley Griswold. . . .* Hartford, Conn., 1798.

Hanson, A. C., ed. *Accurate Report of the Argument on a Motion of Attachment against Baptis Irvine, Editor of the Whig, for a Contempt against the Court of Oyer and Terminer for Baltimore County, by . . . One of the Counsel for the State.* Baltimore, 1808.

[Hanson, Alexander Contee]. *Reflections on the Late Correspondence between Mr. Secretary Smith, and Francis James Jackson, Esq., Minister Plenipotentiary of His Brittanic Majesty.* Baltimore, Md., 1810.

Hench, John B., ed. "Letters of John Fenno and John Ward Fenno, 1779–1800." *Proceedings of the American Antiquarian Society,* n.s., 89 (1980): 299–368, 90 (1980): 163–234.

[Hill, Isaac]. *Brief Sketch of the Life, Character and Services of Major General Andrew Jackson.* Concord, N.H., 1828.

———. *Wise Sayings of the Honorable Isaac Hill.* Concord, N.H., 1828.

Holmes, Isaac. *An Account of the United States of America.* London, 1823.

Hopkins, James F., et al., eds. *The Papers of Henry Clay.* 11 vols. Lexington, Ky., 1959–92.

Hudson, Frederic. *Journalism in the United States, from 1690 to 1872.* 1873. Reprint, New York, 1968.

Hutchinson, William T., William M. E. Rachal, Robert A. Rutland, et al., eds. *The Papers of James Madison.* 17 vols. Vols. 1–10, Chicago, 1962–77; vols. 11–17, Charlottesville, Va., 1977–91.

Jefferson, Thomas. *Writings.* Ed. Merrill D. Peterson. The Library of America, vol. 17. New York, 1984.

———. *The Writings of Thomas Jefferson.* Ed. Paul Leicester Ford. 10 vols. New York and London, 1892–99.

Jensen, Merrill, John P. Kaminski, and Gaspare J. Saladino, eds. 14 vols. to date. *The Documentary History of the Ratification of the Constitution.* Madison, Wisc., 1976–.

Kendall, Amos. *Autobiography of Amos Kendall.* Ed. William Stickney. Boston, 1872.

King, Charles R., ed. *The Life and Correspondence of Rufus King.* 6 vols. New York, 1895.

King, William L. *The Newspaper Press of Charleston, S.C.* Charleston, 1872.

Klein, Philip S., ed. "Memoirs of a Senator from Pennsylvania: Jonathan Roberts, 1771–1854." *Pennsylvania Magazine of History and Biography* 61 (1937): 446–74, 62 (1938): 64–97, 213–48, 361–409, 502–51.

Kline, Mary-Jo, ed. *Political Correspondence and Public Papers of Aaron Burr.* 2 vols. Princeton, N.J., 1983.

Knox, Vicesimus. *The Spirit of Despotism.* 2d American edition. Norristown, Pa. 1807.

Lambert, John. *Travels through Lower Canada, and the United States of America, in the Years 1806, 1807, and 1808.* London, 1810.

Lincoln, William. *History of Worcester, Massachusetts, from Its Earliest Settlement to September, 1836.* Worcester, 1837.

Lodge, Henry Cabot. *Life and Letters of George Cabot.* 1878. Reprint, New York, 1974.

MacAnear, Beverly, ed. "James Parker versus New York Province." *New York History* 22 (1941): 323.

Mason, Jeremiah. "Autobiography." In *Memoir and Correspondence of Jeremiah Mason,* edited by George Stillman Hilliard. Cambridge, Mass., 1873.

Melish, John. *Travels through the United States of America, in the Years 1806 & 1807, and 1809, 1810, & 1811.* Belfast, 1818.

Mencken, H. L. *A Carnival of Buncombe: Writings on Politics,* edited by Malcolm Moos. 1956. Reprint, Chicago, 1984.

Meriwether, Robert L., W. Edwin Hemphill, et al., eds. *The Papers of John C. Calhoun.* 23 vols. to date. Columbia, S.C.: University of South Carolina Press, 1959-.

Merrill, Michael, and Sean Wilentz, eds. *The Key of Liberty: The Life and Democratic Writings of William Manning, "a Laborer," 1747–1814.* Cambridge, Mass., 1993.

Miller, Samuel. *A Brief Retrospect of the Eighteenth Century.* 2 vols. New York, 1803. Reprint, New York, 1970.

Miller, Stephen B. *Historical Sketches of Hudson.* Hudson, N.Y., 1862.

Munsell, J[oel]. *The Typographical Miscellany.* Albany, 1850.

Niles, John M. *The Connecticut Civil Officer.* Hartford, Conn., 1823.

———. *The Life of Oliver Hazard Perry.* 2d ed. Hartford, 1821.

———. "Preface" to *The Independent Whig, or, A Defence of Primitive Christianity.* . . . 1st American from 6th London ed. Hartford, Conn., 1816.

———. *Speech of Hon. J. M. Niles, of Connecticut, on the Compromise Bill.* Washington, D.C., 1848.

———. *Speech of Hon. John M. Niles, of Connecticut, on the War with Mexico.* Washington, D.C., 1848.

———. *Speech of Mr. Niles, of Connecticut, on the Oregon Question.* Washington, D.C., 1846.

———. *Speech of Mr. Niles, of Connecticut, on the Petition of a Society of Friends in Pennsylvania, Praying for the Abolition of Slavery in the District of Columbia.* Washington, D.C., 1836.

Palmer, William P., et al., eds. *Calendar of Virginia State Papers and Other Manuscripts.* 11 vols. Richmond, Va., 1875–93.

Parker, Freddie L., ed. *Stealing a Little Freedom: Advertisements for Slave Runaways in North Carolina, 1791–1840.* New York and London, 1994.

Parrington, Vernon Louis, ed. *The Connecticut Wits.* 1926. Reprint, New York, 1969.

Partridge, Isaac M. "The Press of Mississippi—Historical Sketch." *De Bow's Review* 29, no. 4 (1860): 500–9.

Pennsylvania Archives. 9 series, 120 vols. Philadelphia, 1852–56; Harrisburg, Pa., 1874–1935.

Randolph, Thomas Jefferson. *Memoir, Correspondence, and Miscellanies, from the Papers of Thomas Jefferson.* Charlottesville, Va., 1829.

Ritchie, Thomas. "Unpublished Letters of Thomas Ritchie." Ed. Charles H. Ambler. *The John P. Branch Historical Papers of Randolph-Macon College* 3 (1911): 199–252.

Rogers, Thomas J., ed. *A New American Biographical Dictionary; or, Remembrancer of the Departed Heroes, Sages, and Statesmen, of America.* 3d ed. Easton, Pa., 1824.

———. *Thomas J. Rogers, having purchased the English Printing Office . . . Easton, November 12, 1805.* Broadside, LCP.

Rush, Benjamin. *The Autobiography of Benjamin Rush: His "Travels through Life" together with his "Commonplace Book" for 1789–1813.* Ed. George W. Corner. Princeton, N.J., 1948.

Sawvel, Franklin B., ed. *The Complete Anas of Thomas Jefferson.* New York, 1903.

Schwartz, Bernard, ed. *The Bill of Rights: A Documentary History.* 2 vols. New York, 1971.

[Shepherd, Charles], ed. *A Report on the Trial of Andrew Wright, Printer of the 'Republican Spy,' on an Indictment for Libels against Governor Strong . . . .* Northampton, Mass., 1806.

Speeches at Full Length in the Cause of the People Against Harry Croswell. 1804. Reprint., New York, 1970.

Stewart, Ethelbert, ed. *Documentary History of the Early Organizations of American Printers*. Indianapolis, Ind., 1907.

Swift, Zephaniah. *A System of the Laws of the State of Connecticut*. Windham, Conn., 1795.

Syrett, Harold C., and Jacob E. Cooke, eds. *The Papers of Alexander Hamilton*. 27 vols. New York, 1961–87.

Thale, Mary, ed. *Selections from the Papers of the London Corresponding Society, 1792–1799*. Cambridge, U.K., 1983.

Thomas, Isaiah. *The History of Printing in America*. 2 vols. Worcester, Mass., 1810.

———. *The History of Printing in America*. Ed. Marcus A. McCorison. New York, 1970.

Tocqueville, Alexis de. *Democracy in America*. Ed. J. P. Mayer. Trans. George Lawrence. New York, 1969.

———. *Journey to America*. Ed. J. P. Mayer. Trans. George Lawrence. 1971. Reprint, Westport, Conn., 1981.

To the Republicans of the County of Hunterdon. By a Democratic Republican. Philadelphia, 1812. Shaw/Shoemaker.

Trial of Alexander Contee Hanson, Esq., a Lieutenant in a Company of Militia. . . . Baltimore, Md., 1809.

Tudor, William. *Letters on the Eastern States*. New York, 1820.

Van Buren, Martin. *Autobiography of Martin Van Buren*. Edited by John C. Fitzpatrick. 1920, Reprint, New York, 1983.

Washburn, Charles Grenfill, ed. "Letters of Thomas Boylston Adams to William Smith Shaw, 1799–1823." *Proceedings of the American Antiquarian Society*, n.s., 27 (1917): 83–176.

Watterson, Henry. *"Marse Henry": An Autobiography*. 2 vols. New York, 1919.

Weber, Max. "Politics as a Vocation." In *From Max Weber: Essays in Sociology*, edited and translated by H. H. Gerth and C. Wright Mills, 77–128. New York, 1946.

Weed, Thurlow. *The Autobiography of Thurlow Weed*. Ed. Harriet A. Weed. Boston, 1884.

White, William Allen. *The Autobiography of William Allen White*. New York, 1946.

Wiltse, Charles M., et al., eds. *The Papers of Daniel Webster: Correspondence*. 7 vols. Hanover, N.H., 1974–86.

Wright, Andrew. *The Anti-Shepherd-Crat; or, An Appeal to Honest Republicans: An Historical Sketch*. Northampton, Mass., 1811.

SECONDARY SOURCES

Abel, Richard L. *American Lawyers*. New York, 1989.

Adair, Douglass. *Fame and the Founding Fathers*. Ed. Trevor Colbourn. New York, 1974.

Adams, Henry. *The Life of Albert Gallatin*. Philadelphia, 1879.

Adams, James Truslow. *New England in the Republic, 1776–1850*. 1926. Reprint, Gloucester, Mass., 1960.

Alexander, John K. *The Selling of the Constitutional Convention: A History of News Coverage*. Madison, Wis., 1990.

Altschuler, Glenn C. and Stuart M. Blumin. *Rude Republic: Americans and Their Politics in the Nineteenth Century*. Princeton, N.J.: Princeton University Press, 2000.

Ambler, Charles Henry. *Thomas Ritchie: A Study in Virginia Politics.* Richmond, Va., 1913.

Ames, William E. *A History of the 'National Intelligencer'.* Chapel Hill, N.C., 1972.

Ammon, Harry. *James Monroe: The Quest for National Identity.* 1971. Reprint, Charlottesville, Va. 1990.

———. "The Richmond Junto, 1800–1824." *Virginia Magazine of History and Biography* 61 (1953): 395–418.

Anderson, Benedict. *Imagined Communities.* Revised ed. New York, 1991.

Anderson, John R. *Shepard Kollock: Editor for Freedom.* Chatham, N.J., 1975.

Andrews, J. Cutler. *Pittsburgh's Post-Gazette: "The First Newspaper West of the Alleghenies."* 1938, Reprint, Westport, Conn., 1970.

Appleby, Joyce. *Capitalism and a New Social Order: The Republican Vision of the 1790s.* New York, 1984.

Aronson, Sidney H. *Status and Kinship in the Higher Civil Service: Standards of Selection in the Administrations of John Adams, Thomas Jefferson, and Andrew Jackson.* Cambridge, Mass., 1964.

Ashley, Perry J., ed. *American Newspaper Journalists, 1690–1872.* Vol. 43, *Dictionary of Literary Biography.* Detroit, Mich., 1985.

Ashworth, John. *'Agrarians' and 'Aristocrats': Party Political Ideology in the United States, 1837–1846.* Cambridge, U.K., 1987.

Aspinall, Arthur. *Politics and the Press, c. 1780–1850.* 1949, Reprint, Brighton, U.K., 1979.

Austin, Aleine. *Matthew Lyon: "New Man" of the Democratic Revolution, 1749–1822.* University Park, Pa., 1981.

Bailyn, Bernard. *The Ideological Origins of the American Revolution.* Cambridge, Mass., 1967.

Bailyn, Bernard, and John B. Hench, eds. *The Press and the American Revolution.* Boston, 1981.

Baker, Jean H. *Affairs of Party: The Political Culture of Northern Democrats in the Mid-Nineteenth Century.* Ithaca, N.Y., 1983.

Baker, Paula. "The Domestication of American Politics: Women and American Political Society, 1780–1920." *American Historical Review* 89 (1984): 620–47.

Baldasty, Gerald J. *The Commercialization of News in the Nineteenth Century.* Madison, Wis., 1992.

———. "The New York State Political Press and Antimasonry." *New York History* 64 (1983): 260–79.

———. "The Press and Politics in the Age of Jackson." *Journalism Monographs* 89 (1984): 1–28.

Baldasty, Gerald J., and Jeffrey B. Rutenbeck. "Money, Politics and Newspapers: The Business Environment of Press Partisanship in the Late 19th Century." *Journalism History* 15 (1988): 60–69.

Banner James M., Jr. *To the Hartford Convention: The Federalists and the Origins of Party Politics in Massachusetts.* New York, 1970.

Banning, Lance. *The Jeffersonian Persuasion: Evolution of a Party Ideology.* Ithaca, N.Y.: Cornell University Press, 1978.

Beeman, Richard R. *The Old Dominion and the New Nation, 1788–1801.* Lexington, Ky., 1972.

Bell, Earl L., and Kenneth C. Crabbe. *The Augusta Chronicle: Indomitable Voice of Dixie, 1785–1960.* Athens, Ga., 1960.

Berkeley, Edmund, and Dorothy Smith Berkeley. *John Beckley: Zealous Partisan in a Nation Divided.* Memoirs of the American Philosophical Society, 100. Philadelphia, 1973.

Bernhard, Winifred E. A. *Fisher Ames: Federalist and Statesman, 1758–1808.* Chapel Hill, N.C. 1965.

Berns, Walter. "Freedom of the Press and the Alien and Sedition Laws: A Reappraisal." *Supreme Court Review* (1970): 109–59.

Billias, George Athan. *Elbridge Gerry: Founding Father and Republican Statesman.* New York, 1976.

Black, Jeremy. *The English Press in the Eighteenth Century.* London, 1987.

Bloomfield, Maxwell. *American Lawyers in a Changing Society, 1776–1876.* Cambridge, Mass., 1976.

Blumin, Stuart M. *The Emergence of the Middle Class: Social Experience in the American City, 1760–1900.* New York, 1989.

Bogue, Allan G., Jerome M. Clubb, Carroll R. McKibbin, and Santa Traugott. "Members of the House of Representatives and the Processes of Modernization, 1789–1960." *Journal of American History* 63 (1976): 275–302.

Bohmer, David A. "The Maryland Electorate and the Concept of a Party System in the Early National Period." In *The History of American Electoral Behavior,* edited by Joel H. Silbey, Allan G. Bogue, and William H. Flanigan, 146–73. Princeton, N.J. 1978.

———. "Voting Behavior during the First American Party System: Maryland, 1796–1816." Ph.D. diss., University of Michigan, 1974.

Bond, Donovan H., and W. Reynolds McLeod, eds. *Newsletters to Newspapers: Eighteenth-Century Journalism.* Morgantown, W.Va., 1977.

Botein, Stephen. "'Meer Mechanics' and an Open Press: The Business and Political Strategies of Colonial American Printers." *Perspectives in American History* 9 (1975): 127–225.

———. "Printers and the American Revolution." In *Press and the American Revolution,* edited by Bernard Bailyn and John B. Hench. Boston, 1981, 11–57.

Boyce, George, James Curran, and Pauline Wingate, eds. *Newspaper History: From the Seventeenth Century to the Present Day.* Beverly Hills, Calif. 1978.

Briceland, Alan Vance. "Ephraim Kirby, Connecticut Jeffersonian, 1757–1804: The Origins of the Jeffersonian Republican Party in Connecticut." Ph.D. diss., Duke University, 1965.

———. "The Philadelphia 'Aurora,' The New England Illuminati, and The Election of 1800." *Pennsylvania Magazine of History and Biography* 50 (1976): 3–36.

Brigham, Clarence S. *History and Bibliography of American Newspapers, 1690–1820, including Additions and Corrections (1961).* 2 vols. Hamden, Conn., 1962.

———. *Journals and Journeymen: A Contribution to the History of Early American Newspapers.* Philadelphia, 1950.

Brooke, John L. "Ancient Lodges and Self-Created Societies: Voluntary Association and the Public Sphere in the Early Republic." In *Launching the "Extended Republic": The Federalist Era,* edited by Ronald Hoffman and Peter J. Albert, 273–377. Charlottesville, Va., 1996.

Brown, Richard D. *Knowledge is Power: The Diffusion of Information in Early America, 1700–1865.* New York, 1989.

Brownsword, Alan W. "Connecticut Political Patterns, 1817–1828." Ph.D. diss., University of Wisconsin, 1962.

———. "The Constitution of 1818 and Political Afterthoughts, 1800–1840." *Connecticut Historical Society Bulletin* 30 (1965): 1–10.

Brunhouse, Robert L. *The Counter-Revolution in Pennsylvania, 1776–1790.* 1942. Reprint, Harrisburg, Pa., 1971.

Buel, Richard, Jr. "Freedom of the Press in Revolutionary America: The Evolution of Libertarianism, 1760–1820." In *The Press and the American Revolution,* edited by Bernard Bailyn and John B. Hench. Boston, 1981 99–150.

Burnham, Walter Dean. *Critical Elections and the Mainsprings of American Politics.* New York, 1970.

Bushman, Richard L. *The Refinement of America: Persons, Houses, Cities.* New York, 1993.

Calderhead, William L. "A Strange Career in the Young Navy: Captain Charles Gordon, 1778–1816." *Maryland Historical Magazine* 72 (1977): 373–86.

Calhoun, Craig, ed. *Habermas and the Public Sphere.* Cambridge, Mass., 1992.

Carey, James W. *Communication As Culture: Essays on Media and Society.* Boston, 1989.

———. "The Problem of Journalism History." *Journalism History* 1 (1974): 3–5, 27.

Carter, Edward C., II. "Mathew Carey and the 'Olive Branch,' 1814–1818." *Pennsylvania Magazine of History and Biography* 89 (1965): 399–415

———. "The Political Activities of Mathew Carey, Nationalist, 1760–1814." Ph.D. diss., Bryn Mawr College, 1962.

Chambers, William Nisbet. *Old Bullion Benton: Senator from the New West.* Boston, 1956.

———. *Political Parties in a New Nation: The American Experience, 1776–1809.* New York, 1963.

Chambers, William Nisbet, and Walter Dean Burnham, eds. *The American Party Systems: Stages of Political Development.* New York, 1967.

Chartier, Roger. *The Cultural Origins of the French Revolution.* Trans. Lydia G. Cochrane. Durham, N.C., 1991.

Chase, James S. *The Emergence of the Presidential Nominating Convention, 1789–1832.* Urbana, Ill. 1973.

Chroust, Anton-Hermann. *The Rise of the Legal Profession in America.* 2 vols. Norman, Okla., 1965.

Clark, Allan C. *William Duane.* Washington, D.C., 1905.

Clark, Charles E. "The Newspapers of Provincial America." *Proceedings of the American Antiquarian Society,* n.s., 100 (1990): 367–89.

———. *Printers, the People and Politics: The New Hampshire Press and Ratification.* Concord, N.H., 1989.

———. *The Public Prints: The Newspaper in Anglo-American Culture, 1665–1740.* New York, 1994.

Clark, Charles Hopkins, and Everett G. Hill. "Newspapers and Periodicals of Connecticut." In *History of Connecticut,* edited by Norris Galpin Osborn. New York, 1925.

Clark, Thomas D. *The Southern Country Editor.* Reprint, Columbia, S.C., 1991.

Clubb, Jerome M., William H. Flanigan, and Nancy H. Zingale. *Partisan Realignment: Voters, Parties, and Government in American History.* Beverly Hills, Calif., 1980.

Cohen, Michael. "Lawyers and Political Careers." *Law and Society Review* 3 (1969): 563–74.

Cole, Donald B. *Jacksonian Democracy in New Hampshire, 1800–1851.* Cambridge, Mass., 1970.

———. *Martin Van Buren and the American Political System.* Princeton, N.J., 1984.

Colley, Linda. *Britons: Forging the Nation, 1707–1837.* New Haven, Conn., 1992.

Collier, Christopher. *Roger Sherman's Connecticut: Yankee Politics and the American Revolution.* Middletown, Conn., 1971.

Conroy, David W. *In Public Houses: Drink and the Revolution of Authority in Colonial Massachusetts.* Chapel Hill, N.C., 1995.

Cook, Harry Toliver. *The Life and Legacy of David Rogerson Williams.* New York, 1916.

Cooke, Jacob E. *Tench Coxe and the Early Republic.* Chapel Hill, N.C., 1978.

Cotter, Cornelius P., and Bernard C. Hennessey. *Politics without Power: The National Party Committees.* New York, 1964.

Crackel, Theodore J. *Mr. Jefferson's Army: Political and Social Reform of the Military Establishment, 1801–1809.* New York, 1987.

Cranfield, G. A. *The Press and Society: From Caxton to Northcliffe.* New York, 1978.

Crouse, Timothy. *The Boys on the Bus.* 1973. Reprint, New York, 1986.

Cunningham, Noble E., Jr. *The Jeffersonian Republicans: The Formation of Party Organization, 1789–1801.* Chapel Hill, N.C., 1957.

———. *The Jeffersonian Republicans in Power: Party Operations, 1801–1809.* Chapel Hill, N.C., 1963.

———. *The Process of Government under Jefferson.* Princeton, N.J., 1978.

Cutler, Charles L. *Connecticut's Revolutionary Press.* Connecticut Bicentennial Series, booklet no. 14. Chester, Conn., 1975.

Dabney, Virginius. *Pistols and Pointed Pens: The Dueling Editors of Old Virginia.* Chapel Hill, N.C., 1987.

———. *Richmond: The Story of a City.* Revised and expanded ed. Charlottesville, Va., 1990.

Dangerfield, George. *The Awakening of American Nationalism, 1815–1828.* New York, 1965.

———. *The Era of Good Feelings.* 1952. Reprint, Chicago, 1989.

Daniel, Marcus Leonard. "'Ribaldry and Billingsgate': Popular Journalism, Political Culture, and the Public Sphere in the Early Republic." Ph.D. diss., Princeton University, 1998.

Daniels, Bruce C. *The Connecticut Town: Growth and Development, 1635–1790.* Middletown, Conn., 1979.

Darnton, Robert. *The Literary Underground of the Old Regime.* Cambridge, Mass., 1985.

Darnton, Robert, and Daniel Roche, eds. *Revolution in Print: The Press in France, 1775–1800.* Berkeley, Calif., 1989.

Davidson, Cathy N., ed. *Reading in America: Literature & Social History.* Baltimore, 1989.

Davidson, Philip. *Propaganda and the American Revolution, 1763–1783.* New York, 1973.

Davis, Richard. *The Press and American Politics: The New Mediator.* 2d ed. Upper Saddle River, N.J., 1996.

Detweiler, Philip F. "The Changing Reputation of the Declaration of Independence: The First Fifty Years." *William and Mary Quarterly*, 3d ser., 19 (1962): 557–74.

Dexter, Franklin B. "Abraham Bishop, of Connecticut, and His Writings." *Proceedings of the Massachusetts Historical Society*, 2d Ser. 19 (1905): 190–99.

———. *Biographical Sketches of the Graduates of Yale College*. 6 vols. New York, 1885–1912.

Dickerson, Donna Lee. *The Course of Tolerance: Freedom of the Press in Nineteenth-Century America*. Westport, Conn., 1990.

Dill, William A. *The Growth of Newspapers in the United States*. [Lawrence, Kans.], 1928.

Dinkin, Robert J. *Campaigning in America: A History of Election Practices*. Westport, Conn., 1989.

———. *Voting in Provincial America: A Study of Elections in the Thirteen Colonies, 1689–1776*. Westport, Conn., 1977.

———. *Voting in Revolutionary America: A Study of Elections in the Original Thirteen States, 1776–1789*. Westport, Conn., 1982.

Doggett, Marguerite V. *Long Island Printing, 1791–1830*. Brooklyn, 1979.

Duniway, Clyde Augustus. *The Development of Freedom of the Press in Massachusetts*. Cambridge, Mass., 1906.

Dupre, Daniel. "Barbecues and Pledges: Electioneering and the Rise of Democratic Politics in Antebellum Alabama." *Journal of Southern History* 60 (1994): 479–512.

Durey, Michael. "Thomas Paine's Apostles: Radical Émigrés and the Triumph of Jeffersonian Republicanism." *William and Mary Quarterly*, 3d ser., 44 (1987): 661–688.

———. *Transatlantic Radicals and the Early American Republic*. Lawrence, Kans., 1997.

———. *"With the Hammer of Truth": James Thomson Callender and America's Early National Heroes*. Charlottesville, Va., 1990.

Eaton, Clement. *The Freedom-of-Thought Struggle in the Old South*. Revised and enlarged ed. New York, 1964.

Egerton, Douglas R. *Charles Fenton Mercer and the Trial of National Conservatism*. Jackson, Miss., 1989.

Elkins, Stanley, and Eric McKitrick. *The Age of Federalism*. New York, 1993.

Elliott, Robert Neal. *The "Raleigh Register," 1799–1863*. James Sprunt Studies in History and Political Science, Vol. 26. Chapel Hill, N.C., 1955.

Ellis, Harold Milton. *Joseph Dennie and His Circle: A Study in American Literature from 1792 to 1812*. Austin, Tex., 1915.

Ellis, Richard E. *The Jeffersonian Crisis: Courts and Politics in the Young Republic*. New York, 1974.

Emery, Michael, and Edwin Emery. *The Press and America: An Interpretive History of the Mass Media*. 8th ed. Boston, 1996.

Entman, Robert M. *Democracy without Citizens: Media and the Decay of American Politics*. New York, 1989.

Eulau, Heinz, and John D. Sprague. *Lawyers in Politics: A Study in Professional Convergence*. Indianapolis, Ind., 1964.

Evans, Charles, and Clifford K. Shipton. *American Bibliography*. Vols. 1–12, Chicago, 1903–34; Vols. 13–14, Worcester, Mass., 1955–59.

Fallows, James. *Breaking the News: How the Media Undermine American Democracy*. New York, 1996.

Faragher, John Mack. *Sugar Creek: Life on the Illinois Prairie.* New Haven, Conn., 1986.

Fassett, Frederick Gardiner, Jr. *A History of Newspapers in the District of Maine, 1785–1820.* University of Maine Studies, 2d ser., no. 25. Orono, Maine, 1932.

Febvre, Lucien, and Henri-Jean Martin. *The Coming of the Book: The Impact of Printing, 1450–1800.* Trans. David Gerard. London and New York, 1990.

Ferguson, Robert A. *Law and Letters in American Culture.* Cambridge, Mass., 1984.

Ferguson, Russell J. *Early Western Pennsylvania Politics.* Pittsburgh, 1938.

Field, Alston G. "The Press in Western Pennsylvania to 1812." *Western Pennsylvania Historical Magazine* 20 (1937): 231–64.

Filler, Louis. *The Crusade against Slavery, 1830–1860.* New York, 1960.

Fischer, David Hackett. *The Revolution of American Conservatism: The Federalist Party in the Era of Jeffersonian Democracy.* New York, 1965.

Fisher, Josephine. "Francis James Jackson and Newspaper Propaganda in the United States, 1809–1810." *Maryland Historical Magazine* 30 (1935): 93–113.

Foner, Eric. *Tom Paine and Revolutionary America.* New York, 1976.

Formisano, Ronald P. *The Birth of Mass Political Parties: Michigan, 1827–1861.* Princeton, N.J., 1971.

———. "Deferential-Participant Politics: The Early Republic's Political Culture, 1789–1840." *American Political Science Review* 68 (1974): 473–87.

———. "Federalists and Republicans: Parties, Yes—System, No." In *Evolution of American Electoral Systems,* edited by Kleppner, et al., 33–76.

———. "Political Character, Antipartyism and the Second Party System." *American Quarterly* 21 (1969): 683–709.

———. *The Transformation of Political Culture: Massachusetts Parties, 1790s–1850s.* New York, 1983.

Fowler, Dorothy Canfield. *The Cabinet Politician: The Postmasters General, 1829–1909.* New York, 1943.

Frasca, Ralph. "Benjamin Franklin's Printing Network." *American Journalism* 5 (1988): 145–58.

———. "From Apprentice to Journeyman to Partner: Benjamin Franklin's Workers and the Growth of the Early American Printing Trade." *Pennsylvania Magazine of History and Biography* 114 (1990): 229–48.

Friedman, Lawrence M. *A History of American Law.* 2d ed. New York, 1985.

Garnett, James Mercer. "James Mercer." *William and Mary Quarterly,* 1st ser., 17 (1908–1909): 85–91, 219.

Garraty, John A., and Mark C. Carnes, eds. *American National Biography.* 24 vols. New York, 1999.

Gawalt, Gerard W. *The Promise of Power: The Emergence of the Legal Profession in Massachusetts, 1760–1840.* Westport, Conn., 1979.

———. "Sources of Anti-Lawyer Sentiment in Massachusetts, 1740–1840." *American Journal of Legal History* 14 (1970): 283–307.

Gienapp, William E. *Origins of the Republican Party, 1852–1856.* New York, 1987.

Gilpatrick, Delbert Harold. *Jeffersonian Democracy in North Carolina, 1789–1816.* New York, 1931.

Gilsdorf, Joy B., and Robert R. Gilsdorf. "Elites and Electorates: Some Plain Truths for Historians of Colonial America." In *Saints and Revolutionaries: Essays on Early American History,* edited by David D. Hall, John M. Murrin, and Thad W. Tate, 207–44. New York, 1984.

Gilmore, William J. *Reading Becomes a Necessity of Life: Material and Cultural Life in Rural New England, 1780–1835.* Knoxville, Tenn., 1989.

Gleason, Timothy W. "Historians and Press Freedom Since 1800." *American Journalism* 5 (1988): 230–47.

———. *The Watchdog Concept: The Press and the Courts in Nineteenth-Century America.* Ames, Iowa, 1990.

Glickstein, Jonathan A. *Concepts of Free Labor in Antebellum America.* New Haven, Conn., 1991.

Good, L. Douglas. "Theodore Dwight: Federalist Propagandist." *Connecticut Historical Society Bulletin* 39 (1974): 87–96.

Goodman, Paul. *The Democratic-Republicans of Massachusetts: Politics in a Young Republic.* 1964, Reprint, Westport, Conn., 1986.

———. "The First American Party System." In *American Party Systems: Stages of Political Development,* edited by William Nisbet Chambers and Dean Burnham. New York, 56–89.

Granato, Leonard A. "Freneau, Jefferson and Genet: Independent Journalism in the Partisan Press." In *Newsletters to Newspapers: Eighteenth-Century Journalism,* edited by Donovan H. Bond and W. Reynolds McLeod. Morgantown, W.Va., 1977, 291–301.

Grasso, Christopher. *A Speaking Aristocracy: Transforming Public Discourse in Eighteenth-Century Connecticut.* Chapel Hill, N.C., 1999.

Green, Fletcher M. "Duff Green: Militant Journalist of the Old School." *American Historical Review* 52 (1947): 247–64.

Green, James N. *Mathew Carey: Publisher and Patriot.* Philadelphia, 1985.

Griffith, Louis Turner, and John Erwin Talmadge. *Georgia Journalism, 1763–1950.* Athens, Ga., 1951.

Gross, Robert A. "Printing, Politics and the People." *Proceedings of the American Antiquarian Society* 99 (1989): 375–97.

Gutgesell, Stephen, ed. *Guide to Ohio Newspapers, 1793–1973.* Columbus, Ohio, 1974.

Habermas, Jürgen. *The Structural Transformation of the Public Sphere: An Inquiry into a Category of Bourgeois Society.* Trans. Thomas Burger and Frederick Lawrence. Cambridge, Mass., 1991.

Hall, David D. *Worlds of Wonder, Days of Judgment: Popular Religious Belief in Early New England.* Cambridge, Mass., 1990.

Hall, Kermit L. *The Magic Mirror: Law in American History.* New York, 1989.

Hall, Virginius C. "Moses Dawson, Chronic Belligerent." *Bulletin of the Historical and Philosophical Society of Ohio* 15 (1957): 175–89.

Hallin, Daniel C. *The "Uncensored War": The Media and Vietnam.* Berkeley, Calif., 1989.

Hamilton, Milton W. *The Country Printer: New York State, 1785–1830.* 2d ed. New York, 1964.

Handover, P. M. *A History of "The London Gazette."* London, 1965.

Harris, Michael. *London Newspapers in the Age of Walpole.* Teaneck, N.J., 1987.

Hatch, Nathan O. *The Democratization of American Christianity.* New Haven, Conn., 1989.

Heale, M. J. *The Making of American Politics, 1750–1850.* New York, 1977.

———. *The Presidential Quest: Candidates and Images in American Political Culture, 1787–1852.* New York, 1982.

Heideking, Jürgen. "Die amerikanische Presse und die Verfassungsdebatte der Jahre 1787 and 1788." *Amerikastudien (American Studies)* 30 (1986): 398–412.

Heller, William J. *History of Northampton County (Penn.) and the Grand Valley of the Lehigh.* Boston, 1920.

Hench, John B. "The Newspaper in a Republic: Boston's 'Centinel' and 'Chronicle,' 1784–1801." Ph.D. diss., Clark University, 1979.

———, ed. *Three Hundred Years of the American Newspaper.* Worcester, Mass., 1991.

Henderson, Elizabeth K. "The Attack on the Judiciary in Pennsylvania, 1800–1810." *Pennsylvania Magazine of History and Biography* 61 (1937): 113–36.

Henkin, David M. *City Reading: Written Words and Public Spaces in Antebellum New York.* New York, 1998.

Hickey, Donald R. *The War of 1812: A Forgotten Conflict.* Urbana, Ill., 1990.

Higginbotham, Sanford W. *The Keystone in the Democratic Arch: Pennsylvania Politics, 1800–1816.* Harrisburg, Pa., 1952.

Hochman, Steven H. "On the Liberty of the Press in Virginia: From Essay to Bludgeon, 1798–1803." *Virginia Magazine of History and Biography* 84 (1976): 431–45.

Hofstadter, Richard. *The Idea of a Party System: The Rise of Legitimate Opposition in the United States, 1780–1840.* Berkeley, Calif., 1969.

Holt, Michael F. *The Rise and Fall of the American Whig Party: Jacksonian Politics and the Onset of the Civil War.* New York, 1999.

Hooper, Osman Castle. *History of Ohio Journalism, 1793–1933.* Columbus, Ohio, 1933.

Humphrey, Carol Sue. *The Press of the Young Republic, 1783–1833.* Westport, Conn., 1996.

———. "The Revolutionary Press: Source of Unity or Division?" *American Journalism* 6 (1989): 247–56.

———. *"This Popular Engine": New England Newspapers during the American Revolution, 1775–1789.* Newark, Del., 1992.

Hutson, James H. "The Origins of 'The Paranoid Style in American Politics': Public Jealousy from the Age of Walpole to the Age of Jackson." In Hall et al., *Saints and Revolutionaries: Essays on Early American History,* edited by David D. Hall, John M. Murrin, and Thad W. Tate, 332–72. New York, 1984.

Isaac, Rhys. *The Transformation of Virginia, 1740–1790.* Chapel Hill, N.C. 1982.

Iyengar, Shanto, and Richard Reeves, eds. *Do the Media Govern? Politicians, Voters, and Reporters in America.* Thousand Oaks, Calif., 1997.

Jacob, Margaret C. and James R. Jacob. *The Origins of Anglo-American Radicalism.* 1984, Reprint, Atlantic Highlands, N.J., 1991.

John, Richard R. *Spreading the News: The American Postal System From Franklin to Morse.* Cambridge, Mass., 1995.

Jordan, Daniel P. *Political Leadership in Jefferson's Virginia.* Charlottesville, Va., 1983.

Joyce, William B., David D. Hall, Richard D. Brown, and John B. Hench, eds. *Printing and Society in Early America.* Worcester, Mass, 1983.

Kehl, James A. *Ill Feeling in the Era of Good Feeling: Western Pennsylvania Political Battles, 1815–1825.* Pittsburgh, Pa. 1956.

Kerber, Linda K. *Federalists in Dissent: Imagery and Ideology in Jeffersonian America.* Ithaca, N.Y., 1970.

Ketcham, Ralph. *Presidents above Party: The First American Presidency, 1789–1829.* Chapel Hill, N.C. 1984.

Key, V. O. "A Theory of Critical Elections." *Journal of Politics* 18 (1955): 3–18.

Kielbowicz, Richard B. *News in the Mail: The Press, Post Office, and Public Information, 1700–1860s.* Westport, Conn., 1989.

———. "Party Press Cohesiveness: Jacksonian Newspapers, 1832." *Journalism Quarterly* 60 (Autumn 1983): 518–21.

Klaidman, Stephen, and Tom L. Beauchamp. *The Virtuous Journalist.* New York, 1987.

Klein, Philip Shriver. *Pennsylvania Politics, 1817–1832: A Game without Rules.* Philadelphia, 1940.

Kleppner, Paul, Walter Dean Burnham, Ronald P. Formisano, Samuel P. Hays, Richard Jensen, and William G. Shade. *The Evolution of American Electoral Systems.* Westport, Conn., 1981.

Knudson, Jerry W. "Political Journalism in the Age of Jefferson." *Journalism History* 1 (1974): 20–3.

Kobre, Sidney. *The Development of the Colonial Newspaper.* 1944. Reprint, Gloucester, Mass., 1960.

Koch, Adrienne, and Harry Ammon. "The Virginia and Kentucky Resolutions: An Episode in Jefferson and Madison's Defense of Civil Liberties." *William and Mary Quarterly,* 3d ser., 5 (1948): 145–76.

Kohn, Richard H. *Eagle and Sword: The Beginnings of the Military Establishment in America.* New York, 1975.

Konkle, Burton Alva. "Enos Bronson, 1774–1823." *Pennsylvania Magazine of History and Biography* 57 (1953): 355–58.

Koschnik, Albrecht. "Political Conflict and Public Contest: Rituals of National Celebration in Philadelphia, 1788–1815." *Pennsylvania Magazine of History and Biography* 118 (1994): 209–48.

Koss, Stephen. *The Rise and Fall of the Political Press in Britain.* 2 vols. London, 1982–84.

Kousser, J. Morgan. *The Shaping of Southern Politics: Suffrage Restriction and the Establishment of the One-Party South.* New Haven, Conn. 1974.

Kurtz, Stephen G. *The Presidency of John Adams: The Collapse of Federalism, 1795–1800.* New York, 1961.

Lang, Gladys Engel, and Kurt Lang. *The Battle for Public Opinion: The President, the Press, and the Polls during Watergate.* New York, 1983.

Lathem, Edward Connery. *Chronological Tables of American Newspapers, 1690–1820.* Barre, Mass., 1972.

Leary, Lewis. *That Rascal Freneau: A Study in Literary Failure.* New Brunswick, N.J., 1941.

Lee, Alfred McClung. *The Daily Newspaper in America: The Evolution of a Social Instrument.* New York, 1937.

Leonard, Thomas C. *News for All: America's Coming-of-Age with the Press.* New York, 1995.

———. *The Power of the Press: The Birth of American Political Reporting.* New York, 1986.

Levy, Leonard W. *Emergence of a Free Press.* New York, 1985.

———, ed.. *Freedom of the Press From Zenger to Jefferson: Early America Libertarian Theories.* Indianapolis, Ind., 1966.

———. *Jefferson and Civil Liberties: The Darker Side.* 1963, Reprint, Chicago, 1989.

List, Karen K. "The Role of William Cobbett in Philadelphia's Party Press, 1794–1799." *Journalism Monographs* 82 (1983): 1–41.

Lyon, William H. *The Pioneer Editor in Missouri, 1808–1860.* Columbia, Mo., 1965.

McCormick, Richard P. "New Perspectives on Jacksonian Politics." *American Historical Review* 65 (Jan. 1960): 288–301.

McCoy, Drew R. *The Elusive Republic: Political Economy in Jeffersonian America.* 1980. Reprint, New York, 1982.

McCormick, Richard P. *The Second American Party System: Party Formation in the Jacksonian Era.* 1966, Reprint, New York, 1973.

McDonald, Forrest. *The Presidency of Thomas Jefferson.* Lawrence, Kans., 1976.

McGerr, Michael E. *The Decline of Popular Politics: The American North, 1986–1928.* New York, 1986.

McWilliams, Wilson Carey. "Parties as Civic Associations." In *Party Renewal in America: Theory and Practice,* edited by Gerald M. Pomper, 51–68. New York, 1980.

Maier, Pauline. *American Scripture: Making the Declaration of Independence.* New York, 1997.

———. *From Resistance to Revolution: Colonial Radicals and the Development of American Opposition to Britain, 1765–1776.* New York, 1974.

Malone, Dumas. *Jefferson the President: First Term, 1801–1805.* Boston, 1970.

Manning, Richard H. "Herald of the Albany Regency: Edwin Croswell and the 'Albany Argus,' 1823–1854." Ph.D. diss., Miami University, 1983.

Marshall, Lynn LaDue. "The Early Career of Amos Kendall: The Making of a Jacksonian." Ph.D. diss., University of California, Berkeley, 1962.

Martin, James Kirby. *Men in Rebellion: Higher Governmental Leaders and the Coming of the American Revolution.* 1973, Reprint, New York, 1976.

Martis, Kenneth C. *The Historical Atlas of Political Parties in the United States Congress 1789–1989.* New York, 1989.

———. *The Historical Atlas of United States Congressional Districts, 1789–1983.* New York, 1982.

Marvin, Carolyn. "Space, Time, and Captive Communications History." In *Communications in Transition: Issues and Debates in Current Research,* edited by Mary S. Mander, 20–38. New York, 1983.

Mesick, Jane Louise. *The English Traveller in America, 1785–1835.* New York, 1922.

Miller, John C. *The Federalist Era, 1789–1801.* New York, 1960.

Miller, Perry. *The Life of the Mind in America: From the Revolution to the Civil War.* San Diego, Calif., 1965.

Miller, Richard G. *Philadelphia—The Federalist City.* Port Washington, N.Y., 1976.

Mindich, David T. Z. *Just the Facts: How "Objectivity" Came to Define American Journalism.* New York, 1998.

Moran, James. *Printing Presses: History and Development from the 15th Century to Modern Times.* Berkeley, Calif., 1973.

Morgan, Edmund S. *Inventing the People: The Rise of Popular Sovereignty in England and America.* New York, 1988.

Morison, Samuel Eliot. *The Life and Letters of Harrison Gray Otis, Federalist, 1765–1848.* 2 vols. Boston, 1913.

Morse, Jarvis Means. *Connecticut Newspapers in the Eighteenth Century.* Tercentenary Commission of the State of Connecticut, Committee on Historical Publications, Pamphlet 36. New Haven, Conn., 1935.

————. *A Neglected Period of Connecticut's History, 1818–1850.* New Haven, Conn., 1933.

Mott, Frank Luther. *American Journalism.* 3d ed. New York, 1960.

————. *Jefferson and the Press.* Baton Rouge, La., 1943.

Mushkat, Jerome. *Tammany: The Evolution of a Political Machine, 1789–1865.* Syracuse, N.Y, 1971.

Nash, Gary B. "The Philadelphia Bench and Bar, 1800–1861." *Comparative Studies in Society and History* 7 (1965): 203–20.

————. *The Urban Crucible: Social Change, Political Consciousness, and the Origins of the American Revolution.* Cambridge, Mass., 1979.

Nelson, Harold L., ed. *Freedom of the Press From Hamilton to the Warren Court.* Indianapolis, Ind., 1967.

Nerone, John C. *The Culture of the Press in the Early Republic: Cincinnati, 1793–1848.* Dissertations in Nineteenth-Century American Political and Social History. New York, 1989.

————. "The Mythology of the Penny Press." *Critical Studies in Mass Communication* 4 (1987): 376–422.

————. *Violence against the Press: Policing the Public Sphere in U.S. History.* New York, 1994.

Nevins, Allan. *The Evening Post: A Century of Journalism.* New York, 1922.

Newlin, Claude Milton. *The Life and Writings of Hugh Henry Brackenridge.* Princeton, N.J., 1932.

Newman, Simon P. *Parades and the Politics of the Street: Festive Culture in the Early American Republic.* Philadelphia, 1997.

————. "Principles or Men? George Washington and the Political Culture of National Leadership, 1776–1801." *Journal of the Early Republic* 12 (1992): 477–507.

Newmyer, R. Kent. *Supreme Court Justice Joseph Story: Statesman of the Old Republic.* Chapel Hill, N.C., 1985.

Niven, John. *Gideon Welles: Lincoln's Secretary of the Navy.* New York, 1973. Reprint, Baton Rouge, La., 1994.

————. *Martin Van Buren: The Romantic Age of American Politics.* New York, 1983.

Nord, David Paul. "The Evangelical Origins of Mass Media in America, 1815–1835." *Journalism Monographs* 88 (1984): 1–30.

————. "A Plea for *Journalism* History." *Journalism History* 15 (1988): 8–15.

North, S. N. D. *History and Present Condition of the Newspaper and Periodical Press of the United States.* Washington, D.C., 1884.

Orcutt, Samuel. *History of the Towns of New Milford and Bridgewater, Connecticut, 1703–1882.* Hartford, Conn., 1882.

Osborn, Norris G. *History of Connecticut in Monographic Form.* 5 vols. New York, 1925.

Osthaus, Carl R. *Partisans of the Southern Press: Editorial Spokesmen of the Nineteenth Century.* Lexington, Ky., 1994.

Ostrogorski, M. *Democracy and the Organization of Political Parties.* Trans. Frederick Clarke 2 vols. New York, 1902.

Park, Robert E. "The Natural History of the Newspaper," *American Journal of Sociology* 29 (1923): 80–98.

Pasley, Jeffrey L. "'Artful and Designing Men': Political Professionalism in the Early American Republic, 1775–1820." Ph.D. diss., Harvard University, 1993.

————. "The 'Indiscreet Zeal' of John Norvell: Newspaper Publishing and Politics in the Early American Republic." Paper read at the annual meeting of the Organization of American Historians, Atlanta, Ga., 14 April 1994.

———. "'A Journeyman, Either in Law or Politics': John Beckley and the Social Origins of Political Campaigning." *Journal of the Early Republic* 16 (1996): 531–69.

———. "Party Politics, Citizenship, and Collective Action in Nineteenth-Century America: A Response to Stuart Blumin and Michael Schudson." *Communication Review* 4 (2000): 39–54.

Patterson, Thomas E. *Out of Order.* 2d ed. New York, 1994.

Paullin, Charles O. *Atlas of the Historical Geography of the United States.* Washington, 1932.

Pessen, Edward. *Jacksonian America: Society, Personality, and Politics.* Revised ed. Urbana, Ill. 1985.

———. *Riches, Class, and Power: America Before the Civil War.* 2d ed. New Brunswick, N.J., 1990.

Phillips, Kim T. "Democrats of the Old School in the Era of Good Feelings." *Pennsylvania Magazine of History and Biography* 95 (1971): 363–82.

———. "The Pennsylvania Origins of the Jackson Movement." *Political Science Quarterly* 91 (1976): 489–508.

———. "William Duane, Philadelphia's Democratic Republicans, and the Origins of Modern Politics." *Pennsylvania Magazine of History and Biography* 101 (1977): 365–87.

Phillips, Kim Tousley. "William Duane, Revolutionary Editor." Ph.D. diss., University of California, Berkeley, Calif., 1968.

———. *William Duane: Radical Journalist in the Age of Jefferson.* Outstanding Studies in Early American History. New York, 1989.

Polsby, Nelson. "The Institutionalization of the U.S. House of Representatives." *American Political Science Review* 62 (1968): 144–68.

Popkin, Jeremy D. *News and Politics in the Age of Revolution: Jean Luzac's "Gazette de Leyde".* Ithaca, N.Y., 1989.

———. *Revolutionary News: The Press in France, 1789–1799.* Durham, N.C., 1990.

Preston, Dickson J. *Newspapers of Maryland's Eastern Shore.* Queenstown and Centreville, Md., 1986.

Pretzer, William S. "'The British, Duff Green, the Rats and the Devil': Custom, Capitalism, and Conflict in the Washington Printing Trade." *Labor History* 27 (1985–86): 5–30.

———. "Tramp Printers: Craft Culture, Trade Unions, and Technology." *Printing History* 6 (1984): 3–16.

Prince, Carl E. "The Federalist Party and Creation of a Court Press, 1789–1801." *Journalism Quarterly* 53 (1976): 238–41.

———. *The Federalists and the Origins of the U.S. Civil Service.* New York, 1977.

———. "James J. Wilson: Party Leader, 1801–1824." *Proceedings of the New Jersey Historical Society* 83 (1965): 24–39.

———. "John Israel: Printer and Politician on the Pennsylvania Frontier, 1798–1805." *Pennsylvania Magazine of History and Biography* 91 (1967): 46–55.

———. *New Jersey's Jeffersonian Republicans: The Genesis of an Early Party Machine, 1789–1817.* Chapel Hill, N.C., 1967.

———. "The Passing of the Aristocracy: Jefferson's Removal of the Federalists, 1801–1805." *Journal of American History* 63 (1970): 563–75.

Purcell, Richard J. *Connecticut in Transition, 1775–1818.* Washington, D.C., 1918.

Ratcliffe, Donald J. *Party Spirit in a Frontier Republic: Democratic Politics in Ohio, 1793–1821.* Columbus, Ohio, 1998.

Reeder, Frank. *Record of the Family and Descendants of Colonel Christian Jacob Hütter of Easton, Penn'a, 1771–1902.* Easton, Pa., 1906.

Remer, Rosalind. *Printers and Men of Capital: Philadelphia Book Publishers in the New Republic.* Philadelphia, 1996.

Remini, Robert V. *Andrew Jackson and the Course of American Freedom, 1822–1832.* New York, 1981.

———. *The Election of Andrew Jackson.* Philadelphia, 1963.

———. *Martin Van Buren and the Making of the Democratic Party.* New York, 1959.

Renzulli, Libero Marx. *Maryland: The Federalist Years.* Rutherford, N.J., 1972.

Richard, Carl J. *The Founders and the Classics: Greece, Rome and the American Enlightenment.* Cambridge, Mass., 1994.

Richardson, Charles Francis, and Elizabeth Miner (Thomas) Richardson. *Charles Miner: A Pennsylvania Pioneer.* Wilkes-Barre, Pa., 1916.

Ridgway, Whitman H. *Community Leadership in Maryland, 1790–1840: A Comparative Analysis of Power in Society.* Chapel Hill, N.C., 1979.

Riddle, William. *The Story of Lancaster: Old and New.* Lancaster, Pa., 1917.

Ritchie, Donald A. *Press Gallery: Congress and the Washington Correspondents.* Cambridge, Mass., 1991.

Robertson, Andrew W. *The Language of Democracy: Political Rhetoric in the United States and Britain, 1790–1900.* Ithaca, N.Y., 1995.

Robinson, David. *The Unitarians and the Universalists.* Westport, Conn., 1985.

Robinson, William A. *Jeffersonian Democracy in New England.* 1916, Reprint, New York, 1968.

Rock, Howard B., Paul A. Gilje, and Robert Asher, eds. *American Artisans: Crafting Social Identity, 1750–1850.* Baltimore, 1995.

Rodgers, Daniel T. "Republicanism: The Career of a Concept." *Journal of American History* 79 (1992): 11–38.

Roediger, David R. *The Wages of Whiteness: Race and the Making of the American Working Class.* London, 1991.

Roosevelt, Theodore. *Thomas H. Benton.* New York, 1899.

Rorabaugh, W. J. *The Alcoholic Republic: An American Tradition.* New York, 1979.

———. *The Craft Apprentice: From Franklin to the Machine Age in America.* New York, 1986.

Rosenberg, Norman L. "Alexander Addison and the Pennsylvania Origins of Federalist First-Amendment Thought." *Pennsylvania Magazine of History and Biography* 108 (1984): 399–417.

———. "Another World: Freedom of Press in the Eighteenth Century." *Reviews in American History* 16 (1988): 554–59.

———. *Protecting the Best Men: An Interpretive History of the Law of Libel.* Chapel Hill, N.C., 1986.

Rosenfeld, Richard N. *American Aurora: A Democratic-Republican Returns. The Suppressed History of Our Nation's Beginnings and the Heroic Newspaper That Tried to Report It.* New York, 1997.

Rosswurm, Steven A. *Arms, Country, and Class: The Philadelphia Militia and the "Lower Sort" during the American Revolution, 1775–1783.* New Brunswick, N.J., 1987.

Rowe, G. S. *Thomas McKean: The Shaping of an American Republicanism.* Boulder, Colo., 1978.

Russo, David J. "The Origins of Local News in the U.S. Country Press, 1840s–1870s." *Journalism Monographs* 65 (1980).

Rutenbeck, Jeffrey B. "Editorial Perception of Newspaper Independence and the Presidential Campaign of 1872: An Ideological Turning Point for American Journalism." *Journalism History* 17 (Spring 1990–Summer 1990): 13–22.

———. "Newspaper Trends in the 1870s: Proliferation, Popularization, and Political Independence." *Journalism and Mass Communication Quarterly* 72 (Summer 1995): 361–75.

Rutland, Robert Allen. "The First Great Newspaper Debate: The Constitutional Crisis of 1787–1788." *Proceedings of the American Antiquarian Society*, n.s., 97 (1987): 43–58.

Scharf, J. Thomas. *History of Maryland.* 3 vols. 1879. Reprint, Hatboro, Pa., 1967.

Scharf, J. Thomas, and Thompson Westcott. *History of Philadelphia, 1609–1884.* 3 vols. Philadelphia, 1884.

Schauinger, Joseph. "Alexander Contee Hanson, Federalist Partisan." *Maryland Historical Magazine* 35 (1940): 354–64.

Schiller, Dan. *Objectivity and the News: The Public and the Rise of Commercial Journalism.* Philadelphia, 1981.

Schlesinger, Arthur M. *Prelude to Independence: The Newspaper War on Britain, 1764–1776.* 1957. Reprint, Boston, 1980.

Schudson, Michael. *Discovering the News: A Social History of American Newspapers.* New York, 1978.

———. *The Power of News.* Cambridge, Mass., 1995.

———. "Toward a Troubleshooting Manual for Journalism History." *Journalism and Mass Communication Quarterly* 74 (1997): 463–76.

Sellers, Charles. *The Market Revolution: Jacksonian America, 1815–1846.* New York, 1991.

Shade, William G. *Democratizing the Old Dominion: Virginia and the Second Party System, 1824–1861.* Charlottesville, Va. 1996.

Sharp, James Roger. *American Politics in the Early Republic: The New Nation in Crisis.* New Haven, Conn., 1993.

Shaw, Peter. *The Character of John Adams.* Chapel Hill, N.C., 1976.

Shefter, Martin. *Political Parties and the State: The American Historical Experience.* Princeton, N.J., 1994.

Shields, David S. *Civil Tongues and Polite Letters in British America.* Chapel Hill, N.C., 1997.

Shipton, Clifford K. *Isaiah Thomas: Printer, Patriot and Philanthropist, 1749–1831.* Rochester, N.Y., 1948.

Shulim, Joseph I. "John Daly Burk: Irish Revolutionist and American Patriot." *Transactions of the American Philosophical Society*, n.s., 54, part 6 (1964).

Silbey, Joel H. *The American Political Nation, 1838–1893.* Stanford, Calif., 1991.

Silbey, Joel H., Allan G. Bogue, and William H. Flanigan, eds. *The History of American Electoral Behavior.* Princeton, N.J., 1978.

Silver, Rollo G. *The American Printer, 1787–1825.* Charlottesville, Va., 1967.

———. "Aprons instead of Uniforms: The Practice of Printing, 1776–1787." *Proceedings of the American Antiquarian Society*, n.s., 87 (1977): 111–94.

———. "Benjamin Edes, Trumpeter of Sedition." *Papers of the Bibliographical Society of America* 47 (1953): 248–68.

Skeen, C. Edward. "*Vox Populi, Vox Dei:* The Compensation Act of 1816 and the Rise of Popular Politics," *Journal of the Early Republic* 6 (1986): 253–74.

Sloan, William David. "The Early Party Press: The Newspaper Role in American Politics, 1789–1812." *Journalism History* 9 (Spring 1982): 18–24.

———. "Journalism Historians Lost in the Past, Need Direction." *Journalism Educator* 42 (1987): 4–7, 48.

———. "'Purse and Pen:' Party-Press Relationships, 1789–1816." *American Journalism* 6 (1989): 103–127.

———. "Scurrility and the Party Press, 1789–1816." *American Journalism* 5 (1988): 97–112.

Sloan, William David, and Thomas A. Schwartz. "Freedom of the Press, 1690–1801: Libertarian or Limited?" *American Journalism* 5 (1988): 159–77.

Smelser, Marshall. *The Democratic Republic, 1801–1815.* New York, 1968.

Smith, Anthony, ed. *Newspapers and Democracy: International Essays on a Changing Medium.* Cambridge, Mass., 1980.

———. *The Newspaper: An International History.* London, 1979.

Smith, Culver H. *The Press, Politics and Patronage: The American Government's Use of Newspapers, 1789–1875.* Athens, Ga., 1977.

Smith, Elbert B. *Francis Preston Blair.* New York, 1980.

Smith, James Morton. *Freedom's Fetters: The Alien and Sedition Laws and American Civil Liberties.* Ithaca, N.Y., 1956.

Smith, Jeffery A. *Franklin and Bache: Envisioning the Enlightened Republic.* New York, 1990.

———. "Impartiality and Revolutionary Ideology: Editorial Policies of the *South-Carolina Gazette.*" *Journal of Southern History* 44 (1983): 511–26.

———. *Printers and Press Freedom: The Ideology of Early American Journalism.* New York, 1988.

Smith, Jeffery A. *War and Press Freedom: The Problem of Prerogative Power.* New York, 1999.

Smith, J. Eugene. *One Hundred Years of Hartford's "Courant": From Colonial Times through the Civil War.* New Haven, Conn., 1949.

Solomon, William S., and Robert W. McChesney, eds. *Ruthless Criticism: New Perspectives in U.S. Communication History.* Minneapolis, Minn. 1993.

Startt, James D., and William David Sloan, eds. *The Significance of the Media in American History.* Northport, Ala., 1994.

Steele, Ian K. *The English Atlantic, 1675–1740: An Exploration of Communication and Community.* New York, 1986.

Steffen, Charles G. *The Mechanics of Baltimore: Workers and Politics in the Age of Revolution, 1763–1812.* Urbana, Ill., 1984.

Stevens, George A. *New York Typographical Union No. 6: Study of a Modern Trade Union and its Predecessors.* Albany, 1912.

Stevens, Harry R. *The Early Jackson Party in Ohio.* Durham, N.C., 1957.

Stewart, Donald H. *The Opposition Press of the Federalist Period.* Albany, N.Y., 1969.

Stewart, James Brewer. *Holy Warriors: The Abolitionists and American Slavery.* New York, 1976.

Stiles, Henry Reed. *The History and Genealogies of Ancient Windsor, Connecticut, includ-ing East Windsor, South Windsor, Bloomfield, Windsor Locks, and Ellington, 1635–1891.* Hartford, Conn., 1891–92.

Summers, Mark Wahlgren. *The Press Gang: Newspapers and Politics, 1863–1878.* Chapel Hill, N.C., 1994.

Sutherland, James. *The Restoration Newspaper and its Development.* Cambridge, U.K., 1986.

Sweet, Leonard I., ed. *Communication and Change in American Religious History.* Grand Rapids, Mich., 1993.

Swisher, Carl Brent. *Roger B. Taney.* New York, 1935.

Sydnor, Charles S. *Gentlemen Freeholders: Political Practices in Washington's Virginia.* Chapel Hill, N.C., 1952.

Tagg, James D. *Benjamin Franklin Bache and the Philadelphia "Aurora".* Philadelphia, 1991.

————. "Benjamin Franklin Bache's Attack on George Washington." *Pennsylvania Magazine of History and Biography* 100 (1976): 191–230.

Tapley, Harriet Silvester. *Salem Imprints, 1768–1825: A History of the First Fifty Years of Printing in Salem, Massachusetts.* Salem, Mass., 1927.

Taylor, Alan. "'The Art of Hook and Snivey': Political Culture in Upstate New York during the 1790s." *Journal of American History* 79 (1993): 1371–96.

————. "From Fathers to Friends of the People: Political Personas in the Early Re-public." *Journal of the Early Republic* 11 (1991): 465–91.

————. *Liberty Men and Great Proprietors: The Revolutionary Settlement on the Maine Frontier, 1760–1820.* Chapel Hill, N.C., 1990.

————. *William Cooper's Town: Power and Persuasion on the Frontier of the Early Amer-ican Republic.* New York, 1995.

Teeter, Dwight L. "Press Freedom and the Public Printing: Pennsylvania, 1775–83." *Journalism Quarterly* 45 (1968): 445–51.

————. "The Printer and the Chief Justice: Seditious Libel in 1782–83." *Journalism Quarterly* 45 (1968): 235–42, 260.

Thomas, Edmund B., Jr. "Politics in the Land of Steady Habits: Connecticut's First Political Party System, 1789–1920." Ph.D. diss., Clark University, 1972.

Thornton, J. Mills, III. *Politics and Power in a Slave Society: Alabama, 1800–1860.* Baton Rouge, 1978.

Tinkcom, Harry Marlin. *The Republicans and Federalists in Pennsylvania, 1790–1801: A Study in National Stimulus and Local Response.* Harrisburg, Pa., 1950.

Tolles, Frederick. *George Logan of Philadelphia.* New York, 1953.

Travers, Len. *Celebrating the Fourth: Independence Day and the Rites of Nationalism in the Early Republic.* Amherst, Mass., 1997.

Troy, Gil. *See How They Ran: The Changing Role of the Presidential Candidate.* New York, 1991.

Trumbull, J. Hammond. *Historical Notes on the Constitutions of Connecticut, 1639–1818.* Hartford, Conn., 1873.

Tucher, Andie. *Froth and Scum: Truth, Beauty, Goodness, and the Ax Murder in America's First Mass Medium.* Chapel Hill, N.C., 1994.

Twomey, Richard J. *Jacobins and Jeffersonians: Anglo-American Radicalism in the United States, 1789–1820.* New York, 1989.

United States. Congress. *Biographical Directory of the United States Congress, 1774–1989:*

Bicentennial Edition. Ed. Kathryn Allamong Jacob and Bruce A. Ragsdale. Washington, D.C., 1989. Updated version at <http://bioguide.congress.gov>.

Van Deusen, Glyndon G. *Horace Greeley: Nineteenth-Century Crusader.* 1953, Reprint, New York, 1964.

———. *Thurlow Weed: Wizard of the Lobby.* Boston, 1947.

Van Doren, Carl. *Benjamin Franklin.* New York, 1938.

Vickers, Daniel. "Competency and Competition: Economic Culture in Early America." *William and Mary Quarterly,* 3d ser., 47 (1990): 3–29.

Waldstreicher, David. *In the Midst of Perpetual Fetes: The Making of American Nationalism, 1776–1820.* Chapel Hill, N.C., 1997.

———. "Reading the Runaways: Self-Fashioning, Print Culture, and Confidence in Slavery in the Eighteenth-Century Mid-Atlantic." *William and Mary Quarterly,* 3d ser., 56 (1999): 243–72.

———. "Rites of Rebellion, Rites of Assent: Celebrations, Print Culture, and the Origins of American Nationalism." *Journal of American History* 82 (1995): 37–61.

Waldstreicher, David, and Stephen R. Grossbart. "Abraham Bishop's Vocation; or, the Mediation of American Politics." *Journal of the Early Republic* 18 (1998): 617–57.

Wallace, Michael. "Changing Concepts of Party in the United States: New York, 1815–1828." *American Historical Review* 74 (1968): 453–91.

Wallace, Michael L. "Ideologies of Party in the Ante-Bellum Republic." Ph.D. diss., Columbia University, 1973.

Walters, Raymond, Jr. *Alexander James Dallas: Lawyer-Politician-Financier, 1759–1817.* Philadelphia, 1943.

Warner, Michael. *The Letters of the Republic: Publication and the Public Sphere in Eighteenth-Century America.* Cambridge, Mass., 1990.

———. "The Mass Public and the Mass Subject." In *Habermas and the Public Sphere,* edited by Craig Calhoun. Cambridge, Mass., 1992, 377–40

Weaver, David G., and G. Cleveland Wilhoit. *The American Journalist: A Portrait of U.S. News People and Their Work.* 2d ed. Bloomington, Ind., 1991.

Weisenburger, Francis Phelps. "A Life of Charles Hammond: The First Great Journalist of the Old Northwest." *Ohio Archeological and Historical Quarterly* 43 (1934): 337–427.

Weiss, Harry B. *A Graphic Summary of the Growth of Newspapers in New York and Other States, 1704–1820.* New York, 1948.

White, Alain C. *The History of the Town of Litchfield, Connecticut.* Litchfield, Conn., 1920.

White, Leonard D. *The Federalists: A Study in Administrative History.* New York, 1956.

———. *The Jeffersonians: A Study in Administrative History, 1801–1829.* New York, 1951.

Whitney Jr., William T. "The Crowninshields of Salem, 1800–1808: A Study in the Politics of Commercial Growth." *Essex Institute Historical Collections* 94 (1958): 1–36, 79–118.

Wilentz, Sean. *Chants Democratic: New York City & the Rise of the American Working Class, 1788–1850.* New York, 1986.

———. "On Class and Politics in Jacksonian America." *Reviews in American History* 10 (1982): 45–63.

Williamson, Chilton. *American Suffrage: From Property to Democracy, 1760–1860.* Princeton, N.J., 1960.

Wilson, David A. *United Irishmen, United States: Immigrant Radicals in the Early Republic.* Ithaca, N.Y., 1998.

Wilson, Major L. *The Presidency of Martin Van Buren.* Lawrence, Kans., 1984.

————. "Republicanism and the Idea of Party in the Jacksonian Period." *Journal of the Early Republic* 8 (1988): 419–42.

Wolf, Edwin 2d, and Maxwell Whiteman. *The History of the Jews of Philadelphia from Colonial Times to the Age of Jackson.* Philadelphia, 1957.

Wood, Gordon S. "Conspiracy and the Paranoid Style: Causality and Deceit in the Eighteenth Century." *William and Mary Quarterly,* 3d ser., 39 (1982): 401–41.

————. *The Creation of the American Republic, 1776–1787.* 1969, Reprint, New York, 1972.

————. "Interests and Disinterestedness in the Making of the Constitution." In *Beyond Confederation: Origins of the Constitution and American National Identity,* edited by Richard Beeman, Stephen Botein, and Edward C. Carter II, 69–109. Chapel Hill, N.C., 1987.

————. *The Radicalism of the American Revolution.* New York, 1992.

Wright, Esmond. *Franklin of Philadelphia.* Cambridge, Mass., 1986.

Wroth, Lawrence C. *The Colonial Printer.* 2d ed. 1938. Reprint, Charlottesville, Va., 1964.

Yodelis, Mary Ann. "Who Paid the Piper? Publishing Economics in Boston, 1763–1775." *Journalism Monographs* 38 (1975): 1–49.

Youm, Kyo Ho. "The Impact of *People v. Croswell* on Libel Law." *Journalism Monographs* 113 (1989): 1–24.

Young, Alfred F., ed. *The American Revolution: Explorations in the History of American Radicalism.* DeKalb, Ill., 1976.

————. *The Democratic Republicans of New York: The Origins, 1763–1797.* Chapel Hill, N.C., 1967.

————. "The Framers of the Constitution and the 'Genius' of the People." *Radical History Review* 42 (1988): 8–29.

————. "George Robert Twelves Hewes (1742–1840): A Boston Shoemaker and the Memory of the American Revolution." *William and Mary Quarterly,* 3d ser., 38 (1981): 561–623.

Zboray, Ronald J., and Mary Saracino Zboray. "Political News and Female Readership in Antebellum Boston and Its Region." *Journalism History* 22 (1996): 2–14.

INDEX

[Page numbers of illustrations are printed in italics]

Jeffersonian America

Jan Ellen Lewis and Peter S. Onuf, editors
*Sally Hemings and Thomas Jefferson: History, Memory,
and Civic Culture*

Peter S. Onuf
*Jefferson's Empire: The Language of
American Nationhood*

Catherine Allgor
*Parlor Politics: In Which the Ladies of Washington
Help Build a City and a Government*

Jeffrey L. Pasley
*"The Tyranny of Printers": Newspaper Politics in the
Early American Republic*